ANNUAL REVIEW OF ANTHROPOLOGY

ANNUAL REVIEW OF ANTHROPOLOGY

VOLUME 26, 1997

WILLIAM H. DURHAM, *Editor*
Stanford University

E. VALENTINE DANIEL, *Associate Editor*
University of Michigan

BAMBI B. SCHIEFFELIN, *Associate Editor*
New York University

http://www.AnnualReviews.org   science@annurev.org   650-493-4400

ANNUAL REVIEWS INC.   4139 EL CAMINO WAY   P.O. BOX 10139   PALO ALTO, CALIFORNIA 94303-0139

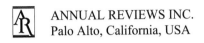

ANNUAL REVIEWS INC.
Palo Alto, California, USA

International Standard Serial Number: 0084-6570
International Standard Book Number: 0-8243-1926-5
Library of Congress Catalog Card Number: 72-821360

The paper used in this publication meets the minimum requirements of American
National Standards for Information Sciences—Permanence of Paper for Printed
Library Materials, ANSI Z39.48-1992

Typesetting by Ruth McCue Saavedra and the Annual Reviews Inc. Editorial Staff

PRINTED AND BOUND IN THE UNITED STATES OF AMERICA

PREFACE

A year ago, in the Preface to Volume 25, I outlined the ways in which each volume of the Annual Review of Anthropology comes to have its particular selection of topics and authors. Here, let me likewise describe the review and editorial procedures that we use in the ARA in an effort to make each review as informative and useful as possible. At the outset, let me admit that the single most important step toward this end is surely the selection, in the first place, of the author (or co-authors) of a given chapter. It is no secret that an author's expertise on a topic, multiplied by his or her creativity and perspective, is the number one ingredient of a successful chapter. We on the Editorial Committee hope that our review and editorial procedures do help, but it is truly the authors themselves who make it work.

That said, our editorial process usually begins shortly after an author has agreed to write a chapter, which is roughly a year to a year-and-a-half before the manuscript is due. At that time, we ask authors to submit a one- or two-page abstract (or "substantive outline") of their contribution, with an additional half-page or so of "landmark" references. These abstracts and references are then vetted by one or more members of the Editorial Committee whose interests and expertise bear on the topic at hand. Suggestions on content and organization, together with any additional key reference suggestions, are sent directly to the author(s) who then has, ideally, a year or so to work them into a draft review.

The second step in the process follows shortly after we receive each chapter. The manuscript is read and reviewed by our Production Editor and then forwarded for a "content reading" to a pertinent member of the Editorial Committee (often the member who previously reviewed the abstract or outline) or to one of our International Correspondents who is knowledgeable on the topic. In most cases, the manuscripts are then returned to authors to allow for revisions and corrections. Occasionally, manuscripts have to be rejected as this stage because they prove overly narrow, dated, too long, or unfairly biased. But as a general rule, once accepted, the revised manuscripts then go back to the Production Editor for copy editing. From there, they go back to a member of the Editorial Committee for a final reading and hence to typesetting and page proofs. Thus to reach publication, not only is each chapter reviewed at the abstract or outline stage, but it is also read and edited in draft at least three times. We believe that the final product is significantly improved by these "extra" steps—a part of our continuing effort to bring you the very best reviews we can.

These procedures have been followed in the volume before you, on a record collection of 25 chapters and two theme sections entitled "Governmentality" and "Religion." In the development of this volume, as well as the previous four, we have benefited enormously from the ever-helpful suggestions and ideas of Michael Little (SUNY, Binghamton) who served as a rotating member of the Editorial Committee. Mike's role in the editorial process will now be carried forward by Ken Weiss (Penn State), whom we welcome enthusiastically to our throng. For two years now it has also been our privilege to work with Peter J. Orne as Production Editor. Peter now moves on to graduate school in journalism, as we welcome Noël Thomas into this important role at ARA. We will all miss Peter's smooth organizational ability, sharp editorial eye, and enduring good cheer even at the deadline. Thanks in part to Peter's encouragement, we inaugurate with this volume the eminently sensible "Harvard style" citation format (i.e. Author, Year, Page) instead of those pesky numerals for which we are justifiably infamous. In addition, we also begin in this volume an ongoing series on "Anthropology and Philosophy," under the intellectual stewardship of Associate Editor E. Valentine Daniel (University of Michigan). I am pleased to report that the series is off to a fine start in these pages with William Roseberry's chapter on "Marx and Anthropology." Chapters on Wittgenstein and Hegel will reward the faithful in subsequent volumes.

William H. Durham
Editor

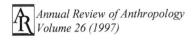

Annual Review of Anthropology
Volume 26 (1997)

CONTENTS

SOME RELATED ARTICLES IN OTHER *ANNUAL REVIEWS*

From the *Annual Review of Genetics*, Volume 31 (1997)

Genetics of Prions, Stanley B. Prusiner and Michael R. Scott
Molecular Genetic Basis of Adaptive Selection, Shozo Yokoyama

From the *Annual Review of Nutrition,* Volume 17 (1997)

Energy and Protein Requirements During Lactation, Kathryn G. Dewey
Evaluation of Methodology for Nutritional Assessment in Children:
  Anthropometry, Body Composition, and Energy Expenditure, Babette
  S. Zemel, Elizabeth M. Riley, Virginia A. Stallings
Taste Preferences and Food Intake, A. Drewnowski

From the *Annual Review of Psychology*, Volume 48 (1997)

Gender, Racial, Ethnic, Sexual, and Class Identities, Deborrah E. S.
  Frable
Discourse Comprehension, Arthur C. Graesser, Keith K. Millis, and Rolf
  A. Zwaan
Language Acquisition: The Acquisition of Linguistic Structure in Normal
  and Special Populations, Janet L. McDonald
Key Issues in the Development of Aggression and Violence from
  Childhood to Early Adulthood, Rolf Loeber and Dale Hay

From the *Annual Review of Public Health,* Volume 18 (1997)

The Public Health Aspects of Complex Emergencies and Refugee
  Situations, Michael J. Toole and R. J. Waldman
Measuring Social Class in US Public Health Research: Concepts,
  Methodologies, and Guidelines, Nancy Krieger, David R. Williams,
  and Nancy E. Moss
The Effects of Poverty on Child Health and Development, J. Lawrence
  Aber, Neil G. Bennett, Dalton Conley, and Jiali Li

From the *Annual Review of Sociology,* Volume 23 (1997)

Feminist Theory and Sociology: Underutilized Contributions for
  Mainstream Theory, Janet Saltzman Chafetz
Sociological Rational Choice Theory, Michael Hechter and Satoshi
  Kanazawa
Culture and Cognition, Paul DiMaggio

ANNUAL REVIEWS INC. is a nonprofit scientific publisher established to promote the advancement of the sciences. Beginning in 1932 with the *Annual Review of Biochemistry,* the Company has pursued as its prinicipal function the publication of high-quality, reasonably priced *Annual Review* volumes. The volumes are organized by Editors and Editorial Committees who invite qualified authors to contribute critical articles reviewing significant developments within each major discipline. The Editor-in-Chief invites those interested in serving as future Editorial Committee members to communicate directly with him. Annual Reviews Inc. is administered by a Board of Directors, whose members serve without compensation.

For the convenience of readers, a detachable order form/envelope is bound into the back of this volume.

Annu. Rev. Anthropol. 1997. 26:1–24

PRACTICING SOCIAL ANTHROPOLOGY IN INDIA

M. N. Srinivas

J.R.D. Tata Visiting Professor, National Institute of Advanced Studies, Bangalore 560012, India; e-mail: mns@hamsadvani.serc.iisc.ernet.in

KEY WORDS: from social philosophy to ethnology, structural-functionalism at Oxford, religion, caste and village, studying own culture, institution-building

ABSTRACT

After completing a BA in social philosophy from Mysore, I went to Bombay to do graduate work in sociology with GS Ghurye, who had been a student of WHR Rivers at Cambridge in the 1920s. At the end of eight years, I became disillusioned with diffusionism and unfocused ethnography. I then went to Oxford, where I worked first with AR Radcliffe-Brown and then EE Evans-Pritchard. At Oxford, I became a structural-functionalist, albeit a somewhat skeptical one. After teaching at Oxford from 1948 to 1951, I returned to India to teach sociology at the University of Baroda. Eight years later, I went to the University of Delhi as Professor of Sociology, and finally moved to Bangalore in 1972 to start, with VKRV Rao, the Institute for Social and Economic Change. As an anthropologist, I am somewhat of a maverick in that I study my own culture and not any distant Other.

INTRODUCTION

My becoming a social anthropologist was largely accidental. After passing the intermediate examination at the University of Mysore in May 1933, I was wondering which subjects to take for the BA course when fate walked in: TLA Acharya, a Marxist and journalist and a friend of my eldest brother, Parthasarathy. Acharya was working for the newspaper *Hitavada* in Nagpur, and

1

he was visiting Mysore on vacation. My brother had borrowed the university handbook so that Acharya would have an idea of the courses available. Acharya thumbed through the pages of the solid volume, and after a while, recommended to me the BA Honors course in social philosophy because, as he put it, it was "humanizing."

The Honors course in social philosophy was not very popular, unlike Honors in economics or history. I applied for a seat and had no difficulty getting in. The program seemed to have been designed to train encyclopedists. It was divided into courses on so-called minor and major subjects. The minor subjects included, in addition to English and a second language, social psychology, social anthropology, comparative politics, and Indian economics, while the major subjects included philosophy of religion, ethics and history of ethics, political philosophy and its history, sociology, Indian social institutions, Indian (Hindu) ethics, Indian (Hindu) political theory, and finally, a course in which I had to write an essay on one of the three or four topics mentioned in a question paper.

I was only 16 when I entered the college in June 1933—too young and immature to benefit from the rich feast of knowledge spread before me. I was taught by conscientious—if underpaid—teachers. I was a diligent student but a poor examinee, passing the course at the level of a high second class.

I had vague ideas of doing graduate studies in sociology in Bombay under GS Ghurye, who had been highly recommended to me by MH Krishna, a historian and archaeologist at Mysore. Sociology, however, was neither popular nor prestigious in India until the 1950s, and anthropology was under a cloud because nationalist Indians regarded the subject as an instrument of colonial rulers who wanted to keep the tribals distinct from the mainstream population. I decided to do a law degree on the side as insurance against unemployment, even though law was poor insurance with too many lawyers chasing too few briefs in the depressed 1930s.

My ideas about pursuing sociology and law in Bombay took shape when the government of Mysore announced in the summer of 1936 that it would hold examinations to select two officers for the Mysore Civil Service. Recruitment to the officer cadre had resumed after a lapse of several years, which meant that everyone who was a graduate and had not crossed the age limit would compete for a position. I knew that many candidates who had obtained the first class level in the BA or BSc program would be in the fray, and that my own record as an examinee was not impressive. Above all, I was sick and tired of taking exams, and highly competitive ones at that. Luckily for me, my eldest brother supported me in my resolve to study sociology and law. I embarked on the long journey by train to Bombay to the disappointment of my mother, who wanted her son to be an officer in the Mysore government.

GRADUATE STUDIES IN BOMBAY

I presented myself before Ghurye at the University School of Economics and Sociology (USES) on the afternoon of June 17, 1936. Ghurye seemed informal. He told me that he had been the examiner of the sociology paper at my Honors examination and that he had given me 66 marks, the highest among the five candidates. This was a surprise because I had answered only four out of the mandatory five questions, and besides, I thought I had done badly in sociology.

I told Ghurye the details of the Honors course, and he told me I should write a thesis. This was music to my ears because I knew I had a better chance at doing well with a thesis than with an examination by papers. Before discussing the topic of the thesis, however, he wanted me to write an essay on LT Hobhouse's *Morals in Evolution*. It was an immense and heavily footnoted tome, and I found it boring. When I met Ghurye after a month or so, he asked me how I was getting on. I told him that I found Hobhouse dull and heavy going. I expected that he would be annoyed, but he was not. Instead, he talked to me about the subject of my research. He suggested that I work on marriage and family among the Kannada-speaking castes of Mysore State. I agreed to undertake the research, in addition to beginning my law degree at the Government Law College.

In the lingo of the Research Hall, where I had been given a table, mine was called a "library thesis." I had to study the ethnographic surveys, gazetteers, and census reports and submit my thesis within three years. Ghurye wrote letters to the university librarian and to the librarian of the Bombay branch of the Royal Asiatic Society requesting that they allow me to use their libraries. I enjoyed my new status as a research student, wandering from one library to another after attending classes in the morning in the Government Law College, which was practically next door to the USES.

In addition to the books and reports recommended by Ghurye, I used material in Kannada folklore and fiction on marriage and family. I printed a questionnaire in English, which I later discarded after a social worker I knew picked holes in it. Fieldwork was fascinating to me, and I visited a village for a few days and witnessed a wedding, which I enjoyed. Village India was terra incognita to me even though my family, absentee landowners, annually received its share of paddy from our tenants. This brief encounter with our tenants had increased my curiosity about villagers and their life and culture.

I had to balance my time between studying law and working on my thesis. During the first year, I paid more attention to law than to sociology, passing the first law exam in May 1937. Then I went all out for my thesis but attended the law college and paid the fees to ensure my eligibility to take the final exam when I would be free to do so. In September 1938, I submitted a 300-page thesis that Ghurye thought, for a brief while, was good enough to be submitted for the PhD.

Ghurye was keen that I should publish my thesis. He secured a grant from the university to pay for the cost and urged me to secure a foreword from the vice chancellor at the University of Mysore in the hope that it might help me to secure a lectureship there. After obtaining the foreword, I went to a local publisher who agreed to publish the book, *Marriage and Family in Mysore* (Srinivas 1942).

I was concerned about how the book would be received, but, to my relief, all the reviews were friendly, including a longish one that appeared in *Nature* (October 1942). Ghurye, who held *Nature* in great esteem, regarded the review as a feather in his cap (Ghurye 1973, pp. 108–9).

After passing the final law exam in October 1939, I started thinking about a suitable theme for PhD research. When I met Ghurye to get his advice, he told me that the university had instituted a research fellowship in sociology and that he would offer it to me if I undertook a field study of the Coorgs. The Coorgs are the dominant ethnic group in Coorg, a montane district then covered with dense forests lying to the southwest of the princely state of Mysore in South India. The Coorgs have a strong martial tradition, and large numbers of them were recruited by the Indian Army during World War II. Their traditional dress, customs, and life-style are different from their neighbors, and their distinctive appearance and customs had been commented upon by outsiders. At the time of my study (1940–1942), the Coorgs were busy defining their collective identity in the Indian subcontinent. They considered themselves Indo-Aryans, descended from the early Aryan invaders, and they interpreted their customs and ritual as derived from the Vedas.

Ghurye's interest in the Coorgs was the result of his having read about their ancestor shrines (*kaimada*) in the *Manual of Coorg* (Richter 1870). He wondered whether the kaimada had been derived ultimately from the Egyptian pyramids. Far-fetched as this may sound to a modern anthropologist, Ghurye's Egypt fixation was inspired by Rivers, who, during the last phase of his undoubtedly remarkable career, had embraced an extreme form of diffusionism under the influence of the anatomist G Elliot-Smith and his colleague, WJ Perry. RH Lowie (1937) summarizes the basic ideas of the diffusionists: "(1) Man is uninventive; hence culture arises only in exceptionally favorable circumstances, practically never twice independently. (2) Such circumstances existed only in ancient Egypt; hence elsewhere culture, except some of its simplest elements, must have spread from Egypt with the rise of navigation. (3) Civilization is naturally diluted as it spreads to the outposts; hence decadence has played a tremendous role in human history" (p. 161).

I did not find any evidence to link Coorg kaimada to the Egyptian pyramids; if anything, they were more likely to have been influenced by the Veerashaivas—popularly known as the Lingayats—who built graves over their dead. Lingayat rajas ruled Coorg from 1633 to 1834, and Coorgs, who formed most of the armies of the rajas, came under Veerashaiva influence. This was especially true of rich and aristocratic Coorgs (Srinivas 1952, pp. 159–60).

Some areas of main concern to Ghurye, during the period I was his student (1936–1944), were kinship, caste, social organization, and tracing the distribution of cultural traits, all of which were derived from Rivers. Ghurye, however, had studied Sanskrit before he took up sociology, and when he became a professor in Bombay he promoted the use of anthropological concepts to interpret ritual, legal, and other material in Sanskrit in the manner of the British Classicists. He did this in his own work and through the work of his students, but the value of his contributions was limited because he did not shake off diffusionism and become familiar with the theoretical advances made by Radcliffe-Brown, Malinowski, and others.

Ghurye, holding as he did a professorship in cosmopolitan Bombay, attracted students from all over the subcontinent, and he directed them, when he could, to update the ethnography of different regions. In this way he retrieved a great deal of information. Further, though he was an armchair anthropologist, he knew the importance of fieldwork in a country as culturally rich and diverse as India at a time when India was beginning to change. His efforts suffered, however, because he remained pre-Malinowskian in his approach. He had not heard of participant observation. Data were collected in interviews of knowledgeable informants, preferably during short field trips. A few of his students also carried out surveys of villages to determine their living conditions.

Ghurye regarded the whole of Indian civilization as his bailiwick, from the tribals of central India and the northeast to the study of Sanskrit literature, the Sadhus or renouncers, the worship of Ganapati, and even Rajput architecture. He realized that no student of Indian culture and society could afford to divide the study of India into two distinct academic fields: social anthropology and sociology. Even the remotest tribes in the subcontinent have some relations with caste Hindus and have been influenced by the ideas of Hinduism, Islam, or Christianity. Equally important but less acknowledged, however, is that tribal ideas and practices may be found among the high castes living in villages and towns, and that they surface particularly during crises.

Relations with Ghurye

In hindsight, I realize that when I first met Ghurye in June 1936, he probably saw in me a student who could promote a few of the goals he had formulated for sociological research in India. After my MA thesis was finished, Ghurye asked me to make an account of the feasts and fasts of the Kannada Brahmins, and then to make a collection of Tamil proverbs translated into English. All this was to be done before I began my fieldwork among the Coorgs in June 1940. My fellowship came to an end, however, in June 1942 and, much to my regret, my fieldwork had to be carried out in short trips because of a severe illness that I contracted during my first stay in Coorg. A few weeks before the fellowship concluded, Ghurye told me that he wanted me to be his research assistant, succeeding CA Hate. I accepted. The research assistantship was a step up from the research fellowship, and it lasted from June 1942 to June 1944.

During the first year of the assistantship I toured the Tamil-speaking areas of Madras Presidency to collect data on kinship and marriage among the various castes, folk songs, and photographs from the Madras Government Museum, which illustrated the varieties of dress worn at different periods in the history of the Tamil people. After I returned to Bombay, my first task was to write up the material on kinship and marriage and then to translate the folk songs. I wrote a paper on Tamil folk songs for publication in the university journal (Srinivas 1943, 1944). In addition to these duties, I had to be available to Ghurye during office hours to hunt up references for a paper or book he was working on. While I was his research assistant, Ghurye was working hard to finish one book so he could begin another.

I toured the Telugu-speaking areas of Madras Presidency in the academic year 1943–1944 to repeat the work I had done in the Tamil-speaking areas. Just before leaving for my tour in August 1943, an interview was held to appoint two lecturers in the department. At Ghurye's urging, I sent in my application. After finishing my tour of the Telugu areas and before returning to Bombay, I briefly visited Mysore, where I learned that I had missed the lectureship. Upon my return, Ghurye was all praise for my fieldwork, and he told me that I was now able to fuse data and theory. I did not show any pleasure at receiving the compliments, however, and further, I expressed my anxiety about not making any progress with my thesis. I told him I needed all my time for my thesis, after writing up the material I had collected in the field. Ghurye seemed to agree.

I worked very hard and completed my tasks, including the paper on Telugu folk songs (Srinivas 1944, 1945) in four or five months after my return. My expectation, however, that I would be allowed to work at my thesis proved to be wrong. Ghurye frequently called me to his room to do one chore or another. Even worse, he started to use me as his amanuensis. He saw that I disliked it, but it did not stop him. One afternoon I told him that I was very anxious about not completing my thesis and that I wanted to be able to devote all my time to it. He at once wrote to CN Vakil, the Director of the School, appointing a colleague of mine to take my place.

Ghurye's termination of my research assistantship was sudden and unexpected. I did not have any money to support myself in Bombay while completing the thesis. My brother, however, wrote from Mysore saying that I should not worry, and that he would send me money. I knew how hard up the family was and felt guilty about taking money from my brother. I worked very hard and managed to submit a two-volume thesis—888 pages—in December 1944. The external examiner was Raymond Firth (now Sir), and he not only passed me but wrote a very favorable report (Ghurye 1973, p. 115).

During the closing months of 1943 and throughout 1944, I was extremely worried about my future. I had no job, nor was there any likelihood that I would procure one. Even more disturbing, I was disillusioned with the kind of sociology I was doing: Tracing Coorg ancestor shrines to ancient Egyptian pyramids seemed to me as absurd an enterprise as tracing the origin of the Coorgs to the Vedas without historical and archaeological evidence. I was bitter that I had begun with the idea of becoming a sociological theorist but had ended up as an antiquarian under Ghurye's tutelage.

In short, I was unemployed and in the midst of an intellectual and moral crisis. It was at this juncture that I came across, quite accidentally, Ruth Benedict's *Patterns of Culture* (1934). I found the book fascinating, and its main idea of looking at cultures holistically and characterizing each culture on the basis of its dominant theme was a refreshing contrast to looking at cultures as assemblages of myriad discrete elements drawn from different parts of the world and across millennia. Benedict had also demonstrated the integral relation between a culture and its members, showing how in each culture some personality types are preferred while others are considered undesirable. It is possible that the marked preference for martial virtues in Coorg culture had made me sensitive to Benedict's thesis, especially because the Lingayats were a thorough contrast to the Coorgs, as were the Brahmins. Benedict appeared to offer me a more fruitful way of looking at culture and society. Looking back, I am surprised that as late as 1944 I was unacquainted with the functionalism of Malinowski or Radcliffe-Brown, even though I had read Malinowski's *Crime and Custom in Savage Society.*

Toward the end of 1943 or slightly thereafter, I began to consider going abroad to study for another PhD. I even mentioned the idea to Ghurye, who not only did not discourage me but recommended Oxford because Radcliffe-Brown was a professor there and because he was a "seeded functionalist," whatever that meant. However, I suspect that his preference for R-B, as Radcliffe-Brown was known, was probably due to R-B having been a student of Rivers. I applied to Oxford and Columbia, and I received an early reply from Oxford, even though England was in the thick of the war. The termination of the research assistantship strengthened my determination to go to Oxford, though I had no clue about how to pay. I applied for a Tata loan scholarship but was turned down.

I did not know at the time I applied that R-B was away in São Paolo and that Daryll Forde was serving in his place. Forde wrote asking me to send him a brief proposal on the theme of my DPhil research. I wrote back stating my reasons for wanting to work on the idea of culture patterns, comparing available material on three South Indian communities—the Coorgs, the Todas, and the Chenchus—about whom C von Fürer-Haimendorf had published a monograph in 1943. Forde approved of my proposal, adding that I would be admitted initially to the BLitt degree with the prospect of transfer to the DPhil at the end of three terms, provided I was found fit for the higher degree.

I went home to Mysore in the first week of January 1945 and spent the time doing the various things necessary to secure a passport and passage to England. The family raised enough money to meet the cost of passage and my stay in Oxford for six months. Things started moving fast, and I learned that my ship would sail from Bombay on April 10, 1945.

I reached Bombay a few days before the departure date. I saw Ghurye and wished him farewell. I thought the meeting would be brief and formal, but it was not. Ghurye told me that I was going to England at the wrong time. There would be no students in British universities because of the war and no intellectual stimulation. He wanted me to stay back: He was going to create a lectureship for me in the department. I was taken aback by Ghurye's talk, and it seemed absurd to think of abandoning my plans on the eve of catching the boat. I told Ghurye that I would return if he created a lectureship for me in the department, and took leave of him.

RESEARCH STUDENT AT OXFORD

After more than a month of wartime sea travel, I presented myself before R-B at the Institute of Social Anthropology in Oxford to learn what was expected of me as a research student. R-B appeared forbidding, and my initial encounters with him were far from propitious. There were many reasons for this, but the most important was probably R-B's antipathy toward Benedict's theoretical stance, of which I was totally ignorant until much later. In addition, even though I was totally disenchanted with diffusionism, my old habits of thought surfaced occasionally during his lectures or supervision sessions, which irritated him.

After the Trinity term ended in July, R-B left for his Welsh village, taking with him my thesis and asking me to write a paper on culture patterns to be shown to him on his return. I worked hard during the summer, becoming familiar with the various libraries in Oxford, and I prepared a longish paper on culture patterns. I discovered that there had been a fair amount of discussion on culture patterns in the United States. During my work I became concerned that I did not have a deep enough grounding in psychology to tackle culture patterns to my satisfaction.

I met R-B soon after his return to Oxford in October. He told me that he had read my thesis during the vacation and that I wrote very well. "Did you go to an English school?" he asked. I told him "no" and handed him the paper on culture patterns, wondering what he would think of it. A few days later he informed me that he was satisfied with the paper and that I could go ahead. I felt greatly relieved, and I then asked him what he thought of my proposal. Sharp came the reply: "It is a waste of time for a man of your scientific talents to work on culture patterns." I then asked him what he thought I should do. He said that there was a considerable amount of material in my thesis on ritual and religion and that I should look at it from the structural-functional point of view. Expecting that he might ask me to go back to Coorg to collect more data, I told him that I had no money, and further, given the war conditions, it was impossible to get a passage to India in the immediate future. He assured me that there was no need for collecting more data. There was plenty of information in my thesis, and he wanted me to look at it from a new point of view.

I then read Durkheim's *Elementary Forms of Religious Life* (1954), R-B's *The Andaman Islanders* (1933), Fustel de Coulanges's *The Ancient City* (1956), Robertson Smith's *The Religion of the Semites* (1927), Evans-Pritchard's *Witchcraft, Oracles and Magic Among the Azande* (1937), and Bateson's *Naven* (1936). I made myself familiar with R-B's many papers on kinship and Evans-Pritchard's *The Nuer* (1940). I read a lot of other literature, too, in an attempt to catch up with recent developments in social anthropology.

The task of looking at the Coorg material from a structural-functional point of view proved to be exciting. It looked as though the material was crying out for such an approach and analysis. I also had the satisfaction of fleshing out a few simple-sounding but key concepts of R-B's, such as "ritual idiom" and "spread" in the analysis of Hinduism. The social structure of Coorgs, when analyzed, fell into clear, distinguishable units, each with its own cult. The cults formed a hierarchy, from the lineage to Pan-Indian Sanskritic Hinduism.

Coorg ideas of purity and impurity were elaborate, and pervasive in their religious and social life. (It was difficult to draw a line between the religious and social.) I regarded ideas of purity and impurity as part of the "ritual idiom" of the Coorgs, along with *mangala,* a complex of ritual acts that was performed on all auspicious occasions. I accepted for heuristic purposes R-B's idea that ritual was a language, and I applied the few rules he had formulated to decode mangala. After I completed my analysis, I felt that I had not probed deeply enough. The feeling remained with me, but two recent verdicts on my effort have been more positive than I could have dared to hope. Milton Singer has commented that my (Singer 1996, p. 20–54)

> chief interest…was in the application of Radcliffe-Brown's theory of ritual to Coorg religious practices and beliefs and their relation to all-India Hindu practices and beliefs. The application goes considerably beyond Radcliffe-Brown's redefinition of the "sacred" in terms of "ritual value," and an analysis of rituals and myths in terms of "symbolic action" and "symbolic thought." It also includes a detailed ethnographic description of the "ritual idiom" and cults of different social units in Coorg—joint family, village, caste; and of the diacritical symbols of age, sex, marital status, caste, sect and other social divisions. His most original contribution to a theory of ritual is his analysis of the hierarchies of ritual purity and ritual pollution among different castes, occupations, and age and sex groups. Srinivas' linking of his analysis to social strategies that different groups adopted for changing their social and "normal ritual status" by changing their ritual practices and beliefs generated the famous theory of "Sanskritization" and "de-Sanskritization" and his later theory of secularization and Westernization.

Jack Goody has written recently that he found the analysis of ritual developed by R-B and me helpful in the analysis of the religion of the LaDagaa in West Africa: "It seemed hardly possible to deal with a rite of passage without building upon Van Gennep's pioneering work, nor did it seem useful to discuss 'symbolic' meanings without recourse to the classic but equally simple techniques developed by Radcliffe-Brown and Srinivas, that is, without being concerned with 'action'" (Goody 1995, p. 125).

Diverse and conflicting elements have gone into the making of Coorg religion, and in my effort to analyze it I used R-B's idea of spread. I had to flesh out the concept, and in the process there emerged such distinctions as local, regional, peninsular, or Sanskritic Hinduism. Sanskritic Hinduism is now widely used by Indianists notwithstanding objections to its usage by some (Fuller 1992, p. 24–28).

The Coorgs regard themselves as a people distinct—even unique—from their neighbors, but they also consider themselves Kshatriyas. In studying their religion I was extending the use of the anthropological approach and concepts to try to understand a world religion and a historic civilization. I embarked on this enterprise without any thought for the difficulties that would be involved, but my naiveté, if not ignorance, paid off. In his foreword to the Coorg book, R-B wrote, "For the student of comparative religion, and particularly for those interested in the sociological study of religion, this book of Dr. Srinivas offers material of exceptional value" (Srinivas 1952, p. ix). Meyer Fortes went further when he said (Fortes 1955): "Even more impressive is Professor

M.N. Srinivas' recent book on *Religion and Society Among the Coorgs of South India* (1952). Here Radcliffe-Brown's methods and theories are ably applied to the religious system of a complex Oriental society. Professor Srinivas shows that there is as close an interlocking of religious institutions, which Frazer would certainly have placed at a higher 'stage' of evolution than Australian totemism, with the family and kinship system, the laws of inheritance and succession, and the principles determining the status of persons, among the Coorgs as among the Australians and Andamanese. He shows how the study of the 'higher' religions can be set free from the crippling trammels of theology, metaphysics and philology and brought within reach of social science." I would, however, qualify Fortes's statement by adding that anthropology ought not to claim that it renders metaphysics, theology, and philology redundant.

R-B retired from his professorship in July 1946, and E-P, as Evans-Pritchard was known, succeeded to the chair in October 1946. I discovered that R-B had spoken well of me to E-P and had suggested that E-P should take over supervising my thesis, which resulted in a brief misunderstanding with Fortes. By October, when E-P took charge as professor, I had more or less broken the back of the conceptual part of the thesis, and only the writing remained. E-P found me too much under the influence of Durkheim and tried to instill some skepticism in me. Apart from this, he approved the draft of my chapters. I submitted my thesis in May 1947, and E-P was present when the DPhil was conferred on me in June. I was his first doctoral student and R-B's last. I regard this as a distinction.

No two persons could be more different than R-B and E-P: E-P was extremely informal and took the trouble to put you at ease, whereas R-B's shyness erected a barrier between himself and others. R-B appeared aloof and distant to most people. He never made small talk, and with anthropological matters he gave the impression that he knew all the answers. E-P had a keen sense of the absurd, which, along with his engaging informality, brought me out of my shyness and diffidence. I could talk to him like an equal across barriers of race, religion, and diversity of cultural background. After I received the DPhil, he congratulated me and then told me that I was his equal(!), and that I should no longer call him "Professor." He requested that I call him E-P.

A few weeks before I was due to sail for India, E-P told me that R-B was visiting Oxford and that he would like to see me in his rooms in All Souls in the evening. When I went there I found R-B and E-P engaged in animated and friendly conversation. Soon after I sat down, R-B said that E-P was planning to create a lectureship for me in Oxford, but before going ahead he wanted to be sure that I would accept it. I was not prepared to hear anything like this, and my initial reaction, I regret to say, was bewilderment. I do not know whether it was interpreted as hesitance. R-B went on to tell me that I was not yet ready to teach in India and that I needed to spend a few more years at Oxford. I then expressed my thanks to E-P and R-B and walked out into the street, happy and confused.

I returned to India in August 1947, a few days before the 15th, when it celebrated its independence. In mid-November, I received a letter from E-P informing me that I had been appointed university lecturer in Indian sociology, beginning January 1, 1948, and that I could spend the first year of my lectureship studying a village of my choice in India. I had mentioned to E-P that I wanted very much to study a multicaste village using the method of participant observation. E-P had remembered it and had generously provided for it. A formal letter of appointment from the registrar of Oxford University soon followed.

I started looking for a suitable village some time in December but settled in one only in February 1948. The assassination of Mahatma Gandhi had delayed my move by a fortnight. The villagers insisted that I should not start my fieldwork during the mourning period for the Mahatma.

Fieldwork in Rampura was a profound experience, influencing my thinking not only about Indian society and culture but about all societies, and even about the nature of sociological understanding itself. I enjoyed my field experience, and it was with reluctance if not sorrow that I bid farewell to the villagers toward the end of November.

TEACHING AT OXFORD

I returned to Oxford in mid-January 1949, in time to start teaching during the Hilary Term. Much water had flowed down the Isis during my absence, and I found the university crowded with students and bustling with excitement. There were several graduate students in the department, including a few from the United States and Africa. A few of E-P's students at Cambridge had followed him to Oxford. The most prominent were Godfrey Lienhardt, Emrys Peters, and David Pocock. Among the students were Mary Douglas, Jack Goody, and John Middleton—all future leaders in anthropology. The Friday seminars were open to outsiders, and after animated discussions in the smoke-filled seminar room, many participants adjourned to the King's Arms to continue discussions in small groups over mugs of beer.

Unlike R-B, E-P was an Oxford man who felt at home in the university, and who knew his way around it in more senses than one. He tapped the Scarborough and Colonial Development and Welfare funds to create lectureships and support field research. He was very keen that anthropology should study non-Western civilizations. E-P's own background in modern history at Oxford and his study of the Sanusi of Cyrenaica (1949), undertaken during the War years, had strengthened his belief in the need for such studies. He was also aware that Oriental Studies commanded considerable prestige at Oxford, and he valued association with the Orientalists.

About these early Oxford years, Jack Goody has written in his memoir on Meyer Fortes: "Together with Evans-Pritchard, Gluckman and Srinivas, they built up a powerful department which attracted students from all over the world at the moment when anthropology, and particularly African anthropology, was expanding rapidly" (Goody 1993, p. 283). Significant contributions to Indian anthropology at Oxford were also made by Louis Dumont and David Pocock. Gluckman went on to Manchester to build an outstanding department, where I was a welcome guest.

It is ironic that Oxford soon proved to be the place where the basic postulates of Radcliffe-Brownian structural-functionalism were rejected. The leader of this move was E-P, who had acknowledged earlier, in his preface to *The Nuer,* Professor AR Radcliffe-Brown, "whose influence on the theoretical side of my work will be obvious to any student of anthropology" (1940, p. viii). The rejection that began in classrooms and seminars found public expression in the six talks on social anthropology that the BBC invited E-P to give. First came the rejection of the idea that social anthropology was a "natural science" (Evans-Pritchard 1951): "Up to the present nothing even remotely resembling what are called laws in the natural sciences has been adduced—only rather naive, deterministic, teleological and pragmatic assertions. The generalizations which have so far been attempted have, moreover, been so vague and general as to be, even if true, of little use, and they have rather easily tended to become mere tautologies and platitudes on the level of commonsense deduction (p. 57)....[S]ocial anthropology studies societies as moral or symbolic systems and not as natural systems, that it is less interested in process than in design, and that it therefore seeks patterns and not laws, demonstrates consistency and not necessary relations between social activities, and interprets rather than explains. These are conceptual and not merely verbal differences (p. 62)." I had reservations about E-P's view that anthropology was "less interested in process."

E-P then went on to reject the other major postulate of functionalism, namely, the irrelevance of history for arriving at a sociological understanding of phenomena. E-P asserted that history was essential for a "fuller understanding of social life" and that social anthropology was "much more like historical branches of scholarships—social history and the history of institutions and of ideas as contrasted with narrative and political history—than it is to any of the natural sciences....[E]ssentially the method of both historiography and social anthropology is descriptive integration, even though anthropological synthesis is usually on a higher plane of abstraction than historical synthesis and anthropology more explicitly than history aims at comparison and generalization" (Evans-Pritchard 1951, p. 61).

E-P returned to the subject in his Marett Memorial Lecture (June 1950), where he was even more scathing in his attack on the natural science view of social anthropology: "The concepts of natural system and natural law, modeled on the constructs of the natural sciences, have dominated anthropology from its beginnings, and as we look back over the course of its growth, I think they have been responsible for a false scholasticism which has led to one rigid formulation after another. Regarded as a special kind of historiography, that is one of the humanities, social anthropology is released from these essentially philosophical dogmas and given the opportunity, though it may be paradoxical to say so, to be really empirical and in the true sense of the word, scientific. This I presume is what Maitland had in mind when he said that 'by and by anthropology will have the choice of being history and being nothing'" (Evans-Pritchard 1962, p. 26).

Where did I stand in this controversy? To me E-P's argument that social anthropologists had produced nothing remotely resembling laws in the natural sciences was self-evident; in addition, I had never really believed in the irrelevance of historical data for sociological explanation. Real history, however, had to be distinguished from conjectural history, and the latter had to be rejected. In addition, sociological explanation did not consist in tracing the origins of institutions. I accepted, however, the functionalist idea of interdependence of institutions and that such interdependence enabled the anthropologist to talk of "social systems." I accepted them only as heuristic devices that enabled me to understand and better analyze social phenomena. Indeed a major consequence of anthropological (or sociological) training ought to be to enable the anthropologist to view institutions in relation to one another, and in relation to the whole, even if the whole happens to be, or is assumed to be, the anthropologist's own construct.

E-P had spent the war years in Sudan, Egypt, and Libya. Freed from the compulsions of academic routine, he had time to think about all aspects of his work, including the postulates of functionalist anthropology. It was during the war years that he became a convert to Roman Catholicism, which profoundly affected his weltanschauung, including his views about the nature of social anthropology. He rejected all forms of determinism, Marxian as well as Durkheimian. He also rejected rationalism, which equated religion to superstition. (He once told me that he felt that he had more in common with the Indian philosopher Sir S Radhakrishnan than with two other Fellows of All Souls, the socialist GDH Cole, and the logical positivist, AM Quinton, both of whom were antireligious.)

RETURN TO INDIA

I left Oxford in June 1951 to take up professorship of sociology in the MS University of Baroda. I was leaving one of the oldest universities in the world to occupy a newly established chair in a new university. Baroda University was a new world to me, but I slowly learned how to go about my work of building a university department that was active in teaching and research. I paid attention throughout my academic career, not only to attract promising students and committed colleagues but to evolve a syllabus in comparative sociology suited to Indian conditions, avoiding parochialism. I also ignored making a distinction between social anthropology and sociology, to the annoyance of some of my anthropological colleagues. I did my utmost to encourage field studies using the method of participant observation. India was changing fast, and chronicling the rich and diverse culture of the country was a major objective of mine.

I had modest success in my endeavor, and I left Baroda early in 1959 for Delhi, where again I was appointed to a newly established chair. Delhi was a far more cosmopolitan city than Baroda, and the atmosphere in the university was propitious for building a first-rate department. Delhi attracted students from all over India, and I also had visiting students and faculty from abroad who added to the liveliness of our weekly seminars. In less than 10 years, my department was recognized by the University Grants Commission as a Center of Advanced Study in Sociology, which meant I got more money for expansion of the faculty, visiting fellows from other universities, scholarships for students, and strengthening the library. I left Delhi in May 1972 to start, along with the distinguished economist and educationist VKRV Rao, the Institute for Social and Economic Change in Bangalore. I am happy that today the department in Delhi continues to be a center of excellence for sociological studies. A great deal of my time and energies have been devoted to building up departments and institutions and promoting my kind of sociology. My own research has suffered much as a result.

SANSKRITIZATION AND WESTERNIZATION

In the late 1940s and early 1950s, Milton Singer, along with Robert Redfield, started to work on an "extended" method for a social anthropology of civilizations. According to Singer, "the suggestion that the field methods and concepts of social anthropology might be extended to a study of the social organization of the Great Traditions of these civilizations was greeted with skepticism. Some Sinologists, Indologists, and Islamicists expressed more confidence in the desirability and feasibility of such a development than did anthropologists. In this climate of opinion the appearance of M.N. Srinivas' *Religion and Society among the Coorgs of South India* in 1952 was a decisive event. It was the first anthropological monograph to show us how a Great Tradition (of Sanskritic Hinduism) could be analyzed within a social anthropological framework, and it set going much of what follows in this volume" (Singer 1972, pp. xii–xiii).

Singer wanted me to prepare a paper on Sanskritization for a seminar he was organizing in Poona in July 1954, and the outcome was "A Note on Sanskritization and Westernization" (Srinivas 1994, pp. 42–62). As it happened, I could not attend the seminar, and I met Singer only much later in Madras. One of the purposes of Singer's stay was to prepare the ground for Redfield's visit to India in 1955, and Singer and I planned, with the help of A Aiyappan of Madras, a seminar to be held in Madras in October 1955. Leading Indian anthropologists, Sanskritists, and others were invited to the seminar. Redfield was present and took an active interest in the discussions. My paper proved incendiary: The Sanskritists condemned my use of the word "Sanskritization." The only people using it at the time were Aiyappan, a non-Sanskritist, and Ed Harper, a young anthropologist from Cornell who was studying a village in Western Karnataka, who remarked that the concept helped him to understand what was happening around him. The term has been uniformly condemned by Sanskritists everywhere, but in spite—or because—of that, Sanskritization has been used extensively by those writing on social and cultural change in South Asia. It has even made its way into the *New Shorter Oxford Dictionary* (1993).

I first used the terms Sanskritization and Westernization in the context of cultural and social change and social mobility. When an individual *jati* (a local endogamous unit of the caste system), or a section of a local jati, captured political power or became wealthy, over a period of time he or the group emulated the customs, ritual, and life-style of a higher caste. Eventually a myth, or *purana,* came into existence claiming noble origins for the caste and changing the caste's name by adding a suffix characteristic of one or another twice-born *varna* [a hierarchical division of Vedic society into four orders: Brahmin (priests), Kshatriya (wariors), Vaishya (traders), and Shudra (menials)]. This is the classic form of Sanskritization.

Sanskritization occurred right from the earliest times in Indian history, and the varna order of Kshatriya has been generally filled by groups that captured power by taking advantage of the fluidity that was characteristic of the political system until the establishment of British rule, which precipitated the end of local and regional political struggles. Similarly, with the development of trade and urban centers in parts of the country, rich traders claimed the rank of Vaishyas, the third twice-born varna.

Thus individual jatis or sections of jatis were able to move up in the caste system by Sanskritizing themselves. That there was provision for individual castes to move up contributed to the survival of caste through millennia. Although individual castes moved up (or down), the system as a whole was stationary. Further, Sanskritization proved to be an instrument for absorbing individual tribes into the Hindu fold, many of them entering the Kshatriya order. Such absorption of tribes occurred everywhere in India, except in the northeast.

In the context of modern India, mobility involves not only Sanskritization but also Westernization. In several parts of the country, the higher castes took the lead in Westernizing their life-style, and while the higher castes were Westernizing, the so-called lower ones were Sanskritizing. This should not be interpreted to mean that the upper castes were throwing out their traditional culture or that the lower were not Westernizing. Both were occurring in each category, but since Western education had spread more widely among the upper castes and more of them were in white-collar jobs, Westernization was more conspicuous among them. The improvement of communications, the activities of holy men, the popularity of pilgrimages, and the spread of education in rural areas all contributed to the increased popularity of Sanskritization.

Since my ideas of Sanskritization and Westernization had created considerable interest among anthropologists and Indianists, I decided to make an overview of social change in modern India using the concepts of Sanskritization and Westernization (Srinivas 1996). One of the features that stood out in my new study was the crucial role played by dominant, landowning castes in the transmission of cultural forms, ideas, and patterns of behavior to the people living within their jurisdiction. They favored the spread of some forms and ideas while they frowned on certain others, and these elements varied from region to region. However, the influence of the dominant castes was occasionally circumscribed by the presence of a nearby monastery, great temple, or center of pilgrimage.

Westernization is a multifaceted concept, and different groups might choose a facet congenial to it. Common to all facets, however, is secularization. Because of Western education, urbanization, and an occupation that required a journey to work and regular working hours, life-styles have undergone rapid changes, along with the decline of ideas of purity-impurity in extramural contexts and the enclaving of ritual. Simultaneously, *sanyasis* (individuals who renounce the world, wearing traditional ochre robes) and heads of monasteries are engaged in social welfare activities promoting education, providing medical relief, undertaking rural development, and building old-age homes. Some of them mix freely with politicians, cultivate the media, and travel abroad to meet their followers and promote religious/sectarian activity. The role of the renouncers seems to have undergone a revolution in India, this world claiming their attention more and more.

India's large and growing middle class is becoming increasingly Westernized. Westernization in one form or another is seen as essential to upward mobility. Consumerism and gadgetry have become tangible symbols of a Westernized life-style. Sanskritization by itself, unaccompanied by a few symbols of Westernization, is considered synonymous with backwardness and poverty.

A most interesting and important feature of recent assertions of equality by the Dalits (ex-Untouchables) is, ironically, through Sanskritization. For instance, Neera Burra, who studied the Mahars of Maharashtra, reports that Mahars "deliberately practiced hitherto forbidden rites and rituals as a means of asserting their right to equality knowing full well that they [the higher castes] could do nothing about it. There was a certain pride in this [assertion of] equality." It is ironical that "As far as upper caste Hindus were concerned, conversion to Buddhism was not resented as much as attempts by Mahars to emulate their customs, ritual and dress" (Burra 1996, p. 168). GK Karanth (1996) reports a similar situation in rural Karnataka.

The Constitution of free India became effective in 1950, and it affirmed the equality of all citizens before the law, abolished Untouchability, and declared its practice in any form an offense punishable by law. The Constitution also provided for the representation of the ex-Untouchables (Scheduled Castes) and tribes (Scheduled Tribes) in legislatures, by reserving seats for them in proportion to their population. The SCs and STs also enjoyed reservation of jobs in government and places in educational institutions. Because of pressure brought in by leaders of the backward castes, the Constitution provided for reservation of places in educational institutions and jobs in government, for the "socially and educationally backward classes" (also referred to as "other backward classes"). The courts have consistently interpreted backward classes as backward castes. In November 1992, in a landmark judgment, the Supreme Court of India declared that the total quantum of reservation of jobs and educational places should not exceed fifty percent of the total.

WHITHER CASTE?

During the early 1950s, the assertion of the equality of all citizens before the law, the abolition of Untouchability, affirmative action on a large scale for "the weaker sections of the society," and the undertaking of a massive and comprehensive program of development all produced a sense of euphoria particularly among the urban intellectuals, who believed that their country was becoming modernized rapidly and that caste, along with Untouchability, was on its way out.

It was in this context that I delivered, in January 1957, my presidential address on "Caste in Modern India" to the Anthropology and Archaeology Section of the Indian Science Congress meeting in Calcutta (Srinivas 1994, pp. 15–41). The speech was read for me because I was at the University of California at Berkeley at that time on a Rockefeller Fellowship. I argued in the address that caste was not on its way out but that it was playing an active role in politics, and that there was rivalry between important castes to capture political power and secure government jobs. I also pointed out that castes were being mobilized by politicians for securing votes. Two years before the address, I had written that "the coming of elections has given fresh opportunities for the crystallization of parties around patrons. Each patron may be said to have a 'vote bank' which he can place at the disposal of a provincial or national party for a consideration which is nonetheless real because it is not mentioned" (Srinivas 1955, p. 31). It is interesting to note that the phrase "vote bank," which emerged from the anthropological study of a village in South India, has become so popular that no journalist reporting an election fails to use it.

Because of the various forces acting on caste during the past hundred years or more and, in particular, since independence, jatis or sections of jatis have broken free from their village or other local cages to form large jati categories straddling large tracts of the country to better compete for such scarce resources as political power, economic opportunity, and education. Success in such efforts results in upward mobility for the jatis that come together. I termed this process "horizontal integration" (Srinivas 1996, p. 115). As political mobilization proceeds apace and more and more castes become aware of the opportunities available to them for securing scarce resources, competition among them will become even more fierce. Such competition offers a total contrast to the cooperation between jati sections living in a village, which so essential to producing the basic needs of the people. Indications are that this cooperation is likely to weaken further. However, with the emergence of large castes competing with one another to secure secular benefits, the weakening of purity-impurity ideas and, finally, the ideological rejection of hierarchy, both in the Constitution and by large sections of the people, all point to a systemic change. As caste as a system begins to break down, individual castes are likely to continue as they secure a variety of benefits for members in addition to giving themselves a sense of identity. As India becomes more urban and heterogeneity becomes the norm, ethnic—including caste—identities are likely to assume much greater importance.

VILLAGE STUDIES

Village studies became a major interest of anthropologists (and sociologists) in India in the 1950s. They greatly enlarged the field of anthropology, and anthropologists presented a more rounded picture of the peasant and his world, unlike other scholars who produced specialized but partial studies of agricultural practices and crop patterns, land tenure systems, subdivision and fragmentation of holdings and their effect on production, deleterious effects of the joint family system, wasteful expenditure at weddings and funerals, and slavery to custom. Again, unlike scholars in other disciplines, anthropologists spent long periods in villages learning the local language, winning the trust of the people, and confirming their facts by carrying out censuses and canvassing questionnaires when necessary. Among the more sensitive accounts of anthropologists there was an attempt to look at the world from the point of view of the villagers. However, what was happening in India was part of a worldwide phenomenon: As Raymond Firth has noted, "the vast middle ground of the peasantry, once the province of the economic historian, is almost overrun by students of modes of production, local and national collectivities, ideological systems, theories of exchange and the politics of reputation, religious movements and cults of saints" (Firth 1975, p. 7).

It is pertinent to note that India had begun to change fundamentally when anthropologists embarked on their intensive studies of villages and tribes. Their studies provide future historians of India with information of a depth and quality not available from any other source. Again, according to Firth, "the significance of anthropological field materials as historical record seems often to be undervalued. It may be that future generations of the peoples we have studied will prize our books, not for the brilliance of our theoretical analyses but for the honesty of our descriptive accounts of their society at a given period" (Firth 1975, p. 20).

Village studies also provided a unique window to the study of Indian civilization. For example, one of my interests when studying Rampura in 1948 was to obtain an accurate account of the ranking of local jatis. I found to my surprise, however, that the rank of each jati was not only not clear but was frequently a matter of dispute. The rank claimed for the jati by a member seemed to be at variance with the rank that a nonmember assigned to it. Further confusion was caused by the peninsular grouping of local jatis into right- and lefthand categories. The former regarded the latter as inferior. In the lefthand category was an artisan caste that wore the sacred thread and considered itself to be Brahmin, but its claim was not conceded by any righthand caste. One particular caste of Brahmins in southern Karnataka was regarded as so low that not even ex-Untouchables would accept cooked food or water from them.

In other words, ambiguity of rank is not confined only to the middle ranges of the system, as Louis Dumont has argued in *Homo Hierarchicus* (1971, p. 74, 78), but is pervasive. While there is no doubt whatsoever that caste represents a hierarchy, at the jati level at least, the rank-order is not clear and is the subject of contentious debate. It was only in the Vedic varna system, which comprised only four caste categories, that mutual rank was not only clear but immutable.

Faced with ambiguity in the ranking of jatis, I had to ask myself the reason behind it: While a clear-cut rank order assumes immutability, ambiguity is a precondition for mobility. What then were the sources of mobility in pre-British caste? A protean source was the pre-British political order, in which fluidity characterized the lower levels, providing opportunities for able and ambitious leaders of dominant castes to capture power during periods of political confusion, and then lay claim to Kshatriyahood. While the political order and opportunities for making wealth were both sources for mobility, Sanskritization provided both the idiom of mobility and its legitimization.

Clearly, then, there was dissonance between varna and jati, between the view of caste obtained from the sacred books and that from the field. I assumed dissonance between the "book view" and "field view" to extend to other institutions and areas, particularly when the books were normative in character. It is not unlikely that such dissonance is not confined to Indian civilization but extends to others as well, though it is probably greater in the former because of the unique character of Hinduism, which does not have a single scripture with overarching authority, one prophet, and one god. In the last 25 years or so, however, the book view has come back with a bang, and complementarity between the book view and field view is taken for granted, whereas it ought to be something to be proved in each empirical case.

THE STUDY OF SELF-IN-THE-OTHER

I am aware that I am an oddball among anthropologists in that all my fieldwork has been carried out in my own country. According to conventional wisdom, anthropology is the study of the Other, and it is widely believed that the study of one's own society is far more difficult than studying an alien society. Another linked proposition is that the study of an alien society enhances the anthropologist's understanding of his own society, if not himself. Finally, if one must study one's society at all, it should be undertaken when one is a seasoned anthropologist with one or two field studies of alien societies under his belt, not when one is a neophyte.

Edmund Leach has argued that the desire to study one's own society, while laudable, is "beset with hazards. Initial preconceptions are liable to prejudice the research in a way that does not affect the work of the naive stranger....[W]hen anthropologists study facets of their own society their vision seems to become distorted by prejudices which derive from private rather than public experience" (Leach 1982). In support of his argument Leach cites the work of four Chinese anthropologists. According to Leach himself, however, three were not studies of own society. The fourth study was by Fei Hsiao Tung, who spent two months (July and August 1936) in a village in the

Yangtze delta about 125 miles southwest of Shanghai. Leach wrote that "the merit of Fei's book lies in its functionalist style. Like all the best work done by social anthropologists it has at its core the very detailed study of the network of relationships operating within a single small-scale community. Such studies do not or should not claim to be 'typical' of anything in particular. They are not intended to serve as illustrations of something more general. And yet the best of such monographs despite the concentration upon a tiny range of human activity, will tell us more about the ordinary social behavior of mankind than a whole shelf-full of general textbooks labeled Introduction to Cultural Anthropology" (Leach 1982, pp. 124–27).

Fei was able to produce within two months a first-rate study of a village in South China, an enterprise that would have taken an outsider several years. Leach has thus contradicted his own thesis about the difficulty of studying one's own society. Was Leach even aware that he was contradicting his thesis?

When an Indian anthropologist is studying a group or community other than his own local group, he is undertaking a study that is both familiar and strange. Over millennia, Indian civilization has penetrated practically every corner of the country, and the influence of the epics, *Mahabharata* and *Ramayana,* has been ubiquitous (they have also influenced people living beyond South Asia). Indian culture, however, is also extraordinarily rich in diversity of all kinds, including regional, linguistic, religious, ethnic, and caste. Over millennia there have been innumerable movements of groups from one part of the country to another, adding to the diversity of each region. One's own backyard often displays such similarities as well as diversity. I once summarized this situation: "[A]s an over-protected Brahmin...boy growing up on College Road, I experienced my first culture shocks not more than fifty yards from the back wall of our house....[T]he entire culture of Bandikeri (the area behind our house where lived a colony of Shepherds, immigrants from their village, located a few miles from Mysore) was visibly and olfactorily different from that of College Road. Bandikeri was my Trobriand Islands, my Nuerland, my Navaho country and what have you. In retrospect it is not surprising that I became an anthropologist, all of whose fieldwork was in his own country" (Srinivas 1992, p. 141).

When an Indian anthropologist is studying a different caste or other group in India, he is studying someone who is both the Other and also someone with whom he shares a few cultural forms, beliefs, and values. That is, he is studying a self-in-the-Other and not a total Other, for both are members of the same civilization, which is extraordinarily complex, layered, and filled with conflicting tendencies.

I consider the study of one's own society not only feasible but essential, for it is best that a culture is studied by both outsiders and insiders. Alone, neither is complete. Each may have its own biases, but the two together may provide a more complete account. Given that anthropologists have no choice but to study other cultures through the prisms of their own, the need for anthropologists from at least two different cultures to study a single culture becomes a necessity. Anthropology has reached a state when such studies ought to be undertaken. The clash of multiple subjectivities would, to my mind, be better than a single subjectivity, whether that of the insider or outsider.

> **Visit the *Annual Reviews home page* at**
> **http://www.AnnualReviews.org.**

Literature Cited

Bateson G. 1936. *Naven: A Survey of the Problems Presented by a Composite Picture of the Culture of a New Guinea Tribe Drawn from Three Points of View.* Cambridge: Cambridge Univ. Press

Benedict R. 1934. *Patterns of Culture.* Boston: Houghton Mifflin

Burra N. 1996. Buddhism, conversion and identity: a case study of village Mahars. See Srinivas 1996, pp. 152–73

Dumont L. 1971. *Homo Hierarchus.* London: Wiedenfeld & Nicolson

Durkheim E. 1954. *The Elementary Forms of the Religious Life.* London: Allen & Unwin

Evans-Pritchard EE. 1937. *Witchcraft, Oracles and Magic Among the Azande.* London: Oxford Univ. Press

Evans-Pritchard EE. 1940. *The Nuer.* Oxford: Clarendon

Evans-Pritchard EE. 1951. *Social Anthropology.* London: Cohen & West

Evans-Pritchard EE. 1949. *The Sanusi of Cyrenaica.* Oxford: Clarendon

Evans-Pritchard EE. 1962. *Essays in Social Anthropology.* London: Faber & Faber

Firth R. 1975. An appraisal of modern social anthropology. *Annu. Rev. Anthropol.* 4: 1–25

Fortes M. 1955. Radcliffe-Brown's contributions to the study of social organization. *Br. J. Sociol.* 6:28–29

Fuller CJ. 1992. *The Camphor Flame: Popular Hinduism and Society in India.* Princeton, NJ: Princeton Univ. Press

Fustel de Coulanges ND. 1956. *The Ancient City: A Study on the Relation, Laws and Institutions of Greece and Rome.* New York: Doubleday Anchor Books

Ghurye GS. 1973. *I and Other Explorations.* Bombay: Popular Prakasan

Goody J. 1993. Meyer Fortes 1906–1983. *Proc. Br. Acad.* 80:283

Goody J. 1995. *The Expansive Moment: Anthropology in Britain and Africa 1918–1970.* Cambridge: Cambridge Univ. Press

Karanth GK. 1996. Caste in contemporary rural India. See Srinivas 1996, pp. 87–109

Leach E. 1982. *Social Anthropology.* New York: Oxford Univ. Press

Lowie RH. 1937. *The History of Ethnological Theory.* New York: Rinehart & company

New Shorter Oxford Dictionary. 1993. Oxford: Oxford Univ. Press

Radcliffe-Brown AR. 1933. *The Andaman Islanders.* London: Cambridge Univ. Press

Richter G. 1870. *Manual of Coorg: A Gazetteer.* Mangalore

Robertson Smith W. 1927. *Lectures on the Religion of the Semites—The Fundamental Institutions.* London: Black

Singer M. 1996. On the semiotics of ritual: Radcliffe-Brown's legacy. In *Social Structure and Change: Theory and Method,* ed. AM Shah, BS Baviskar, EA Ramaswamy pp. 20–54. New Delhi: Sage

Singer M. 1972. *When a Great Tradition Modernizes.* New York: Praeger

Srinivas MN. 1942. *Marriage and Family in Mysore.* Bombay: New Book

Srinivas MN. 1943. Some Tamil Folksongs—Part I. *J. Univ. Bombay* 7(1): 48–82

Srinivas MN. 1944. Some Tamil Folksongs—Part II. *J. Univ. Bombay* 7(4): 48–82

Srinivas MN. 1944. Some Telugu Folksongs—Part I. *J. Univ. Bombay* 8(1): 66–86

Srinivas MN. 1945. Some Telugu Folk-songs—Part II. *J. Univ. Bombay* 8(4): 15–30

Srinivas MN. 1952. *Religion and Society Among the Coorgs of South India.* Oxford: Clarendon

Srinivas MN. 1992. *On Living in a Revolution and Other Essays.* New Delhi: Oxford Univ. Press

Srinivas MN. 1955. The social system of a Mysore village. In *Village India: Studies in the Little Community,* ed. M Marriott, p.

31. Chicago: Univ. Chicago Press

Srinivas MN. 1994. *Caste in Modern India and Other Essays.* Bombay: Media Promot. Publ.

Srinivas MN. 1995. Sociology in Delhi. In *The Delhi School of Economics,* ed. D Kumar, D Mookherjee, pp. 31–52. New Delhi: Oxford Univ. Press

Srinivas MN, ed. 1996. *Caste: Its Twentieth Century Avatar.* New Delhi: Viking

von Fürer-Haimendorf C. 1943. *The Chenchus: Jungle Folk of the Deccan.* London: Macmillan

Annu. Rev. Anthropol. 1997. 26:25–46

MARX AND ANTHROPOLOGY

William Roseberry

Department of Anthropology, Graduate Faculty, New School for Social Research, New York, NY 10003; e-mail: roseberr@newschool.edu

KEY WORDS: theory, philosophy, history, political anthropology, materialism, capitalism

---

ABSTRACT

This essay explores the continuing relevance of Marx's work in anthropological theory by examining three dimensions of his thought, concentrating on a central text in each: historical materialism (*The German Ideology*), the analysis of capitalism (Volume 1 of *Capital*), and political analysis (*The Eighteenth Brumaire*). Each of these dimensions is related to present-day discussions in anthropological and social theory, but the emphasis remains on an interpretation of Marx's work.

INTRODUCTION

In his eleventh thesis on Feuerbach, Marx (1970a) claimed, "The philosophers have only *interpreted* the world, in various ways; the point is to *change* it" (p. 123). Today both ends of this thesis point to problems. Most marxist-inspired or -organized attempts to "change" the world have been discredited, and there are few activists who will now mount a political program in his name. Moreover, many scholars contend that a central reason for the failure of marxist-inspired attempts to change the world lies in marxist interpretations of it. That is, as an attempt to understand the making of the modern world, marxism was embedded within, and shared basic assumptions of, other modes of thought that interpreted the rise of capitalism. It was, in short, modernist, and it approached history and politics with a positivistic commitment to interpretive schemes that subsumed different societies and histories within a common overarching scheme—a grand or master narrative.

0084-6570/97/1015-0025$08.00

A central figure in this line of critique was Foucault (1980), who began with a rejection of what he called "global, *totalitarian theories*" (p. 80) (he mentioned specifically marxism and psychoanalysis) and counterposed what he called "local" and "subjugated" knowledges—knowledge of relations, struggles, and effects that are denied or suppressed by "totalitarian" theories. Such knowledge therefore undercuts or subverts the "tyranny of globalising discourses" (p. 83).

A consideration of the relevance of Marx's thought for anthropology must begin with a recognition of the political failure of most marxist-inspired movements and the influential intellectual critique that seems to speak to it. A radical disjuncture must also be recognized between the interpretive schemes of those marxisms that came to power and those of Marx himself. The criticism of "globalizing" or "totalizing" theories can more easily be leveled at these marxisms than at Marx himself. This is not to deny that elements in Marx's thought can be found to support the more closed, mechanical, and evolutionistic schemes that came to dominate marxist thought for much of this century. But Marx's thought was not a closed system, and he did not see the historical and materialist framework or outlook he devised in the 1840s as a universal scheme (or "master narrative") in terms of which a range of historical, political, and philosophical problems could be resolved. It contained inconsistencies and contradictions, and it was capable of development and modification through analysis and interpretation of particular events and processes. Indeed, Marx warned against the mechanical application of his ideas or the construction of grand historical schemes (e.g. Marx 1983, p. 136).

My aim in returning to some of Marx's texts is not to claim that there is nothing to criticize. Rather, I engage some of Marx's texts to suggest that he dealt creatively with a number of issues that remain active concerns in anthropological work, and that he proposed resolutions or modes of approach to some of those issues that continue to influence current thought. My strongest claim is that these ideas and modes of analysis deserve to be part of the discussion.

I develop this claim across three thematic areas, in each of which I concentrate on a central text: Marx's materialism (in which I consider *The German Ideology*), the analysis of capitalism (Volume 1 of *Capital*), and the historical and political surveys (*The Eighteenth Brumaire of Louis Bonaparte*). Unlike other commentaries on anthropology and Marx, I do not concentrate on anthropologists' subsequent appropriations of Marx or evaluate Marx's assertions in light of more recent anthropological understandings (see Bloch 1985; Donham 1990; Kahn & Llobera 1981; Sayer 1987, 1991; Vincent 1985; Wessman 1981). In each thematic area I deal with issues that have received anthropological attention, but the emphasis remains on the texts themselves.

HISTORICAL MATERIALISM

The Framework

In *The German Ideology,* Marx and Engels began not with nature or with material "conditions" but with a collectivity of humans acting in and on nature, reproducing and transforming both nature and material conditions through their actions (Marx & Engels 1970). The starting point of Marx's materialism was the social, conceived as material. Individuals within the social collectivity were seen as acting upon nature and entering into definite relations with each other as they did so, in providing for themselves. The process of provisioning was not limited to the problem of basic subsistence but to the reproduction of a "whole mode of life" (Marx & Engels 1970), taking Marx and Engels back to the specific collectivity of individuals with which they began. Yet the process of provisioning, of interacting with nature and individuals through labor, was seen to transform both nature and the collectivity of individuals.

Marx had emphasized that labor was organized by and in a specific, "empirically perceptible" (Marx & Engels 1970, p. 47) social collectivity. Thus labor as human process, the nature upon which humans acted, and the social collectivity that organized labor were historically situated and differentiated. Marx and Engels related all intellectual and philosophical problems to a material/productive history, and they moved quickly from a statement of philosophical principles to a discussion that would otherwise seem to be a diversion—a preliminary account of the history of forms of ownership and property (pp. 43–46). One finds, first, an emphasis on materiality in the form of transforming, creative labor, in specific conditions; second, a statement of the historicity of both the conditions and the labor; and, third, a referencing of all philosophical problems to this material history. As Marx expressed it, "The human essence is no abstraction inherent in each single individual. In its reality it is the ensemble of the social relations" (p. 122).

Thus a range of philosophical problems were given both practical and historical resolutions. There was little room in this framework for universal truths. The human essence Marx had earlier located—labor (see Marx 1964)—led in turn to an emphasis on historical difference, as particular modes of organizing and appropriating labor were seen as the *differentia specifica* of historical epochs. This philosophical stance required investigation of particular social collectivities and their modes of life, particular "ensembles of social relations," or particular forms of property in history. This was what *The German Ideology* proceeded to do.

Marx and Engels made a number of moves that were to influence their later work, as well as subsequent marxisms. First, their treatment of labor had various temporal dimensions. While one involved a long-term, epochal or evolutionary sweep across various forms of property broadly conceived, another involved a concentration on more specific forms and the processes of their reproduction or transformation (Marx & Engels 1970, pp. 62–63).

Second, as they considered long-term history, they emphasized two aspects that were to become central to most definitions of "modes of production": the productive forces (or the material conditions and instruments upon which and with which labor acts and is organized) and the "forms of intercourse" (or the ensemble of social relations through which labor is mobilized and appropriated, understood elsewhere as "relations of production"; pp. 86–87).

Third, their placement of philosophical issues within material and historical forms and processes led them to a clearly stated determinism (pp. 46–47). A number of deterministic statements were made in *The German Ideology,* from the general claim that social being determines social consciousness to strong claims of the material determination of the form of the state, ideas, and beliefs. Some of these statements can be read in terms of the polemical context in which the text was written, and the intellectual and political excitement the authors must have felt as they criticized and rejected a range of philosophical texts, experimented with a new form of materialism that seemed to undercut prior conceptions of materialism and idealism, and considered a range of historical, political, and philosophical projects their approach both required and made possible. There are, nonetheless, a number of problematic dimensions that require comment.

Nature

One of the strengths of the text is its historicization of "nature." Marx and Engels criticized the separation of nature and history, "as though these were two separate 'things' and man did not always have before him an historical nature and a natural history" (pp. 62, 63). Nonetheless, "always" had a more limited meaning for them than it should have. Thus, by the end of the passage in which they made this claim they had begun to retreat, envisioning a natural time before or outside of history—"except perhaps on a few Australian coral-islands of recent origin" (p. 63). Their exception gives pause, because it includes within the nature that preceded human history a social world, made natural.

Earlier, the implications of this exception were made clear when they presented a thumbnail sketch of forms of property (pp. 43, 44). Here one finds two kinds of naturalization that subsequent generations of anthropologists have effectively undercut: a first of "the tribe" and a second of "the family." In this early text, Marx and Engels were not radically historical enough in their consideration of the family.

"Ideological Reflexes and Echoes"

The basic framework itself can also be questioned. Consider the frequent references to "real premises" and "real individuals," which can be "verified in a purely empirical way." Or, in one of their most famous passages: "[W]e do not set out from what men say, imagine, conceive, nor from men as narrated, thought of, imagined, conceived, in order to arrive at men in the flesh. We set out from real, active men, and on the basis of their real life-process we demonstrate the development of the ideological reflexes and echoes of this life-process" (p. 47).

Here three elements of a necessary unity (what men say or imagine, how they are narrated, and men in the flesh) were separated, and one of those elements (men in the flesh) was treated as before the others. The central contribution of Marx's materialism was to stress that men as they imagine themselves and as narrated or imagined by others could not be separated from men in the flesh. The reverse point, however, can also be made against most materialisms: Men in the flesh cannot be separated from men as they imagine or are imagined. Sahlins (1976) criticized all philosophies that begin with practice for ignoring the mediation of a conceptual scheme. That is, all action occurs within, and is understandable in the context of, socially and culturally conditioned frames of reference. This does not necessarily mean, as Sahlins claimed, that a kind of priority needs to be reestablished, with "conceptual scheme" seen as superior to "action." The danger of any simple materialism that would assert the alternate priority (men in the flesh) is that its inadequacy in the face of both action and meaningful frameworks will almost require the assertion of a reverse priority (what men say, imagine, conceive).

. Similarly, the recent emphasis on the discursive constitution of the historical and social sciences has made students much more aware of how the objects of social scientific and historical inquiry are "constructed" through the process of investigation and, especially, the writing of texts. Here the emphasis shifts from what men say, imagine, and conceive to how they are narrated, imagined, and conceived by other "men," and how these narrations are shaped and constrained by literary, interpretive, and investigative conventions. This emphasis on how narrative and investigative conventions "constitute" certain objects of inquiry offers a necessary correction to naive empiricism. Yet the danger here, too, is that a kind of priority might be given to the narrative conventions of the texts, and the "real individuals" or "men in the flesh" will disappear.

Together, the twin emphases on conceptual scheme and narrative conventions undercut any materialism that takes as its basic premises "real individuals" in "purely empirical" relationships making "real history." "Real history" is made by men and women acting within and upon socially, politically, and culturally constituted relationships, institutions, and conventions, reproducing some and changing others. As they do so, they have certain understandings and images of who they are and what they are doing (Marx 1974b, p. 146). Similarly, "our" understanding of "their" history is constructed and conveyed in texts that emphasize certain "real individuals" and not others, or certain "purely empirical" relationships and actions and not others.

To the extent that the materialist method in *The German Ideology* calls up a naive realism or empiricism, it is untenable. Yet the text can also be read, more modestly, as claiming that imagination (conceptual scheme), narration (texts), and "real individuals" (or "men in the flesh") constitute an indissoluble unity. In this sense, the text offers a fundamental criticism both of the young Hegelians of the 1840s and much of the cultural anthropology of the 1980s and 1990s.

To say that these dimensions constitute a unity is not to say that they are indistinguishable. The three points of the Marx and Engels quote indicate three aspects of "real history," and the tension and relation among them needs to be maintained. Williams's emphasis on mutual construction, or the way in which language, for example, is both constituting and constituted, is important here. We could then revisit Sahlins's claim that all practice is mediated by conceptual scheme and argue that the conceptual scheme is itself shaped by action, by "real individuals" who live and act within an "ensemble of social relations." Similarly, we could accept the new historicists' emphasis on the narrative construction of history while insisting that there are definite limits to such construction and that those limits are created by "real individuals" and what they "say, imagine, conceive."

History and Evolution

There are two dimensions that are necessary for a claim of indissoluble unity: (*a*) a starting point in a social collectivity, made "material," and the specific "conditions" in which they live (including the "nature" they confront, the tools and instruments they use to work on them, the ensemble of social relations, institutions and relations of power, and the images and conceptions actors have of nature, instruments, ensembles, and institutions); and (*b*) a temporal dimension that stresses both the constitution of subjects within this complex of "conditions" and the formation of those "conditions" by generations of subjects.

This temporal dimension was emphasized by Marx himself. Yet there is a tension in Marx's work between two kinds of temporal dimension, both of which can be called "historical." Williams has usefully distinguished between "epochal" and "historical" analysis, the first characterizing long-term epochs in human history and the second examining particular societies at specific moments (Williams 1977, p. 121; cf White 1945). One could easily substitute the word "evolutionary" for "epochal" in that the temporal dimension involved is the *longue durée,* the succession of human epochs (such as feudalism or capitalism) in history and the analysis of their basic characteristics, structures, and dynamics. This evolutionary dimension is present in much of Marx's work (Marx 1970b, Marx & Engels 1970), conceived as a succession of modes of production.

Yet Marx also attended to historical analysis in the more specific and particular sense suggested by Williams. The two kinds of analysis must be distinguished; each is appropriate for different kinds of problem. Yet they are also interconnected. On one hand, most historical changes and processes are not part of epochal transformations, although our understanding of historical processes is enhanced by placing them within an epochal time and space. On the other hand, epochal transformations also, and always, take place in historical times and places, and proper understanding of the development of capitalism (say) requires detailed knowledge of complex and changing social fields in Leicester, Nottingham, Manchester, or Leeds—and Charleston, the Gold Coast, and Bombay.

THE ANALYSIS OF CAPITALISM

The Formal Analysis

Marx's method led him to concentrate on the organization, mobilization, and appropriation of labor. Class relations could be characterized according to an opposition between producers and nonproducers, and relations between them were based on the appropriation by nonproducers of a portion of the labor, or the surplus labor, of the producers. Different historical epochs and modes of production could be characterized according to different forms of appropriation and the property relations that made them possible (Marx 1967, pp. 791–92).

Given this general framework, Marx devoted most of his analysis to the inner workings of capitalism. In one sense, an epochal and definitional one, Marx's analysis in *Capital* can be quickly summarized. Capitalism depends, first, on a situation in which working people have been stripped of ownership or control of means of production (and stripped from a community of producers as well) and must work for wages to survive. Second, capitalism involves the accumulation of means of production in the hands of a few, who employ those means in production by hiring members of the propertyless mass. In short, capitalism depends on free wage labor.

In his analysis of capitalism, Marx critically engaged the literature of classical political economy, especially Smith, Ricardo, and Mill. Despite Smith's well-known emphasis on the "free hand" of competition, the classical economists were also concerned with the production and distribution of wealth among three classes (labor, capital, and landlords, which depended on three different sources of income: wages, profits, and rent). Where later economists began with exchange and circulation occurring in a world of asocial and classless individuals, the classical economists considered the production, distribution, and circulation of wealth in a differentiated social and political world.

Their theory of value was based on labor rather than the circulation of commodities among consumers. Although terminology differed among authors, the classical economists made a distinction between value and price, or between "natural" and "market" price. Value was seen as something that inhered in a commodity, around which market prices oscillate; value was determined in, and as a result of, production whereas price was determined in the market.

In this sense, Marx was a classical economist, working within while writing against the basic assumptions of the political economy of the day. This was most clear in the treatment of value and price, and the assumption that value was determined by the labor time that inhered in the commodity. While Marx shared the classical emphasis on production, however, he actually began *Capital* with commodities and the circulation of commodities (Marx 1977).

A commodity is defined by Marx as a product of human labor that can be alienated through a particular kind of exchange, in which one product of labor can be placed in quantitatively comparable relation to another product of labor. What makes commodities comparable in this sense is that both are products of human labor. While they are different as useful things, and may be valued differently by those individuals who use them, they have in common the fact that they are products of labor. To the extent that qualitatively different kinds of labor can be compared at all or made equivalent, in Marx's view (and that of classical political economy), they can be measured in terms of time—the average number of hours or days that go into making a particular commodity. Thus the value of a commodity is determined by the average "socially necessary" time that goes into its production.

A central task of the first section of *Capital* is to provide a formal analysis of the appropriation of labor under capitalism, using the assumptions of classical political economy. That is, if labor is the source of all value, and if commodities are purchased and sold at their values, how does profit emerge, and how is "surplus value" (appropriated by capital) created? Marx resolved this by introducing a distinction between labor power and labor: In the wage relation, capital purchased not labor but the worker's capacity to work, for a limited period. Capital then had use of that capacity, as actual labor, during which labor generated enough value to reproduce the cost of labor power plus additional ("surplus") value, which could be appropriated by the purchaser of the commodity labor power (that is, by capital). At a formal level, and within the assumptions of classical political economy, the production and appropriation of surplus value through the wage relation was "a piece of good luck for the buyer, but by no means an injustice towards the seller" (p. 301).

Questions Suggested by the Formal Analysis

Marx's framework suggests certain questions, only some of which were addressed by Marx himself. First, as he recognized, "exchange" value was not the only kind that one could discern in a product of human labor. There was also a subjective component in that products must be considered useful by the person purchasing or exchanging for them; they must satisfy a felt need. All commodities were therefore seen to have two kinds of value: use value (that is, they satisfy felt needs on the part of purchasers) and exchange value (that is, they are comparable in exchange as products of average quantities of human labor). Marx stressed that both aspects were necessary for a product of labor to be a commodity. On the one hand, not all kinds of useful products are commodities in that they never become alienable exchange values. They are produced for the use of those who have made them, or they change hands through mechanisms other than market exchange (gifts, tribute, etc). On the other hand, a product of human labor placed on the market must be considered useful by someone, or it fails as a commodity. Thus, for a product to have an exchange value, it must first be felt to be useful.

This apparently simple distinction raises a number of interesting dimensions for analysis, most of which Marx ignored. One is evolutionary, questioning the relationship between use values and exchange values (or use values and commodities) at various stages in human history before the dominance of capitalism (seen as a particular kind of commodity economy in which commodity exchanges have come to dominate all social relations). A related historical question concerns the relationship between capitalist and noncapitalist spheres in a world economy, and the flow of particular products between these spheres (use values in one sphere, commodities in the other), or the introduction of commodified relations and valuations in formerly noncommodified relations and valuations. Still another concerns the construction of felt needs, or the manipulation of "usefulness."

Each of these questions has received important attention (e.g. Collins 1990, Ohmann 1996, Palerm 1980, Taussig 1980, Trouillot 1988, Wolf 1982), and they remain central issues for most anthropological extensions of Marx's ideas toward an analysis of culture and power in capitalist as well as noncapitalist settings. That Marx chose to ignore these questions has nonetheless been the starting point for two contrasting, facile commentaries—one, written by critics of marxism suggesting that the fact that Marx neglected these questions invalidates marxism as a whole, and the other, written by the watchdogs of orthodoxy, contending that because Marx did not address these questions they lay outside the domain of marxian inquiry altogether.

Another question concerns the reduction of qualitatively distinct kinds of human labor to the common denominator of measurable time, which requires a number of historical processes with cultural effects. A central transformation is in the understanding of time itself; a second is in the reduction of qualitatively different thought and work processes to a number of relatively simple and common operations that can be performed across various branches of human activity [what a later literature has called "deskilling" (Braverman 1975)]; another concerns the loss of control over the work process, and the means of production, by people performing the basic work of production. For most of human history, working people did not live and work under such circumstances. The development of capitalism involves, in part, a transformation of work and the conditions of work that includes these three dimensions, all of which are necessary for the imposition of a new kind of work discipline and control. The imposition of discipline, in turn, is necessary for the rational calculation and comparison of different labors in terms of a common, "socially necessary" standard.

Marx recognized this, though he had little to say about time, and he stressed the historical uniqueness of capitalism and of the concepts useful for the analysis of capitalism. Following this line of reasoning, the labor theory of value could only be relevant under capitalism, in a situation in which qualitatively different kinds of labor have been reduced, socially and economically, to a common standard (Marx 1977, pp. 152, 168).

Historical Analysis

On the basis of the formal analysis of the wage relation, Marx pursued a range of economic implications. But formal analysis also made possible and required historical and political commentaries and investigations. That is, having pursued the theory of value in a fictitious world of commodity producers and merchants in which all transactions are fairly conducted among equals, Marx arrived at a social world divided between two classes, in which a uniquely positioned commodity was offered for sale on the market. On the one hand, remaining within the confines of value theory and a fictitious world of equality and equity, he said the fact that one of those classes appropriates the value produced by the other class was "by no means an injustice." Yet several hundred pages later, he returned to a more evaluative mode and condemned an economic system that makes, "an accumulation of misery a necessary condition, corresponding to the accumulation of wealth" (Marx 1977, p. 799). The movement from the one view to the other can only be understood by recognizing that Marx placed the historical and political development of capitalist social relations at the center of his analysis, not as a mere appendage to a more rigorous and logically satisfying formal analysis.

The first move toward history came when Marx postulated a new kind of commodity, labor power. As Marx noted, however, this commodity does not exist in nature; it is produced, under specific conditions. For labor power to exist as a commodity, it must be "free" to be sold, in two senses. First, the person who possesses the capacity to work (the laborer) must be free to sell it on a limited, contractual basis to the possessor of capital. That means he or she must not be encumbered by ties of bondage or slavery that restrict his or her independent action on the market. Second, he or she must have been "freed" from ownership or control of means of production, and from participation in a community of producers, and must therefore sell his or her capacity to work to survive.

Marx insisted that most working people in human history have not been "free" in this dual sense and have therefore not been in a position to sell their capacity to work, a necessary condition for capitalist social relations. In *Capital* and elsewhere, he pursued two kinds of retrospective analysis to stress the uniqueness of capitalism and the commodity form of labor power. One, which we might call epochal, looked to prior modes of organizing and mobilizing labor. At various points in *Capital,* he briefly pointed to earlier forms (pp. 169–75; see also Marx 1973, 1989). Second, in an analysis we can call historical, Marx examined the proletarianization of peasants in England through the enclosure movements (Marx 1977, part 8). Here, his aim was to show that force was required, and we are far removed from the formal analysis with which *Capital* began.

Another occasion for historical and political analysis was provided by the relationship between capital and labor (as classes, rather than as political economic categories) over the level of surplus value. Marx first presented surplus value as a category, and as an unproblematic sum appropriated by capital. He soon emphasized that it points to a relationship marked by negotiation and struggle. Marx made a distinction between absolute and relative surplus value, suggesting that there are two ways in which capital can increase the amount of surplus value it captures in the production process. The first, assuming a constant level of productivity and rate of surplus value, increases the amount of surplus value by lengthening the working day, or the period of time living labor can be used when the commodity—labor power—has been purchased. Assuming here that the value of labor power is recovered in the same amount of time, increasing the amount of work increases the quantity of surplus value. This method appropriates and increases absolute surplus value. Relative surplus value, alternatively, increases the rate of surplus value appropriation, lowering the portion of the working day required to recover the value invested in labor power. This can be done by increasing productivity, or by cheapening the value of labor power itself.

All these issues push Marx toward history. In his consideration of absolute surplus value, he examined the history of English legislation and agitation over the length of the working day. In his discussion of relative surplus value, he moved toward a history of English industrialization and an examination of work and health conditions in English mills, especially with the employment of women and children. In this, he focused primarily on increasing productivity and (with one important exception) did not pay much attention to mechanisms by means of which the value of labor power itself could be decreased.

This remains a rich area for analysis, however. Marx had stressed that the value of labor power did not represent a bare subsistence minimum but a level that was historically and culturally determined. The level of subsistence, then, is subject to a different kind of historical process and political struggle than that associated with the expropriation of peasants from the land. Changing working-class diets could cheapen the value of labor power (Thompson 1966, pp. 319–49; Mintz 1985).

Population Dynamics

Finally, Marx linked demographic structure and dynamics to the historical and cultural determination of the value of labor power. He claimed that population growth was not subject to natural or universal laws but that each mode of production produced its own laws of population (Marx 1977, p. 784). This in itself is not surprising from an author who explicitly rejected any sort of abstract, universal "laws" or dynamics. The historically specific "laws" he pointed to here do not develop mechanically but through the action of human agents. That is, he indicated certain characteristic relationships under capitalism and explored the ways in which people might act within these relationships.

With regard to population dynamics under capitalism, Marx stressed that capitalist production occurs within social spaces that include what we might call structural centers and peripheries: active mills and mines that regularly employ workers but do not regularly employ the same numbers of workers. In economic cycles of boom and bust, they sometimes employ relatively more, sometimes employ relatively fewer. The working population is divided into segments composed of those who are routinely employed across economic cycles, those who are routinely not employed across economic cycles, and those who are sometimes employed, sometimes underemployed, and sometimes unemployed. The second and third groups compose what Marx called a "disposable industrial reserve army" (p. 784), which he divided into various segments. The first he called the "floating" reserve army, composed of proletarianized workers who are alternately employed and unemployed. Their labor power is a commodity, but they have difficulty selling it on a routine basis. The second is the "latent," composed of people who are not employed but also not unemployed. That is, they may be independent producers (e.g. in agriculture) who have not been proletarianized (or whose labor power is not a commodity) who may become proletarianized and employed as part of the general expansion of capitalist production. The third, the "stagnant," is composed of people who have been proletarianized but who find employment with difficulty, workers who have been passed over ("have become redundant," p. 796) by the social and technological development of capitalism. The dynamic relation between the employed and unemployed across economic cycles serves as a check on the activities of laborers and can decrease the value of labor power.

This model remains a suggestive source for historical and anthropological analysis. When one considers the kinds of ethnic, racial, and gendered markers through which such human segments are created in any social setting, for example, we see that Marx's model went well beyond a simple two-class model. Students fascinated by the recent emergence of flexible labor schemes and who think that this marks a "postmodern" world that is also "postcapitalist" would do well to read this brief section of *Capital* (pp. 781–802). Indeed, Harvey's (1989, pp. 150–55) analysis of sectorial distinctions among the workforce under flexible accumulation is explicitly indebted to Marx's treatment. Scholars on both sides of a growing employment crisis in the academy (those with jobs and those without, those with tenure and those without) might find insight here as well (Roseberry 1996).

Critical Reflections

Reading *Capital* critically, one notices, first, the narrowing of his approach to labor. While the early Marx saw labor as human essence and criticized an economic process that channeled workers into specialized, repetitive tasks, thus only partially developing a fuller human capacity, *Capital* concentrates on labor primarily in its relationship to capital. Marx was also exclusively concerned with "productive" labor, in the language and assumption of classical political economy, leaving aside other kinds of labor that fell "outside the domain of political economy" (Collins 1990, Marx 1964, Sayer 1991, Young et al 1981).

There is, further, the question of what kind of sociological work the analysis in *Capital* can, and cannot, be made to do. Marx claimed that the manner in which surplus labor is pumped out of direct producers "reveals the innermost secret" of the social structure (Marx 1967, p. 791). While this "secret" provided the basis of a powerful analysis of fundamental relationships and processes under capitalism, the "secret" of a social structure cannot stand in for an adequate description of it. For this we need much more specification and detail.

We might therefore return to *Capital* and ask what has been left out. All that was specified was a relationship between capital and labor power. At a structural level alone, much more specification is necessary. Beginning with the "nonproducer," or capital, end of the bipolar model, we find a mechanism for the production of surplus value, and an indication of its conversion into "capital." But surplus value is sectorially subdivided into, say, industrial, merchant, financial, and landed capitals, which figure both in the distribution and production of value. At the least, these are tied to different social and spatial configurations, material interests and projects, and so on. Similar differences concern small and large capitals, or regional and sectorial hierarchies. At the "direct producer," or labor, end, we need a more expansive conception of labor, one not wedded to the classical economists' distinction between productive and unproductive labor. We should consider as well a variety of differences among workers—skilled and unskilled, employed and unemployed, male and female, adult and child, old and young. Marx provided a basis for such analysis in his model of the relative surplus population under capitalist accumulation. But the divisions among floating, latent, and stagnant sections of the "reserve army of labor" need to be fit within regional, spatial and social hierarchies. We need also to see how ethnic, racial, or gendered labels are assigned—socially and politically—to these sections. In short, a thick sociology and history can, and must, be built up on the "innermost secret" of the relationship between capital and labor.

THE HISTORICAL AND POLITICAL SURVEYS

The Texts

A number of essays develop Marx's methodological framework for more straightforward historical analysis. In these surveys, Marx did not attempt to force recalcitrant events and movements into a preconceived and formulaic model or grand narrative. He applied a materialist conception to these events and movements, posing questions about class formation, structure, and interests, the position of various groups in relation to each other structurally, spatially, and historically, and the structure and role of states. He also attended to less predictable issues such as individual careers and strategies, parliamentary debates and party platforms, and the texts of constitutions.

The surveys include *Class Struggles in France* (1974a), *The Eighteenth Brumaire of Louis Bonaparte* (1974b), *The Civil War in France* (1934), and a number of brief pieces written about the peasant commune in Russia and its fate in the aftermath of an agrarian reform (Shanin 1983). Some preliminary observations concerning the surveys are necessary. First, they cover the entire period of Marx's writing career. The first two were written during and immediately after the mid-century European revolutions, the last two during the last 12 years of his life. *The Civil War* was a response to the Paris commune of 1871, and the discussions of Russian peasantries, written shortly before his death, were a response to inquiries from and a debate among Russian activists about the revolutionary potential of the *mir,* or peasant commune. The middle decades of his writing life were dominated by the work on *Capital,* but even here he attended to specific historical and political issues in England, Germany, France, India, and the United States.

Second, the surveys directly responded to the imperative of the eleventh thesis on Feuerbach in that they were commentaries on and attempts to shape the direction of movements to "change [the world]." They, more than the general methodological essays or even *Capital,* constitute the most important texts in which to evaluate the philosopher who hoped both to understand and change the world he encountered.

Here a remarkable aspect of these surveys is how little they respond to or reflect a "grand narrative." This is most clearly seen in his discussion of Russian peasantries. Marx was asked his view on a debate among Russian activists about the specific history of Russia in relation to the more general history of world capitalism. Reflecting the evolutionist spirit of the time, one group (hoping to monopolize the claim to "marxism") contended that Russia would have to recapitulate the history of western European capitalism, that the Russian peasantry would have to suffer a process of "primitive accumulation," and that Russia would have to enter a long "stage" of capitalism before entering a socialist future. Their opponents saw in the commune a possible cell form for a future socialist society. They hoped Russia could avoid capitalism altogether and that the commune would serve as the social bridge that would make this possible.

Marx's attempts to respond gave little comfort to either group. With regard to the first, he rejected any evolutionist understanding of world history or capitalist development, calling such schemes "supra-historical" attempts to find a universal master-key (Marx 1983, Shanin 1983). The populists' position, however, was both evolutionist (the question had to do with skipping stages, not rejecting stage schemes altogether) and romantic, in that their vision of the commune removed it from its specific history and structural relations to landlords, merchants, and the Russian state. Marx turned his attention to these questions, producing a more detailed and realistic account of late-nineteenth-century Russian peasants.

The Eighteenth Brumaire

In *The Eighteenth Brumaire,* instead of the two great classes Marx and Engels had postulated in theory (capital and labor), there are a number of historically and politically specific class fractions. There is also an analysis of a particular spatial and political constellation of classes and class fractions, within Paris and between Paris and the rest of the country. Moreover, we find a detailed narrative analysis of a specific political process—the 1848 Revolution and subsequent processes of reaction, state formation, and petty and personal intrigue. I consider three dimensions of this survey: his approach to the French state, his understanding of the peasantry, and his use of class analysis.

Marx's analysis of the French state was complex. It included an attempt to understand politics in terms of the actions, interests, and strategies of classes, and he claimed that one can discern certain kinds of material interest behind more flowery claims of principle and program. But he also saw important gaps between interest and program. One gap occurred in the separation of the bourgeoisie (or particular fractions thereof) and its parliamentary representatives, who, in addition to representing broader class interests, pursued their own careers and strategies. The postulation of a "republican faction of the bourgeoisie" (1974b, p. 157), then, provided an analytic bridge for the representation of certain class interests in parliamentary debates and processes, but it also introduced the possibility of tensions and contradictions between factions, in which general class interests would be badly represented or sacrificed.

He also explored the structural relationship between state and society in France, arguing for what later generations would call the "relative autonomy" of the state (p. 238). Surveying the structure of the French state from the Old Regime through the Revolution of 1789 to the Revolution of 1848, Marx saw continuity. Despite major economic and social upheavals, state institutions remained intact and became more ramified and developed over time. Thus the state became a growing power in and over society. It was not simply an inert set of institutions to be captured by a particular class so that the state might serve that class's interests. Instead, the state, and the people who staffed it across revolutionary upheavals, might have their own interests not reducible to those of any particular class. The French state, then, was "a frightful parasitic body, which surrounds the body of French society like a caul and stops up all its pores." In it, "[e]very *common* interest was immediately detached from society, opposed to it as a higher, *general* interest, torn away from the self-activity of the individual members of society and made a subject for governmental activity, whether it was a bridge, a schoolhouse, the communal property of a village community, or the railways, the national wealth and the national university of France" (pp. 237–38).

Marx, however, also observed that the French state "does not hover in mid-air" (p. 238). By 1852 it was grounded in, and enjoyed the support of, the peasantry. We here encounter some of Marx's most often quoted and least understood claims. The French peasantry, in his view, constituted an "immense mass" of similarly structured but socially isolated households; they could only be considered as a group "by the simple addition of isomorphous magnitudes, much as potatoes in a sack form a sack of potatoes." Moreover, in analyzing them politically, he considered two questions: whether they shared common material interests, and whether their common interests promoted the formation of a political organization or shared "feeling of community" (p. 239). Finding common interest but no possibility of community, he concluded that the peasants were "incapable of asserting their class interest in their own name," and: "They cannot represent themselves; they must be represented" (p. 239). Their representative in 1852 was Bonaparte himself, a strong executive power before whom "all classes fall on their knees, equally mute and equally impotent, before the rifle butt" (p. 236).

To these claims, two kinds of question might be posed. One deals with them as historical analysis: Is this an adequate account and interpretation of the positions and roles of French peasants in the Revolution of 1848 and its aftermath? A second treats them as epochal analysis: Is this Marx's view of the positions and roles of peasants in revolutionary movements in general? Unfortunately, generations of marxists subjected the passage (along with his analysis of the state) to a systematic, epochal misreading. In this misreading, Marx was examining not the French state or the French peasantry, but "the" state and "the" peasantry in general.

Yet in Marx's discussion, the references were specific and historical. Marx moved from his general observation regarding the French peasants as a sack of potatoes to a discussion of concrete issues: the creation of small proprietorship as a result of the Revolution of 1789, and then the experience of "two generations" of peasants in the face of exactions placed on their parcels—mortgages imposed by urban merchants and creditors, and taxes imposed by the state. The "immense mass" of households, as "isomorphous magnitudes," was a relatively recent political product, which had as one consequence the creation of a class (in one sense) of producers with none of the mediating institutions, either of community or of aristocracy, that had characterized the Old Regime (p. 243).

Critical Reflections

This, in turn, raises a final question concerning *The Eighteenth Brumaire,* one that points toward a critical assessment. Throughout the text, Marx pursued a class analysis that took him in at least two different directions. First, he interpreted political positions and programs in terms of material interests. In discussing the division between the Orleanist and Bourbon royal houses, he linked the two factions to two different forms of property—capital and landed property. He contended further that the passions these groups brought to politics—their "old memories, personal enmities, fears and hopes, prejudices and illusions, sympathies and antipathies, convictions, articles of faith and principles" (p. 173)—were only their imagined starting points of activity. One could find the "real" starting points in "the division between their interests" (p. 174).

This claim needs to be placed next to Marx's discussion of the French peasantry as a class, in which he posed two questions—one concerning the peasantry's positions and material interests in relation to other classes, the other concerning the peasantry's (lack of a) feeling of community. In his earlier discussion of class and politics, he did not ask the second question and concentrated on the first. Yet it is interesting that in both cases he referred to certain "feelings"—"modes of thought and views of life" in one case, and feelings "of community" in the other. He recognized that these were separate from, and in many ways counter to, the class interests and identifications he posited. But in one case he dismissed them as "illusions" or imagined starting points of activity; in the other he saw the "feeling of community" as necessary for the very definition of a class.

Marx was outlining the basis for two distinct forms of class analysis, then, one that would separate "real," material interests from imagined (implicitly false) ones, and the other that might take the cultural construction of community as a central problem for class analysis. Yet the second remained little more than a suggestion, picked up by a later marxist tradition (Thompson 1966, 1978). The first undergirded most of Marx's analysis in *The Eighteenth Brumaire* and had a dominant influence on the later development of marxisms. Despite the move from a two-class model toward one that saw several class fractions in a particular social and political space, the definition of class was tied to material interest, and the "tradition and upbringing" of individuals and groups were relegated to the secondary realm of illusion.

This ignored the materiality of "tradition and upbringing," and even of "memories, personal enmities, fears and hopes, prejudices and illusions,"

along lines suggested above (pp. 7–10). Here three dimensions require emphasis. The first concerns the social formations and communities through which
individuals and collectivities identify themselves as subjects (e.g. as "proletarians," "cobblers," "tailors"; or as "Parisians" or "the people"; as "peasants"
or "Burgundians"; and so on). It is interesting to note, for example, that French
working people had only begun to see and organize themselves as a working
class with the Revolution of 1848. Earlier, they had grouped themselves by
particular and separate trades (Sewell 1983). Second, just as these modes of association and identity are material, they are also formed in fields of power, including state power. Third, the formation of individuals, as subjects, in relation
to particular communities, modes of identity, and material interest will often
involve multiple sites and modes of distinction (Althusser 1971, Laclau &
Mouffe 1985).

CONCLUSION

Among the many marxisms that have laid claim to Marx's work, two grand traditions can be delineated: one that makes Marx's framework a science of society and history, positing an evolutionary teleology; and another that uses a historical materialist framework to grasp both the "innermost secret" of social
structures in terms of the appropriation of labor and the specific structured
constellations of power that confront working people in particular times and
places (Roseberry 1993, p. 341; Thompson 1978, pp. 188–90). The first can be
unproblematically subsumed within a wider range of evolutionary philosophies of the nineteenth and twentieth centuries. The second remains a valuable
and creative tradition despite the political defeat of the first tradition. Indeed,
that political defeat might be considered a condition of possibility for the further development of the second.

Stripped of evolutionist "grand narratives," Marx's work stands in critical
relation to much that is now dominant in social theory. It is, first, materialist, in
its broad assumption that social being determines social consciousness and its
more specific assertion that the forms and relations through which humans
produce their livelihoods constitute fundamental, and determining, relations in
society. It is, second, realist, in its confidence that these forms and relations
have a material existence and can be described and understood in thought and
text. It is, third, structural, in that it envisions these forms and relations as consolidated over time in classes, powers, and institutions. Fourth, among the
most important structures Marx analyzed are those of class. Fifth, he saw these
institutions exercising a determining influence over human action. This does
not mean that Marx ignored the transforming capacities of human action: aside
from the opening passage of *The Eighteenth Brumaire* or the eleventh thesis on

Feuerbach, a confidence in such transforming capacities infused his work. He nonetheless saw the real, material structures he had delineated as exerting a shaping power over, and setting limits upon, human action.

Marx's understanding of power is worth some concluding comment. While I have contended that recent readers have been wrong to place Foucault, say, and Marx on different sides of a philosophical divide because of the former's search for local knowledges and the latter's faith in grand narratives, their understandings of power were starkly different. Foucault was therefore correct to identify Marx as one of the influential thinkers who thought of power as concentrated in particular structural or institutional locations or centers. Marx would almost certainly have rejected Foucault's emphasis on a more diffuse and "capillary" understanding of power; he might even have suggested that Foucault's was the more "global, totalitarian theor[y]" (Foucault 1980, p. 80). Yet I wish to conclude not by pointing out obvious differences and then taking sides but by indicating ways in which these different positions can speak to, and "supplement" (Dirks et al 1994), gaps or weaknesses in other positions.

Of critical importance in Foucault's work was his concentration on the formation of certain kinds of subjects within and by regimes and rituals of rule (Althusser 1971; Corrigan & Sayer 1985; Foucault 1982, 1991; Laclau & Mouffe 1985). This is missing in most of Marx's discussions of class, as we have seen, leading him to ignore both the materiality and power dimensions in other modes of association and community. Here Foucault's more complex model of power, permeating a range of institutions and relationships, with multiple sites and modalities, is important.

Yet it is here that Marx remains insightful and important. Clearly one does not want to resort to a simple power grid, akin to a corporate or military hierarchy. But by placing power in specific locations, he also understood that it is limited and subject to change, even as his political surveys emphasized the overwhelming resistance of, say, the state to change despite other kinds of social transformation and revolution (see Corrigan & Sayer 1985). It is in this sense, above all, that Marx's thought resisted becoming a "totalizing" or "totalitarian" theory, and it is here that his own writings nurtured a critical tradition that undercut official marxisms.

Literature Cited

Althusser L. 1971. Ideology and ideological
state apparatuses (notes toward an investi-
gation). In Lenin and Philosophy and
Other Essays, pp. 127–86. New York/Lon-
don: Monthly Review
Bloch M. 1985. Marxism and Anthropology.
Oxford/New York: Oxford Univ. Press
Braverman H. 1975. Labor and Monopoly
Capital. New York: Monthly Review
Collins J. 1990. Unwaged labor in compara-
tive perspective: recent theories and unan-
swered questions. In Work Without Wages,
ed. J Collins, M Gimenez, pp. 3–24. Al-
bany: State Univ. NY Press
Corrigan P, Sayer D. 1985. The Great Arch:
English State Formation as Cultural Revo-
lution. Oxford: Blackwell
Dirks N, Eley G, Ortner S. 1994. Introduction.
In Culture/Power/History: A Reader in
Contemporary Social Theory, ed. N Dirks
et al, pp. 3–45. Princeton, NJ: Princeton
Univ. Press
Donham D. 1990. History, Power, Ideology:
Central Issues in Marxism and Anthropol-
ogy. Cambridge/New York: Cambridge
Univ. Press
Fernbach D, ed. 1974. Karl Marx: Surveys
from Exile. Political Writings, Vol. II.
New York: Vintage
Foucault M. 1980. Power/Knowledge. New
York: Pantheon
Foucault M. 1982. The subject and power. In
Michel Foucault: Beyond Structuralism
and Hermeneutics, ed. HL Dreyfus, P Ra-
binow, pp. 208–26. Chicago: Univ. Chi-
cago Press
Foucault M. 1991. Governmentality. In The
Foucault Effect: Studies in Governmental-
ity, ed. G Burchell, Gordon C Miller, pp.
87–104. Chicago: Univ. Chicago Press
Harvey D. 1989. The Condition of Postmoder-
nity. Oxford/Cambridge: Blackwell
Kahn J, Llobera J, eds. 1981. The Anthropol-
ogy of Pre-Capitalist Societies. London:
Macmillan
Laclau E, Mouffe C. 1985. Hegemony and So-
cialist Strategy. London: Verso
Marx K. 1934. The Civil War in France. Chi-
cago: Kerr
Marx K. 1964. The Economic and Philosophi-
cal Manuscripts. New York: International
Marx K. 1967. Capital, Vol. 3. New York: In-
ternational
Marx K. 1970a. Theses on Feuerbach. See
Marx & Engels 1970, pp. 121–23
Marx K. 1970b. Preface. In A Contribution to

the Critique of Political Economy, ed. M
Dobb, pp. 19–23. New York: International
Marx K. 1973. Grundrisse. New York: Pen-
guin
Marx K. 1974a. Class struggles in France. See
Fernbach 1974, pp. 35–142
Marx K. 1974b. The Eighteenth Brumaire of
Louis Bonaparte. See Fernbach 1974, pp.
143–249
Marx K. 1977. Capital, Vol. 1. New York:
Vintage
Marx K. 1983. Letter to the Editorial Board of
Otechestvennye Zapiski. See Shanin 1983,
pp. 134–37
Marx K. 1989. Pre-Capitalist Economic For-
mations. New York: International
Marx K, Engels F. 1970. The German Ideol-
ogy, ed. CJ Arthur. New York: Interna-
tional
Mintz S. 1985. Sweetness and Power. New
York: Viking/Penguin
Ohmann R. 1996. Selling Culture. London/
New York: Verso
Palerm A. 1980. Antropologia y Marxismo.
Mexico City: Nueva Imagen
Roseberry W. 1993. Beyond the agrarian ques-
tion in Latin America. In Confronting His-
torical Paradigms, by F Cooper, A Isaac-
man, F Mallon, W Rosemerry, S Stern, pp.
318–68. Madison: Univ. Wis. Press
Roseberry W. 1996. The unbearable lightness
of anthropology. Radic. Hist. Rev. 65:5–25
Sahlins M. 1976. Culture and Practical Rea-
son. Chicago: Univ. Chicago Press
Sayer D. 1987. The Violence of Abstraction.
Oxford/New York: Blackwell
Sayer D. 1991. Capitalism and Modernity: An
Excursus on Marx and Weber. London/
New York: Routledge
Sewell W. 1983. Work and Revolution in
France. Cambridge/New York: Cam-
bridge Univ. Press
Shanin T, ed. 1983. Late Marx and the Russian
Road: Marx and "The Peripheries of
Capitalism." New York: Monthly Review
Taussig M. 1980. The Devil and Commodity
Fetishism in South America. Chapel Hill:
Univ. N. C. Press
Thompson EP. 1966. The Making of the Eng-
lish Working Class. New York: Vintage
Thompson EP. 1978. The Poverty of Theory
and Other Essays. New York: Monthly
Review
Trouillot MR. 1988. Peasants and Capital.
Baltimore/London: Johns Hopkins Univ.
Press

Vincent J. 1985. Anthropology and Marxism: past and present. *Am. Ethnol.* 12:137–47

Wessman J. 1981. *Anthropology and Marxism*. Cambridge: Schenkman

White L. 1945. History, evolutionism, and functionalism: three types of interpretation of culture. *Southwest. J. Anthropol.* 1: 221–48

Williams R. 1977. *Marxism and Literature.* New York/Oxford: Oxford Univ. Press

Wolf E. 1982. *Europe and the People Without History.* Berkeley: Univ. Calif. Press

Young K, Walkowitz C, McCullagh R. 1981. *Of Marriage and the Market.* London: CSE Books

Annu. Rev. Anthropol. 1997. 26:47–71

RELIGIOUS LANGUAGE

Webb Keane

Department of Anthropology, University of Pennsylvania, Philadelphia,
Pennsylvania 19104

KEY WORDS: text and context, intentionality, agency, interaction, language ideology

---

ABSTRACT

The effort to know and interact with an otherworld tends to demand highly marked uses of linguistic resources. In contrast to less marked speech situations, in religious contexts the sources of words, as well as the identity, agency, authority, and even the very presence of participants in an interaction, can be especially problematic. Different religious practices alter any of a variety of formal and pragmatic features of everyday language in response to their distinctive assumptions about the world, otherworlds, and the beings they contain. These practices are also mediated by speakers' assumptions about the nature and workings of language. Because such assumptions bear on the presumed nature of human and nonhuman subjects, religious debates often dwell on details of verbal and textual practice. The study of religious language touches on more general problems concerning relations among performance, text, and context. It also reveals chronic tensions between transcendence and the situated nature of practices, with implications for the nature of agency and belief.

RELIGION AND MARKED LANGUAGE PRACTICES

Religion, according to William James (1902; cf Wallace 1966, p. 52), is founded on the subjective experience of an invisible presence. A similar assumption seems to underlie EB Tylor's assertion that prayers begin as spontaneous utterances and degenerate into traditional formulas (Tylor 1873, p. 371). An approach, however, to the study of religion that begins with subjective experience encounters certain difficulties. One is epistemological, because the observer can only have access to other people's experiences and beliefs through objective manifestations. The difficulty, however, is due not only to the skepticism or positivism of the outsider. To presume that religious practice derives from prior experiences or beliefs is to play with theologically loaded dice. An emphasis on subjective experience involves

47

presuppositions and entailments that are not shared by all religious traditions (Asad 1993). Moreover, concrete activities such as speaking, chanting, singing, reading, writing—or their purposeful suppression—can be as much a condition of possibility for the experience of the divine as a response to it (Ferguson 1985). This can be especially evident, for instance, in the context of proselytization and conversion, in which language may help make the supernatural believable (Harding 1987) or induce certain religious dispositions in the worshiper (Rafael 1992, cf Foucault 1980). In general, analytic approaches that stress the public rather than the subjective character of culture (Rappaport 1979, Schieffelin 1985, Urban 1991) are also likely to concur with Clifford Geertz's observation that it is "out of the context of concrete acts of religious observance that religious conviction emerges on the human plane" (1973, pp. 112–13).

Religious observance tends to demand highly marked and self-conscious uses of linguistic resources. In this article [bear in mind that the analytic coherence, discreteness, and universality of the category religion are problematic (Asad 1993)], religious language will be provisionally defined in terms of the perceived distinctiveness of certain interactions, textual practices, or speech situations. To the extent that participants consider religious language different from everyday speech, this distinctiveness seems to respond to some of the common semiotic and pragmatic questions they face: By what means can we, and in what manner ought we, talk with invisible interlocutors? How can we get them to respond? How should we talk about them? By what marks do we know that some words originate from divine sources? Are these words true, fitting, efficacious, or compelling in some special way? These questions touch on more general problems concerning the relations among performance, text, and context. They also involve the relations among experience, concrete practices, and what is culturally construed to lie beyond ordinary experience, whether that be in the past, the future, at a spatial distance, or across an ontological divide. The problems of communication between this world and another, or of handling authoritative words derived from distant sources, are critical to many religious practices: Not only do they impose special semiotic difficulties on human practitioners, but their language must sometimes contend with the fact that the very presence of the deity, spirits, or ancestors cannot be taken for granted.[1]

[1]This review is confined largely to issues that have been raised in empirical studies of the role of language in religious practice. I have written little about the extensive literature on belief statements, the logic of religious discourse, myth, hermeneutics and scriptural interpretation, conversion narratives, feminist critiques of religious rhetoric, or the more scattered discussions of oaths, blessings, and uses of writing as material artifact. The review also does not address research at the intersection between language and music. It does, however, cast the net broadly to include practices such as divination and so-called "magic," which some definitions of religion exclude (often on theologically parochial and historically shifting grounds). Throughout, citations are limited to works available in English.

Language is one medium by which the presence and activity of beings that are otherwise unavailable to the senses can be made presupposable, even compelling, in ways that are publically yet also subjectively available to people as members of social groups. However, no single set of formal or pragmatic features is diagnostic of religious as opposed to other marked uses of language, such as poetic or ceremonial speech. Rather, different religious practices seem to select from among the entire spectrum of linguistic possibilities (Murray 1989, Sherzer 1990, Tedlock 1983). They suspend or alter certain aspects of everyday ways of speaking (even when religious language is taken to be prior to the everyday) in response to problems posed by their particular otherworlds and their assumptions about the everyday. Religious language is deeply implicated with underlying assumptions about the human subject, divine beings, and the ways their capacities and agencies differ. At the same time, religions face chronic dilemmas posed by the tensions between transcendence and the situated and concrete nature of verbal practices. So much depends on these assumptions and tensions that much religious debate dwells on linguistic forms (Bauman 1990; Bowen 1989, 1993; Ferguson 1985; Samarin 1973). The review begins with one common denominator among many varieties of religious language, the problems raised by interaction with invisible beings. It then addresses linguistic form and pragmatics. The final two sections consider the emerging scholarly interest in entextualization and the dilemmas posed for practitioners by otherworldly authority and agency.

Invisibility and Interaction

That the peculiarity of certain speech situations can support religious interpretation is famously evident in Augustine's conversion to Christianity (Augustine 1961, pp. viii, 6–10). Upon hearing the words "take and read, take and read" (*tolle lege, tolle lege*) spoken in a "sing-song" voice by an unseen child from the other side of a wall, Augustine understood them to be a command from God. Opening the Bible, he took the words he encountered to be another moment of communication. Two features of the speech situation permitted this. First, the invisibility of the speaker allowed Augustine to wonder about the true source of the words. Second, the fact that words written in one context can be taken up and read in another allowed him to see himself as their addressee. This episode illustrates the importance both of participant roles and of the tension between text and context in understanding the efficacy of religious language. Moreover, the repetitiveness and assonance that drew Augustine's attention to the child's utterance hint at the power of linguistic form as well.

Such speech situations are made possible by general properties of language that allow otherwise nonperceptible beings to play a role in human societies, interactions that some scholars view as defining religion (Boyer 1994). To the extent that religion does involve interaction with invisible and intangible entities (or even, say, visible but silent icons), it poses certain practical difficulties. This is implicit in Hanks's remark that "it is distorting to describe a shaman...as acting alone simply because his spirit others are nowhere visible to the untrained observer" (1996a, p. 167). Invisibility, however, may pose dilemmas for even the trained observer, as suggested in the words of a practitioner, which form the title to an ethnography of prayer: "Where are you spirits?" (Metcalf 1989).

Religious speech situations can differ from the familiar parameters of everyday speech in several respects. In doing so, they can challenge ordinary habits as well as the theoretical models of speech that are predicated on them. If everyday conversation is a joint production that depends on the participants sharing certain default assumptions (Hanks 1996a, p. 168; cf Sperber & Wilson 1995), such as who is participating and what counts as the relevant context of "here" and "now," religious speech frequently occurs in situations in which those assumptions must be suspended (Howell 1994). In contrast to the face-to-face encounters of conversation analysis, the presence, engagement, and identity of spiritual participants in the speech event cannot always be presupposed or guaranteed. Prayer often seeks to bring about interaction between human beings and other kinds of beings that would (or should) not otherwise occur (Atkinson 1989; Gill 1981; Hanks 1990, 1996a; McCreery 1995; Shelton 1976). In some traditions, human beings must be reassured by aural means "that the ancestors and spirits have not forsaken us" (Peek 1994, p. 475). Even belief in the omnipresence of divinity does not assure that one can interact with it (KH Basso 1990, Peacock & Tyson 1989). Spirits may be the real audience, even of performances not explicitly directed to them as addressees (Becker 1979, McDowell 1983), and even practitioners who agree on how to pray may disagree on who their prayers actually address (Frisbie 1980a).

In contrast to everyday conversation, where such matters can be tacitly assumed, addressing invisible interlocutors may require that the participants in the speech event or even its location be clearly referred to (Gill 1981, Hanks 1996a, McCreery 1995, Metcalf 1989, Schipper 1974, Thomas & Afable 1994). The need to be explicit may also extend to the nature and purpose of the speech act being undertaken. Much of the content of spells and prayers is *metapragmatic,* that is, it reflexively refers to the very actions it is undertaking (Silverstein 1976; cf Jakobson 1971). One reason is presumably that the supposed participants do not all share the same spatiotemporal context, or do not share it in quite the same way. Metcalf observed of one Berawan prayer that half the verses are devoted to "trying to ensure that the recently dead man whom he addresses knows exactly what is happening and why" (1989, p. 266). Such meta-pragmatic means may help effect communication with the spirit world or permit a textual world to direct concrete actions (Atkinson 1989, Bell 1987, Bowen 1993, Gill 1981, Hanks 1996a, Malinowski 1965, Sherzer 1990, Tambiah 1970). Some Gayo spells center on passages from the Qur'an that describe events in which certain powers were granted to characters in the text (Bowen 1993). By reciting these passages, the speaker may obtain those powers in turn. This appears to work by recontextualizing narratives as metapragmatic statements: Their linguistic form remains the same, but their function shifts. Rather than being construed as accounts of actions that were carried out in the past, the words are taken as reports on and directives for the action they themselves carry out in the moment of speaking.

The problem of presence is often compounded by another feature of otherworldly beings. If these beings are sufficiently transcendent, then the ordinary means by which people speak of or to entities in the world of everyday experience may be ruled out in principle. Some traditions, fearing hubris or blasphemy, index the transcendence of divinity by enjoining name avoidance or circumlocution (Janowitz 1989, 1993). Reflexive reference to the very prohibition itself—e.g. the "unspoken name" (Keane 1997a, p. 131)—may serve to refer to a deity. As fully developed—for example, in negative theology and many mystical traditions—the concept of transcendence leads to the dilemma that even to say that the divine lies beyond discourse is already to reduce it to discursive form, which should therefore be eschewed (Clooney 1987, Lopez 1990, Sells 1994, Wright 1993; cf Katz 1992). The divine may be avoided not just as an object of discourse. According to some Jewish traditions, the power of the divine name lies in the fact that, because the deity Himself utters it, it is "the most important token" of divine speech (Janowitz 1989, p. 85; 1993). The prohibition on speaking the divine name thus prevents human beings from presuming to take on a speaking part reserved for God. Prohibition may also serve not only to protect the speakers from otherworldly dangers, it may also serve to bound off an entire sacred code from the effects of secular contexts (Kroskrity 1992). To protect the status of Hebrew in Israel, where it is also the language of secular affairs, Ultraorthodox Jews will not speak it outside liturgical settings (Glinert & Shilhav 1991, Kantor 1992). From a pragmatic perspective, this preserves the presupposition that any actual instance of speaking Hebrew will in fact be sacred.

Most religious traditions, however, do require practitioners to engage with the invisible world in some respect, and they provide the linguistic means to do so. What in their own speech activities enables people to have interactions with divine or spirit beings? Wherein lies the efficacy of religious language? Answering these questions requires examination of formal characteristics of speech performance and the explicit beliefs or implicit assumptions that accompany them.

Form

Some of the richest work on religious language can be divided into that which focuses on meaning and that which focuses on form, though the two are usually closely linked. Studies that focus on meaning, especially as conveyed by metaphor (Calame-Griaule 1986; Fernandez 1982, 1986; Wagner 1986; Weiner 1991; Witherspoon 1977), tend to stress the richness and polyvalent qualities of religious language (although often only according to semantic content). Conversely, studies of form often ascribe to ritual language a certain semantic poverty. Here I concentrate on questions of form, which have been more central to those interested in verbal practices per se.

It is unusual for religious language not to bear some formal marks of its special character. Even the so-called plain speech of Quakers is recognizable by certain stylistic features (Bauman 1990, Irvine 1982, Maltz 1985; cf Coleman 1996). In her pioneering work, Reichard (1944) sought the "compulsive" force of Navajo prayer in its formal patterns. Developing the theme, Gill (1981) claimed that it is a general characteristic of the language of prayer that its repetition and formal elaboration are far out of proportion to the message, construed as denotation. One evident function of this elaboration, he proposes, is to signal a special frame of interpretation. Virtually any means, including changes in phonology, morphology, syntax, prosody, lexicon, and entire linguistic code can frame a stretch of discourse as religious. Shifts in phonology can mimic shifts in language code. I have observed Indonesian Christians take on Arabic-inflected pronunciations to index the religious (albeit not Muslim) character of a speech event. Linguistic form is multifunctional, however, and such devices are likely to entail more than just a shift of frames. For example, when practitioners of local religions in the Indonesian backcountry take words from the prayers of their Muslim neighbors, they are also trying to tap into the power held by politically dominant groups and to claim some of the status associated with spatially distant sources of knowledge (Atkinson 1989, Metcalf 1989, Tsing 1993).

A useful summary of characteristics commonly found in ritual speech is provided by Du Bois (1986). Du Bois's list can be divided into features of performance and of text, and an associated belief that ritual speech replicates how the ancestors spoke. The performance features consist of marked voice quality, greater fluency relative to colloquial speech, stylized and restricted intonational contours, gestalt knowledge (speakers often learn texts as a whole and cannot recite them in parts), personal volition disclaimer (crediting a traditional source for one's words), avoidance of first and second person pronouns, and mediation through several speakers. Du Bois argues that these features tend to shift apparent control over speech from the individual proximate speaker, who is bodily present at the moment of speaking, to some spatially, temporally, or ontologically more distant agent (see also Urban 1989). This shift of control and thus responsibility is reinforced by the textual features, including the use of a ritual register (different lexical items for the same words in colloquial and ritual speech), archaistic elements (including words and grammatical forms that speakers believe to be archaic), elements borrowed from other languages, euphemism and metaphor, opaqueness of meaning, and semantic-grammatical parallelism (the latter having inspired an especially large literature, e.g. EB Basso 1985, Boyer 1990, Fox 1975, 1988, Gossen 1974, Jakobson 1960, Keane 1997a, Kratz 1994, Kuipers 1990, Sherzer 1990, Urban 1991).

Boyer (1990) proposed to explain the special forms taken by ritual speech on the grounds that listeners always assume that those forms are somehow caused by their divine sources and are thus evidence of the workings of forces that are otherwise imperceptible. Du Bois's survey of ritual speech, however, suggests that the authority ritual speech holds for its hearers need not require us to attribute implicit theories of causality to them. The formal properties listed above have such effects as playing down the indexical grounding of utterances in the context of the specific speech event, increasing the perceived boundedness and autonomous character of certain stretches of discourse, and diminishing the apparent role of the speaker's volitional agency in producing them. The resulting decentering of discourse (Bauman & Briggs 1990; Silverstein & Urban 1996a, p. 15), can encourage the perception that the words come from some source beyond the present context. For example, each recitation of Zuni prayer should be an exact repetition of words "according to the first beginning" (Bunzel 1932a, p. 493). But the participants' sense that such prayers do indeed repeat primordial words need not rely merely on their acceptance of some explicit doctrine. Rather, the decentering effects produced by the formal properties of prayers help support this belief as an intuition that is reinforced by each performance.

A second influential approach focuses on sociopolitical effects of linguistic form. One version of this approach builds on Durkheim's observation (1915; cf Briggs 1988, Kratz 1994) that ritual form can create a unified congregation by regimenting vocal and bodily movements and, by its emotional effects, may transform individuals' subjective states (Davis 1985, George 1996, Goodman 1972, Lawless 1988, Maltz 1985, Nelson 1985, Pitts 1993, Roseman 1991, Titon 1988). Another approach looks at how linguistic form can restrict access to the circulation of discourse (Briggs 1993, McDowell 1983, Urban 1996; cf KH

Basso 1990). To the extent that their use demands esoteric knowledge, religious speech genres or lexicons can become scarce resources (Bledsoe & Robey 1986, Carpenter 1992, Frisbie 1980a, Irvine 1989, Lindstrom 1990). Their distinctive aesthetic and semantic character is then sometimes projected onto those who command them. Those who customarily speak refined or sacred words may themselves be credited with essential qualities of refinement or sacredness (Bourdieu 1991, Buckley 1984).

If those who emphasize metaphor are often inclined to see religious language as richer than ordinary speech, another approach sees it as more impoverished. Bloch (1975, 1989) claimed that the formal structure of ritual speech leads to diminished propositional meaning and in other ways restricts the range of what can be said (cf Rappaport 1979). By these effects, highly formal speech comes to serve the perpetuation of authority. Bloch has drawn criticism, both for his account of language and for the conclusions he draws from it, even from some who concur with aspects of his thesis (Boyer 1990, McDowell 1983). Formality, redundancy, and repetition are not incompatible with semantic meaning (Briggs 1988, Janowitz 1989). As Gill (1981) pointed out, formality only looks noncreative when we take texts in isolation rather than as components of larger actions. In a fundamental challenge to Bloch, Irvine (1979) showed that he had grouped together a heterogeneous set of properties under the rubric of formality, conflating linguistic properties, kinds of events, and aspects of social order, when demonstrably formality of one does not necessarily follow from the other. Thus, rigid poetic canons may correlate with political hierarchy but leave performers powerless (Metcalf 1989), whereas flexible speech norms in relatively egalitarian societies may reinforce individual differences of social status (Atkinson 1989). We need to be careful, then, about what aspect of society is being correlated with the formality of its ritual speech (Brenneis & Myers 1984).

Few would be willing to claim that the linguistic and pragmatic properties of ritual speech are without effect. A third approach has been to link these properties to the actions that ritual speech is supposed to undertake. In an influential paper, Silverstein (1981) argued that ritual speech is persuasive in part because of the mutually reinforcing ways in which its form, at multiple linguistic levels, serves as a metapragmatic figure for the accomplishment of the successive stages of the action being undertaken. For example, the sequence of verbs in Navajo prayers moves from plea for expected future actions to description of actions taking place to description of result of accomplished actions (Gill 1981; cf Vitebsky 1993). Thus, over the course of the actual time of the speech event the portrayal of time by the grammatical tense system shifts, until finally the outcome is implicitly taken to be something already accomplished.

Such analyses focus on the effects of form on the consciousness of hearers, speakers, or readers. The forms taken by ritual speech also reflect the participants' assumptions about agency or about what is required to communicate effectively across (or even talk about) (Wright 1993) the semiotic and ontological gap between human beings and invisible interlocutors (Gill 1987). If human beings cannot be sure their addressees share the same language, wordless song (EB Basso 1985) may be the best way to communicate with them; conversely, spirits may manifest their presence by producing unintelligible sounds (Hinton 1980) or changes in voice quality (Howell 1994, Irvine 1982, Schieffelin 1985) in possessed human beings. When people use a sacred language, such as Arabic, they may debate matters of pronunciation in the effort to reproduce the sound of revelation (Nelson 1985). Sonic form itself can be seen as divine (Alper 1988, Buckley 1984, Dusenbery 1992, JD Hill 1993, Janowitz 1993, Lopez 1990, Sullivan 1988, Witherspoon 1977). If the utterance of mantra is tantamount to divine presence (Staal 1990), the speaker's intention and semantic intelligibility become irrelevant. Conversely, those who receive part of their scripture in translation (e.g. from Hebrew to the Greek of some early Christians) may find the "spirit" to lie in semantics, in contrast with the "fleshly" linguistic form (Janowitz 1993, p. 400; cf Stock 1996).

At issue in the formal character of religious language, therefore, are not just aesthetic, emotional, or social functions, but also assumptions about who is actually speaking and listening in any given speech event. Closely bound up with these are local assumptions about how language works. These questions can be addressed in turn as problems of intentionality, participant roles, and authorship.

Intentionality and Responsibility

The means by which human beings communicate with invisible beings tend to reflect underlying assumptions about the nature of these beings, of the human subject, and of the social relations between them (Buckley 1984, Bunzel 1932a, Gossen 1974, Rosaldo 1982). In some traditions prayers are shaped by human deference toward the beings addressed (Robson 1994); others, like the Zuni, "do not humble themselves before the supernatural; they bargain with it" (Bunzel 1932b, p. 618). Some forms of speech seek to persuade, flatter, or please the listener (Calame-Griaule 1986) or influence the spirits by displaying the speaker's privileged knowledge of their names or origins (Atkinson 1989, Bowen 1993, Lambek 1981, Sherzer 1990). It is precisely the assumptions about the participants implicit in linguistic form that are often at issue when religious reformers seek to transform or forbid certain speech practices. One complaint by reformers is that if God is all-powerful, then cajoling words are arrogant, and magical words—to the extent that they seek to act directly upon their addressee—a denial of divine agency. Another complaint is that persuasive words that seem to be addressed to offerings, sacralia, or altars thereby inappropriately impute subjectivity to an inanimate listener and are effectively a form of fetishism (Keane 1996).

Similar concerns about the role of speakers as agentive, volitional, and intending subjects animate debates in the academic study of language. Religious language raises difficulties, for example, for the view that the meaning of utterances depends on the listener's construal of the speaker's intentions (Grice 1957, Sperber & Wilson 1995). Do shamans or worshippers necessarily address beings from whom they expect recognition of their intentions? Do glossolalia (Goodman 1972, Samarin 1972), the use of a language unknown to the addressee (Bauman 1990), or other esoteric or unintelligible speech (Hinton 1980) communicate an intention, and if so, whose? Must I impute intentions to spirits when seeking signs from them in return? In collective worship, must every participant share the same intentions or assumptions about what is happening?

Religious practices have played a central role in scholarly efforts to understand language as a form of action (Malinowski 1965; cf Lienhardt 1961, p. 238), notably under the influence of Austin's concept of speech acts (Austin 1975; see Ahern 1979; Du Bois 1992; Finnegan 1969; Gill 1981, 1987; Rappaport 1979; Tambiah 1979; Wheelock 1982). Models of action typically require some account of actors' intentions; for example, in the case of language, those of speakers', as is evident in Searle's (1969) version of speech act theory. In response, ethnographic counterexamples—largely drawn from ritual contexts—have been adduced against the models of speech that give central place to the intentionality of individual speakers (Duranti 1993, Rosaldo 1982). In his debate with Searle, Derrida (1982) stressed the degree to which language is independent of the intentions of its speakers. What Derrida calls the *iterability* of language means that because any given utterance must draw on a preexisting linguistic system and thus can never be fully determined by or confined to the specific circumstances in which it is uttered, it is always vulnerable to being taken out of context, being cited rather than used, taken in jest rather than in seriousness, and so forth. Derrida can be criticized for overlooking the social character of speech, because over the course of a given interaction participants tend to work together to limit the possible interpretations of their utterances (Borker 1986, Brenneis 1986, Duranti & Brenneis 1986, Tedlock & Mannheim 1995). In many religious speech situations, however, the possibilities for such interactive work are highly restricted: Because the spirits are not full coparticipants in the shaping of meaning in the same way other sorts of conversation partners are, the ambiguities due to language's iterability can be especially prominent.

Du Bois (1992) argued that divination works by suppressing speaker intentionality, distinguishing between the propositional content of questions formulated by human beings and the pragmatic force carried by the oracle's answers. By restricting imputed intentionality to only one component of the communicative event, divination allows people to avoid responsibility for what is said. Still, Du Bois's analysis appears to take intentionality to be the default assumption in speech and fails to explain why suppression of intentions should be more successful than the ascription of intentions to, say, oracular devices or hidden spirits (for an alternative approach, see the following section).

Speaker intentionality is a central issue in the debates among Indonesian Muslims discussed in detail by Bowen (1989, 1993). Some modernists demand that believers pray with sincere intentions by uttering the words with a "powerful depictive imagination" of their goal (1993, p. 84). As this example shows, intentionality can be crucial even when the words used are highly formulaic and thus not subject to manipulation by speakers. As an element of particular *language ideologies* (culturally specific assumptions about the relations between language form and function) (Woolard 1992), the concept of intentionality can produce effects in its own right. Swedish Evangelicals, for example, emphasize the intentionality of the individual speaker. According to Stromberg (1993), however, because speech can express unacknowledged aims, there will be occasions of stress when they find themselves saying things they have not consciously meant. To explain such utterances, which their language ideology renders mysterious, they ascribe them to divine agency. Similarly, Catholic Charismatics tell rounds of stories that often develop a thematic unity over the course of a gathering. Because the collective product is outside the volition of any particular storyteller, the participants take this unity to manifest the presence of a single divine source (Szuchewycz 1994; cf Borker 1986). This conclusion seems to be predicated on their assumption that any agency that lies beyond the level of the individual is not likely to be human. The role of intentionality across the range of known speech practices remains subject to debate. But these examples show that any theory of intentions must consider both extraordinary interactions and the mediating role of language ideologies.

Participant Roles

In Du Bois's view, divinatory procedures work in part by distributing responsibility for different components of speech among the several participants in the communicative event. Notice, however, that what Du Bois takes to be the suppression of individual intentionality can also be described as an expansion of the presupposed speaking subject beyond the level of the individual (Keane 1997a) and a fostering of collaborative authorship and interpretation (Brenneis

1986, Lambek 1981). This expansion can be effected through the elaboration of participant roles. Erving Goffman (1981, cf Irvine 1996) distinguished several roles involved in speech events, including the *principal* who bears responsibility for what is said, the *author* who formulates the actual words, the *animator* who utters them, the proximal *addressee* of the utterance, the *target* to whom the words are ultimately directed, and the *overhearer*. To treat a spirit as the addressee of words is to impute to it a different sort of presence, and perhaps agency, than that of an overhearer. Roles that can be held in combination by one person may also be distributed among several incumbents (e.g. priests who, in the name of ritual sponsors, utter words attributed to spirit authors). Distribution of roles may serve to displace responsibility away from particular individuals or diffuse it among many. Elaborations of participant roles may help invoke sources of authority that are not limited to the perceptible here and now, so that, for instance, the speech event makes plausible the presence of invisible and inaudible spirits (Hanks 1996a). Religious belief thus finds support in the concrete forms of speech practices as much by what they presuppose as by what they depict.

If some speech events distribute participant roles among many persons, others combine several roles in one physical individual (Hill & Irvine 1992, Silverstein & Urban 1996a). This is evident in possession (Boddy 1994), in which the deity or spirit and the human being both use the same body, and in Pentecostal speaking in tongues or glossolalia (Goodman 1972, Maltz 1985, Mueller 1981, Samarin 1972). In possession, however, linguistic forms may not be sufficient to determine what being has entered the scene (Goodman 1972, Whyte 1990), or for that matter, whether the speaker is simply insane: The ultimate decision may be determined as much by the politics of interpretation as by the character of the speech (Irvine 1982).

An important kind of religious transformation consists of taking on a new role as speaker. The conversion narrative of preachers is often about the call to preach (Titon 1988), and full conversion may entail being transformed from the listener to the speaker in acts of "witnessing" (Harding 1987, Lawless 1988, Peacock & Tyson 1989, Titon 1988) or developing "attunement" with a teacher's discourse patterns (Trix 1993). As such studies show, the speaker's religious identity is approached not only or most usefully as an object of discourse (as in the "life-history"), but also as an inhabitable speaking role (Kratz 1994, McDowell 1983), with all the discursive and moral possibilities that may entail.

Authorship

The analysis of participant roles calls into question who counts as present in any given event, and to whom the words manifested in any event are to be attributed. Of particular importance in many situations is the question of authorship. One speech genre in a single ritual can encompass quite different kinds of authors; an Episcopal service can include prayers whose sources are both local (that for Congress) and divine (the Lord's Prayer, as taught by Christ). In Boyer's (1990) hypothesis, listeners take the special forms of ritual speech to index a divine source. The hypothesis, however, does not fully account for the role played by the human animator who utters words imputed to otherworldy authors or principals. Often participants are primarily interested in the social relationships along which speech is transmitted from otherworld to manifest actors. Shamans, for instance, are commonly said to develop individual relationships with spirits who then provide them with songs or chants (Atkinson 1989; Briggs 1993; LR Graham 1995; Hanks 1990, 1996a; Howell 1994; Lambek 1981; Roseman 1991; Sullivan 1988). For listeners who are aware of this, the performance itself will be sufficient to index the existence of the relationship, and the relationship in turn provides the warrant for the performance. In addition, the efficacy of ritual or sacred speech may stem from the fact that it originates from those to whom it speaks, something that gives the speaker special authority or persuasiveness, or places the listener under special obligations (Bledsoe & Robey 1986, Briggs 1993).

When the author of words is distinct from their animator, relationships between the two can display significant variation. Yucatec Mayan shamans receive speech in dreams or from other shamans, but each individual continues to "beautify" this speech throughout a lifetime, leading Hanks to ask "what kind of speaker is this?" (1996a, p. 161–62). Warao shamans receive chants in dreams that are induced by tobacco that has been received from an older shaman (Briggs 1993). In this case, the chant appears to index two sources, both the spirit's authorship (of linguistic form) and the teacher's authorization (of pragmatic capacity). Distinctions among participant roles can have political consequences: Lawless (1988) argued that divinely inspired testimony allows Pentecostal women in patriarchal communities to exert influence that would not be available to them were they to claim full responsibility for their words. Howell (1994) correlated distinctions of authorship with sociopolitical principles. Whereas the egalitarian Chewong treat spirits and shamans as coproducers of the text, ritual speakers of the more hierarchical Lio are not supposed to innovate (see also Atkinson 1989, Metcalf 1989). What these examples show is that the handling of imputed authorship may have more general implications for local assumptions about agency. At one extreme, if words are compulsively effective in themselves, then anyone would be able to use them, regardless of the speaker's personal character or intentions, and without consequences for personal status—unless, like early Quakers, one is the chosen but relatively empty receptacle for God's words (Bauman 1990). At the other extreme, if one's words are supposedly only one's "own voice" (Metcalf 1989), the speaker takes on considerable responsibility and risk.

A single performance can manifest a range of speaker control and a variety of presumed presences and actors, visible and invisible. Many rituals take advantage of this "heteroglossic" variability by undergoing, for example, a shift over performance time from what Bakhtin (1981) called relatively "dialogic" toward more "monologic" and authoritative speech forms (Kuipers 1990). In the process, the identity of the presupposed author can shift by degrees along a wide spectrum. For example, Baptist preachers work toward a climactic stage marked by a staggered stanza pattern created by breath groups bounded by audible gasps or nonsense syllables (Pitts 1993; cf Davis 1985, Rosenberg 1970, Titon 1988). Participants take this final stage to be evidence of the divine speaking through the preacher because "no mortal could possibly project such a design so far in advance, and so consistently, upon what appears to be spontaneous speech" (Pitts 1993, p. 165). When Xavante narrate their dreams, according to Laura Graham, pronoun use, altered voice quality, and other features come to identify the speaker with the spirits (LR Graham 1995). This exemplifies Urban's (1989; cf Besnier 1995, JD Hill 1993, Kroskrity 1992, Lawless 1988) thesis that during a performance, animators can shift between fuller and lesser identification with the narrated speaker, positioning themselves as commentators on the spirits, who thereby remain relatively absent from the present event, or performing as a spirit, thereby bringing their world relatively close to the present, while also distancing the speaker from the self of everyday speech. A shift in presumed author entails a shift in the animator's relationship to his or her words. Falling short of full possession, in which one socially recognized identity can supplant the other, is what Hymes (1981) called the "breakthrough" by which a speaker may shift from report (taking some distance on his or her words) to performance (fully identifying with the role of authoritative animator, even if not that of author).

Shifts in performance may thus restructure relations between the speech event and an otherworld. As a preacher shifts into divinely inspired speech, not only does an otherworldly author become present in the context of the particular speech event, but the speech event may come to be projected into another, scriptural, context (Davis 1985, Peacock & Tyson 1989). The relative dominance of text and context can vary, as shown in Briggs's (1988) analysis of New Mexican Catholicism: Whereas everyday Biblical allusions bring scriptural passages to bear on a here-and-now context that itself remains the center of attention (cf Meigs 1995), the mass may collapse the distinction between Biblical text and ritual context.

Quotation

Because not every society provides explicit, doctrinal explanations of the sources of ritual words, it may lie primarily with linguistic form to make the spirit world manifest, inferable, or presupposable for the participants. In addition to the linguistic and paralinguistic cues already noted, one means of making evident that words have otherworldly sources is the use of quotation. Shamanistic speech seems to fall ambiguously between that of priests and of the possessed. The distinction lies in whether performance is taken to be a kind of quotation or whether the spirits are speaking through the performer. Words that are framed as reported speech can thereby be portrayed as originating outside the present context in which they are being reported (Buckley 1984). The Sufi teacher's authority comes in part from animating the words of others who have actually seen the other world (Trix 1993). When Baptists hear the voice of the Spirit in the inward self, the only evidence lies in the public act of talking about it, a common reason for quoting divine speech (Titon 1988). Jewish, Christian, and Islamic scriptures abound in reported speech of God (Wolterstorff 1995).

The different ways in which the quoted words are framed by the quoting speech can have entailments for their respective authority. What is quoted might be the original moment in which the words were received (LR Graham 1995), previous performances (Hanks 1996a, Howell 1994), or words formulated by other participants in the same speech event. Because the reported speech given in the rabbinic text analyzed by Janowitz (1989; cf Trix 1993) consists of past didactic dialogues, the reader, as addressee of that reported speech, becomes one more link in the chain of transmission. Simultaneously, the authority of those words is displayed by quotation frames that show them to have their origins in the past. The relations between quoter and quoted speaker may be subject to contestation and historical reconfiguration. According to William Graham (1977, 1987), early Islam did not differentiate the authority of divine words and the prophetic words ascribed to Muhammed. The divine words found in the Qur'an are quotation, God's words framed as reported in the words of the Prophet. Conversely, the Prophet's words bear divine authority as utterances of God's appointed. Subsequent efforts to distinguish "prophetic speech" from "revelation" in effect sharpen the boundary between author and animator, and thus between reported text and reporting context, thereby keeping the original prophecy at a greater, potentially more authoritative, remove from subsequent events.

What distinguishes direct from indirect quotation is the purported resemblance of form between the words as they occurred in the original speech event and their reoccurrence in the subsequent, quoting, speech event (Vološinov 1973). In contrast with direct quotation, indirect quotation grants to the person reporting the original words responsibility for interpreting them from the perspective of the subsequent speech event (Lucy 1993). Whereas direct quotation separates animator (the person doing the quoting) from author (the person being quoted), indirect quotation combines the two roles (because the person doing the quoting indicates that the original words have been rephrased), while still locating the principal—the speaker responsible for the original utterance—in some previous context. Consequently, people often feel direct quotation to be more deferential to the original speaker because it maintains a clearer distinction between the voices of quoted and quoting speakers, does not presume to interpret another's words, and does not superimpose the speaker's indexical frame of reference onto that of the original speech event (Hanks 1996b, p. 211; cf Urban 1989). Vološinov points out that such differences in form reflect the relative authority of the reported words and their authors: "The stronger the feeling of hierarchical eminence in another's utterance, the more sharply defined will its boundaries be, and the less accessible will it be to penetration by reporting and commenting tendencies from outside" (1973, p. 123). As William Graham's (1977) discussion of prophetic speech suggests, however, direct quotation can also come to identify animator with author. For example, Janowitz (1989) argued that the hymns given by a rabbinic ascent text are supposed to be identical to the words sung by angels in heaven. Because these hymns are replicas of angelic speech, the human being who recites them in effect joins the heavenly chorus, "collapsing the distance between heaven and earth" (p. 91). Differences in how reported speech is framed are evidence for a range of ways in which the animator is thought to benefit from or identify with the divine sources of the reported words (Irvine 1996, p. 150; Meigs 1995; Urban 1989). Thus, questions about religious authority and ritual efficacy can demand a closer examination of the relations between text and context.

Entextualization and Contextualization

As the question of authorship demonstrates, there is a wide range of forms by which speech can manifest the presence of divine or spirit beings in concrete events or cast particular circumstances as instances of eternal or originary truths. This variation can be seen in terms of agency, as shown above, and it can also be viewed in relation to the definition and transformation of context (Schieffelin 1985, Wheelock 1982). The emphasis on the textual aspects of ritual is, more specifically, part of a growing scholarly interest in the particular ways by which the transformation of context comes about, and a move away from an earlier anthropological tendency to privilege "face-to-face" interaction and oral performance (Blackburn 1988, Boyarin 1993). A key concept is *entextualization,* "the process of rendering discourse extractable,…[so that] it can be lifted out of its interactional setting" (Bauman & Briggs 1990, p. 73; cf Silverstein & Urban 1996b). This process can be affected by anything that emphasizes the internal cohesion and autonomy of a stretch of discourse, permitting it to form a text (whether oral or written) that is perceived to remain constant across contexts (Bauman & Briggs 1990). The process can include linguistic and performance devices, such as the formal features listed by Du Bois (1986), that diminish the speaker's control over the utterance. Entextualization is thus an ubiquitous feature of language use [cf Jakobson's (1960) poetics and Derrida's notion of iterability]. For example, it is one means by which animator can be distinguished from author, because it permits stretches of discourse to be removed from one context and resituated in another as reported speech.

Note, however, that text is one moment in a dialectical process through which words undergo both contextualization and entextualization (Bell 1987). (Re)contextualization, the (re)insertion of text into a context, may, for example, take the form of reading aloud, reciting formulaic verse, or quoting another's words (Becker 1983, Boyarin 1993, Janowitz 1993, Meigs 1995, Silverstein 1996). When scripture is believed to report the actual words of divine revelation, the act of reading aloud effectively closes the circuit from utterance in context to written text and back to utterance again (Janowitz 1989, pp. 102–3). To the extent that a scriptural text merges with a context, it can be taken as making divinity present (Nelson 1985, Peacock & Tyson 1989). Recitations, however, often retain some marked linguistic or performance features (Blackburn 1988, Rabin 1976, Silverstein 1996), which testifies to their persistent connection to and difference from the prior—and distant—context. Thus, to the extent that performance permits a distinction between text and context to remain perceptible (e.g. by reading with an exaggerated monotone), it provides material substantiation for the participants' intuitions that the present interaction stands out against a more authoritative source that is in some way absent (Besnier 1995, George 1996, Valentine 1995). The relation, however, between text and context can also be understood as an instance of a pervasive dilemma for many religions, that the divine is in practice entangled with the concrete human acts it should transcend (Lopez 1990, Lutgendorf 1991, Nelson 1985). Groups that seek immediate access to divinity tend to be suspicious of any overtly textual mediation, including not only actual written artifacts such as prayerbooks or notes (Bauman 1990, Maltz 1985, Peacock & Tyson 1989, Pitts 1993, Stock 1996, Titon 1988), but also memorized, formalized, or aesthetically appealing words, the use of which can be seen as inauthentic and idolatrous (Coleman 1996, Janowitz 1993, Keane 1997b, Nelson 1985, Prell 1989).

The concept of entextualization means that context is not the court of final appeal for any analysis, or something residual that must only be taken into account. Rather, what is relevant to context—and even whether context is to be considered relevant—is the result of ongoing social processes, genre expectations, and language ideologies. Because entextualization tends to decenter the

event (Bauman & Briggs 1990, p. 70), reorienting it around a prior or otherwise absent origin, what counts as context becomes problematic. This would
seem to support Bloch's (1989) contention that ritual suppresses this world in
favor of the otherworldly. Ritual, however, need not serve only one function.
To the extent that entextualization and contextualization exist in a dialectic relation to each other, neither can serve as a final ground for analysis. Because
language use moves between the poles of entextualization and contextualization, speech events can also stress the boundary between text and context—as
when ritual language remains incomprehensible to listeners—maintaining the
separation between worlds. To the extent that texts can move across contexts,
they allow people to create the image of something durable and shared, independent of particular realizations such as readings, interpretations, or performances or their historical transformations (Barth 1990; Urban 1991, 1996). One
effect of the transportability of texts is the identification of spatial with temporal distance: Local practitioners may find the authority of both the scriptures
and the practices they ordain to derive simultaneously from their global reach
and their ancient origins (Bledsoe & Robey 1986, Bowen 1993, Briggs 1988,
Pitts 1993).

Dilemmas of Belief and Agency

The ways in which different religious practices handle language can shed light
on some general dilemmas of belief and agency. One implication follows from
the challenge these practices pose to any strong version of linguistic determinism. Irvine (1982) argued that a diagnosis of spirit possession is never determined directly by how the possessed person speaks but requires some degree
of social negotiation. Others point out that linguistic form alone cannot tell us
what people take their words to be doing, where they believe those words
originate, or even whether they consider the language to be intelligible (Briggs
1988; Irvine 1982, p. 243). Practitioners themselves may remain in some doubt
about these matters (Goodman 1972). An important consequence of the underdetermined relationship between linguistic form and function is that existing
ritual forms can take on new functions and meanings during periods of religious reform, in the name either of change or of continuity (Bowen 1989, 1993;
Keane 1995; Tambiah 1979).

A second implication concerns belief. Academic discussions of belief have
tended to presuppose the view characteristic of conversion-oriented religions,
that one either believes or does not, and often that co-religionists can be assumed to possess a high degree of shared belief. But matters need not be so
clear-cut: If linguistic form and function are not mechanically bound together,
then particular practices need not require particular beliefs (Boyer 1990,
Favret-Saada 1980). In fact, some language practices seem designed to permit

people to carry on without demanding an explanation of what is happening (Du Bois 1992). Moreover, in contrast to Bloch's thesis that ritual speech is successful only to the extent that it brooks no deviation, some religious speech practices may be effective precisely because they can support ambivalent or contradictory beliefs in the practitioner. This is one implication of Rafael's (1992) view that Tagalog speech practices in the confessional were simultaneously ways of converting to Catholicism and of fending off missionaries' demands for belief. Ivy (1995), using the psychoanalytic model of the fetish, proposes that Japanese spirit mediums provide members of a highly industrialized society with the solace of communication with the dead without needing to fully persuade them that such communication has been achieved.

Religious language also raises questions about agency. In studies of ritual, performance, and conversation, attention has increasingly shifted from formal patterns to the emergence and negotiation of meanings over the course of interaction (Bauman & Briggs 1990, Kratz 1994, Schieffelin 1985, Silverstein & Urban 1996b, Tedlock & Mannheim 1995). Wary of the determinism alleged of some varieties of structuralism, analytic approaches that stress interaction often give great weight to the agency of participants. The problem of agency becomes especially acute, however, in circumstances that are supposed to involve otherworldly agents, and in practices that impose severe constraints on the human practitioner. Religious language frequently puts the role of the apparent performers into question and situates the more efficacious, moral, or liberating agency in all sorts of other loci, such as sounds, canonical words, teachers, deities, divinatory mechanisms, congregations, or books.

That language practices presuppose certain constructions of agency helps explain why religious reform movements give so much attention to the proper uses of words. Reformers in several religions (Bauman 1990, Bowen 1993, Maltz 1985) often attack existing speech practices as either granting human beings too much agency (relative to divine beings), or too little (relative to false idols or objectified words). Traditionalists may in turn defend themselves by asserting their superior respect for forebears or accusing reformers, who seek unmediated access to the divine, of excessive pride. At stake is the relationship between the exteriority of language and its implications for the interiority of speakers (Keane 1997b). As has often been observed, language can seem both deeply subjective (as an apparent medium of inner thought), and eminently social (as a preexisting system and a medium of communication). Those who stress sincerity or direct access to divinity tend to be suspicious of language, to the extent that its concrete forms bear evidence of its conventional or social origins outside the individual speaker. Those who stress the distance or difficulty of access to the divine often lay great weight on the mediating power or intersubjectivity provided by those same properties of language. In one view, speakers should shape their words; in another, sacred words should offer something to speakers that they would not otherwise have. Implicit in these differing stances is a broader point, that human agency is not always something people want entirely to celebrate or claim for themselves; they may prefer to find agency in other worlds. To the extent, however, that their access to other worlds is mediated by language, it involves persistent tensions between transcendence and the pragmatic present. Those tensions sustain a wide range of certainties, ambivalences, and ambiguities and thereby keep open a host of historical possibilities.

ACKNOWLEDGMENTS

John Lucy, Adela Pinch, Michael Silverstein, and Stephen F Teiser generously commented on versions of this article. I thank Jacqueline Fewkes, Matthew Tomlinson, and Jeremy Wallach for research assistance, and colleagues too numerous to list here for references.

> Visit the *Annual Reviews home page* at
> **http://www.AnnualReviews.org.**

Literature Cited

Ahern EM. 1979. The problem of efficacy: strong and weak illocutionary acts. *Man* (NS) 14(1):1–17

Alper HP, ed. 1988. *Understanding Mantras.* Albany: SUNY Press

Asad T. 1993. *Genealogies of Religion: Discipline and Reasons of Power in Christianity and Islam.* Baltimore/London: Johns Hopkins Univ. Press

Atkinson JM. 1989. *The Art and Politics of Wana Shamanship.* Berkeley/Los Angeles/Oxford: Univ. Calif. Press

Austin JL. 1975. *How to Do Things with Words.* Cambridge, MA: Harvard Univ. Press

Bakhtin MM. 1981. *The Dialogic Imagination: Four Essays,* Transl. C Emerson, M Holquist, ed. M Holquist. Austin: Univ. Tex. Press

Barth F. 1990. The guru and the conjurer: transactions in knowledge and the shaping of culture in Southeast Asia and Melanesia. *Man* 25:640–53

Basso EB. 1985. *A Musical View of the Universe: Kalapalo Myth and Ritual Performances.* Philadelphia: Univ. Penn. Press

Basso KH. 1990. (1973). A Western Apache writing system: the symbols of Silas John. In *Western Apache Language and Culture: Essays in Linguistic Anthropology,* pp. 25–52. Tucson: Univ. Ariz. Press

Bauman R. 1990. (1983). *Let Your Words be Few: Symbolism of Speaking and Silence among Seventeenth-Century Quakers.* Prospect Heights, IL: Waveland Press

Bauman R, Briggs CL. 1990. Poetics and performance as critical perspectives on language and social life. *Annu. Rev. Anthropol.* 19:59–88

Becker AL. 1979. Text-building, epistemology, and aesthetics in Javanese shadow theatre. In *The Imagination of Reality: Essays in Southeast Asian Coherence Systems,* ed. A Yengoyan, AL Becker, pp. 211–43. Norwood, NJ: Ablex

Becker AL. 1983. Biography of a sentence: a Burmese proverb. In *Text, Play, and Story: The Construction and Reconstruction of Self and Society,* ed. EM Bruner, pp. 135–55. Washington, DC: Am. Ethnol. Soc.

Bell C. 1987. Ritualization of texts and the textualization of ritual. *Hist. Relig.* 27:366–92

Besnier N. 1995. *Literacy, Emotion, and*

Authority: Reading and Writing on a Polynesian Atoll. Cambridge: Cambridge Univ. Press

Blackburn SH. 1988. *Singing of Birth and Death: Texts in Performance.* Philadelphia: Univ. Penn. Press

Bledsoe CH, Robey KM. 1986. Arabic literacy and secrecy among the Mende of Sierra Leone. *Man* 21:202–26

Bloch M. 1975. Introduction. In *Political Language and Oratory in Traditional Society,* ed. M Bloch, pp. 1–28. New York: Academic

Bloch M. 1989. (1974). Symbols, song, dance, and features of articulation: Is religion an extreme form of traditional authority? In *Ritual, History, and Power: Selected Papers in Anthropology,* pp. 19–45. London/Atlantic Highlands, NJ: Athlone

Boddy J. 1994. Spirit possession revisited: beyond instrumentality. *Annu. Rev. Anthropol.* 23:407–34

Borker RA. 1986. "Moved by the spirit": constructing meaning in a Brethren Breaking of Bread service. See Duranti & Brenneis 1986, pp. 317–37

Bourdieu P. 1991. *Language and Symbolic Power,* ed. JB Thompson. Transl. G Raymond, M Adamson. Cambridge, MA: Harvard Univ. Press

Bowen JR. 1989. *Salāt* in Indonesia: the social meaning of an Islamic ritual. *Man* (NS) 24:600–19

Bowen JR. 1993. *Muslims Through Discourse: Religion and Ritual in Gayo Society.* Princeton, NJ: Princeton Univ. Press

Boyarin J. 1993. Voices around the text: the ethnography of reading at Mesivta Tifereth Jerusalem. In *The Ethnography of Reading,* ed. J Boyarin, pp. 212–37. Berkeley: Univ. Calif. Press

Boyer P. 1990. *Tradition as Truth and Communication: A Cognitive Description of Traditional Discourse.* Cambridge: Cambridge Univ. Press

Boyer P. 1994. *The Naturalness of Religious Ideas: A Cognitive Theory of Religion.* Berkeley: Univ. Calif. Press

Brenneis DL. 1986. Shared territory: audience, indirection and meaning. See Duranti & Brenneis 1986, pp. 339–47

Brenneis DL, Myers FR. 1984. Introduction. In *Dangerous Words: Language and Politics in the Pacific,* ed. DL Brenneis, FR Myers, pp. 1–29. New York: New York Univ. Press

Briggs CL. 1988. *Competence in Performance: The Creativity of Tradition in Mexicano Verbal Art.* Philadelphia: Univ. Penn. Press

Briggs CL. 1993. Generic versus metapragmatic dimensions of Warao narratives: Who regiments performance? See Lucy 1993, pp. 179–212

Buckley T. 1984. Yoruk speech registers and ontology. *Lang. Soc.* 13:467–88

Bunzel RL. 1932a. Introduction to Zuni ceremonialism. *Rep. Bur. Am. Ethnol., 47th, 1929–1930.* Washington, DC: Smithson. Inst. Press

Bunzel RL. 1932b. Zuni ritual poetry. *Rep. Bur. Am. Ethnol., 47th, 1929–1930.* Washington, DC: Smithson. Inst. Press

Calame-Griaule G. 1986. (1965). *Words and the Dogon World.* Philadelphia: Inst. Study Hum. Issues

Carpenter D. 1992. Language, religion, and society: reflections on the authority of the Veda in India. *J. Am. Acad. Relig.* 60(1):57–78

Clooney FX. 1987. Why the Veda has no author: language as ritual in early Mīmā sā and post-modern theology. *J. Am. Acad. Relig.* 55(4):659–84

Coleman S. 1996. Words as things: language, aesthetics and the objectification of Protestant evangelicalism. *J. Mater. Cult.* 1(1):107–28

Davis GL. 1985. *I Got the Word in Me and I Can Sing It, You Know: A Study of the Performed African-American Sermon.* Philadelphia: Univ. Penn. Press

Derrida J. 1982. (1972). Signature event context. In *Margins of Philosophy.* Transl. A Bass, pp. 307–30. Chicago: Univ. Chicago Press

Du Bois JW. 1986. Self-evidence and ritual speech. In *Evidentiality: The Linguistic Coding of Epistemology,* ed. W Chafe, J Nichols, pp. 313–36. Norwood, NJ: Ablex

Du Bois JW. 1992. Meaning without intention: lessons from divination. See Hill & Irvine 1992, pp. 48–71

Duranti A. 1993. Truth and intentionality: an ethnographic critique. *Cult. Anthropol.* 8(2):214–45

Duranti A, Brenneis DL, eds. 1986. The audience as co-author. *Text* 6(3):239–347

Durkheim E. 1915. *The Elementary Forms of the Religious Life.* Transl. JW Swain. London: George Allen & Unwin

Dusenbery VA. 1992. The word as Guru: Sikh scripture and the translation controversy. *Hist. Relig.* 31(4):385–402

Favret-Saada J. 1980. *Deadly Words: Witchcraft in the Bocage.* Transl. C Cullen. Cambridge: Cambridge Univ. Press

Ferguson CA. 1985. The study of religious discourse. In *Language and Linguistics: The Interdependence of Theory, Data, and*

Application, pp. 205–13. Washington, DC: Georgetown Univ. Press

Fernandez JW. 1982. *Bwiti: An Ethnography of the Religious Imagination in Africa.* Princeton, NJ: Princeton Univ. Press

Fernandez JW. 1986. *Persuasions and Performances: The Play of Tropes in Culture.* Bloomington: Indiana Univ. Press

Finnegan R. 1969. How to do things with words: performative utterances among the Limba of Sierra Leone. *Man* 4:537–52

Foucault M. 1980. *The History of Sexuality,* Vol. 1, *An Introduction.* Trans. R Hurley. New York: Vintage

Fox JJ. 1975. On binary categories and primary symbols: some Rotinese perspectives. In *The Interpretation of Symbolism,* ed. R Willis, pp. 99–132. London: Malaby

Fox JJ, ed. 1988. *To Speak in Pairs: Essays on the Ritual Languages of Eastern Indonesia.* Cambridge: Cambridge Univ. Press

Frisbie CJ. 1980a. Ritual drama in the Navajo House Blessing ceremony. See Frisbie 1980b, pp. 161–98

Frisbie CJ, ed. 1980b. *Southwestern Indian Ritual Drama.* Albuquerque: Univ. N. M. Press

Geertz C. 1973. (1966). Religion as a cultural system. In *The Interpretation of Cultures,* pp. 87–125. New York: Basic Books

George KM. 1996. *Showing Signs of Violence: The Cultural Politics of a Twentieth-Century Headhunting Ritual.* Berkeley: Univ. Calif. Press

Gill SD. 1981. *Sacred Words: A Study of Navajo Religion and Prayer* (Contrib. Intercult. Compar. Stud., No. 4). Westport, CT/London: Greenwood Press

Gill SD. 1987. *Native American Religious Action: A Performance Approach to Religion.* Columbia, SC: Univ. S. C. Press

Glinert L, Shilhav Y. 1991. Holy land, holy language: a study of Ultraorthodox Jewish ideology. *Lang. Soc.* 20:59–86

Goffman E. 1981. Footing. In *Forms of Talk,* pp. 124–59. Philadelphia: Univ. Penn. Press

Goodman FD. 1972. *Speaking in Tongues: A Cross-Cultural Study in Glossolalia.* Chicago: Univ. Chicago Press

Gossen GH. 1974. To speak with a heated heart: Chamula canons of style and good performance. In *Explorations in the Ethnography of Speaking,* ed. R Bauman, J Sherzer, pp. 389–413. Cambridge: Cambridge Univ. Press

Graham LR. 1995. *Performing Dreams: Discourses of Immortality among the Xavante of Central Brazil.* Austin: Univ. Tex. Press

Graham WA. 1977. *Divine Word and Prophetic Word in Early Islam: A Reconsideration of the Sources with Special Reference to the Divine Saying or Ḥadîth Qudsî.* The Hague/Paris: Mouton

Graham WA. 1987. *Beyond the Written Word: Oral Aspects of Scripture in the Hisotry of Religion.* Cambridge: Cambridge Univ. Press

Grice HP. 1957. Meaning. *Philos. Rev.* 64: 377–88

Hanks WF. 1990. *Referential Practice: Language and Lived Space among the Maya.* Chicago: Univ. Chicago Press

Hanks WF. 1996a. Exorcism and the description of participant roles. See Silverstein & Urban 1996b, pp. 160–200

Hanks WF. 1996b. *Language and Communicative Practices.* Boulder, CO: Westview

Harding SF. 1987. Convicted by the holy spirit: the rhetoric of fundamentalist Baptist conversion. *Am. Ethnol.* 14(1):167–81

Hill JD. 1993. *Keepers of the Secret Chants: The Poetics of Ritual Power in an Amazonian Society.* Tucson: Univ. Ariz. Press

Hill JH, Irvine JT, eds. 1992. *Responsibility and Evidence in Oral Discourse.* Cambridge: Cambridge Univ. Press

Hinton L. 1980. Vocables in Havasupai song. See Frisbie 1980b, pp. 275–307

Howell S. 1994. Singing to the spirits and praying to the ancestors: a comparative study of Chewong and Lio invocations. *l'Homme* 132, 34(4):15–34

Hymes D. 1981. *"In Vain I Tried to Tell You": Essays in Native American Ethnopoetics.* Philadelphia: Univ. Penn. Press

Irvine JT. 1979. Formality and informality in communicative events. *Am. Anthropol.* 5: 651–74

Irvine JT. 1982. The creation of identity in spirit mediumship and possession. In *Semantic Anthropology,* ed. D Parkin, pp. 241–60. London: Academic

Irvine JT. 1989. When talk isn't cheap: language and political economy. *Am. Ethnol.* 16(2):248–67

Irvine JT. 1996. Shadow conversations: the indeterminacy of participant roles. See Silverstein & Urban 1996b, pp. 131–59

Ivy M. 1995. *Discourses of the Vanishing: Modernity, Phantasm, Japan.* Chicago: Univ. Chicago Press

Jakobson R. 1960. Closing statement: linguistics and poetics. In *Style in Language,* ed. TA Sebeok, pp. 350–77. Cambridge, MA: MIT Press

Jakobson R. 1971. (1957). Shifter, verbal categories, and the Russian verb. In *Selected Writings of Roman Jakobson,* 2:130–47. The Hague: Mouton

James W. 1902. *The Varieties of Religious Experience: A Study in Human Nature.* New York: Longman Green

Janowitz N. 1989. *Poetics of Ascent: Theories of Language in a Rabbinic Ascent Text.* Albany, NY: SUNY Press

Janowitz N. 1993. Re-creating Genesis: the metapragmatics of divine speech. See Lucy 1993, pp. 393–405

Kantor H. 1992. Current trends in the secularization of Hebrew. *Lang. Soc.* 21:603–9

Katz ST, ed. 1992. *Mysticism and Language.* New York: Oxford Univ. Press

Keane W. 1995. The spoken house: text, act, and object in eastern Indonesia. *Am. Ethnol.* 22:102–24

Keane W. 1996. Materialism, missionaries, and modern subjects in colonial Indonesia. In *Conversion to Modernities: The Globalization of Christianity,* ed. P van der Veer, pp. 137–70. New York: Routledge

Keane W. 1997a. *Signs of Recognition: Powers and Hazards of Representation in an Indonesian Society.* Berkeley: Univ. Calif. Press

Keane W. 1997b. From fetishism to sincerity: on agency, the speaking subject, and their historicity in the context of religious conversion. *Comp. Stud. Soc. Hist.* In press

Kratz CA. 1994. *Affecting Performance: Meaning, Movement, and Experience in Okiek Women's Initiation.* Washington, DC: Smithson. Inst. Press

Kroskrity PV. 1992. Arizona Tewa kiva speech as a manifestation of linguistic ideology. *Pragmatics* 2:297–309

Kuipers JC. 1990. *Power in Performance: The Creation of Textual Authority in Weyewa Ritual Speech.* Philadelphia: Univ. Penn. Press

Lambek M. 1981. *Human Spirits: A Cultural Account of Trance in Mayotte.* Cambridge: Cambridge Univ. Press

Lawless EJ. 1988. *Handmaidens of the Lord: Pentecostal Women Preachers and Traditional Religion.* Philadelphia: Univ. Penn. Press

Lienhardt G. 1961. *Divinity and Experience: The Religion of the Dinka.* Oxford: Clarendon

Lindstrom L. 1990. *Knowledge and Power in a South Pacific Society.* Washington, DC: Smithson. Inst. Press

Lopez DS. 1990. Inscribing the Bodhisattva's speech: on the *Heart Sūtra's* mantra. *Hist. Relig.* 29:351–72

Lucy JA, ed. 1993. *Reflexive Language: Reported Speech and Metapragmatics.* Cambridge: Cambridge Univ. Press

Lutgendorf P. 1991. *The Life of a Text: Performing the Ramācritmānas of Tulsidas.* Berkeley: Univ. Calif. Press

Malinowski B. 1965. (1935). *Coral Gardens and Their Magic (2): The Language of Magic and Gardening.* Bloomington: Indiana Univ. Press

Maltz DN. 1985. Joyful noise and reverent silence: the significance of noise in Pentecostal worship. In *Perspectives on Silence,* ed. D Tannen, M Saville-Troike, pp. 113–37. Norwood, NJ: Ablex

McCreery JL. 1995. Negotiating with demons: the uses of magical language. *Am. Ethnol.* 22(1):144–64

McDowell JH. 1983. The semiotic constitution of Kamsá ritual language. *Lang. Soc.* 12:23–46

Meigs A. 1995. Ritual language in everyday life: the Christian right. *J. Am. Acad. Relig.* 63(1):85–103

Metcalf P. 1989. *Where Are You Spirits? Style and Theme in Berawan Prayer.* Washington, DC: Smithson. Inst. Press

Mueller T. 1981. A linguistic analysis of glossolalia: a review article. *Concordia Theol. Q.* 45:185–91

Murray DW. 1989. Transposing symbolic forms: actor awareness of language structures in Navajo ritual. *Anthropol. Ling.* 31(3–4):195–208

Nelson K. 1985. *The Art of Reciting the Qur'an* (Mod. Middle East Ser. No. 11). Austin: Univ. Tex. Press

Peacock JL, Tyson RW. 1989. *Pilgrims of Paradox: Calvinism and Experience among the Primitive Baptists of the Blue Ridge.* Washington, DC/London: Smithson. Inst. Press

Peek PM. 1994. The sounds of silence: cross-world communication and the auditory arts in African societies. *Am. Ethnol.* 21(3): 474–94

Pitts WF. 1993. *Old Ship of Zion: The Afro-Baptist Ritual in the African Diaspora.* New York/Oxford: Oxford Univ. Press

Prell R. 1989. *Prayer and Community: The Havurah in American Judaism.* Detroit: Wayne State Univ. Press

Rabin C. 1976. Liturgy and language in Judaism. See Samarin 1976, pp. 131–55

Rafael VL. 1992. (1988). *Contracting Colonialism: Translation and Christian Conversion in Tagalog Society under Early Spanish Rule.* Durham, NC/London: Duke Univ. Press

Rappaport RA. 1979. The obvious aspects of ritual. In *Ecology, Meaning, and Religion,* pp. 173–221. Berkeley: North Atlantic Books

Reichard GA. 1944. *Prayer: The Compulsive*

Word. Monogr. Am. Ethnol. Soc. 7. New York: Augustin

Robson SO. 1994. Speaking to God in Javanese. *l'Homme* 132, 34(4):133–42

Rosaldo MZ. 1982. The things we do with words: Ilongot speech acts and speech act theory in philosophy. *Lang. Soc.* 11: 203–37

Roseman M. 1991. *Healing Sounds from the Malaysian Rainforest: Temiar Music and Medicine.* Berkeley/Los Angeles/Oxford: Univ. Calif. Press

Rosenberg BA. 1970. *The Art of the American Folk Preacher.* New York: Oxford Univ. Press

Samarin WJ. 1972. *Tongues of Men and Angels: The Religious Language of Pentecostalism.* New York: Macmillan

Samarin WJ. 1973. Protestant preachers in the prophetic line. *Int. Yearb. Sociol. Relig.* 8:243–57

Samarin WJ, ed. 1976. *Language in Religious Practice.* Ser. Socioling., Georgetown Univ./Cent. Appl. Ling. Rowley, MA: Newbury House

Schieffelin EL. 1985. Performance and the cultural construction of reality. *Am. Ethnol.* 12(4):707–24

Schipper KM. 1974. The written memorial in Taoist ceremonies. In *Religion and Ritual in Chinese Society,* ed. AP Wolf, pp. 309–24. Palo Alto: Stanford Univ. Press

Searle J. 1969. *Speech Acts: An Essay in the Philosophy of Language.* Cambridge: Cambridge Univ. Press

Sells MA. 1994. *Mystical Languages of Unsaying.* Chicago/London: Univ. Chicago Press

Shelton AJ. 1976. Controlling capricious gods. See Samarin 1976, pp. 63–71

Sherzer J. 1990. *Verbal Art in San Blas: Kuna Culture Through Its Discourse.* Cambridge: Cambridge Univ. Press

Silverstein M. 1976. Shifters, linguistic categories, and cultural description. In *Meaning in Anthropology,* ed. KH Basso, H Selby, pp. 11–56. Albuquerque: Univ. N. M. Press

Silverstein M. 1981. Metaforces of power in traditional oratory. Lect. Dep. Anthropol., Yale Univ., New Haven, CT

Silverstein M. 1996. The secret life of texts. See Silverstein & Urban 1996b, pp. 81–105

Silverstein M, Urban G. 1996a. The natural history of discourse. See Silverstein & Urban 1996b, pp. 1–17

Silverstein M, Urban G, eds. 1996b. *Natural Histories of Discourse.* Chicago: Univ. Chicago Press

Sperber D, Wilson D. 1995. *Relevance: Communication and Cognition.* Oxford: Blackwell. 2nd ed.

Staal F. 1990. *Rules Without Meaning: Ritual, Mantras and the Human Sciences.* Toronto Studies in Religion, Vol. 4. New York: Lang

St. Augustine. 1961. *Confessions.* Transl. RS Pine-Coffin. Harmondsworth, UK: Penguin

Stock B. 1996. *Augustine the Reader: Meditation, Self-Knowledge, and the Ethics of Interpretation.* Cambridge, MA: Harvard Univ. Press

Stromberg PG. 1993. *Language and Self-Transformation: A Study of the Christian Conversion Narrative.* Cambridge: Cambridge Univ. Press

Sullivan LE. 1988. *Icanchu's Drum: An Orientation to Meaning in South American Religions.* New York: Macmillan

Szuchewycz B. 1994. Evidentiality in ritual discourse: the social construction of religious meaning. *Lang. Soc.* 23:389–410

Tambiah S. 1970. *Buddhism and the Spirit Cults in North-East Thailand.* Cambridge: Cambridge Univ. Press

Tambiah S. 1979. A performative approach to ritual. *Proc. Br. Acad.* 65:113–69

Tedlock D. 1983. *The Spoken Word and the Work of Interpretation.* Philadelphia: Univ. Penn. Press

Tedlock D, Mannheim B, eds. 1995. *The Dialogic Emergence of Culture.* Urbana/Chicago: Univ. Ill. Press

Thomas PL, Afable PO. 1994. Kallahan invocations to the dead. *l'Homme* 132, 34(4): 89–99

Titon JT. 1988. *Powerhouse for God: Speech, Chant, and Song in an Appalachian Baptist Church.* Austin: Univ. Tex. Press

Trix F. 1993. *Spiritual Discourse: Learning with an Islamic Master.* Philadelphia: Univ. Penn. Press

Tsing AL. 1993. *In the Realm of the Diamond Queen: Marginality in an Out-of-the-Way Place.* Princeton, NJ: Princeton Univ. Press

Tylor EB. 1873. *Primitive Culture, Vol 2.* London: Murray.

Urban G. 1989. The "I" of discourse. In *Semiotics, Self, and Society,* ed. B Lee, G Urban, pp. 27–51. Berlin: Mouton de Gruyter

Urban G. 1991. *A Discourse-Centered Approach to Culture: Native South American Myths and Rituals.* Austin: Univ. Tex. Press

Urban G. 1996. *Metaphysical Community: The Interplay of the Senses and the Intellect.* Austin: Univ. Tex. Press

Valentine LP. 1995. *Making It Their Own: Severn Ojibwe Communicative Practices* Toronto/Buffalo/London: Univ. Toronto Press

Vitebsky P. 1993. *Dialogues with the Dead: The Discussion of Mortality among the Sora of Eastern India.* Cambridge: Cambridge Univ. Press

Vološinov VN. 1973. (1930). *Marxism and the Philosophy of Language.* Transl. L Matejka, IR Titunik. New York/London: Seminar

Wagner R. 1986. *Symbols That Stand for Themselves.* Chicago/London: Univ. Chicago Press

Wallace AFC. 1966. *Religion: An Anthropological View.* New York: Random House

Weiner JF. 1991. *The Empty Place: Poetry, Space, and Being among the Foi of Papua New Guinea.* Bloomington/Indianapolis: Indiana Univ. Press

Wheelock WT. 1982. The problem of ritual language: from information to situation. *J. Am. Acad. Relig.* 50(1):49–71

Whyte SR. 1990. Uncertain persons in Nyole divination. *J. Relig. Africa* 20(1):41–62

Witherspoon G. 1977. *Language and Art in the Navajo Universe.* Ann Arbor: Univ. Mich. Press

Wolterstorff N. 1995. *Divine Discourse: Philosophical Reflections on the Claim that God Speaks.* Cambridge: Cambridge Univ. Press

Woolard KA. 1992. Language ideology: issues and approaches. *Pragmatics* 2:235–50

Wright DS. 1993. The discourse of awakening: rhetorical practice in classical Ch'an Buddhism. *J. Am. Acad. Relig.* 61(1):23–40

Annu. Rev. Anthropol. 1997. 26:73–85

LANGUAGE POLICIES AND LANGUAGE RIGHTS

Christina Bratt Paulston

Department of Linguistics, University of Pittsburgh, Pittsburgh, Pennsylvania 15260;
e-mail: paulston@vms.cis.pitt.edu

KEY WORDS: individual vs collective rights, linguistic human rights, linguistic minorities, principles of territoriality vs personality

ABSTRACT

This review is an overview of the newly developing field of language rights. It distinguishes between (*a*) historical/descriptive studies where language rights are treated as the resultant variable with no attempt to predict consequences, and (*b*) exhortatory and ideologically based studies in which language rights are considered a causal variable. An attempt at definitions follows, set within the field of language planning. Principal concerns, such as territoriality versus personality principles and individual versus collective rights, are discussed.

The review ends with an argument to consider language rights as emic rights, which is to say culture-language-context–specific rights, rather than to consider linguistic human rights from a universal rights perspective which overstates issues and masks rights *to* as also being rights *against*. We need a careful exploration of the nature of language rights and their consequences.

INTRODUCTION

"Major language legislation in the area of language policy is evidence, within certain political contexts, of contracts, conflicts and inequalities among languages used within the same territory" (Turi 1994, p. 111). So does Turi begin his essay "Typology of Language Legislation." He further states that the fundamental goal of all legislation about language is to resolve the linguistic problems which stem from these language conflicts and inequalities by legally establishing and determining the status and use of the concerned languages. It is a good capsule description of the study of language rights, a new field that has

73

developed recently within language planning and sociolinguistics, because language rights is basically about the legislation—or absence of legislation—for the rights and privileges of languages and their speakers.

A quick glance at any on-line library catalog will verify the newness of this topic. In a library search at the University of Pittsburgh, of the 81 book titles found using the keyword phrase "language rights," 48 were written in the past decade. For the phrase "linguistic rights," all 18 were written since 1979 (with 15 in the 1990s), and for "linguistic human rights," all were written in the 1990s (one is an update of a United Nations report from 1979). Most of these writings concern conditions in Europe and North America; in Europe, these are mostly directly traceable to the European Union and a concern for its minority languages (e.g. Coulmas 1991, Rouland et al 1996) and to the collapse of the Soviet empire. In Canada, they focus on the long-impending and now acute crisis in Quebec. In the United States, the interest can be traced to the Civil Rights Act of 1964 and the Voting Rights Act of 1965 (Leibowitz 1982, Teitelbaum & Hiller 1977), not only because of the zeitgeist that led to their enactment but primarily because these acts form the legal precedent to most subsequent language legislation in the United States. Also an important impetus for this new interest has been increased immigration from the third world, the Bilingual Education Act of 1968, and the backlash English-Only movement. Formerly colonized areas and nations continue to show a concern for language rights, but this concern typically surfaces under other headings, such as official languages, medium of instruction, or language standardization.

The literature on language policies as language rights and linguistic human rights falls into two major camps. First are the historical and present-day descriptive accounts of official or nonofficial language policies in practice. Some of the best of these have been written by lawyers—not necessarily easy to read (e.g. De Witte 1993)—historians [Giordan (1992) and Vilfan (1993) are my personal favorites], and political scientists. Typically these accounts are descriptive and atheoretical, and language rights are mostly treated as a dependent or resultant variable. There is no attempt—or perhaps even interest—to predict the consequences of language rights. Language rights are often considered as individual rights, according to the legal situation.

The other camp is exhortatory—at times quite wildly so—and often ideologically biased and can range from ethnic nationalism—e.g. in the Baltic States—to federalist extremism—e.g. in Quebec. These writings are basically concerned with social change or future developments in which language rights is clearly the independent or causal variable. Linguists, anthropologists, politicians, and educators all figure prominently here—some, of course, also belong to the first camp. In the majority, the rights advocated here are based on the notion of group or collective rights.

There is also a middle camp between the two—and a useful literature it is—formed by special-interest groups and organizations such as the Mexican American Legal Defense Fund (MALDEF), the Puerto Rican Legal Defense and Education Fund (PRLDEF), the National Association of Bilingual Education (NABE), and the Center for Applied Linguistics, all of which have distinguished publication lists (see also Domínguez & López 1995). In addition, there is a nonideological and rather nostalgic concern for endangered and disappearing languages, mostly on the part of linguists (Hale et al 1992, Robins & Uhlenberg 1991). The Endangered Language Fund, Inc, newly founded, is dedicated to the scientific study of endangered languages. The following message, part of its formal statement, on Linguist List (Vol. 7-1595, Nov. 11, 1996), strikes me, though surely it is not intended to, as consumer rights cast as language rights: "Languages have died off throughout history, but never have we faced the massive extinction that is threatening the world right now. As language professionals, we are faced with a stark reality: Much of what we study will not be available to future generations."

DEFINITIONS

Three terms commonly used in the literature to denote the field are "language rights," "linguistic rights," and "linguistic human rights." There is a remarkable lack of definitions in the literature; the three terms are commonly used synonymously. In addition, they may differ in the law from country to country, resulting in no generally accepted standard legal definition, as Joseph Lo Bianco, Chief Executive of the National Languages and Literacy Institute of Australia, pointed out at the Comparative Education Societies' World Congress in 1996. Language rights and linguistic rights usually do mean the same thing. The latter form is presumably influenced by *derechos linguisticos* and *droits linguistiques,* as they are known in Spanish and French, respectively. Language rights, in the sense of the German *Sprachenrecht,* may be interpreted, according to Vilfan (1993; for an interesting review, see Ager 1994), as the legal regulation of the use of languages in public life as part of the arrangements dealing with interethnic regulations in a country with a mixed ethnic structure. Other areas of regulation deal with language use in schooling and religious life, the political representation of ethnic groups, and the international protection of minority groups, as well as the rights of members of nondominant ethnic groups in using their particular language in administrative and judicial legal procedures. One objective of language rights for a nondominant ethnic group is the recognition of that group's existence. This implies "the degree of status sought by the group as part of its efforts to overcome a feeling of inferiority acting to hamper members of such a nondominant group in their endeavours both to maintain their ethnic identity and advance in terms of social mobility" (Vilfan 1993).

In his US *Federal Recognition of the Rights of Minority Language Groups,* Leibowitz (1982) does not define language rights outright but does so indirectly in terms of access—political, legal, economic [especially employment (Piatt 1993)], and educational—in a narrative summary of the legislative, administrative, and judicial efforts made to recognize the needs and secure the civil rights [sic] of minority-language citizens. In addition, one may add the concern over access to social policies and health care (Hamel 1997a).

Turi (1994) commented that language legislation is typically aimed at the speakers of a language rather than at the language itself unless that legislation is clearly a public policy law. As an exception, he cited the France Quick Case in which Cour d'appel de Paris in 1984 acquitted a firm of using terms such as "bigcheese" and "hamburger" on the grounds that the French consumers understood them. This ruling was overturned by France's Cour de cassation, which argued that "French language legislation protected the French language rather than francophones," Turi (1994) adds cryptically "without entering into much detail." Some cases cannot help but strike an anglophone as quite amusing.

Linguistic human rights (LHRs), however, is a different concept. Its awkward stylistic tautology—if it is linguistic it must, of course, already be human—derives from the attempt to link language with human rights, i.e. to reframe the issues of language rights in terms of human rights, now a generally accepted notion. "The challenge to lawyers, politicians and language professionals is to see how a human rights perspective can support efforts to promote linguistic justice," wrote Phillipson et al (1994) in a recent and first major publication on *Linguistic Human Rights: Overcoming Linguistic Discrimination.*

The expression "human rights" is relatively new. It takes the place of "natural rights" and has come into general parlance only since World War II and the atrocities of Nazi Germany. Forerunners to the United Nations' *Universal Declaration of Human Rights* (1948) "as a common standard of achievements for all peoples and all nations" (*Encyclopedia Britannica* 1993) were the US Declaration of Independence, in which it is written that "We hold these truths to be self-evident, that all men are created equal, that they are endowed by their creator with certain inalienable rights, that among these are Life, Liberty and the Pursuit of Happiness" (1776), and the French Declaration of the Rights of Man and the Citizen, which states that "men are born and remain free and equal in rights" these being "Liberty, Property, Safety and Resistance to Oppression" (1789).

The moot point whether language rights are individual or collective (see discussion below) has its roots in the conjunction of Roman law (individual) with Germanic tribal law (collective) at the collapse of the Roman empire. To-day LHRs proponents tend to take for granted that both individual and collective rights apply. Human rights are often discussed in terms of "three generations of human rights" proposed by the French jurist Karel Vasak, based on the themes of the French revolution: liberté, égalité, and fraternité. Liberty represents "freedom from"; equality represents individual and collective "rights to" (language rights, had he thought of them, would fit here); and fraternity represents collective "solidarity rights" such as self-determination, economic and social development, and benefit from the common heritage of mankind (e.g. earth-space resources). The latter emerged from the claims of the so-called third-world nations in the postcolonial period, the legitimacy of these being a function of context.

The human rights of the first two "generations" are typically conceived as "quintessentially general or universal in character, in some sense equally possessed by all human beings everywhere, including in some instances even the unborn. In stark contrast to the 'Divine Rights of Kings' and other such conceptions of privilege, human rights extend, in theory, to every person on Earth without discrimination irrelevant to merit" (*Encyclopedia Britannica* 1993). It is precisely this notion of *droits universels* of LHRs which becomes the basic problem with this putative concept (see also Capotorti 1991).

The question of language rights concerns ethnic minorities in most cases, and a word of caution is due here. "Minority" implies quantitative differences only, but as a number of writers (Giordan 1992, Paulston 1994, Vilfan 1993) have pointed out, the most salient difference is that of a superordinate/subordinate status relationship. As Vilfan discusses, it is more correct to speak about privileged or dominant and nonprivileged or nondominant ethnic groups. Dominance, or its lack, depends "upon numerous circumstances, for instance social structure, the dispersion of social groups, the electoral system, historical traditions and the respective prestige of the 'historical nations' involved" (Vilfan 1993).

LANGUAGE RIGHTS AND LANGUAGE POLICIES AS LANGUAGE PLANNING

Language policies are probably best considered as a subset of language planning, an important field of sociolinguistics that emerged in the 1960s, triggered by real-world problems (Fishman et al 1968, Whiteley 1971). This new field of language planning found itself consistently dealing with language policies for linguistic minorities. Even the absence of explicit policy, as Heath (1976) pointed out, is in itself an act of language policy.

This is not to say that historians and political science people do not also write about language policies. They do so, and very well, but they typically deal with them as events (i.e. case studies) or as contextual or dependent variables. For a theoretical understanding of the consequences of language rights, of the causal effect of language rights as language policy, the field of language planning is probably the most rewarding approach to pursue (see e.g. Grabe 1994).

The term "language planning" is usually limited to "the organized pursuit of solutions to language problems, typically at the national level" (Fishman 1973). A recent framework that integrates earlier scholarship is Hornberger's (1994) work on theoretical approaches to language planning and language policy, discussed again in Ricento & Hornberger (1996). Nancy Hornberger considers policy (concerning matters of society and nation) and cultivation (relating to language and literacy at the microscopic level) planning [Neustupny's (1974) terms originally]. She also uses Cooper's (1989) distinction of three types of planning, which Cooper adapted from Kloss (1969): status planning (about uses of language), acquisition planning (about users of language), and corpus planning (about language). Most language policy relating to language rights falls under status planning, e.g. recent choice of national languages as in South Africa, or under acquisition planning, e.g. choice of medium of instruction.

Ricento & Hornberger point out that planning often results in unintended outcomes. [Fishman (1973) had earlier termed such failure "unexpected system linkages."] Implementation may be poor and evaluation nonexistent or dependent on the values of who does the evaluating. They list some issues in the ongoing development of language planning of which the following are of interest here (see e.g. Tollefson 1991, 1995): (a) the investigation of specific language policies in specific contexts to provide "richer" explanation (the importance of the context is stressed throughout the article and from my viewpoint rightly so); (b) the shift of interest from the nation building and modernization in third-world countries to language rights globally and the perpetuation of structural socioeconomic inequalities and language revitalization; and (c) the discovery by English-language teaching (ELT) professionals of critical theory and the historical-structural approach:[1] (i) Language policies represent the interests of those in power. (ii). Such interests serve to maintain the socioeconomic interests of the elites.(iii). These ideologies permeate society at all levels and all its institutions. (iv). Individuals do not have freedom of language choice, neither in education nor in social life. They go on to point out that none

---

[1]There is in the United States a marked lack of academic intercourse between ELT and bilingual education (BE) professionals. The issues Ricento & Hornberger discuss were all written about in the 1970s by scholars working in the field of (bilingual) education. See my chapter "The Conflict Paradigm," in Paulston (1980).

of the theoretical approaches of language planning policies they discuss can "predict the consequences of a particular policy or show a clear cause/effect relationship between particular policy types...and observed outcomes" (Ricento & Hornberger 1996). To which I would add, as they also do later: "Language policy must be evaluated not only by official policy statements or laws on the books but by language behavior and attitudes in *situated,* especially institutional *contexts*" (italics mine; Ricento & Hornberger 1996).

It is indeed the major argument of this review that any real insight into the nature of language rights can only be reached if we consider such rights emic rather than universal. Linguistic human rights is a tempting and facile conceptualization for advocacy purposes, but it holds little explanatory power and may ultimately backfire in that its claims are too strong and therefore more easily dismissed.

PRINCIPAL CONCERNS

The Territoriality Versus the Personality Principles

Officially bilingual or multilingual nations often resort to either the territoriality or the personality principle in their language legislation. McRae (1983), who has written about many multilingual countries, discussed these principles in an early, excellent article. According to McRae (1975), "[t]he principle of territoriality means that the rules of language to be applied in a given situation will depend solely on the territory in question." Belgium or Switzerland would be examples. "[T]he principle of personality means that the rules will depend on the linguistic status of the person or persons concerned" (McRae 1975). Federal, if not provincial, Canadian legislation affirms the right to services in French or English regardless of territory (see Nelde et al 1992). After a lengthy discussion of the historical development, McRae adds three further dimensions of language policy, namely the distinction between linguistic equality and minority status, the degree of domain comprehensiveness, and the degree of centralization in decision making. He goes on to demonstrate how these dimensions, combined with the territoriality-personality axis, afford a basis for the analysis and evaluation of language policies in a number of selected countries. "The criteria for the choice of a particular combination of options can be seen as resting on two groups of factors: (1) a set of given environmental factors, including in particular the relative numbers of the language groups, their geographical distribution, economic and social status, levels of political development, and so on and (2) a combination of goals based on the value structure of the society concerned or of one of its constituent groups" (McRae 1975). He concludes that the number of relevant variables seems large enough that no two linguistic situations will be alike in all significant aspects; therefore, one cannot generalize about the relative merits of territoriality or personality per se as alternative principles of language planning. McRae's arguments are worth keeping in mind when one considers universal language rights.

In a more recent discussion, based on the situations in Belgium, Canada, and Quebec, Nelde et al (1992) argue basically the same point: "Because of the inappropriateness of adopting either a model based upon the territoriality or the personality principles and given the essential need for compromise in most concrete situations, the measures we formulate are located somewhere in between both principles." [For a similar discussion of Catalonia, see Woolard (1985).] They acknowledge state intervention in language planning in legislative functions (promulgation of laws), executive functions (writing and implementation of laws), administrative functions (introduction and assurance of respect for laws), and judiciary functions (arbitration on the constitutionality and on the respecting of laws)—a distinction of functions I find quite helpful. They go on to point out, however, that "the motor of linguistic planning" is made up of collectivities, i.e. special-interest groups, not necessarily based on territorial linguistic communities. For example, francophones in Quebec were both for and against the latest referendum vote on sovereignty for Quebec. This leads the authors to consider the personality principle in terms of individual and collective rights. They cite Woehrling (1989), in translation: "Language is a collective possession which can only be used and maintained in a group....The collective nature of these rights does not disappear simply because they are legally attributed to individuals and they can individually claim the benefit." The resultant three concepts—territorial, individual, and collective rights—prevail in linguistic rights, by which I presume the authors mean they are the primary legal bases or foundations for language rights. There is a sizable literature on these concepts—territoriality, personality, individual, collective—but I have found the Nelde-Labrie-Williams model to be the most helpful. They conclude inter alia that language planning should "genuinely take into account the situational and contextual characteristics of the linguistic groups" (Nelde et al 1992), a common argument in the language rights literature.

It is interesting in this context to consider the Bord na Gaeilge (1988) report *The Irish Language in a Changing Society*. The report mentions that legislation inevitably interprets rights as attaching to individuals rather than to groups or collectivities and that non-Irish speakers are allowed to build houses in Gaeltacht areas and so become a threat to the survival of the minority language: "Individual rights become a threat to the common good" (Bord na Gaeilge 1988, p. 95). Compare the Irish situation to that of Åland, a set of islands in the Baltic which is an autonomous region of Finland but is Swedish speaking. The European Union recently approved the so-called Ålandprotocol, which grants as exception the right that only Ålanders can buy land and farm the soil (Berglund 1995). No reason is given in the report for this legislation, but if anything is based on territorial rights, this certainly is—especially in contrast with the Irish legislation. Whatever the intention of the law, it will certainly serve to maintain Swedish on the islands (the rest of Finland shows shift from Swedish to Finnish).

Universal Versus Emic Language Rights

The leading proponents of LHRs are Tove Skutnabb-Kangas and Robert Phillipson (1994—see especially the bibliography; see also Gomes de Matos 1993). A fairly succinct introduction to this topic is the article "Linguistic Rights and Wrongs" (Phillipson & Skutnabb-Kangas 1995), in which they recapitulate their basic arguments: Linguistic rights are one type of human rights, part of a set of inalienable, universal norms for just enjoyment of one's civil, political, economic, social, and cultural rights (p. 483). After a review of human rights and LHRs, they make the generalization that lack of linguistic rights is one of the causal factors in certain conflicts, and that linguistic affiliation is a rightful mobilizing factor in conflicts with multiple causes where power and resources are unevenly distributed along linguistic and ethnic lines (1995). They end their article with what a Universal Declaration of Linguistic Human Rights "should guarantee, in our view:

"A. everybody can: 1. identify with their mother tongue(s) and have this identification accepted and respected by others; 2. learn the mother tongue(s) fully, orally (when physiologically possible) and in writing (which presupposes that minorities are educated through the medium of their mother tongue(s)); 3. use the mother tongue in most official situations (including schools).

"B. everybody whose mother tongue is not an official language in the country where s/he is resident, can become bilingual (or trilingual, if s/he has 2 mother tongues) in the mother tongue(s) and (one of) the official language(s) (according to his or her own choice).

"C. any change of mother tongue is voluntary, not imposed."

It is interesting to compare Phillipson & Skutnabb-Kangas (1995) with the Declaration of Linguistic Rights, which was actually signed in June 1996 in Barcelona and co-chaired by UNESCO and CIEMEN (a Barcelona-based organization specializing in linguistic rights issues), and which is ultimately headed for the United Nations. The following (from Argemi 1996) is an extract from the Declaration, Article 3 (note the "may" in point 2):

"1. This Declaration considers the following to be inalienable personal rights which may be exercised in any situation: the right to be recognized as a member of a language community; the right to use one's own language in private and in public; the right to the use of one's own name; the right to interrelate and associate with other members of one's language community of origin; the right to maintain and develop one's own culture and all the other rights related to language which are recognized in the International Covenant on Civil and Political Rights of 16 December 1966 and the International Covenant on Economic, Social and Cultural Rights of the same date.

"2. This Declaration considers that the collective rights of language groups may include the following, in addition to the rights attributed to the members of language groups in the foregoing paragraph, and in accordance with the conditions laid down in paragraph 2.2: the right for their own language and culture to be taught; the right of access to cultural services; the rights to an equitable presence of their language and culture in the communications media; the right to receive attention in their own language from government bodies and in socio-economic relations.

"3. The aforementioned rights of persons and language groups must in no way hinder the interrelation of such persons or groups with the host language community or their integration into that community. Nor must they restrict the rights of the host community or its members to the full public use of the community's own language throughout its territorial space."

By emic (but see Harris 1976 for a range of meanings possible but not intended here) rights I intend nothing more than culture-, language-, and context-specific rights. It is not a term used in the literature on language rights, if close at hand for a linguist; nor is it discussed at all as a contrast to universal rights. The thought first occurred to me as discussant at a session on Minority and International Perspectives on Linguistic Human Rights at the AAA meeting in 1994. Ana Celia Zentella (1997) had argued the rights for the minority language (Spanish in Puerto Rico), followed later by a presentation by Ina Druviete proclaiming the rights of the national language (Latvian in Latvia with undeniable—and understandable—overtones against the now barely minority Russian). On the notion that rights *to* are at the same time rights *against* something (Hamel 1997b), I merely pointed out that their claims were contradictory and that we needed to resolve them, as it seemed to me that both were right. They later conferred and informed me that I was wrong in saying they disagreed, because they did not. Hence stems my fledgling thought that language rights are not universal, and my concern that such universal claims merely serve to weaken potential rights since many claimed rights patently cannot be enforced in some situations, echoing Lo Bianco: "rights are always modified by the pragmatic capacity of their enforcement" (personal communication, 1996). In addition, as Nelde et al (1992) point out, it is an accepted fact in the legal domain in Canada that linguistic rights are based on political compromise and therefore must be interpreted by the courts with more discretion than is usually the case for other fundamental rights (1992).

Courtney Cazden somewhere has discussed the event of a child erasing a blackboard: It may be in punishment, it may be as reward, or it may be the routine of that particular classroom, but until you have an emic understanding, you will not understand what is happening. On the whole, the notion of emic understanding, where the same event may have different significance in different cultures, or where different events/phenomena may have the same significance, is ignored in the discussions of language rights. The more important is Hamel's "Language conflict and linguistic human rights in indigenous Mexico: a sociolinguistic framework" (1997a), where he argues for the necessity to relate LHRs to a sociolinguistic analysis, which takes into account not only the surface structures of language but also the cultural schemes and patterns, similar to Dell Hymes's communicative competence construct. He argues convincingly that to deal with an Indian minority in matters of the Mexican judicial system, using concepts and notions of the Western world will still be bewildering even if it is done in the Indian language. Surface structure of language is not enough. I do not expect that Hamel intended his work as an argument against universal language rights, but nevertheless that is its effect.

CONCLUSION

What should follow here is a discussion in terms of language rights of the English-Only/English Plus movement (Adams & Brink 1990, Cazden & Snow 1990, Crawford 1992, Gomez de Garcia 1996, Lang 1995, Wiley & Lukes 1996, Wong 1988); of the Canadian situation and the Quebec secession movement (Corson & Lemay 1996, Coulombe 1995, Edwards 1995); Australian language policies (Baldauf & Luke 1990, Herriman 1996, Lo Bianco 1987); the Arctic and Saami movements (Blom et al 1992, Collis 1990, Corson 1995, Nordisk Kontakt 1993); and so on, i.e. language rights issues in specific localities around the world; but space does not permit a mapping of this diversity.

According to Giordan (1992), "the optimal development of the linguistic and cultural riches constituted by this diversity is a major condition for the realization of a democratic society capable of guaranteeing peace in this geopolitical space" (my translation). Giordan is writing about Europe, but he could just as well have meant the world. Language rights is an important new topic for us, because their existence usually reveals past and present injustice or exploitation against the weak in the world. Our responsibility as academics is the careful exploration of the nature of language rights and their consequences.

Literature Cited

Adams K, Brink D, eds. 1990. *Perspectives on Official English: The Campaign for English as the Official Language of the USA.* Berlin: Mouton de Gruyter

Ager D. 1994. Review of *Ethnic Groups and Language Rights,* ed. S Vilfan with G Sandvik, L Wils. Aldershot: Dartmouth

Argemi A. 1996. Universal Declaration of Linguistic Rights: responding to a need. *Contact Bull. Eur. Bur. Lesser Used Lang.* 13:3–4

Baldauf RB, Luke A, eds. 1990. *Language Planning and Education in Australasia and the South Pacific.* Clevedon, Engl: Multilingual Matters

Berglund J-E. 1995. Ålandsprotokollet ändras ej av EUs regeringskonferens (The Åland protocol not changed by EU's government conference). *Nord. Kontakt tema* 2:12–13

Blair P. 1994. *The Protection of Regional or Minority Languages in Europe.* Fribourg: Inst. Féd. Fribg. Suisse

Blom G, Graves P, Kruse A, Thomsen BT, eds. 1992. *Minority Languages: The Scandinavian Experience.* Oslo: Nord. Lang. Secr.

Bord na Gaeilge. 1988. *The Irish Language in a Changing Society: Shaping the Future.* Dublin: Bord na Gaeilge

Capotorti F. 1991. *Study of the Rights of Persons Belonging to Ethnic, Religious, and Linguistic Minorities.* New York: United Nations

Cazden CB, Snow CE, eds. 1990. English plus: issues in bilingual education. *Ann. Am. Acad. Polit. Soc. Sci.* 508. Newbury Park, CA: Sage

Collis DRF, ed. 1990. *Arctic Languages: An Awakening.* Paris: UNESCO

Cooper R. 1989. *Language Planning and Social Change.* Cambridge: Cambridge Univ. Press

Corson D. 1995. Norway's 'Sámi language act: emancipatory implications for the world's aboriginal peoples. *Lang. Soc.* 24:493–514

Corson D, Lemay S. 1996. *Social Justice and Language Policy in Education: The Canadian Research.* Toronto: OISE Press

Coulmas F, ed. 1991. *A Language Policy for the European Community.* Berlin: Mouton de Gruyter

Coulombe PA. 1995. *Language Rights in French Canada.* New York: Lang

Crawford J. 1992. *Hold Your Tongue: Bilingualism and the Politics of "English-only".* Reading, MA: Addison-Wesley

De Witte B. 1993. Conclusion: a legal perspective. In *Ethnic Groups and Language Rights,* ed. S Vilfan, pp. 303–14. Aldershot: Dartmouth

Domínguez F, López N. 1995. *Sociolinguistic and Language Planning Organizations.* Lang. Int. World Dir. Amsterdam: Benjamins

Druviete I. 1997. Linguistic human rights in the Baltic States. In *Linguistic Human Rights from a Sociolinguistic Perspective,* ed. RE Hamel. *Int. J. Sociol. Lang.* 127

Edwards J. 1995. Monolingualism, bilingualism, biculturalism and identity. *Curr. Issues Lang. Soc.* 2:5–57

Encyclopedia Britannica. 1993. Human rights. 20:656–64

Fishman JA. 1973. Language modernization and planning in comparison with other types of national modernization and planning. *Lang. Soc.* 2:23–42

Fishman JA, Ferguson CA, das Gupta J, eds. 1968. *Language Problems of Developing Nations.* New York: Wiley

Giordan H. 1992. *Les minorités en Europe: droits linguistiques et Droits de l'Homme.* Paris: Kimé

Gomes de Matos F. 1993. Ten years' work in linguistic rights: a selected bibliography. *Sociolinguist. Newsl.* 7:52–53

Gomez de Garcia J. 1996. Official English and the Native American: another tribe heard from. *Appl. Linguist. Forum* 16:5–7

Grabe W, ed. 1994. Language policy and planning. *Annu. Rev. Appl. Linguist.,* Vol. 14. Cambridge: Cambridge Univ. Press

Hale K, Krauss M, Watahomigie L, Yamamoto A, Craig C, et al. 1992. Endangered languages. *Language* 68:1–42

Hamel RE. 1997a. Language conflict and language shift: a sociolinguistic framework for linguistic human rights. *Int. J. Sociol. Lang.* 127

Hamel RE, ed. 1997b. Linguistic human rights from a sociolinguistic perspective. *Int. J. Sociol. Lang.* 127

Harris M. 1976. History and significance of the emic/etic distinction. *Annu. Rev. Anthropol.* 5:329–50

Heath SB. 1976. A National Language Academy? *Int. J. Sociol. Lang.* 11:9–43

Herriman M. 1996. Language policy in Australia. In *Language Policies in English Dominant Countries,* ed. M Herriman, B

Burnaby, pp. 35–61. Clevedon: Multilingual Matters

Hornberger NH. 1994. Literacy and language planning. *Lang. Educ.* 8:75–86

Kloss H. 1969. *Research Possibilities on Group Bilingualism: A Report.* Quebec: Int. Cent. Res. Bilingual.

Lang P. 1995. *The English Language Debate: One Nation, One Language?* Springfield, NJ: Enslow

Leibowitz AH. 1982. *Federal Recognition of the Rights of Minority Language Groups.* Rosslyn, VA: Natl. Clgh. Biling. Educ.

Lo Bianco J. 1987. *National Policies on Languages.* Canberra: Aust. Gov. Publ. Serv.

McRae KD. 1975. The principle of territoriality and the principle of personality in multilingual states. *Int. J. Sociol. Lang.* 4: 33–54

McRae KD. 1983. *Conflict and Compromise in Multilingual Societies.* Waterloo, Ont: Laurier

Nelde PH, Labrie N, Williams CH. 1992. The principles of territoriality and personality in the solution of linguistic conflicts. *J. Multiling. Multicult. Dev.* 13:387–406

Neustupny J. 1974. Basic types of treatment of language problems. In *Adv. Lang. Plan.,* ed. JA Fishman, pp. 37–48. The Hague: Mouton

Nordisk Kontakt. 1993. Arktis. Engl. summ., Vol. 2

Paulston CB. 1980. *Bilingual Education: Theories and Issues.* Rowley, MA: Newbury House

Paulston CB. 1994. *Linguistic Minorities in Multilingual Settings.* Amsterdam: Benjamins

Phillipson R, Rannut M, Skutnabb-Kangas T. 1994. Introduction. In *Linguistic Human Rights.* Berlin: Mouton de Gruyter

Phillipson R, Skutnabb-Kangas T. 1995. Linguistic rights and wrongs. *Appl. Linguist.* 16:483–504

Piatt B. 1993. *Language on the Job: Balancing Business Needs and Employee Rights.* Albuquerque: Univ. N. M. Press

Ricento TK, Hornberger NH. 1996. Unpeeling the onion: language planning and policy and the ELT professional. *TESOL Q.* 30: 401–27

Robins HR, Uhlenberg EM, eds. 1991. *Endangered Languages.* Oxford: Berg

Rouland N, Pierre-Caps S, Poumarede J. 1996. *Droits des Minorités et des Peuples Autochtones.* Paris: Presses Univ. Fr.

Skutnabb-Kangas T, Phillipson R, eds. 1994. *Linguistic Human Rights.* Berlin: Mouton de Gruyter

Teitelbaum H, Hiller RJ. 1977. *The Legal Perspective: Bilingual Education,* Vol. 3. Arlington, VA: Cent. Appl. Linguist.

Tollefson J. 1991. *Planning Language, Planning Inequality: Language Policy in the Community.* London: Longman

Tollefson J, ed. 1995. *Power and Inequality in Language Education.* Cambridge: Cambridge Univ. Press

Turi J-G. 1994. Typology of language legislation. See Skutnabb-Kangas & Phillipson 1994, pp. 111–19

Vilfan S, ed. 1993. *Ethnic Groups and Language Rights.* Aldershot: Dartmouth

Whiteley WH, ed. 1971. *Language Use and Social Change: Problems with Multilingualism with Special Reference to Eastern Africa.* Oxford: Oxford Univ. Press

Wiley TG, Lukes M. 1996. English-only and standard English ideologies in the US. *TESOL Q.* 30:511–35

Woehrling J. 1989. Les droits linguistiques des minorités et le projet de modification de la Constitution du Canada. In *Langue et Droit,* ed. P Pupier, J Woehrling. Montreal: Wilson & Lafleur

Wong S-LC. 1988. Educational rights of language minorities. In *Language Diversity: Problems or Resource?,* ed. SL McKay, S-LC Wong, pp. 367–86. New York: Newbury House

Woolard KA. 1985. Catalonia: the dilemma of language rights. In *Language of Inequality,* ed. N Wolfson, J Manes, pp. 91–109. Berlin: Mouton de Gruyter

Zentella AC. 1997. The Hispanophobia of the official English movement in the USA. In *Linguistic Human Rights from a Sociolinguistic Perspective,* ed. RE Hamel. *Int. J. Sociol. Lang.* 127

Annu. Rev. Anthropol. 1997. 26:87–108

COMMERCE AND CULTURE IN SOUTH ASIA: Perspectives from Archaeology and History

Kathleen D. Morrison

Department of Anthropology, University of Chicago, Chicago, Illinois 60637

KEY WORDS: trade, urbanism, Buddhism, archaeology, South Asia

ABSTRACT

This review examines aspects of the trajectory of economic change in South Asia, particularly the development of markets, money, commercial production, and certain specialized economic institutions, in light of the longer historical experience of posturban polities. A review of archaeological and historical evidence from the Early Historic (500 BC–AD 500) through the Middle Period (AD 500–1600) highlights several consistent themes: urbanization and related transformation of settlement; monetization and the increasing role of production for markets; the volatile relationship between long-distance exchange and local political and economic structure; the intensification of production; and the shifting roles of religious and other institutions such as monasteries, temples, and guilds.

INTRODUCTION

In a recent review of the role of mercantile activity in the development of South Asia's social and political structure during the Early Modern period (sixteenth to eighteenth centuries), Subrahmanyam & Bayly (1990, p. 242) discuss the role of what they term "portfolio capitalists," entrepreneurs who, as they put it, "were able to straddle the worlds of commerce and political participation." This recognition of the interpenetration of commerce and state power and, one might add, of both with strategies and structures of production, moves

87

beyond simple oppositions of "merchants," "markets," and "states" in the precolonial context. Expanding the scope of Subrahmanyam & Bayly's review, this paper suggests that the trajectory of economic change in South Asia, particularly the development of markets, money, commercial production, and specialized economic institutions, is best understood in light of the longer historical experience of posturban polities. It is possible to follow several important strands of economic change from the "second urbanization" of the Early Historic up to the Early Modern, a chronological division increasingly referred to as the Middle Period of South Asian history.

Recent archaeological and historical scholarship on the Middle Period points to both a high degree of regional diversity in political and economic organization and a fluctuating degree of interregional commercial and political connectivity. Nevertheless, several consistent themes emerge: urbanization and related transformations of settlement; monetization and the increasing role of production for markets; the volatile relationship between long-distance exchange and local political and economic structure; the intensification of production; and the shifting roles of such specialized institutions as monasteries, temples, and guilds. In this review, I highlight these critical issues and, in particular, situate these economic transformations in the dynamics of political and social power and in the changing religious landscape of South Asia.

The disciplinary matrix of Middle Period South Asia is diverse, with historians, art historians, and anthropologists staking out intellectual territories. I seek here to integrate some contributions of archaeology into broader issues of commerce and culture, and to consider what additional questions and insights might derive from analysis of the material record. Specific contributions lie in the areas of regional settlement patterns, urban layout and spatial structure of built environments, human modification of the natural landscape, contexts of production of a range of agricultural and nonagricultural goods, and the tracking of specific raw materials, manufactures, and media of exchange across space and time. Data from archaeological survey and excavation become relatively less abundant as we move through time, while historical data present a complementary distribution.

Lurking behind any discussion of networks of exchange, politics, and society in South Asia or the Indian Ocean region more generally is a consideration of European colonialism and domination, and of the emergence and inevitability (or not) of the "World System" and of capitalism (Dale 1994; Chase-Dunn & Hall 1991; Chaudhuri 1985, 1990; Pearson 1988; Perlin 1983; Schneider 1977; Subrahmanyam 1990a,c; Wallerstein 1974). Was there—is there?—a World System? Were there "precapitalist" world systems? Were Asian economies headed toward capitalism at the time of colonization? Is there an Asian mercantilism that was not or could not become capitalist? Were states in Asia uninterested and uninvolved in trade? What role did markets play in precolonial economies and to what extent was money a part of how they functioned? Did European involvement in trade and later in governance fundamentally restructure Asian states, economies, and their regional linkages? Is there a structuring role here for cultural difference? Even for the study of very early periods, these concerns have tended to implicitly structure anthropological and historical research. There are two dimensions to this structuring role: 1. Precolonial and precapitalist periods are seen as the "seeds," "roots," or "stems" of colonialism and capitalism; the burden of the less recent past is to become the more recent past. 2. Colonial understandings of Asia and models of economic organization derived from contemporary capitalist societies have tended to structure our views of the past itself. I do not pretend to answer or even systematically address all these questions here, but it is imperative not to ignore this intellectual shadow behind even what seems to be straightforward empirical research. My strategy, then, is to highlight some substantive patterns in the Indian Ocean trade with an explicit focus on three themes or abstractions: "commerce," "culture," and "the state."

THE EARLY HISTORIC

Urbanism and Trade

Scholarship on the Early Historic period (ca 500 BC–AD 500) has concentrated on the Gangetic plain, the region with the first evidence for cities after the end of Harappan urbanism in the second millennium BC (but see Shaffer 1986). This period also marks the advent of decipherable written language in South Asia, a shift with implications for both the period and its scholarship (Morrison 1995b, pp. 206–7). The Gangetic "second urbanization" has been a major focus of archaeological research in South Asia since its beginnings under British colonialism (Chakrabarti 1988). In the past century, excavations have been carried out at urban sites such as Hastinapura (Lal 1955), Ahichchatra (Ghosh & Panigrahi 1946), Atranjikhera (Gaur 1983), Kausambi (Sharma 1960, 1969), Rajghat (Narain & Roy 1976, 1977; Narain & Singh 1977), Vaisali (Krishna Deva & Misra 1961, Sinha & Roy 1969), Rajagriha (Ghosh 1951, Chakrabarti 1976), Sringaverapura (Lal 1993), Mathura (Joshi 1989), Pataliputra (Sinha & Narain 1970), and Ujjain (Banerjee 1965), among many others. Chakrabarti (1995a) and Ghosh (1989a) provide concordances of the roughly 130 sites dating to between 200 BC and AD 300 that have been excavated (Sharma 1994, p. 13). Allchin (1995) provided the most recent synthesis of Early Historic archaeology in north India.

Among the similarities in material culture and urban form at these sites are the presence of fortifications and ramparts, cast copper and punch-marked silver coins (Cribb 1985), and the increasingly common use of iron (Allchin 1995). All these features set Early Historic cities apart from earlier settlements in the region and point to significant changes in political, economic, and social organization over this period. As noted below, settlements of this period also contain indicators (texts, exotic ceramics, beads, coins, glass, and sculpture) of substantial long-distance connections within and beyond the subcontinent (Lahiri 1992, Ray 1995).

The initial appearance of cities in what was previously a landscape of scattered small and medium-sized settlements separated by tracts of forest (Lal 1986, Sharma 1994) was followed by an overall expansion in both the number and size of settlements through time. Regional field studies are distressingly few; important exceptions include Makkan Lal's (1984) survey in the western and Erdosy's (1988) in the central Gangetic plain. Lal (1984) found continuity between the earlier (but overlapping) Painted Grey Ware (PGW) (Tripathi 1976) and the later (Early Historic) NBP "horizons." NBP, or NBPW, is shorthand for Northern Black Polished Ware, a ceramic ware whose distribution is centered on the Gangetic plain but which has a wide, if thin, distribution across South Asia.

This sketchy regional archaeological picture, along with evidence from texts, suggests a landscape of variable population density, with nodal cities playing key roles as political capitals and loci of production, exchange, and consumption (Sharma 1994). Nevertheless, in spite of the robust archaeological and textual evidence for vibrant urban centers, a nagging prejudice against seeing Indian cities as being "really" urban, a prejudice clear from Marx onward (Morrison 1994, O'Leary 1989), persists in the archaeological literature. Erdosy (1988), for example, claims that Early Historic cities "never met the criteria set by Weber for truly urban settlements in spite of their transitory magnificence. Society remained correspondingly inert in the absence of the stimulus expected from its largest congregations of populations" (p. 152). He goes on to claim (1988) that cities could not "free themselves [presumably he refers to people or institutions within cities] from the political powers that created them in the first place" (p. 152).

These orientalist notions of Asiatic lassitude (see e.g. Breckenridge & van der Veer 1993, O'Leary 1989, Wittfogel 1957) and of the inexorable dependence of social, economic, and cultural dynamics on politics (the inevitability of despotism) are clearly not supportable (cf Misra 1994). Commitment to this line of thought, however, has had the effect of deflecting archaeological attention from investigating the actual organization of production, distribution, and consumption within urban sites and their degree of autonomy or dependence on political structure or patronage. If Subrahmanyam & Bayly's (1990) portfolio capitalists had antecedents in the Early Historic period, archaeology would thus be of little use in elucidating this. Fortunately, historians have had much to say on the organization of both politics and exchange; this scholarship reveals a dynamic arena of exchange in which organized groups of traders, generally glossed as "guilds" (Ray 1986, Thapar 1995a) operated largely autonomously of political institutions. Rulers did, however, interest themselves in exchange, as indicated by texts describing coastal trading cities and networks (e.g. Huntingford 1980).

Empire and Region: *Archaeological and Historical Patterns*

The early urban societies of the Gangetic plain supported a number of nascent, competing state polities (Thapar 1966, 1984), polities eventually engulfed by the expansive Mauryan empire (321–185 BC). The geographical extent of Mauryan claims to supremacy is truly impressive. However, if these rather extravagant territorial claims, particularly under its most famous ruler, Aśoka, were indeed justified in terms of actual control, this would mean that the earliest South Asian empire was also the largest and most tightly integrated (Schwartzberg 1992). A systematic treatment of the Mauryan empire lies beyond the scope of this review, but it is important to mention the distributions of two material forms thought to be associated with Mauryan political expansion and to note their problematic interpretation.

The first class of objects are texts, the Aśokan rock and pillar edicts (Sircar 1979). These are the oldest deciphered texts in South Asia and can be divided into major and minor edicts on the basis of content and length (Irwin 1983, Thapar 1988). The distribution of Aśokan edicts (Figure 1) centers around the Gangetic home of the empire, with peripheral examples in or near major cities of the northwest, east, and west and a significant cluster in the south, in northern Karnataka (Kotraiah 1983). Clearly, such representations make both direct and implied claims to power and hegemony (Thapar 1995a), claims that must, however, be treated with caution, particularly in outlying areas such as the Karnataka cluster.

A different class of material, but one sometimes similarly interpreted, is the fine slipped black ceramic, Northern Black Polished (NBP) Ware. This ceramic ware was probably limited in its distribution across social classes, representing a "deluxe" (Ray 1994b; see also Banerjee 1965, Roy 1986) rather than utilitarian ware. Although technological source analysis is urgently needed, the distribution of NBP (Figure 1) suggests one or more manufacturing locales on the Gangetic plain. Its extensive distribution outside this area (usually in very small quantities), however, has suggested to archaeologists an association with Mauryan political expansion, so much so that NBP is sometimes seen as a marker of Mauryan imperialism (e.g. Allchin 1995, p. 133; Ray 1986, p. 52; cf Margabandhu 1985). Such an interpretation illustrates the impact on archaeo-

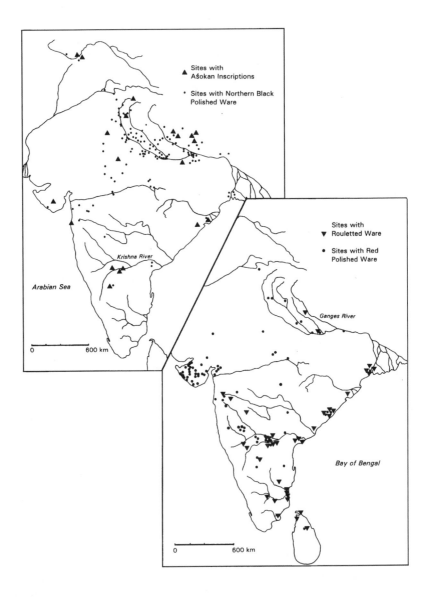

Figure 1   South Asia. Distribution of Aśokan Inscriptions and Northern Black Polished Ware (NBP) ceramics, distributions of Rouletted Ware and Red Polished Ware ceramics (data from Begley 1992, Morrison 1995b, Orton 1992, Schwartzberg 1992).

logical systematics of the implied primacy of political power in South Asian history critiqued above and seems more properly a proposition to be evaluated than an assumption on which to build. Interpretations of NBP can also be seen as uncritical archaeological transformations of arguments by historians about the primacy of the Gangetic plain as an exporter of "civilization" to central and southern India, arguments that range from a notion of simple cultural and political "influence" to outright control (e.g. Kosambi 1989, Pannikar 1956).

Cities and states in both the Deccan and the far south do appear later than those of the Gangetic plain and, far from representing independent developments, these sites contain indisputable evidence of contact with the states, empires, and religious institutions of the north. Older studies of urbanization stressed exogenous factors in the development of complex political organization in the region (Kosambi 1989, Pannikar 1956; see Thapar 1984), which with trade has been viewed as the raison d'etre for the political and economic changes immediately before and coincident with the establishment of the Satavahana polity in the Deccan. Institutional Buddhism has also been assigned a key role in this trade expansion. This view of southern passivity and retardation has been increasingly challenged (Parasher 1994, Parasher-Sen 1993). Significant changes in agricultural organization and settlement appear to predate the Early Historic, and existing Megalithic or Iron Age settlements show a degree of status differentiation and economic sophistication that belies their rather poor image (Morrison 1995b, Parasher-Sen 1993).

The most dynamic contemporary scholarship, in fact, is associated with the south, with work that integrates archaeological and textual data increasingly the norm (Begley & DePuma 1992, Parasher-Sen 1993, Ray 1986, 1994a,b). Early excavations at key sites in the greater Deccan, including Ter (Chapekar 1969), Nagarjunakonda (Subrahmanyam et al 1975), Bhokardan (Deo 1974), Nasik (Sankalia & Deo 1955), Maheshwar and Navdatoli (Sankalia et al 1958), and Nevasa (Sankalia et al 1960), and the south such as Brahmagiri (Wheeler 1947) and Arikamedu (Wheeler et al 1946), among others, have been supplemented by more recent work at Satanikota (Ghosh 1986), Mantai (Sri Lanka, Carswell 1992), Sannati, Thotlakonda (Krishna Sastry et al 1992), and Bavikonda (Prasad 1994), and by reexcavation at Arikamedu (Begley 1983, 1992). This research shows a dynamic pattern of urban growth in the western Deccan, the Krishna valley and delta (Krishna Sastry 1983) and in the Palghat-Coimbatore region (Soundara Rajan 1994, p. 4), where settlement density was very high. Elsewhere, urban settlements were widely spaced, and many peninsular residents lived outside the immediate sphere of urban society. Notably, putatively earlier Megalithic burial/memorial sites and ceramic forms continued to be produced alongside Buddhist structures and Early Historic ceramic forms.

Recent research on long-distance exchange has also challenged Wheeler's (1955) widely cited ideas about the presence of Roman trading colonies in southeast India; such colonies were previously thought to have sparked "civilization" in the south (Maloney 1968, Warmington 1928). Recent analyses of Mediterranean amphorae (Slane 1992, Will 1992), glass (Stern 1992), terra sigillata ceramics (restricted to Arikamedu, Comfort 1992), bronzes (DePuma 1992), and other objects (Deo 1992) have indicated a wide range of production locales and a variety of distribution patterns (Begley 1992). This research has definitively shown an active pre-Roman trade and has failed to substantiate the presence of substantial foreign colonies in south India (Ray 1994b). These new perspectives have prompted inquiry into the variable social and ethnic identity of *yavanas* [foreigners, sometimes identified as Greeks or Indo-Greeks (Cimino 1994, Karttunen 1994, Parasher 1991)] mentioned in texts and implicated in exchange networks, giving Early Historic urbanism and exchange a decidedly more indigenous feel in contemporary scholarship.

One example of this recent improvement in archaeological understanding of exchange networks can be illustrated with reference to the distributions of two ceramic wares (Figure 1), Red Polished Ware (RPW) (Orton 1992) and Rouletted Ware (Begley 1983, 1986, 1992). Both of these wares were once thought to be either imported or Mediterranean inspired. Distributions of these wares suggest, first, that RPW was produced in Gujarat (though to my knowledge no sourcing analysis has been done), and that vessels made their way as far south as Anuradhapura, Sri Lanka (Deraniyagala 1972, 1986), as well as to the Gangetic plain and the northwest. Rouletted Ware is distributed entirely differently, found along the shores of the Bay of Bengal and in such key transpeninsular regions as the Krishna basin. It is thus possible to suggest separate spheres of exchange for the east and west coasts of the peninsula (Begley 1992). Further, recent X-ray fluorescence studies of Rouletted Ware indicate, contrary to previous expectations (Begley 1992, Wheeler et al 1946), that this ware was produced at several locations in the lower Ganges, with an epicenter at the sites of Tamluk and Chandraketugarh in Bengal (Gogte 1997), a finding that calls for radical recentering of our ideas about exchange networks in South and Southeast Asia (and see Carswell 1992, Liu 1988). Distributions of Roman coins also indicate differences in distribution between the east and west coasts (Ray 1986); more systematic work on coins is called for.

Buddhism: Creed, Monastery, and Connection

The establishment of institutionalized religions during the Early Historic, especially the "heterodox sects" of Buddhism and Jainism, has been linked by many writers to the nascent urbanism and the growing power of states and empires during this period as well as to the apparent rise in the volume of long-distance exchange (Heitzman 1984, Ray 1986). I draw specific attention to the special role Buddhism has been assigned in facilitating trade. Buddhism, in this view, overcame many of the problems Brahminical Hinduism presented to merchants, including strict rules of commensality, limited avenues for social advancement, and a prohibition against overseas travel (Liu 1988; Ray 1986, 1995). Further, Buddhism has been seen as an urban and missionary religion, seeming to account both for its rapid spread to Southeast and East Asia (for a review, see Barnes 1995) and for its apparent dynamism relative to Hinduism. It is worth noting that British colonial scholarship on the Early Historic fixed on a notion of Buddhism as a (positive) alternative to a negatively portrayed Hinduism (Chakrabarti 1988), and that orientalist scholarship more generally often blamed India's "backwardness" on Hinduism.

This particular argument is strikingly similar to later arguments about the spread of Islam and its putative affinity with merchants, cities, and trade (Risso 1995; but cf Eaton 1993). As the following sections show, however, empirical trends in South Asian commerce appear more complex than could be accounted for by such a simple cultural correlation. Finally, it is worth noting here recent scholarship that actively contests the putative antibusiness character of Hinduism. First, Dale's (1994) recent study of Indian (mostly Hindu) merchants in Central Asia and Iran in the seventeenth and eighteenth centuries points to their financial clout (partly related to their religiously sanctioned ability to charge interest). Rudner's (1994) analysis of the Nattukottai Chettiars, a merchant banking caste, provides a similar counterperspective for a later period.

The spectacular rock-cut Buddhist monastic "cave" complexes of the Deccan, an architectural form that persisted until the twelfth century AD (Nagaraju 1981), have been a focus of study for over 100 years (Burgess 1883, Dehejia 1972, Nagaraju 1981). Over 800 rock-cut caves are known in the western Deccan alone, ranging from isolated cells to large, elaborate complexes. As discussed below, Hindu temples in Middle period South India had political and economic significance in addition to their more evident functions as ritual and scholarly centers. Buddhist monks and monastic complexes, similarly, may have been involved in both exchange and politics. Many scholars, for example, have noted that Buddhist monastic complexes are situated along trade routes (passes) leading through the western Ghat mountain chain (Dehejia 1972, Nagaraju 1981, Sarao 1990), and some have suggested that monasteries thus played an active role in regional exchange. Monastic complexes, however, were also located in cities (Chakrabarti 1995b), and the location of monasteries might also be partly understood with reference to the needs of the nonproducing Buddhist religious to have access to agricultural produce (Morrison 1995b).

That monastic complexes were supported by the gifts of merchants, including residents of far-away towns, is clear from the inscriptional record (Ray 1986, Sarao 1990). However, merchants are only a part of a record of prestation in which agriculturalists, small-scale craftspeople, and other nonelites, including women (Willis 1992), are prominently featured. This pattern of "collective patronage" (Dehejia 1992) contrasts markedly with later inscriptions that derive largely from elites of various sorts (cf Morrison & Lycett 1994). In a few cases, endowments were invested with merchant guilds in order to provide a perpetual income flow to the monastery (Chakrabarti 1995b). Thus, it is hard to avoid the conclusion that producer and distributor guilds must have had some influence in the affairs of the monasteries. However, these guilds appear to have themselves been relatively independent of state control (Kulke & Rothermund 1986, p. 102; Ray 1986; Thapar 1984).

Neither did political leaders control the Buddhist assembly, or *sangha,* a pattern that contrasts with the control later exercised by Thai monarchs over Buddhist monasteries (Ishii 1993, cf Gunawardana 1979). However, the expansion of Buddhism across South Asia was not divorced from the actions of elites. One thinks, for example, of the emperor Aśoka's famous conversion to Buddhism and subsequent support for Buddhist beliefs and institutions. Outside its Gangetic homeland, the spread of Buddhism was also associated with the extension of state power and state sponsorship (Heitzman 1984, p. 131). Pre-Satavahana *stupas* do occur in the Deccan (Ray 1986, p. 52), but in the Satavahana period the number of Buddhist structures increased dramatically. Although the Satavahana rulers were themselves not Buddhists (Chakrabarti 1995b), they nevertheless provided significant material and other support to Buddhist institutions. Most striking is the close association between the tempo of cave-cutting and the political fortunes of the Satavahanas. As Ray (1986, p. 87) noted, there were two major periods of monastery construction, the first between ca 100 and 20 BC and the second between AD 50 and 200. The 70-year lull in construction coincides with a period in which Satavahana political fortunes were waning.

The Early Historic period is one of the most active arenas of integrated research in South Asian archaeology and history. Much work remains to be done, however, on the contexts of production of a range of agricultural and nonagricultural goods, and more specific studies tracking specific raw materials, manufactures, and media of exchange across space and time are required. Studies of consumption have barely begun. Our best distributional data at the moment come from coins, beads, and ceramics, but even our understanding of these is bound to change as material science approaches are joined with more synthetic studies.

Merchants, markets, and the state in the Early Historic were linked in complex and somewhat unclear ways. That merchant (and producer) guilds constituted strong structures, relatively independent of state power, seems clear. Markets and marketplaces were multiple (ports, urban markets, exchange within monasteries for the subsistence of monks) and variously organized. Buddhist monastic institutions were linked to the exercise and spread of state power, and, to some extent, exchange to Buddhism, but the role of particular states in exchange is unclear. Economies do not seem to have been generally monetized, in spite of the appearance of the first coins, but there were clearly sophisticated financial instruments that allowed long-distance exchange and that facilitated investment of specie. The proposed special role of Buddhism in trade and urban expansion, however, seems overstated both in light of later developments and in consideration of the continued religious diversity of the period.

THE FIRST PART OF THE MIDDLE PERIOD

The early Middle period (AD 500–1200), sometimes referred to as the Early Medieval, is rather arbitrarily set off from the Early Historic. In north India, this has been characterized as a period in which both trade and centralized state power declined, thus the parallel to feudal Europe (on this hotly debated topic, see e.g. Kulke 1995b, Mukhia 1995, Sharma 1995). This period is one of great regional diversity in polity and economy, with no simple way to characterize change across the entire subcontinent (see overviews by Kulke & Rothermund 1986, Nilakanta Sastri 1975; and critical reviews by Habib 1995, Heitzman 1995, Inden 1990, Kulke 1995b, Subrahmanyam 1986, Wink 1990, among others). Archaeological research focusing on this period is minimal, and synthetic treatments of archaeological data rare (see Ghosh 1989b). For the sake of brevity, I restrict my discussion to one small part of the period and to the Chola empire in south India (AD 850–1200), focusing on archaeological research.

Buddhism, Hinduism, Islam: Institutional Religion and the World of Commerce

The first millennium AD saw the beginnings of the decline of Buddhism across India. Buddhism's eclipse was a highly variable process, and Buddhist institutions survived in South India until the latter part of the Middle period (Abraham 1988, Nilakanta Sastri 1975) and, of course, never died out in Sri Lanka and parts of Southeast and East Asia. In South India, (Hindu) Śaivism and Vaiśnavism largely replaced Buddhism as objects of royal patronage (Champakalakshmi 1995). Debates about the causes of Buddhism's decline (Ray

1994b) are rather inconclusive, but again association with elite patronage appears to be one important factor.

This period also saw the phenomenal expansion of Islam in the Indian Ocean region (Chaudhuri 1985, Wink 1990). The expansion of Islam as doctrine was felt primarily in the coastal regions (e.g. Dale 1990), although political expansion by Muslim-led polities certainly had an impact on the south. It is worth noting again that many arguments about the dramatic spread of Islam stress its special affinity to trade and traders (Risso 1995, and see Ibrahim 1990, Reid 1993b) and its urban character (cf Eaton 1993). In this we see a structural echo of accounts of expanding Buddhism. As outlined below, however, the Chola period was one of active trade and expanding cities (Champakalakshmi 1994) in spite of the "Hindu renaissance" (Nilakanta Sastri 1975) of the period. Jainism continued to have local importance, especially in Karnataka.

Polity and Economy: The Chola Empire

Although the Cholas of the Tamil country of southeast India were mentioned in Early Historic Sangam poetry, it was not until AD 850 that the Chola polity (re)emerged to claim hegemony over much of the south. There is an immense historical literature on this period; active debate centers particularly on the nature of Chola political organization. Stein's (1980, 1995) model of the "segmentary state" challenged earlier conceptions (cf Nilakanta Sastri 1975, 1955) of a powerful, centralized, bureaucratic state (see Champakalakshmi 1981, Kulke 1995b). This debate both grew out of and led to (e.g. Heitzman 1987, 1995; Talbot 1991) careful and detailed analyses of texts, particularly inscriptions. Unfortunately, archaeological research has not kept pace with this historical scholarship.

Inscriptional data make clear the important role of Hindu temples in this period, not only for ritual and scholarship, but also as economic centers with considerable political influence, particularly in royal legitimation. Temples appear as beneficiaries of gifts, especially livestock and cash (Spencer 1983), and thus as holders of considerable wealth (Stein 1980). However, Hindu temples were only one of several types of religious institutions, all of which played economic and political roles. These included *brahmadeyas,* settlements of Brahmins with their own assemblies (Jha 1985, Stein 1980), as well as Buddhist and Jain temples. Temples, along with their wealth, were managed by committees, which could be variously composed of land-controlling agriculturalists, Brahmins, merchants, or others (Nilakanta Sastri 1955, Stein 1980).

Unlike studies of religious institutions, there are few specific studies of merchants and trade (but see Mines 1984). The most thorough analyses are those of Abraham (1988), Ramaswamy (1985a), and Hall (1980), who describe well-organized merchant guilds with links to associations of producers such as potters, weavers, leather workers, market gardeners, and farmers. Different types of merchants operated on either a regional or an international scale, marketing such products as iron, textiles, livestock, and forest products including spices (Abraham 1988, Hall 1980). According to Hall (1980), local merchant guilds had monopolistic power within their own marketing territory, power that was negotiated with political leaders and could include landholding, management of temple finances and land, collection of taxes for the state, and even local political administration. Some guilds supported private armies (Hall 1980, Mines 1984). Inscriptional data show merchant support for, as well as occasional administration of, both Hindu and Jain temples (Abraham 1988, pp. 97–98). Abraham (1988, p. 10) noted the dramatic explosion of all forms of trade in the thirteenth century, the end of this period, but it is important to note that both local and long-distance exchange prospered under the Cholas (and see Bandaranayaka et al 1990), that Chola rulers had an active interest (Hall 1980) in trade but were unable or unwilling to closely control it, and that merchants appear to have had both economic and political clout.

Historians describe periodic markets and fairs, as well as permanent urban marketplaces; media of exchange seem to have varied in different contexts. In some cases, "barter" (Abraham 1988, p. 123) was employed; in others equivalencies in rice were set, apparently by merchant groups (Hall 1980). Coined money, however, was employed in long-distance trade (Abraham 1988, pp. 123–24), and some luxury goods had prices fixed in gold. These smaller markets were dwarfed by the great port cities, with the Pandya port of Mammalapuram playing a secondary role to the Chola royal port, Kaveripattinam.

Recently published excavations from Kaveripattinam (Soundara Rajan 1994) describe the long occupation of this port city from the third century BC to the thirteenth century AD (Soundara Rajan 1994, pp. 132–33). The earlier occupation included the temporally overlapping Megalithic or Iron Age and Early Historic periods, when Rouletted Ware and Red Slipped Ware were found, as well as Buddhist structures and a wharf, the latter radiocarbon dated to 300–200 BC, uncalibrated (Soundara Rajan 1994, p. 140). The latter Middle Period occupation represented two "sizable towns" (Soundara Rajan 1994, p. 132) in which Chola coins and at least one Hindu temple were located. Dense modern occupation made it difficult to expose much residential architecture. Chinese Celadon ceramics and Vijayanagara coins mark the end of the occupation sequence. On a regional scale, the Kaveripattinam project brought to light an impressive number of habitation sites across the Kaveri delta (Soundara Rajan 1994, pp. 135–39), with an apparently continuous temporal range from the Iron Age through the latter Middle period. Several of these sites have surface artifact assemblages that point to the possibility of bead production or large-scale exchange.

The Kaveripattinam excavations—and a very few others (see Ramachandran 1980)—are the exception, however, to the general archaeological emphasis on art and architecture. Most scholarly attention has been paid to Chola bronze sculptures and temple architecture; outstanding recent work includes the French Institute's monumental study of the temple complex at Tiruvannamalai (Guilmoto et al 1989, Hernault et al 1989, Reiniche 1989, Srinivasan & Reiniche 1989) that integrates epigraphy, architecture, and ethnography. In general, these studies come from a very different research tradition than that of research on earlier periods. There has been, to date, little archaeological focus on regional analysis and even less on the material remains of nonelites, of domestic contexts, or of economies (Sri Lanka is an exception to this; recent archaeological research is described by Coningham 1995, Coningham & Allchin 1992, Myrdal-Runebjer 1994, Prickett-Fernando 1990, Weisshaar & Wijeyapala 1994).

THE LATTER PART OF THE MIDDLE PERIOD

Expansion and Change: Temples, Trade, and Empire

The so-called Late Medieval or Precolonial period (AD 1200–1600) was one of dramatic change in settlement dynamics, regional and long-distance economies, and political organization. Only a few of these important trends can be noted here. First, the expansion of cities and settlement density more generally was quite marked, with agricultural expansion keeping pace. According to Stein (1980), this agricultural expansion across South Asia mostly took the form of permanent plough cultivation pushing back areas used under other land-use regimes; swidden cultivation, hunting and gathering, pastoralism. Both urban and agricultural expansion have been linked to Hindu temples, for whom there now seem to be fewer institutional competitors. Temple economies and their varied roles in agriculture, politics, ritual, craft production, and investment, particularly under the expansionist Vijayanagara empire (fourteenth to early seventeenth centuries) are described by Breckenridge (1985), Karashima (1992), Stein (1992), and Talbot (1991), among others. Significantly, this was also a period of continued change in Hindu practice, with *bhakti* or devotional sects, sometimes taking a rather antiauthoritarian cast (cf Narayana Rao 1990) expanding across South India (for a review, see Verghese 1995). Simultaneously, elite culture—and courtly architecture (Michell 1992)—was increasingly modeled, even in "Hindu" states, after patterns of conduct, dress, and deportment established by Deccani and north Indian "Muslim" polities (Wagoner 1995).

Stein (1980, 1995) also applied his "segmentary state" model to the Vijay-anagara polity, and there exists a substantial literature, most of it critical, pointing out that Vijayanagara kings exercised a greater degree of control over material resources than Stein allows (Champakalakshmi 1981, Inden 1990, Palat 1987). On a more local scale, archaeological work has shown this control to have been highly contextually variable (Sinopoli & Morrison 1995).

As many scholars have noted, the latter part of the Middle Period brought with it an unprecedented expansion in the volume of international exchange, not just in India but across the Indian Ocean (e.g. Chaudhuri 1985, Reid 1993a, Subrahmanyam 1990). Some, but not all (Dale 1994), of this expansion grew out of the expanded participation of European traders and trade organizations in the region; a vast historical literature explores many dimensions of these exchange relationships (e.g. Arasaratnam 1986, Bouchon 1988, Subrahmanyam 1990a). The fact that this period saw the beginnings of sustained European involvement in South Asian markets and, ultimately, South Asian affairs, however, has tended to change the character and even analytical focus of historical research (with its flood of new textual data) so that coastal regions and European activity form the focus of most research. The most thorough review of both land- and sea-based trade in South India in this period is that of Subrahmanyam (1990a).

As Subrahmanyam (1990a) and others (e.g. Abraham 1988) noted, the strong merchant guilds of the Chola period appear at this time to have lost much of their influence, and many either disappear from textual notice or seem to have been drastically reorganized (and see Mines 1984). At the same time, these groups are replaced by individual merchants such as the newly emergent "master weavers" who controlled both production and distribution of some textiles (Ramaswamy 1985b). It has also been argued that the sixteenth century finally saw the monetization of the Vijayanagara economy (Palat 1987), and discussions about the payment of some taxes in cash (e.g. Breckenridge 1985, Palat 1987) suggest that this process was closely tied to the exercise of state or local political power. The expansion of trade networks, the participation of new groups of traders, and the political volatility of the period, especially after the fall of Vijayanagara (Narayana Rao et al 1992) created the contexts in which Subrahmanyam's (1990a) portfolio capitalists—Arasaratnam's (1986) "political merchants"—emerged in the seventeenth century.

Archaeological Research: The Vijayanagara Empire

Recent archaeological work on this period outstrips the effort expended on the former part of the Middle Period but is overshadowed by research on the Early Historic. Excavated sites in the south include the fortified settlement of

Daulatabad (Devgiri) in western India (Mate 1985) and Champaner in Gujarat (Mehta 1977), both political capitals. However, the most extensive archaeological work has taken place in or near the city of Vijayanagara, the capital of the eponymous empire (Devaraj & Patil 1991a,b; Fritz et al 1985; Morrison 1995a; Nagaraja Rao 1983, 1985; Narasimaiah 1992; Sinopoli 1993). This work has not, by in large, addressed issues of marketing and exchange (but see Morrison & Sinopoli 1992), concentrating instead on problems of religious architecture and iconography (Dallapiccola et al 1992, Verghese 1995, Wagoner 1991) and urban layout (Fritz 1986). The layout of the city of Vijayanagara, with its long "bazaar" streets associated with great temple complexes seems to accord well with textual descriptions of specialized market places and with historical understanding of the economic role of temples (Ismail 1984).

Ongoing surveys and test excavations in the city's hinterland document the massive expansion and intensification of agriculture in the fourteenth and, more dramatically, the sixteenth centuries (Morrison 1995a). Work both in the city and this larger region indicates the presence of numerous small-scale workshops producing utilitarian earthenware ceramics (Sinopoli 1993, Sinopoli & Morrison 1995), products that did not participate in large regional distribution networks. The most visible artifactual markers of long-distance exchange are imported ceramics, of which Chinese Celadon and porcelains make up the vast majority. In the region surrounding the city of Vijayanagara, porcelains have been found in a number of contexts outside the elite residential area of the city—where the largest number of these Chinese imports are found (Morrison 1990, Sinopoli 1986)—including small settlements, roads, and gateways. Thus, this luxury ware did move in a small way outside the orbit of the large cities. However, the quantity of porcelain at this populous inland capital is dwarfed by that found in contemporaneous port cities in East Africa, such as Kilwa (Chittick 1974), and in Red Sea and Persian Gulf ports (Rougeulle 1994). Further studies of Chinese ceramic material from Vijayanagara (Bailey-Goldschmidt 1995) promise to add to our understanding of these distributions.

CONCLUSION

Without indulging in "potentialities" arguments (Subrahmanyam 1990c, pp. 3–4) about what might have happened to the structure of South Asian trade had the European trading companies not appeared and had they not been followed by programs of colonial incorporation, it seems clear that a long view of South Asian commerce and culture indicates a degree of historical depth and sophistication in both local and interregional production and distribution that belies orientalist suppositions about the stagnant or solely agrarian character of

South Asian civilization. Without minimizing the important economic and political changes that began in the sixteenth century, changes that have been in some sense reified into a rigid World System, a long-term view of both material culture and texts shows a profound degree of South Asian commercial and cultural participation in the far-flung Indian Ocean trading world.

This participation is manifest in the distributions of exotic ceramics, precious and semiprecious stones, coins, and beads, and in the cultural forms and systems of belief expressed in art and architecture. The potential to learn a great deal more through archaeological analysis about the location and organization of production of a range of products and about their distribution remains high, with studies on Early Historic material currently on the forefront. Research on Vijayanagara archaeology has shown the degree of potential variation in productive organization of a range of goods (Sinopoli 1988, Sinopoli & Morrison 1995); these detailed local studies that integrate, for example, settlement history and agriculture with what is usually called by archaeologists "craft" production, point the way to a fuller understanding of local economic dynamics. A dynamic historical and anthropological scholarship on South Asia is currently exploring dimensions of commerce and culture that move beyond simple oppositions between merchants, markets, states, ideologies, and religions to consider their complex interpenetration and connection. Archaeology has, to now, lagged somewhat behind these intellectual developments, but it clearly has the potential to inform on dimensions of these issues uniquely visible in the archaeological record.

> **Visit the *Annual Reviews home page* at**
> **http://www.AnnualReviews.org.**

Literature Cited

Abraham M. 1988. *Two Medieval Merchant Guilds of South India.* Delhi: Manohar

Allchin FR. 1995. *The Archaeology of Early Historic South Asia: The Emergence of Cities and States.* Cambridge: Cambridge Univ. Press

Arasaratnam S. 1986. *Merchants, Companies and Commerce on the Coromandel Coast 1650–1740.* Delhi: Oxford Univ. Press

Bailey-Goldschmidt J. 1995. Vijayanagara and the commodity economy: porcelain as an indicator of international trade. *Presented at Annu. Conf. S. Asia, 24th,* Madison, Wis.

Bandaranayaka S, Dewaraja L, Silva R, Wimalaratne KDG, eds. 1990. *Sri Lanka and the Silk Road of the Sea.* Colombo: Sri Lanka Natl. Comm. UNESCO/Cent. Cult. Fund

Banerjee NR. 1965. *The Iron Age in India.* Delhi: Munshiram

Banga I, ed. 1994. *The City in Indian History.* Delhi: Manohar

Barnes GL. 1995. An Introduction to buddhist archaeology. *World Archaeol.* 27(2): 165–82

Begley V. 1983. Arikamedu reconsidered. *Am. J. Archaeol.* 87:461–68

Begley V. 1986. From Iron Age to Early Historical in South Indian archaeology. See Jacobsen 1986, pp. 297–319

Begley V. 1992. Ceramic evidence for pre-*Periplus* trade on the Indian coasts. See Begley & DePuma 1992, pp. 157–96

Begley V, DePuma RD, eds. 1992. *Rome and India: The Ancient Sea Trade.* Delhi: Oxford Univ. Press

Bouchon G. 1988. *"Regent of the Sea": Cannanore's Response to Portuguese Expansion, 1507–1528.* Delhi: Oxford Univ. Press

Breckenridge CA. 1985. Social storage and the extension of agriculture in South India 1350 to 1750. In *Vijayanagara: City and Empire,* ed. AL Dallapiccola, pp. 41–72. Wiesbaden: Franz Steiner

Breckenridge CA, van der Veer P, eds. 1993. *Orientalism and the Postcolonial Predicament.* Philadelphia: Univ. Pa. Press

Burgess J. 1883. *Report on the Buddhist Cave Temples and their Inscriptions.* Delhi: ASI Rep., N. S. 4

Carswell J. 1992. The Port of Mantai, Sri Lanka. See Begley & DePuma 1992, pp. 197–203

Chakrabarti DK. 1976. Rajagriha. *World Archaeol.* 7:261–68

Chakrabarti DK. 1988. *A History of Indian Archaeology from the Beginning to 1947.* Delhi: Munshiram

Chakrabarti DK. 1995a. *The Archaeology of Ancient Indian Cities.* Delhi: Oxford Univ. Press

Chakrabarti DK. 1995b. Buddhist sites across South Asia as influenced by political and economic forces. *World Archaeol.* 27(2): 185–202

Champakalakshmi R. 1981. Peasant state and society in medieval South India: a review article. *Ind. Econ. Soc. Hist. Rev.* 18: 411–26

Champakalakshmi R. 1994. Urban processes in early medieval Tamil Nadu. See Banga 1994, pp. 47–68

Champakalakshmi R. 1995. State and economy: South India, Circa AD 400–1300. See Thapar 1995b, pp. 266–308

Chapekar BN. 1969. *Report on the Excavation at Ter.* Pune: Latkar

Chase-Dunn C, Hall TD, eds. *Core/Periphery Relations in Precapitalist Worlds.* Boulder: Westview

Chaudhuri KN. 1985. *Trade and Civilisation in the Indian Ocean: An Economic History from the Rise of Islam to 1750.* Cambridge: Cambridge Univ. Press

Chaudhuri KN. 1990. *Asia Before Europe: Economy and Civilisation of the Indian Ocean from the Rise of Islam to 1750.* Cambridge: Cambridge Univ. Press

Chittick N. 1974. *Kilwa: An Islamic Trading City on the East African Coast.* Nairobi: Br. Inst. East. Afr.

Cimino RM. 1994. The *Yavanas* (Westerners). In *Ancient Rome and India,* ed. RM Cimino, pp. 64–74. Delhi: Inst. Ital. Medio Est. Oriente

Comfort H. 1992. Terra Sigillata at Arikamedu. See Begley & DePuma 1992, pp. 134–50

Coningham R. 1995. Monks, caves, and kings: a reassessment of the nature of early Buddhism in Sri Lanka. *World Archaeol.* 27(2):222–42

Coningham R, Allchin FR. 1992. Anuradha Citadel Archaeological Project: preliminary report of the third season of Sri Lankan–British excavations at Salgaha Watta. *S. Asian Stud.* 8:155–67

Cribb J. 1985. Dating India's earliest coins. See Schotsmans & Taddei 1985, pp. 535–54

Dale SF. 1990. *Islamic Society on the South Asian Frontier: The Mappilas of Malabar 1498–1922.* Oxford: Clarendon

Dale SF. 1994. *Indian Merchants and Eurasian Trade, 1600–1750.* Cambridge: Cambridge Univ. Press

Dallapiccola AL, Fritz JM, Michell G, Rajasekhara S. 1992. *The Ramachandra Temple.* Delhi: AIIS/Manohar

Dehejia V. 1972. *Early Buddhist Rock Temples: A Chronological Study.* London: Thames/Hudson

Dehejia V. 1992. Collective and popular bases of early Buddhist patronage: sacred monuments, 100 BC–AD 250. See Miller 1992, pp. 35–45

Deo SB. 1974. *Excavations at Bhokardan (Bhogavardhana).* Nagpur: Aurangabad

Deo SB. 1992. Roman trade: archaeological discoveries in Western India. See Begley & DePuma 1992, pp. 39–45

DePuma RD. 1992. The Roman bronzes from Kohlapur. See Begley & DePuma 1992, pp. 82–112

Deraniyagala S. 1972. The Citadel of Anuradhapura 1969: excavations in the Gedige area. *Anc. Ceylon* 2:48–170

Deraniyagala S. 1986. Excavations in the Citadel of Anuradhapura: Gedige 1984. *Anc. Ceylon* 6:39–47

Devaraj DK, Patil CS, eds. 1991a. *Vijayanagara: Progress of Research 1984–87.* Mysore: Dir. Archaeol. Mus.

Devaraj DK, Patil CS, eds. 1991b. *Vijayanagara: Progress of Research 1987–88.* Mysore: Dir. Archaeol. Mus.

Eaton R. 1993. *The Rise of Islam and the Bengal Frontier 1204–1760*. Berkeley: Univ. Calif. Press

Erdosy G. 1988. *Urbanisation in Early Historic India*. Oxford: BAR Int. Ser. 430

Fritz JM. 1986. Vijayanagara: authority and meaning of a South Indian imperial capital. *Am. Anthropol.* 88:44–55

Fritz JM, Michell G, Nagaraja Rao MS. 1985. *Where Kings and Gods Meet: The Royal Centre at Vijayanagara*. Tucson: Univ. Ariz. Press

Gaur RC. 1983. *Excavations at Atranjikhera: Early Civilization of the Upper Ganga Basin*. Delhi: Motilal

Ghosh A. 1951. Rajgir 1950. *Anc. India* 7: 66–78

Ghosh A, ed. 1989a. *Encyclopedia of Indian Archaeology*. Delhi: Munshiram

Ghosh A. 1989b. Late historical. See Ghosh 1989a, pp. 151–63

Ghosh A, Panigrahi KC. 1946. Pottery of Ahichchhatra (U.P.). *Anc. India* 1:37–59

Ghosh NC. 1986. *Excavations at Satanikota, 1977–78*. Delhi: ASI Mem. 82

Gogte VD. 1997. Chandraketurgarh-Tamluk region of Bengal: the source of early historic Rouletted Ware from India and Southeast Asia. *Man Environ.* 32(1)

Guilmoto C, Reiniche M-L, Pichard P. 1989. *Tiruvannamalai: A Śaiva Sacred Complex of South India*. La Ville, 5. Pondicherry: Inst. Fr. Pondichéry

Gunawardana RALH. 1979. *Robe and Plough: Monasticism and Economic Interest in Early Medieval Sri Lanka*. Tucson: Univ. Ariz. Press

Habib I. 1995. *Essays in Indian History: Towards a Marxist Perception*. Delhi: Tulika

Hall KR. 1980. *Trade and Statecraft in the Age of the Colas*. Delhi: Abhinav

Heitzman J. 1984. Early Buddhism, trade, and empire. In *Studies in the Archaeology and Palaeoanthropology of South Asia*, ed. KAR Kennedy, G Possehl, pp. 121–37. Delhi: Oxford/IBH

Heitzman J. 1987. Temple urbanism in medieval South India. *J. Asian Stud.* 46:791–826

Heitzman J. 1995. State formation in South India, 850–1280. See Kulke 1995a, pp. 162–94

Hernault F, Pichard P, DeLoche J. 1989. *Tiruvannamalai: A Śaiva Sacred Complex of South India: L'Archéologie du Site*, Vol. 2. Pondicherry: Inst. Fr Pondichéry

Huntingford GWB. 1980. *The Periplus of the Erythraean Sea*. London: Hakluyt Soc. (From Greek)

Ibrahim M. 1990. *Merchant Capital and Islam*. Austin: Univ. Texas Press

Inden R. 1990. *Imagining India*. London: Blackwell

Irwin J. 1983. The true chronology of Aśokan Pillars. *Art. Asiae* 44(4):247–65

Ishii Y. 1993. Religious patterns and economic change in Siam in the sixteenth and seventeenth centuries. See Reid 1993a, pp. 180–96

Ismail K. 1984. *Karnataka Temples: Their Role in Socio-Economic Life*. Delhi: Sundeep

Jacobsen J, ed. 1986. *Studies in the Archaeology of India and Pakistan*. Delhi: Oxford/IBH

Jha DN. 1985. Relevance of "peasant state and society" to Pallava-Cola times. In *Indus Valley to Mekong Delta: Explorations in Epigraphy*, ed. N Karashima, pp. 103–40. Madras: New Era

Joshi MC. 1989. Mathurā as an ancient settlement. See Srinivasan 1989, pp. 165–70

Karashima N. 1992. *Toward a New Formation: South Indian Society Under Vijayanagar Rule*. Delhi: Oxford/IBH

Karttunen K. 1994. Yonas, Yavanas and related matters in Indian Epigraphy. See Parpola & Koskikallio 1994, pp. 329–36

Kosambi DD. 1989. *The Culture and Civilisation of Ancient India in Historical Outline*. Delhi: Vikas

Kotraiah CTM. 1983. Hampi before founding of Vijayanagara. In *Srinidhi: Perspectives in Indian Art and Archaeology*, ed. KV Raman, KG Krishnan, MS Ramaswami, N Karashima, AV Narasimha Murty, et al, pp. 381–88. Madras: New Era

Krishna Deva, Misra VK. 1961. *Vaiśalī Excavations 1950*. Vaisali: Vaisali Sangh

Krishna Sastry VV. 1983. *The Proto and Early Historical Cultures of AP*. Hyderabad: Gov. Andhra Pradesh

Krishna Sastry VV, Subrahmanyam B, Rama Krishna Rao N. 1992. *Thotlakonda (A Buddhist Site in Andhra Pradesh)*. Hyderabad: Gov. Andhra Pradesh

Kulke H, ed. 1995a. *The State in India 1000–1700*. Delhi: Oxford Univ. Press

Kulke H. 1995b. Introduction: the study of the state in pre-modern India. See Kulke 1995a, pp. 1–47

Kulke H, Rothermund D. 1986. *A History of India*. New York: Dorsett

Lahiri N. 1992. *The Archaeology of Indian Trade Routes*. Delhi: Oxford Univ. Press

Lal BB. 1955. Excavation at Hastinapura and other explorations in the Upper Ganga and Sutlej Basin 1950–52. *Anc. India* 10–11: 5–151

Lal BB. 1993. *Sringavarapura Excavations*. Delhi: ASI Mem. 88

Lal M. 1984. *Settlement History and Rise of Civilization in the Ganga-Yamuna Doab, from 1500 BC to 300 AD.* Delhi: BR

Lal M. 1986. Iron tools, forest clearance and urbanisation in the Gangetic Plain. *Man Environ.* 10:83–90

Liu X. 1988. *Ancient India and Ancient China: Trade and Religious Exchanges AD 1–600.* Delhi: Oxford Univ. Press

Maloney C. 1968. *The effects of early coastal sea traffic on the development of civilization in South India.* PhD thesis. Univ. Pa.

Margabandhu C. 1985. *Archaeology of the Satavahana Ksatrapa Times.* Delhi: Sundeep

Mate MS. 1985. Daulatabad. In *Recent Advances in Indian Archaeology,* ed. SB Deo, K Paddayya, pp. 110–12. Pune: Deccan Coll.

Mehta RN. 1977. *Prehistoric Champaner.* Vadodara: MS Univ. Baroda

Michell GA. 1992. *The Vijayanagara Courtly Style.* Delhi: AIIS/Manohar

Miller BS, ed. 1992. *The Powers of Art: Patronage in Indian Culture.* Delhi: Oxford Univ. Press

Mines M. 1984. *The Warrior Merchants: Textiles, Trade, and Territory in South India.* Cambridge: Cambridge Univ. Press

Misra SC. 1994. Urban history in India: possibilities and perspectives. See Banga 1994, pp. 1–8

Morrison KD. 1990. Patterns of urban occupation: surface collections at Vijayanagara. In *South Asian Archaeology 1987,* ed. M Taddei. Rome: Inst. Ital. Medio Est. Oriente

Morrison KD. 1994. States of theory and states of Asia: regional perspectives on states in Asia. *Asian Perspect.* 33(2):183–96

Morrison KD. 1995a. *Fields of Victory: Vijayanagara and the Course of Intensification.* Berkeley: Contrib. Archaeol. Res. Facility 52

Morrison KD. 1995b. Trade, urbanism, and agricultural expansion: Buddhist monastic institutions and the state in the early historic western Deccan. *World Archaeol.* 27(2):203–21

Morrison KD, Lycett MT. 1994. Centralized power, centralized authority? Ideological claims and archaeological patterns. *Asian Perspect.* 32:327–50

Morrison KD, Sinopoli CM. 1992. Economic diversity and integration in a precolonial Indian empire. *World Archaeol.* 23: 335–52

Mukhia H. 1995. Was there Feudalism in Indian history? See Kulke 1995a, pp. 86–133

Myrdal-Runebjer E. 1994. Vävala väva—Sigiri Mahavava irrigation system: prelimi-

nary results from an archaeological case study. See Parpola & Koskikallio, pp. 551–62

Nagaraja Rao MS, ed. 1983. *Vijayanagara: Progress of Research 1979–83.* Mysore: Dir. Archaeol. Mus.

Nagaraja Rao MS, ed. 1985. *Vijayanagara: Progress of Research 1983–84.* Mysore: Dir. Archaeol. Mus.

Nagaraju S. 1981. *Buddhist Architecture of Western India (c. 250 BC–c. AD 30).* Delhi: Agam Kala

Narain AK, Roy TN. 1976. *Excavations at Rajghat, Part I.* Varanasi: Banaras Hindu Univ.

Narain AK, Roy TN. 1977. *Excavations at Rajghat, Part II.* Varanasi: Banaras Hindu Univ.

Narain AK, Singh P. 1977. *Excavations at Rajghat, Part III.* Varanasi: Banaras Hindu Univ.

Narasimaiah B. 1992. *Metropolis Vijayanagara: Significance of Remains of Citadel.* Delhi: Book India

Narayana Rao V. 1990. *Siva's Warriors: The Basava Purāna of Pālkuriki Somanātha.* Princeton, NJ: Princeton Univ. Press (From Telugu)

Narayana Rao V, Shulman D, Subrahmanyam S. 1992. *Symbols of Substance: Court and State in Nāyaka Period Tamil Nadu.* Delhi: Oxford Univ. Press

Nilakanta Sastri KA. 1955. *The Cōlas.* Madras: Univ. Madras

Nilakanta Sastri KA. 1975. *A History of South India.* Delhi: Oxford Univ. Press. 4th ed.

O'Leary B. 1989. *The Asiatic Mode of Production.* London: Blackwell

Orton NP. 1992. Red polished ware in Gujarat: a catalogue of twelve sites. See Begley & DePuma 1992, pp. 46–81

Palat R. 1987. The Vijayanagara empire: reintegration of the agrarian order of medieval South India. In *Early State Dynamics,* ed. HJM Claessen, P van der Velde, pp. 170–86. Leiden: EJ Brill

Pannikar KM. 1956. *A Survey of Indian History.* Bombay: Asia Publ. House. 3rd ed.

Parasher A. 1991. *Mlecchas in Early India.* Delhi: Munshiram

Parasher A. 1994. Social structure and the economy of settlements in the Central Deccan (200 BC–AD 200). See Banga 1994, pp. 19–46

Parasher-Sen A. 1993. Culture and civilization: the beginnings. In *Social and Economic History of Early Deccan,* ed. A Parasher-Sen, pp. 66–114. Delhi: Manohar

Parpola A, Koskikallio P, eds. 1994. *South*

Asian Archaeology 1993. Helsinki: Suomalainen Tiedeakatemia

Pearson MN. 1988. *Before Colonialism: Theories on Asian-European Relations 1500–1750.* Delhi: Oxford Univ. Press

Perlin F. 1983. Proto-industrialization and precolonial South Asia. *Past Present* 98: 31–95

Prasad NRV. 1994. *Bavikonda: A Buddhist Site in North Coastal Andhra Pradesh.* Hyderabad: Dep. Archaeol. Mus.

Prickett-Fernando M. 1990. Durable goods: the archaeological evidence of Sri Lanka's role in the Indian Ocean Trade. See Bandaranayaka et al 1990, pp. 60–84

Ramachandran KS. 1980. *Archaeology of South India—Tamil Nadu.* Delhi: Sundeep

Ramaswamy V. 1985a. *Textiles and Weavers in Medieval South India.* Delhi: Oxford Univ. Press

Ramaswamy V. 1985b. Artisans in Vijayanagara Society. *Ind. Econ. Soc. Hist. Rev.* 22(4):417–43

Ray HP. 1986. *Monastery and guild: commerce under the Satavahanas.* Delhi: Oxford Univ. Press

Ray HP. 1994a. The Western Indian Ocean and the early maritime links of the Indian subcontinent. *Ind. Econ. Soc. Hist. Rev.* 31(1):65–88

Ray HP. 1994b. *The Winds of Change: Buddhism and the Maritime Links of Early South Asia.* Delhi: Oxford. Univ. Press

Ray HP. 1995. Trade and contacts. See Thapar 1995b, pp. 142–75

Roy TN. 1986. a study of northern black polished ware culture. Delhi: Ramanand Vidya Bhawan

Reid A, ed. 1993a. *Southeast Asia in the Early Modern Era: Trade, Power, and Belief.* Ithaca: Cornell Univ. Press

Reid A. 1993b. Islamization and Christianization in Southeast Asia: the critical phase, 1550–1650. See Reid 1993a, pp. 151–79

Reiniche M-L. 1989. *Tiruvannamalai: a Saiva Sacred Complex of South India: La Configuration Sociologique du Temple Hindou,* Vol. 4. Pondicherry: Inst. Fr. Pondichéry

Risso P. 1995. *Merchants and Faith: Muslim Commerce and Culture in the Indian Ocean.* Boulder: Westview

Rougeulle A. 1994. Medieval trade networks in the Western Indian Ocean: some reflections from the distribution pattern of Chinese imports in the Islamic world. In *Tradition and Archaeology: Early Maritime Contacts in the Indian Ocean,* ed. HP Ray, J-F Salles, pp. 159–80. Delhi: Manohar

Roy TN. 1986. *A Study of Northern Black Polished Ware Culture: An Iron Age Culture of India.* Delhi: Ramanand Vidya Bhawan

Rudner DW. 1994. *Caste and Capitalism in Colonial India: the Nattukottai Chettiars.* Berkeley: Univ. Calif. Press

Sankalia HD, Deo SB. 1955. *Report on the Excavations at Nasik and Jorwe 1950–1951.* Poona: Deccan Coll.

Sankalia HD, Deo SB, Ansari ZD, Ehrhardt S. 1960. *From History to Pre-History at Nevasa (1954–1956).* Poona: Deccan Coll. 6

Sankalia HD, Subbarao B, Deo SB. 1958. *The Excavations at Maheshwar and Navdatoli 1952–1953.* Pune & Baroda: Deccan Coll. and MS Univ. Publ. 1

Sarao KTS. 1990. *Urban Centres and Urbanisation as Reflected in the Pali Vinaya and Sutta Pitakas.* Delhi: Vidyanidhi Orient

Schneider J. 1977. Was there a precapitalist world-system? *Peasant Stud.* 6(1):20–29

Schotsmans J, Taddei M, eds. 1985. *South Asian Archaeology 1983.* Naples: Inst. Univ. Orientale

Schwartzberg JE. 1992. *A Historical Atlas of South Asia. Second Impression.* New York: Oxford Univ. Press

Shaffer JG. 1986. Cultural development in the Eastern Punjab. See Jacobson 1986, pp. 195–236

Sharma GR. 1960. *The Excavations at Kausambi 1957–1959.* Allahabad: Allahabad Univ. Publ. No. 1

Sharma GR. 1969. *Excavations at Kausambi 1949–1950.* Delhi: ASI Mem. 74

Sharma RS. 1994. Urbanism in early historic India. See Banga 1994, pp. 9–18

Sharma RS. 1995. How feudal was Indian feudalism? See Kulke 1995a, pp. 48–85

Sinha BP, Narain LA. 1970. *Pataliputra Excavation: 1955–1956.* Patna: Dir. Archaeol. Mus.

Sinha BP, Roy SR. 1969. *Vaiśā Excavations 1958–62.* Patna: Dir. Archaeol. Mus.

Sinopoli CM. 1986. *Material patterning and social organization: a study of ceramics from Vijayanagara.* PhD thesis. Univ. Mich., Ann Arbor

Sinopoli CM. 1988. The organization of craft production at Vijayanagara, South India. *Am. Anthropol.* 90:580–97

Sinopoli CM. 1993. *Pots and Palaces.* Delhi: AIIS/Manohar

Sinopoli CM, Morrison KD. 1995. Dimensions of imperial control: the Vijayanagara capital. *Am. Anthropol.* 97(1):83–96

Sircar DC. 1979. *Aśokan Studies.* Calcutta: Indian Mus.

Slane KW. 1992. Observations on Mediterranean amphoras and tablewares found in India. See Begley & DePuma 1992, pp. 204–15

Soundara Rajan KV. 1994. *Kaveripattinam Excavations 1963–73 (A Port City on the Tamilnadu Coast).* Delhi: ASI Mem. 90

Spencer GW. 1983. *The Politics of Expansion: The Chola Conquest of Sri Lanka and Sri Vijaya.* Madras: New Era

Srinivasan DM, ed. 1989. *Mathurā: The Cultural Heritage.* Delhi: Manohar and AIIS

Srinivasan PR, Reiniche M-L. 1989. *Tiruvannamalai: a Śaiva sacred complex of South India: Inscriptions,* Vol. 1.1, 1. 2. Pondicherry: Inst. Fr. Pondichéry

Stein B. 1980. *Peasant State and Society in Medieval South India.* Delhi: Oxford Univ. Press

Stein B. 1992. Patronage and Vijayanagara religious foundations. See Miller 1992, pp. 160–67

Stein B. 1995. The segmentary state: interim reflections. See Kulke 1995a, pp. 134–61

Stern M. 1992. Early Roman export glass in India. See Begley & DePuma 1992, pp. 113–24

Subrahmanyam R, Banerjee KD, Khare MD, Rao BV, Sarkar H, et al. 1975. *Nagarjunakonda (1954–1960).* Delhi: ASI Mem. 75

Subrahmanyam S. 1986. Aspects of state formation in South India and Southeast Asia, 1550–1650. *Ind. Econ. Soc. Hist. Rev.* 23: 358–77

Subrahmanyam S. 1990a. *The Political Economy of Commerce: Southern India, 1500–1650.* Cambridge: Cambridge Univ. Press

Subrahmanyam S, ed. 1990b. *Merchants, Markets, and the State in Early Modern India,* Delhi: Oxford Univ. Press

Subrahmanyam S. 1990c. Introduction. See Subrahmanyam 1990b, pp. 1–17

Subrahmanyam S, Bayly CA. 1990. Portfolio capitalists and the political economy of early modern India. See Subrahmanyam 1990b, pp. 242–65

Talbot C. 1991. Temples, donors, and gifts: patterns of patronage in thirteenth century South India. *J. Asian Stud.* 50:308–40

Thapar R. 1966. *A History of India,* Vol. 1. London: Penguin

Thapar R. 1984. *From Lineage to State.* Bombay: Oxford Univ. Press

Thapar R. 1988. *The Mauryas Revisited.* Calcutta: KP Bagchi

Thapar R. 1995a. The first millennium BC in Northern India. See Thapar 1995b, pp. 80–141

Thapar R, ed. 1995b. *Recent Perspectives of Early Indian History.* Bombay: Popular Prakashan

Tripathi V. 1976. *The Painted Grey Ware—An Iron Age Culture of Northern India.* Delhi: Concept

Verghese A. 1995. *Religious Traditions at Vijayanagara.* Delhi: Manohar/AIIS

Wagoner PB. 1991. Architecture and mythic space at Hemakuta Hill: a preliminary report. See Devaraj & Patil 1991b, pp. 142–48

Wagoner PB. 1995. *"Sultan Among Hindu Kings": Dress, Address, and the Islamicization of Hindu Culture at Vijayanagara.* Presented at Triang. S. Asia Consort, Durham, Univ. North Carolina

Wallerstein I. 1974. *The Modern World-System I: Capitalist Agriculture and the Origins of the European World-Economy in the Sixteenth Century.* San Diego: Academic

Warmington EH. 1928. *The Commerce between the Roman Empire and India.* Cambridge: Cambridge Univ. Press

Weisshaar HJ, Wijeyapala W. 1994. The Tissamaharama project 1992–1993 (Sri Lanka): metallurgical remains of the Akurugoda Hill. See Parpola & Koskikallio 1994, pp. 803–14

Wheeler REM. 1947. Brahmagiri and Chandravalli 1947: megalithic and other cultures in the Chitaldurg District, Mysore State. *Anc. India* 4:181–309

Wheeler REM. 1955. *Rome Beyond the Imperial Frontiers.* Harmondworth: Penguin

Wheeler REM, Ghosh A, Krishna Deva. 1946. Arikamedu: an Indo-Roman trading station on the East Coast of India. *Anc. India* 2:17–124

Will EL. 1992. The Mediterranean shipping amphoras from Arikamedu. See Begley & DePuma 1992, pp. 151–56

Willis JD. 1992. Female patronage in Indian Buddhism. See Miller 1992, pp. 46–53

Wink A. 1990. *Al-Hind. The Making of the Indo-Islamic World,* Vol. 1: *Early Medieval Expansion of Islam, 7th–11th Century.* Leiden: Brill

Wittfogel KA. 1957. *Oriental Despotism: A Comparative Study of Total Power.* New Haven: Yale Univ. Press

Annu. Rev. Anthropol. 1997. 26:109–28

GESTURE

Adam Kendon

43 West Walnut Lane, Philadelphia, Pennsylvania 19144; e-mail:
adamk@nwfs.gse.upenn.edu

KEY WORDS: cultural differences, language, sign languages, communication, speech

ABSTRACT

The integration of gesture with speech production is described, and the various
ways in which—in conversational settings—gesture functions in relation to
spoken discourse are discussed. Cultural differences in gesture use are outlined, and the possible relationship between these differences and language
differences, on the one hand, and the microecology of social life, on the other,
are considered. Conventionalization in speech-associated gestures and in gestures that can be used without speech is discussed. Various kinds of "gesture
systems" and sign languages used in speaking communities (alternate sign languages) are described along with their relationships to spoken language. Fully
autonomous sign languages, as developed among the deaf, are briefly considered in regard to how signs and signing may be related to gestures and gesturing.

INTRODUCTION

According to the Oxford English Dictionary, in contemporary English the
word "gesture" refers to "a movement of the body or of any part of it" that is
"expressive of thought or feeling." A degree of voluntarism is always implied,
however. If someone starts at a sudden explosion, or bursts out laughing at
something said, or if, on being told bad news, tears well up, these expressions
are not usually regarded as gestures. Nevertheless, it is not possible to specify
where to draw the line between what is gesture and what is not. Although
someone making the "thumbs up" gesture, gesticulating while speaking, or using a sign language is using gesture in the sense in which the word is commonly understood, it is sometimes difficult to be certain whether a postural adjustment, an object manipulation, or a hair pat are gestures (see Scheflen
1965). In this review only actions that are treated by coparticipants in interac-

109

tion as part of what a person meant to say will be included: Conventional gestures, gesticulations, and signing are included, but posture shifts, self-touchings, and incidental object manipulations are not (for more on defining gesture, see Kendon 1981b, 1985a).

In the West, gesture has been a topic of interest since antiquity. It first received systematic treatment by Quintilian in AD 100 (Graf 1992, Lamedica 1984, Magli 1980, Quintilian 1924). Its importance was recognized in the middle ages (Schmitt 1990), and treatises devoted to it began to appear at the beginning of the seventeenth century (Angenot 1973). A philosophical interest in gesture developed in the eighteenth century, especially in France. It seemed that its study might reveal the nature of thought (Diderot 1904) or throw light on the origin of language (Wells 1987), or that it could form a basis for a universal language (Knowlson 1965). In the nineteenth century, prominent discussions of gesture included those by Tylor (1865), Mallery (1972), and Wundt (1973). These authors regarded it as providing important insights into the nature of symbolic processes and, for Mallery and Wundt especially, as providing clues to the problem of language origins. For much of this century, however, gesture has been little studied, despite the interest in nonverbal communication that developed after 1950 (Kendon 1982). Only within the past fifteen years, as gesture has come to be seen as relevant to theoretical issues in cognition, language acquisition, and conversational processes, has it once again begun to receive serious attention (see also Schmitt 1984).

In this review, I focus on adult gesture use in conversation, emphasizing communicative and semiotic aspects. Because of space, I leave aside studies of the development of gesture (Volterra & Erting 1990), neurological studies (reviewed in Feyereisen & de Lannoy 1991), and gesture in nonhuman primates (see Tanner & Byrne 1996 and references therein). Studies of gesture by archaeologists and historians of art (Barasch 1976, 1987; de Jorio 1832; Durand 1990; Sittl 1890), law (Hibbitts 1992), or everyday life (Bertellie & Centanni 1995, Bremmer & Roodenburg 1992, Schmitt 1990) receive passing mention. Sign language studies, though connected to gesture studies, are beyond the present scope (see Baker & Cokely 1980, Emmorey & Reilly 1995, Isenhath 1990, Klima & Bellugi 1979, Kyle & Woll 1985, Volterra 1987, Yau 1992), though they will be briefly referred to in the section on "Sign, Gesture, and Language." The relevance of gesture to theories of language origins is also left aside (for recent discussions, see Armstrong et al 1994, 1995).

GESTURE IN RELATION TO SPEECH

The microanalysis made possible by audiovisual recording technology of the relationship between speech and bodily movement reveals that speech and gesture are produced together, and that they must therefore be regarded as two aspects of a single process (Kendon 1972, 1980a; McClave 1991; McNeill 1985, 1992; Nobe 1996; Schegloff 1984). Speakers combine, as if in a single plan of action, both spoken and gestural expression. Two examples are given by way of illustration.

In a telling of the story of Little Red Riding Hood (Kendon 1990a, 1993a), at one point the speaker gestured as if swinging a hatchet. She did this in association with the sentence: "And he took his hatchet and with a mighty sweep sliced the wolf's stomach open." This arm-swing action, however, was performed precisely in association with the verb "sliced." The speaker began to lift her hands into position above her right shoulder in the brief pause that immediately preceded the entire sentence. The hands reached this position by the completion of the word "hatchet" and were held there during "and with a mighty sweep." The precise timing of the arm-swing with the pronunciation of "sliced" could not have been achieved unless the speaker had begun to organize her gestural action in advance. That she did so shows that here gestural action and speech must have been organized together. It is only by commencing the movements for the gesture in advance of the speech that the synchrony of arm swing and "sliced" could have been achieved.[1]

In this example, the arm-swing action, co-occurring as it does with the verb "sliced," serves to make the meaning of the verb more precise. Note that the character of the act of "slicing" depends on what is being sliced and the instrument used. To say "sliced the wolf's stomach open" says nothing about this, but by combining gesture and spoken verb the speaker can create a more specific expression.

This combination of gesture and speech, by which a verb or other linguistic expression is given greater specificity, has been noted by Bavelas (1992), McNeill (1987, 1992), Müller (1994), and others. Gestures also provide meanings beyond those expressed linguistically (see examples in Bavelas et al 1992, de Fornel 1992, McNeill 1992). In a dinner party conversation [recorded in 1991 near Salerno, Italy (see Kendon 1997)], the discussion had turned to pear trees and the problem of how their branches were to be held up when loaded with fruit. One speaker said: "No, ci mettono le mazze sotto (No, they put staves under there)." As he said "le mazze (staves)" he held his forearm in a

---

[1]The tendency for gesture phrases to begin before that part of the spoken expression with which the phase of the gesture phrase deemed to carry semantic import [the "stroke" in Kendon (1980a)] appears to be related [termed "lexical affiliate" by some, following Schegloff (1984)] has been variously interpreted. Space limitations exclude a review here, but see Beattie & Aboudan (1994), Butterworth & Beattie (1978), McNeill (1985, 1992), Morrel-Samuels & Krauss (1992), Nobe (1996), and Rimé & Schiaratura (1991).

vertical position, the hand—with fingers drawn together in a bunch—also directed upward, as if it were an extension of the forearm. The arm in this position was moved upward vertically during the first syllable of "mazze," it was then lowered slightly, and was again moved upward during "sotto." Thereafter it was lowered to rest in his lap.

In this example, too, the speaker prepared his gesture in advance: He started to move his forearm and hand into vertical position as he began saying, "No, ci mettono." Consider, however, what this gesture expresses. The vertical position renders visible the idea of the vertical position of the "mazze," and the upward movements give the idea of something acting to hold something up. In this way the speaker makes clear how the "mazze" are placed underneath the branches, and by the upward movements of his forearm he conveys an idea of their function. Neither of these aspects is to be found in his words.

As in the previous example, the gestures provide a visual representation of things that can be observed ("iconic" in McNeill's terminology). In this second example, however, in the twice-repeated upward movement of the vertical forearm, the speaker uses muscular action to refer to the function of the staves as supports for heavily laden branches. Staves, however, do not do anything to prevent laden branches from falling down. The action of twice lifting the forearm is a metaphorical expression of the idea that the staves support the branches.

With gestures, speakers use a mode of expression that renders in visible form part of what is meant by the utterance. There are different ways in which this may be done. These include enactment (first example), the use of body parts as models of things (second example), and the use of moving hands as if they are sketching diagrams or shapes in the air (for a discussion of types of representation in gesture, see Kendon 1980b, Mandel 1977, Müller 1996, and Wundt 1973). Speakers can also point to things, persons, or locations as a way of bringing these in as referents (Haviland 1993). These visible expressions can be used both to represent aspects of literal reality and to provide images for abstract ideas, and in pointing, as McNeill et al (1993) have shown, abstract ideas can be given locations in space.

McNeill (1992) has referred to the use of gestures to render abstract ideas in visible form as "metaphoric." He provides many examples that show how the conduit metaphor (Reddy 1979); metaphors for seeing as an active, penetrating process; the representation of abstract processes as dynamic patterns; and the like are commonly displayed in gestures. Calbris (1985) and Kendon (1993b) have discussed how spatial metaphors for time are shown in gesture.

Gestures have other functions besides expressing aspects of utterance content. They can provide a visible indication of different "levels" of discourse structure and can also function in relation to aspects of interaction management. McNeill (1992) described how simple rhythmic hand movements (which he terms "beats") mark "new" in contrast to "given" information in certain discourse contexts. He also described "cohesive" gestures, which, in narrative discourse, indicate logical connections between different parts of the discourse. Other gestures mark contrast between discourse that advances a narration and discourse that provides background information. Kendon (1995a), studying naturally occurring conversations recorded near Salerno, has described conventionalized gestures with discourse marking functions, such as distinguishing "topic" from "comment" or marking that part of a discourse that is pivotal to the speaker's argument.

Gestures can also express the type of "move" or "speech act" of a speaker. Streeck & Hartge (1992), in a study of Ilokano (Philippines) conversations, described a gesture indicating the type of talk a speaker will engage in once a turn is granted. Kendon (1995a) described gestures that mark certain kinds of questions. These can also be used on their own so that, by simply using one of these "illocutionary marker" gestures, a person can indicate that it is a plea or a critical question that is being expressed (see also Kendon 1992, Poggi 1983, Ricci-Bitti & Poggi 1991). Gestures also play a role in various aspects of conversational interchange management. Bavelas and her colleagues (Bavelas et al 1992, 1995) gave an account of "interactive gestures" which, among other functions, cross-reference the content of a current speaker's utterance to the theme of the conversation, indicate a participant's understanding of another's contribution, and serve in the management of turn distribution in a conversation.

WHEN SPEAKERS GESTURE AND WHY

Speakers do not gesture every time they speak. Furthermore, the kinds of gesturing employed and the role gesture plays in relation to what is being said or in relation to the interaction situation varies. Few studies, however, have directly considered what occasions gesture.

In some studies, gesture use has been compared in circumstances in which interlocutors can or cannot see each other. Cohen & Harrison (1973) and Cohen (1977) showed that speakers, when giving route directions, used far fewer gestures when speaker and interlocutor were not mutually visible than when they were. Rimé (1982), however, found that rates of gesture in pairs of speakers conversing with a partition between them were only slightly reduced in comparison to when there was no partition. Bavelas and colleagues (Bavelas et al 1992, Bavelas 1994) have conducted similar experiments. They showed that when speakers could not see each other they did not use "interactive" gestures, although they continued to use "topic" gestures [i.e. gestures which express aspects of utterance content (Bavelas 1992)].

Some experimental work suggests that the apparently nonstandardized "spontaneous" gestures that speakers produce while talking convey little or no information to recipients (Krauss et al 1991). Because of this and because speakers—even when invisible to their interlocutor—sometimes use "topic" gestures, it has been suggested that such gestures function primarily for the speaker. They are thought to aid verbal formulation, perhaps because they help the speaker to keep complex concepts in mind while seeking to talk about them (Freedman 1977), or perhaps because they play a role in lexical retrieval (Butterworth & Beattie 1978, Krauss et al 1996, Morrel-Samuels & Krauss 1992). Such "internal" functions, if there are such, would not, however, necessarily contradict any communicative functions they might have, and other experimental studies show that recipients do gain information from gestures of this type (Goldin-Meadow et al 1992, McNeill et al 1994; for a review, see Kendon 1994).

To more fully understand what is entailed in the occasioning and functioning of gesture in conversation, collections of specific instances of gesture use in different conversational situations are required. These instances must then be analyzed to determine how gestures contribute to the way participants make sense of the interactional moves of which they are a part. Work of this type already published shows how speakers deploy gestures in a wide variety of ways and accomplish a wide variety of communicative purposes in doing so. For instance, gestures can play a role in how interactants regulate each others' patterns of attention (Goodwin & Goodwin 1986, Heath 1992); participants in nonspeaker roles may use gestures to indicate their assessment or understanding of another's utterance (de Fornel 1992, Goodwin & Goodwin 1992, Heath 1992, Streeck 1994); gestures may be incorporated into discourse as objects of deictic reference (Goodwin 1986, Heath 1986, Streeck 1993), and gestures may be used in alternation with spoken elements in discourse, partnering words as syntactic elements (Jarmon 1996, Kendon 1997, Marslen-Wilson et al 1992, Sherzer 1972, Slama-Cazacu 1993). Gestures may serve to project the nature of the speaker's next turn, or the next part of the discourse (Schegloff 1984, Streeck & Hartge 1992), and they can play an important role in how conversational participants may collaborate in reaching understanding when a spoken expression is momentarily lacking (Schlegel 1997, Streeck 1993).

Consequently, no simple generalization about how gestures are used in conversation is possible. Together with speech, gestures are used as an available resource for the construction of the units of action out of which a conversation is fashioned. Analytically, our task is to show how they are so used, and to

show how the particular properties that gestures have as an expressive medium—for example, that they are silent, are a form of physical action, and can
serve as a means for creating visual representations of things—make them
adapted for a variety of communicative functions (Kendon 1985b). That conversation is a "multimedia" process has been sufficiently demonstrated. We
now need to understand how its various "media" are articulated in relation to
one another. The studies listed above provide some good beginnings.

CULTURAL DIFFERENCES IN GESTURE

Cultural differences in gesture have long been recognized. The greater propen-
sity for the inhabitants of southern Italy to use gesture compared with those in
nothern Europe has been noted at least since the seventeenth century (Burke
1992, Roodenburg 1992). There is, however, only one systematic study of cultural differences in gesture. Efron (1972), who first published this study in
1941, described marked differences in various aspects of gesture use between
Jewish Yiddish-speaking immigrants and Italian-speaking immigrants from
southern Italy in New York City. He found, however, that these differences
were much less marked or virtually absent in the assimilated descendants of
these two groups. Efron also discussed the history of gesture use in England
and France. In England, whereas, already in the mid-nineteenth century, restraint in gesture was considered a virtue, 100 years or more before, in the London of Steele and Hogarth, gesturing in public conversation, in speech-
making, or in preaching was elaborate and lively. In France, between the sixteenth and the nineteenth centuries, there were marked changes in what was
considered appropriate in the use of gesture.

It appears that except for movements of the most restricted and carefully
controlled sort, gesture has often been viewed as uncultivated. Since the fifteenth century, at least, and even in Classical times, restraint in gesture has
been regarded as a virtue (Bremmer & Roodenburg 1992, Schmitt 1990). It is
interesting to note that this view is found not only in Europe. To give but one
unrelated example, Levinson (1996b) noted that the Tenejapan Tzeltal (of
Mexico) are highly restrained in their gesturing in formal interactions.

Language Differences and Differences in Gesture

Some aspects of cultural differences in gesture may follow from language differences, whether in prosody, syntactic patterning, or the way a language describes things. Creider (1978, 1986) compared gesticulation in speakers of
three East African languages—the Nilotic languages Luo and Kipsigis and the
Bantu language Gusii—and showed that how the peak of the action of the gesture phrase [the "stroke" in Kendon (1980a)] is placed within a tone unit varies

in relation to differences between these languages in the patterning and function of linguistic stress.

Languages also differ, of course, in the way they express things, and where and how a speaker deploys gesture may differ accordingly. Talmy (1985) has compared languages according to how the semantic components of a "motion event"—i.e. something moving from one place to another, how it does so, and the path it takes through space—are packaged linguistically. For example, the motion verbs in a language may incorporate information about the path and manner of movement (so-called verb-framed languages), or these aspects may be conveyed by verb "satellites"—particles and prepositions—instead (so-called satellite-framed languages). Recently, interest has focused on the way a speaker uses gesture in describing a motion event. Does this differ according to whether the language is verb framed or satellite framed? Perhaps. Müller (1994, 1996), who compared Spanish and German, and Kita (1993), who compared English and Japanese, both suggested that what gains representation in gesture can be influenced by what, besides mere motion, a motion verb encodes. For example, Müller found that speakers of German, which incorporates motion in the verb root, tended to use manner gestures more than speakers of Spanish, which does not incorporate manner of motion in the verb. In Kita's study, all the English speakers showed the path of the motion event they were describing, also using a verb ("swing") which incorporates the path of motion. Only some of the Japanese speakers in the study showed path in their gesture when describing the same motion event, however. Kita suggested that this may be because in Japanese there is no verb of motion like "swing" that incorporates reference to the shape of the movement path. Neither of these studies suggests a very strict relationship between how a language represents a motion event and how a speaker represents it when using both language and gesture, but they may indicate some influence.

Another difference between languages that may influence gesture is in how location is specified using coordinate systems (Levinson 1996a). According to Levinson (1996a), coordinate systems may be intrinsic (coordinates established in relation to asymmetries in shape and function of the reference object), relative (coordinates established in relation to the speaker as reference point), or absolute (coordinates based on a system of cardinal directions such as compass points). It has been suggested that speakers of "absolute" languages use gesture differently from speakers of "relative" languages. Examples of languages using absolute systems are Guugu Yimithirr in Australia (Haviland 1979, Levinson 1992) or Tzeltal in Mexico (Levinson 1996b). Levinson (1996b) compared features of gesture observed in both Tzeltal speakers and Guugu Yimithirr speakers. He examined recordings in which traditional stories were told that had actual geographical locations (Tzeltal) or, in the Australian case, a story of a personal incident that happened years before that also had actual geographical locations. Levinson found that both the Tzeltal and Gugu Yimithirr speakers show many similarities in how they use gesture. He argued that, where an "absolute" coordinate system is in use, consistency in spatial reference is essential. Gestures become tied to this, and their directionality bears important information. In this respect they may differ from gestures used by speakers of English or Dutch, which are "relative" rather than "absolute" languages. (Note that there is no systematic study by which this possibility can be checked.)

Cultural Differences in Gesture, Cultural Values, and Communication Ecology

Much contemporary work on gesture remains focused on the individual speaker, with an emphasis on the value of studying it for what it may reveal of the cognitive styles that speakers of given languages may have. Gesturing, however, like speaking, is part of how individuals both "give" and "give off" information to one another (Goffman 1963) and is thus a part of the "expressive strategy" of participants in interaction. As such, gesturing, like speech, is influenced by cultural values and historical tradition, and its usage is adjusted according to the setting, social circumstance, and micro-organization of any given occasion of interaction. Accordingly, to understand cultural differences in gestural usage requires comparative in situ investigations of gestural practice in conversation.

It is also necessary to consider the history of communication conduct and of the behavior settings within which gesturing occurs in the regions to be compared. Historical anthropologists such as Elias (1978–1982), Burke (1987, 1992, 1993), Schmitt (1990), Hibbitts (1992), and others (see Bremmer & Roodenburg 1992) have discussed changes in conversational practice, shifts in moral attitudes to gesture and the etiquette of body management, and changes in the role of formal gesture in legal transactions, which have taken place in Europe between antiquity, the middle ages, and the modern era. Their work shows how the prominence and importance of gesture in conversation can change markedly with historical circumstances (see also Efron 1972). From such studies it is possible to develop hypotheses about how communicational style—and the role of gesture within this—and the ecology of everyday life "in public" (Goffman 1963) may be related. For example, in a city such as Naples, the particular combination of climatic conditions, built environment, social structure, and economy that have come to prevail there over more than two millennia has created communication circumstances in which gesture would be particularly valuable. It may be inferred, for example, from travelers' accounts and descriptions of popular theatre and from contemporary prints that gesture has always been important in everyday life. It is useful both for conspicuous display and for inconspicuous communication, for communicating at a distance and when noise levels are high. It has been suggested (Kendon 1995b) that the special elaboration of gesture for which the inhabitants of Naples have long been famous can be understood partly in terms of how the systems of communication in interaction in common use have been adapted over many centuries to the communication ecology of that city, acquiring in the process the force of a cultural tradition.

Conventionalization in Gesture

Among southern Italians many patterns of gesture have become conventionalized within the community as a sort of vocabulary. Thus Efron (1972, p. 123) noted that it was possible "to draw a more or less exhaustive inventory of the 'bundle of pictures' that a 'traditional Italian' usually carries in his hands." Many users can "quote" at least some items from this inventory out of context and offer verbal glosses for them. Efron referred to the gestures in this inventory as "emblematic." Since the work of Ekman & Friesen (1969), partly an adaptation of Efron's classification, gestures distinguishable as part of a shared inventory and that are "quotable" (Kendon 1992) have been called "emblems." Gestures of this type have often been treated as though they were a distinct species, highly conventionalized and contrasted with "illustrators," which are generally regarded as spontaneous and idiosyncratic.

Many studies of gesture have been confined to emblems. When they are compared from one culture to another, cultural differences in gesture can be readily discerned (see, for example, Morris et al 1979, Saitz & Cervenka 1972). A number of publications list gestures of this sort for different communities [Payrató (1993) has a good bibliography]. Comparative studies of existing lists, using the glosses provided (Kendon 1981a), or studies classifying gesture glosses elicited from informants into semantic and pragmatic categories (Payrató 1993), suggest that the semantic range and pragmatic functions of these gestures tend to be restricted. For example, Payrató shows for Catalan quotable gestures that they serve mainly to convey messages of interpersonal control (orders, commands, threats) as a component of an interaction ritual, or as evaluative expressions of the personal state of the self or of others.

Most studies of emblems have simply provided descriptions of the forms of the gestures, with glosses attached. Excluding Sparhawk (1978) and Payrató (1993), there is usually no information about how the descriptions were obtained or from whom they were obtained, and almost never any material providing examples of how these forms are used in context, who uses them, or in what situations (exceptions are Driessen 1992; Sherzer 1972, 1991, 1993).

Kendon (1995a), in a study of gesture use in conversations in coastal Campania, analyzed the contexts of use of four well-known and highly conventionalized gestures. He showed that speakers draw as freely upon these forms as they do upon more spontaneous gesturings, simply as it suits their purposes. According to this study, emblems and illustrators do not behave in fundamentally different ways. Rather there are a range of forms that vary in their degree of conventionalization. Emblems are simply those gestural expressions that, for reasons that are not at all well understood in most cases, have become stable in form and tend to be more readily recalled as a result.

Many gestural patterns are intermediate in the degree to which they are conventionalized, however. Calbris's (1990) study of movement patterns and handshapes in French gesticulation strongly suggests considerable consistency in form-meaning relationships in gesture. This is also clear in later work by Webb (1996). Webb examined the uses of metaphoric gestures [in McNeill's (1992) sense of this term] in recordings of speakers in several different settings. She found that the majority of the metaphoric gestures produced had stable form-meaning relationships and that these relationships were the same from speaker to speaker. For example, the handshape in which the tip of the thumb makes contact with the tip of the index finger (or sometimes with the middle finger), forming a sort of ring, with the other fingers partially extended and spread apart, recurs in contexts in which the speaker is seeking to make a precise point or a clear distinction. Webb also showed that in some cases gestures can be analyzed into components; that is, a given gesture can be regarded as being composed of a combination of features. For example, a gesture involving the ring handshape may be performed in a location near the side of the head, and its reference to a "precise point" may be combined with a reference to mental processes. When performed close to the center of the speaker's chest it may combine with references to the "self," or possibly to emotions. In this way, a single gesture phrase may retain the meaning and form of each of its constituent components.

Webb's findings appear to confirm the idea that we can speak of a "morphology" of gesture, and they support Calbris's (1990) position. Webb suggests that, to some degree, gestural expressions are constructed from a repertory of component features that have stable, though highly abstract, meanings.

This work needs to be extended. Especially valuable will be studies that compare data from diverse cultures and languages, for they may reveal the extent to which these consistencies in gestural form-meaning relationships result from social tradition or from parallel invention. For example, the contexts of use of ring handshape gesture as a marker of "precision" in discourse in the United States, as noted by Webb, are described likewise by Kendon (1995a) for southern Italy and similarly by Jones & Morey (1932) in their comments on gesture forms depicted in the miniatures illuminating the early medieval manuscripts of the Roman playwright Terence. We also find this meaning attributed to it by de Jorio (1832) for Neapolitan.

Morris et al (1979), who interpreted this handshape in a like manner, suggested that it derives from the "precision grip" and expresses the idea that when specifying something or making something precise it is as though one is seizing upon or picking up a very small object (for a discussion of how forms of action in gesture may be related to practical action, see also Rozik 1992, Streeck 1996). If so, this metaphor appears to be common at least to both Italians and Americans, and it appears to have been employed for many centuries. Is the metaphor shared widely in Western European culture and spread by tradition? Or is it universal and therefore used in similar contexts in unrelated cultures?

GESTURE SYSTEMS AND ALTERNATE SIGN LANGUAGES

As suggested above, certain kinds of communication economies may provide circumstances in which gesture tends to be "foregrounded" in interaction and is more frequently relied upon in communication. In these conditions, patterns of gesture may be widely shared, as they are, for example, in Naples and surrounding areas.

If circumstances that make speech difficult or impossible are routine, and gesture is used as a replacement, then it is rapidly codified and may develop into a "gesture system." This has been demonstrated experimentally. When people are asked to use only gesture to tell stories or to describe something, they can do so readily, and they can create, even within the space of one short session, a stable gesture vocabulary. Gestures that are elaborate when first invented soon became abbreviated and stylized. Consistencies in sequencing also develop, suggesting a rudimentary syntax (Goldin-Meadow et al 1996; McNeill 1992, pp. 65–71).

In settings such as broadcasting studios, auctions, racecourses, sawmills, and certain factories, where workers have to remain in communication with one another but can do so only by sight, gesture systems sometimes become established (Barakat 1969, Brun 1969). Meissner & Philpott (1975) described a system of this type in a sawmill in British Columbia. Workers in the mill were positioned in full view of one another but were too far away to talk. A system of specialized gestures had been devised to handle essential aspects of coordinating the mill's operations, and this had been elaborated into a more complex system, allowing for brief exchanges about such topics as sports, weather, women, and boss-worker relations. The gesture sequences used in these exchanges tended to be fixed, however, and the system was not used outside the work setting.

Work-setting gesture systems probably all have this limited character, but further descriptions are much needed. Where speech becomes unavailable as a matter of routine in all settings, however, gesture systems may become highly productive. Thus there are certain European monastic orders in which speech is foregone for religious reasons in most everyday situations. A restricted official vocabulary of essential gestures is permitted, but within each monastery, local gesture systems—often quite complex—have commonly developed (Barakat 1975, Kendon 1990b, Rijnberk 1954, Umiker-Sebeok & Sebeok 1987).

The most complex versions of systems of this type are found in those societies where speech is foregone in all situations of everyday life, in the first place as a matter of ritual. Among the Australian Aborigines of the north central desert, such as the Warlpiri or the Warumungu, it is the practice for mature women to forego the use of speech for prolonged periods (sometimes for a year or more) when they are bereaved of their spouse or certain other male relatives. Among women in these societies, highly complex "alternate" sign languages have developed that fulfill virtually all the functions of spoken language (Kendon 1988).

Complex alternate sign languages also developed among the Native Americans from northern Mexico to the Plains. A version of one of these came into widespread use in the nineteenth century and served as a means of intertribal communication. West (1960) provided a detailed account of the linguistic structure of one version. For earlier accounts, see Mallery (1972) and Sebeok & Umiker-Sebeok (1978). Farnell (1995) has described how certain older Assiniboine speakers make extensive use of elements from one of these sign languages (called Plains Sign Talk) as an integral part of their everyday expression.

SIGN, GESTURE, AND LANGUAGE

A point of particular interest with these gesture systems is the extent and nature of their relationship to the spoken languages of their users. The simplest systems seem to show little relationship to spoken language. In the sawmill system referred to above, however, English morphology played some role in sign formation. English syntax influenced the construction of sign sentences in the Cistercian system described by Barakat (1975) for a monastery in Massachusetts. Kendon (1988) showed that for the Warlpiri and adjacent peoples, in the most sophisticated versions of the sign languages they used, signs were employed as if they were the equivalents of the morphemes of the spoken languages, including many bound morphemes, such as semantic case-endings.

West (1960), however, found that the version of Plains Indian Sign Language he studied was structurally independent of any spoken language. He found that it used many of the grammatical devices, such as spatial inflection, later described for primary sign languages (such as American Sign Language). This structural autonomy may partly be because the system studied by West was a lingua franca, whereas the Australian sign languages studied by Kendon do not function in this way. Furthermore, Australian languages such as Warlpiri and Warumungu have a thoroughgoing "agglutinative" morphology, so that expressions can readily be assembled as sequences of signs for morphemes. The languages of the Plains Indians have "synthetic" morphologies, which could not be represented with signs as morpheme equivalents.

Gesture systems that develop into sign languages among the deaf show, not surprisingly, only an indirect relationship to spoken language, and they use modes of expression that fully exploit the potential of the spatial-visual medium in which they are elaborated. Since Stokoe (1960), studies have demonstrated that the systems established in deaf communities (such as American Sign Language) are full-fledged languages. Still not resolved, however, is the way modes of expression in such primary sign languages may be related to those found in gesture in speaker-hearers.

Some developmental studies support the view that gesturing that comprises signing is distinct from nonsigning gesture. For example, in a study of the use of deictic gestures in two very young deaf children, Pettito (1990) found that their use in person reference shows a distinct and later development, comparable to the development of the use of personal pronouns in speaking children. Reilly et al (1990) reported that deaf children learn to use those facial actions that are optional in signing but that have important syntactic functions in a manner that is distinct from the development of their use of facial actions as expressions that give emotional color to what they are saying. Of special importance here, however, is the work of Kegl et al (1997) on the emergence of a sign language in Nicaragua, where it is only within the past twenty years that a deaf community has come into being. Kegl et al show that the gesture systems developed in families of isolated deaf are variable and labile. A more stable and widely shared system emerged once home sign users came into contact with one another in schools. They found, however, that the first cohort of very young deaf children to attend school where the shared system was used transformed this system and introduced into it distinct grammatical features as though they had created a new, more complex, and consistent system. Kegl and her colleagues compared this to the process of "language creation" described by Bickerton (1981) in his studies of the development of creoles.

On the basis of studies of this sort, it has been argued that a sharp distinction should be drawn between gesture, as it is found in hearing people, and "sign" as it is found in sign languages. It seems incorrect, however, to characterize all the gestural activities of speaker-hearers as "nonlinguistic." As noted above, gestures used by speaker-hearers often play an important role in making what is being said more specific or providing additional features of meaning. Further, as noted in particular by Slama-Cazacu (1993), speakers may use gestures as if they are the functional equivalents of lexical units in spoken language, alternating them with spoken elements within a sentence. From a functional point of view, therefore, gestures can be regarded as "part of language."

It has been said that most of the gestures used by speakers at the same time as they speak cannot be considered "linguistic" because they appear to be improvised and cannot be decomposed into elements that can be recombined (McNeill 1992). However, Calbris (1990) and Webb (1996)—noted above— have provided grounds for believing that gestures of this sort may, after all, have a morphology and may show compositionality at least to some extent. Furthermore, as noted in the discussion of conventionalization in gesture, there are gestures used by speaker-hearers—so-called emblems—that have have structural characteristics that suggest they have been shaped by processes quite similar to those that operate to produce signs in sign language.

From the point of view of formal organization, thus there may be in gesture a spectrum of forms, more or less linguistic, rather than a sharp break. If a distinction is to be drawn between linguistic gesture and nonlinguistic gesture, it seems that this does not separate "signers" from "speaker hearers" in as clear a way as might be expected. Only with further research, however, will it be possible to clarify the domains in which we may observe linguistic gesture in speakers and the precise conditions in which it is likely to be found.

CONCLUSION

In 1832, at the beginning of his treatise on Neapolitan gesture, Andrea de Jorio asked: "Is there anything more readily observable, more common and more elementary than the gesturing of man?" He invited his readers to "consider its vast extent" and to look at it carefully in all its aspects. Then, he continued, it will be seen "how little is known of the power of gestural expression, and how much more there is to observe" (de Jorio 1832, pp. iii–iv). Despite the recent upsurge in interest in gesture, to say nothing of the long tradition this is heir to, we can still say the same today. Notwithstanding the marginal position gesture so often seems to occupy in our experience, and notwithstanding its character as something seemingly light-weight, ephemeral, even comic, its study can contribute to our understanding of issues of general importance such as symbol formation, the boundaries of language, and communication practice. Surely the agenda ahead is exciting, and there is worthwhile work to be done.

ACKNOWLEDGMENTS

I wish to thank Jürgen Streeck for numerous suggestions and comments, which have led to many improvements wherever I have heeded them.

> Visit the *Annual Reviews home page* at
> http://www.AnnualReviews.org.

Literature Cited

Angenot M. 1973. Les traités de l'éloquence du corps. *Semiotica* 8:60–82

Armstrong DF, Stokoe WC, Wilcox SE. 1994. Signs of the origin of syntax. *Curr. Anthropol.* 35:349–68

Armstrong DF, Stokoe WC, Wilcox SE. 1995. *Gesture and the Nature of Language.* Cambridge: Cambridge Univ. Press

Auer P, di Luzio A, ed. 1992. *The Contextualization of Language.* Amsterdam/Philadelphia: Benjamins

Baker C, Cokely D. 1980. *American Sign Language. A Teacher's Resource Text on Grammar and Culture.* Silver Spring, MD: T. J. Publ.

Barakat RA. 1969. Gesture systems. *Keyst. Folkl. Q.* 14:105–21

Barakat RA. 1975. *Cistercian Sign Language.* Kalamazoo, MI: Cistercian Publ.

Barasch M. 1976. *Gestures of Despair in Medieval and Early Renaissance Art.* New York: NY Univ. Press

Barasch M. 1987. *Giotto and the Language of Gesture.* Cambridge: Cambridge Univ. Press

Bavelas JB. 1992. Redefining language. Nonverbal linguistic acts in face-to-face dialogue. *B Aburey Fisher Mem. Lect.* Salt Lake City: Univ. Utah, Dep. Commun.

Bavelas JB. 1994. Gestures as a part of speech: methodological implications. *Res. Lang. Soc. Interact.* 27:201–21

Bavelas JB, Chovil N, Coates L, Roe L. 1995. Gestures specialized for dialogue. *Pers. Soc. Psychol. Bull.* 21:394–405

Bavelas JB, Chovil N, Lawrie DA, Wade A. 1992. Interactive gestures. *Discourse Processes* 15:469–89

Beattie G, Aboudan R. 1994. Gestures, pauses and speech: an experimental investigation of the effects of changing social context on their precise temporal relationships. *Semiotica* 99:239–72

Bertellie S, Centanni M, ed. 1995. *Il gesto nel rito e nel cermoniale dal mondo antico ad oggi.* Firenze: Ponte alle Grazie

Bickerton D. 1981. *The Roots of Language.* Ann Arbor: Karoma

Bremmer J, Roodenburg H, eds. 1992. *A Cultural History of Gesture.* Ithaca, NY: Cornell Univ. Press

Brun T. 1969. *The International Dictionary of Sign Language.* London: Wolfe

Burke P. 1987. *The Historical Anthropology of Early Modern Italy: Essays in Perception and Communication.* Cambridge: Cambridge Univ. Press

Burke P. 1992. The language of gesture in early modern Italy. See Bremmer & Roodenburg 1992, pp. 71–83

Burke P. 1993. *The Art of Conversation.* Ithaca, NY: Cornell Univ. Press

Butterworth B, Beattie GW. 1978. Gesture and silence as indicators of planning in speech. In *Recent Advances in the Psychology of Language: Formal and Experimental Approaches,* ed. R Campbell, P. Smith, pp. 347–60. New York: Plenum

Calbris G. 1985. Espace-temps: expression gestuelle du temps. *Semiotica* 55:43–73

Calbris G. 1990. *Semiotics of French Gesture.* Bloomington: Indiana Univ. Press

Cohen AA. 1977. The communicative functions of hand gestures. *J. Commun.* 27: 54–63

Cohen AA, Harrison RP. 1973. Intentionality in the use of hand illustrators in face-to-face communication situations. *J. Pers. Soc. Psychol.* 28:276–79

Creider CA. 1978. Intonation tone groups and body motion in Luo conversation. *Anthropol. Linguist.* 20:327–39

Creider CA. 1986. Interlanguage comparisons in the study of the interactional use of gesture. *Semiotica* 62:147–63

de Fornel M. 1992. The return gesture: some remarks on context inference and iconic gesture. See Auer & di Luzio 1992, pp. 159–76

de Jorio A. 1832. *La mimica degli antichi investigata nel gestire napoletano.* Naples: Fibreno

Diderot D. 1904. Lettre sur le sourds et muets—Letter on deaf mutes. In *Diderot's Early Philosophical Works,* ed. Jourdain H, pp. 160–218. Chicago: Open Court

Driessen H. 1992. Gestured masculinity: body and sociability in rural Andalusia. See Bremmer & Roodenburg 1992, pp. 237– 49

Durand J-L. Gesture and rituality in ancient Greek imagery. See Moerman & Nomura 1990, pp. 141–65

Efron D. 1972. (1941). *Gesture Race and Culture.* The Hague: Mouton

Ekman P, Friesen W. 1969. The repertoire of nonverbal behavior: categories, origins, usage and coding. *Semiotica* 11:49–98

Elias N. 1978–1982. *The Civilizing Process: Sociogenetic and Psychogenetic Investigations,* Vol. 1, *The History of Manners,* Vol. 2, *Power and Civility.* Oxford: Blackwell

Emmorey K, Reilly J, eds. 1995. *Language, Gesture and Space.* Hillsdale NJ: Erlbaum

Farnell B. 1995. *Do You See What I Mean?: Plains Indian Sign Talk and the Embodiment of Action.* Austin: Univ. Tex. Press

Feldman R, Rimé B, eds. 1991. *Fundamentals of Nonverbal Behavior.* Cambridge: Cambridge Univ. Press

Feyereisen P, de Lannoy J-D. 1991. *Gesture and Speech: Psychological Investigations.* Cambridge: Cambridge Univ. Press

Freedman N. 1977. Hands, words and mind: on the structuralization of body movements during discourse and the capacity for verbal representation. In *Communicative Structures and Psychic Structures: A Psychoanalytic Approach,* ed. N Freedman, S Grand, pp. 109–32. New York/ London: Plenum

Goffman E. 1963. *Behavior in Public Places.* New York: Free Press

Goldin-Meadow S, McNeill D, Singleton J. 1996. Silence is liberating: removing the handcuffs on grammatical expression in the manual modality. *Psychol. Rev.* 103: 34–55

Goldin-Meadow S, Wein D, Chang C. 1992. Assessing knowledge through gesture: using children's hands to read their minds. *Cogn. Instr.* 9:201–19

Goodwin C. 1986. Gesture as a resource for the organization of mutual orientation. *Semiotica* 62:29–49

Goodwin C, Goodwin MH. 1992. Context activity and participation. See Auer & di Luzio 1992, pp. 77–99

Goodwin MH, Goodwin C. 1986. Gesture and co-participation in the activity of searching for a word. *Semiotica* 62:51–75

Graf F. 1992. Gestures and conventions: the gestures of Roman actors and orators. See Bremmer & Roodenburg 1992, pp. 36–58

Haviland JB. 1979. Gugugu Yimidhirr. In *Handbook of Australian Languages,* Dixon RW, Blake B, ed. 1:27–182. Canberra: Aust. Natl. Univ. Press

Haviland JB. 1993. Anchoring iconicity and orientation in Guugu Yimithirr pointing gestures. *J. Linguist. Anthropol.* 3:3–45

Heath CC. 1986. *Body Movement and Speech in Medical Interaction.* Cambridge: Cambridge Univ. Press

Heath CC. 1992. Gesture's discrete tasks: multiple relevancies in visual conduct in the contextualization of language. See Auer & di Luzio 1992, pp. 102–27

Hibbitts BJ. 1992. "Coming to our senses": communication and legal expression in performance cultures. *Emory Law J.* 41: 873–960

Isenhath JO. 1990. *The Linguistics of American Sign Language.* Jefferson, NC: McFarland

Jarmon LH. 1996. *An ecology of embodied interaction: turn-taking and interactional syntax in face-to-face encounters.* CD-ROM. PhD thesis. Univ. Tex., Austin

Jones LW, Morey CR. 1932. *The Miniatures of the Manuscripts of Terence Prior to the Thirteenth Century,* Vols. 1, 2. Princeton, NJ: Princeton Univ. Press

Kegl J, Senghas A, Coppola M. 1997. Creation through contact: sign language emergence and sign language change in Nicaragua. In *Comparative Grammatical Change: The Intersection of Language Acquisition, Creole Genesis and Diachronic Syntax,* M DeGraff, ed. Cambridge, MA: MIT Press. In press

Kendon A. 1972. Some relationships between body motion and speech. An analysis of an example. In *Studies in Dyadic Communication,* ed. A Siegman, B Pope, pp. 177–210. Elmsford, NY: Pergamon

Kendon A. 1980a. Gesticulation and speech: two aspects of the process of utterance. In *The Relationship of Verbal and Nonverbal Communication,* ed. MR Key, pp. 207–27. The Hague: Mouton

Kendon A. 1980b. A description of a deaf-mute sign language from the Enga Province of Papua New Guinea with some comparative discussion. Part II. The semiotic functioning of Enga signs. *Semiotica* 32: 81–117

Kendon A. 1981a. Geography of gesture. *Semiotica* 37:129–63

Kendon A. 1981b. Introduction: current issues in the study of "nonverbal communication." In *Nonverbal Communication Interaction and Gesture,* ed. A Kendon, pp. 1–53. The Hague: Mouton

Kendon A. 1982. The study of gesture: some observations on its history. *Rech. Sémiot./Semiot. Inq.* 21:45–62

Kendon A. 1985a. Behavioural foundations for the process of frame attunement in face-to-face interaction. In *Discovery Strategies in the Psychology of Action,* ed. GP Ginsburg, M Brenner, M von Cranach, pp. 229–53. London: Academic

Kendon A. 1985b. Some uses of gesture. In *Perspectives on Silence,* ed. D Tannen, M Saville-Troike, pp. 215–34. Norwood, NJ: Ablex

Kendon A. 1988. *Sign Languages of Aboriginal Australia: Cultural Semiotic and Communicative Perspectives.* Cambridge: Cambridge Univ. Press

Kendon A. 1990a. Gesticulation, quotable gestures and signs. See Moerman & Nomura 1990, pp. 53–77

Kendon A. 1990b. Signs in the cloister and elsewhere. *Semiotica* 79:307–29

Kendon A. 1992. Some recent work from Italy on quotable gestures ('emblems'). *J. Linguist. Anthropol.* 21:72–93

Kendon A. 1993a. Human gesture. In *Tools, Language and Cognition in Human Evolution,* ed. KR Gibson, T Ingold, pp. 43–62. Cambridge: Cambridge Univ. Press

Kendon A. 1993b. Space time and gesture. *Degrès* 7(4):3A–16

Kendon A. 1994. Do gestures communicate? A Review. *Res. Lang. Soc. Interact.* 27: 175–200

Kendon A. 1995a. Gestures as illocutionary and discourse structure markers in Southern Italian conversation. *J. Pragmat.* 23: 247–79

Kendon A. 1995b. Andrea De Jorio: the first ethnographer of gesture? *Vis. Anthropol.* 7:375–94

Kendon A. 1997. Alcuni modi di usare i gesti nella conversazione. *Atti Congr. Soc. Linguist. Italiana, 27th,* ed. F Lo Piparo. In press

Kita S. 1993. *Language and thought interface: a study of spontaneous gestures and Japanese mimetics.* PhD thesis. Univ. Chicago, IL

Klima EA, Bellugi U. 1979. *The Signs of Language.* Cambridge, MA: Harvard Univ. Press

Knowlson JR. 1965. The idea of gesture as a universal language in the 17th and 18th centuries. *J. Hist. Ideas* 26:495–508

Krauss RM, Chen Y, Chawla P. 1996. Nonverbal behavior and nonverbal communica-

tion: What do conversational hand gestures tell us? In *Adv. Exp. Soc. Psychol.,* ed. M Zann, 38:389–450. New York: Academic

Krauss RM, Morrel-Samuels P, Colasante C. 1991. Do conversational gestures communicate? *J. Pers. Soc. Psychol.* 61:743–54

Kyle JG, Woll B. 1985. *Sign Language: The Study of Deaf People and Their Language.* Cambridge: Cambridge Univ. Press

Lamedica N. 1984. *Oratori Filosofi Maestri di Sordomuti.* Cosenza: Pellegrini Editore

Levinson SC. 1992. Language and cognition: cognitive consequences of spatial description in Guugu Yimithirr. *Work. Pap. No. 13.* Cogn. Anthropol. Res. Group, Max Planck Inst. Psycholinguist., Nijmegen

Levinson SC. 1996a. Language and space. *Annu. Rev. Anthropol.* 25:353–82

Levinson SC. 1996b. The body in space: cultural differences in the use of body-schema for spatial thinking and gesture. *Work. Pap. No. 39.* Cogn. Anthropol. Res. Group, Max Planck Inst. Psycholinguist., Nijmegen

Magli P. 1980. *Corpo e Linguaggio.* Rome: Espresso Strumenti

Mallery G. 1972. (1881). *Sign Language among North American Indians compared with that among other peoples and deafmutes.* The Hague: Mouton

Mandel M. 1977. Iconic devices in American sign language. In *On the Other Hand: New Perspectives on American Sign Language,* pp. 57–108. New York: Academic

Marslen-Wilson W, Levy E, Tyler LK. 1992. Producing interpretable discourse: the establishment and maintenance of reference. *Speech, Place and Action: Studies in Deixis and Related Topics,* ed. Jarvella RJ, Klein W, pp. 339–78. Chichester: Wiley

McClave EZ. 1991. *Intonation and gesture.* PhD thesis. Georgetown Univ., Washington, DC

McNeill D, Cassell J, Levy ET. 1993. Abstract deixis. *Semiotica* 95:5–19

McNeill D, Cassell J, McCullough K-E. 1994. Communicative effects of speech mismatched gestures. *Res. Lang. Soc. Interact.* 27:223–37

McNeill D. 1985. So you think gestures are nonverbal? *Psychol. Rev.* 92:350–71

McNeill D. 1987. *Psycholinguistics: A New Approach.* New York: Harper & Row

McNeill D. 1992. *Hand and Mind.* Chicago: Univ. Chicago Press

Meissner M, Philpott SB. 1975. The sign language of sawmill workers in British Columbia. *Sign Lang. Stud.* 9:291–308

Moerman M, Nomura M, eds. 1990. *Culture Embodied. Senri Ethnol. Stud. No. 27.* Osaka: Natl. Mus. Ethnol.

Morrel-Samuels P, Krauss RM. 1992. Word familiarity predicts temporal asynchrony of hand gestures and speech. *J. Exp. Psychol.: Learn. Mem. Cogn.* 18:615–22

Morris D, Collett P, Marsh P, O'Shaughnessy M. 1979. *Gestures: Their Origins and Distribution.* London: Cape

Müller C. 1994. Semantic structure of motional gestures and lexicalization patterns in Spanish and German descriptions of motion-events. *CLS* 30(1):281–95

Müller C. 1996. *Gestik in kommunikation und interaktion.* PhD thesis. Freie Univ. Berlin, Berlin

Nobe S. 1996. *Cognitive rhythms gestures and acoustic aspects of speech.* PhD thesis. Univ. Chicago, IL

Payrató L. 1993. A pragmatic view on autonomous gestures: a first repertoire of Catalan emblems. *J. Pragmat.* 20:193–216

Pettito LA. 1990. The transition from gesture to symbol in American Sign Language. See Volterra & Erting 1990, pp. 153– 61

Poggi I. 1983. La mano a borsa: analisi semantica di un gesto emblematico olofrastico. In *Communicare senza Parole,* ed. G Attili, PE Ricci-Bitti, pp. 219–38. Rome: Bulzoni

Quintilian MF. 1924. *Institutio Oratoria,* Vol. 4. Transl. HE Butler. London: Heinemann (from Latin)

Reddy M. 1979. The conduit metaphor: a case of frame conflict in our language about language. In *Metaphor and Thought,* A Ortony, pp. 284–324. Cambridge: Cambridge Univ. Press

Reilly JS, McIntire ML, Bellugi U. 1990. Faces: the relationship between language and affect. See Volterra & Erting 1990, pp. 128–49

Ricci-Bitti PE, Poggi I. 1991. Symbolic nonverbal behavior: talking through gestures. See Feldman & Rimé 1991, pp. 433–57

Rijnberk GV. 1954. *Le Langage par Signes Chez les Moines.* Amsterdam: North Holland

Rimé B, Schiaratura L. 1991. Gesture and speech. See Feldman & Rimé 1991, pp. 239–81

Rimé B. 1982. The elimination of visible behaviour from social interactions: effects on verbal nonverbal and interpersonal variables. *Eur. J. Soc. Psychol.* 12:113–29

Roodenburg H. 1992. The 'hand of friendship': shaking hands and other gestures in the Dutch Republic. See Bremmer & Roodenburg 1992, pp. 152–89

Rozik E. 1992. Metaphorical hand gestures in the theatre. *Assaph C: Stud. Theat.* 8: 127–52

Saitz RL, Cervenka EJ. 1972. *Handbook of Gestures: Columbia and the United States.* The Hague: Mouton

Scheflen AE. 1965. Quasi-courting behavior in psychotherapy. *Psychiatry* 28 245–57

Schegloff EA. 1984. On some gestures' relation to talk. In *Structures of Social Action: Studies in Conversation Analysis.* ed. JM Atkinson, J Heritage, pp. 266–96. Cambridge: Cambridge Univ. Press

Schlegel J. 1997. Finding words, finding meanings: collaborative learning and distributed cognition. In *Language Practices of Older Children,* ed. S Hoyle, CT Adger. Oxford: Oxford Univ. Press. In press

Schmitt J-C. 1984. Introduction and general bibliography. *Hist. Anthropol.* 1:1–28

Schmitt J-C. 1990. *Il gesto nel medioevo.* Rome: Laterza. (from French)

Sebeok TA, Umiker-Sebeok DJ. 1978. *Aboriginal Sign Languages of the Americas and Australia.* New York: Plenum

Sherzer J. 1972. Verbal and nonverbal deixis: the pointed lip gesture among the San Blas Cuna. *Lang. Soc.* 21:117–31

Sherzer J. 1991. The Brazilian thumbs-up gesture. *J. Linguist. Anthropol.* 12 189–97

Sherzer J. 1993. Pointed lips, thumbs up and cheek puffs: some emblematic gestures in social interactional and ethnographic context. *Symp. Lang. Soc.* (SALSA) I, pp. 196–211

Sittl K. 1890. *Die Gebärden der Griechen und Römer.* Leipzig: Teubner

Slama-Cazacu T. 1993. Les composantes non verbales de la communication orale et le concept de "syntaxe mixte": une synthèse. *Degrés* 7:4–24E

Sparhawk CM. 1978. Contrastive-identificational features of Persian gesture. *Semiotica* 24:49–86

Stokoe WC. 1960. Sign language structure. *Stud. Linguist. Occas. Pap. No. 8.* Buffalo: Univ. Buffalo

Streeck J. 1993. Gesture as communication. I. Its coordination with gaze and speech. *Commun. Monogr.* 60:275–99

Streeck J. 1994. Gesture as communication. II. The audience as co-author. *Res. Lang. Soc. Interact.* 27:239–67

Streeck J. 1996. How to do things with things: objets trovés and symbolization. *Hum. Stud.* 19:365–84

Streeck J, Hartge U. 1992. Previews: gestures at the transition place. See Auer & di Luzio 1992, pp. 135–57

Talmy L. 1985. Lexicalization patterns: semantic structure in lexical forms. In *Language Typology and Syntactic Description. Grammatical Categories and the Lexicon,* ed. T Shopen, 3:57–149. Cambridge: Cambridge Univ. Press

Tanner JE, Byrne RW. 1996. Representation of action through iconic gesture in a captive lowland gorilla. *Curr. Anthropol.* 37: 162–73

Tylor EB. 1865. *Researches into the Early History of Mankind and the Development of Civilization.* London: Murray

Umiker-Sebeok DJ, Sebeok TA, eds. 1987. *Monastic Sign Languages.* Berlin: Mouton

Volterra V, ed. 1987. *La Lingua Italiana dei Segni: La comunicazione visivo-gestuale dei sordi.* Bologna: Il Mulino

Volterra V, Erting CJ, ed. 1990. *From Gesture to Language in Hearing and Deaf Children.* Berlin/New York: Springer

Webb R. 1996. *Linguistic features of metaphoric gestures.* PhD thesis. Univ. Rochester, Rochester, NY

Wells GA. 1987. *The Origin of Language: Aspects of the Discussion from Condillac to Wundt.* La Salle, IL: Open Court

West LM, Jr. 1960. *The Sign Language: An analysis.* PhD thesis. Indiana Univ., Bloomington, IN

Wundt W. 1973. (1921). *The Language of Gestures.* Transl. JS Thayer, CM Greenleaf, MD Silberman. The Hague: Mouton (from Ger.)

Yau S-C. 1992. *Creations gestuelle et debuts du langage: Creation de langues gestuelles chez des sourds isoles.* Paris: Editions Langages Croisés

Annu. Rev. Anthropol. 1997. 26:129–61

STATE AND SOCIETY AT TEOTIHUACAN, MEXICO

George L. Cowgill

Department of Anthropology, Box 872402, Arizona State University, Tempe, Arizona 85287-2402; e-mail: cowgill@asu.edu

KEY WORDS: archaeology, Mesoamerica, early states, governmentality, ideology

ABSTRACT

Between 100 BCE and 200 CE, the city of Teotihuacan grew rapidly, most of the Basin of Mexico population was relocated in the city, immense civic-religious structures were built, and symbolic and material evidence shows the early importance of war. Rulers were probably able and powerful. Subsequently the city did not grow, and government may have become more collective, with significant constraints on rulers' powers. A state religion centered on war and fertility deities presumably served elite interests, but civic consciousness may also have been encouraged. A female goddess was important but probably not as pervasive as has been suggested. Political control probably did not extend beyond central Mexico, except perhaps for some outposts, and the scale and significance of commerce are unclear. Teotihuacan's prestige, however, spread widely in Mesoamerica, manifested especially in symbols of sacred war, used for their own ends by local elites.

INTRODUCTION

Teotihuacan is an immense prehistoric city in the semi-arid highlands of central Mexico. It rose in the first or second century BCE and lasted into the 600s or 700s (Figure 1 outlines the ceramic chronology). Its early growth was rapid, and by the 100s it covered about 20 km^2 with a population estimated to be around 60,000–80,000 (Cowgill 1979, p. 55; Millon 1992, p. 351). Subsequently, there was little change in area, and population grew more slowly, ap-

129

parently reaching a plateau of 100,000 or more by the 300s or earlier. No other Mesoamerican city had such a large and dense urban concentration before Aztec Tenochtitlan, in the late 1400s. By the 200s Teo (as I will henceforth call it) also had the largest integrated complex of monumental structures in Mesoamerica: the gigantic Sun Pyramid (with a base area close to that of the largest Egyptian pyramid), the Moon Pyramid, the 16-ha Ciudadela enclosure with its Feathered Serpent Pyramid, and the broad 5-km-long Avenue of the Dead, along whose northern 2 km these and many other pyramids, platforms, and elite residences are arranged (Figure 2).

Millon et al (1973) published map sheets of the whole city at a scale of 1:2000, based on an intensive surface survey. A 1:40,000 version appears in Millon (1973, 1974, 1976, 1981, 1988a). Articles by Millon (1981, 1988a, 1992) and Cowgill (1992a,b) include reviews of research and literature on Teo. I concentrate here on publications since the mid-1960s that bear especially on state and society. I emphasize relatively accessible sources and do not always identify earliest publications of specific ideas. Edited volumes with papers on a wide range of Teo topics include Berlo (1992a), Berrin (1988), Berrin & Pasztory (1993), Cabrera Castro et al (1982a,b, 1991a), Cardós (1990), de la Fuente (1995), Diehl & Berlo (1989), McClung de Tapia & Rattray (1987), Rattray et al (1981), Sanders (1994-1996), Sociedad Mexicana de Antropología (1967, 1972), and special sections of *Ancient Mesoamerica* [1991, Vol. 2(1,2)] and *Arqueología* (1991). The proceedings of a 1993 Instituto Nacional de Antropología e Historia (INAH) workshop on Teo chronology, edited by Cabrera and Brambila, are in press, and a book by Pasztory (1997) has just appeared. Sugiyama has created a web site: http://archaeology.la.asu.edu/vm/mesoam/teo.

METHOD AND THEORY

We still only glimpse the outlines of polity and society in the city and the state it dominated. Surviving inscriptions are few, brief, and hard to read. Teo society was destroyed by the 700s or earlier, and to the Aztecs, about whom we have a wealth of ethnohistoric data, Teo was a place of mysterious ruins; more mythical than historical. These problems mean that theoretical preconceptions and methodological assumptions play a large role in determining which interpretations seem intrinsically plausible or even empirically well founded. Sanders et al (1979) and Santley (1983, 1984, 1989) are strongly cultural-materialist and favor interpretations and explanations in terms of environmental and economic factors, relatively neglecting warfare and nearly excluding religion and other ideational aspects and the agency of individual actors. Others give more weight to ideation and individual agency.

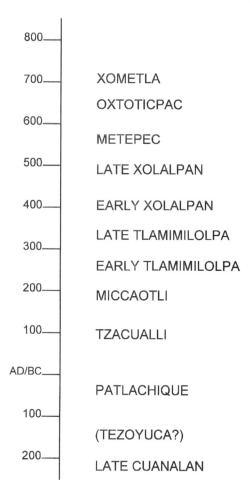

Figure 1 Teotihuacan ceramic chronology.

Teo is in a challenging twilight zone for direct historical approaches; close enough to the 1500s to make it wasteful to neglect evidence from later societies, yet distant enough to make it unsound to project ethnohistoric data uncritically. Linguistic evidence suggests that Nahua speakers were absent or at least not influential in the Basin of Mexico before the decline of Teo (Justeson et al 1983). The Aztecs and other Nahua in-migrants adopted much from earlier central Mexican traditions, but the possibility of significant ethnic discontinuity adds to the uncertainties of direct historical projections. Kubler (1967) went

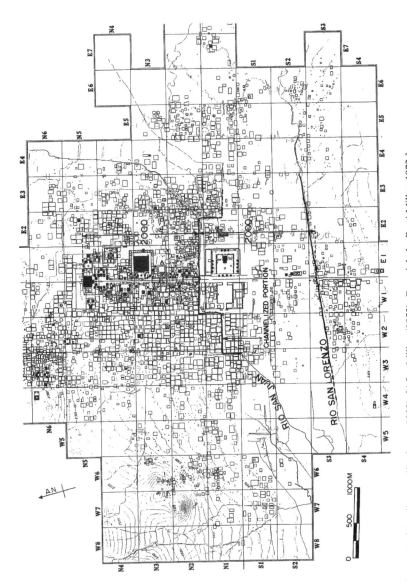

Figure 2   Most of Teotihuacan (Sugiyama 1993). [After Millon (1973). Copyright by René Millon 1972.]

to a skeptical extreme; Pasztory (1992) has returned to this extreme and favors a "semiotic" approach. López Austin et al (1991) and Coe (1981) are at the opposite pole. A more nuanced approach is preferable to either extreme. Using knowledge from the 1500s to understand Teo is neither impossible nor easy, and it is best to proceed piecemeal, case by case. Many Teo images have no obvious later counterparts. Others do but must be used cautiously; meanings and clusters of meanings may have shifted.

GROWTH OF THE CITY

It is notoriously difficult to derive accurate population estimates from archaeological data. Millon (1973) estimated the Xolalpan Phase population by using sizes, layouts, and inferred uses of rooms in excavated apartment compounds to infer that a 60×60-m compound would have housed about 60 to 100 people. His surface survey indicated that over 2000 such compounds were occupied during Xolalpan times. Making allowances for those larger or smaller than 60 $\times 60$ m, he arrived at an estimate of 100,000 to 200,000 for the whole city, with 125,000 a reasonable middle value (Millon 1992, p. 344). Architectural data for other phases are less clear, so Cowgill (1974, 1979) extrapolated the Xolalpan estimate by comparing quantities of phased sherds collected by the Mapping Project, with adjustments for estimated phase durations, assuming that per capita sherd production remained approximately constant. He did not find a Xolalpan peak. Instead, early rapid growth was followed by a long plateau. By ca 1 BCE the city covered about 8 km^2 and probably had a population of 20,000 to 40,000 (Cowgill 1979, p. 55). In the century before any known monumental structures were built, Teo was already a city of exceptional size. During the Tzacualli phase (ca 1–150 CE) increase continued to around 60,000–80,000, aided by movement into the city of most people in the Basin of Mexico. After that, growth was much slower. Urban population may have reached its maximum by the Miccaotli phase, ca 200 CE. Perhaps Teo had reached a ceiling imposed by difficulties in provisioning a larger city with the resources and means of transportation available. Most of the farming population was concentrated in and near the city, and Teo seems to have underutilized the southern Basin, including the lands most suited for *chinampa* cultivation.

It is also possible, if Storey's (1985, 1992) estimates for one low-status compound can be generalized, that very high infant and child mortality rates set a limit to the city's growth. In any case, Teo's population seems to have been fairly stable for several centuries. This suggests that whatever environmental degradation may have occurred must have been gradual.

EXTENT OF TEOTIHUACAN RULE

Teo was the capital of an important state, but we know little about it. Teo is in the northeastern part of the Basin of Mexico, about 45 km from modern Mexico City. The Basin is about 80×50 km, ca 5000 km^2, ringed on most sides by volcanoes and high mountains, but more open to the north and northeast, so Teo was well situated for movement in and out. The Basin is high (ca 2250 m) but relatively flat and generally suitable for growing maize, beans, and other food crops, though tracts suitable for canal irrigation are limited and localized, a major one being a few thousand hectares just west of the city. Teo clearly dominated the Basin politically, as shown by its drastic interference with the settlement system.

Very likely Teo's administrative control extended somewhat beyond the Basin of Mexico, but perhaps not much beyond. It covered at least 25,000 km^2 (Millon 1988a), a radius of about 90 km, and may have reached considerably farther. Beyond that, Teo probably concentrated on controlling key settlements and routes between them, rather than solid blocks of territory; "hegemonic" in Hassig's (1992, pp. 57–59) terms. Teo's immense prestige, however, surely exceeded its political sphere, and we still know little about specific outposts. Hassig's lucid account is a fascinating source of conjectures to be tested, but it presents much as fact that is highly uncertain or sometimes wrong. Studies such as Kurtz's (1987) and Algaze's (1993) also fit ambiguous or problematic data into preconceived patterns.

Relations between Teo and Cholula, 90 km away, in the next major upland plain to the southeast, are unclear (McCafferty 1996), though the weight of evidence suggests it may have been independent. Cantona, further northeast, on the way to the Gulf lowlands, may also have resisted Teo (García Cook 1994). Teo moved south to control the eastern Valley of Morelos where, unlike the Basin of Mexico, cotton could be grown, a key resource for a textile industry (Hirth 1978, 1980; Hirth & Angulo Villaseñor 1981).

Northwest, there is a Teo presence in the area around Tula, Hidalgo, notably at the site of Chingú (Díaz Oyarzábal 1980). It is uncertain how far Teo influence went west or north of Tula. Aveni et al (1982) argued for Teo presence at Alta Vista, in Zacatecas. Some features at Alta Vista have astronomical significance, and its location on the Tropic of Cancer is probably intentional. We should not assume, however, that local people were unlikely to make the needed observations without tutelage from Teo "merchant-scientists-priests." Ceramic resemblances suggest only remote, indirect connections. A cross-in-circle petroglyph motif is shared with Teo, but it is widespread in Mesoamerica; its occurrence need not mean Teo presence. Teo may have received minerals from this area, but its impact on local societies is unclear.

In Oaxaca, the Zapotec state was independent and maintained diplomatic relations with Teo (Marcus & Flannery 1996). Some sort of Teo presence is known for Matacapan in southern Veracruz (Santley 1989), Mirador in Chiapas (Agrinier 1975), Kaminaljuyú, and other sites in highland and Pacific coastal Guatemala (Berlo 1983, 1984, Demarest & Foias 1993, Kidder et al 1946, Sanders & Michels 1977). Santley's (1989; Santley et al 1987) exaggerated claims about a Teo outpost at Matacapan have created much confusion. Most of the Matacapan ceramics are strikingly different (Arnold et al 1993), and the Teo impact seems weaker than at Kaminaljuyú. Matacapan cylinder tripod vases, for example, show generic resemblances to Teo forms, but very few, if any, are specific Teo subtypes. Small, relatively crude twin-chambered incense burners (candeleros) are a stronger point of similarity. A relief from Soyoltepec in a style closely similar to Teo shows a figure with flaming torches and a rattlesnake headdress, suggesting military action in the lowlands (Sugiyama 1989b, von Winning 1987).

A Teo connection is manifest at Altun Ha in Belize by the early 200s (Pendergast 1990), but most Teo influences in the Maya lowlands do not seem earlier than the late 300s, which suggests that the spread of Teo prestige occurred considerably later than the rapid rise of the city. They are especially strong at Tikal (Kowalski 1997, Laporte & Fialko 1990) but are unlikely to represent control by Teo. Many reflect adoption of a limited number of Teo-related symbols by local elites for their own purposes (Stone 1989, Demarest & Foias 1993).

WRITING AND LITERACY

Teo had nothing like the writing systems of the contemporary Lowland Maya or earlier neighbors in Veracruz, though some Teotihuacanos must have been aware of these systems. There is ample evidence, however, of standardized signs and a notational system comparable to those of the Aztecs, though few specific signs are shared (Berlo 1989). Langley (1986) provided an indispensable study and catalog of signs, whereas his later works deal with specific clusters and compounds (Langley 1991, 1992). Cowgill (1992c) identified a sign cluster ("red bone-flower") semantically equivalent to a term used by Aztecs. However, no examples of phoneticism have been identified, nor any grammatical elements, so, even when meanings can be inferred, the signs have not helped to identify the dominant language or languages of the city.

A remarkable find in recent work in the La Ventilla district directed by Rubén Cabrera, not far southwest of the Great Compound, consists of over 30 signs and sign clusters painted on the floor of a patio (de la Fuente 1995). They stand alone, unassociated with representational scenes. They were made quickly and show a control of line that bespeaks an experienced hand. Their meaning and purpose are obscure, but there can no longer be any doubt that Teotihuacanos had a notational system adequate for the information-handling needs of their society. What remains noteworthy is the sparing use of this system in sculpture, mural painting, and decorated ceramics; one aspect of the near lack of public celebration of named specific individuals.

Pasztory (1992) suggested that Teo was almost secretive and made a point of being different from other Mesoamerican societies. It is easy for us, in our frustration, to feel they were deliberately being difficult, but I suspect most meanings of their scenes and signs were intended to be clear to the average Teotihuacano, and we have trouble only because we still lack many keys. They seem, however, not to have been very interested in exotic ideas. Some fine foreign ceramics were imported, but most exotic goods were raw materials intended for working by Teo artisans. The contrast with the Aztec interest in finished products from afar, seen in the Templo Mayor offerings (Matos Moctezuma 1988), is striking. Persons in other societies adopted Teo symbols for their own ends, but there was little flow in the opposite direction; Teotihuacanos seem to have been satisfied with their local style and symbols (Pasztory 1990, p. 187). The great value placed on the exotic in many societies (Helms 1993) is not evident at Teo.

One exception is adoption of interlocking scroll motifs from the lowlands of central Veracruz (Stark 1995). The earliest cylinder tripod vases were probably imports from this region (Bennyhoff 1967, p. 26). Teotihuacanos, however, may have recognized an affinity with Gulf lowland neighbors, and the adoptions occurred during Miccaotli and/or Early Tlamimilolpa, when Teo may have been more receptive to new ideas than it was later.

PERSONALITY AND SOCIALIZATION

Approaches that take serious account of individual agency imply that we should also take account of individual personality. Archaeologists, however, have done little along this line, and there is almost no explicit discussion of this topic for Teo. Foucault's notion of governmentality looks useful but has not yet been applied. Pasztory (e.g. 1992) characterizes the art as remote and impersonal, and Cowgill (1993, pp. 564–68) touches on the topic of personality. No scenes glorify specific individuals, and human beings are shown subordinate only to deities, not to other human beings. This has implications about the political system, or about how the system was represented, but it also suggests something about socialization of children and about preferred character traits.

Beginning as early as the repeated images on the Feathered Serpent Pyramid (FSP), identical figures are repeated in numerous copies. Some scenes (especially of fierce animals) convey tension and vibrant power, as in the "Mythological Animals" mural (de la Fuente 1995, pp. 93–101), and elsewhere (e.g. Berrin 1988, p. 187), but much of the art is stiff, and human faces look expressionless to modern viewers. Sometimes small human figures are shown simply clad, in free and playful poses, as in a scene from Tepantitla that reminds us how small a fraction of Teotihuacano life was depicted in Teo art. Most scenes show human beings so loaded with clothing and insignia that faces and other body parts are barely visible. Emphasis is on acts rather than actors; on offices rather than office-holders. This, together with the multiplicity of identical scenes, suggests an ethos in which individuals were interchangeable and replaceable. These properties are found not only in sculpture and paintings that must have been elite sponsored, but also in ubiquitous objects such as composite censers and clay figurines. Whether or not impersonality and multiplicity were deliberately encouraged by state policy, they are themes that pervaded all classes and social sectors. No evidence of resistance or dissent has been recognized so far.

NONELITE ELEMENTS OF THE SOCIETY

Households and Apartment Compounds

We know little of Teo housing during the early centuries when the great temples were being built. In the 200s and 300s, more than 2000 "apartment compounds" were built to house nearly the whole city, of all socioeconomic statuses. Millon uses "apartment" because each building contains several distinct suites of rooms, indicating occupation by multiple domestic units, and "compound" rather than "complex" because they are bounded by thick outer walls with few entrances and are separated from one another, often by narrow streets. Contrary to widespread belief, in many districts compound sizes are not highly standardized, and they vary widely around an average of roughly 60 × 60 m. Internal layouts are diverse, although the core of most apartments is a patio surrounded by rooms and platforms. Yet the facts that compounds are so substantially built (of rubble walls faced with thick concrete covered with lime plaster) and approximate the canonical Teo orientation of 15.5° east of true north, even in outlying areas where they are widely spaced, suggest some sort of state interest. Possibly the state aided in their construction. Very likely occupants of a compound formed an important sociopolitical unit, composed of several households but smaller than a neighborhood (Millon 1976). Societies with most of the population organized in units of this size are not common.

Construction quality and size of rooms vary considerably, between compounds and within single compounds. Some have spacious rooms and abundant mural paintings [e.g. Zacuala "Palace" (Séjourné 1959)]; others are far more modest [e.g. Tlajinga 33 (Storey 1985, 1991, 1992; Widmer 1991; Widmer & Storey 1993]. When less was known about the compounds it seemed reasonable to call some of them "palaces," but over-broad application of the term has been misleading. Millon (1976) suggests at least six socioeconomic levels, with uppermost elite residences in the Ciudadela and elsewhere near the Avenue of the Dead. He would put Zacuala "Palace" in about the third level from the top. Sempowski (1994) has tabulated information on offerings in Teo burials, mostly in apartment compounds, and her analyses suggest status differences and changes over time in these differences.[1] Spence's (1974, 1994) studies of nonmetric skeletal traits suggest a preference for patrilocal postmarital residence in most compounds.

It is unclear whether there was any distinct material gap between the elite and the merely prosperous, and proportions of residences of varying quality are also unclear. Further analyses of Mapping Project surface collections may clarify these questions (Robertson 1997). Even the proportion of compounds with mural paintings is debatable. Fine murals were not common, and many compounds had only white-plastered walls, with at most a few borders outlined in red. Most floors were plaster over concrete; some were of cobbles or earth.

We need excavations of many more compounds using the best methods and concepts of household archaeology. Good examples already exist, in a residential area in the Oztoyahualco district (Manzanilla 1993, 1996; Manzanilla & Barba 1990), in the Oaxaca enclave (Spence 1989, 1992), in the "Merchants' Barrio" (Rattray 1989, 1990), and in the Tlajinga 33 ceramic and lapidary residential workshop. Manzanilla and her colleagues have used chemical analyses of residues on plaster floors to infer highly localized activities within rooms.

Barrios, Enclaves, and Districts

Occupants of the city must have recognized distinct neighborhoods. Millon (1976, p. 225) said that many spatial clusters of apartment compounds can be identified. Some, such as the block that includes the Tepantitla compound (Figure 2, NE part of square N4E2), look clear. Craft workshops often form spatial clusters. Unambiguous distinct small neighborhoods, however, seem hard to define in much of the city. Most freestanding pyramids are not plausible barrio temples, and they are absent in large tracts of the city. The excavated plan of one compound, Yayahuala, suggests that it may have housed a barrio headman (Millon 1976) but other examples would be hard to recognize without excavation. J Altschul (personal communication) suggests that the impor-

---

[1] Rattray (1992) also provided data on burials and offerings. See Millon's corrections in Sempowski & Spence (1994).

tance of apartment compounds as multihousehold social and political units may have meant that small neighborhoods were not very important administrative units.

There are at least two enclaves with foreign affiliations. Toward the western edge of the city, centered in square N1W6, is a cluster of about a dozen compounds with Oaxacan affinities (Rattray 1993; Spence 1989, 1992). Architecture and most ceramics are typically Teo. A small percentage of the ceramics, however, mostly locally made, are Late Monte Albán II (formerly called II/IIIA transition) in style, and a few vessels are imports. Stratigraphic evidence suggests that this early style continued to be used from Tlamimilolpa through Metepec times, which implies either remarkable conservatism (Spence 1992) or some unresolved problem in ceramic chronology. A further Oaxacan tie is collective tombs, quite different from the Teo pattern of individual inhumations beneath floors. Socioeconomic status of the enclave occupants looks no more than average. Their role in Teo society is unclear, but similar ceramics in a lime-producing district near Tula (Crespo & Mastache 1981) suggest they may have been masons.

Another enclave with foreign ties is the "Merchants' Barrio" on the eastern edge of the city. Most ceramics are Teo, but some are imports from the Gulf lowlands, and a smaller number are from the Maya lowlands. Some structures are Teo-like, but others are circular, a form associated with the lowlands (Rattray 1989, 1990). Probably the enclave specialized in lowlands imports, including perhaps cotton and other perishable materials.

It is not clear whether Teo was as ethnically diverse as is often suggested. The early influx from within the Basin would have brought in people with different local affinities, but they may not have differed much in language or culture. Later, foreigners seem to have been handled by spatial segregation, to judge from the enclaves described above. Even without ethnic frictions, factions would have posed sociopolitical management problems.

Aztec Tenochtitlan was divided into four quarters that were important sociopolitical units. Teo is divided into quarters by the Avenue of the Dead and "East" and "West" Avenues, whose axes pass through the Great Compound and the Ciudadela. Sugiyama (1993, p. 110) questions the existence of the east and west avenues, but Millon's survey found ample evidence of them. They differ sharply, however, from the northern part of the Avenue of the Dead in not being lined by pyramids, platforms, or other obviously special structures. Teo has no long and architecturally prominent east-west alignments comparable to the north-south Avenue of the Dead. Division of the city is more bipartite than quadripartite.

There is evidence for socially meaningful districts larger than barrios and enclaves, but smaller than whole quarters (Altschul 1987, Cowgill et al 1984).

Freestanding walls bound a number of precincts, especially near the Avenue of the Dead. They are 1–2 m thick at their bases, but nearly all have been eroded to ground level. A Mapping Project excavation (TE5) found that the top of one wall joined the northwest corner of the Moon Pyramid at a height of about 5 m. Other walls are much farther from the ceremonial center. Starting at the "Plaza One" three-pyramid complex in square N5W2 (Figure 2), a wall can be traced eastward for more than 1 km and southward for nearly 1 km. Traces of other walls several 100 m long are at the east edge of N5W4 and near the south edge of N6W3. There is no suggestion that the city was enclosed by walls, and walls may or may not have been militarily significant. They, however, as well as watercourses, would have strongly affected movement within the city.

Some abrupt changes in density of apartment compounds coincide with walls outside the central ceremonial district, but changes in socioeconomic status indicators have not been obvious. A possible exception is the so-called "Old City," centered in square N6W3. Millon (1973) recognized during the 1960s survey that structures in this area were different from most apartment compounds, and excavations by Manzanilla (1993) bear this out. Millon suggested that the apartment compound innovation and concomitant social changes did not spread to this area, which preserved an earlier style of housing. I am not sure whether it was earlier or just different, but it is unlike most of the city. It is outside the outermost known walls, population density was high, and it has two of the largest three-pyramid complexes outside the city center. Some artifact categories, such as composite censers, occur in unusually high proportions, but no categories unique to this district have been recognized. A search for distinctions at the microtradition level might be rewarding.

The Tlajinga district, in S3W2, S3W1, S4W2, and S4W1, is near the southern extreme of the city, separated from the rest by the Río San Lorenzo. The Mapping Project survey found exceptional proportions of San Martín Orange, a utility ware, on a number of sites, and excavations at one of these, Tlajinga 33, have confirmed its manufacture there (Sheehy 1992, Storey 1991, Widmer & Storey 1993). This was probably a district of low-status artisans. Specialized ceramic production was plausibly situated in this remote area to shield higher-status Teotihuacanos from the smoke of pottery firing.

Lineages?

Even modest apartment compounds or room complexes, such as Tlajinga 33 and Tlamimilolpa (Linné 1942) tend to have one or a few relatively richly stocked graves, which may have been those of founders (e.g. Millon 1976, Headrick 1996). Millon points out that the inflexible sizes of compounds with fixed outer walls are ill-suited to the inevitable fluctuations of strictly unilineal descent groups, and Spence (1974) cites one case in which shared nonmetric skeletal traits suggest a group of related women who stayed home while their husbands moved in from elsewhere. Nevertheless, consistent with most of Spence's findings, each apartment compound probably was associated with a core of individuals claiming descent from a common ancestor, plus others whose rights to residence were based on marriage, some more tenuous kin tie, or a wide variety of special circumstances, perhaps including servants and apprentices.

Headrick (1996) proposed that descent groups at the apartment compound level may have been hierarchically organized into much larger groups, whose heads would have been of elite status. Different apartment compound groups may have been roughly ranked according to the degree to which they could claim connection with the apical ancestor through senior links. Many such systems exist elsewhere in the world. If such higher-level units existed, many of their head families may have resided on or near the Avenue of the Dead, while member lineages may have been dispersed in various districts, rather than being spatially concentrated. A few three-pyramid complexes in the northwest part of the city, not associated with the Avenue, could be headquarters for more independent lineages, although other interpretations are possible (Cowgill et al 1984).

Household Religion and Ritual

Pasztory (1992) argued that a good deal of village-level religion persisted in urban Teo. Assuredly, much was distinct from the "state" religion, but it dealt with domestic and familial concerns that would have persisted no matter how large and complex the state became. Many such rituals may have been of no interest to the state. Others, however, may reflect the "long arm" of the state imposing itself at the household level. I know of nothing that suggests conscious resistance to the state.

Standardized stone bowls supported on the back of a thin and bent old man, ubiquitous in apartment compounds of all socioeconomic statuses, probably belong to a cult of the hearth. They are called "Huehueteotls," but use of this Aztec term is problematic; an Aztec revival of the form (López Luján 1989, Umberger 1987) reinterprets it and shows that Aztecs did not recognize its Teo meaning. Except that the state had an interest in promoting domestic tranquillity, it is unlikely that these stone carvings had much political significance.

Composite censers are also ubiquitous. These are built from coarse flowerpot-like bowls, often on a high pedestal base, with a similar inverted bowl as a lid, from which rises a tubular chimney. Panels, frames, and a profusion of appliqué ornaments largely conceal the chimney. Often the central element is a human face. From Late Tlamimilolpa onward, faces and other ornaments are moldmade. Some censers are associated with burials, but many are not. Nevertheless, they were probably used in rituals commemorating the dead. Headrick (1996) and others have argued that Teo stone masks were attached to mortuary bundles containing remains of deceased elites. Composite censers were probably an equivalent for commemorating honored but less illustrious compound residents. As such, it might seem that the state would have little interest in them. One of the clearest instances of a state-related workshop at Teo, however, is in the large enclosure attached to the north side of the Ciudadela, where great numbers of censer ornaments and molds for their manufacture were found (Múnera 1985). Múnera and Sugiyama have prepared an unpublished catalog of these finds. The nature of the state interest in composite censers will become clearer through further studies of the multitude of standard signs on their ornaments.

Another indication that beliefs and practices associated with composite censers may have been connected with the Teo state is that they disappear with the collapse of that state. Dominant post-Teo censer forms are ladles, much more portable and adapted for quite different activities. The shift, however, may simply reflect ethnic discontinuity. This may also be the case with twin-chambered "candeleros," small, simple, and often crude incense burners that occur in great numbers at Teo but that do not survive the city. They are ubiquitous but are less common in the city center. Probably they were for modest household or individual rituals. Twin-chambered Teo-like varieties occur rarely in Maya sites and elsewhere in Mesoamerica, but are not scarce at Matacapan.[2]

Pasztory (1992) also linked "Tlaloc" jars with popular religion. Some occur in sites of no obvious prominence, but they are more abundant in high-status contexts, such as the FSP. Most are well-polished, elaborately hand-modeled, and represent (by Teo standards) a high level of skill and manufacturing effort. In murals, the Storm God often carries similar jars, and they are probably associated with state religion.

Infants' burials are often associated with patio altars. It is not clear whether any were sacrificial victims; high infant mortality probably accounts for the number observed. In recent Tlaxcala they are seen as especially effective intermediaries between human beings and the supernatural because they have spent so little time in this world (Headrick 1996, Nutini 1988). This analogy makes great sense of the Teo data.

Designs pecked on rocks or impressed in plaster floors are common at Teo. These include rectangles, Maltese crosses, and other forms, but many consist of a cross and two concentric circles. This motif is widespread, from north of Alta Vista (Zacatecas) to Uaxactun. Among the first found at Teo were a pair,

---

[2] F Bove (personal communication) finds them in Pacific coast Guatemalan sites that also have composite censers.

several kilometers apart, that formed a perpendicular to the Avenue of the Dead, suggesting that they were important in astronomical alignments and city planning. So many more have since been found at Teo, often within buildings where long-distance sightings would have been unfeasible, that their use for astronomy and surveying has become uncertain. Some consist of approximately 260 dots, and the case is better for a connection with the 260-day sacred calendar, perhaps divination, and possibly gaming. Many outside the city are on prominences suitable for distant sightings, but within the city many are in seemingly unremarkable buildings. This, plus their abundance and simplicity, makes state involvement somewhat unlikely. Pecked cross-&-circles and other motifs are especially profuse in a recently uncovered floor near the Sun Plaza, but even here they could reflect a popular cult.

The term "temple" has been used at Teo to refer to freestanding pyramids and also to the platforms that are ubiquitous in apartment compounds. The former must represent public religion, whether at the state or at some intermediate level. The latter are standard Teo "talud-tablero" platforms, which usually support a room fronted by a portico. Typically there are three such platforms, on the north, east, and south sides of a patio to which they connect by short stairways and in whose center there is often an altar; the eastern platform is most prominent. Millon (1976) suggested that a patio-platform group in the Yayahuala compound, because of its size and accessibility, may have served as a barrio temple, and the compound may have housed a barrio headman. Many of these patio-platform groups, however, were more likely used only by compound occupants, and often there is more than one such group in a single compound. They are architecturally substantial, and they were probably used for some mundane activities as well as for ceremonial occasions.

CRAFT PRODUCTION AND TRADE

We have learned much about Teo technology, but scale and organization of craft production are still poorly understood. Depopulation of the countryside implies that farming was a major activity of many households. Earlier estimates on the order of 400 obsidian workshops have been revised downward. Clark (1986) thinks the scale of production and exchange was much smaller. He overstates his case and perhaps underestimates the immense quantities of obsidian debitage at Teo. Assessments of the obsidian industry by Spence (1981, 1984, 1987, 1996) are more reasonable. The Mapping Project made test pits in or near obsidian and lapidary workshops, but more extensive excavations of obsidian and other workshops are needed.

Obsidian from the nearby Otumba source is of moderate quality and was used mainly for local consumption. Teo controlled the Pachuca source of superior green obsidian. Much was consumed in the city, and it is found in small amounts widely in Mesoamerica. There is good evidence, however, that Teo did not monopolize obsidian production and exchange (Drennan et al 1990). Sources unlikely to have been controlled by Teo continued to export obsidian (Stark et al 1992). Teo emissaries could be backed by the city's prestige and could carry fine stucco-decorated ceramics and perhaps perishable manufactures, but green obsidian was the only locally obtained valuable raw material they could offer abroad, which may account for its wide distribution. Commerce in obsidian and other materials may have been fairly important, although we have recognized no evidence of a distinct merchant class [Manzanilla (1992) doubts that one existed], but the scale of trade postulated by Santley (1983, 1984; Santley et al 1986) is not supported by evidence. Emphasis on trade alone underplays military and ideational bases for Teo's wide influence.

Sheehy (1992) and Hopkins (1995) have studied Teo ceramic production techniques, and the late Paula Krotser began a review of Mapping Project evidence for production sites, but we still lack a comprehensive picture of the organization and spatial distribution of pottery making. San Martín Orange utility ware was a specialization in the Tlajinga district. Other utility wares, such as burnished ollas and cazuelas, may have been made on a smaller scale in less specialized households. Significant state involvement seems unlikely, except for the mold-made censer parts noted above.

Turner (1987, 1992) reported on a barrio of lapidary craftsmen on the eastern outskirts of the city, and other evidence suggests some lapidary work in fine stone and marine shell under state sponsorship. Lapidary work at Tlajinga 33 (Widmer 1991) was probably not state directed. An obsidian concentration in a walled precinct just west of the Moon Pyramid (Spence 1981, 1984, 1987) implies at least part-time work sponsored by temple or state. This, as well as the censer ornament workshop in the enclosure attached to the Ciudadela, indicates that some craftsmen worked outside household contexts at least part of the time. Some may have been attached specialists, but most or all may have been providing periodic labor services. A great deal of production seems household based, however, possibly taxed and regulated to some degree by the state but not state sponsored.

WAR AND THE MILITARY

By the 1960s it was clear that Teo was not a very peaceable society (C Millon 1973, R Millon 1976). Recognized military symbolism, however, was mostly late, and it seemed that emphasis on military elements increased over time. New finds and reinterpretations of old data now show that military emphasis began early. About 200 persons were sacrificed as part of the FSP construction activities, ca 200 CE (Cabrera Castro et al 1991b; Sugiyama 1989a,b, 1992, 1995; *Arqueología* 1991, Vol. 6). Many, but not all, were in military garb and accompanied by weapons. Two large pits, underneath the pyramid and at the foot of its stairway, may have contained bodies of Teo rulers, but they were looted anciently, so it is not clear whether the victims accompanied a dead ruler. In any case, victims and grave goods were arranged in highly structured patterns, which Sugiyama (1995) argued were related to the calendar and creation symbolism. The victims may have been enemies or low-status Teotihuacanos dressed as soldiers and dignitaries, but I suspect they belonged to the royal household and that the soldiers were elite guardsmen. Anatomical, chemical, and cultural studies of bones, teeth, and grave goods, now under way, may resolve these issues.

Many now see the symbolism of the FSP facade as associated with war (Carlson 1991; López Austin et al 1991; Sugiyama 1989b, 1995; Taube 1992). For most, the Feathered Serpent itself reflects sacred Venus-related war; Taube makes the connection by interpreting the figure that alternates with the Feathered Serpent as a solar fire/war serpent.

"Portrait" clay figurines are abundant at Teo. Their heads, stamped in molds, are anything but portraits of individuals. Their contorted body positions have been puzzling (Figure 3). W Barbour (in Berrin & Pasztory 1993, p. 228) suggested convincingly that they are poised to hurl a spear (of perishable material) in the right hand and held a shield in the left hand. They probably wore perishable clothing. These figurines also point to the salience of war in Teo thought.

It is unlikely that Teo could have gained preeminence—however aided by its sacred significance, location on a strategic trade route, and proximity to canal-irrigated fields—unless it had been able to overcome armed resistance from rival centers. Defensible locations of sites of the poorly understood Tezoyuca phase (Sanders et al 1979) suggest warring polities in the Basin of Mexico just before or early in Teo's rise. Pasztory (1990, 1993, p. 138) thinks Teo emphasis on war was mainly symbolic, but it was probably very real, at least initially. Hassig (1992) argued convincingly that Teo armies were highly effective not only because of their atlatl-propelled darts and other weapons but because they fought in disciplined masses, using many commoners as well as elites. This is consonant with everything else we know of Teo. It is less clear that organization was what Hassig (1992) calls "meritocratic," i.e. that commoners were motivated by the chance for upward mobility if they performed well; this view underestimates the power of ideology.

Berlo (1983, 1984) emphasizes military symbolism in Teo-derived composite censers in Pacific coastal Guatemala, and war is prominent in Teo symbolism adopted by the lowland Maya (Schele & Freidel 1990, Stone 1989).

Figure 3   A "portrait" figurine (after Pasztory 1997).

Conquest of the lowland Maya is unlikely, but the city's military prestige trav-
eled well. Teo weapons and possibly some tactics seem to have been adopted
by the Maya, at least for a while. But military successes would have been attributed at least as much to potency of the Teo War God as to weapons and tactics, and this would have been a powerful incentive for adopting elements of
Teo religion. Teo's military prestige may have lasted long after its real military
effectiveness waned.

   Teo soldiers were associated with fierce animals, especially rattlesnakes,
jaguars, coyotes, and raptorial birds. There were probably military orders
something like the Aztec eagle and jaguar knights, as suggested by C Millon
(1973, 1988) and argued especially by Headrick (1996). These may have been
sodalities that crosscut kin ties and provided politically important cohesive institutions. The earliest prominent fierce animal is the Feathered Serpent, depicted as a rattlesnake, though with avian feathers and a feline snout. Many
nose pendants of the "butterfly" type (Figure 4b) were in the burial at the center of the FSP. Oralia Cabrera Cortés (1995) recognized that they are not but-
terflies (prominent in other Teo war symbolism), but final segments of rattlesnake rattles. Wearers of this type of nose pendant were identified with the
Feathered Rattlesnake. Whether there was such a sodality is unclear.

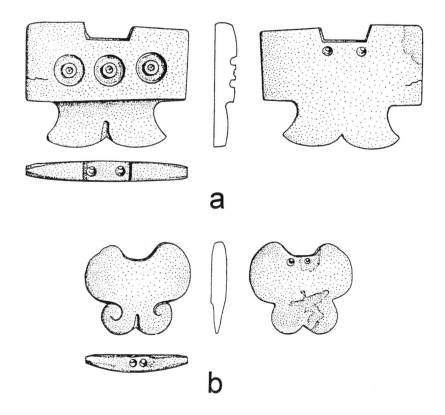

Figure 4   Teo nose pendants: (*a*) "Tlaloc" type from FSP grave 13; (*b*) a so-called "butterfly" nose pendant. Actually it represents the final element of a rattlesnake tail (from Cabrera Cortés 1995).

Canid jaws were worn by a few sacrificed soldiers at the FSP, and a few eagle and felid bones were found. Symbolic importance of these animals seems to have increased over time, since they are shown more centrally and more engaged in activities in later murals, where serpents occur mainly in bordering frames. Serpents seem to have a (literally) overarching importance, whereas human beings and symbolic animals carry out the actions. In the West Plaza Group of the Avenue of the Dead Complex, an earlier balustrade of the central pyramid stairway has projecting monumental heads that are serpent-like, replaced in a later stage by more feline heads (Morelos García 1993). Many war birds have been identified as owls, but most may be eagles. There may have been an early period, until the mid-200s, dominated by the Feathered Rattle-snake, followed by growing emphasis on coyote, jaguar, and owl/eagle orders. This may reflect the rise of military sodalities that limited the power of the ruler.

C Millon (1973, 1988) has recognized a distinctive tasseled headdress as a symbol of high war-related office, probably approximately what we would call "general." It may represent a level above the postulated sodalities.

STATE/PUBLIC RELIGION

State interests were probably represented by a few major deities. One was the Feathered Serpent, discussed above. Like all Teo deities, it had multiple aspects, and besides its military associations it often occurs associated with vegetation and the fruitful earth. Another reptilian being was prominent and is represented by the head-like object that pairs with the Feathered Serpent in the FSP facades. This is often called "Tlaloc," but it shows few traits of that god. Sugiyama (1993, p. 116) and Taube (1992) argued that it is a headdress. Drucker (1974), Sugiyama (1989b), and López Austin et al (1991) linked it to Aztec Cipactli, the Primordial Crocodile and the beginning of calendrical time, whereas Taube linked it with the Xiuhcoatl solar fire serpent.

The Storm/War God

This deity is identifiable by his fangs, distinctive upper lip, receding or absent lower jaw, and goggles around the eyes. Other attributes, such as aquatic vege-tation in the mouth, a distinctive headdress, and a lightning bolt in the hand, are more variable and emphasize different aspects. Pasztory's (1974) distinction between "Tlaloc A" and "Tlaloc B" no longer seems clearcut, but she rightly pointed out a range of contexts and meanings for this god. He is associated with beneficent rain and fertility, but also with lightning, thunderstorms, and the crop-devastating hail that often accompanies them. Sometimes weapons associate him with warfare. The state would have had a profound interest in maintaining good relations with this god in all his aspects. He may differ in de-tails but is broadly similar to Aztec Tlaloc and to other Mesoamerican deities such as Zapotec Cociyo and Maya Chac.

Death and Underworld Gods

Several large skull carvings come from within or near the Sun Plaza (Berrin & Pasztory 1993, p. 168; Millon 1973). Possibly these and jaguar sculptures from the Sun Plaza pertain to death, the underworld, and the night sun, and they may be related to the cave under the Sun Pyramid. The pyramid may have been associated with a sun god, in day and night aspects.

The "Great Goddess" and Rulership

Pasztory (1977) identified certain images, characterized by a nose pendant and a bird in the headdress, as a goddess. Others tend to agree (C Millon 1988; Berlo 1983, 1992b; Taube 1983; von Winning 1987). Pasztory (1992, p. 281) says there is a near consensus that there was a single Great Goddess with several aspects, including a military persona, whose image became progressively more important from about 200 CE, who is shown superior to the Storm God, and who was apparently the major deity of Teo.

Among the multiplicity of Teo images of deities it has not been possible to decide how many distinct individuals there are, and how many iconographic complexes represent aspects of a single deity. Teotihuacanos may not have felt a need to settle this question. Gender identification is also a problem. Most Teo figures are too heavily clad for biological sex to be inferred from physical features, so usually we must rely on costume to infer socially constructed gender. One deity with female dress is the "Diosa de Agua" found near the Moon Pyramid (Pasztory 1992), which is 3.9 m high and weighs 22 tons. Some much

Figure 5 Frieze from the West Plaza Group of the Avenue of the Dead Complex. It has been identified as the Great Goddess by some scholars, but it probably represents rulership (from Berlo 1992a:282).

smaller stone figures wearing female dress may also be deities (Berlo 1992b, p. 138, Figure 11, p. 144, Figure 18; Pasztory 1992, p. 309, Figure 23). None of these figures in female dress has nose pendants or other supposed Great Goddess diagnostics. The unfinished and somewhat damaged Colossus of Coatlinchan (moved in the 1960s to the front of the Museo Nacional), which weighs 180 tons and is over 7 m tall (Berlo 1992b, p. 138, Figure 10) is said to wear female clothing, but I find its dress ambiguous.

A female goddess with multiple aspects was certainly important in the state religion, but I am not convinced that she was as important or pervasive as Pasztory and others argue. The difficulty is that attributes that may be only diacritical are treated as diagnostic. For example, a goddess is shown in a mural at Tepantitla, wearing a distinctive nose pendant consisting of a bar in which there are three circles, and from which fangs depend (Berlo 1992b, p. 130, Figure 1; Langley 1986, p. 277, No. 153, type E nose pendant). Rather than treating the pendant as a diacritical element that emphasizes some aspect of the goddess, it is treated as a diagnostic that marks any other figure that bears it as a manifestation of the Great Goddess. This, as well as a headdress with birds, is what led Pasztory (1992) to identify a frieze from the West Plaza Group in the Avenue of the Dead Complex as probably a depiction of the Goddess (Figure 5). If one does not take the nose pendant or the birds in the headdress as diagnostic of the Goddess, however, nothing else in the figure proves it to be female. Further doubts are raised by the discovery of very similar nose pendants of green stone in Burial 13 of the FSP (Figure 4a), one of them associated with an unusually robust male.

The figure in this frieze holds a torch in each hand, from which flames and smoke emerge, together with budding plant stalks. The torches are wrapped rods with "year-sign" variants on their fronts. Torches were symbols of rulership in Preclassic Mesoamerica (Grove 1987). The frieze probably symbolizes rulership rather than the Great Goddess (Cowgill 1992a,b). Linda Schele (personal communication) has independently reached a similar conclusion.

One could read the frieze as an example of the Great Goddess's identification with rulership. Pasztory (1992) (in one of the few explicit considerations of gender ideology at Teo) suggested that a female was chosen as the supreme deity because a female could be seen as benevolent, maternal, and impartially transcending factions associated with male heroes. This makes assumptions about Teo social construction of gender that are plausible but need further testing. I think any connection between this frieze and the Great Goddess is questionable.

This is not to say that the frieze represents a specific individual. Morelos García (1993, Figure F.2) illustrated additional fragments of two more figures from the same context, apparently identical to the relatively complete one. It seems that the idea or office of rulership, rather than any specific rulers, is represented. It is interesting that this frieze comes from the West Plaza Group of the Avenue of the Dead Complex, which I think may have been a setting for top-level government activities (Cowgill 1983).

The colossal figure in female dress that was found near the Moon Pyramid might be connected with the moon. This would be consonant with the idea, developed most fully by Sugiyama (1993), that the Sun and Moon Pyramids and the Venus-related Ciudadela represent a triad of astral deities, a concept widespread in Mesoamerica.

THE NATURE OF TEOTIHUACAN RULERSHIP

Palaces

The Ciudadela apartment compounds flanking the FSP have been interpreted as residences of the heads of the Teo state (Armillas 1964, Coe 1981, Cowgill 1983, Millon 1973, Taube 1992). Sugiyama (1993, pp. 110, 123) appears to be skeptical, perhaps because he believes the Ciudadela was associated with the underworld, while administrative centers for the "present" world would more likely have been near the Sun and Moon and/or along the Avenue of the Dead. The Ciudadela and the Great Compound, however, are very different from any other Teo complexes, which suggests that they served unique purposes. Nevertheless, the Ciudadela is unlike many better-known royal palaces, such as those in Tenochtitlan when the Spaniards arrived. The Templo Mayor shows the practice of rebuilding a temple on the same spot, each new structure enlarging on and covering its predecessors. In sharp contrast, Aztec rulers tended to build new palaces; in 1519 Axayacatl's was still standing, not far from that of Motecuhzoma II. Aztec palaces were luxurious, with numerous facilities for large staffs and a wide range of civic and private activities.

The Aztec pattern is similar to many palaces in European and other traditions. Frequent major changes are most likely when rulers have relatively unrestricted control over a large fraction of state resources and can command the construction of residences as much for their personal glorification as for the state. When heads of state directly control fewer resources, and especially if their residence cannot be viewed as family property, as, for example, the US White House, major changes are less likely.

The Ciudadela fits this second pattern better (Cowgill 1983). It is about three fourths the volume of the Sun Pyramid, but most of the mass is in the great outer platforms and the FSP. The total area of apartments would only accommodate a few hundred occupants. To begin with, there seems to have been little differentiation among apartments. Probably it was designed to serve a ruler who could command great resources but was accustomed to operating with a small staff. The South Palace remained nearly unchanged, but some doorways in the North Palace were blocked to make it less public, it was enlarged by another room complex that projected into the great plaza of the Ciudadela, and it had relatively good access to the large walled compound immediately to the north, where specialists in moldmade censer adornos and perhaps other artisans worked. These look like features intended to facilitate administrative purposes at relatively low cost and without too drastically changing outward appearances.

Another macrocomplex that may have been used for high-level government and may possibly have housed rulers is the "Avenue of the Dead Complex" (Cowgill 1983). It straddles the Avenue of the Dead, is partially enclosed by large walls, extends about 350 × 350 m, and has many groups of rooms, apartment compounds, pyramids, platforms, and plazas. Their number and variety would have provided for more administrative activities than could easily be accommodated by the Ciudadela. It includes the luxurious Viking Group compound, the Superposed Buildings group, and, in its west center, the "West Plaza Group" (Morelos García 1993). Much remains unexcavated. Earliest major structures are probably a little later than the Ciudadela, although we need greater chronological precision. Major rebuildings followed. Perhaps the rulers' residence shifted to the Avenue of the Dead Complex during the political changes that may have occurred somewhere between 250 and 350 CE.

An Oligarchic Republic?

Supreme Teo political authority may not always have been strongly concentrated in a single person or lineage. R Millon (1976) suggested that Teo might have been an oligarchic republic. The case now seems stronger, though not yet overwhelming. Rulership in early states was not always monarchic. It is no longer widely thought that states arose as responses to social and/or environmental problems and benefited commoners as well as elites. The main explanations, however, of how elites could exploit the rest are that they could threaten force and that they promoted ideologies in which the gods and the very nature of the universe made inequality right, or at least unavoidable. Undoubtedly force and religious ideology were used by the Teo state. However, a more mundane civic consciousness, a sense of the virtue of "good citizenship," may also have been a factor. Given the prominence of this theme in modern societies, it is surprising that ancient Mesoamericans are not often credited with such perceptions and sentiments.

Pasztory's (1992) concept of a "utopian" society touches on similar issues, but I do not think Teo was utopian in any reasonable sense. Nevertheless, civic pride and a sense of citizenship, and not just submission to overawing deities and overpowering rulers, may explain much about Teo's stability and why there was no abundance of self-glorifying rulers. Blanton et al (1996) are probably correct in considering the Teo state "corporate,"[3] at least in its later stages.

An oligarchic republic is not necessarily democratic or egalitarian. There are many Old World examples. Romila Thapar (1966) described republics in early India. Other cases are the city states of Classical Greece, Rome before the Empire, and some of the small states of Medieval and Renaissance northern Italy. Venice is a notable example.

Venice

Venice differed greatly from Teo (Muir 1981), yet it is interesting to compare. By the 800s this island city was ruled by a duke subject to the Byzantine emperor in Constantinople. Over time, Venice gained its independence and the duke (called "doge"; "ducal" is the adjective) was chosen by popular acclamation. By around 1300 this was formalized in a system that lasted until the Napoleonic conquest of 1797, wherein the adult males of specified elite families comprised a "Great Council," whose members were the only ones eligible to elect the doge and to hold that and a number of other high offices. The doge was elected for life by an intricate system of balloting and lottery intended as much to counteract factionalism (a recognized problem in other Italian states) as to ensure representation of elite majority will. The office circulated widely among leading families. Venetians thought themselves remarkably free of factions, and many outsiders saw them that way. Factions were probably more important than Venetians liked to admit, but they seem to have been less divisive than in other Italian states.

Many restrictions were imposed on doges' use of public funds or their private resources; for example, gift giving was sharply restricted. In Eisenstadt's (1969) terms, doges commanded limited "free-floating resources." Some doges tried to subvert the system and gain more personal power, but with little success. The elite were also relatively successful in keeping popular resistance under control; some disturbances occurred but the masses never overthrew regimes, as they sometimes did in other Italian states.

Individual doges were more celebrated than Teo rulers appear to us, but their pedigrees seem to have been unimportant, as long as they belonged to elite Great Council families. There are numerous portraits of doges, and many

[3]Millon (1992) noted that "corporate state" commonly refers to systems and ideologies that glorify personal rule and the cult of the leader—the opposite of how Mesoamericanists have used the term. "Collective" would be preferable, but "corporate," in the sense of collective, may be too entrenched to be changed easily.

had fine tombs (at least one was criticized for living and dying too simply), but these seem by way of keeping up a certain dignity for the prestige of the state, and I do not believe any ducal tombs or images became important in state ritual and myth (as did the relics of various saints, especially St. Mark). If we had as little data on Venice as we do on Teo, visibility of the doges would probably be low.

The doge's palace immediately adjoins the basilica of St. Mark, the principal religious structure of the state. An earlier ducal palace on this site was destroyed by fire, but the present one has persisted for many centuries. Occasional efforts to move the ducal residence to another site were successfully resisted. Each new doge would move his immediate family and household furnishings into the palace, but upon his death the survivors had only a few days to remove themselves and their goods. Although various doges renovated or modified the palace, its location and basic structure remained unchanged for a long time. It sounds something like the Ciudadela palaces.

Early Autocracy?

How much did the Teo political system change over time? Teo probably never emphasized inheritance and validation of rulership through pedigree as much as the Classic Maya, yet early rulers may have been powerful and self-glorifying. All the awe-inspiring monuments are early, and they represent an audacious plan imposed on several square kilometers of landscape. Millon (1992) thinks the layout developed over time in several stages, beginning shortly after the concentration of most of the population of the Basin of Mexico in the city around 1 CE. Sugiyama (1993) argued that all major elements of the layout were probably envisioned as an integrated plan from the beginning, although it may have taken some time to complete the construction project. He relies most strongly on key linear dimensions of structures and distances between them, which he feels translated key calendrical numbers into a unified spatial pattern, and he downplays ceramic evidence for the length of time that elapsed between the earliest Sun Pyramid and the Ciudadela.

Whoever is more nearly correct about how much of the present pattern was fully conceived from its inception, the layout of the monumental part of Teo was created in two centuries or less. Teo began its urban growth in the last centuries BCE and already covered about 8 km^2, with a population of 20,000–40,000, before anything very monumental was constructed. The great surge of building does not seem to represent the thought of weak rulers or of persons strongly beholden to advisory councils. Moreover, it is just at the beginning of this interval that virtually the entire population disappeared elsewhere in the Basin of Mexico (Sanders et al 1979). People were evidently resettled in Teo. The official ideology may or may not have been collective, but in any case it looks as if there were a few very powerful, very able, and very imaginative rulers, who were probably not self-effacing persons. The immense structures were probably seen as lasting monuments to these rulers, who needed no inscriptions and no statues to reinforce the messages of the buildings. Sugiyama (1993) and Millon (1992) suspect that a royal tomb is associated with the Sun Pyramid; Millon suspects one also at the Moon Pyramid.

Absence of different plans for different city districts contrasts significantly with many other Mesoamerican centers, where there is coordinated planning within large segments but no single plan that encompasses all segments. Imposition of one plan for almost the whole city is another sign of early strength of the central authority at Teo and suggests relative weakness of intermediate social units, such as large lineages.

A Shift to More Collective Governance?

In the ensuing centuries, from about the middle of the 200s to the 600s or 700s, the city's population remained high and the total volume of monumental construction was quite large. It consisted, however, of enlargements and modifications of existing complexes. It was also at this time that architecturally substantial apartment compounds were built. These soon housed nearly all residents, of low as well as intermediate and high status. Emphasis on building apartment compounds rather than new pyramids may have been part of a conscious shift to greater concern for general well-being than for individual glory.

There is evidence that this change began violently. Our 1988–1989 excavations revealed that the FSP and the temple atop it were burned in a hot fire, and large fragments of modeled clay walls and other debris from the temple were used as part of the fill for the stepped platform ("Plataforma Adosada") that covered (and preserved) most of the front of the FSP. Instead of being buried by some grander pyramid, most of the ruined FSP was left exposed, perhaps a reminder to any future ruler tempted to overstep, and it suffered further damage[4]. It was probably at this time that looters tunneled into the FSP and removed most contents of the largest pits. If these events happened soon after the FSP was built, and if FSP victims were in fact loyal high-status Teotihuacanos, it may be that elites saw the sacrifices as excessive and reacted strongly (Millon 1988b, Pasztory 1988). Identities of the victims, however, are not yet established, and incomplete ceramic analyses suggest that a century or more may have elapsed before the Plataforma Adosada was built. Perhaps several autocratic rulers succeeded the one responsible for the FSP and the sacrifices, and perhaps it was some time before a less able ruler made revolt possible.

---

[4]Conceivably this was when work on the idol of Coatlinchan halted; it may have been a ruler's try at personal glorification.

Whether reaction was swift or delayed, it seems to have initiated a period of more collective rule. There may have been a consciously new theory of governance. Possibly, however, Teo political theory always favored collective rule, and the time of powerful rulers may have been seen as a tyrannical aberration. If so, the reaction would have been perceived as the restoration of traditional government.

Teotihuacanos living from infancy in sight of the great pyramids may no longer have been overawed by them, but they must have taken immense pride in them; one likely reason for their disinterest in things foreign.

The scarcity of obvious boasting by Teo rulers has prompted comparisons with the Harappan civilization of the Indus Valley. Teo differs markedly, however. Harappan sites do not have the monumental civic-religious structures of Teo nor the wealth of pictorial art, and settlement patterns are very different.

DECLINE AND COLLAPSE

Metepec-Period Decline?

During Teo's last century the city's population may have declined significantly. The extent of decline, however, will not be clear until there is more agreement on Metepec period ceramic diagnostics. Some households remained quite prosperous, but disparities among households may have been increasing (Sempowski 1994). Centers such as Xochicalco and Cacaxtla possibly developed only after the fall of Teo but may have begun earlier, as a declining Teo lost its ability to punish upstarts. Better control of the chronology of Teo's decline and the rise of other central Mexican sites is crucial. It is easy to imagine ways in which Teo government and society might have been in trouble, through some combination of bureaucratic proliferation; failure to adapt to "Epiclassic" styles of government, commerce, and religion that were developing elsewhere; and possibly environmental problems. Without new income from new conquests and without crises posed by outside threats, rulers may have found it hard to break free of increasingly stultifying constraints and unable to adjust to changes even if they had the will and wisdom (Cowgill 1992a, Millon 1988b).

Fiery (But Selective) Destruction

The Teo state was physically destroyed by the burning of temples and elite residences and the smashing of idols, especially in the central part of the city. Millon emphasizes how selective the destruction was. It was intended to destroy the artifacts and physical facilities of the Teo state. Millon (1988a) believes it could only have been done by insiders, but I think surrounding societies may have gained power and numbers to the point where they, or some combination, perhaps including dissident insiders, could have defeated a weakened and no longer well-led city. A sizable population, perhaps 40,000, survived or resettled the city, which has remained a town of some importance ever since. But Teo was never again the capital of a regional state.

ACKNOWLEDGMENTS

Preparation of this article was aided by work on a manuscript in press, during a 1992–1993 Fellowship at the Center for Advanced Study in the Behavioral Sciences, Stanford, California. I am grateful for financial support provided by NSF grant SES-9022192. Oralia Cabrera Cortés, John E Clark, René Millon, Ian Robertson, Barbara L Stark, and Saburo Sugiyama made useful suggestions on an earlier draft, but I am solely responsible for this version.

Visit the *Annual Reviews home page* at http://www.AnnualReviews.org.

Literature Cited

Agrinier P. 1975. *Mounds 9 and 10 at Mirador, Chiapas, Mexico.* New World Archaeol. Found., Pap. 39, Provo, UT

Algaze G. 1993. Expansionary dynamics of some early pristine states. *Am. Anthropol.* 95:304–33

Altschul JH. 1987. Social districts of Teotihuacan. See McClung de Tapia & Rattray 1987, pp. 191–217

Armillas P. 1964. Northern Mesoamerica. In *Prehistoric Man in the New World*, ed. JD Jennings, E Norbeck, pp. 291–321. Chicago: Univ. Chicago Press

Arnold PJ, Pool CA, Kneebone RR, Santley RS. 1993. Intensive ceramic production and Classic-period political economy in the sierra de los Tuxtlas, Veracruz, Mexico. *Anc. Mesoam.* 4(2):175–91

Aveni AF, Hartung H, Kelley JC. 1982. Alta Vista (Chalchihuites), astronomical implications of a mesoamerican ceremonial outpost at the tropic of Cancer. *Am. Antiq.* 47(2):316–35

Bennyhoff JA. 1967. Chronology and change in the Teotihuacan ceramic tradition. See Sociedad Mexicana de Antropología 1967, pp. 19–29

Berlo JC. 1983. The warrior and the butterfly: central Mexican ideologies of sacred warfare and Teotihuacan iconography. In *Text and Image in Pre-Columbian Art*, ed. JC Berlo, pp. 79–117. Br. Archaeol. Rep. Int. Ser. 180, Oxford

Berlo JC. 1984. *Teotihuacan Art Abroad.* Br. Archaeol. Rep. Int. Ser. 199, Oxford

Berlo JC. 1989. Early writing in central Mexico: *in tlilli, in tlapalli* before A. D. 1000. See Diehl & Berlo 1989, pp. 19–47

Berlo JC, ed. 1992a. *Art, Ideology, and the City of Teotihuacan.* Washington, DC: Dumbarton Oaks

Berlo JC. 1992b. Icons and ideology at Teotihuacan: the Great Goddess reconsidered. See Berlo 1992a, pp. 129–68

Berrin K, ed. 1988. *Feathered Serpents and Flowering Trees: Reconstructing the Murals of Teotihuacan.* San Francisco: The Fine Arts Museums of San Francisco

Berrin K, Pasztory E, eds. 1993. *Teotihuacan: Art from the City of the Gods.* New York: Thames & Hudson

Blanton RE, Feinman GM, Kowalewski SA, Peregine PN. 1996. A dual-processual theory for the evolution of Mesoamerican civilization. *Curr. Anthropol.* 37(1): 1–14

Cabrera Castro R, Rodríguez I, Morelos N, eds. 1982a. *Teotihuacan 80–82: Primeros Resultados.* Mexico City: Inst. Nac. Antropol. Hist.

Cabrera Castro R, Rodríguez I, Morelos N, eds. 1982b. *Memoria del Proyecto Arqueológico Teotihuacan 80–82.* Mexico City: Inst. Nac. Antropol. Hist.

Cabrera Castro R, Rodríguez I, Morelos N, eds. 1991a. *Teotihuacan 1980–1982: Nue-*

vas Interpretaciones. Mexico City: Inst. Nac. Antropol. Hist.

Cabrera Castro R, Sugiyama S, Cowgill GL. 1991b. The Templo de Quetzalcoatl project at Teotihuacan. *Anc. Mesoam.* 2(1): 77–92

Cabrera Cortés MO. 1995. *La lapidaria del Proyecto Templo de Quetzalcoatl 1988–1989.* Licentiate thesis. Esc. Nac. Antrop. Hist., Mexico City

Cardós A, ed. 1990. *La Epoca Clásica.* Mexico City: Inst. Nac. Antropol. Hist.

Carlson JB. 1991. *Venus-Regulated Warfare and Ritual Sacrifice in Mesoamerica: Teotihuacan and the Cacaxtla "Star Wars" Connection.* College Park, MD: Cent. Archaeoastron., Tech. Publ. 7

Clark JE. 1986. From mountains to molehills: a critical review of Teotihuacan's obsidian industry. See Isaac 1986, pp. 23–74

Coe MD. 1981. Religion and the rise of mesoamerican states. In *The Transition to Statehood in the New World,* ed. GD Jones, RR Kautz, pp. 157–71. Cambridge: Cambridge Univ. Press

Cowgill GL. 1974. Quantitative studies of urbanization at Teotihuacan. See Hammond 1974, pp. 363–96

Cowgill GL. 1979. Teotihuacan, internal militaristic competition, and the fall of the Classic Maya. In *Maya Archaeology and Ethnohistory,* ed. N Hammond, GR Willey, pp. 51–62. Austin: Univ. Tex. Press

Cowgill GL. 1983. Rulership and the Ciudadela: political inferences from Teotihuacan architecture. In *Civilization in the Ancient Americas,* ed. RM Leventhal, AL Kolata, pp. 313–43. Cambridge, MA: Univ. N. M. Press & Peabody Mus., Harvard Univ.

Cowgill GL. 1992a. Toward a political history of Teotihuacan. In *Ideology and Pre-Columbian Civilizations,* ed. AA Demarest, GW Conrad, pp. 87–114. Santa Fe, NM: Sch. Am. Res. Press

Cowgill GL. 1992b. Social differentiation at Teotihuacan. In *Mesoamerican Elites: An Archaeological Assessment,* ed. DZ Chase, AF Chase, pp. 206–20. Norman: Univ. Okla. Press

Cowgill GL. 1992c. Teotihuacan glyphs and imagery in the light of some early colonial texts. See Berlo 1992a, pp. 231–46

Cowgill GL. 1993. Distinguished lecture in archeology: beyond criticizing New Archeology. *Am. Anthropol.* 95(3):551–73

Cowgill GL, Altschul JH, Sload RS. 1984. Spatial analysis of Teotihuacan: a mesoamerican metropolis. In *Intrasite Spatial*

Analysis in Archaeology, ed. HJ Hietala, pp. 154–95. Cambridge: Cambridge Univ. Press

Crespo AM, Mastache AG. 1981. La presencia en el área de Tula, Hidalgo, de grupos relacionados con el barrio de Oaxaca en Teotihuacan. See Rattray et al 1981, pp. 99–106

de la Fuente B, ed. 1995. *La Pintura Mural Prehispánica en México I: Teotihuacan. Tomo 1: Catálogo.* Mexico City: Inst. Investigaciones Estéticas, Univ. Nac. Autón. Méx.

Demarest AA, Foias AE. 1993. Mesoamerican horizons and the cultural transformation of Maya civilization. In *Latin American Horizons,* ed. DS Rice, pp. 147–91. Washington, DC: Dumbarton Oaks

Díaz Oyarzábal CL. 1980. *Chingú: un sitio clásico del área de Tula, Hgo.* Mexico City: Inst. Nac. Antropol. Hist.

Diehl RA, Berlo JC, eds. 1989. *Mesoamerica After the Decline of Teotihuacan.* Washington, DC: Dumbarton Oaks

Drennan RD, Fitzgibbons PT, Dehn H. 1990. Imports and exports in Classic Mesoamerican political economy: the Tehuacan Valley and the Teotihuacan obsidian industry. *Res. Econ. Anthropol.* 12:177–99

Drucker RD. 1974. *Renovating a reconstruction: The Ciudadela at Teotihuacan, Mexico.* PhD thesis. Univ. Rochester

Eisenstadt SN. 1969. *The Political Systems of Empires.* New York: Free Press

García Cook A. 1994. *Cantona.* Mexico City: Salvat

Grove DC. 1987. Torches, "knuckle dusters" and the legitimization of Formative Period rulership. *Mexicon* 9(3):60–65

Hammond N, ed. 1974. *Mesoamerican Archaeology: New Approaches.* London: Duckworth

Hassig R. 1992. *War and Society in Ancient Mesoamerica.* Berkeley: Univ. Calif. Press

Headrick A. 1996. *The Teotihuacan Trinity: unMASKing the political structure.* PhD thesis. Univ. Tex., Austin

Helms M. 1993. *Craft and the Kingly Ideal.* Austin: Univ. Tex. Press

Hirth KG. 1978. Teotihuacan regional population administration in eastern Morelos. *World Archaeol.* 9(3):320–33

Hirth KG. 1980. *Eastern Morelos and Teotihuacan.* Nashville, TN: Vanderbilt Univ. Publ. Anthropol. 25

Hirth KG, ed. 1984. *Trade and Exchange in Early Mesoamerica.* Albuquerque: Univ. N. M. Press

Hirth KG, Angulo Villaseñor J. 1981. Early

state expansion in central Mexico: Teotihuacan in Morelos. *J. Field Archaeol.* 8(2):135–50

Hopkins MR. 1995. *Teotihuacan cooking pots: scale of production and product variability.* PhD thesis. Brandeis Univ., Waltham, MA

Isaac BL, ed. 1986. *Economic Aspects of Prehispanic Highland Mexico.* Greenwich, CT: JAI Press

Justeson JS, Norman WM, Campbell L, Kaufman T. 1983. The foreign impact on lowland Mayan language and script: a summary. See Miller 1983, pp. 147–58

Kidder AV, Jennings JD, Shook EM. 1946. *Excavations at Kaminaljuyu, Guatemala.* Washington, DC: Carnegie Inst. Wash.

Kowalski JK. 1997. Natural order, social order, political legitimacy and the sacred city: the architecture of Teotihuacan. In *Mesoamerican Architecture as a Sacred Symbol,* ed. JK Kowalski. New York/Oxford: Oxford Univ. Press

Kubler G. 1967. *The Iconography of the Art of Teotihuacan.* Washington, DC: Dumbarton Oaks

Kurtz DV. 1987. The economics of urbanization and state formation at Teotihuacan. *Curr. Anthropol.* 28(3):329–53

Langley JC. 1986. *Symbolic Notation of Teotihuacan.* Br. Archaeol. Rep. Int. Ser. 313, Oxford

Langley JC. 1991. The forms and usage of notation at Teotihuacan. *Anc. Mesoam.* 2(2): 285–98

Langley JC. 1992. Teotihuacan sign clusters: emblem or articulation? See Berlo 1992a, pp. 247–80

Laporte JP, Fialko V. 1990. New perspectives on old problems: dynastic references for the Early Classic at Tikal. In *Vision and Revision in Maya Studies,* ed. FS Clancy, PD Harrison, pp. 33–66. Albuquerque: Univ. N. M. Press

Linné S. 1942. *Mexican Highland Cultures.* Stockholm: Ethnog. Mus. Sweden

López Austin A, López Luján L, Sugiyama S. 1991. The Temple of Quetzalcoatl at Teotihuacan: its possible ideological significance. *Anc. Mesoam.* 2(1):93–105

López Luján L. 1989. *La Recuperación Mexica del Pasado Teotihuacano.* Mexico City: Inst. Nac. Antropol. Hist.

Manzanilla L. 1992. The economic organization of the Teotihuacan priesthood: hypotheses and considerations. See Berlo 1992a, pp. 321–38

Manzanilla L, ed. 1993. *Anatomía de un Conjunto Residencial Teotihuacano en Oztoyahualco,* 2 Vols. Mexico City: Inst. Investigaciones Antropol., Univ. Nac. Autón. Méx.

Manzanilla L. 1996. Corporate groups and domestic activities at Teotihuacan. *Lat. Am. Antiq.* 7(3):228–46

Manzanilla L, Barba L. 1990. The study of activities in classic households. *Anc. Mesoam.* 1:41–49

Marcus J, Flannery KV. 1996. *Zapotec Civilization.* London: Thames & Hudson

Matos Moctezuma E. 1988. *The Great Temple of the Aztecs.* London: Thames & Hudson

McCafferty GG. 1996. Reinterpreting the great pyramid of Cholula, Mexico. *Anc. Mesoam.* 7(1):1–17

McClung de Tapia E, Rattray EC, eds. 1987. *Teotihuacan: Nuevos Datos, Nuevas Síntesis, Nuevos Problemas.* Mexico City: Inst. Investigaciones Antropol., Univ. Nac. Autón. Méx.

Miller AG, ed. 1983. *Highland-Lowland Interaction in Mesoamerica.* Washington, DC: Dumbarton Oaks

Millon C. 1973. Painting, writing, and polity in Teotihuacan, Mexico. *Am. Antiq.* 38(3): 294–314

Millon C. 1988. A reexamination of the Teotihuacan tassel headdress. See Berrin 1988, pp. 114–34

Millon R. 1973. *Urbanization at Teotihuacan, Mexico,* Vol. 1, *The Teotihuacan Map. Part 1: Text.* Austin: Univ. Tex. Press

Millon R. 1974. The study of urbanism at Teotihuacán, Mexico. See Hammond 1974, pp. 335–62

Millon R. 1976. Social relations in ancient Teotihuacan. In *The Valley of Mexico,* ed. ER Wolf, pp. 205–48. Albuquerque: Univ. N. M. Press

Millon R. 1981. Teotihuacan: city, state, and civilization. In *Supplement to the Handbook of Middle American Indians,* Vol. 1, *Archaeology,* ed. JA Sabloff, pp. 198–243. Austin: Univ. Tex. Press

Millon R. 1988a. The last years of Teotihuacan dominance. In *The Collapse of Ancient States and Civilizations,* ed. N Yoffee, GL Cowgill, pp. 102–64. Tucson: Univ. Ariz. Press

Millon R. 1988b. Where *do* they all come from? The provenance of the Wagner murals from Teotihuacan. See Berrin 1988, pp. 78–113

Millon R. 1992. Teotihuacan studies: from 1950 to 1990 and beyond. See Berlo 1992a, pp. 339–429

Millon R, Drewitt RB, Cowgill GL. 1973. *Urbanization at Teotihuacan, Mexico,* Vol. 1, *The Teotihuacan Map. Part 2: Maps.* Austin: Univ. Tex. Press

Morelos García N. 1993. *Proceso de Producción de Espacios y Estructuras en Teotihuacán*. Mexico City: Inst. Nac. Antropol. Hist.

Muir E. 1981. *Civic Ritual in Renaissance Venice*. Princeton, NJ: Princeton Univ. Press

Múnera LC. 1985. *Un Taller de Cerámica Ritual en la Ciudadela, Teotihuacan*. Licentiate thesis. Esc. Nac. Antrop. Hist., Mexico City

Nutini HG. 1988. *Todos Santos in Rural Tlaxcala*. Princeton, NJ: Princteon Univ. Press

Pasztory E. 1974. *The Iconography of the Teotihuacan Tlaloc*. Washington, DC: Dumbarton Oaks

Pasztory E. 1977. (1973). The gods of Teotihuacan. In *Int. Congr. Am., 40th, Rome-Genoa, 1972*. 1:147–59. Reprinted in *Pre-Columbian Art History*, ed. A Cordy-Collins, J Stern, pp. 81–95. Palo Alto, CA: Peek

Pasztory E. 1988. A reinterpretation of Teotihuacan and its mural painting tradition. See Berrin 1988, pp. 45–77

Pasztory E. 1990. El poder militar como realidad y metáfora en Teotihuacan. See Cardós 1990, pp. 181–204

Pasztory E. 1992. Abstraction and the rise of a utopian state at Teotihuacan. See Berlo 1992a, pp. 281–320

Pasztory E. 1993. An image is worth a thousand words: Teotihuacan and the meanings of style in Classic Mesoamerica. In *Latin American Horizons*, ed. DS Rice, pp. 113–45. Washington, DC: Dumbarton Oaks

Pasztory E. 1997. *Teotihuacan: An Experiment in Living*. Norman: Univ. Okla. Press

Pendergast DM. 1990. *Excavations at Altun Ha, Belize, 1964–1970*, Vol. 3. Toronto: R. Ont. Mus.

Rattray EC. 1989. El barrio de los comerciantes y el conjunto Tlamimilolpa. *Arqueología* 5:105–29

Rattray EC. 1990. The identification of ethnic affiliation at the Merchants' barrio, Teotihuacan. In *Etnoarqueología: Primer Coloquio Bosch-Gimpera*, ed. Y Sugiura, MC Serra, pp. 113–38. Inst. Investigaciones Antropol., Univ. Nac. Autón. Méx.

Rattray EC. 1992. *The Teotihuacan Burials and Offerings*. Nashville: Vanderbilt Univ. Publ. *Anthropol*. 42

Rattray EC. 1993. *The Oaxaca Barrio at Teotihuacan*. Puebla: Univ. Américas, Monogr. Mesoam. 1

Rattray EC, Litvak J, Díaz C, eds. 1981. *Interacción Cultural en México Central*. Mexico City: Inst. Investigaciones Antropol., Univ. Nac. Autón. Méx.

Robertson I. 1997. Thematic mapping of empirical Bayesian parameter estimates at Teotihuacan, Mexico. *J. Quant. Anthropol*. In press

Sanders WT, ed. 1994–1996. *The Teotihuacan Valley Project Final Report*, Vol. 3, *The Teotihuacan Period Occupation of the Valley*. 4 Parts. University Park: Matson Mus. Anthropol., Pa. State Univ. Press

Sanders WT, Michels JW, eds. 1977. *Teotihuacan and Kaminaljuyu*. University Park: Pa. State Univ. Press

Sanders WT, Parsons JR, Santley RS. 1979. *The Basin of Mexico*. New York: Academic

Santley RS. 1983. Obsidian trade and Teotihuacan influence in Mesoamerica. See Miller 1983, pp. 69–124

Santley RS. 1984. Obsidian exchange, economic stratification, and the evolution of complex society in the Basin of Mexico. See Hirth 1984, pp. 43–86

Santley RS. 1989. Obsidian working, long-distance exchange, and the Teotihuacan presence on the south Gulf Coast. See Diehl & Berlo 1989, pp. 131–51

Santley RS, Kerley JM, Kneebone RR. 1986. Obsidian working, long-distance exchange, and the politico-economic organization of early states in central Mexico. See Isaac 1986, pp. 101–32

Santley RS, Yarborough C, Hall B. 1987. Enclaves, ethnicity, and the archaeological record at Matacapan. In *Ethnicity and Culture*, ed. R Auger, M Glass, S MacEachern, P McCartney, pp. 85–100. Calgary: Univ. Calgary

Schele L, Freidel D. 1990. *A Forest of Kings*. New York: Morrow

Séjourné L. 1959. *Un Palacio en la Ciudad de los Dioses*. Mexico City: Inst. Nac. Antropol. Hist.

Sempowski M. 1994. Mortuary practices at Teotihuacan. See Sempowski & Spence 1994, pp. 1–314

Sempowski ML, Spence MW, eds. 1994. *Mortuary Practices and Skeletal Remains at Teotihuacan*. Salt Lake City: Univ. Utah Press

Sheehy JJ. 1992. *Ceramic production in ancient Teotihuacan, Mexico: a case sudy of Tlajinga 33*. PhD thesis. Pa. State Univ.

Sociedad Mexicana de Antropología. 1967. *Teotihuacan, Onceava Mesa Redonda*. Mexico City

Sociedad Mexicana de Antropología. 1972. *Teotihuacan, XI Mesa Redonda*. Mexico City

Spence MW. 1974. Residential practices and the distribution of skeletal traits in Teotihuacan, Mexico. *Man* 9(2):262–73

Spence MW. 1981. Obsidian production and the state in Teotihuacan. *Am. Antiq.* 46(4): 769–88

Spence MW. 1984. Craft production and polity in early Teotihuacan. See Hirth 1984, pp. 87–114

Spence MW. 1987. The scale and structure of obsidian production in Teotihuacan. See McClung de Tapia & Rattray 1987, pp. 429–50

Spence MW. 1989. Excavaciones recientes en Tlailotlacan, el barrio oaxaqueño de Teotihuacan. *Arqueología* 5:82–104

Spence MW. 1992. Tlailotlacan, a Zapotec enclave in Teotihuacan. See Berlo 1992a, pp. 59–88

Spence MW. 1994. Human skeletal material from Teotihuacan. See Sempowski & Spence 1994, pp. 315–445

Spence MW. 1996. Commodity or gift: Teotihuacan obsidian in the Maya region. *Lat. Am. Antiq.* 7(3):21–39

Stark BL. 1995. Estilos de volutas en el período clásico. In *Rutas de Intercambio en Mesoamérica,* ed. EC Rattray. Mexico City: Univ. Nac. Autón. Méx. In press

Stark BL, Heller L, Glascock MD, Elam JM, Neff H. 1992. Obsidian-artifact source analysis for the Mixtequilla region, south-central Veracruz, Mexico. *Lat. Am. Antiq.* 3(3):221–39

Stone A. 1989. Disconnection, foreign insignia, and political expansion: Teotihuacan and the warrior stelae of Piedras Negras. See Diehl & Berlo 1989, pp. 153–73

Storey R. 1985. An estimate of mortality in a pre-Columbian urban population. *Am. Anthropol.* 87:519–35

Storey R. 1991. Residential compound organization and the evolution of the Teotihuacan state. *Anc. Mesoam.* 2(1):107–18

Storey R. 1992. *Life and Death in the Ancient City of Teotihuacan.* Tuscaloosa: Univ. Ala. Press

Sugiyama S. 1989a. Burials dedicated to the Old Temple of Quetzalcoatl at Teotihuacan, Mexico. *Am. Antiq.* 54(1):85–106

Sugiyama S. 1989b. Iconographic interpretation of the Temple of Quetzalcoatl at Teotihuacan. *Mexicon* 11(4):68–74

Sugiyama S. 1993. Worldview materialized in Teotihuacan, Mexico. *Lat. Am. Antiq.* 4(2):103–29

Sugiyama S. 1995. *Mass Human Sacrifice and Symbolism of the Feathered Serpent Pyramid in Teotihuacan, Mexico.* PhD thesis. Ariz. State Univ., Tempe

Taube KA. 1983. The Teotihuacan Spider Woman. *J. Lat. Am. Lore* 9(2):107–89

Taube KA. 1992. The Temple of Quetzalcoatl and the cult of sacred war at Teotihuacan. *Res* 21:53–87

Thapar R. 1966. *A History of India,* Vol. 1. New York: Penguin

Turner MH. 1987. *The lapidary industry of Teotihuacan, Mexico.* PhD thesis. Univ. Rochester

Turner MH. 1992. Style in lapidary technology. See Berlo 1992a, pp. 89–112

Umberger E. 1987. Antiques, revivals, and references to the past in Aztec art. *Res* 13:61–105

von Winning H. 1987. *La Iconografía de Teotihuacan.* Mexico City: Univ. Nac. Autón. Méx.

Widmer RJ. 1991. Lapidary craft specialization at Teotihuacan: implications for community structure at 33:S3W1 and economic organization in the city. *Anc. Mesoam.* 2(1):131–41

Widmer RJ, Storey R. 1993. Social organization and household structure of a Teotihuacan apartment compound: S3W1:33 of the Tlajinga barrio. In *Prehispanic Domestic Units in Western Mesoamerica,* ed. RS Santley, KG Hirth, pp. 87–104. Boca Raton: CRC Press

Annu. Rev. Anthropol. 1997. 26:163–83

THE ANTHROPOLOGY OF COLONIALISM: Culture, History, and the Emergence of Western Governmentality

Peter Pels

Research Centre Religion and Society, University of Amsterdam, 1012 DK Amsterdam, The Netherlands; e-mail: ppels@pscw.uva.nl

KEY WORDS: ethnography, literary theory, modernity, travel, reflexive anthropology

ABSTRACT

The study of colonialism erases the boundaries between anthropology and history or literary studies, and between the postcolonial present and the colonial past. From the standpoint of anthropology, it is also reflexive, addressing the colonial use and formation of ethnography and its supporting practices of travel. Since the 1960s, the study of colonialism has increasingly presented a view of colonialism as struggle and negotiation, analyzing how the dichotomous representations that Westerners use for colonial rule are the outcome of much more murky and complex practical interactions. By thus treating Western governmentality as emergent and particular, it is rewriting our histories of the present.

> The art of government lies in knowing nothing at the proper moment.
>
> Edgar Wallace (1912)

> [T]here is too much hypocrisy in East Africa today. The European official and the European settler rule and maintain their prestige mainly by hypocrisy, their inner motives would hardly stand examination; the Indian trader makes his living by downright dishonesty or at best by sheer cunning which is hypocrisy; the African clerk or laborer often disregards fulfilling his part of a contract and even a very educated African will pretend to love the European whereas his heart is nearly bursting with envy and hatred.
>
> Julius Kambarage Nyerere (1952)

0084-6570/97/1015-0163$08.00

Alles Verstehen ist daher immer zugleich ein Nicht-Verstehen, alle Übereinstimmung
in Gedanken und Gefühlen zugleich ein Auseinandergehen.
                                    Wilhelm von Humboldt (quoted in Fabian 1995)

INTRODUCTION

The anthropology of colonialism is neither the exclusive province of anthropologists nor restricted to colonialism. Therefore, this review often penetrates
noncolonial territory and colonizes terrain first settled by historians and literary theorists by indulging in the conceit that a subdiscipline such as the anthropology of colonialism can be outlined. This conceit can be legitimized because, from the point of view of anthropology, the study of colonialism presents a unique view and commands a peculiar sense of engagement. For anthropologists, more than for any other type of scholar, colonialism is not a historical object that remains external to the observer. The discipline descends from
and is still struggling with techniques of observation and control that emerged
from the colonial dialectic of Western governmentality.

Anthropologists mostly think of colonialism in three ways: as the universal,
evolutionary progress of modernization; as a particular strategy or experiment
in domination and exploitation; and as the unfinished business of struggle and
negotiation. All these views, in both positive and negative versions, were common colonial currency. Anthropological views of colonialism commonly
stressed a combination of the three. A standard conception of professionaliz-
ing anthropology between the wars was that, to avoid colonial struggle—race
conflict, indigenous revolt—one should follow a colonial strategy based on
anthropological knowledge and planning to achieve the desired evolutionary
progress cheaply and without bloodshed (e.g. Malinowski 1929). Around
1970, anthropologists often told their colleagues to shun collaboration with the
powerful in neocolonial planning and strategy. Instead, they were supposed to
support "indigenous" peoples in their struggles, to help the latter achieve the
modernization that the legacy of colonialism—a perfidious combination of an
ideology of modernization and a strategy of exploitation—denied them.

That is, reinventions of anthropology often used images of colonialism as
their cutting edge. Only in the past 25 years, however, have such critique and
reflexivity become structural, owing to the increasing stress on the third view
of colonialism, as a struggle that constantly renegotiates the balance of domination and resistance (Dirks 1992b, Guha 1989, Stoler & Cooper 1997). Because one cannot simply demarcate a past colonialism from struggles in the
present (Dirks 1992b, Thomas 1994), the anthropology of colonialism systematically interrogates contemporary anthropology as well as the colonial circumstances from which it emerged. The anthropology of colonialism is also

always an anthropology of anthropology, because in many methodological, organizational, and professional aspects the discipline retains the shape it received when it emerged from—if partly in opposition to—early twentieth-century colonial circumstances. Studying colonialism implies studying anthropology's context, a broader field of ethnographic activity that existed before the boundaries of the discipline emerged and that continues to influence the way they are drawn (Pels & Salemink 1994).

Anthropology, therefore, needs to be conceptualized in terms of governmentality (Wright 1995), as an academic offshoot of a set of universalist technologies of domination—a *Statistik* or "state-craft" at least partly based on ethnography—that developed in a dialectic between colonial and European states (Cohn 1987, 1996; Stagl 1995). These forms of identification, registration, and discipline emerged in tension and in tandem with technologies of self-control that fostered notions of cleanliness, domesticity, ethnicity, and civilization (Chakrabarty 1994, Stoler 1995a). Anthropology, in negotiating ethnic, civilized, and savage identities, was at the juncture of these technologies of domination and self-control. It precariously straddled a world of paradox and contradiction in which notions of race were universalistically shunned at the same time that they particularistically helped constitute the nation-state's civilities (Stoler 1995a, Stoler & Cooper 1997). Both anthropology and colonialism projected seemingly universal and Manichean essentializations of Us and Them, which in practice had to give way to much more complex and particularist negotiations of rule (Pels & Salemink 1994, Stoler & Cooper 1997).

ANTHROPOLOGY OF COLONIALISM: GENEALOGIES

The social-scientific study of colonial society predates the 1960s (Balandier 1963, Mair 1938, Malinowski 1945). After decolonization, however, a set of interests started to converge that can now be regarded as constituting a new departure. Ethnohistory questioned the boundaries between anthropology and history (Cohn 1968, Sturtevant 1966). Those who had been colonized raised doubts about the relevance of anthropology (Deloria 1969, p'Bitek 1970). Neo-Marxist and feminist approaches to peasant societies and their modes of production and the economy of the household fueled an interest in economic change, and consequently in colonialism (Etienne & Leacock 1980, Hafkin & Bay 1976, Meillassoux 1964, Wolf 1982; for an overview, see Stoler 1995b). Critical approaches to classical anthropology questioned the nature of the knowledge required for colonial rule and the involvement of anthropologists in its production and paved the way for some of the analytics of knowledge and power that matured later on (Asad 1973, Gough 1968, Hymes 1974). The historical and sociological turn of the Kuhnian philosophy of science helped raise doubts about the claim to scientific independence from colonial circumstances that had been made by anthropologists since the early twentieth century.

From the late 1970s onward, this set of interests was further developed by the increasing realization that many features of the discourses developed under and for colonial rule were still operative in present-day anthropology. A critical hermeneutics, sometimes informed by a more epistemologically inclined neo-Marxism, elaborated the continuities between colonial and postcolonial constructions of anthropology's object (Clifford 1982, Fabian 1983, Webster 1982). Analyses of the political role of textual representation, developed by literary theorists (Williams 1977), entered anthropology through the critique of orientalism and other forms of colonial discourse (Barker et al 1985, Bhabha 1994, Clifford & Marcus 1986, Clifford 1983, Said 1978). By the 1990s, these developments resulted in a paradoxical situation: While the historicizing political economy approaches of the 1970s were criticized because of their lack of a cultural critique (Coronil 1996, Stoler & Cooper 1997, Taussig 1989), the notions of "culture" and "ethnography" themselves were also criticized for their contribution to colonial and postcolonial essentializations of ethnic entities (Dirks 1992b, Fabian 1983, Pels & Salemink 1994, Thomas 1994).

Since the early 1990s, anthropologists have moved away from the 1980s impact of literary theory, feeling that colonial discourse inadequately defines historical anthropology's object of critique (Dirks 1992b, Stoler & Cooper 1997, Thomas 1994). The analysis of the textual strategies of colonial discourse is increasingly replaced by an effort at contextualization that implies reading ethnographic texts and colonial archives as sites of struggle, and setting them against the practical conditions of the encounter that produced these texts and archives (Dirks 1993a, Stoler 1992, Pels & Salemink 1994, Stocking 1991, Taussig 1992). The publication of a number of textbooks shows that the anthropology of colonialism has settled down (Cooper & Stoler 1997, Dirks 1992b, Schwartz 1994, Thomas 1994). But however settled it may be in its own terms, it is often unsettling to other anthropologists, for it tends to destabilize disciplinary identity by questioning anthropology's methods and redefining its contexts.

METHODS AND CONTEXTS; CULTURE AND HISTORY

Classical anthropologists already suggested that one should study culture contact holistically (Malinowski, in Mair 1938) and study colonizers in the same way as the colonized (Schapera, in Mair 1938). Their emphasis, however, remained on the study of "the changing native," betraying that anthropologists' theories and fieldwork methods were predominantly meant to serve as instruments of governmental planning (Malinowski, in Mair 1938). The culture of the colonizer became systematically subject to anthropological scrutiny only after the opportunities for fieldwork among colonizers had disappeared. Now that anthropologists of colonialism find themselves in the realm of history, their notions of method and culture themselves turn out to have had specific colonial uses. To the dismay of some and the delight of others, the concepts of ethnography, fieldwork, participant observation, and even culture and history themselves have to be put in historical context.

Such methodological inquiry has, despite some promising departures, barely begun. Method has, since the late 1960s, silently dropped off the agenda of academic anthropology. Most innovations have come from other disciplines, from history and literary theory in particular. Investigation into the cultural history of method and the political tasks it performed has, despite the early efforts of Walter Ong, only recently gained momentum (Cohn 1996, Fabian 1983, Ludden 1993, Ong 1958, Stagl 1995). Yet it has already made a number of unsettling suggestions. Professional ethnography, for instance, may be better regarded as a specific offshoot of a wider field of colonial intelligence rather than, as most historians of anthropology implicitly assumed, the fulfillment of an intellectual goal to which colonial ethnographies vainly aspired (Pels & Salemink 1994). Fieldwork is subject to the way local colonial circumstances shaped the field (Schumaker 1996) but also to a history of colonial sciences such as geography, botany, and ethnography, which set up the exotic as a field to be observed (Grove 1995; see below). Observation, participant or not, reflects centuries of so-called visualist bias in the culture of Western science, to which the role of other sensory registers in producing knowledge was subordinated (Fabian 1983). In fact, empiricism in general may be seen to have a political agenda (Ludden 1993), and colonialism is also a set of empirical "investigative modalities" (Cohn 1996).

If ethnography as method is something subject to historical critique, then the concept of culture itself can also be contextualized. As indicated above, the anthropological concept of culture—which enables us to say that colonialism needs to be analyzed as culture—has at least partly emerged as an instrument of colonial control (Dirks 1992b). This argument can, of course, be turned around: Not only can the concept of culture be deconstructed by setting it in the context of a history of colonial control, "history" itself needs to be deconstructed by asking which stories it culturally privileges (Chakrabarty 1992, Prakash 1992). History and culture stand in a supplemental relationship where the one is both necessary for and subversive of the thrust of the other (NB Dirks, unpublished manuscript). To actually realize how culture supplements history and vice versa, we need not only to find out how classifications of culture functioned within strategies of colonial governmentality but how historiography provided governmentality with an ontological underpinning (Cohn

1996). We require more analyses of alternative histories, not just those "from below" (Fabian 1990, Stoler 1995b) or those analyzing non-European colonialism (Robertson 1995) but those that challenge historiographical "hierarchies of credibility" (Stoler 1992) because they derive from street art, spirit possession, oral tradition, rumor, gossip, and other popular or subaltern forms of knowledge production (Fabian 1996, Kramer 1993, Lambek 1995, Vansina 1985, White 1993).

Much of the search for other histories has been pioneered by historians of Asian, African, or European workers and peasants, and their methodological arsenal has been assiduously plundered by historical anthropologists. Especially the historians of the Subaltern Studies collective (Arnold 1993; Chakrabarty 1992, 1994; Chatterjee 1989, 1993; Guha 1983; Guha et al 1982-1994; Pandey 1990; Prakash 1992) and their Africanist colleagues (Boahen 1987; Cooper 1992, 1996; Feierman 1990, 1993; Kimambo 1991; Ranger 1983, 1989, Vaughan 1991, 1994) have provided anthropologists of colonialism with analytics and exemplars. A new phase in the debate between anthropologists and historians has been achieved by the predominantly anthropological argument that the historians' inclination to remain close to the ground of a specific archive needs to be countered by more attention to the archive's cultural construction in past or present (Comaroff & Comaroff 1992, Dirks 1993a, Stoler 1992).

Historians and anthropologists often agree on the holistic intuition that, above all, one should be sensitive to context. Here, literary theory introduced a peculiar methodological innovation that may last longer than the brief vogue of textual experimentation it bequeathed on anthropology in the 1980s: the need to "[bracket] particular questions of historical accuracy and reliability in order to see the text whole, to gauge the structure of its narrative, and chart the interplay of its linguistic registers and rhetorical modalities" (Hulme 1992). To understand a discourse, one must step back and compare tropes and *topoi* derived from disparate times and places, that is, decontextualize first to better understand the relevant context of a specific set of utterances or symbols (see also Dirks 1996, Fabian 1995, Thornton 1988, White 1987).

This is indeed a "scandalous" operation (Hulme 1992). It violates the disciplinary boundaries by which many orientalists, historians, or anthropologists felt protected from political challenges. It brings together cultural stereotypes from different contexts—political domination, popular prejudice, academic scholarship—to inquire whether and to what extent they are founded on a similar history of colonial violence. Often such political challenges are fended off by the argument that the likes of Edward Said commit the sin of historical, cultural, or literary de(con)textualization (Boyarin & Boyarin 1989, Lewis 1993, Otterspeer 1989, Shokeid 1992). Yet the power of discourse analysis is precisely to show the extraordinary redundancies produced by colonial common-places across the lines that divide political, economic, religious, and cultural contexts and the disciplines that study them. These redundancies not only explain some of the self-evidence acquired by Western governmentality in its development, their study also gives a new lease of life to cultural analysis [something not always appreciated by anthropologists (see Rosaldo 1994)]. They allow one to trace continuities that go beyond the West's occidental self-images (Carrier 1995): continuities between past colonial and today's professional ethnography (Fabian 1983; Pels & Salemink 1994; Pratt 1985, 1992; Stewart 1994), or between nineteenth-century reinventions of ethnicity and their present-day deployment (Appiah 1993; Dirks 1992a, 1995; Mudimbe 1988).

In recent years, however, some anthropologists have become impatient with the historical and literary preoccupation with texts, and they have turned away from an exclusively textual notion of culture. Some suspect the culture of literacy that informed Western representations of self and other (Fabian 1983). While studies of the textual strategy of colonial representation have significantly advanced our understanding of its grassroots operation (Mitchell 1991), they insufficiently grasp the contradictions and paradoxes of specific micro-physics of colonial struggle, encounter, (knowledge) production, and exchange (Hirschkind 1991, Pels 1996a, Stoler & Cooper 1997). Analyses of colonialism increasingly stress the nonverbal, tactile dimensions of social practice: the exchange of objects, the arrangement and disposition of bodies, clothes, buildings, and tools in agricultural practices, medical and religious performances, regimes of domesticity and kinship, physical discipline, and the construction of landscape (Arnold 1993, Cohn 1996, Comaroff 1985, Comaroff & Comaroff 1997, Eves 1996, Mangan 1986, Pels 1996b, Schumaker 1996, Stoler 1995a, Vaughan 1991). This makes the study of colonialism more anthropological, as older methods of museum studies, physical anthropology and archaeology, or the classical British functionalist injunction to add what people do to what they say about it are reinvented and made relevant to new pursuits.

HOMES, FIELDS, AND THE TRAVELS IN BETWEEN

If, however, the study of nonverbal practices makes the analysis of colonialism more anthropological, it will also challenge the dichotomous image of twentieth-century anthropology. The dyad of anthropologist and informants and of an academic home juxtaposed to a "field" of research breaks down once one brings the physical work necessary to maintain these dichotomies into the analysis—the work of traveling, making a temporary dwelling, or constructing ethnographic occasions or a "field" in colonial circumstances (Clifford 1992, Pels & Salemink 1994, Schumaker 1996, Stocking 1991). The erasure of these practical conditions also deleted colonial and postcolonial governments and made them external to the self-conception of anthropology. Just such an erasure of a much more multisided, contradictory, and paradoxical practice by a dichotomous world view characterized colonialism in general (Stoler & Cooper 1997). The study of colonial discourse may have done much to outline the ambivalent dichotomies between self and other, its tendency to reduce colonial struggle to a form of governmentality that marks out a subject nation in pejorative terms (Bhabha 1994) ignores many of the contradictions, paradoxes, and negotiations that accompany colonial rule (Thomas 1994). For every imaginary opposition of home and field, one must study the hybrid work of travel that links them up.

Conquests and Expeditions

Given that the view of colonialism as struggle has only recently come to predominate its study, it is not surprising that anthropologists, unlike historians, rarely researched the violent beginnings of colonial occupation. Yet conquests, other colonial wars, and their routines of reconnaissance have a peculiar relationship to colonial mythology and the subsequent structuration of colonial rule. Studies of "first contact" often produced remarkable instances of diverging cultural interpretations of the same events (Connoly & Anderson 1987, Sahlins 1985, Schieffelin & Crittenden 1991). Military intelligence employed most colorful and ruthless anthropologists (such as Richard Burton, Christiaan Snouck Hurgronje, or Colonel Creighton in Kipling's *Kim*). The cultural organization of military prowess and its relative lack of success vis-á-vis colonial armies often left a legacy of ethnic distinctiveness under later phases of colonial rule (Forster 1994, West 1994).

It is well known that indigenous religious and magical conceptions played a crucial role in the process and subsequent reinterpretation of successful conquests by Europeans (Connoly & Anderson 1987; Reid 1994; Sahlins 1985, 1995; Wiener 1995). Such images, however, of the European as god or powerful magician were also recurrent themes of colonial mythology and have, at least in the history of Mexico and Peru, been "unmasked" as second- and third-generation (re)inventions of tradition (Adorno 1994, Gillespie 1989, Lockhart 1994). Do images of cultural difference between conqueror and conquered obscure rather than illuminate the outcome of violent exchanges (the issue of debate between Obeyesekere 1992, Sahlins 1995)? Some cases suggest different conceptualizations of otherness on the part of the conquered (Lockhart 1994). Further accounts suggest that the main difference between Europeans and others was the former's extreme capacity for violence, whether technological (Reid 1994) or cultural and emotional (De Silva 1994). The study of colonial conquest will be crucial in rethinking the relationship of culture and violence.

Military or other expeditions often forged novel oriental and occidental identities, for the simple reason that the two parties in the encounter were accumulating the experiences that would make them decide whether and how to apply a self/other dichotomy to a much more multisided set of relationships (Thornton 1995). We have as yet, however, no clear view of the precise sociohistorical conditions within which a *bricolage* of tactical engagements gave way to colonial strategies based on fairly stable conceptions of otherness. We have very few anthropologically informed studies of the tactical engagements themselves (but see Byrnes 1994, Connoly & Anderson 1987). Anthropologists of colonialism seem to have taken the military struggle for granted as a material event, forgetting that even a single blow requires cultural preparations. Similarly, barring one excellent exception, we have very few studies of the symbolic process that accompanies colonial violence (Taussig 1992). Other expeditions, which depend on a tactical *bricolage* similar to military ones, have also yet to receive the attention they deserve, though the study of some of their aspects such as the circulation of objects (Thomas 1991) or the creation of linguistic knowledge (Fabian 1986) provide tantalizing insights.

Translation, Conversion, and Mission

The study of Christian missionaries has been a major area of innovation in the anthropology of colonialism. Initial interest, however, was raised by the suspicion of missionaries cultivated by anthropologists since the 1930s. The anthropological *Feindbild* of missionaries as exemplary colonialist indoctrinators defined the former's activity as an essentially harmless curiosity, and this view informed some of the earliest work on the topic (Beidelman 1981). The study of missions, however, soon complicated that image and contributed some of the more exciting approaches in the anthropology of colonialism.

Much of this work concentrates on how the different worlds of missionary and potential convert are related through language. Urged by the necessity to communicate the Gospel, missionaries did probably more substantial recording of unknown languages than all anthropologists taken together. Because learning a language implies learning cultural competence, they also had to cope with the relations of power that are constructed by and expressed in hierarchies between languages, their notation and translation, and the conversations that occurred on that basis. All colonial relationships require a language of command, and often its dictionary and grammar were provided by missionaries (Cohn 1996, Fabian 1986). While the indeterminacies of translation gave missionaries much trouble, they also provided potential converts with a certain liberty of meaning (Rafael 1988, 1992). The conversation that developed on this basis was essential for the development of a colonial structure from hitherto separate European and indigenous routines (Comaroff 1985; Comaroff & Comaroff 1991, 1997).

These studies have shown that it is impossible to separate the missionary movement from broader processes of propagating modernity, anthropology included. Missionaries were central to the emergence and professionalization of ethnology and anthropology in Britain and in the way Britain envisaged its role in the colonies (Dirks 1995, Pels & Salemink 1994). Missionary education was a crucial factor in the emergence of secularizing strategies in colonial India (Viswanathan 1989), and it often spread the language on which, later, the state's identification of ethnic identities was based (Dirks 1995, Ranger 1989). Religious and secular colonization, therefore, occupy common ground (Fabian 1986, Van der Veer 1995). Yet it is possible to identify differences in attitude between missionaries and colonial administrators. Because of their generally assimilationist attitude, missionaries are less prone to essentialize, because for them, otherness is preferably already in the past. Moreover, they are often engaged with individual converts rather than whole groups, and ethnic and racial essentializations do not occupy the structural position in their texts that one sees in other colonizers' (Pels 1994, Thomas 1994).

Thus, the combination of religious teaching, massive involvement in colonial education, and relative autonomy from the practice of colonial control gave missionaries a special position at the juncture of colonial technologies of domination and self-control. Individually, missionaries often resisted collaboration with colonial authorities, but they supported them by education and conversion. For the colonized, education and conversion became technologies of self-control that enabled subordination at the same time that they structured resistance to Christianity, colonialism, and their trappings. "Conversion to modernity" was the prime locus where technologies of the self and of colonial domination converged (Van der Veer 1995). One should treat the concept of conversion with caution, however. Earlier uses of the term within a theory of modernization (e.g. Horton 1971) carry the idealist connotations of the Protestantism from which it emerged, and this may cause us to ignore the media and alternative cultural interpretations of the transformation (Comaroff & Comaroff 1991). Such transformations are also accomplished by changes in family and gender patterning; corporeal regimes like clothing, dances, and initiation; and agricultural and domestic objects and spaces (Comaroff & Comaroff 1997, Eves 1996, Jolly & MacIntyre 1989, Pels 1996b).

Settlers, Plantations, and Labor

The study of settler culture was also central to the anthropology of colonialism, partly because plantation economies featured prominently in the *marxisant* anthropology of the 1970s (see Stoler 1995b), but more importantly because such studies subsequently deepened our understanding of the composition of colonial culture. Caused, on the one hand, by a largely feminist-inspired discovery of colonial domesticity and, on the other, by rethinking the organization of plantation labor violence, this highlighting of the "tensions of empire" much advanced the interpretation of colonialism as a constant struggle rather than as a singular and coherent strategy (Cooper & Stoler 1997).

By the mid-1980s, feminists had added the study of European women to that of the study of the consequences of colonialism for the colonized (Callaway 1987, Strobel 1991). The study of colonial domesticity showed that to maintain colonial authority along the lines of race, European women had to submit to far stricter rules than was common in the metropole. The colonial state engaged in the racial policing of class boundaries as well (Stoler 1991, 1995a). Similarly, gender distinctions were monitored in the attempt of colonial states to regulate working classes, though such constructions may have been beyond the limits of colonial and in the sphere of self-control (Cooper 1992, White 1990). Colonial authority was bolstered by the often mistaken assumption that European women were less oppressed than indigenous ones, making so-called emancipation a legitimation for intervention (Hafkin & Bay 1976, Mani 1990). Miscegenation was a major preoccupation of colonial discourse (Wolfe 1994). Occidentalist distinctions between public and private became technologies of self when the colonized introduced them into the public performance of domestic life (Chakrabarty 1994), while in the metropole such technologies of self were developed in reference to the colonies (Davin 1978).

Settler colonialism was, of course, based on expropriation of land, and recent innovative work shows that the cultural consequences of concomitant doctrines of *terra nullius* have not yet been sufficiently researched (Wolfe 1991, 1994). Because of their attempts at permanent establishment, settlers left some of the most lasting legacies of colonialism (Thomas 1994), legacies that we often fail to recognize as colonial because they are the product of an internal colonialism in which discussion of the colonized has given way to discussion of minority ethnic groups (Barth 1969, Hechter 1975). Plantations and forced labor were at the root of European colonialism and provided the model for other, non-European practices of exploitation by slavery (Sheriff 1987). Settlers' desire for cheap labor often led them to argue that indigenous workers needed different treatment—by force—than those back in the metropole. This was a crucial feature of the development of late colonial rule (Cooper 1996) and often led to opposition to settlers' concerns by the administrative interest in a colony's strategic stability (Salemink 1991). Ethnology itself emerged from the protest against ethnocidal policies of settler colonies and the consequent need for salvage ethnography (Rainger 1980, Stocking 1971).

To further study colonial culture, it seems especially important to continue interrogating how the boundaries and relationships between public and private were constructed—where they required the rescheduling of rhythms of domestic and work time (Cooper 1992), the redrawing of standards of public performance [as evidenced by colonial notions of corruption (Pels 1996a)], the rebuilding of towns and cities (Al Sayyad 1992), or the redecorating of the home and the self through consumption (Comaroff & Comaroff 1997). Public and private are also involved in the forms of classificatory kinship peculiar to colonialism—as yet rarely studied in themselves—such as the Indian colonial administrator's *ma-bap* or father-mother role, the ubiquitous infantilizing of the colonized, and the peculiar role of so-called universal brotherhood of diverse forms of colonial and anticolonial propaganda and protest. We have only just begun to study the culture of labor regimes and their ascriptions of ethnic essences to coolies, migrant laborers, and former slaves (but see Breman 1989, Thomas 1994, Stoler 1995b).

ETHNICIZATION AND ITS FRAGMENTS

In the preceding section, trade was not addressed. Mercantile capitalism prefigured Western technologies of government and their ethnic categorizations in general. William Pietz shows how Dutch merchants were among the first ethnographers to produce non-Christian alterities, articulated on the normal and abnormal exchange of objects. He shows how the concept of fetish, formerly functional within the hybrid relationships of global trade, was made to define the essence of African society. His work should be made paradigmatic for the study of the processes of essentialization that characterize the production of ethnography (Pietz 1985, 1987, 1988). Mercantile ethnicizations also pioneered the imagination of European self and nation-state. Here, too, merchants prefigured modern governmentality by creating the first images of national community (Helgerson 1992) and pioneering the insurance technologies from which probability and statistics would emerge (Hacking 1990). Their metaphors of the ship and the island helped to shift the notion of economy from family relationships to the more abstract concept of population, a development that is the major marker of the new discourse on government (Foucault 1991; Grove 1995). Although the seventeenth and eighteenth centuries were constitutive of both empires and nations and their tensions and fragments (Cooper & Stoler 1997, Chatterjee 1993), they have rarely been researched by anthropologists of colonialism.

Statistics and Ethnography

Statistics and ethnography were the carriers of modern classifications of race, nation, and ethnicity, and fortunately we have an excellent account of the transformations of the art of travel from which they emerged (Stagl 1995). The epistemological shift from the incorporating cosmology of crusade, pilgrimage, and mission to the distancing cosmology of exploration made implicit practices of traveling subject to explicit, written classifications of knowledge that were the methodological predecessors of statistical questionnaires and the anthropologists' *Notes and Queries* (Fabian 1983). Human beings were simultaneously redefined as analogous to animal and plant species, as ethnic types to be slotted in the pigeonholes of such questionnaires (Thomas 1994). Taxonomy was also at the heart of the new "art of government," based, as La Perrière said, on the "right disposition of things, arranged to lead to a convenient end" (cited in Foucault 1991). Europeans seem to have learned the taxonomic management of "things" particularly in governing bounded, isolated units of goods and personnel such as ships (Foucault 1991) and islands (Grove 1995). Such a culture of objects to be managed characterized early trading relationships (Pietz 1985, 1987, 1988) as well as later forms of exploration (Thomas 1991) and became a basic feature of European self-conceptions by laying the groundwork for a museum culture through the curiosity cabinet—where it, again, ties in with the history of anthropology. If, however, the outlines of such a reinterpretation of European colonial culture(s) are there, much more research needs to be done.

What line such research can take can partly be understood from the history of botany, which was both a revolutionary activity in scientific terms and a most practical one in terms of researching the possibilities for colonial revenue from agriculture. From the time of the La Condamine scientific expedition of 1735 onward, Linnean botany had helped to create an international network of scientists (Pratt 1992). It provided, for instance, Dutch, British, or Russian expeditions with German naturalists, creating a circuit for the exchange of knowledge in which much colonial intelligence could be passed on from one empire to another (Slezkine 1994, Thomas 1991). The network of scientific societies and botanical gardens was specifically colonial—rather than metropolitan—and even the knowledge it disseminated was a hybrid of, among other things, Indian and European botanical classifications (Grove 1995). Botanists pioneered the colonial deployment of statistics (Vicziany 1986). Anthropologists of colonialism, however, still need to catch up with the recent advances made in the (colonial) history of science and research its significance for the development of colonial rule. Since most colonial naturalists were medical men, this is obviously also a history of colonial conceptions of the body and disease, the more important because before the rise of the clinic in the nine-teenth century the confrontation of European and other medical systems was one between more or less equally effective practices of curing.

The study of colonial statistics can also yield more results. It is clear that governmental notions of population and economy, and the "numbering" they necessarily imply, were pioneered in the colonies (Appadurai 1993, Hacking 1990). While some of the best work in the anthropology of colonialism has shown the importance of census and statistics in establishing colonialism and modern governmentality (Anderson 1991, Cohn 1987), much research is needed on how they emerged from colonial insurance and political arithmetic. Moreover, while we assume that ethnography and statistics, after having been coined together in the late eighteenth century (Stagl 1995), parted company at the beginning of the twentieth century (Asad 1994), little research has been done on how this happened, on the role colonial experience played in this de-velopment (see Dirks 1996), and on the possibility of comparing nineteenth-century ethnography and statistics with twentieth-century anthropological sur-veys such as the Human Relations Area Files (Cohn 1996).

Inventions of Tradition and Modernity

Seventeenth- and eighteenth-century exemplars developed technologies of domination that have recently been studied: the regime of representation (Mitchell 1991, Rabinow 1989); the rise of environmentalism, crucial to utili-tarianism and functionalism (Grove 1995) as well as to the emergence of sani-tation (Arnold 1993, Thomas 1994); colonial map-making (Noyes 1992); the agricultural and social improvement of villages necessary for colonial revenue (Breman 1988, Dewey 1972, Guha 1989); or the development of colonial po-licing (Arnold 1993, Dirks 1996). It is still unusual for researchers to fully es-cape the dichotomy of colonial state and oppressed and/or resistant others, and to realize how much colonial empires were fragmented by other tensions (Stoler & Cooper 1997). Empires were maintained by ethnic soldiers that fought the colonized at the same time that they colonized themselves (Fox 1985), or by white women subordinating their domestic staff while they were acting out their own subordination (Stoler & Cooper 1997). The present em-phasis on governmentality as a pervasive form of power should not obscure that one's hegemony was often the other's coercion. Surely, governmentality should be understood as a power dispersed through the social body. It cannot be regarded as a singular colonial strategy, and we should study the struggles going on among groups of colonizers and the colonized and between them, not only over the control of governmental technologies but also over their appro-priateness, application, and desirability.

The most influential argument in this respect is that of the invention of tradition under colonial circumstances: the use of an image of tribal or traditional government within strategies of indirect rule (Ranger 1983). Such an image of other government and its tension with ethnocentric definitions of modern government were crucial to any form of colonial rule (Mamdani 1996). The contradiction between other and modern government was founded on a similar infrastructure of representation (Mitchell 1991). However, the notion of invented tradition privileged European agency and regarded the tradition too much as an ideology imposed on, rather than coauthored with or resisted by, sections of colonized groups (Dirks 1993b, Pels 1996a, Thomas 1992).

Moreover, we cannot restrict ourselves to inventions of tradition; modernity itself needs to be imagined and constructed as well. It is here that analytic perspectives on alternative imaginings of history, of the public/private or work/home dichotomies, or of Christianity (Chakrabarty 1994, Cooper 1992, Mbembe 1992, Pels 1996b, White 1993) may prove to be important to future developments in the anthropology of colonialism. They shall, for instance, raise the question of the extent to which governmentality is synonymous with Western culture as such, whether it can be regarded as a whole, or whether it is a set of technologies that lend themselves to selective adoption into alternative governmentalities. Similarly, they should address to what extent colonialism has triggered subaltern processes of global communication such as black culture, rumor, art, or possession (Appiah 1993, Kramer 1993, Pels 1992).

CONCLUSION: HISTORIES OF THE PRESENT

The mottoes at the beginning of this review argue that colonialism was a contradictory project. Like modern anthropology, it tends to bracket out part of the self to know and/or rule the other, or vice versa. If Mr. Commissioner Sanders should know nothing of the cruel measures his African "indirect ruler" needed to keep Sanders's peace, it is clear from Nyerere's statement that this hypocrisy of domination penetrated the self-control of all participants in the colonial process. Anthropology, too, has often denied that it knew anything of colonialism, to the point of making colonialism into the definition of what anthropology is not (e.g. Beidelman 1981). If we are now in a position to overcome that denial by doing the anthropology of colonialism as an anthropology of anthropology, this indicates that, after Humboldt, we are capable or in need of separating ourselves from a phase in which anthropology and colonial rule were part of the same social formation: the world of modernity, development, and the welfare state.

This makes the anthropology of colonialism a historiography of the present. After colonialism comes the postmodern; the latter cannot be understood except as postcolonial (Appiah 1993, Thomas 1994). Postcolonial societies are mainly based on development regimes constructed under colonial rule (Ludden 1992), regimes that inherited the colonial inclination to excise politics from economic and administrative practice (Ferguson 1990, Fields 1985, Pels 1996a). Governmentality was, like social science, a political technology meant to prevent coercion and politics (Malinowski 1929; Rabinow 1989). The bifurcation, however, of colonial polities into traditional and modern often functioned to facilitate coercive practices such as forced labor (Cooper 1996) or tribalism, communalism, and apartheid (Mamdani 1996, Pandey 1990). We are not only in need of more studies of the simultaneous emergence of modernity and colonialism in the seventeenth and eighteenth centuries, but of more ethnographies of decolonization, focusing on the continuity between present and past practices of development, welfare, and good governance, and the way they were constituted by anthropology, economics, and political science. If we are ever going to be capable of disengaging anthropology from colonialism, we first need to reflexively blur the boundaries between colonialism and our present anthropology.

ACKNOWLEDGMENTS

I thank Peter van der Veer and the Editorial Committee of the *Annual Review of Anthropology* for encouraging me to write this review. Much of its inspiration has been derived from several years of conversation on the topic with Oscar Salemink, and from a sojourn among staff and students of the University of Michigan's anthrohistory program in 1995, made possible by UM's International Institute and the Dutch Royal Academy of Sciences. I am grateful to Nicholas Dirks, Johannes Fabian, Lynette Schumaker, Nicholas Thomas, and Peter van der Veer for their comments on an earlier draft of the review.

Visit the *Annual Reviews home page* at http://www.AnnualReviews.org.

Literature Cited

Adorno R. 1994. The indigenous ethnographer: the "indio ladino" as historian and cultural mediation. See Schwartz 1994, pp. 378–402

Al Sayyad N, ed. 1992. *Forms of Dominance. On the Architecture and Urbanism of the Colonial Enterprise.* Aldershot: Avebury

Anderson B. 1991. *Imagined Communities. Reflections on the Origin and Spread of Nationalism.* London: Verso. 2nd ed.

Appadurai A. 1993. Number in the Colonial Imagination. See Breckenridge & Van der Veer 1993, pp. 314–39

Appiah KA. 1993. *In My Father's House. Africa in the Philosophy of Culture.* London: Methuen

Arnold D. 1993. *Colonizing the Body. State Medicine and Epidemic Disease in Nineteenth-Century India.* Berkeley: Univ. Calif. Press

Asad T, ed. 1973. *Anthropology and the Colonial Encounter*. London: Ithaca Press

Asad T. 1994. Ethnography and statistical representation. *Soc. Res.* 6:55–88

Balandier G, ed. 1963. (1955). *Sociologie Actuelle de l'Afrique Noire*. Paris: Press. Univ. France

Barker F, Hulme P, Iversen M, Loxley D, eds. 1985. *Europe and Its Others*. Colchester: Univ. Essex

Barth F, ed. 1969. *Ethnic Groups and Boundaries*. Bergen/London: Univ. Forlaget/Allen & Unwin

Beidelman TO. 1981. *Colonial Evangelism*. Bloomington: Indiana Univ. Press

Bhabha HK. 1994. *The Location of Culture*. London/New York: Routledge

Boahen AA. 1987. *African Perspectives on Colonialism*. Baltimore: Johns Hopkins Univ. Press

Boyarin D, Boyarin J. 1989. Toward a dialogue with Edward Said. *Crit. Inq.* 15: 626–33

Breckenridge CA, Van der Veer P, eds. 1993. *Orientalism and the Postcolonial Predicament. Perspectives on South Asia*. Philadelphia: Univ. Pa. Press

Breman JC. 1988. *The Shattered Image: Construction and Deconstruction of the Village in Colonial Asia*. Dordrecht: Foris/CASA

Breman JC. 1989. *Taming the Coolie Beast. Plantation Society and the Colonial Order in Southeast Asia*. Delhi: Oxford Univ. Press

Burchell G, Gordon C, Miller P, eds. 1991. *The Foucault Effect. Studies in Governmentality*. Chicago: Univ. Chicago Press

Byrnes G. 1994. 'The imperfect authority of the eye': Shortland's southern journey and the calligraphy of colonialism. See Pels & Salemink 1994, pp. 207–35

Callaway H. 1987. *Gender, Culture and Empire. European Women in Colonial Nigeria*. Oxford: Macmillan

Carrier JG, ed. 1995. *Occidentalism. Images of the West*. Oxford: Clarendon

Chakrabarty D. 1992. Postcoloniality and the artifice of history: Who speaks for 'Indian' pasts? *Representations* 37:1–26

Chakrabarty D. 1994. The difference-deferral of a colonial modernity: public debates on domesticity in British India. *Subaltern Stud.* 8:50–88

Chatterjee P. 1989. *Nationalist Thought and the Colonial World: A Derivative Discourse?* London: Zed Books

Chatterjee P. 1993. *The Nation and Its Fragments. Colonial and Postcolonial Histories*. Princeton, NJ: Princeton Univ. Press

Clifford J. 1982. *Person and Myth: Maurice Leenhardt in the Melanesian World*. Berkeley: Univ. Calif. Press

Clifford J. 1983. On ethnographic authority. *Representations* 2:118–46

Clifford J. 1992. Traveling Cultures. *Cult. Stud.* New York/London: Routledge

Clifford J, Marcus G, eds. 1986. *Writing Culture. The Poetics and Politics of Ethnography*. Berkeley: Univ. Calif. Press

Cohn BS. 1968. Ethnohistory. *Int. Enc. Soc. Sci.* 5:440-48. New York: Macmillan/Free Press

Cohn BS. 1987. *An Anthropologist Among the Historians and Other Essays*. Delhi: Oxford Univ. Press

Cohn BS. 1996. *Colonialism and Its Forms of Knowledge. The British in India*. Princeton, NJ: Princeton Univ. Press

Comaroff J. 1985. *Body of Power, Spirit of Resistance. The Culture and History of a South African People*. Chicago: Univ. Chicago Press

Comaroff J, Comaroff J. 1991. *Of Revelation and Revolution*, Vol. 1. Chicago: Univ. Chicago Press

Comaroff J, Comaroff J. 1992. *Ethnography and the Historical Imagination*. Chicago: Univ. Chicago Press

Comaroff J, Comaroff J. 1997. *Of Revelation and Revolution*, Vol. 2. Chicago: Univ. Chicago Press

Connolly B, Anderson R. 1987. *First Contact. New Guinea's Highlanders Encounter the Outside World*. Harmondsworth: Penguin

Cooper F. 1992. Colonizing time: work rhythms and labour conflict in colonial Mombasa. See Dirks 1992b, pp. 209–45

Cooper F. 1996. *Development and African Society. The Labor Question in French and British Africa*. Cambridge: Cambridge Univ. Press

Cooper F, Stoler AL, eds. 1997. *Tensions of Empire. Colonial Cultures in a Bourgeois World*. Berkeley: Univ. California Press

Coronil F. 1996. Beyond Occidentalism: toward nonimperial geohistorical categories. *Cult. Anthropol.* 11(1):1–37

Davin A. 1978. Imperialism and motherhood. *Hist. Workshop* 5:9–57

Deloria V. 1969. *Custer Died For Your Sins. An Indian Manifesto*. New York: Avon

De Silva CR. 1994. Beyond the Cape: the Portuguese encounter with the peoples of South Asia. See Schwartz 1994, pp. 295–322

Dewey C. 1972. Images of the village community: a study in Anglo-Indian ideology. *Mod. Asian Stud.* 6:291–328

Dirks NB. 1992a. Castes of mind. *Representations* 37:56–78

Dirks NB, ed. 1992b. *Colonialism and Culture.* Ann Arbor: Univ. Mich. Press

Dirks NB. 1993a. Colonial histories and native informants: biography of an archive. See Breckenridge & Van der Veer 1993, pp. 279–313

Dirks NB. 1993b. *The Hollow Crown. Ethnohistory of an Indian Kingdom.* Ann Arbor: Univ. Michigan Press. 2nd ed.

Dirks NB. 1995. The conversion of caste: location, translation and appropriation. See Van der Veer 1995, pp. 115–36

Dirks NB. 1996. Reading Culture. Anthropology and the Textualization of India. In *Culture/Contexture. Explorations in Anthropology and Literary Studies,* ed. EV Daniel, JM Peck. Berkeley: Univ. Calif. Press

Etienne M, Leacock E, eds. 1980. *Women and Colonization. Anthropological Perspectives.* New York: Praeger

Eves R. 1996. Colonialism, corporeality and character: Methodist missions and the refashioning of bodies in the Pacific. *Hist. Anthropol.* 10:85–138

Fabian J. 1983. *Time and the Other: How Anthropology Makes Its Object.* New York: Columbia Univ. Press

Fabian J. 1986. *Language and Colonial Power: The Appropriation of Swahili in the Former Belgian Congo, 1880–1938.* Cambridge: Cambridge Univ. Press

Fabian J. 1990. *History from Below: The "Vocabulary of Elisabethville" by André Yav. Texts, Translation, and Interpretive Essay.* Amsterdam/Philadelphia: Benjamins

Fabian J. 1995. Ethnographic misunderstanding and the perils of context. *Am. Anthropol.* 97:41–50

Fabian J. 1996. *Remembering the Present. Painting and Popular History in Zaire.* Berkeley: Univ. Calif. Press

Feierman S. 1990. *Peasant Intellectuals. Anthropology and History in Tanzania.* Madison: Univ. Wis. Press

Feierman S. 1993. African histories and the dissolution of world history. In *Africa and the Disciplines. The Contribution of Research in Africa to the Social Sciences and Humanities,* ed. R Bates, V Mudimbe, J O'Barr, pp. 167–212. Chicago: Univ. Chicago Press

Ferguson J. 1990. *The Anti-Politics Machine: "Development", Depoliticization and Bureaucratic Power in Lesotho.* Cambridge: Cambridge Univ. Press

Fields KE. 1985. *Revival and Rebellion in Colonial Central Africa.* Princeton, NJ: Princeton Univ. Press

Forster P. 1994. Politics, ethnography and the 'invention of tradition': the case of T. Cullen Young of Livingstonia Mission, Malawi. See Pels & Salemink 1994, pp. 299–320

Foucault M. 1991. Governmentality. See Burchell et al 1991, pp. 87–104

Fox RB. 1985. *Lions of the Punjab. Culture in the Making.* Berkeley: Univ. Calif. Press

Gillespie SD. 1989. *The Aztec Kings. The Construction of Rulership in Mexica History.* Tucson: Univ. Arizona Press

Gough K. 1968. Anthropology: child of imperialism. *Mon. Rev.* 19(11):12–27

Grove R. 1995. *Green Imperialism. Colonial Expansion, Tropical Island Edens and the Origin of Environmentalism, 1600–1860.* Cambridge: Cambridge Univ. Press

Guha R. 1983. *Elementary Aspects of Peasant Insurgency in Colonial India.* Delhi: Oxford Univ. Press

Guha R. 1989. Dominance without hegemony and its historiography. In *Subaltern Studies,* ed. R Guha, 6:210–309. Delhi: Oxford Univ. Press

Guha R, Arnold D, Chatterjee P, Hardiman D, Pandey G, eds. 1982–1994. *Subaltern Studies.* Delhi: Oxford Univ. Press

Hacking I. 1990. *The Taming of Chance.* Cambridge: Cambridge Univ. Press.

Hafkin NJ, Bay EG, eds. 1976. *Women in Africa. Studies in Social and Economic Change.* Stanford: Stanford Univ. Press

Hechter M. 1975. *Internal Colonialism. The Celtic Fringe in British National Development, 1536–1966.* Berkeley: Univ. Calif. Press

Helgerson R. 1992. Camões, Hakluyt, and the Voyages of Two Nations. See Dirks 1992b, pp. 27–63

Hirschkind C. 1991. 'Egypt at the exhibition': reflections on the optics of colonialism. *Crit. Anthropol.* 11:279–98

Horton R. 1971. African conversion. *Africa* 41:85–108

Hulme P. 1992. *Colonial Encounters. Europe and the Native Caribbean 1492–1797.* London/New York: Routledge

Hymes D, ed. 1974. *Reinventing Anthropology.* New York: Vintage

Jolly M, MacIntyre M, eds. 1989. *Family and Gender in the Pacific.* Cambridge: Cambridge Univ. Press

Kimambo I. 1991. *Penetration and Protest in Tanzania.* London/Dar es Salaam/Nairobi/Athens: Currey/Tanzania Publ. House/Heinemann/Ohio Univ. Press

Kramer F. 1993. *The Red Fez. Art and Spirit Possession in Africa.* London: Verso

Lambek M. 1995. The poiesis of Sakalava history. Presented at 11th Satterthwaite Symp. Afr. Rel. Ritual, Satterthwaite, UK

Lewis B. 1993. *Islam and the West.* Oxford: Oxford Univ. Press

Lockhart J. 1994. Sightings: initial Nahua reactions to Spanish culture. See Schwartz 1994, pp. 218–48

Ludden D. 1992. India's development regime. See Dirks 1992b, pp. 247–87

Ludden D. 1993. Orientalist empiricism. See Breckenridge & Van der Veer 1993, pp. 250–78

Mair L, ed. 1938. *Methods in the Study of Culture Contact.* Oxford: Oxford Univ. Press

Malinowski B. 1929. Practical anthropology. *Africa* 2:22–38

Malinowski B. 1945. *The Dynamics of Culture Change.* New Haven: Yale Univ. Press

Mamdani M. 1996. *Citizen and Subject. Contemporary Africa and the Legacy of Late Colonialism.* Princeton, NJ: Princeton Univ. Press

Mangan JA. 1986. *The Games Ethic and Imperialism.* New York: Viking Penguin

Mani L. 1990. Contentious traditions: the debate on *sati* in colonial India. In *Recasting Women: Essays in Indian Colonial History,* ed. K Sangari, S Vaid. New Brunswick: Rutgers Univ. Press

Mbembe A. 1992. Provisional notes on the postcolony. *Africa* 62:3–37

Meillassoux C. 1964. *Anthropologie économique des Gouro de Côte d'Ivoire.* Paris: Mouton

Mitchell T. 1991. *Colonizing Egypt.* Berkeley: Univ. Calif. Press. 2nd ed.

Mudimbe V. 1988. *The Invention of Africa.* Bloomington: Indiana Univ. Press

Noyes J. 1992. *Colonial Space. Spatiality in the discourse of German South West Africa, 1884–1914.* Chur, Reading: Harwood

Nyerere JK. 1966. (1952). *Freedom and Unity.* Dar es Salaam: Oxford Univ. Press

Obeyesekere G. 1992. *The Apotheosis of Captain Cook: European Mythmaking in the Pacific.* Princeton, NJ: Princeton Univ. Press

Ong W. 1958. *Ramus: Method and the Decay of Dialogue.* Cambridge: Harvard Univ. Press

Otterspeer W. 1989. The ethical imperative. In *Leiden Oriental Connections, 1850–1940,* ed. W Otterspeer. Leiden: Brill

Pandey G. 1990. *The Construction of Communalism in Colonial North India.* Delhi: Oxford Univ. Press

p'Bitek O. 1970. *African Religions in Western Scholarship.* Nairobi: Kenya Lit. Bur.

Pels P. 1992. *Mumiani:* the white vampire. A neo-diffusionist analysis of rumour. *Etnofoor* 5(1–2):165–87

Pels P. 1994. The construction of ethnographic occasions in late colonial Uluguru. See Pels & Salemink 1994, pp. 321–51

Pels P. 1996a. The pidginization of Luguru politics. Administrative ethnography and the paradoxes of indirect rule. *Am. Ethnol.* 23(4):738–61

Pels P. 1996b. *Kizungu* rhythms. Luguru Christianity as *Ngoma. J. Rel. Afr.* 26(2): 163–201

Pels P, Salemink O, eds. 1994. *Colonial Ethnographies. Hist. Anthropol.* 8:1–352

Pietz W. 1985. The problem of the fetish. I. *Res* 9:5–17

.Pietz W. 1987. The problem of the fetish. II The origin of the fetish. *Res* 13:23–45

Pietz W. 1988. The problem of the fetish. III. Bosman's Guinea and the enlightenment theory of fetishism. *Res* 16:105–123

Prakash G. 1992. Writing post-Orientalist histories of the Third World: Indian historiography is good to think. See Dirks 1992b, pp. 353–88

Pratt ML. 1985. Scratches on the face of the country, or: What Mr. Barrow saw in the land of the bushmen. *Crit. Inq.* 12:119–43

Pratt ML. 1992. *Imperial Eyes. Travel Writing and Transculturation.* London/New York: Routledge

Rabinow P. 1989. *French Modern. Norms and Forms of the Social Environment.* Cambridge, MA: MIT Press

Rafael VL. 1988. *Contracting Colonialism. Translation and Christian Conversion in Tagalog Society under Early Spanish Rule.* Ithaca, NY: Cornell Univ. Press

Rafael VL. 1992. Confession, conversion and reciprocity in early Tagalog colonial society. See Dirks 1992b, pp. 65–88

Rainger R. 1980. Philanthropy and science in the 1830s: the British and Foreign Aborigines' protection society. *Man* (NS) 15: 702–17

Ranger TO. 1983. The invention of tradition in colonial Africa. In *The Invention of Tradition,* ed. E Hobsbawm, TO Ranger. Cambridge: Cambridge Univ. Press

Ranger TO. 1989. Missionaries, migrants and the Manyika: the invention of ethnicity in Zimbabwe. In *The Creation of Tribalism in Southern Africa,* ed. L Vail, pp. 118–50. London/Berkeley: Currey/Univ. Calif. Press

Reid A. 1994. Early Southeast Asian categories of Europeans. See Schwartz 1994, pp. 268–94

Robertson J. 1995. Mon Japon: the revue theater as a technology of Japanese imperialism. *Am. Ethnol.* 22:970–96

Rosaldo R. 1994. Whose cultural studies? *Am. Anthropol.* 96:524–29

Sahlins M. 1985. *Islands of History.* Chicago/London: Univ. Chicago Press

Sahlins M. 1995. *How "natives" think. About Captain Cook, for example.* Chicago: Univ. Chicago Press

Said E. 1978. *Orientalism.* Harmondsworth: Penguin

Salemink O. 1991. *Mois* and *Maquis.* The invention and appropriation of Vietnam's Montagnards from Sabatier to the CIA. See Stocking 1991, pp. 243–84

Schieffelin EL, Crittenden R, eds. 1991. *Like People You See in a Dream. First Contact in Six Papuan Societies.* Stanford: Stanford Univ. Press

Schumaker L. 1996. A tent with a view: colonial officers, anthropologists, and the making of the field in Northern Rhodesia. *Osiris.*11:237–58

Schwartz SB, ed. 1994. *Implicit Understandings. Observing, Reporting, and Reflecting on the Encounters Between Europeans and Other Peoples in the Early Modern Era.* Cambridge: Cambridge Univ. Press

Sheriff A. 1987. *Slaves, Spices and Ivory in Zanzibar. Integration of an East African Commercial Enterprise into the World Economy, 1770–1873.* London/Nairobi/Dar es Salaam/Athens: Currey/Heinemann/Tanzania Publ. House/Ohio Univ. Press

Shokeid M. 1992. Commitment and contextual study in anthropology. *Cult. Anthropol.* 7:464–77

Slezkine Y. 1994. Naturalists versus nations: eighteenth-century Russian scholars confront ethnic diversity. *Representations* 47:170–95

Stagl J. 1995. *A History of Curiosity. The Theory of Travel 1550–1800.* Chur: Harwood Acad.

Stewart S. 1994. *Crimes of Writing.* Durham: Duke Univ. Press

Stocking GW. 1971. What's in a name? The origins of the Royal Anthropological Inst. *Man* (NS) 6:369–90

Stocking GW, ed. 1991. *Colonial Situations. Essays on the Contextualization of Ethnographic Knowledge. History of Anthropology, Vol. 7.* Madison: Univ. Wis. Press

Stoler AL. 1991. Carnal knowledge and imperial power. gender, race, and morality in colonial Asia. In *Gender at the Crossroads of Knowledge: Feminist Anthropology in the Postmodern Era,* ed. M Di Leonardo, pp. 51–101. Berkeley: Univ. Calif. Press

Stoler AL. 1992. 'In cold blood': hierarchies of credibility and the politics of colonial narratives. *Representations* 37:151–89

Stoler AL. 1995a. *Race and the Education of Desire. Foucault's* History of Sexuality *and the Colonial Order of Things.* Durham, NC: Duke Univ. Press

Stoler AL. 1995b. [P]refacing capitalism and confrontation in 1995. In *Capitalism and Confrontation in Sumatra's Plantation Belt, 1870–1979,* ed. AL Stoler, pp. vii–xxxiv. Ann Arbor: Univ. Mich. Press. 2nd ed.

Stoler AL, Cooper F. 1997. Between metropole and colony. Rethinking a research agenda. See Cooper & Stoler 1997, pp. 1–56

Strobel M. 1991. *European Women and the Second British Empire.* Bloomington: Indiana Univ. Press

Sturtevant WB. 1966. Anthropology, history and ethnohistory. *Ethnohistory* 13:1–51

Taussig M. 1989. History as commodity in some recent American (anthropological) literature. *Crit. Anthropol.* 9:70–23

Taussig M. 1992. Culture of terror—space of death: Roger Casement's Putumayo report and the explanation of torture. See Dirks 1992b, pp. 135–73

Thomas N. 1991. *Entangled Objects. Exchange, Material Culture and Colonialism in the Pacific.* Cambridge, MA: Harvard Univ. Press

Thomas N. 1992. The inversion of tradition. *Am. Ethnol.* 19:213–32

Thomas N. 1994. *Colonialism's Culture. Anthropology, Travel and Government.* London: Polity Press

Thornton RJ. 1988. The rhetoric of ethnographic holism. *Cult. Anthropol.* 3:285–303

Thornton RJ. 1995. The colonial, the imperial, and the creation of the 'European' in Southern Africa. See Carrier 1995, pp. 192–217

Vansina J. 1985. *Oral Tradition as History.* London: Currey

Van der Veer P, ed. 1995. *Conversion to Modernities: The Globalization of Christianity.* New York/London: Routledge

Vaughan M. 1991. *Curing Their Ills: Colonial Power and African Illness.* Cambridge/Stanford: Polity Press & Stanford Univ. Press

Vaughan M. 1994. Colonial discourse theory and African history, or has postmodernism passed us by? *Soc. Dyn.* 20(2):1–23

Vicziany M. 1986. Imperialism, botany and statistics in early nineteenth-century India: the surveys of Francis Buchanan (1762–1829). *Mod. Asian Stud.* 20(4): 625–60

Viswanathan G. 1989. *Masks of Conquest. Literary Study and British Rule in India.* New York: Columbia Univ. Press

Wallace E. 1912. *The People of the River.* London: Ward, Lock & Co.

Webster S. 1982. Dialogue and fiction in ethnography. *Dialect. Anthropol.* 7:91–114

West A. 1994. Writing the Nagas. A British Officers' Ethnographic Tradition. In Pels & Salemink 1994, pp. 58–88

White H. 1987. *The Content of the Form.* Baltimore: Johns Hopkins Univ. Press

White L. 1990. *The Comforts of Home. Prostitution in Colonial Nairobi.* Chicago: Univ. Chicago Press

White L. 1993. Cars out of place: vampires, technology, and labour in East and Central Africa. *Representations* 43:27–50

Wiener M. 1995. *Visible and Invisible Realms. Power, Magic and Colonial Conquest in Bali.* Chicago: Chicago Univ. Press

Williams R. 1977. *Marxism and Literature.* Oxford: Oxford Univ. Press

Wolf E. 1982. *Europe and the People without History.* Berkeley: Univ. Calif. Press

Wolfe P. 1991. On being woken up: the dreamtime in anthropology and in Australian settler culture. *Comp. Stud. Soc. Hist.* 33:197–224

Wolfe P. 1994. White man's flour. doctrines of Virgin birth in evolutionist ethnogenetics and Australian state-formation. See Pels & Salemink 1994, pp. 165–205

Wright S. 1995. Anthropology: still the uncomfortable discipline? In *The Future of Anthropology,* ed. A Ahmed, C Shore, pp. 65–93. London: Athlone

Annu. Rev. Anthropol. 1997. 26:185–210

MAKING BEHAVIORAL AND PHYLOGENETIC INFERENCES FROM HOMINID FOSSILS: Considering the Developmental Influence of Mechanical Forces

Daniel E. Lieberman

Department of Anthropology, Rutgers University, New Brunswick, New Jersey 08903-0270; e-mail: danlieb@rci.rutgers.edu

KEY WORDS: bone, hominid, phylogeny, functional morphology, evolution

---

ABSTRACT

Fossils pose special problems for making phylogenetic and functional inferences about evolution. One reason is that bones have numerous functions and grow through a variety of processes, some of which are under strong genetic control, but many of which are highly influenced by external stimuli. Analyses of the angular kinetics, cross-sectional geometries, and microstructural properties of bones reveal information not only about the forces generated by habitual activities but also about osteogenic responses to such forces. Consequently, comparisons of osseous characters are at best an indirect and frequently misleading source of systematic information. By integrating functional and phylogenetic studies of the skeleton with analyses of how bones develop, we may find a useful solution to these problems.

INTRODUCTION

When asked why he wanted to climb the world's highest mountain, George Leigh Mallory (who perished near its summit) responded, "Because it is there." Likewise, many biological anthropologists test the majority of their evolutionary hypotheses with bones for the same reason. Bones preserve well

185

in the fossil and archaeological records, and often they are the only source of information with which to make inferences about life histories, habitual behaviors, and evolutionary relationships. That's a lot to ask of one tissue. The purpose of this review is to ask how well bones live up to these numerous and potentially conflicting epistemological demands.

Bone is not an ideal source of data for making and testing hypotheses about human evolution. Contrary to its immutable appearance, bone is a dynamic, multifunctional tissue that changes constantly during life through a variety of processes. Bone's primary function is to be *stiff* in order to provide rigidity for movement and to support and protect other structures (Currey 1984). Consequently, bones also need *strength* to maintain their integrity and remain adequately stiff. Bones also function as a calcium storehouse, they often create marrow cavities for the production of red blood cells, and they need to have the capacity to alter their shape, size, and structure throughout life. The volume of the human skull, for example, expands from about 400 cm^3 at birth to approximately 1350 cm^3 by age six (Tobias 1971). During this time the bones of the cranial vault and base must enlarge rapidly, in some cases quadrupling in size, while maintaining precise spatial relationships with the many nerves and vessels that supply the brain, and providing sufficient stiffness and strength to protect these vital tissues from possibly fatal injuries. Finally, successful adaptation requires that bones be able to respond to new mechanical environments by altering their external and internal configurations.

As recently noted by Churchill (1996), there is a tendency to regard osseous morphologies as either independent features with a predominantly genetic basis that are governed largely by the forces of natural selection, or as the result of primarily nongenetic or epigenetic interactions between bones and their environment. Neither of these extreme views, of course, is completely correct. The many functions and processes that influence bone growth mean that numerous factors influence the shape of any given region of bone. Such a complex system is the developmental basis for morphological integration that is essential for proper function. Genes regulate many aspects of bone growth and morphology, but it would be impossible to preprogram any osseous feature to know what shape it should be at various times from infancy to senescence. Life's unpredictability and the countless interactions between anatomical structures require that bones be able to respond to nongenetic signals from neighboring tissues, from mechanical forces, and from myriad local growth factors and systemic hormones. The multifactorial basis for osseous morphologies, however, means that they often defy simple interpretations, obscuring crucial information on their developmental histories. If we wish to make inferences about evolutionary relationships among fossils, then we want to use features that have a strong genetic basis and which therefore provide accurate information about ancestor-descendant relationships. In contrast, if we wish to test hypotheses about behavioral or life-history variations, then we want to compare features that are either very plastic or that have important functional roles. These conflicting epistemological demands often contribute to the vastly different conclusions that are drawn from analyses of the same bones and/or fossils. Frequently, we unwittingly use osseous characters to test hypotheses for which they provide inadequate or sometimes misleading data.

To explore this problem, this review summarizes recent research on how bones grow and respond to mechanical forces, particularly those aspects of bone growth that are most relevant to testing functional and phylogenetic hypotheses about human evolution. There are many other aspects of bone biology important to anthropology—including bone chemistry and the use of skeletal variations to sex and age skeletons—but I concentrate on the consequences of mechanical loading for making behavioral and phylogenetic inferences from skeletal variations because force is probably the most potent nongenetic influence on bone growth. Many but not all of the examples below come from the skull because of the special importance of variations in cranial morphology for defining species and hence evaluating their evolutionary relationships.

BONE AS A DYNAMIC TISSUE

Composition and Properties

Bone is a composite material that is approximately 60% organic and 40% mineral by dry weight. The major organic constituent of bone is collagen, a long, three-stranded protein that forms a triple helix. Individual collagen fibrils bundle together into rope-like fibers that play many roles. Structurally, collagen fibers give bone flexibility and the ability to resist tension along their long axes, and they organize bone by providing sites for the deposition of calcium phosphate mineral (Lowenstam & Weiner 1989). The mineral component of bone provides rigidity and the ability to withstand compression. Bone thus grows in a two-step process in which bone cells (osteoblasts) first produce collagen, which they subsequently mineralize. The collagen structure of bone determines its many possible histological variations (see Figure 1). Bone tissue that grows very rapidly, known as woven bone, tends to have an unorganized collagen matrix, like a tangled mass of rope. More slowly deposited bone tends to have more structure, usually in the form of layers—lamellae—in which the collagen fibers are oriented in the same direction within each lamella but vary between lamellae (Figure 1a). Lamellae sometimes encircle the bone on its outside (periosteal) and inside (endosteal) surfaces, but they can also grow as *osteons* in circumferential lamellae around neurovascular channels that run through bones (Figure 1*b*). Osteons are especially important because they provide the major mechanism by which new bone tissue replaces old tissue. In this process, known as *Haversian remodeling,* bone-removing cells (osteoclasts) first tunnel through old bone; they are then followed by osteoblasts that lay down new bone in circumferential lamellae surrounding the channel (for details, see Martin & Burr 1989).

The mechanical properties of bone, which is both flexible and strong, are essential to understanding its responses to forces. Figure 2 summarizes the relationship between stiffness and strength by plotting stress, which is defined as force applied per unit area, against strain, which is defined as deformation per unit length, a dimensionless unit that can be either positive (tension) or negative (compression). Bone tissue remains stiff at low stresses but begins to deform above 30–50 MPa and typically fractures above 53–135 MPa (Turner & Burr 1993). Other loading factors, however, also need to be considered including the number, rate, and frequency of loading events. Schaffler et al (1990a,b), for example, demonstrated that bone tissue initially loses some strength when subjected to moderate levels of strain within normal physiological ranges, presumably from microfracturing that occurs, but that bone stabilizes when subjected to repeated loading events as the tissue's microstructure halts the propagation and accumulation of these fractures. In addition, bone is an anisotropic material on both the macroscopic and microscopic levels, which means that its mechanical properties vary with the direction of loading. Bone tissue is inherently strongest when loaded under compression, it is less strong when loaded under tension, and even less so under shearing and twisting forces

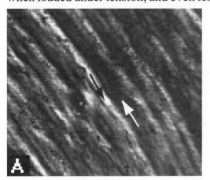 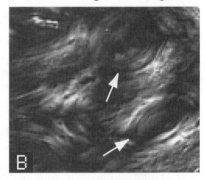

Figure 1   Variations in bone histology, seen in cross-polarized light, which highlights the contrasting orientation of collagen fibers between layers. (*a*) Periosteal, circumlamellar bone. (*b*) Haversian systems (secondary osteons), which consist of concentric lamellae surrounding a neurovascular channel. Haversian remodeling is the major means by which new bone tissue replaces old bone tissue.

(Martin & Burr 1989, Reilly & Burstein 1975). Consequently, the macrostructural strength of a bone depends to a large extent on the orientation of the loads it experiences relative to its microstructural organization.

Responses to Force

Of the many nongenetic stimuli that influence bone growth activity, mechanical loading has such dominant effects that the phenomenon was described over 100 years ago as Wolff's Law (Wolff 1892). Wolff's Law states that bones modify their internal and external configuration in response to their mechanical environments. Despite ample evidence for Wolff's Law, attempts to apply it to skeletal morphologies are often frustrating because of the highly variable nature of bone responses to forces. Applied forces of similar magnitude and frequency can cause bones to grow thicker, to change shape, or to alter their internal structure. Experimentally controlled increases in loading in mammals

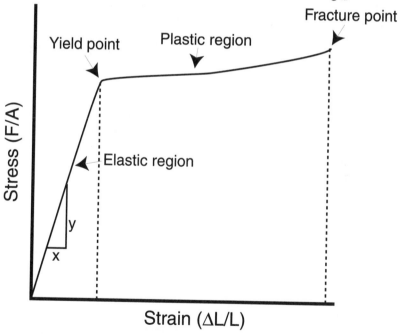

Figure 2   Stress-strain curve for cortical bone. The y-axis is stress (force, *F*, per unit area, *A*), the x-axis is strain (changes in length, ΔL, per unit length, *L*). Both stiffness and strength can be determined from this type of load deformation curve. The stiffness of the tissue, Young's modulus of elasticity, is given by the slope of the stress-strain curve (*y/x*). Note that for stresses below the bone's yield point, Young's modulus remains constant; higher stresses cause the tissue to yield and ultimately fail.

have been shown to cause periosteal growth (Raab et al 1991; Rubin & Lanyon 1984, 1985), to inhibit endosteal resorption (Woo et al 1981), and to induce higher rates of Haversian remodeling (Bouvier & Hylander 1981, 1997; Burr et al 1985; Mori & Burr 1993). Higher levels of loading, however, do not always stimulate bone growth (Carter et al 1981a), and it remains unclear how variations in the nature of strain (e.g. magnitude, orientation, rate, duration) elicit variable responses (Bertram & Swartz 1991, Martin & Burr 1989). Therefore, before discussing how to consider the potential effects of force on osseous morphologies to evaluate their evolutionary significance, it is useful to review how forces can result in diverse possible changes in the shapes of any given bone.

Figure 3 illustrates a hierarchical model from Lieberman & Crompton (1998) of the intermediate mechanisms that cause bones to adapt in various ways to mechanical loading. Force applied to a bone can produce two major categories of response: *modeling,* in which the bone adds new tissue, and *remodeling,* in which the bone replaces or removes old tissue, thereby changing its microstructure and/or shape. Bone responses to force are variable because at least three major kinds of intermediate processes and constraints mediate the degree and nature of modeling and remodeling: structural, transductional, and design.

STRUCTURAL RESPONSES   As noted above, stress causes strain, which appears to be the most important effect of force (Biewener & Taylor 1986, Lanyon et al

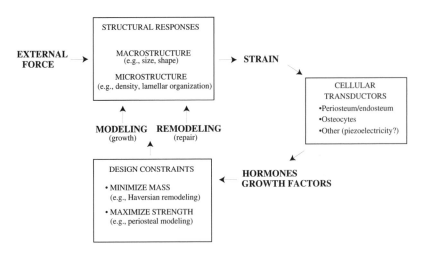

Figure 3   Hierarchical responses of bone tissue to applied forces. See text for explanation.

1982) because it causes the accumulation and growth of small fractures that eventually lead to mechanical failure (Carter & Hayes 1976a,b, 1977a,b; Carter et al 1981a,b; Schaffler et al 1990a,b). The most basic level of bone responses to force are, therefore, *structural* because variations in a bone's size and shape (its macrostructure), as well as many of its microstructural and material properties (such as lamellar orientation or mineral density) all contribute to determine the degree and nature of strain within a bone. A thicker or more heavily mineralized bone, for example, usually experiences less strain per unit of force than a thinner or less mineralized bone. In addition, a bone whose long axis is aligned in the direction of loading will experience less strain than a bone of similar size and thickness whose mass distribution is different. For this reason, one of the simplest ways to strengthen a bone is to increase the amount or distribution of its mass in the planes in which forces generate strain (discussed below). Just as a floor beam resists vertical bending through its height, a mandible resists sagittal (vertical) bending strains by being sagittally thick. Many microstructural properties also help determine how much strain a given force elicits. Young bone, for example, is more elastic than old bone, and primary lamellar bone has a higher tensile strength than Haversian bone (Schaffler & Burn 1988).

TRANSDUCTIONAL RESPONSES   The second, *transductional* level of response consists of the cellular processes by which bones actually detect and respond to strain. Strain transduction may occur through the activation of nerve receptors in the periosteum and/or the endosteum membranes that cover the outside and inside of bones, respectively, like a sleeve. Because these densely innervated and highly vascular membranes are tightly anchored to the bone's surface by bundles of collagen fibers, they experience the same types of strain as the outer and inner surfaces of the bone when force is applied, thereby activating bone cells (Taylor 1992). In addition, cells within the bone, known as *osteocytes,* also appear to sense strain and subsequently trigger various cellular responses to mechanical forces. Osteocytes have long processes, cannaliculi that communicate with each other and with the periosteum (Doty 1981), and which contain compressible fluid that may enable them to detect and transmit information about strain or microfractures (Watson 1991, Weinbaum et al 1994). Osteocytes show increased chemical activity after a bone is strained in vivo, apparently leading to periosteal bone growth (Lanyon 1993, Pead et al 1988). Bone may also detect and mediate strain through the tiny electrical currents (piezoelectricity) generated by collagen deformation (Spadaro 1991).

DESIGN CONSTRAINTS   The third, least understood level of intermediate responses includes *design constraints.* Most bones perform a variety of non-mechanical functions, such as red blood cell production, that influence their shape. In addition, some bones need to grow to specific dimensions, have special structural properties, or perhaps conserve mass. The cranial vault bones, for example, are much stronger than most bones relative to the forces they normally experience, presumably because of the magnitude of attendant selection pressures (a broken skull is usually fatal; Lieberman 1996). Likewise, bones toward the distal end of a limb tend to be thinner, and thus weaker, than bones at the proximal end of a limb, presumably because it costs exponentially more energy to move a heavy foot than a light foot (Alexander 1977). One way that bones achieve varied responses to strain is through the modulation of modeling versus remodeling activity. Controlled experiments on goats and pigs (Lieberman & Crompton 1998) demonstrated that regions of the skeleton such as the foot or the jaw joint, where spatial constraints or energy costs prohibit the addition of too much mass, tend to respond to strain more through high levels of Haversian remodeling than through growth (modeling). In such cases Haversian remodeling appears to function to repair damaged bone tissue without adding mass or changing the bone's dimensions (see below). In contrast, more proximal regions of the skeleton such as the femur or humerus, where mass increases are less costly or where strength is paramount, tend to respond to strain through modeling rather than Haversian remodeling.

Bones grow and change their shape because of differential cellular activity in discrete *growth field* regions in the periosteal and endosteal membranes that envelop the surface of bones. Growth fields are either *depository,* in which they consist of osteoblasts that lay down new tissue; *resorptive,* in which they consist of osteoclasts that remove preexisting tissue; or *resting,* in which the cells along the surface are quiescent (Boyd 1980, Bromage 1987). Four factors, therefore, govern variations in bone shape: (*a*) whether the growth fields are depository, resorptive, or quiescent; and relative differences in the (*b*) onset, (*c*) rate, and (*d*) duration of activity within each field (Enlow 1990). Combinations of these activities account for all aspects of gross morphological variation. Some bones, such as those of the upper cranial vault, can only become thicker because their internal and external surfaces are only depository (Lieberman 1996); other bones, such as those of the face, can literally "move" without becoming thicker through *drift* if one surface is depository and its opposite surface is resorptive.

MAKING INFERENCES ABOUT BEHAVIOR

The task of discovering how bones respond to applied forces is inextricably linked with efforts to infer habitual behaviors and functions from morphology. Although there are many ways in which to examine function from skeletal morphology, I focus here on three commonly used approaches—angular kinetics, cross-sectional geometry, and microstructural analysis—all of which are especially important for the skull and which require consideration of how applied forces that result from habitual behaviors influence morphology, and vice versa. For an excellent review of the relationships between body size and both bone shaft dimensions and joint morphology, see Ruff & Runestad (1992).

Angular Kinetics

Bones mainly act as fixed levers that rotate around joints as the result of contractile forces exerted by muscles at discrete locations. Consequently, the musculo-skeletal system lends itself readily to analyses of mechanical efficiency using basic principles of angular kinetics. Force that generates rotation—*torque*—is the product of applied force times the distance between the joint and the point where the force is applied (the moment arm). For each joint-muscle system, one can calculate the torque of the *lever arm* (or in-lever), defined as the product of the force produced by the muscle and its moment arm distance to the joint; the torque of the *load arm* (or out-lever) is the product of the mass being moved and its moment arm distance to the joint. There is a trade-off between torque and acceleration so that the same system cannot maximize both speed and power: Increasing the lever/load arm ratio enhances torque at the expense of acceleration, and increasing the lever/load arm ratio enhances acceleration at the expense of torque. Since muscles rarely exert force in an orientation perpendicular to their actual osseous load arms, one can simplify matters somewhat by calculating the normal component of the lever and load arms perpendicular to the instantaneous center of rotation. Figure 4 illustrates an important example, the effect of the adductor muscles in just the sagittal plane on elevating the mandible to chew a bolus of food at the second molar (M_2). Assuming that the temporo-mandibular joint (TMJ) only rotates around a medio-lateral axis (and ignoring the nonnormal and nonsagittal forces), the load arm of this system is the perpendicular distance from the vector of bite force at M_2 to the TMJ, while the normal component of the lever arm is the perpendicular distance from the average adductor resultant vector to the TMJ (illustrated in Figure 1*b*). As Spencer (1995) has noted, increases in the vertical height of the jaw below the TMJ by means of a taller ramus cause the adductor muscles' lever arm to become proportionately longer relative to their load arm if the bite force resultant is antero-superiorly oriented (Figure 4*c*). In contrast, by solely increasing jaw length, hence load arm length, the adductor muscles exert less torque at M_2 but cause the mandible to close more rapidly (Figure 4*d*).

Although the length of lever and load arms can be estimated from many fossils, little information is typically available about the actual forces produced by

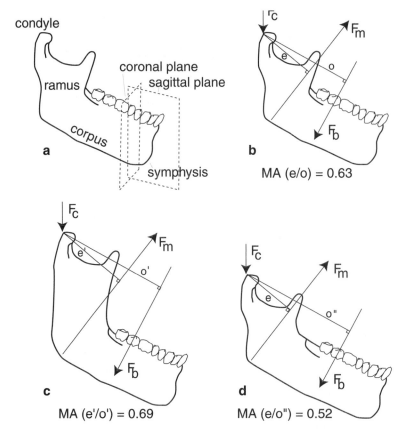

Figure 4 (*a*) Normal human mandible showing location of corpus, ramus, symphysis, and condyle, as well as orientation of sagittal and coronal planes. (*b*) Normal sagittal plane mechanical advantage (MA), the ratio of the normal lever (*e*) to load (*o*) arm lengths, for a chew at the second molar. F_m is the resultant vector of adductor muscle force in the sagittal plane; F_b is the force generated at the point of bite; F_c is the condylar reaction force. (*c*) Note that by solely increasing the height of the ramus, the antero-superior orientation of the adductor resultant increases the length of the lever arm (*e′*) relatively more than the load arm (*o′*), augmenting the system's MA. (*d*) By solely elongating the mandibular corpus, the lever arm remains constant but the load arm (*o″*) is increased, decreasing the system's MA.

the muscles that move them. Consequently, many biomechanical analyses of fossils merely address the ratio of lever arm to load arm length (mechanical efficiency) without incorporating data on the forces applied to the system. Demes (1985), for example, has suggested that the long nuchal plane of *Homo erectus* and archaic human beings such as Neanderthals may have been an adaptation for increasing the mechanical efficiency of the neck muscles because it increases lever arm length relative to load arm length. Such analyses are useful but remain partially unsatisfactory because they lack estimates of muscle force, hence torque. Human beings, for example, have shorter jaws than chimpanzees and thus greater mechanical efficiency of the masseter muscle (the muscle that runs from the cheekbone to the jaw); yet human beings apparently produce absolutely *less* occlusal force than chimpanzees because we have even less muscle mass (Demes et al 1986). In this case, what does it mean in terms of behavioral reconstruction to say that the genus *Homo* has a more efficient masticatory system than *Pan*? One could argue that selection has decreased jaw length to make hominids more efficient chewers in terms of kinetic energy; alternatively, one could argue that chewing muscles in *Homo* do not grow to the size of those of *Pan* because their mechanical action is more efficient. A third possibility is that masseter muscle size was much larger in many fossil hominids than in recent human beings so that their chewing forces were as great or greater than those of *Pan*. Muscle size, hence force production, can rapidly be altered with use. One recent study (Ingervall & Bitsanis 1987), for example, showed that 13 Greek children who chewed hard, resinous gum for two hours a day for a year were able to produce significantly more masticatory force than control samples.

Given the potential pitfalls of reconstructing habitual behaviors solely from calculations of mechanical efficiency, several researchers have sought new ways to incorporate force estimates in analyses of fossil morphology. One important approach is to use skeletal clues to estimate muscle mass size, and hence muscle force. For most muscles, contractile force is proportional to its average cross-sectional area perpendicular to the muscle's line of action (McMahon 1984). Demes & Creel (1988) employed this principle by using cranial landmarks to estimate masseter and temporalis (the two major chewing muscles) cross-sectional areas to calculate actual bite force equivalents for a variety of fossil hominids and extant hominoids. Their results reveal that, in comparison with living hominoids, only the robust australopithecines probably generated huge bite forces relative to body weight [although Lucas et al (1988) showed that these extrapolations probably yielded underestimates]. More recently, Spencer & Demes (1993) employed a somewhat similar approach in which they examined the location of muscle resultants to compare bite forces produced in the anterior and posterior dentition of Neanderthals and Inuit. Although some researchers (e.g. Anton 1994, Rak 1986, Smith & Paquette 1989, Trinkaus 1987) have suggested, on the basis of calculations of mechanical efficiency, that the prognathism and posterior position of the zygomatic in Neanderthals decreased their ability to produce high bite forces, Spencer & Demes were able to show that Neanderthals probably generated higher occlusal bite forces in the anterior and posterior dentitions than early modern human beings.

In most cases, little information is available about the actual forces generated in fossils because data on cross-sectional muscle area, hence muscle force, are usually unavailable. Although some researchers have attempted to extrapolate cross-sectional muscle size from the size of the muscles' origin and attachment areas (e.g. Caspari 1991), these provide unreliable estimates because the size of muscle origin or insertions are highly variable and largely independent of the size of the muscle belly itself. In addition, one comprehensive study (Hannam & Wood 1989), which used magnetic resonance imaging techniques to gather cephalometric and cross-sectional data on human beings, found that too many biomechanically important parameters exist to relate accurately muscle forces with their mechanical efficiency. For the time being, there seems little hope of estimating forces directly from skeletal features; however, finite element modeling studies that relate muscle areas, orientations, and skeletal architecture with electromyogram (EMG) and strain gauge data from bones may potentially yield some advances.

An additional consideration for inferences based on angular kinetics is the effect of mechanical forces on the actual dimensions used to calculate lever and load arms. As noted above, applied forces tend to stimulate bone growth in regions of high strain. Such growth can influence the mechanical advantage of muscles, blurring the distinction between biomechanical configurations selected to produce high forces with those that result from counteracting such forces. Mandibular dimensions, again, provide an interesting example. While increasing the height of the mandible increases the maximum load arm for the chewing muscles, it elongates even more the lever arm length for those muscles with an oblique orientation (as shown in Figure 4b). A number of controlled experiments have demonstrated that chewing strains can influence mandibular height and sometimes length, thereby altering lever/load arm ratios. Corruccini & Beecher (1982, 1984), for example, compared the mandibular dimensions of adult squirrel monkeys (*Saimiri sciureus*) and baboons (*Papio cynocephalus*) raised on hard and soft food diets. In both species, the animals raised on hard food had significantly more vertical and lateral growth of the mandible, presumably in response to strains in the sagittal and coronal planes, respectively. (The sagittal plane divides the left and right side of the body. The coronal plane divides the front and back of the body.) Such growth efficiently counteracts strains, but it also may have the effect of increasing the mechanical efficiency of the chewing muscles slightly. Similar results were obtained for rhesus macaques by Bouvier & Hylander (1981) and for rats by Kiliaridis et al (1985). Such studies suggest that the substantial decreases in mandibular ramus height between preindustrial and modern Finns (Varrela

1992) and in mandibular length and height between hunter-gatherer and farmer Nubians (Carlson 1976, Carlson & Van Gerven 1977) may have been caused to some extent by decreased in vivo responses to chewing forces. Epigenetic rather than natural selection forces may also account for many of the morphological differences in mandibular and facial dimensions among fossil human populations (e.g. Frayer 1984).

Cross-Sectional Geometry

A complementary means of inferring behavior from bone morphology is to examine how osseous morphologies function to counteract the forces generated by movement. The most important macrostructural responses to mechanical loading are changes in the amount and distribution of mass. Since force per unit area (stress) generates potentially damaging strain, bones can augment their mass in the planes in which they are deformed, thereby limiting the magnitude of strain elicited by a given force. Studies by van der Meulen and colleagues (1993, 1995, 1996) demonstrate that the developmental determinants of bone cross-sectional geometry in living human beings and other mammals are almost entirely the consequence of skeletal responses to biophysical forces rather than intrinsic genetic factors. There are many excellent, well-documented examples of these phenomena for the postcranium, including a famous study (Jones et al 1977), recently reanalyzed by Trinkaus et al (1994) and Ruff et al (1994), of professional tennis players' arms. When a tennis player hits a ball, his or her humerus is bent along its long axis, causing high strain. The humerus apparently responds to such repeated strains through a number of mechanisms (described above) including more periosteal growth and less endosteal resorption (Ruff et al 1993). Consequently, the cortical area (CA) in cross-sections of a tennis player's humeral midshaft on the playing side was up to 40% thicker than the nonplaying side, with higher proportions of asymmetry in individuals who started playing at a younger age (Ruff et al 1994). Ruff et al (1994) also found an age-related difference in the responsiveness of endosteal and periosteal surfaces to strain, with more periosteal growth occurring in childhood and more endosteal growth occurring during adulthood. Although increases in CA act to counteract strains, note that it is the distribution of area rather than the total area of bone that really counts. Cross-sectional resistance to deformation is calculated as the second moment of area (SMA), which is the product of unit areas of a bone times their squared moment arm distance to the central axis around which the deformation occurs [the moment arm is squared because it is used to calculate a moment of inertia, the resistance of an object to a change in angular motion; for details, see Wainright et al (1976); Ruff & Hayes (1983); Ruff (1992)]. SMAs (sometimes called area moments of inertia) can be derived for bones from cut cross-sections, radiographs, or CT scans. Because the SMA is a fourth-power function, bones with small CAs but larger diameters can provide considerably more resistance to bending than thicker bones with smaller diameters (illustrated in Figure 5).

Techniques for measuring bone cross-sectional geometry and their mechanical consequences in fossil and recent human beings have been developed and applied to a large extent by Ruff and colleagues to test behavioral hypotheses using inferences from postcranial limb shaft dimensions. Ruff (1992), for example, compared femoral cross-sections in archaeological populations, concluding that the femora of more sedentary farmers tend to be rounder, with less antero-posterior elongation generated by in vivo responses to mobility. Ruff (1987) and Larsen & Ruff (1994), moreover, documented a decline in sexual dimorphism of femoral cross-sections with the transition from hunting and gathering to increased agricultural sedentism in the American Southeast, suggesting that a greater proportion of long-distance mobility was undertaken by males in earlier populations. In one intriguing recent study, Trinkaus et al (1997) compared the cross-sectional geometries in the upper and lower limbs of Neanderthals with those of roughly contemporary Middle Paleolithic anatomically modern human beings. When corrected for limb length, the cross-sectional geometries of Neanderthal and modern human lower limbs appear to be adapted for similar levels of loading activity; in contrast, their upper limbs differ significantly, providing substantial evidence that Neanderthals used their upper bodies much more, perhaps for spear throwing and other forms of manipulative behavior (Churchill 1994). These researchers conclude that levels of mobility were similar in both populations but that their pattern of resource exploitation differed substantially.

Cortical thickness: 3.5 mm
Cortical area: 342 mm^2
Polar moment of inertia (J): 7.8 x 10^{4}mm^4

Cortical thickness: 7.0 mm
Cortical area: 353 mm^2
Polar moment of inertia (J): 2.2 x 10^{4}mm^4

Figure 5   Cross-sectional geometric properties of two idealized "bones." The bone on the left has half the thickness and slightly less cortical area, hence mass, than the bone on the right. Because the mass in the left bone lies farther from the central (neutral) axis, it has a correspondingly higher resistance to bending and twisting, as measured by its polar moment of inertia (*J*).

SMAs and other measurements of mass distribution have also been used to analyze cranial morphologies. Again, the mandible provides a useful illustration. Although researchers have long appreciated that the large mandibles of robust australopithecines suggest that they chewed a mechanically demanding diet, Hylander (1988), Daegling (1989), and Daegling & Grine (1991) have shown that the distribution of mass in the mandibles of these fossils corresponds to resistance to elevated chewing forces. In particular, the vertical depth of their mandibles would have resisted unusually high vertical (sagittal) bending forces, and their wide, hence round, mandibular corpora would have effectively resisted enormous transverse bending and twisting forces, respectively. In addition, the transverse width of the symphysis probably counteracted high levels of wishboning (lateral transverse bending) caused by enormous medially directed grinding forces (Hylander 1988). To what extent these morphological variations were genetically heritable adaptations or in vivo responses to strains remains an important problem for future research.

There are some potential problems, however, with using bone mass distributions to infer habitual forces uncritically, because there may not always be a simple correspondence between these parameters. Daegling (1993) has suggested this to be the case for the hominoid mandible. Although the symphysis and the posterior regions of the corpus near the second and third molars are most likely subjected to the highest bending stresses in the mandible (Hylander 1979, 1984), these regions may not always be the strongest in terms of their cross-sectional geometry (Daegling 1993). Biknevicius & Ruff (1992), however, showed that the variations in cross-sectional properties of the mandibular corpus in carnivores correspond well with their inferred mechanical loading patterns. Primates may therefore be unusual in this regard because they have nonstereotypical and/or more complex loading patterns than other mammals, which may not be modeled adequately using beam theory. Similar dissociations may exist for many postcranial limb geometries, both near epiphyses and in distal element midshafts. In most species adapted for running, distal elements tend to be thinner, hence structurally weaker than proximal elements as a mass-saving adaptation in spite of equivalent forces (see below). The human lower limb, in which the large SMA of the tibia makes it nearly as strong as the femur, is a probable and unusual exception to this rule. Most animals such as pigs, however, probably compensate for decreased distal limb bone strength by having proportionately shorter distal elements, thereby minimizing bending strains (Alexander 1977); specialized runners with long limbs such as horses, moreover, appear to counteract these forces by reorienting their limbs during peak loading so they are loaded more axially, making them structurally stronger than if they were primarily bent (Biewener 1990; Biewener et al 1983, 1988). The only way to resolve such relationships between behaviorally induced loading and bone morphology is to integrate kinematic analyses of bones as they are loaded with in vivo strain data. As noted above, such studies have been done for the primate skull by Hylander and others, but, for understandable reasons, have not been investigated much for the human postcranial skeleton (see, however, Carter 1978).

Microstructure

Bones respond to force not only through the macrostructural changes described above, but also through microstructural modifications. Consequently, another potential means of assessing the effects of force on bone growth is through the analysis of bone histology, although this remains an underused and poorly understood approach for behavioral reconstruction. Microstructural responses to loading are diverse, but include changes in mineral density, cellularity, vascularization, and collagen organization (data summarized in Martin & Burr 1989). Perhaps the most important is Haversian remodeling (HR). HR is the process by which osteoclast cells tunnel out preexisting bone, which osteoblasts then replace by depositing bone tissue in concentric lamellae around a central vascular channel (Frost 1986; Parfitt 1979, 1984), forming a secondary osteon or Haversian system (see Figure 1b).

HR density has been used for many years to make inferences about age of death from bones because there appears to be a reasonable predictive linear relationship between age and the density of Haversian systems at a number of specific locations in the skeleton (e.g. Stout & Lueck 1995, Stout & Paine 1992). Such relationships, however, are indirect and often highly variable (Burr 1992) because they are mediated primarily by mechanical loading. HR is probably the major repair mechanism that strengthens bone by removing weakened tissue and/or reorienting its structure (Martin & Burr 1982). Although Haversian bone is weaker than young, primary bone, it is apparently stronger than old, microcrack-damaged primary bone. Not surprisingly, there is a large body of evidence that loading significantly increases HR rates (Bouvier & Hylander 1981, 1997; Burr et al 1985; Hert et al 1972; Lieberman & Crompton 1997; Schaffler & Burr 1984). HR, however, has some significant disadvantages, the most notable of which is that the vascular channels of Haversian systems, if sufficiently large, can weaken bones by increasing porosity, contributing to osteoporosis (Martin 1995, Parfitt 1988).

Several studies have recently begun to examine how HR can be used to assess certain behavioral aspects of archaeological populations. Burr et al (1990) compared HR rates and dimensions from the anterior femoral midshafts of Pecos Native Americans with modern Europeans. Although both populations were overall very similar histologically, the Pecos population had a higher density of Haversian systems, which, in women, had thicker walls with smaller vascular channels. These results indicate that increased levels of mechanical loading from exercise result in higher remodeling rates but lower porosity, which is consistent with data from archaeological and cross-sectional analyses of the Pecos sample (Ruff & Hayes 1983). More recently, Abbott et al (1996) compared these results with histological sections from femoral fragments of ten Late Pleistocene samples from the Middle East and Africa. In comparison with recent human beings, the Pleistocene sample had significantly lower HR rates, but with Haversian systems that are approximately 25% smaller and with larger vascular channels. Unfortunately, the histological sections from the fossils were sampled (by necessity) from different locations in the femur, making the results difficult to interpret (see below). Abbott et al (1996) nevertheless suggested that the lower rate of HR activity in the Pleistocene fossils compared with the Pecos sample may have resulted from extremely high strain levels that, according to Frost (1986), preferentially induce periosteal and endosteal growth (modeling) rather than remodeling.

While histological studies have much potential for testing anthropological hypotheses about fossils, the diversity of osteological responses to loading highlights the importance of integrating behavioral inferences from both the gross structural and microstructural aspects of bones. As noted above, mechanical stimuli induce modeling and/or remodeling, but we have little understanding of what mechanisms modulate these alternative responses. Recall that HR, unlike modeling, may often function as a repair mechanism to remove microcrack damage in bones and can thereby alter a bone's strength by modifying its histology but without significantly altering its mass or external shape. Such HR responses to loading may explain why cross-sectional analyses of bones sometimes fail to predict their mechanical environments. Several researchers (e.g. Frost 1986, Martin 1995) have suggested that modeling and remodeling are activated at different strain energies, but these models so far have little empirical support. Lieberman & Crompton (1998) have proposed that the distribution of modeling and remodeling in the skeleton varies to some extent according to variations in their relative costs and benefits. According to this trade-off model, strains high enough to cause microdamage are predicted to induce modeling in proximal regions of the skeleton where the cost of moving additional mass is low, whereas remodeling may be favored in more distal regions of the skeleton, such as toward the ends of limbs, in which the kinetic energy costs of mass increases are exponentially higher. Therefore, modeling preferentially occurs as a growth response to strain in regions of the skeleton in which there is a low cost to additional mass increases, but HR is favored as a repair mechanism to fracture damage in regions such as the distal elements of the limb where mass increases impose an exponentially higher energetic cost. This mechanism may explain to some extent why distal limb bones tend to be

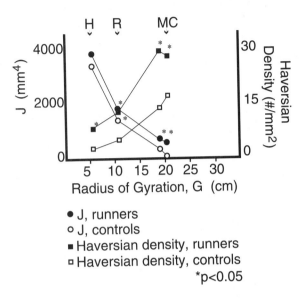

Figure 6   Comparison of element strength, measured as the polar moment of inertia (*J*), and Haversian remodeling density at the midshafts of the humerus (*H*), radius (*R*), and third and fourth metacarpals (*MC*) in three pairs of exercised vs unexercised young swine. Note that as the midshafts become increasingly distant from the hip joint (measured at midstance as the radius of gyration, *G*), the cross-sectional strength of the bones declines but the percentage of Haversian remodeling increases. For experimental details, see Lieberman (1996); Lieberman & Crompton (1998).

thinner and weaker than proximal bones (see also Biewener 1990). This hypothesis has yet to be tested on human populations, but it is supported by a study of exercised swine (Lieberman & Crompton 1998) which demonstrates that, within limbs, the percentage area of bone tissue modeled and remodeled relative to total cross-sectional area varies inversely as a function of the moment arm length of each bone (measured from radiographs as the maximum mid-stance distance from the hip to the element's midshaft). As Figure 6 shows, more distal elements have a significantly higher percentage of remodeling than modeling, and these differences are exaggerated by exercise.

So far, such an approach has yet to be applied to human or hominid skeletons. Design constraints certainly exist in bones, but we currently have much to learn about the intermediate transductional mechanisms by which the skeleton apparently modulates modeling and remodeling responses to loading.

MAKING INFERENCES ABOUT SYSTEMATICS

Considering how bones respond to mechanical loading is essential not only for biomechanical analyses of fossils but also for testing taxonomic and phylogenetic inferences from skeletons. Phylogenetic analyses based on skeletal data are typically achieved by dividing bones into discrete units, called *characters,* whose variations can be compared among and between specimens (Fristrup 1992). Most characters describe shape and/or size. Two logical techniques exist for comparing morphological characters: phenetic analyses that compare overall similarity, and cladistic analyses that compare only characters that are evolutionary novelties (so-called derived characters). Both approaches have advantages and disadvantages. Phenetics is convenient for analyzing continuous characters like the shape and size of bones, but it fails to distinguish between primitive characters (ancestral retentions) and derived characters. Since evolution is the process by which descendants inherit derived characters (novelties) from their ancestors, it follows logically that only derived characters that have changed provide reliable information about ancestor-descendant relationships (Hennig 1966). Cladistics is logically superior but is often practically more difficult to accomplish, especially for closely related taxa.

There is much debate over how to apply phenetic and cladistic techniques to hominid phylogeny (see Lieberman 1995, including comments) to a large extent because both yield unsatisfactory results. With few exceptions, phylogenetic analyses of bone morphological characters yield numerous different trees that have an almost equal probability of being correct. Lieberman et al (1996), for example, compared 48 cranial characters commonly used to examine the evolutionary relationships among early species of the genus *Homo.* These characters supported one most parsimonious cladogram that was substantially different from at least 44 other cladograms that were only marginally less parsimonious. Moreover, altering the data set by one or two characters yielded very different, often contradictory cladograms. The proximate cause for these variable, hence inconclusive, results is the phenomenon of *character-conflict* in which two characters support alternative phylogenies. Typically, only about 60–70% of the osseous characters in hominid phylogenetic analyses support the most parsimonious cladogram. Consequently, a given set of characters yields many cladograms of approximately equal length, rendering the results highly subject to error and, therefore, inconclusive.

One important reason for the high percentage of character conflict in phenetic and cladistic analyses of skeletal material is that both techniques suffer from the same basic problem: how to define osseous characters that provide apparently reliable information about ancestor-descendant relationships. A consideration of how mechanical forces influence bone growth may help to resolve this impediment. Many researchers (e.g. Strait et al 1997) attribute high frequencies of character conflict to *homoplasy* (often called convergence or parallelism), the process by which evolutionary novelties evolve independently. Homoplasy certainly occurs; however, it should be evident that the multifactorial processes by which bones grow and respond to external stimuli have the potential to contribute substantially to character-conflict by obscuring ancestor-descendant relationships. Ideally, phylogenetic analyses should be based solely on genetically heritable characters that are passed from one generation to the next (see Feldman 1992). Many osseous characters are, therefore, probably inappropriate for use in phylogenetic analyses for two interrelated reasons. First, we do not inherit our bones from our ancestors; we inherit only DNA base pairs that play some role in their growth. Second, because bone is a dynamic tissue with diverse functions, most osseous characters are influenced by a variety of nongenetic stimuli that do not necessarily reflect ancestor-descendant relationships. That is, we should expect that osseous similarities (morphological homologies) between two taxa to occur through more than one process. Two taxa, for example, might share a similar-shaped jaw through common inheritance or parallel evolution of the same DNA base pairs that code for the processes by which the jaw grows; but their similarities may also result from using their jaws in the same way so that they grow and respond to forces similarly. Such effects are demonstrated by the dramatic differences between normal human mandibles and those of individuals who suffer from diseases, such as myotonic dystrophy, that impair muscle function (Kiliaridis et al 1989). Most morphological homologies result from a complex combination of genetic and nongenetic factors, which we must dissociate to find phylogenetic homologies (Cartmill 1994).

Bone thickness is an excellent example of how the processes by which bones grow often render them inappropriate for testing phylogenetic hypotheses. Bone thickness or robusticity is commonly used in phylogenetic analyses because it fits many criteria for a good character: It is morphologically homologous, straightforward to measure, and varies among taxa. Recent modern human beings, for example, have significantly thinner skulls and limb bones than those of Neanderthals and *Homo erectus* (Lieberman 1996, Ruff et al 1994, Twiesselmann 1941). Cranial and postcranial robusticity have therefore been used in a number of phylogenetic analyses (e.g. Stringer 1987, Wood 1991). From a developmental perspective, however, bone thickness is clearly a poor character for phylogenetic analyses because it is influenced substantially by nongenetic stimuli. In a recent experiment, Lieberman (1996) compared the cranial and postcranial bones of miniature swine exercised on a treadmill for three months with unexercised sibling controls. The exercised animals had not only 23% thicker tibial midshafts but also 20–30% thicker frontal and parietal bones. These differences, which obviously do not have a pure genetic basis, are roughly equivalent to those between modern and archaic human beings, indicating that robusticity as a character is more useful for testing hypotheses about habitual behaviors than evolutionary relationships.

Although osseous characters are always likely to be less reliable for testing phylogenetic hypotheses than are genetic ones, some might be more heritable than others. Our challenge is to integrate functional and developmental analyses with phylogenetic analyses in an effort to select or define characters whose developmental basis reflects nongenetic stimuli as little as possible. Lieberman and colleagues (1996) have suggested that, for skulls, the shape of the basicranium may be a more reliable indicator of phylogenetic relationships than most neurocranial and facial dimensions because many parts of the cranial base are apparently under tighter genetic control and are morphologically more conservative (De Beer 1937). In addition, variations in cranial base morphology appear to exert important developmental constraints on neurocranial dimensions and facial width, but not vice versa. Articular morphologies may be another potential source of useful phylogenetic information because it is possible that their shapes may be more constrained functionally and genetically than other regions of the skeleton (Ruff et al 1994, Trinkaus et al 1994). Such hypotheses, however, need to be tested rigorously using extant taxa whose phylogenetic relationships are already known through molecular studies (for such an approach, see Yoder 1994).

CONCLUSION AND SUMMARY

Bones unquestionably yield important information for testing hypotheses about behavior and phylogenetic relationships from skeletal material. Morphological analyses of bones, however, do not always provide a straightforward source of evolutionary information because the developmental processes by which bones grow and change are extremely complex and multifactorial. Like most tissues, bones have numerous functions and respond to a huge array of genetic and nongenetic stimuli. Consequently, analyses of the angular kinetics, cross-sectional geometries, and microstructural properties of the skeleton not only reveal information about the forces generated by habitual activities but also include information about osteogenic responses to such forces as well. Likewise, comparisons of osseous characters are at best an indirect and frequently misleading source of information on phylogenetic relationships because of the low degree of heritability of most skeletal characters.

The resolution to these problems is to integrate functional and phylogenetic studies of the skeleton with analyses of how bones develop. Since the morphologies of bones are the consequence of a variety of developmental processes, it follows that the real "information" in bones is not so much their shapes but the processes by which those shapes were created. Genetically heritable processes reveal useful information about ancestor-descendant relationships, and osteogenic responses to load-bearing activities contain useful information about habitual behaviors. In other words, we can best evaluate the epistemological utility of a given character by asking how it grew. One of the most exciting and potentially rewarding challenges of paleoanthropology is, therefore, to integrate analyses of development with those of function and phylogeny to provide a more satisfying understanding of the meaning of morphological variations in the skeleton.

ACKNOWLEDGMENTS

I am grateful to S Churchill, R McCarthy, C Ruff, and D Strait for their cogent comments and suggestions on a draft of this paper.

Visit the *Annual Reviews home page* at
http://www.AnnualReviews.org.

Literature Cited

Abbott S, Trinkaus E, Burr DB. 1996. Dynamic bone remodeling in later Pleistocene fossil hominids. *Am. J. Phys. Anthropol.* 99:585–601

Akazawa T, Aoki K, Bar-Yosef O, eds. 1997. *Neanderthals and Modern Humans in Western Asia.* In press

Alexander RM. 1977. Terrestrial locomotion. In *Mechanics and Energetics of Animal Locomotion,* ed. RM Alexander, G Goldspink, 7:168–203. London: Chapman & Hall

Anton SC. 1994. Mechanical and other perspectives on Neandertal craniofacial morphology. In *Integrative Paths to the Past: Palaeoanthropological Advances in Honor of F. Clark Howell,* ed. RS Corruccini, RL Ciochon, 29:677–95. Englewood Cliffs, NJ: Prentice Hall

Bertram JEA, Swartz SM. 1991. The 'Law of Bone Transformation': A case of crying Wolff? *Biol. Rev.* 66:245–73

Biewener AA. 1990. Biomechanics of mammalian terrestrial locomotion. *Science* 250:1097–103

Biewener AA, Taylor CR. 1986. Bone strain: a determinant of gait and speed? *J. Exp. Biol.* 123:383–400

Biewener AA, Thomson J, Lanyon LE. 1988. Mechanics of locomotion and jumping in horse *Equus;* in vivo stress in the tibia and metatarsus. *J. Zool. London* 214:547–65

Biewener AA, Thomson J, Lanyon LE. 1983. Mechanics of locomotion and jumping in the forelimb of the horse *Equus; in vivo* stress in the radius and metacarpus. *J. Zool. London* 201:67–82

Biknevicius AR, Ruff CB. 1992. The structure of the mandibular corpus and its relationship to feeding behaviours in extant carnivorans. *J. Zool. Soc. London* 228:479–507

Bouvier M, Hylander WL. 1981. Effect of bone strain on cortical bone structure in macaques *Macaca mulatta. J. Morphol.* 167:1–12

Bouvier M, Hylander WL. 1997. The function of secondary osteonal bone: mechanical or metabolic? *Arch. Oral Biol.* 41:941–50

Boyd A. 1980. Electron microscopy of the mineralizing front. *Metab. Bone Dis. Relat. Res.* 2:69–78

Bromage TG. 1987. The scanning microscopy/replica technique and recent applications to the study of fossil bone. *Scanning Electron Microsc.* 1:607–13

Burr DB. 1992. Estimated intracortical bone turnover in the femur of growing macaques: implications for their use as models in skeletal pathology. *Anat. Rec.* 232: 180–89

Burr DB, Martin RB, Schaffler MB, Radin EL. 1985. Bone remodeling in response to *in vivo* fatigue microdamage. *J. Biomech.* 18: 189–200

Burr DB, Ruff CB, Thompson DD. 1990. Patterns of skeletal histologic change through time: comparison of an archaic Native American population with modern populations. *Anat. Rec.* 226:307–13

Carlson DS. 1976. Temporal variation in prehistoric Nubian crania. *Am. J. Phys. Anthropol.* 45:467–84

Carlson DS, Van Gerven DP. 1977. Masticatory function and post-Pleistocene evolution in Nubia. *Am. J. Phys. Anthropol.* 46: 495–506

Carter DR. 1978. Anisotropic analysis of strain rosette information from cortical bone. *J. Biomech.* 11:199–202

Carter DR, Caler WE, Spengler DM, Frankel VH. 1981a. Fatigue behavior of adult cortical bone—the influence of mean strain and strain range. *Acta Orthop. Scand.* 55: 481–90

Carter DR, Caler WE, Spengler DM, Frankel VH. 1981b. Uniaxial fatigue of human cortical bone. The influence of tissue physical characteristics. *J. Biomech.* 14:460–70

Carter DR, Hayes WC. 1976a. Fatigue life of compact bone. I. Effects of stress amplitude, temperature and density. *J. Biomech.* 9:27–34

Carter DR, Hayes WC. 1976b. Bone compressive strength: the influence of density and strain rate. *Science* 194:1174–76

Carter DR, Hayes WC. 1977a. Compact bone fatigue damage—a microscopic examination. *Clin. Orthop. Relat. Res.* 127:265–74

Carter DR, Hayes WC. 1977b. Compact bone fatigue damage. I. Residual strength and stiffness. *J. Biomech.* 10:323–37

Cartmill M. 1994. A critique of homology as a morphological concept. *Am. J. Phys. Anthropol.* 94:111–23

Caspari R. 1991. *The evolution of the posterior cranial vault in the Central European Upper Pleistocene.* PhD thesis. Univ. Michigan

Churchill SE. 1994. *Human upper body evolution in the Eurasian later Pleistocene.* PhD thesis. Univ. New Mexico

Churchill SE. 1996. Particulate versus integrated evolution of the upper body in late Pleistocene humans: a test of two models. *Am. J. Phys. Anthropol.* 100:559–83

Corruccini RS, Beecher RM. 1982. Occlusal variation related to soft diet in a nonhuman primate. *Science* 218:74–76

Corruccini RS, Beecher RM. 1984. Occlusofacial morphological integration lowered in baboons rasied on soft diet. *J. Craniofac. Genet. Dev. Biol.* 4:135–42

Currey JD. 1984. *The Mechanical Adaptations of Bones.* Princeton, NJ: Princeton Univ. Press

Daegling DJ. 1989. Biomechanics of cross-sectional size and shape in the hominoid mandibular corpus. *Am. J. Phys. Anthropol.* 80:91–106

Daegling DJ. 1993. The relationship of *in vivo* bone strain to mandibular corpus morphology in *Macaca fascicularis. J. Hum. Evol.* 25:247–69

Daegling DJ, Grine FE. 1991. Compact bone distribution and biomechanics of early hominid mandibles. *Am. J. Phys. Anthropol.* 86:321–39

De Beer G. 1937. *The Development of the Vertebrate Skull.* Oxford: Oxford Univ. Press

Demes B. 1985. Biomechanics of the primate skull base. *Adv. Anat. Embryol. Cell Biol.* 94:1–59

Demes B, Creel N. 1988. Bite force, diet, and cranial morphology of hominids. *J. Hum. Evol.* 17:657–70

Demes B, Creel N, Preuschoft H. 1986. Functional significance of allometric trends in the hominoid masticatory apparatus. In *Primate Evolution,* ed. JG Else, PC Lee, 3:229–37. Cambridge: Cambridge Univ. Press

Doty SB. 1981. Morphological evidence of gap junctions between bone cells. *Calcif. Tissue Int.* 33:509–12

Enlow DH. 1990. *Facial Growth.* Philadelphia: Saunders. 3rd ed.

Feldman M. 1992. Heritability: some theoretical ambiguities. See Keller & Lloyd 1992, pp. 151–57

Frayer DW. 1984. Biological and cultural change in the European late Pleistocene and early Holocene. In *The Origin of Modern Humans: A Survey of the World Evidence,* ed. FH Smith, F Spencer, pp. 211–50. New York: Liss

Fristrup K. 1992. Character: current usages. See Keller & Lloyd 1992, pp. 45–51

Frost HM. 1986. *Intermediary Organization of the Skeleton.* Boca Raton: CRC Press

Hannam AG, Wood WW. 1989. Relationships between the size and spatial morphology of human masseter and medial pterygoid muscles, the craniofacial skeleton, and jaw biomechanics. *Am. J. Phys. Anthropol.* 80: 429–45

Hennig W. 1966. *Phylogenetic Systematics.* Urbana: Univ. Ill. Press

Hert J, Prybylová E, Liskova M. 1972. Reaction of bone to mechanical stimuli, Part 3. Microstructure of compact bone of rabbit tibia after intermittent loading. *Acta Anat.* 82:218–30

Hylander WL. 1979. An experimental analysis of temporomandibular joint reaction force in macaques. *Am. J. Phys. Anthropol.* 51: 433–56

Hylander WL. 1984. Stress and strain in the mandibular symphysis of primates: a test of competing hypotheses. *Am. J. Phys. Anthropol.* 64:1–46

Hylander WL. 1988. Implications of *in vivo* experiments for determining the structural significance of "robust" australopithecine jaws. In *Evolutionary History of the Robust Australopithecines,* ed. FE Grine, 3: 55–83. New York: Aldine de Gruyter

Ingervall B, Bitsanis E. 1987. A pilot study on the effect of masticatory muscle training on facial growth in long-face children. *Eur. J. Orthod.* 9:15–23

Jones HH, Priest JD, Hayes WC, Tichenor CC, Nagel DA. 1977. Humeral hypertrophy in response to exercise. *J. Bone Joint Surg. A* 59:204–8

Keller EF, Lloyd EA, eds. 1992. *Keywords in Evolutionary Biology.* Cambridge: Harvard Univ. Press

Kiliaridis S, Engström C, Thilander B. 1985. The relationship between masticatory muscle function and craniofacial morphology. I. A cephalometric longitudinal analysis in the growing rat fed a soft diet. *Eur. J. Orthod.* 7:273–83

Kiliaridis S, Mejersjö C, Thilander B. 1989. Muscle function and craniofacial morphology: a clinical study in patients with myotonic dystrophy. *Eur. J. Orthod.* 11: 131–38

Lanyon LE. 1993. Osteocyte, strain detection, bone modeling and remodeling. *Calcif. Tissue Int.* 53:S102–7

Lanyon LE, Goodship AE, Pye CJ, MacPhie H. 1982. Mechanically adaptive bone remodeling. *J. Biomech.* 15:141–54

Larsen CS, Ruff CB. 1994. The stresses of conquest in Spanish Florida: structural adaptation and change before and after contact. In *In the Wake of Contact: Biological Responses to Conquest,* ed. CS Larsen, GR Milner, pp. 21–34. New York: Wiley-Liss

Lieberman DE. 1995. Testing hypotheses about recent human evolution from skulls: integrating development, function, and phylogeny. *Curr. Anthropol.* 36:159–97

Lieberman DE. 1996. How and why recent humans grow thin skulls: experimental evidence for systemic cortical robusticity. *Am. J. Phys. Anthropol.* 101:217–36

Lieberman DE. 1997. Neanderthal and early modern human mobility patterns: comparing archaeological and anatomical evidence. See Akazawa et al 1997. In press

Lieberman DE, Crompton AW. 1998. Responses of vertebrate bones to stress. In *Diversity in Biological Design: Symmorphosis—Fact or Fancy?,* ed. E Weibel, CR Taylor, L Bolis. Cambridge: Cambridge Univ. Press. In press

Lieberman DE, Wood B, Pilbeam D. 1996. Homoplasy and early *Homo:* an analysis of the evolutionary relationships of *H. habilis sensu stricto* and *H. rudolfensis. J. Hum. Evol.* 30:97–120

Lowenstam H, Weiner S. 1989. *On Biomineralization.* Oxford: Oxford Univ. Press

Lucas P, Peters CR, Arrandale SR. 1988. Seed-breaking forces exerted by orangutans with their teeth in captivity and a new technique for estimating forces produced in the wild. *Am. J. Phys. Anthropol.* 94:339–63

Martin RB. 1995. Mathematical model for repair of fatigue damage and stress fracture in osteonal bone. *J. Orthoped. Res.* 13: 309–16

Martin RB, Burr DB. 1982. A hypothetical mechanism for the stimulation of osteonal remodeling by fatigue damage. *J. Biomech.* 15:137–39

Martin RB, Burr DB. 1989. *Structure, Function, and Adaptation of Compact Bone.* New York: Raven

McMahon TA. 1984. *Muscles, Reflexes and Locomotion.* Princeton, NJ: Princeton Univ. Press

Mori S, Burr DB. 1993. Increased intracortical remodeling following fatigue damage. *Bone* 16:103–9

Parfitt AM. 1979. Quantum concept of bone remodeling and turnover: implications for the pathogenesis of osteoporosis. *Calcif. Tissue Int.* 28:1–5

Parfitt AM. 1984. The cellular basis of bone remodeling: the quantum concept reexamined in light of recent advances in the cell biology of bone. *Calcif. Tissue Int.* 36: S37–45

Parfitt AM. 1988. Bone remodeling: relationship to the amount and structure of bone, and the pathogenesis and prevention of fractures. In *Osteoporosis: Etiology, Diagnosis and Management,* ed. BL Riggs, LJ Melton, pp. 45–93. New York: Raven Press

Pead MJ, Skerry TM, Lanyon LE. 1988. Direct transformation from quiescence to bone formation in the adult periosteum following a single brief period of bone loading. *J. Bone Miner. Res.* 3:647–56

Raab DM, Crenshaw TD, Kimmel DB, Smith EL. 1991. A histomorphometric study of cortical bone activity during increased weight-bearing exercise. *J. Bone Miner. Res.* 6:741–49

Rak Y. 1986. The Neanderthal: a new look at an old face. *J. Hum. Evol.* 15:151–64

Reilly DT, Burstein AH. 1975. The elastic and ultimate properties of compact bone tissue. *J. Biomech.* 8:393–405

Rubin CT, Lanyon LE. 1984. Regulation of bone formation by applied dynamic loads. *J. Bone Joint Surg.* 66:397–402

Rubin CT, Lanyon LE. 1985. Regulation of bone mass by mechanical strain magnitude. *Calcif. Tissue Int.* 37:411–17

Ruff CB. 1987. Sexual dimorphism in human lower limb bone structure: relationship to subsistence strategy and sexual division of labor. *J. Hum. Evol.* 16:391–416

Ruff CB. 1992. Biomechanical analyses of archaeological human skeletal samples. In *Skeletal Biology of Past Peoples: Research Methods*, ed. SR Saunders, A Katzenburg, pp. 37–58. New York: Wiley-Liss

Ruff CB, Hayes WC. 1983. Cross-sectional geometry of Pecos Pueblo femora and tibiae—a biomechanical investigation. I. Method and general patterns of variation. *Am. J. Phys. Anthropol.* 60:359–81

Ruff CB, Runestad JA. 1992. Primate limb bone structural adaptations. *Annu. Rev. Anthropol.* 21:407–33

Ruff CB, Trinkaus E, Walker A, Larsen CS. 1993. Postcranial robusticity in *Homo*. I. Temporal trends and mechanical interpretation. *Am. J. Phys. Anthropol.* 91:21–53

Ruff CB, Walker A, Trinkaus E. 1994. Postcranial robusticity in *Homo*. III. Ontogeny. *Am. J. Phys. Anthropol.* 93:35–54

Schaffler MB, Burr DB. 1984. Primate cortical bone microstructure: relationship to locomotion. *Am. J. Phys. Anthropol.* 65: 191–97

Schaffler MB, Burr DB. 1988. Stiffness of compact bone: effects of porosity and density *J. Biomech.* 21:13–16

Schaffler MB, Radin EL, Burr DB. 1990a. Mechanical and morphological effects of strain rate on fatigue of compact bone. *Bone* 10:207–14

Schaffler MB, Radin EL, Burr DB. 1990b. Long-term fatigue behavior of compact bone at low strain magnitude and rate. *Bone* 11:321–26

Smith FH, Paquette SP. 1989. The adaptive basis of Neanderthal facial form with some

thoughts on the nature of modern human origins. In *The Emergence of Modern Humans*, ed. E Trinkaus, pp. 181–210. Cambridge: Cambridge Univ. Press

Spadaro JA. 1991. Bioelectrical properties of bone and response of bone to electrical stimuli. In *Bone*, ed. BK Hall, 3:109–39. Boca Raton, FL: CRC Press

Spencer MA. 1995. *Masticatory system configuration and diet in anthropoid primates*. PhD thesis. State Univ. NY Stony Brook

Spencer MA, Demes B. 1993. Biomechanical analysis of masticatory system configuration in Neanderthals and Inuits. *Am. J. Phys. Anthropol.* 91:1–20

Stout S, Lueck R. 1995. Bone remodeling rates and skeletal maturation in three archaeological skeletal populations. *Am. J. Phys. Anthropol.* 98:161–71

Stout S, Paine RR. 1992. Histological age estimation using rib and clavicle. *Am. J. Phys. Anthropol.* 87:111–15

Strait DS, Grine FE, Moniz MA. 1997. A reappraisal of early hominid phylogeny. *J. Hum. Evol.* 32:17–82

Stringer CB. 1987. A numerical cladistic analysis for the genus *Homo*. *J. Hum. Evol.* 16:135–46

Taylor JF. 1992. The periosteum and bone growth. In *Bone*, ed. BK Hall, 6:21–52. Boca Raton: CRC Press

Tobias PV. 1971. *The Brain in Hominid Evolution*. New York: Columbia Univ. Press

Trinkaus E. 1987. The Neandertal face: evolutionary and functional perspectives on a recent hominid face. *J. Hum. Evol.* 16: 429–43

Trinkaus E, Churchill SE, Ruff CB. 1994. Postcranial robusticity in *Homo*. II. Humeral bilateral asymmetry and bone plasticity. *Am. J. Phys. Anthropol.* 93:1–34

Trinkaus E, Ruff CB, Churchill SE. 1997. Upper limb versus lower limb loading patterns among Near Eastern Middle Palaeolithic hominids. See Akazawa et al 1997. In press

Turner CH, Burr DB. 1993. Basic biomechanical measurements of bone: a tutorial. *Bone* 14:595–608

Twiesselmann F. 1941. Méthode pour l'évaluation de l'épaisseur des parois cranienne. *Bull. Mus. R. Hist. Nat. Belg.* 17:1–33

van der Meulen MCH, Ashford MW Jr, Kiralti BJ, Bachrach LK, Carter DH. 1996. Determinants of femoral geometry and structure during adolescent growth. *J. Orthop. Res.* 14:22–29

van der Meulen MCH, Beaupré GS, Carter DR. 1993. Mechanobiologic influences in long bone cross-sectional growth. *Bone* 14:635–42

van der Meulen MCH, Carter DH. 1995. Developmental mechanics determine long bone allometry. *J. Theor. Biol.* 172: 323–27

Varrela J. 1992. Dimensional variation of craniofacial structures in relation to changing masticatory-functional demands. *Eur. J. Orthodot.* 14:31–36

Wainright SA, Biggs BA, Currey JD, Gosline JM. 1976. *Mechanical Design in Organisms*. Princeton, NJ: Princeton Univ. Press

Watson PA. 1991. Function follows form: generation of intracellular signals by cell deformation. *FASEB* 5:2013–19

Weinbaum S, Cowin SC, Zeng Y. 1994. A model for the excitation of osteocytes by mechanical loading-induced bone fluid shear stresses. *J. Biomech.* 27:339–60

Wolff J. 1892. *Das Gesetz der Transformation der Knochen*. Berlin: Hirschwald

Woo SLY, Kuei SC, Amiel D, Gomez MA, Hayes WC, et al. 1981. The effect of prolonged physical training on the properties of long bone: a study of Wolff's law. *J. Bone J. Surg.* 63:780–87

Wood B. 1991. *Koobi Fora Research Project*, Vol. 4, *The Hominid Cranial Remains*. Oxford: Oxford Univ. Press

Yoder AD. 1994. Relative position of the Cheirogaleidae in Strepsirhine phylogeny: a comparison of morphological and molecular methods and results. *Am. J. Phys. Anthropol.* 94:25–46

Annu. Rev. Anthropol. 1997. 26:211–34

THE ARTS OF GOVERNMENT IN EARLY MESOAMERICA

J. E. Clark

Department of Anthropology, Brigham Young University, Provo, Utah 84602

KEY WORDS: Olmec, governmentality, kingship, ritual, ideology

---

ABSTRACT

This review addresses issues of governmentality for Mesoamerica's earliest kingdoms. About 3200 years ago the Olmecs instituted stratified society based upon sacred kingship. Supervision of public works projects, the creation and deployment of monumental art, and control of ritual and ideology were the kings' principal means of governance within their kingdoms. Evidence for Olmec governance outside their region is equivocal. Olmecs may have conquered the societies of the Mazatan region, but they interacted with societies in the Mexican Highlands on a less coercive and more equitable basis.

Need raised up Thrones; the Sciences and Arts have made them strong.
JJ Rousseau (1981, p. 5)

INTRODUCTION

Rousseau's aphorism aptly describes the formula for success of Mesoamerica's first kingdoms, which arose among the Olmecs about 3200 years ago. Although the causes of the evolution of Olmec kingdoms from rank societies remain to be determined, it is clear that the subsequent flowering and spread of Olmec civilization for the next half millennium was intimately tied to the creation, display, and manipulation of monumental and portable art objects. How did this art make these early Olmec kingdoms strong and aid in their governance? In this review I address this question of early Olmec governmentality for the period from 1200 to 900 BC (all dates in radiocarbon years).

211

The title of this review is a deliberate play on Foucault's (1991) definition of "governmentalilty" as the "arts of government," meaning the techniques and procedures employed by governments to create docile, obedient subjects (Gordon 1991, Simons 1995). In the Olmec case, the creation and deployment of "art," as narrowly defined, promoted governance through covert control of foundational ideologies. Public art legitimated privileged access to supernatural forces and powers by marking a leader's exclusive access to revered ancestors, supernatural spirits, or deities.

Although no specialist has explicitly applied Foucault's notion of governmentality to the Olmec, a few studies have been sympathetic to its emphases on the "hows" of governance. Currently, prevailing opinion is that arts of governance involved political rituals and manipulation of belief systems which granted supernatural charter to some individuals to lead and, at the same moment, convinced others to follow (Drennan 1976, Grove & Gillespie 1992b). Control of mind and heart was more important than governmental discipline of the body. Thus, early polities are thought to have comprised communities of obedient believers, with physical force being either unnecessary or illegitimate. This position will probably prove facile, but it arises from the current analytical emphasis on art as the primary means of addressing questions of ideology and power.

In a practical sense, fundamental Olmec arts of government entailed production of art to convey ultimate sacred propositions (Drennan 1976). Royal sponsorship of art and its deployment in periodic public rituals reinforced basic cultural belief systems and social roles, with their attendant allocation of privileges and responsibilities. Internalization of these cosmic propositions fostered self-discipline critical to the smooth operation of each community and minimized the need for coercive government. As Flannery & Marcus (1996, p. 351) stress, ideology comprises the "principles, philosophies, ethics, and values by which human societies are governed." Giving these ideologies material expression was one of the principal arts of Olmec governance.

As Foucault frequently demonstrated, governmental power to influence individual conduct can be exerted at the minute interstices of social life. Given the nature of archaeological data, however, few microsociological details of everyday Olmec life will ever be available, and therefore issues of governance must deal with a macroperspective. With current data, most considerations of governmentality are necessarily speculative, as is my treatment of the two fundamental issues of concern here: (a) practices of governance within individual Olmec kingdoms, and (b) possible Olmec hegemony within the greater Mesoamerican region. To provide context for this discussion I first briefly introduce the archaeological Olmecs.

THE EARLY OLMECS

The term "Olmec" is generally used to refer to a "people," but it more appropriately describes a political phenomenon that began about 1150 BC in the tropical lowlands of the Gulf Coast of modern-day Veracruz and Tabasco, Mexico (Figure 1). This water-logged region of meandering rivers was occupied continuously from at least 1500 BC to the Spanish Conquest, arguably by the same people, but "Olmec" refers only to that period in their history when they created and deployed a spectacular art style and developed novel governmental practices based upon social stratification and kingship. Their earliest monumental sculptures included massive stone thrones and naturalistic, 3-D depictions of rulers, carved as either colossal heads or full-figures (Coe 1965b; see Figure 2). Portable arts included solid and hollow, hand-molded ceramic figurines, predominantly of men. Depictions of supernatural creatures or "dragons" were carved on ceramic vessels and perhaps other perishable media. The term "dragon" has fallen from grace in recent debate, but it still well describes the composite representations of the biologically impossible crocodilian-bird-jaguars or serpent-birds portrayed. Such creatures, lacking

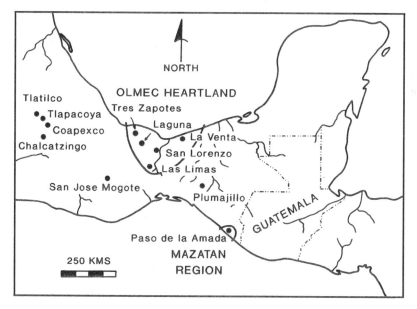

Figure 1 Map of early Mesoamerica showing the locations of sites and regions mentioned in the text.

real-world referents, are thought to depict Olmec supernatural beings, perhaps even gods (Joralemon 1976).

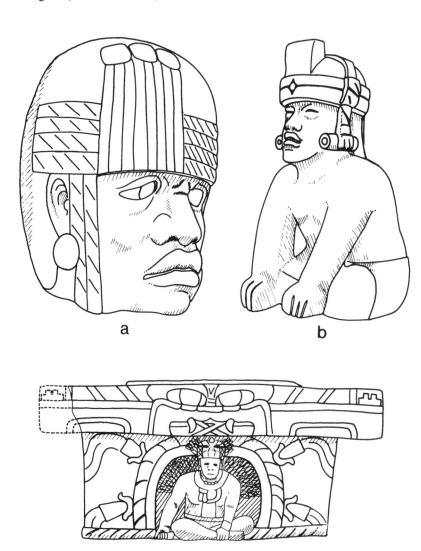

Figure 2 Early Olmec sculpture; not to scale. (*a*) Colossal head, Monument 4, San Lorenzo, Veracruz (1.78 m high, ca 6 tons); (*b*) full-figure sculpture, "The Prince," Cruz del Milagro, Veracruz (1.30 m high, 0.7 tons); (*c*) Table-top throne, Altar 4, La Venta, Tabasco (3.19 m. long, ca 21 tons).

Later Olmec art, dating to the ninth to the fifth centuries BC, was iconographically more complex and has provided greater purchase for modern speculations on ancient Olmec beliefs and practices. At this time, stone carving shifted from 3-D forms to high- and low-relief narrative carvings on relatively flat stone surfaces. Much of this art may portray divine kings dressed in the costume of corn deities (Taube 1996). Other small stone statuettes are thought to depict kings in shamanic transformation (Reilly 1989, 1990). However, there is no clear indication among earlier Olmec representations of either concept.

Four inferences concerning early Olmec history provide a basis for addressing issues of governmentality. 1. Olmec civilization was an indigenous development from the horticultural and fishing societies that inhabited the heartland zone (Stark 1997). 2. These peoples instituted the first stratified society in Middle America and the techniques and practices to sustain it (Coe 1981). 3. Some of the critical props in quotidian governance were stone sculptures, ceramic figurines, and carved pottery that depicted rulers and supernaturals. 4. The phenomenon known as Olmec civilization represented a set of beliefs and practices or lifestyle; these were adopted, whole or in part, by different peoples living outside the heartland zone. The distribution of Olmec-style pots and figurines across early Mesoamerica suggests a rapid spread of Olmec artistic canons—and possibly accompanying Olmec practices of governance. The likelihood of this possibility is the central question of current research.

The past 30 years of debates about Olmec civilization concern its essence and functioning, issues directly linked to questions of governance. What was the nature of Olmec polities? What catalytic impact, if any, did Olmecs have on other societies in Mesoamerica? Essentialist arguments of identity oscillate among designations of the Olmecs as a civilization, complex chiefdom, kingdom, state, or empire (for a summary, see Grove 1997). I prefer the term "kingdom" to designate stratified societies ruled by kings; these can be either complex chiefdoms or states, as the ethnographic records of Polynesia and Africa clearly demonstrate. In kingdoms, the king embodies the body politic and is its principal political force. Lost in most arguments about correct attribution of Olmec polities is the fact that such designations depend on assessments of how these polities actually operated or, in a word, governmentality. Did early Olmec polities exercise coercive force over others, thereby meriting the "state" label, or did they lack such power?

Processual questions of possible Olmec influence are the obverse of the essentialist debates. Mesoamerica as a cultural area began in the twelfth century BC with the development of complex sociopolitical formations based on social stratification. Two rival birth narratives claim to offer Mesoamerica's true history. The "mother culture" narrative sees the Olmecs of the Gulf lowlands as the creators of Mesoamerican civilization and as the purveyors of its institutions to neighboring societies (Coe 1965b, 1968a). The "sister cultures" view envisions multiple sources for the origins of basic Mesoamerican institutions rather than one root source in an Olmec mother culture (Hammond 1988). Instead, complex society arose from the interactions of societies at similar levels of sociopolitical complexity. From the sister cultures perspective, the Olmecs were just one of many societies that contributed to the formulation of the Mesoamerican way of life. Each peer polity retained its independence from the others—before, during, and after the emergence of civilization (Demarest 1989; Flannery & Marcus 1994; Grove 1989, 1996; Grove & Gillespie 1992a,b; Marcus 1989; Niederberger 1996).

The mother culture narrative sees a single, Olmec source for the fundamental institutions that constituted Mesoamerican civilization. The boundaries of Mesoamerica expanded through time as more and more societies adopted basic Olmec institutions surrounding social stratification and kingship (Clark & Perez 1994). The origins and enlargement of Mesoamerica were thus linked historic processes that began about 1150 BC in the Olmec heartland and spread from then and there to other regions. The processes by which Olmec institutions spread to other regions are thought to have involved various techniques of Olmec intervention in neighboring, hinterland regions. Colonization, conquest, ideological persuasion (that is, spread of an Olmec cult), control of long-distance trade, and emulation by local populations of their sophisticated, Olmec neighbors have all been proposed. The mother culture model claims (*a*) temporal priority for Olmec civilization and, by logical implication, (*b*) greater organizational complexity of the Olmecs as compared with their contemporaries. The sister cultures model rejects both claims and views Olmec civilization as neither temporally nor organizationally precocious. I assess these claims in the following sections by addressing questions of early Olmec governance at home and abroad.

OLMEC GOVERNANCE AT HOME

Current evidence indicates that the earliest complex polity in the Olmec region arose at the community now known as San Lorenzo, Veracruz (Coe 1981, Coe & Diehl 1980). San Lorenzo was the first city and stratified society in Mesoamerica. Although its early history has yet to be determined, by the tenth century BC San Lorenzo covered about 690 hectares (Cyphers 1996, p. 67) and was 10 to 20 times larger than any contemporaneous community in Mesoamerica. Current investigators refrain from estimating San Lorenzo's population, pending collection of better data on residential spacing and site limits, but conservative demographic constants of 15 to 25 persons per hectare for tropical lowland communities yields an estimated minimum population of 10,500 to 17,500 people.

San Lorenzo is the only community of the twelfth century BC known to have sponsored the creation of numerous stone monuments. Colossal stone heads, multiton table-top thrones (Figure 2), and lesser monuments were dragged through the tropical rainforest to San Lorenzo from stone outcrops located 60–70 km away. The fabrication and transport of these colossi represented an impressive outlay of resources and labor (Coe 1968b). Other public works projects concerned the construction of San Lorenzo itself. The central portion of the site is a natural, 50-m-high plateau that was intensively and extensively modified in pre-Olmec and early Olmec times by constructing a series of massive, residential terraces that stepped up from the surrounding plain to the summit (Coe & Diehl 1980, Cyphers 1996). Millions of person-hours of labor are represented in these construction projects.

Most discussions of Olmec civilization presume sequential capitals in the heartland, with unified decision-making involved for each. The assumption of solitary, unified polities will probably prove to be incorrect. During the twelfth to tenth centuries BC, the heartland may have had two to five independent, contemporaneous kingdoms (i.e. San Lorenzo, Laguna de los Cerros, La Venta, Las Limas, and Tres Zapotes; Figure 1), with San Lorenzo being the largest (Drucker 1981, Lowe 1997). The presence of other kingdoms must have affected the possibilities and techniques of governance in each. More importantly, kings did not govern alone. San Lorenzo was the capital of a kingdom that had secondary centers and tertiary villages, hamlets, and special function sites (Grove 1997, Symonds 1995). Satellite centers to San Lorenzo were probably administered by princes. Monumental sculpture at these subsidiary centers is less frequent and more restricted in theme than that at San Lorenzo, consisting only of small thrones and sculptures of seated princes (Clark & Perez 1994; see Figure 2b).

San Lorenzo was clearly a hierarchical society consisting of an elite class of a king, nobles, priests, and perhaps craftspersons and traders and a nonelite class of other craftspersons, farmers, hunters, fishers, and carriers (cf Drucker 1981). Slaves may have also been present. The principal means of governing the commoners was to reiterate through ritual drama and oratory the naturalness of class differences and of the superiority of nobles and their rights to rule as entailed in creation myths (Coe 1972), and to inspire a sense of awe, and perhaps fear, for royal power. As a class, the nobility needed to be mindful of the subservience and loyalty of commoners, and sacralized arguments about superior blood or access to supernatural forces sufficed to instill this divisive ideology. As high sovereign, however, the king had to control both the commoners and the nobility. But any ideology about superior essence would have been of little effect among those believed to share it. How, then, did successive San Lorenzo kings simultaneously govern the nobles and commoners and maintain order in the kingdom? Current data suggest that sponsorship of public works and political rituals and control of ideology were all critically important.

Public Works and Largesse as Governance

At San Lorenzo, one can reasonably infer the following kingdom-sponsored activities, each of which may have concerned techniques of governance: public works projects for the construction of massive terraces, plazas, elite residences, platforms, and systems of elaborate stone drains (Coe 1981, Cyphers 1996, Grove 1997); fabrication and transport of an assortment of colossal stone monuments and miscellaneous stone objects such as house pillars, drain stones, and step covers (Cyphers 1996); significant but perhaps ephemeral constructions and activities associated with dragging the largest monuments, including cutting swaths through the jungle, building roads, bridges, and ramps, and constructing rafts and docks (Lowe 1997); periodic movement of multiton monuments within San Lorenzo itself to compose narrative scenes at its different plazas for state rituals (Cyphers Guillen 1994); tribute to accumulate needed foods and supplies to sponsor several thousand people for two or three months as they inched colossal sculptures to San Lorenzo from distant workshops (Clark 1994c); long-distance trade for rare stones and minerals such as obsidian, jade, and iron ores (magnetite and ilmenite), and probably many perishable goods such as cacao and cotton (Coe 1965a, 1968a; Cyphers 1996; Lowe 1989); production of goods for export such as carved wooden bowls, textiles, and some pottery and figurines; and sponsorship of state-rituals and activities such as the ballgame.

The frequency of public works and monument-moving projects at San Lorenzo was truly prodigious. Each represented mobilization of resources and clarion demonstrations of royal might. The labor force deployed in the largest projects would have involved 2000 to 3000 people, a temporary work party roughly the size of the largest neighboring polities to the Olmecs (see below). Ideological motivations for the laborers could have been some notion of reciprocal service due the king for his ritual activities in maintaining prosperity within his kingdom and in interceding with the gods to assure cosmic order and abundant crops (Heizer 1960). It is probable that the king also had the means of extracting his due by force should the occasion arise. In truth, however, we do not know who the servile personnel involved in these activities were nor the motivations compelling them; they may have been anyone from devoted cultists to slaves captured in raids on neighboring polities. The latter situation would have required greater supervision by nobles and enforcers. The obvious exercise of discipline and power in projects involving hundreds of people at one time and in one place would have generated its own self-evident truths of royal right and might, and periodic projects would have kept these truths in the public eye.

The logical complement of public works projects was royal tribute of food and supplies extracted on a regular basis. Commoners probably complied with periodic demands for goods, food, and services. The delegation of authority within each kingdom to princes and lesser nobles may have been to insure the timely collection of tribute and labor service from dependent communities. Again, the potential to apply royal muscle would have been important. Such power could have been exercised to pillage outlander villages. Authorized raiding, no matter how infrequent, would have served to keep distant, dependent villagers loyal to the kingdom, lest they become a target of aggression. The evidence of cannibalism at San Lorenzo (Coe 1994, p. 69) could indicate such aggressive behavior. Raiding would also have provided nobles a means of winning booty and glory in service to their king.

Not all production for export and trade was controlled by the king, but some probably was. One major trade item was small drilled ilmenite cubes. These iron-ore cubes were imported to San Lorenzo from Plumajillo in central Chiapas (Agrinier 1984, Lowe 1989) by the tens of thousands, and most used and broken pieces were subsequently horded in massive caches at San Lorenzo (Cyphers Guillen 1994), which indicates their value and the perceived need to control their distribution. Lowe (1997) argued that Plumajillo was a small, specialized, indigenous community supervised by a minority of elites from San Lorenzo. If true, it would indicate direct Olmec supervision of the production of at least one valuable good in the hinterland.

Specialized imported goods controlled by Olmec kings may have been used as largesse to be distributed among elites to curry their favor. Fine obsidian blades imported from highland Guatemala and central Mexico would have been especially prized as ritual bloodletters and may have been dispersed in this manner (Clark 1987). Whatever their utilitarian function, if any, the ilmenite cubes may have served as bride wealth or a standard medium of exchange (Clark 1994c, 1996) and thus have made particularly valuable gifts.

The activities mentioned above touch on several stratagems for keeping a potentially restless elite in check. The highest-born elite, those with claims to the throne, represented the greatest threat to the king's rule. Olmec kings at San Lorenzo appear to have exercised at least two options for governing the nobility: keeping them busy and buying their loyalty. Royal largesse of foreign goods, tributed foodstuffs and handicrafts, lands, rights to labor services of servants or slaves, and possibly granting of titles at royal banquets or appropriate rituals. The king also installed nobility in administrative positions in satellite centers, and perhaps distant centers (see below), and possibly made them priests and other functionaries of the royal house, directors of construction projects, supervisors of monument carving and moving projects, or perhaps in charge of specialized workshops for the production of sumptuary goods. Of course, royal strategies for retaining supreme power by sharing discrete portions of it fostered the conditions for undermining it completely. In this light, possible evidence of palace revolts and changes in kingship at San Lorenzo (Coe 1967b) is of special interest. These involved destruction or mutilation of stone monuments associated with the king.

Ritual Use and Abuse of Monuments as Regal Legitimacy

When it comes to Olmec rituals, exuberant speculation has greatly outstripped the data. We currently lack concrete evidence of the public rituals that sanctified kings' rights to reign, such as succession rituals, enthronement ceremonies, building dedications, ritual peregrinations around kingdom borders, or even mortuary rites. Conjectures about the types of rituals that may have been present include ritual bloodletting with stingray spines, jade awls, or obsidian blades by rulers for the benefit of their people (Flannery & Marcus 1976, p. 380); possible human sacrifice (Ortiz & Rodriguez 1994); votive offerings around monuments, in springs, and on mountain tops (Ortiz & Rodriguez 1994); axe offerings (Coe 1967a, p. 1399; Ortiz & Rodriguez 1994); empowerment or succession rituals in caves (Coe 1972, Grove 1973); ritual enactments of primal myths (Coe 1972); and drug-induced shamanic trances (Reilly 1994b). Given the paucity of data, it is ironic that the supposed clearest case for early ritual ("decommissioning" of monuments) may actually relate to antiritual—desecration of sources of royal power—rather than rituals to perpetuate the institution of rulership.

The majority of Olmec full-figured statuary is of seated males (de la Fuente 1996), and almost all of these have been decapitated. Early investigators speculated that this monument mutilation resulted from conquest by outsiders (Stirling 1940, p. 334), destruction by Olmec revolutionaries (Coe 1967b, p. 25), iconoclastic destruction by disillusioned believers (Heizer 1960), or mutilation by later peoples (Drucker et al 1959, p. 230). In a provocative essay, Grove (1981) considered the pattern of monument mutilation "as a key to meaning." The basic pattern for monument mutilation includes the following: Monument mutilation was not confined to the Olmec heartland; destruction and defacement of monuments spanned at least six centuries (1200 to 600 BC); and thrones and full-figure representations of elite males received the worst abuse, colossal heads incurred ceremonial damage but not major breakage or defacement, and explicitly religious monuments with supernatural beings received little mutilation (Grove 1981).[1] According to Grove, the spatial and temporal extent of monument mutilation, as well as its thematic selectivity, is not due to conquest or revolution because these are infrequent and localized events. How, then, to account for the broad patterns?

Relying on ethnographic analogy, Grove (1981) posited that the personal objects associated with sacred chiefs (considered kings here) were infused with their power, and this power had to be neutralized upon each chief's death to prevent it from running amok and undermining the social order. Consequently, the most powerful objects had to be broken and buried as part of the mortuary rites of the deceased chief; the more powerful the objects, the more necessary their neutralization. Assuming a direct correlation between the degree of mutilation and the power of the monument, Grove found that thrones were the most powerful objects, followed by full portraits of rulers; the colossal stone heads showed surprisingly little damage.

I believe Grove is correct in relating mutilation to the power of the object and in equating breakage with its neutralization, but I question the reason for such acts. Personalized thrones and statues of kings were the principal targets of breakage, while images of supernaturals, presumably also of great power, were left relatively untouched. In short, monuments with cosmological power were spared while monuments with personalized, political power were not. Grove's intriguing conclusion fails to account for all of the evidence because not all kingly portraits and thrones were destroyed (see Figure 2b). If breakage of statuary occurred as an integral act of royal mortuary rites, why would any have been spared?

A model based on factional politics suggests that the monuments destroyed were tied to explicit claims of legitimacy for particular rulers. One could dethrone a king by actually destroying his throne and statue. If true, this raises the possibility that the unmutilated colossal heads were generally portraits of deceased kings and that their destruction may not have been politically expedient. Preservation of these monuments, as well as carvings of deities, may have been desirable. As sources of power and potential legitimacy, monuments and the accouterments of rulership would have been major sources of contention

---

[1]Mutilation of early Olmec monuments varied in kind and degree. Most of the colossal heads show extensive, intentional pitting and grooving, perhaps to deface the monument, but no significant breakage. Given their massive size and roundish shape, however, they would have been particularly difficult to break (M Coe, personal communication, 1997). If intentional pitting of the colossal heads were meant as ritual defacement analogous to the decapitation of full-figure monuments, then any speculations based upon the postulated lack of significant mutilation of these monuments are erroneous.

among heirs to a throne. A secondary heir had nothing to gain and much to lose by destroying monuments of his deceased father or grandfathers but could well benefit by desecrating those of his reigning older brother or cousin. Recarving the throne of one's rival into a colossal head [at least two were so transformed (Porter 1989)] would have been a particularly fitting way to establish one's new claim to kingship and a royal line.

As mentioned above, San Lorenzo may have experienced several revolts before its eventual collapse; it may also have suffered from outside raids (Coe 1994, p. 69). The temporal pattern of monument destruction documented by Grove (1981) may indicate that factional competition for the throne was a recurring phenomenon and that Olmec nobility did not take governance well. The later Maya believed that stone monuments of their kings shared a literal spiritual essence or identity with the kings portrayed (Houston & Stuart 1997). If a similar notion existed among the Olmecs, decapitation of the king's portrait statue represented literal regicide, and the detached head may have been taken away as a trophy and sign of conquest. I anticipate that the missing heads from monuments will be found in elite contexts, as is the case for the severed head recovered in an elite grave at Chalcatzingo (Grove 1981, p. 58).

Iconography as Ideologies of Supernatural Monopoly

Native rhetoric at the time of the Spanish Conquest portrayed rulership as exemplary kingship, with kings being models of comportment for their subjects. Metaphorically, kings were honorifically addressed as magnificent shade trees that protected their people, mirrors for reflecting the divine, flutes that relayed the messages of the gods, or burden bearers who willingly bore the onerous weight of government on their backs (Sahagun 1969). Kings were responsible for the well-being of their subjects and interceded with the gods to ensure annual abundance.

Although not all these concepts can be traced back in time, visual representations of earlier kings suggest that some post-Classic metaphors have a deep history. Classic Maya kings were associated with mirrors and cosmic trees (Schele 1996); and earlier Olmec kings were portrayed in similar fashion (Coe 1972). During the ninth to fifth centuries BC, Olmec kings were depicted in regalia that included elaborate dress, jewelry, scepters, and headdresses. Images of trees, corn plants, or cosmic center (quincunx) designs adorned their headdresses and clothing, suggesting that kings were symbolizing their mediating cosmic roles as *axis mundi* (Reilly 1994a,b, 1996; Schele 1996; Taube 1996). The ability to monopolize access to the supernatural realm is thought to have been the principal source of power of early kings and the reason for their sway over their subjects. It is worth noting that pervasive loyalty among his subjects would have been a king's principal social resource in governing the nobility;

common support for the king would have provided sufficient incentive to lesser nobles to publicly acknowledge the king's supernatural superiority, thereby compromising their own possibilities for Machiavellian maneuvering.

A variant of the theme of royal power derives from a different corpus of middle Olmec statuettes that appear to depict sequential moments in the shamanic transformation of an adult male into a jaguar (Furst 1996; Reilly 1989, 1990). Other art suggests that kings attired themselves as avian deities with shamanic powers (Kappelman 1997; see Figure 2c). In both cases, the king in transformation traverses the portal to the nether world. Kingly power was thus tied to the ability to effect a trance state and to commune with supernaturals (Reilly 1994b). Such abilities could have been claimed rhetorically and artistically or dramatized through public rituals on frequent occasions and could have promoted general belief in their actuality.

The time of the first Olmec kings lies between the earlier period of figurine complexes, interpreted as evidence for village shamans-chiefs (Clark 1991), and the middle Olmec period of divine kings with shamanic powers (Reilly 1994a,b, 1996). With this convenient bracketing, one would expect a logical progression from early village shaman-chiefs to later Olmec shaman-kings, but such does not appear to have been the case. Representations of the earliest Olmec rulers are naturalistic portrayals of adult males wearing simple headgear and ear ornaments (Figure 2a,b), neither of which appears to signal shamanic garb or divine costume.

Iconographically, there appears to be a clear discontinuity during the early Olmec period in the representation of rulers, and this may, in fact, represent a real discontinuity in conception and not just portrayal. Early Olmec kings were depicted as ballplayers or warriors rather than shamans or gods (Coe 1968a, Taube 1992). Minor support for this inference comes from the high frequency of clay figurines of ballplayers in the Olmec heartland at this time (Coe & Diehl 1980). It is also of interest that the most convincing representations of early leaders in the Basin of Mexico, after Olmec contact, were portrayed in elaborate ballplaying gear and headdresses (Bradley & Joralemon 1993, Niederberger 1987). If the Olmecs had a creation myth similar to the Maya epic *Popul Vuh,* self-portrayals as ballplayers would have linked the rulers metaphorically to the creation of the world. Early Olmec kings visually stressed a different metaphor of power than later Olmec and Maya Kings, and one that evoked physical prowess rather than access to the supernatural. This may correspond to a greater role of coercion in Olmec governance than is commonly thought.

Lack of clear evidence in portraiture of privileged access to spiritual forces does not, of course, necessarily signal its absence. There remains the evidence of dragon pots. The images on these pots are thought to represent Olmec gods

(Coe 1989; Joralemon 1976, 1996) or supernatural forces (Marcus 1989). The temporal and spatial distribution in Mesoamerica of vessels with Olmec supernaturals suggests that they were adopted for socially significant reasons. If such vessels were used in rituals to invoke the supernatural entities depicted on them, their wide distribution could be evidence of alliances between Olmec rulers and hinterland clients who sought greater status by tapping into Olmec sources of political and ritual power.

OLMEC GOVERNANCE ABROAD

Before the formative twelfth century, proto-Mesoamerica was populated by small, independent village societies that interacted with one another, as clearly apparent in the distribution of trade goods. Later, most of these same societies experienced significant interaction with the Olmecs, as evident by the presence of Olmec-style figurines and dragon pots in hinterland regions about 1100–1000 BC. As noted, the "supernatural" motifs on these vessels suggest that some critical cosmological ideas may have been communicated and powers conferred. In each region for which data are adequate, the appearance of these artifacts corresponded precisely to a significant change in the organization and/or size of local populations and their possible level of sociopolitical complexity (Figure 3). The question of a causal connection between Olmec contact and local evolution is thus unavoidable. The nature of Olmec interaction with hinterland societies is most easily checked by comparing developmental histories of societies in the heartland with those from adjacent regions. Here I compare developmental histories of hinterland communities to that of San Lorenzo discussed above.

A Comparison of Early Mesoamerican Communities

During its apogee in the tenth century BC, the Olmec capital at San Lorenzo encompassed an area of nearly 7 km², possibly with upward of 14,000 inhabitants. In contrast, Coapexco, the largest known community in the Mexican highlands at this time, covered 10 ha and had an estimated, dense population of 1420–1640 persons (Tolstoy 1989, p. 95); Tlatilco and Tlapacoya, two neighboring centers, are estimated respectively at 30 and 25 ha (Niederberger 1987, pp. 701–2). San José Mogote, the largest community in the highlands of Oaxaca, covered 60–70 ha at 900 BC and had an estimated 1000 inhabitants (Marcus & Flannery 1996, p. 106). In the Pacific lowlands of Chiapas, Paso de la Amada, the largest community at 1300 BC, was over 50 ha in size and accommodated an estimated 1500 persons (Clark 1994b, p. 380). In terms of simple demographics, San Lorenzo appears to have been qualitatively different from its neighbors.

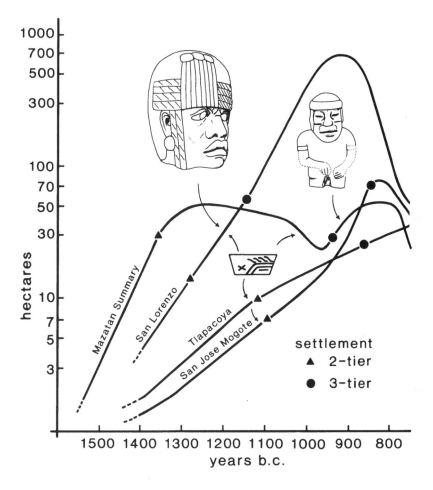

Figure 3   Comparative summary of changes in community sizes, settlement size-hierarchies, and Olmec influence in early Mesoamerica. The log scale of the vertical axis allows juxtaposition of San Lorenzo on the same graph with its smaller contemporaries. The horizontal axis represents radiocarbon years. Olmec influence is indicated by the earliest occurrence of carved "dragon" pots in each sequence (represented by the central trapezoid icon). "Settlement" refers to size hierarchies rather than inferred administrative hierarchies; changes in the settlement hierarchy are a rough surrogate measure of shifts in sociopolitical complexity. The Mazatan line summarizes sequential centers rather than one because the largest centers were abandoned with the advent of Olmec hegemony in the region. The early parts of the slopes of community size for San Lorenzo, San José Mogote, and Tlapacoya are hypothetical pending more secure data.

Evaluations of residences and public buildings at these same communities lead to a similar conclusion. During the eleventh century BC, San José Mogote lacked residences that were clearly elite (Marcus & Flannery 1996, p. 103; Winter 1989), and public structures were small, one-room, rectangular buildings constructed of mud-covered pine poles and thatch and with crushed rock floors covered with plaster (Flannery & Marcus 1990, p. 23–29; Marcus & Flannery 1996, pp. 87, 109). Large platforms for public buildings were erected at the site in the tenth to ninth centuries BC (Marcus & Flannery 1996, p. 109). Basal mounds for public buildings are also reported for Tlapacoya and Tlatilco in the Basin of Mexico and Chalcatzingo in Morelos (Niederberger 1987, p. 702). These platforms were of modest size (for Chalcatzingo, 2 m high and more than 15 m long) and probably supported perishable superstructures (Grove 1996, p. 108). Public buildings are unknown for Paso de la Amada (Clark 1994b; contra Marcus & Flannery 1996, p. 91), but this community did have an early ballcourt that measured 80 m in length and would have required 30 people 25 days to construct (Hill 1996). The impressive chiefly residence at this same site required similar amounts of labor to build (Blake 1991).

The total combined labor invested in public and elite architecture at all five hinterland centers mentioned, however, would be the equivalent of one terrace at San Lorenzo. It is worth noting that one, 12-m-long apsidal elite dwelling at San Lorenzo was raised on a 2-m-high basal platform measuring 50 by 75 m. A recently discovered residence had a massive 3.5-m tall central basalt pillar to support roof beams, as well as carved stone step covers, stone benches, an elaborate stone drain, and plastered and painted walls, both inside and out (Cyphers 1996, p. 66). San Lorenzo was an order of magnitude beyond its contemporaries in terms of labor investments in public and domestic architecture, stone monuments, public works, and community size. Mesoamerica would not see another city of the disproportionate magnitude of San Lorenzo for another millennium [e.g. El Mirador, Peten, Guatemala (Hansen 1990)].

Arguments for interaction among relatively equal partners in early Olmec times and lack of disparities among them are based upon (a) recourse to old data that underestimated the size of San Lorenzo at 53 ha (essentially its elite ward on the plateau), and (b) dismissal of its stone monuments, either by arguing that they are not as early as was thought (Graham 1989, Hammond 1988) or as socially significant as claimed (Flannery & Marcus 1994; Grove 1993; Grove & Gillespie 1992a,b; Marcus & Flannery 1996). Recent research demonstrates that the monuments are indeed early and present in greater frequencies than thought (Cyphers 1996, Grove 1997) and socially significant (Clark 1994c, 1996).

The striking disparities among early communities were actually greater than suggested. Most of the preceding comparisons involve eleventh or tenth century hinterland communities that, without exception, evince clear Olmec influence (Figure 3); thus, their size and complexity at that time may have benefited from an Olmec stimulus. More appropriate comparisons would be of these same communities at 1250 BC, before significant Olmec contact. In this time frame, possibilities for organizational parity evaporate. In the Basin of Mexico, only Tlapacoya has a documented pre-Olmec occupation, and none of its modest public platforms had yet been constructed. Nor is there any indication of rank society at this time in all of the highlands.

The Olmecs and Their Neighbors

In the 1950s, Olmec-style artifacts were seen as evidence of colonization or conquest of highland peoples by Olmec lowlanders (Covarrubias 1946, 1950). Later research demonstrated clear continuity of local populations in each suspected colonized locale. Local populations merely adopted Olmec-style artifacts and iconography and were not replaced by colonists or invaders (Niederberger 1987). Flannery (1968) proposed that Olmec-style objects in the highlands signaled asymmetrical but mutually beneficial trade relationships between these societies and the Olmecs. The lowland Olmecs gained access to desired highland resources, and the highlanders received ritually charged, prestige goods that they used to pursue higher status in their own local systems. Flannery & Marcus (1994) have since modified this view and now see the highland peoples of the Valley of Oaxaca as true peers with the Olmecs of San Lorenzo. The Oaxaca peoples adopted the supposed Olmec motifs, as did all societies in the early interaction sphere, but these motifs of supernaturals were put to local use to mark lineage membership and were not prestige goods signaling Olmec connections as once thought.

The observation that Olmec-style artifacts appear to have been used idiosyncratically in different hinterland regions (see Grove 1989, Marcus 1989, Tolstoy 1989) reveals nothing about specific Olmec connections. Why were these artifacts and symbols adopted by non-Olmec peoples in the first instance? Unfortunately, data from highland sites are currently not fine-grained enough to differentiate between two critical processes conflated in this pattern of artifact distribution: the initial adoption of foreign artifacts and their subsequent local use and modification once adopted. Such a distinction is critical, however, for sorting out the question of possible Olmec impact on hinterland regions. The critical processes may have occurred in less than a decade, but scholars attempt to evaluate them by monitoring time in two- to three-century segments. Recent data from the Mazatan region provide a finer-grained chronology (Blake et al 1995) and do allow a better appraisal of Olmec influence in one hinterland region.

The Mazatan case represents a severe challenge to the mother culture model as rank and simple chiefdom societies (indicated by the two-tiered settlement hierarchy in Figure 3) in this lowland region antedate their presence in the Olmec heartland. The Olmecs may have received their initial stimulus to develop complex society from the coastal dwellers of the Soconusco region (Clark & Blake 1989). Similarities in basic artifact inventories indicate sustained interaction between the two groups beginning by 1500 BC (Coe 1994).

The emergence of simple chiefdom societies in Mazatan appears to have been a local process aided by the manipulation of foreign contacts and long-distance exchange. Numerous goods were procured through trade, including obsidian, jade, mica, and greenstone; cacao was probably exported in return. By 1350 BC, the Mazatan region was home to half a dozen or more small, independent village chiefdoms (Clark & Blake 1994). Paso de la Amada was the seat of the largest chiefdom that had a population of 3000 to 5000 people (Clark 1994b). At about 1100 BC, significant contact with the Gulf Coast Olmecs became evident in the presence of imported ceramic vessels (*sans* dragon designs) and human figurines. These served as templates for producing local copies of these imported forms. Thus, the initial period of clear Olmec influence in the Soconusco involved trade and emulation by a thriving, independent society (Clark 1990).

In the first half of the eleventh century, the Mazatan region underwent radical reorganization that can be attributed to intervention by Olmecs. All the formerly independent simple chiefdoms were consolidated into one complex chiefdom directed from a new regional center established in the middle of the region. Most of the former head villages of the traditional simple chiefdoms were abandoned, and their inhabitants were relocated to newly founded villages nearby, testimony of forced abandonment of former seats of political legitimacy. Most artifacts indicate a significant shift to Olmec-style utensils; ceramic vessels (now including dragon pots), figurines, and grinding stones are clearly similar to those from the Olmec heartland. Monumental stone sculpture in the regional center was also in the Olmec style (Figure 3). In short, the new Mazatan polity overtly signaled its connections to the heartland Olmecs in a range of media, from domestic cooking vessels and figurines to public art (Clark 1993, 1994a; Clark & Blake 1989).

Two phenomena related to reorganization are of interest. First, local consumption of foreign, imported goods outside the new regional center declined dramatically (Clark 1990). Second, there appears to have been a significant population decline (Clark 1994b). Coupled with preceding observations, these data appear to indicate an aggressive takeover of the Mazatan region by their former trade allies, the Olmecs. The ethnic base population in Mazatan remained the same, with the likely addition of some Olmec elites at the apex of a now more complex political system based on social stratification rather than rank (Clark 1993, 1994a). Olmec influence in Mazatan varied in kind and intensity through time, beginning with trade and emulation and ending in coercion and the actual presence of some Olmecs in the region. The processes for insinuating Olmec hegemony into Mazatan remain the topic of research, but I suspect that it was the age-old situation of one faction of competing aggrandizers in the Mazatan zone supplicating their trade partners for help in gaining political clout locally, with the eventual consequence being that their Olmec allies came and helped—and then helped themselves.

More data are needed to corroborate changing patterns of settlement and artifact use, but it appears plausible that an Olmec king controlled the Mazatan region by dispatching a contingent of elites and bodyguards to govern in his name. Alternatively, dissident nobles may have fled the heartland zone and forged an alliance with a local, Mazatan chief (or an aspiring chief), gained control over the region, and reorganized it like their mother polity. The canonic Olmec symbolism used at the time signaled close ties to San Lorenzo, suggesting that the Mazatan region was ultimately directed from afar rather than by Olmec separatists. The particular interest in governing Mazatan may have been to control the cacao trade and to monitor the transshipment of the obsidian and jade being exported to the heartland from highland Guatemala. Given the logistical difficulties of governing Mazatan from a 400-km distance, any heartland control must have been loose and perhaps have consisted merely of periodic shipments of tribute goods and laborers, or even slaves, from Mazatan to the Olmec heartland. Most governance would have been local, with the reigning Olmec prince having considerable flexibility in Mazatan.

It is worth stressing that Olmec hegemony in Mazatan implies nothing about other regions. The Olmecs, for example, may not have troubled themselves with the small social groups in the semi-arid highlands with whom there may have been language barriers. Early monumental Olmec sculpture is unknown in highland regions, and local artifact inventories retained a local character, with overt Olmec-style objects being limited to carved bowls, figurines, and cylinder seals. These observations suggest the likelihood that Olmec interaction with hinterland societies took a variety of forms depending on the particular partner involved. Mazatan appears to have come under Olmec control, but the highlanders may have retained their independence, with Olmec objects there resulting from trade and emulation.

CONCLUSIONS

The obvious conclusion suggested by my summary of research on early Olmec governance, and by my speculative treatment of the most recent data, is that much more research will be required before the principal issues of early governmentality can be addressed adequately. Future investigations need to consider additional Olmec sites and other hinterland regions. Of critical importance will be the alignment of regional sequences to assess the comparative histories of events and institutionalized practices, both within and between polities. My preliminary attempt at such an analysis here suggests that the basic claim of the mother culture theory is correct, namely, that the heartland Olmec were organizationally precocious in early Mesoamerica. The Olmec instituted a political economy based on social stratification and kingship well before any of their peers. The impact of this historic event was felt throughout early Mesoamerica to varying degrees.

In light of current debates concerning Olmec governmentality, my assessment of the data is ambivalent. The early comparative history of Mesoamerica supports the basic assumptions of the mother culture model but some of the conclusions of the sister cultures model. The Olmecs were the strongest polity in the neighborhood, but they did not subjugate all their neighbors. The ambivalence arising between the two models lies in the difference between ability and action, or in potential influence and actual influence. Many mother culture models mistake the potential for influence for its actuality. In turn, all sister cultures models take the lack of clear evidence of influence as evidence for its absence, and for the absence of its potential. Such reductionist assumptions are inappropriate. Interactions between the Olmecs and their neighbors need to be assessed on a case by case basis to determine the nature of the interaction, the level of complexity of each polity, the contributions to the interaction by both parties, and the significance of the interaction for each. Currently, the data suggest that the Olmecs forcibly took over the Mazatan region and controlled it for their own purposes. In contrast, their foreign relations with other hinterland polities appear to have been of a different sort. In some cases, hinterland peoples may have emulated the sophisticated Olmecs; in others, neighboring polities may merely have traded with the Olmecs or ignored them altogether.

Within their own kingdoms, Olmec rulers governed through a variety of means. Most discussions of Olmec governance stress the role of ideology and ritual power in the orderly operation of these early polities. Here I suggest that more mundane activities may have played an equally important part. In particular, the mobilization of labor for public works projects may have been a principal means of instilling concepts of good citizenry into one's subjects through simple physical toil. Control of the manufacture and deployment of monumental art was another means, both in terms of the actual physical carving and portage of monuments as well as in the ability to control its thematic content and meaning (Clark 1996). Other activities of the political economy, such as the production and exchange of precious goods, were probably also of major importance.

Given the data, it would be premature to claim resolution of any questions of early Olmec governance. I am hopeful that all the speculative claims made here will be contested by those whose interests they do not serve. In future debates over the adequacy of various data and their parsimonious interpretation, Foucault's (1991) concept of governmentality and his genealogical method of careful historic documentation will serve the field well by providing a framework for discussion and a method for research.

ACKNOWLEDGMENTS

The content and argumentative tone of this paper have greatly benefited from comments from Michael Blake, Elizabeth Brumfiel, Kent Flannery, David Grove, Stephen Houston, Gareth Lowe, Joyce Marcus, and Barbara Stark. I appreciate their interest and candid advice.

> Visit the *Annual Reviews home page* at
> http://www.AnnualReviews.org.

Literature Cited

Agrinier P. 1984. *The Early Olmec Horizon at Mirador, Chiapas, Mexico. Pap. New World Archaeol. Found., No. 48.* Provo: Brigham Young Univ. Press

Benson EP, ed. 1968. *Dumbarton Oaks Conference on the Olmec.* Washington, DC: Dumbarton Oaks

Benson EP, ed. 1981. *The Olmec and Their Neighbors: Essays in Memory of Matthew W. Stirling.* Washington, DC: Dumbarton Oaks

Benson EP, ed. 1996. *The Olmec World: Ritual and Rulership.* Princeton, NJ: The Art Museum, Princeton Univ.

Benson EP, de la Fuente B, eds. 1996. *Olmec Art of Ancient Mexico.* Washington, DC: National Gallery of Art

Blake M. 1991. An emerging early formative chiefdom at Paso de la Amada, Chiapas, Mexico. See Fowler 1991, pp. 27–46

Blake M, Clark JE, Voorhies B, Michaels G, Love MW. 1995. Radiocarbon chronology for the late archaic and formative periods on the Pacific Coast of southeastern Mesoamerica. *Anc. Mesoam.* 6:161–83

Bradley DE, Joralemon PD. 1993. *The Lords of Life: The Iconography of Power and Fertility in Preclassic Mesoamerica.* South Bend: Snite Mus. Art, Univ. Notre Dame

Burchell G, Gordon C, Miller P, eds. 1991. *The Foucault Effect: Studies in Governmentality.* Chicago: Univ. Chicago Press

Clark JE. 1987. Politics, prismatic blades, and Mesoamerica civilization. In *The Organization of Core Technology,* ed. JK Johnson, CA Morrow, pp. 259–84. Boulder: Westview

Clark JE. 1990. Olmecas, Olmequismo y Olmequización en Mesoamerica. *Arqueologia* 3:49–56

Clark JE. 1991. The beginnings of Mesoamerica: apologia for the Soconusco Early Formative. See Fowler 1991, pp. 13–26

Clark JE. 1993. Una Reevaluación de la Entidad Política Olmeca: ?Imperio, Estado o Cacicazgo? In *Segundo y Tercer Foro de Arqueología de Chiapas,* ed. TA Lee Jr, pp. 159–69. Tuxtla Gutierrez: Inst. Chiapaneco Cult.

Clark JE. 1994a. Antecedentes de la cultural Olmeca. See Clark 1994d, pp. 31–41

Clark JE. 1994b. *The development of early formative rank societies in the Soconusco, Chiapas, Mexico.* PhD thesis. Univ. Michigan, Ann Arbor. 593 pp.

Clark JE. 1994c. El Sistema Económico de los primeros Olmecas. See Clark 1994d, pp. 189–201

Clark JE, ed. 1994d. *Los Olmecas en Mesoamerica.* Mexico: Equilibrista

Clark JE. 1996. Craft specialization and Olmec civilization. In *Craft Specialization and Social Evolution: In Memory of V. Gordon Childe, Univ. Mus. Monogr. 93,* ed. B Wailes, pp. 187–99. Philadelphia: Univ. Mus. Archaeol. Anthropol.

Clark JE, Blake M. 1989. El origen de la civilización en Mesoamérica: los Olmecas y Mokaya del Soconusco de Chiapas, Mexico. In *El Preclásico o Formativo: Avances y Perspectivas,* ed. M Carmona Macias, pp. 385–403. Mexico City: Museo Nacl. Antropol.

Clark JE, Blake M. 1994. The power of prestige: competitive generosity and the emergence of rank societies in lowland Mesoamerica. In *Factional Competition and Political Development in the New World,* ed. EM Brumfiel, JW Fox, pp. 17–30. Cambridge: Cambridge Univ. Press

Clark JE, Perez T. 1994. Los Olmecas y el Primer Milenio de Mesoamérica. See Clark 1994d, pp. 261–75

Coe MD. 1965a. *The Jaguar's Children: Preclassic Central Mexico.* New York: Mus. Primit. Art

Coe MD. 1965b. The Olmec style and its distribution. In *Handbook of Middle American Indians: Archaeology of Southern Mesoamerica,* ed. R Wauchope, 3:739–75. Austin: Univ. Tex. Press

Coe MD. 1967a. Olmec civilization, Veracruz, Mexico: dating of the San Lorenzo phase. *Science* 155:1399–401

Coe MD. 1967b. Solving a monumental mystery. *Discovery* 3:21–26

Coe MD. 1968a. *America's First Civilization.* New York: Am. Heritage

Coe MD. 1968b. San Lorenzo and Olmec Civilization. See Benson 1968, pp. 41–71

Coe MD. 1972. Olmec jaguars and Olmec kings. In *The Cult of the Feline: A Conference in Pre-Columbian Iconography,* ed. EP Benson, pp. 1–18. Washington, DC: Dumbarton Oaks

Coe MD. 1981. San Lorenzo Tenochtitlan. In *Supplement to the Handbook of Middle American Indians: Archaeology,* ed. JA Sabloff, pp. 117–46. Austin: Univ. Tex. Press

Coe MD. 1989. The Olmec heartland: evolution of ideology. See Sharer & Grove 1989, pp. 68–82

Coe MD. 1994. *Mexico: From the Olmecs to the Aztecs.* London: Thames & Hudson. 4th ed.

Coe MD, Diehl RA. 1980. *In the Land of the Olmec: The Archaeology of San Lorenzo Tenochtitlán.* Austin: Univ. Tex. Press

Covarrubias M. 1946. El arte Olmeca o de La Venta. *Cuad. Am.* 4:154–79

Covarrubias M. 1950. Tlatilco: el arte y la cultura preclasica del Valle de Mexico. *Cuad. Am.* 9:149–62

Cyphers A. 1996. Reconstructing Olmec life at San Lorenzo. See Benson & de la Fuente 1996, pp. 61–71

Cyphers Guillen A. 1994. San Lorenzo Tenochtitlan. See Clark 1994d, pp. 43–67

de la Fuente B. 1996. Homocentrism in Olmec monumental art. See Benson & de la Fuente 1996, pp. 41–49

Demarest AA. 1989. The Olmec and the rise of civilization in Eastern Mesoamerica. See Sharer & Grove 1989, pp. 303–44

Drennan RD. 1976. Religion and social evolution in formative Mesoamerica. In *The Early Mesoamerican Village,* ed. KV Flannery, pp. 345–64. New York: Academic

Drucker P. 1981. On the nature of Olmec polity. See Benson 1981, pp. 29–47

Drucker P, Heizer RF, Squier RJ. 1959. Excavations at La Venta, Tabasco, 1955. *Smithsonian Institution, Bureau of American Ethnology, Bull. 170.* Washington, DC: US Gov. Print. Off.

Flannery KV. 1968. The Olmec and the Valley of Oaxaca: a model for interregional interaction in formative times. See Benson 1968, pp. 79–117

Flannery KV, Marcus J. 1976. Formative Oaxaca and the Zapotec Cosmos. *Am. Sci.* 64:374–83

Flannery KV, Marcus J. 1990. *Borrón, y Cuenta Nueva:* setting Oaxaca's archaeological record straight. In *Debating Oaxaca Archaeology. Anthropol. Pap. No. 84,* ed. J Marcus, pp. 17–69. Ann Arbor: Mus. Anthropol., Univ. Mich.

Flannery KV, Marcus J. 1994. *Early Formative Pottery of the Valley of Oaxaca, Mexico. Mem. Mus. Anthropol. No. 27.* Ann Arbor: Mus. Anthropol., Univ. Michigan

Flannery KV, Marcus J. 1996. Cognitive archaeology. In *Contemporary Archaeology in Theory: A Reader,* ed. RW Preucel, I Hodder, pp. 350–63. Oxford: Blackwell

Foucault M. 1991. Governmentality. See Burchell et al 1991, pp. 87–104

Fowler WR, ed. 1991. *The Formation of Complex Society in Southeastern Mesoamerica.* Boca Raton: CRC Press

Furst PT. 1996. Shamanism, transformation, and Olmec art. See Benson 1996, pp. 69–81

Gordon C. 1991. Governmental rationality: an introduction. See Burchell et al 1991, pp. 1–51

Graham J. 1989. Olmec diffusion: a sculptural view from Pacific Guatemala. See Sharer & Grove 1989, pp. 227–46

Grove DC. 1973. Olmec altars and myths. *Archaeology* 26:128–35

Grove DC. 1981. Olmec monuments: mutilation as a clue to meaning. See Benson 1981, pp. 49–68

Grove DC. 1989. Olmec: What's in a name? See Sharer & Grove 1989, pp. 8–14

Grove DC. 1993. "Olmec" horizons in formative period Mesoamerica: Diffusion or social evolution? In *Latin American Horizons,* ed. DS Rice, pp. 83–111. Washington, DC: Dumbarton Oaks

Grove DC. 1996. Archaeological contexts of Olmec art outside of the gulf coast. See Benson & de la Fuente 1996, pp. 105–17

Grove DC. 1997. Olmec archaeology: a half century of research and its accomplishments. *J. World Prehist.* 11(1):51–101

Grove DC, Gillespie SD. 1992a. Archaeological indicators of formative period elites: a perspective from central Mexico. In *Mesoamerican Elites: An Archaeological Assessment,* ed. DZ Chase, AF Chase, pp. 191–205. Norman: Univ. Okla. Press

Grove DC, Gillespie SD. 1992b. Ideology and evolution at the prestate level. In *Ideology and Pre-Columbian Civilizations,* ed. AA Demarest, GW Conrad, pp. 15–36. Santa Fe, NM: Sch. Am. Res. Press

Hammond N. 1988. Cultura hermana: reappraising the Olmec. *Q. Rev. Archaeol.* 9(4):1–4

Hansen RD. 1990. *Excavations in the Tigre Complex, El Mirador, Peten, Guatemala. Pap. New World Archaeol. Found., No. 62.* Provo, UT: Brigham Young Univ. Press

Heizer RF. 1960. Agriculture and the theocratic state in lowland southeastern Mexico. *Am. Antiq.* 26:215–22

Hill WD. 1996. *Mesoamerica's earliest ballcourt and the origins of inequality.* Presented at Annu. Meet. Am. Archaeol. Soc., 61, New Orleans

Houston SD, Stuart DS. 1997. The presentation of self in royal life: personhood and portraiture among the classic Maya. *Res: Anthropol. Aesthet.* In press

Joralemon PD. 1976. The Olmec dragon: a study in pre-Columbian iconography. In *Origins of Religious Art and Iconography in Preclassic Mesoamerica,* ed. HB Nickolson, pp. 27–71. Los Angeles: Latin Am. Cent. Publ. Ethnic Arts Counc. Los Angeles, Univ. Calif.

Joralemon PD. 1996. In search of the Olmec cosmos: reconstructing the world view of Mexico's first civilization. See Benson & de la Fuente 1996, pp. 51–59

Kappelman JG. 1997. *Of Macaws and men: late preclassic cosmology and political ideology in Izapan-style monuments.* PhD thesis. Univ. Tex., Austin. 565 pp.

Lowe GW. 1989. The heartland Olmec: evolution of material culture. See Sharer & Grove 1989, pp. 33–67

Lowe GW. 1997. *Los Olmecas: Diez Preguntas.* Mexico City: Univ. Nac. Autón. Méx.

Marcus J. 1989. Zapotec chiefdoms and the nature of formative religions. See Sharer & Grove 1989, pp. 148–97

Marcus J, Flannery KV. 1996. *Zapotec civilization: how urban society evolved in Mexico's Oaxaca Valley.* London: Thames & Hudson

Niederberger C. 1987. *Paleopaysages et Archeologie Preurbaine du Bassin de Mexico. Collection Etudes Mésoaméricaines,* Vol. 11. Mexico: Cemca

Niederberger C. 1996. The Basin of Mexico: a multimillennial development toward cultural complexity. See Benson & de la Fuente 1996, pp. 95–103

Ortiz P, Rodriguez MC. 1994. Los espacios sagrados Olmecas: el Manatí, un caso especial. See Clark 1994d, pp. 68–91

Porter JB. 1989. Olmec colossal heads as recarved thrones: "mutilation," revolution and recarving. *Res: Anthropol. Aesthet.* 17–18:23–29

Reilly FK III. 1989. The shaman in transformation pose: a study of the theme of rulership in Olmec art. *Rec. Art Mus., Princeton Univ.* 48:4–21

Reilly FK III. 1990. Cosmos and rulership: the function of Olmec-style symbols in formative period Mesoamerica. *Vis. Lang.* 24: 12–37

Reilly FK III. 1991. Olmec iconographic influences on the symbols of Maya rulership: an examination of possible sources. In *Sixth Palenque Round Table, 1986,* ed. VM Fields, pp. 151–65. Norman: Univ. Okla. Press

Reilly FK III. 1994a. Cosmologia, soberanismo y espacio ritual en la Mesoamerica del formativo. See Clark 1994d, pp. 239–59

Reilly FK III. 1994b. *Visions of another world: art, shamanism, and political power in middle formative Mesoamerica.* PhD thesis. Univ. Tex., Austin. 526 pp.

Reilly FK III. 1996. Art, ritual, and rulership in the Olmec world. See Benson 1996, pp. 27–45

Rousseau JJ. 1981. *The First and Second Discourses together with the Replies to Critics and Essay on the Origin of Languages,* ed. & tranl. V Gourevitch. New York: Harper & Row (From French)

Sahagun B. 1969. *Florentine Codex: Book 6: Rhetoric and Moral Philosophy.* Transl. CE Dibble, AJO Anderson. Salt Lake City: Univ. Utah Press (From Nahuatl)

Schele L. 1996. The Olmec mountain and tree of creation in Mesoamerican cosmology. See Benson 1996, pp. 105–17

Sharer RJ, Grove DC, eds. 1989. *Regional Perspectives on the Olmec.* Cambridge: Cambridge Univ. Press

Simons J. 1995. *Foucault and the Political.* London: Routledge

Stark B. 1997. Framing the Gulf Olmec. In *Olmec Art and Archaeology: Developments in Formative Period Social Complexity,* ed. JE Clark, ME Pye. Washington, DC: National Gallery of Art. In press

Stirling MW. 1940. Great stone faces of the Mexican jungle. *Natl. Geogr. Mag.* 78: 309–34

Symonds SC. 1995. *Settlement distribution and the development of cultural complexity in the lower Coatzacoalcos drainage, Veracruz, Mexico: an archaeological survey at San Lorenzo Tenochtitlan.* PhD thesis. Vanderbilt Univ., Nashville. 1142 pp.

Taube KA. 1992. Uses of sport: review of the Mesoamerica ballgame. *Science* 256: 1064–65

Taube KA. 1996. The Olmec maize god: the face of corn in formative Mesoamerica. *Res: Anthropol. Aesthet.* 29/30:39–81

Tolstoy P. 1989. Coapexco and Tlatilco: sites with Olmec materials in the Basin of Mexico. See Sharer & Grove 1989, pp. 85–121

Winter M. 1989. *Oaxaca: The Archaeological Record.* Mexico City: Editorial Minutiae Mexicana

Annu. Rev. Anthropol. 1997. 26:235–61

PASTORALISM: GOVERNANCE AND DEVELOPMENT ISSUES

Elliot Fratkin

Department of Anthropology, Smith College, Northampton, Massachusetts 01063;
e-mail: efratkin@sophia.smith.edu

KEY WORDS: conservation, Maasai, Mongolia, political ecology, tragedy of the commons

ABSTRACT

Pastoralist societies face more threats to their way of life now than at any previous time. Population growth; loss of herding lands to private farms, ranches, game parks, and urban areas; increased commoditization of the livestock economy; out-migration by poor pastoralists; and periodic dislocations brought about by drought, famine, and civil war are increasing in pastoralist regions of the world. Mongolia and China, however, have seen a revitalization of pastoral production with decollectivization. This review examines problems of pastoral governance and development including the "tragedy of the commons" debate, threats to common property rights, the effects of commercial ranching on pastoral economies, decollectivization in the former socialist countries, and the current state of development policies of Western donor countries. Case examples from the Maasai and Barabaig of East Africa and pastoralists of Mongolia and China illustrate these changes.

INTRODUCTION

The practice of pastoralism, where human populations live on the products of their domestic animals in arid environments or areas of scarce resources, shows a remarkable resilience. Pastoral populations continue to herd their animals in the arid lands of Africa, the Mideast, Central Asia, Mongolia, highland Tibet and the Andes, and arctic Scandinavia and Siberia. Pastoral production is increasing in China and Mongolia as these economies decentralize and expand

235

their markets. Nevertheless, pastoralists throughout the world today face more constraints on their economies than at any previous time, threatened by growth of human and livestock populations; loss of herding lands to private farms, ranches, game parks, and urbanization; out-migration by poor pastoralists; increased commoditization of the livestock economy; and periodic dislocations caused by drought, famine, and civil war.

In the 1970s and 1980s, pastoralist research was dominated by the cultural ecology framework of adaptation, particularly as anthropologists and ecologists sought to understand how pastoralists responded to drought and environmental change. This was also a period of large-scale development projects by the international donor community, many of whose policies, driven by the "tragedy of the commons" thesis, emphasized privatization of the range, commercial ranching, and sedentarization of nomads, particularly in Africa. Increasingly, there has been a shift in theoretical understanding of development that has moved from *cultural* ecology to *political* ecology, as anthropologists critique development policies using models of political encapsulation, hegemony of the national state, and decline in pastoral autonomy and mobility. Human-livestock-land interactions are explained less in terms of "carrying capacity" or "desertification" and more in terms of loss of common property rights, increased economic differentiation and social stratification, and incorporation and domination of tribal pastoral groups by larger state systems.

The literature on pastoralism is large and growing. In preparing this review, over 600 articles, books, and reports about pastoralism and development were examined, nearly all written in the past ten years. Almost half dealt with issues of ecology, with topics ranging from arid land management to species diversity to household organization of labor. A significant number focused on political and economic change, including problems of loss of communal grazing lands, sedentarization and urban migration, and rapid commoditization in a market economy.

This review considers several key problems of pastoral governance and development, including the debate on the tragedy of the commons, common property regimes, effects of commercial ranching in formerly subsistence-based economies, collectivization and decollectivization in formerly socialist countries, and the current state of development policies of Western donor countries. Several cases, including the Maasai and Barabaig of East Africa and pastoralists of Mongolia and China, illustrate these problems.

LITERATURE ON PASTORALISM

Following a period of relatively few but notable ethnographies on pastoral organization (Evans-Pritchard 1940, Stenning 1959), research on pastoralist societies took off in the 1970s and 1980s, particularly from Africa and the Mideast (cf overviews by Barfield 1993, Dyson-Hudson & Dyson-Hudson 1980). With the publication of *Nomads and the Outside World,* Khazanov (1994) bridged the gap between Soviet and Western scholarship by providing a remarkable synthesis and analysis of pastoralist history and ethnography worldwide.

Increased drought and famine during the 1970s and early 1980s, particularly in West and East Africa, led to major discussions about the future of pastoralism (Équippe Écologie 1979, Fabietti & Salzman 1996, Galaty et al 1981, Galaty & Bonte 1991, Galaty & Johnson 1990, Salzman 1980, Salzman & Galaty 1990, Swift 1977). In the past ten years, anthropologists have looked more intensely at the consequences of development efforts by international donors and national governments in pastoralist regions (e.g. Bennett 1988, Hogg 1992a, Horowitz & Little 1987). Three interrelated themes dominate the literature: ecological adaptability of pastoral systems, problems of governance and relations with agricultural states, and the effects of international development policies on pastoralist populations.

Ecological Literature

Ecological research about pastoralist systems followed Dyson-Hudson's (1972) remark that "to understand herders, one must understand herding." Researchers were urged to provide more empirical studies of ecology that looked at specific behaviors rather than at pastoral types (Dyson-Hudson & Dyson-Hudson 1980). Dahl & Hjort's (1976) *Having Herds* provided a manual for researchers on herd growth and its relation to household labor and economy. Subsequent studies adhered to an adaptation model, emphasizing a pastoralist rationality to land use in marginal lands that was based on herd flexibility, diversity, and mobility of the human and animal populations, particularly in studies from Africa (Baumann et al 1993, Bekure et al 1991, Dahl 1979, Dyson Hudson & McCabe 1985, Fratkin 1986, Fratkin & Roth 1990, Manger et al 1996, McCabe 1990, Oba 1994, Roth 1996, Schwartz 1993, Sperling & Galaty 1990), but also from the Andes (Kuznar 1991), Lappland (Ingold 1980), and India (Casimir & Rao 1985, 1992; Gooch 1992; Köhler-Rollefson 1992). Models were proposed for herd diversity, maximization, and recovery following drought (Behnke & Scoones 1992, Behnke et al 1993, Dahl & Hjort 1976, Dyson-Hudson & Dyson-Hudson 1982, Roth 1990, Scoones 1992) and for correlations between population density, resource variability, and territoriality (Dyson-Hudson & Smith 1978). Several studies describe variations in household wealth, organization of production and importance of kinship and redistribution of livestock (Fratkin 1987, 1989; Herren 1990; Potkanski 1994; Roth 1996; Sperling 1985). Several large interdisciplinary projects combined ecological, economic, and anthropological research including the decade-long South Turkana Ecosystem Project in Kenya (Dyson-Hudson & McCabe 1985, Little & Leslie 1997), the UNESCO–Integrated Project in Arid Lands (Integrated Project in Arid Lands 1984, O'Leary 1984), the International Livestock Center for Africa's program in Ethiopia (Coppock 1993), and the Institute of Development Studies (University of Sussex) program in Mongolia (Swift & Mearns 1993).

One tendency in ecological research followed Garret Hardin's thesis in "Tragedy of the Commons" (1968), which upheld that common property resources shared by pastoralists led to overgrazing and environmental degradation. Pastoral practices including the tendency of individual herders to maximize their herds, coupled with growing populations of both herders and their animals, was viewed as promoting desertification, the expansion of desert regions brought about by human mismanagement (Lamprey 1976, UNCOD 1977). This position followed the Lotka-Volta model of predator-prey oscillations, emphasizing that so-called unnatural increases of the predator population (cattle) will ultimately destroy the prey population (forage) until starvation reduces the predator population. Pastoralists living in and exploiting arid areas were seen as disturbances in the system rather than as a long-term part of the same larger ecosystem (Little 1994a). A variant of this theme discusses competition between herders and wildlife, particularly in the game parks of Africa where pastoralists such as the Maasai are seen as environmental stressors who should be excluded from grazing their livestock in formerly shared ecosystems (Prins 1992).

Other ecologists argue that pastoral systems are able to respond to fluctuating and patchy resources with cultural behaviors that include flexibility, mobility, and diversity of species (Coughenour et al 1985, Ellis & Swift 1988, Hjort 1981, Homewood & Rodgers 1991). Furthermore, herd growth cannot be indefinitely maintained because herds are periodically decimated by drought and disease, and because they are limited by the labor they can provide (Dahl & Hjort 1976, Fratkin & Smith 1994). Ellis & Swift (1988) criticized development efforts that regard rangelands in stable equilibrium unless disrupted by overstocking and overgrazing of domesticated animals. They argued that rangelands are inherently unstable because of large climatic factors and that development should enhance traditional pastoral practices because they are more appropriate for arid ecosystems than those based on ranch management paradigms.

Political Organization and Governance

A second approach in pastoralist research focuses on political processes of internal organization and dealings with other groups, particularly larger state structures. This literature comes largely out of Middle East (and particularly Iranian) ethnography (e.g. Beck 1986, Bradburd 1990, Marx 1977, Salzman 1974, Tapper 1979), which points to long-term interactions between tribal pastoralist confederacies and sedentary agricultural states.

Meir (1988) distinguished the *centrifugal* ideology of nomads seeking autonomy and mobility from the *centripetal* ideology of the sedentary state that strives for dominance and encapsulation, as illustrated by the relations of Negev Bedouins to Ottoman, British, and Israeli rule. Over time, either of these forces may be ascendant. Mearns (1996) distinguished *governance* from *government,* defining the former as the exercise of legitimate authority within a local group through endogenously evolved sets of rules, and the latter as the formal exercise of control, through law and coercion, over a community by a constituted state. Pastoral/sedentary relations are often ones of conflict, particularly because the aims and objectives of pastoral groups are at variance with sedentary, agricultural states. The history of relations between the two, particularly during the twentieth century, is one of encapsulation of pastoral communities rather than incorporation.

An example is the Yarahmadzai Baluch of Iran who, before the successful military campaign of Reza Shah in 1936, were an independent tribe, governing itself through a council of household heads and collective responsibility of lineages. Local chiefs (*sardar*) had a role limited to internal mediation and represented the tribe to outsiders. Following encapsulation by the Shah's regime, raiding was suppressed, and arms were confiscated. The *sardar*'s position increased in importance as he took the role of middleman and ultimately as administrator of the Shah's government in Baluchistan (Salzman 1974). Salzman (1979) notes political encapsulation of pastoralist groups occurring more readily when the tribe is centralized, as are the Baluch, than when it is decentralized, such as the Yomut Turkmen (Irons 1979). A distinction is made between *tribal* pastoralists, independent political entities made up of similar local groups of primary producers, which characterizes many East African pastoralists, are distinguished from *peasant* pastoralists, local groups that have been incorporated into an agrarian regime controlled by a ruling class with political, military, and ritual power, as in the Middle East (Salzman 1996).

Khazanov (1994) argued that stratification within pastoralist groups seldom results from internal processes but is caused by external contact and control by larger states, as in the case of the continental empires of Russia, China, and Ottoman Turkey, which encroached upon the territories of mobile pastoralists. This land was taken for agricultural, military, and trade purposes. Today this encapsulation continues as industrial states expand commercial production in arid lands, forcing pastoralists into sedentary or urban communities (Khazanov 1994).

Development Literature

Increasing efforts by multilateral and bilateral assistance organizations (e.g. United Nations, World Bank, United States Agency for International Development) implementing programs in arid lands has led to a large literature on pastoral development. Many of these writings are found in the "gray" literature of international donors and nongovernmental organizations (NGOs), and several bibliographies have been assembled (Jowka 1991, Oxby 1975, Scholz 1992, Scoones 1988). Other works, particularly by cultural anthropologists, have described the effects—often negative—of development efforts on pastoralists (Anderson & Broch-Due 1997, Baxter 1991, Baxter 1993, Baxter & Hogg 1990, Charnley 1996, Fratkin 1991, Horowitz 1979, Horowitz & Little 1987, Little 1994a, Peters 1994, Sandford 1983) and pastoralist women (Dahl 1987, Ensminger 1987, Fratkin & Smith 1995, Horowitz & Jowka 1992, Talle 1988).

THE TRAGEDY OF THE COMMONS

Garret Hardin's "Tragedy of the Commons," published in *Science* in 1968, played an enormous role in environmental studies and development policies. His thesis is straightforward:

> The tragedy of the commons develops in this way. Picture a pasture open to all. It is to be expected that each herdsman will try to keep as many cattle as possible on the commons....As a rational being, each herdsman seeks to maximize his gain....The rational herdsman concludes that the only sensible course for him to pursue is to add another animal to his herd. And another; and another....But this is the conclusion reached by each and every rational herdsman sharing a commons. Therein is the tragedy. Each man is locked into a system which compels him to increase his herd without limit—in a world that is limited. Ruin is the destination towards which all men rush, each pursuing his own interest in a society that believes in the freedom of the commons. Freedom in a commons brings ruin to all" (Hardin 1968, p. 1244).

Hardin's thesis had a large impact on public understanding and scientific research concerned with famine and environmental degradation in arid lands. Some environmentalists saw "pastoral mismanagement" leading to desertification, defined as human-induced desiccation that was contributing to the Sahara Desert moving farther south each year. Solutions were proposed to limit or dismantle common property regimes, which were seen as key to the problem of degradation (Lamprey 1983, UNCOD 1977).

"Desertification" emerged as a major environmental issue in the 1970s following the prolonged Sahelian drought. The United Nations sponsored a Conference on Desertification in 1976 in Nairobi and established a desertification branch at the newly formed United Nations Environment Programme (UNEP). Funding for research projects on desertification by world donors followed, leading to the UNESCO–Integrated Project in Arid Lands (IPAL) in North Kenya (IPAL 1984). Over ten years, IPAL integrated range, livestock, and meteorological research and attempted programs to encourage local pastoralists to sell more livestock and reduce grazing pressures. The project leaders rarely listened to the advice of their own social scientists or the complaints of local Rendille and Gabra pastoralists, and by the mid-1980s IPAL disbanded without having had much impact in the area (Fratkin 1991, 1992; Little 1994a; O'Leary 1990).

Hardin's thesis also provided a rationalization for World Bank programs calling for sweeping privatization of land and commercialization of livestock production. Development planners and agronomists agreed that a major problem in Africa was one of increasing livestock productivity to feed Africa's growing population. They saw the problem not so much as improving livestock productivity (through capital improvements in water facilities, disease control, or range improvement, which had been tried with varying success in the colonial and postcolonial period in Africa), but one of limiting the size of herds on rangeland, which could best be achieved by increased livestock marketing, using Western models of individual commercial ranches (Simpson & Evangelou 1984).

Simpson & Sullivan (1984) argued that the African livestock sector was worse off in the 1980s than at any time in history, despite investments of about $1 billion between 1970 and 1984. They attributed this to growing human and livestock populations, with animals providing decreasing amounts of milk and meat because of depleting resources. They concluded that development projects should focus on ending common property land tenure and increasing privatization because it promoted more rational land use for livestock production. "If there are no charges or regulations, such resources will come to be used excessively and…result in deterioration and even destruction of the resource" (Simpson & Sullivan 1984, pp. 64–65)

Critiques of Hardin's tragedy thesis emerged from two directions: social scientists who worked with pastoral populations and natural scientists measuring the effects of traditional herding practices on environmental resources. Social scientists criticized Hardin's assumption that communally held resources meant no restriction on use. They argued that communal tenure systems in dry regions regulate access to users and sanction abusers, have mechanisms in place to conserve resources at certain times of the year to guard against mismanagement, and are more effective than exclusive and private forms of ownership (Behnke & Scoones 1992, Bromley 1992, McCabe 1990, Peters 1994, Turner 1993). While land degradation does occur in pastoralist regions, it is due not to generalized overpopulation but uneven population distribution, made worse by excessive population concentrations around mechanized bore holes and small towns (Little 1994a). Furthermore, bore holes and irrigation projects promote overcrowding by both farmers and herders, leading to inter-pastoralist as well as farmer-vs-pastoralist competition and conflict (Broken-sha & Little 1988, Hogg 1987, Little 1987a).

Bromley & Cernea (1989) argued that empirical work is not inherent to common property regimes but is caused by an absence of common property rules, and that the tragedy of the commons should be labeled the "tragedy of open access." Although development planners and government officials are uncomfortable with traditional forms of collective land tenure, which they feel lack defined rules about how resources are used, customary tenure systems are often quite specific about who may or may not use grazing and water resources (IDS 1988, Juul 1993).

Natural scientists began to question the ecological evidence in the tragedy thesis. Climatologists argued that figures on the southward advancement of desert had been exaggerated and that the extensive droughts of the 1970s and 1980s could be attributed to large climatic disruptions such as those brought about by El Niño/Southern Oscillation (ENSO) events (Glantz 1987, Nichol-son 1986). Dryland ecologists show that arid and semiarid environments are inherently unstable, where stocking rates and human population densities rise and fall in response to climatic stress, and that the concept of "carrying capac-ity" fails to recognize the variability and patchiness of arid lands ecology (Behnke 1994, Behnke & Scoones 1992, Behnke et al 1993, Coughenour et al 1985, Ellis & Swift 1988, Homewood & Rodgers 1991).

Despite these arguments, Hardin's critics were largely ignored during the heyday of arid lands development in the 1970s and 1980s (Dyson-Hudson 1991, Sandford 1983). In a USAID discussion paper about pastoral develop-ment projects in Africa's Sahel, Horowitz (1979, p. 27) wrote:

> So many documents, officials, and even scientists repeat the assertion of pas-toral responsibility for environmental degradation that the accusation has achieved the status of a fundamental truth, so self evident a case that mar-shaling evidence in its behalf is superfluous if not in fact absurd, like trying to satisfy a skeptic that the earth is round or the sun rises in the East.

MAASAI OF EAST AFRICA

The situation of Maasai pastoralists of Kenya and Tanzania illustrates the ef-fects of loss of customary grazing rights to land that is now—under state sanc-tion—being yielded to farmers, commercial estates, and national game parks.

Maasai society and history have been extensively studied recently (e.g. Galaty 1993, Spear & Waller 1993, Spencer 1988), with particular studies focusing on the development of group and individual ranches (Campbell 1984, Galaty 1992), conservation strategies and the effects of game parks (Homewood 1995, McCabe et al 1992), and commercial livestock projects (Bennett 1988, Jacobs 1980, Hodgson 1997). Never a single political entity, the Maasai, who today number about 350,000, are composed of a dozen independent groups including the Kisongo of Tanzania and the Purko, Loita, Matapato, and Kaputei of Kenya (Galaty 1993a). Before colonial rule (1885–1963), Maasai cattle herders occupied the Rift Valley savanna plains from Lake Turkana in northern Kenya to the Maasai Steppe in Central Tanzania. An international border divided the Maasai into German Tanganyika and British Kenya in 1885. In 1911, Kenyan Maasai saw their lands reduced by 60% when the British evicted them from north central Kenya to make room for settler ranches, confining the Maasai to the present-day Kajiado and Narok districts. Maasai lands in both countries were further reduced with the creation of game parks, including the Amboseli, Nairobi, and Mara Masai parks in Kenya and the Serengeti National Park (14,760 km^2) in Tanzania. Maasai were prohibited from grazing their herds in the park because government administrators felt that cattle competed for resources with wildlife, which were becoming an increasingly important source of foreign revenue through tourism (Homewood 1995).

In addition to loss of herding lands to game parks, Maasai in Kenya and Tanzania have faced competition for land from agriculturalists, including wheat-growing and beef-producing commercial enterprises. In 1962, the Maasai constituted 78% of Kenya's Kajiado District but less than 60% in 1984, owing mainly to immigration of non-Maasai farmers (Campbell 1984). In the neighboring Narok District, 320,000 ha of land were sold to land speculators and farmers in the 1980s, primarily to grow wheat. Much of this land has been leased, rented, or sold outright by Maasai owners, who can no longer graze their animals on their former lands (Campbell 1993, Galaty 1994).

The ability of Kenyan Maasai to transfer land individually is a recent phenomenon brought about when the government encouraged citizens to title their own land in the 1960s. In traditional Maasai society, no Maasai can "own" grazing or water resources; rights to graze are shared by all members of the territorial section (*olosho*), although educated and influential members of the community have sought title to individual sections of land. In 1968, with support from USAID and the World Bank, Kenya proposed "group ranches" which conferred formal and legal land tenure to a community of coresidents. Many Maasai accepted the group ranch concept as a means to prevent further agricultural encroachment and to acquire legal tenure enabling owners to qualify for loans for bore holes and cattle dips (Campbell 1984). By the mid-1980s,

Kenya was titling common lands in the semiarid regions to individual owners, particularly to small holders growing maize and other market crops. There was a stampede for land claims, especially in the Maasai areas, as both Kikuyu farmers and Maasai rushed to claim title to some land, lest they lose it all. John Galaty (1992) wrote that it is now land, not cattle, that is the most important resource in Maasailand.

In Tanzania, the socialist policy of *ujamaa* villagization was unsuccessful among Maasai, but the Nyerere government did create "livestock villages" controlling grazing and water resources. The USAID and World Bank funded the Maasai Livestock and Range Management Project between 1969 and 1979. Its $23 million budget was used to create cattle dips, dams, wells, and roads designed to increase livestock productivity and encourage the Maasai to sell more animals for beef. The project did not result in any substantial increase in livestock sales, especially in Tanzania, and the water and road development contributed to the large numbers of immigrant farmers, as in Kenya. Forced onto marginal lands or concentrated near the bore holes, pastures quickly became overgrazed. Predicting disaster, USAID finally terminated the project (Homewood 1995, Jacobs 1980).

Elsewhere in Tanzania, local Maasai were given joint use of Ngorongoro Conservation Area (8292 km^2) in exchange for evacuation of the Serengeti Plain. However, the Maasai are now restricted from grazing their cattle in the national park, although wildebeest and other wild animals move freely among Maasai herds, transmitting diseases and competing for pasture (McCabe et al 1992). Homewood argues that declines in cattle productivity have resulted in nutritional declines, leading to efforts by Maasai to supplement herding with farming, which is prohibited in the conservation area (Homewood 1992).

Countering Hardin's formulation of the "prisoner's dilemma" in stocking decisions, Galaty (1993b, p. 110) described the "pastoralists' dilemma," who, seeing "their land treated as an alienable free good, demand their privatized shares before that share disappears. The 'pastoralist's dilemma' occurs not when rangeland is controlled by communities, but when community control is undermined by state or private interests."

SAAMI AND BARABAIG LAND CASES

Pastoralist communities have increasingly gone to court to defend their rights to communally held property, particularly in countries that recognize some form of customary land tenure. In Norway in the 1970s, Saami (Lapps) sought to stop the construction of a series of hydroelectric dams on the Alta River. The case was tried in the Norwegian courts, where the Saami asked for legal protection as an indigenous minority to resolve land and water rights, using as legal precedent the Saami Codicil of 1751 which established Saami collective rights. Although these collective rights were upheld by the Norwegian Supreme Court, the Saami lost the case to stop the hydroelectric program. In another legal battle lasting fifteen years in the 1960s and 1970s, the Saami demanded land and water rights to the Taxed Mountains of Sweden, including rights to the forests and deer. Again, their usufructory rights as a collective group were upheld, but they lost the particular case (Svensson 1992).

Another important legal struggle is the Barabaig land case in Tanzania. The Barabaig are cattle pastoralists who live around Mt. Hanang near Arusha. In 1968, the Barabaig saw 70,000 ha (later expanded to 100,000 ha) of their land taken over by the parastatal National Agriculture and Food Corporation (NAFCO) to grow commercial wheat on seven state farms. This project was funded in large part by the Canadian International Development Agency (CIDA), which provided US$60 million in assistance mainly to pay for Canadian expertise and mechanized equipment. Barabaig herders were evicted from these lands and forbidden from crossing farm boundaries to reach grazing and water resources. Trespassers were punished with beatings and fines, despite protests by Barabaig elders that Tanzanian law recognizes customary rights to land. Elders also complained that they were denied access to the graves of their ancestors located on the farm property (Lane 1996).

The Barabaig challenged the legality of their land alienation in Tanzanian courts in 1981, claiming that neither local Barabaig nor the village council were consulted when NAFCO acquired land for a Malbadaw wheat farm (one of seven NAFCO farms). They wanted restoration of grave sites, action to arrest soil erosion, restoration of traditional rights of way across the farms, and damages of Tsh. 100 million (US$1 million in 1986, US$125,000 in 1994) (Lane 1994).

NAFCO did not deny their acquisition of land but claimed it had authority to acquire it "in the public interest." The Tanzanian High Court ruled in favor of the Barabaig by declaring that their customary claims were valid under the Tanzanian constitution and that proper legal procedures for acquiring land were not followed by NAFCO. However, the victory was limited by a technical flaw. The court ruled that all 788 plaintiffs were not properly notified and awarded only the six plaintiffs who appeared in court. The six plaintiffs were compensated for 300 ha of land (but not the actual land) totaling US$1200. This judgment, however, was overturned on appeal in 1986 because not all the plaintiffs were considered "natives" within the definition of the 1923 Land Ordinance, because several were Somali descendants. This defeat was a major setback for the Barabaig and led to an increase in NAFCO aggression toward the Barabaig and expansion of the wheat scheme in the 1980s. Furthermore, the Tanzanian government set in motion a series of laws attempting to extinguish customary rights in land and prohibit the payment of compensation for such extinctions (Lane 1994). Frustrated by the slow pace of the courts, the Barabaig began an international campaign in the 1980s, which included the publication of an open letter in Canadian newspapers demanding that "indigenous pastoral communities have customary rights to the land they occupy so that their future livelihoods may be protected by the law of the land" (Lane 1996).

AGRICULTURAL EXPANSION, SEDENTARIZATION, AND URBAN MIGRATION

Pastoralists worldwide are experiencing the effects of increased agricultural expansion into arid lands, of increased urban migration and sedentarization by former nomads, and of increased participation in the market economy which includes both greater sales of their products (beef, dairy, wool, skins, and livestock), and also an increasing proletarianization of labor. These processes, while categorically distinct, are interrelated and have varying effects on pastoralists.

Herder-Farmer Relations

Pastoralists have interacted with sedentary farmers for millennia, with established practices of trade and symbiotic production such as the grazing of livestock on farmers' fields before planting seasons. However, both population growth and increasing commodity production have led to the expansion of agriculturalists on formerly shared grazing lands, and have increased tension and conflict between these groups in many parts of the world (Van den Brink et al 1995), including Sudan (Manger 1988, Mohamed-Salih 1992), Somalia (Unruh 1991), West Africa (Waters-Bayer & Bayer 1994), Azerbaijan (Yamskov 1991), and among Bedouins in Israel (Kressel et al 1991, Marx & Shmueli 1984, Meir 1996).

Sedentarization

Pastoralists are settling down at a rapid rate, both to take up farming or to live in or near towns. This process is occurring in response to loss of lands and livestock, but also to the attraction of new opportunities in marketing and wage labor. In some situations, resettlement is involuntary, as among pastoralists displaced by dams (Ayeni et al 1994, Schmitz 1993), famine, and civil war (Ammons 1996, Doornbos et al 1992, Hitchcock & Twedt 1995, Schlee 1995, Shipton 1990). For most pastoralists, however, settlement is voluntary. Urban migration, especially to smaller towns, is occurring throughout arid regions in Africa and the Mideast, and many pastoralists are settling in towns (Mohamed-Salih et al 1995).

Several studies report negative social and economic consequences of pastoral sedentarization, including poorer nutrition, inadequate housing, and lack of clean drinking water (Galvin et al 1994, Hill 1985). In Kenya, settled Rendille children were three times more likely to be malnourished than nomadic Rendille children during the drought year of 1992 (Nathan et al 1996), which the authors attributed to greater access to camel's milk by nomadic communities. However, sedentarized populations have better health care, including higher rates of vaccinations and disease interventions. In Mali, nomadic pastoral populations have higher rates of tuberculosis, brucellosis, syphilis, and trachoma and higher child mortality than settled agricultural groups. The settled populations, however, have higher rates of malaria, anemia, bilharzia, and intestinal parasites (Chabasse 1985). Several studies are currently pointing to increased AIDS among settled pastoralists, as among Barabaig and Maasai of Kenya (Klepp et al 1994).

Several studies have pointed to changing economic opportunities, particularly for women, associated with pastoral sedentarization. Women have entered the commodity market trade, particularly selling milk (Fratkin & Smith 1995, Little 1994b, Waters-Bayer 1985). However, dairy marketing is often taken over by men, as in the case of the Hawazma of Sudan (Michael 1987). Urbanization may offer new opportunities for poor pastoralist women as maids and cooks, as well as illegal or low-status employment such as charcoal making, beer brewing, and prostitution (Dahl 1987, Talle 1987, 1988).

Commoditization of the Livestock Economy

Pastoralists have traded or exchanged livestock products for grains, tools, clothing, and other commodities with agricultural or urban societies since the beginning of recorded history. In the seventeenth and eighteenth centuries, Middle Eastern herders produced "Persian wool" for British trading companies, provided animals and labor for caravan trades, and traded livestock products in large regional economies (Chang & Koster 1994). Today, wage labor as well as livestock are sold as part-time herders take jobs in construction, road building, and truck driving and join the armed forces in large numbers in Arabia, Kenya, and Iran (Cole 1975, Lancaster 1986, Sperling 1987).

Amanor (1995) argued against the "substantivist" view of pastoralists as subsistence herders in West Africa, showing the high numbers of male animals produced for sale in the long-term regional export markets in West Africa. This supposedly subsistence-oriented nomadic economy supplies all the major urban centers of West Africa with a steady flow of meat (Swift 1988). Throughout Africa, pastoralists regularly sell 5–10% of their herds annually to local or urban markets, mainly to purchase grains, teas, and sugar (Ensminger 1992, Kerven 1992, Little 1987b, O'Leary 1990).

Commercialization of the livestock economy usually occurs in terms favorable to the ruling sedentary elite, as in Mauritania where transfer of lands to traders, civil servants, and wealthy farmers has deprived local herders of grazing resources (Galaty & Bonte 1991). Ranches are now replacing pastoral households as main commercial producers in many parts of the pastoral world. Mohamed-Salih (1991) showed how in Sudan Baggara, Kababish, and Rufa'a, small producers were forced out of livestock markets by subsidization of large-scale capital-intensive projects. Farmers are now buying more livestock, increasing herds from 33–50% in some regions. In Burkina Faso and Côte d'Ivoire, Fulani are becoming agro-pastoral, and farmers are raising more livestock, both in response to commoditization (Zuppan 1994).

MONGOLIA AND CHINA

A different situation of market integration is emerging in the formerly socialist economies of Asia, particularly in Mongolia and China.

Mongolia

Mongolia is a vast (1.6 million km^2) but underpopulated country of 2.2. million people owning 25 million animals. Mongolia has historically relied on pastoral production including the herding of camels, goats, and sheep in the southern Gobi Desert; cattle, yaks, and sheep in the northern steppes; and horses throughout. Until decollectivization in 1991, half of the Mongolian population lived in the capital of Ulanbaatar and a few other towns while 40% of Mongolians were engaged directly in pastoral production. In the 1980s, pastoralism provided over half of GDP and 40% of total exports. Milk and meat consumption are among the highest in the world (Potkanski 1993).

Mongolia became the world's second communist state in 1921, with technical, financial, and ideological support from the Soviet Union. After a disastrous attempt at forced collectivization in 1929–1931, which was quickly abandoned, communal cooperatives (*negdel*) were encouraged on a voluntary basis in the 1950s. These cooperatives were welcomed by wealthier stock owners who had large labor needs, and where herding households were enabled to pool funds to bore wells, buy haymaking equipment, and build winter shelters for animals. In 1954, there were 198 *negdels* with 15,400 members and one million livestock, and by 1989 all Mongolian herding households were in collectives. The collectives furnish transport for nomadic moves and supplementary feed for winter and spring, clear snow from pastures, and provide veterinary and specialized animal breeding services (Mearns 1996).

Following the collapse of the Soviet Union in 1991, Mongolia underwent significant economic and political reform. The state retreated from direct involvement in production, and prices were freed from previous controls. Following World Bank recommendations to increase privatization, *negdel* cooperatives transformed into joint stock companies, which quickly fragmented into privatized companies and household enterprises. With increased sales of beef and wool to China, the pastoral economy grew. Urban wage earners, many no longer employed by state bureaucracies or enterprises, moved back to the countryside to join their pastoral families. Where in 1990 state collectives owned 68% of all livestock, by 1994, 90% of the animals were privately owned (Mearns 1996).

This period has seen a renewed strengthening of the *khot ails,* the prerevolutionary herding groups of two to ten households, who are related by kinship, who act again as a basic social and economic group in Mongolian society. The *khot ail* acts as a social safety net for poorer rural households, providing forms of mutual assistance and pooling risk between households, including sharing food resources as well as long-term loans of livestock. Mongolians have also developed grass-roots organizations (*khorshoo*) that are neither customary nor state-inspired institutions but are marketing cooperatives seeking transport and trade with China and elsewhere (Potkanski 1993).

While pastoral production is firmly back in the hands of independent household groups, pastoral land is specifically excluded from private ownership. Of Mongolia's total land, 79% is under pasture, forming the largest area of common grazing land in the world (Mearns 1996). It is this continued public ownership of grazing resources, combined with private ownership of livestock, that distinguishes Mongolia from other pastoralist regimes, particularly in Africa and the Mideast.

There have been several problems associated with the rapid decollectivization in Mongolia, including increased wealth differentiation between herding households and the inability of poor *khot ails* to support all members. Cooper (1993) noted that while customary institutions are currently supporting weaker members, one might see in the future negative wage labor relationships with richer households. Templer et al (1993) argued that without adequate external provision of safety nets, environmental risks will increase for poor households. While there was an increase in offtake and livestock marketing following the 1991 liberalization, current offtake is declining, and the Mongolian government is seeking new ways to develop markets and increase herders' incomes (Edstrom 1993).

Chinese and Tibetan Decollectivization

Similar processes of decentralization have occurred in the pastoral regions of China and Tibet. A long-term study of Tibetan and Hui pastoralists of Menyuan Horse Farm in Qinghai Province in NW China was conducted between 1984–1991 (Cincotta et al 1992). After decades of fully collectivized ownership of agricultural capital, the rights to land and livestock were transferred to producers after 1979 through contractual systems of "household responsibility." By 1984, livestock was divided among individual households, but the former brigade leadership (now constituted as "farm management") were retained for service functions and as economic middlemen. Importantly, summer and autumn pastures are still held in common, without restrictions on grazing numbers, because management expected that livestock numbers would reach a "natural maximum" based on limits of private winter forage.

Farm management receives a fixed amount of sheep wool and meat from each producing household, at less than market value. This "tax" is sold to pay for construction, transportation, meat storage, education, and health and veterinary care for the collective farm. Any surplus is sold on the market, often for double the prices paid by the farm management. Results of this arrangement have led to increases by 25% of summer herds, most of which are sold before winter. Local pastoralists credited privatization for their herd growth, because it enabled them to fence their summer hay fields (keeping trespassing herds off) and to buy hay in the winter (Cincotta et al 1992). These processes of decentralization and privatization, coupled with communal grazing rights, have also occurred in Tibet and Inner Mongolia (Goldstein & Beall 1991, Li et al 1993).

India

The situation has not been as favorable to pastoralists of South Asia, particularly among groups like the Gujars of northwest India. In Gujarat, 250,000 pastoralists annually migrate with herds of small ruminants to and from Saurashtra. As common pastures shrink because of agricultural expansion and high population density (210 people/km^2), poor small ruminant herders live in squalid camps, producing manure (i.e. waste products) and wool for sale to settled populations. Today, Gujarat farmers are driving out pastoralists altogether (Cincotta & Pangare 1994). Cincotta & Pangare (1994, p. 19) wrote that, "Not until pastoralism impinges upon economic and public health factors that touch the elite, will their situation be recognized. This is unlikely to occur."

The neglect of the Gujars, as well as the Raikas and Himalayan pastoralists by the Indian government, has been documented by several anthropologists (Gooch 1992, Köhler-Rollefson 1992, Vira 1993).

INTERNATIONAL DEVELOPMENT POLICY

Sandford (1983, pp. 11–19) described a "mainstream" view about pastoral development held by a majority of government and development officials: 1.

Most of the world's rangelands are suffering from desertification. 2. In most cases, it is caused by overgrazing by domestic animals, which in turn is caused by an increase in the number of animals. 3. The technology is available to combat desertification but is not applied because the traditional economic and social systems of pastoralists, and especially their systems of communal land tenure, militate against this. 4. The solution involves privatized tenure, such as commercial ranches or grazing blocks, where pasture use follows scientific advice about stocking levels and grazing rotation, implemented through a centralized bureaucratic organization.

Privatization is not only touted as more efficient, but it is part of a larger modernization framework of free enterprise and entrepreneurship strongly advocated by the World Bank and its major funders from United States, Japan, and the European Community. Development policies aimed at pastoralists have undergone several transformations, as summarized by Dyson-Hudson (1991). Under colonial rule, policies began as small-scale efforts to improve water supplies, improve breeds, and establish fixed or rotational grazing. In the 1960s and 1970s, governments attempted to transform localized subsistence pastoralism into market-oriented commercial ranching on a national scale, particularly in Africa. Large-scale assistance was provided by the World Bank and bilateral agencies as fixed-term interventions, usually of highly capitalized infrastructural inputs including roads, slaughter houses, railway transport, mechanized bore holes, dipping facilities, and feed lots, planned by outside technical experts for implementation by national government officers. As in the Maasai case in Kenya, these projects also supported privatization and individuation of common herding lands (Galaty 1992).

These government interventions, ostensibly for economic development and for improving range management and livestock, have been uniformly negative and frequently disastrous. As Swift (1991, p. 34) wrote,

> The record of this type of policy in Africa has been dismal, as any review of livestock projects shows. Land degradation, where it is taking place, has not been halted and has sometimes increased, livestock productivity has not grown although economic inequality has, and vulnerability to food insecurity and loss of tenure rights has increased. Faced with the failure of their policies, many major donors have stopped investing in livestock projects, and some now argue for a policy of benign neglect toward the dry areas on the grounds that little can be done there....

Pastoral production demands mobility, the sine qua non of dryland cattle keeping, yet the actions of governments have curtailed mobility through alienation of land, demarcation of new political boundaries, the establishment of tribal grazing units, and mechanization of bore holes. Moreover, governments have displaced local authority over range and water use, decreased effectiveness of sanctions, and facilitated manipulation by the wealthy and influential (Little 1987a, Brokensha & Little 1988, Schlee 1990).

The World Bank has recently modified its approach to pastoral development away from Western ranching models (which are successful only in areas with adequate rainfall and pasturage) to more "integrated natural resource management," which attempts to involve local pastoralists in the implementation process (de Haan 1994). Cernea (1994) described World Bank projects in Senegal, for example, that created a user-based system of range and water management in a 1.3 million–ha project by promoting users organizations, state protection of tenurial rights, technical experts to improve sustainable resource use, and a literacy program for 4000 pastoralists.

Some anthropologists remain skeptical of larger development projects, however. Paul Baxter (1994) concluded that most attempts to develop or improve traditional pastoralism have failed and that pastoralists are growing poorer. In his view, development interventions continue to aim at sedentarizing pastoralists, controlling their movements through grazing blocks, and steering their integration into the commercial economy to supply cheap meat to the cities.

Pastoralists, however, are moving into the twenty-first century with less ability to maintain their subsistence livestock economies than at any time in their past. Following a seven-year project among Boran of southern Ethiopia, the International Livestock Center for Africa (ILCA) concluded that human populations were growing faster than livestock, whose reproductive and dairy productivity were declining because of increasing competition for forage, echoing concerns raised earlier by Simpson & Sullivan (1984). In the absence of any development intervention, ILCA predicted that the Boran would face increasing food energy deficits, approaching declines of 60% by the turn of the century. These deficits, in turn, would lead to permanent and expanding efforts to cultivate, to the following increases in the offtake of cattle to buy grain, the out-migration of young men (leading to key labor shortages), wealth stratification, population of peri-urban poor dependent on dairy sales for survival, and a decline in the maintenance of traditional rights and responsibilities (Coppock 1993).

Recognition of the limits and constraints on traditional pastoralism leads to two opposing solutions. One view, articulated in the environmental journal *Ambio* (Steen 1994), recommends abandoning pastoralism altogether and encouraging former herders to plant forage crops, cereals, and fodder to raise livestock in sedentary settings and to integrate into an industrialized, market-based economy. An opposing view emphasizes restoring or protecting traditional pastoralism through recognition of legal rights to water and pasture resources, rights of way for herds to travel through cultivated lands during migration periods, rights to unhindered passage across international borders, recognition of pastoralist knowledge of water, pasture, and herd management, an end of propaganda to sedentarize, the right to fair prices and water, and, finally, the right to run their own local affairs (Baxter 1993, Charnley 1996, Hjortaf Ornäs 1990, Horowitz 1986).

DEVELOPMENT ALTERNATIVES

Grassroots Organizations

A new direction in pastoral development is necessary, one that is rooted in pastoral peoples' strategies and that recognizes environmental variability and the need for mobility and flexibility (Scoones & Graham 1994). This is occurring to a degree with the development of pastoralist associations, organizations of increased representation by pastoralists themselves in the development process. Pastoralist associations have developed in Senegal, Mali, Chad, Burkina Faso, Mauritania, and Sudan, where they manage water points, run veterinary drugstores for profit, and secure labor for absentee owners (Bruggeman 1993, Cullis 1992, Köhler-Rollefson 1995, Vedeld 1992, Waters-Bayer & Bayer 1994).

There are problems, however, when Western NGOs take the lead in these initiatives. CARE and OXFAM programs in Kenya and Ethiopia, for example, focus on small-scale communities and fail to address larger problems of rangeland, population growth, and declining resource base. Furthermore, they fail to collect baseline information on traditional pastoral systems, monitor progress in achieving project objectives, and work with governments (Hogg 1992b). As Hogg noted in this article, however, NGOs can play an important role through informing policy makers about local, national, and international processes increasing the vulnerability of pastoralists to drought, and can help design and implement effective interventions to reduce this vulnerability in the future.

Financial and Veterinary Self-Help

An important area of pastoralist development concerns development of banking and credit associations, as in Ethiopia, where ILCA recommends converting some cattle into savings accounts. "While older male cattle have traditional value as storage, they compete with milk cows for range. Banking livestock capital is keystone intervention for managing the system out of famine, poverty, and increasing risk of environmental degradation" (Coppock 1993, p. 6). Other low-cost and participatory recommendations include promoting monetization, the maintenance of wells and ponds using heavy machinery, promoting

grazing management schemes, and veterinary improvements including vaccinations and treatments for common but deadly diseases. Many of these services can be achieved by education and training within the pastoralist communities themselves (Coppock 1993).

SUMMARY

The future of pastoralist populations is far from certain. While nomadic or mobile livestock herding has been a successful food production system in arid
lands, the problems of population growth, competition for land with other pastoralists, farmers, commercial estates, game parks, and urban areas are increasingly preventing pastoral producers from traditional mobility and flexibility
necessary to survive. While commoditization of the livestock economy, as
well as sedentarization and agro-pastoralism, have increased throughout pastoral regions in the world, these do not seem to threaten livestock production in
and of itself, although they have contributed to an increased economic differentiation including the creation of absentee herdowners and wage-working
herders (Beck 1980, Little 1985, Rao 1995). The growth of farms and towns,
however, does provide an outlet for population growth in the pastoral areas, as
well as a market source for increased livestock offtake, which helps conserve
pastoral resources.

For pastoral populations to continue to live off their herds, however, several
changes in development policy must occur. First and foremost, herders must
have rights to pasture and water, rights that may include communal, village-
based, or cooperative tenure guaranteed by law. Mongolia's success in revital-
izing its livestock system is due not just to the individual privatization of their
herds but to national policies guaranteeing shared grazing resources, access to
markets, and access to veterinary care. Conversely, the greatest impediment to
Maasai or Barabaig pastoralism in Africa is the enclosure, privatization, and
fencing of grazing lands that exclude former owners from their traditional
lands. Recognition of customary land tenure is essential to the continuation of
pastoralism in most parts of the world.

Another development should include the recognition by international development donors that pastoral livestock management in arid lands is productive, rational, and an essential way of utilizing scarce and patchy resources.
Pastoral strategies of herd diversity, pastoral mobility, and residential flexibility offer a means to convert patchy, seasonal, and scarce vegetation into calories and protein for human consumption in arid or marginal lands.

The needs of pastoral populations should not be pitted against wildlife conservation, as is happening in Africa, India, and other regions. Pastoral production is not necessarily harmful to wildlife conservation. Instead, it may be an

important component of rangeland ecology. Evicting pastoralists from game parks does not solve the problem of range use but creates greater problems by forcing pastoralists into greater competition with agricultural or other pastoral populations. Wildlife policy needs to be coordinated with pastoral needs, preferably though direct meetings between governments and pastoralists and by mutual sharing of rewards such as tourism revenues.

Finally, pastoralists need better access to credit and savings institutions to improve animal husbandry, pay for school fees, purchase veterinary medicines, and improve water sources through low-cost dams and catchments. Pastoralism remains an important food production system in vast areas of the world. It has the potential to provide meat, leather, wool, and milk to growing towns and cities in the developing world and should be encouraged—not discouraged—by development planners and national governments.

ACKNOWLEDGMENTS

I am very grateful to Tiffany Sher-Mei Wu and to Smith College for their assistance in the production of this review.

> Visit the *Annual Reviews home page* at
> http://www.AnnualReviews.org.

Literature Cited

Amanor KS. 1995. Dynamics of herd structures and herding strategies in West Africa: a study of market integration and ecological adaptation. *Africa* 65(3):351–94

Ammons L. 1996. Consequence of war on African countries: social and economic development. *Afr. Stud. Rev.* 39(1):67–82

Anderson D, Broch-Due V, eds. 1997. *Poverty Matters: Rich and Poor Among Pastoralists in Eastern Africa.* London: Curry

Ayeni JSO, Roder W, Ayanda JO. 1994. The Kainji lake experience in Nigeria. *World Bank Tech. Pap.* 227:111–24

Barfield TJ. 1993. *The Nomadic Alternative.* Englewood Cliffs, NJ: Prentice-Hall

Baumann MPO, Janzen J, Schwartz HJ, eds. 1993. *Pastoral Production in Central Somalia.* Eschborn, Ger: Dtsch. Ges. Tech. Zs.arb. Schr.reihe GTZ, No. 237

Baxter PTW, ed. 1991. *When the Grass is Gone: Development Intervention in African Arid Lands.* Uppsala: Scand. Inst. Afr. Stud.

Baxter PTW. 1993. The 'new' east African pastoralism: an overview. In *Conflict and the Decline of Pastoralism in the Horn of Africa,* ed. J Markakis, pp. 143–62. London: Macmillan

Baxter PTW. 1994. Pastoralists are people: Why development for pastoralists, not the development of pastoralism? *Rur. Ext. Bull. (Univ. Sussex)* 4:3–8

Baxter PTW, Hogg R, eds. 1990. *Property, Poverty, and People: Changing Rights in Property and Problems of Pastoral Development.* Manchester, UK: Univ. Manchester

Beck L. 1980. Herd owners and hired shepherds: the Qashqa'i of Iran. *Ethnology* 19(3):327–51

Beck L. 1986. *The Qashqa'i of Iran.* New Haven, CT: Yale Univ. Press

Behnke R. 1994. Natural resource management in pastoral Africa. *Dev. Pol. Rev.* 12(1):5–27

Behnke RH, Scoones I. 1992. *Rethinking*

Range Ecology: Implications for Rangeland Management in Africa. Env. Work. Pap. 53. Washington, DC: World Bank

Behnke R, Scoones I, Kerven C. 1993. *Range Ecology at Disequilibrium: New Models of Natural Variability and Pastoral Adaptation in African Savannas.* London: Overseas Dev. Inst.

Bekure S, de Leeuw PN, Grandin BE, Neate PJH, eds. 1991. *Maasai Herding: An Analysis of the Livestock Production System of Maasai Pastoralists in Eastern Kajiado District, Kenya.* ILCA Syst. Stud., No. 4. Addis Ababa: Int. Livestock Cent. Afr.

Bennett JW. 1988. The political economy and economic development of migratory pastoral societies in Eastern Africa. In *Power and Poverty Development and Development Projects in the Third World,* ed. DT Attwood, TC Bruneau, JG Galaty, pp. 31–60. Boulder: Westview

Bradburd D. 1990. *Ambiguous Relations.* Washington, DC: Smithson. Press

Brokensha DW, Little PD, eds. 1988. *Anthropology of Development and Change in East Africa.* Boulder: Westview

Bromley DW. 1992. *Making the Commons Work: Theory, Practice, and Policy.* San Francisco: ICS

Bromley DW, Cernea MM. 1989. *The Management of Common Property Natural Resources: Some Conceptual and Operational Fallacies.* Washington, DC: World Bank

Bruggeman H. 1993. *Pastoral Associations in Chad: Experiences from an Oxfam Project.* Oxfam Res. Pap. 7. Oxford: Oxfam

Campbell DJ. 1984. Responses to drought among farmers and herders in southern Kajiado district, Kenya. *Hum. Ecol.* 12(1): 35–64

Campbell DJ. 1993. 'Land as ours, land as mine'. See Spear & Waller 1993, pp. 258–72

Casimir MJ, Rao A. 1985. Vertical control in the Western Himalayas: some notes on the pastoral ecology of the nomadic Bakrwal of Jammu and Kashmir. *Mount. Res. Dev.* 5(3):221–32

Casimir MJ, Rao A, eds. 1992. *Mobility and Territoriality: Social and Spatial Boundaries Among Foragers, Fishers, Pastoralists and Peripatetics.* Providence: Berg

Cernea MM. 1994. Environmental and social requirements for resource-based regional development. *Region. Dev. Dialogue* 15(1):186–98

Chabasse D, Roure C, Abdoulaye R, Ranque P, Quilici M. 1985. The health of nomads

and semi-nomads of the Malian Gourma: an epidemiological approach. In *Population, Health and Nutrition in the Sahel,* ed. AG Hill, pp. 319–39. London: Routledge & Kegan Paul

Chang C, Koster HA, eds. 1994. *Pastoralists at the Periphery: Herders in a Capitalist World.* Tucson: Univ. Ariz. Press

Charnley S. 1996. Pastoralism and the demise of communal property in Tanzania. *Cult. Surv. Q.* 20(1):41–44

Cincotta RP, Pangare G. 1994. Population growth, agricultural change, and natural resource transition: pastoralism amidst the agricultural economy of Gujarat. In *Rajasthan and Gujarat.* Past. Dev. Netw. Pap. 36a:17–35. London: Overseas Dev. Inst.

Cincotta RP, Zhang YQ, Zhou XM. 1992. Transhumant alpine pastoralism in Northeastern Qinghai Province: an evaluation of livestock population response during China's agrarian economic reform. *Nomadic Peoples* 30:3–25

Cole DP. 1975. *Nomads of the Nomads: The Al Murrah Bedouin of the Empty Quarter.* Arlington Heights, IL: Harlan Davidson

Cooper L. 1993. Patterns of mutual assistance in the Mongolian pastoral economy. *Nomadic Peoples* 33:153–62

Coppock DL. 1993. *The Borana Plateau of Southern Ethiopia: Synthesis of Pastoral Research, Development and Change, 1980–91.* Addis Ababa: Int. Livestock Cent. Afr.

Coughenour MB, Ellis JE, Swift DM, Coppock DL, Galvin K, et al. 1985. Energy extraction and use in a nomadic pastoral ecosystem. *Science* 230:619–25

Cullis A. 1992. *Taking the Bull by the Horns: NGOs and Pastoralists in Coalition.* Past. Dev. Net. Pap. 33rd. London: Overseas Dev. Inst.

Dahl G. 1979. *Suffering Grass: Subsistence and Society of Waso Borana.* Stockholm: Dep. Soc. Anthropol. Stockholm: Univ. Stockholm

Dahl G. 1987. Women in pastoral production: some theoretical notes on roles and resources. *Ethnos* 52(1):246–79

Dahl G, Hjort A. 1976. *Having Herds: Pastoral Herd Growth and Household Economy.* Stockholm: Dep. Soc. Anthropol. Stockholm: Univ. Stockholm

de Haan C. 1994. *An Overview of the World Bank's Involvement in Pastoral Development.* Past. Dev. Net. Pap. 36b:1–6. London: Overseas Dev. Inst.

Doornbos M, Cliffe L, Ahmed AGM, Markakis J, eds. 1992. *Beyond Conflict in the*

Horn: Prospects for Peace, Recovery and Development in Ethiopia, Somalia and the Sudan. London: Currey

Dyson-Hudson N. 1972. The study of nomads. *J. Afr. Asian Stud.* 7(1–2):2–29

Dyson-Hudson N. 1991. Pastoral production systems and livestock development projects: an East African perspective. In *Putting People First: Sociological Variables in Rural Development,* ed. MM Cernea, pp. 219–56. New York: World Bank/Oxford Univ. Press. 2nd ed.

Dyson-Hudson N, Dyson-Hudson R. 1982. The structure of East African herds and the future of East African herders. *Dev. Change* 13:213–38

Dyson-Hudson R, Dyson-Hudson N. 1980. Nomadic pastoralism. *Annu. Rev. Anthropol.* 9:15–61

Dyson-Hudson R, McCabe JT. 1985. *South Turkana Nomadism: Coping with an Unpredictably Varying Environment.* New Haven, CT: HRAFLEX

Dyson-Hudson R, Smith EA. 1978. Human territoriality: an ecological reassessment. *Am. Anthropol.* 80:21–41

Edstrom J. 1993. The reform of livestock marketing in Mongolia: problems for a food secure and equitable market development. *Nomadic Peoples* 33:137–52

Ellis J, Swift DM. 1988. Stability of African pastoral ecosystems. *J. Range Manage.* 41:450–59

Ensminger J. 1987. Economic and political differentiation among Galole Orma women. *Ethnos* 52(1–2):28–49

Ensminger J. 1992. *Making a Market: The Institutional Transformation of an African Society.* New York: Cambridge Univ. Press

Équippe Écologie Anthropologie Societés Pastorales. 1979. *Pastoral Production and Society.* Cambridge: Cambridge Univ. Press

Evans-Pritchard EE. 1940. *The Nuer.* Oxford: Oxford Univ. Press

Fabietti U, Salzman PC, eds. 1996. *The Anthropology of Tribal and Peasant Pastoral Societies: The Dialectics of Social Cohesion and Fragmentation.* Pavia-Como: Ibis

Fratkin E. 1986. Stability and resilience in East Africa pastoralism: the Rendille and the Ariaal of Northern Kenya. *Hum. Ecol.* 14(3):269–86

Fratkin E. 1987. Age sets, households and the organization of pastoral production. *Res. Econ. Anthropol.* 8:295–314

Fratkin E. 1989. Household variation and gender inequality in Ariaal Rendille pastoral production: results of a stratified time allocation survey. *Am. Anthropol.* 91(2):45–55

Fratkin E. 1991. *Surviving Drought and Development: Ariaal Pastoralists of Northern Kenya.* Boulder: Westview

Fratkin E. 1992. Drought and development in Marsabit District, Kenya. *Disasters* 16(2):119–30

Fratkin E, Galvin KA, Roth EA, eds. 1994. *African Pastoralist Systems: An Integrated Approach.* Boulder: Lynne Rienner

Fratkin E, Roth EA. 1990. Drought and economic differentiation among Ariaal pastoralists of Kenya. *Hum. Ecol.* 18:385–402

Fratkin E, Smith K. 1994. Labor, livestock, and land: the organization of pastoral production. See Fratkin et al 1994, pp. 91–112

Fratkin E, Smith K. 1995. Women's changing roles with pastoral sedentarization: varying strategies in alternative Rendille communities. *Hum. Ecol.* 23:433–54

Galaty JG. 1992. "The Land is Yours": social and economic factors in the privatization, sub-division and sale of Maasai ranches. *Nomadic Peoples* 30:26–40

Galaty JG. 1993a. Maasai Expansion and the New East African Pastoralism. See Spear & Waller 1993, pp. 61–86

Galaty JG. 1993b. The Pastoralist's Dilemma: Common Property and Enclosure in Kenya's Rangeland. In *Food Systems Under Stress in Africa,* ed. R Vernooy, pp. 100–13. Ottawa: Int. Dev. Res. Cent.

Galaty JG. 1994. Rangeland tenure and pastoralism in Africa. See Fratkin et al 1994, pp. 185–204

Galaty JG, Aronson D, Salzman PC, Chouinard A, eds. 1981. *The Future of Pastoral Peoples.* Montreal: International Development Research Centre

Galaty JG, Bonte P, eds. 1991. *Herders, Warriors, and Traders: Pastoralism in Africa.* Boulder: Westview

Galaty JG, Johnson DL, eds. 1990. *The World of Pastoralism.* New York: Guilford

Galvin K, Coppock DL, Leslie PW. 1994. Diet, Nutrition, and the Pastoral Strategy. See Fratkin et al 1994, pp. 113–32

Glantz MH, ed. 1987. *Drought and Hunger in Africa: Denying Famine a Future.* Cambridge Univ. Press

Goldstein MC, Beall CM. 1991. Change and continuity in nomadic pastoralism on the Western Tibetan Plateau. *Nomadic Peoples* 28:105–22

Gooch P. 1992. Transhumant pastoralism in Northern India: the Gujar case. *Nomadic Peoples* 30:84–96

Hardin G. 1968. The tragedy of the commons. *Science* 162:1243–48

Herren UJ. 1990. Socioeconomic stratification and small stock production in Mukogodo Division, Kenya. *Res. Econ. Anthropol.* 12:111–48

Hill AG, ed. 1985. *Population, Health, and Nutrition in the Sahel.* London: Routledge & Kegan Paul

Hitchcock RK, Twedt TM. 1995. Physical and cultural genocide of various indigenous peoples. In *Genocide in the Twentieth Century,* ed. S Totten, WS Parsons, IW Charny, pp. 483–534. New York: Garland

Hjort A. 1981. A critique of "ecological" models of pastoral land use. *Ethnos* 46(3–4): 171–89

Hjort af Ornäs A. 1990. Pastoral and environmental security in East Africa. *Disasters* 14:115–22

Hodgson DL. 1997. Images and interventions: the 'problems' of 'pastoralist' development. See Anderson & Broch-Due 1997. In press

Hogg R. 1987. Settlement, pastoralism and the commons. In *Conservation in Africa: People, Policies and Practices,* ed. D Anderson, RH Grove, pp. 293–306. Cambridge: Cambridge Univ. Press

Hogg R. 1992a. Should pastoralism continue as a way of life? *Disasters* 16:131–37

Hogg R. 1992b. NGOs, pastoralists and the myth of community: three case studies of pastoral development from East Africa. *Nomadic Peoples* 30:122–46

Homewood KM. 1992. Development and the ecology of Maasai pastoralist food and nutrition. *Ecol. Food. Nutr.* 29:61–80

Homewood KM. 1995. Development, demarcation and ecological outcomes in Maasailand. *Africa* 65(3):331–50

Homewood KM, Rodgers WA. 1991. *Maasailand Ecology: Pastoralist Development and Wildlife Conservation.* Cambridge: Cambridge Univ. Press

Horowitz MM. 1979. *The Sociology of Pastoralism and African Livestock Project.* AID Prog. Eval. Discuss. Pap. 6. Washington, DC: USAID

Horowitz MM. 1986. Ideology, policy, and praxis in pastoral livestock development. In *The Anthropology of Rural Development in West Africa,* ed. MM Horowitz, T Painter, pp. 251–72. Boulder: Westview

Horowitz MM, Jowka F. 1992. *Pastoral Women and Change in Africa, the Middle East and Central Asia.* New York: Inst. Dev. Anthropol., IDA Work. Pap. 91

Horowitz MM, Little PD. 1987. African pastoralism and poverty: some implications for drought and famine. See Glantz 1987, pp. 59–82

IDS (Institute of Development Studies). 1988. *Pastoral Land Tenure in East Africa.* Brighton UK: Inst. Dev. Stud.

IPAL (Integrated Project in Arid Lands). 1984. *Integrated Resource Assessment and Management Plan for Western Marsabit District, Northern Kenya.* IPAL Tech. Rep. A-6. Nairobi: UNESCO

Ingold T. 1980. *Hunters, Pastoralists, and Ranchers: Reindeer Economies and Their Transformations.* Cambridge Univ. Press

Irons W. 1979. Political stratification among pastoral nomads. See Equippe Ecologie 1979, pp. 361–74

Jacobs AH. 1980. Pastoral development in Tanzanian Maasailand. *Rural Afr.* 7:1–14

Jowka F, ed. 1991. *Gender Relations of Pastoral/Agropastoral Production: A Bibliography with Annotations.* Binghamton, NY: Inst. Dev. Anthropol.

Juul K. 1993. Pastoral tenure problems and local resource management: the case of Northern Senegal. *Nomadic Peoples* 32: 81–90

Kerven C. 1992. *Customary Commerce: A Historical Reassessment of Pastoral Livestock Marketing in Africa* ODI Agr. Occas. Pap. 15. London: Overseas Dev. Inst.

Khazanov AM. 1994. *Nomads and the Outside World.* Madison, WI: Univ. Wis. Press. 2nd ed.

Klepp K-I, Biswalo PM, Talle A. 1994. *Young People at Risk: Fighting Aids in Northern Tanzania.* Oslo: Scand. Univ. Press

Köhler-Rollefson I. 1992. The Raika dromedary breeders of Rajasthan: a pastoral system in crisis. *Nomadic Peoples* 30:74–83

Köhler-Rollefson I. 1995. Rajasthan's camel pastoralists and NGOs: the view from the bottom. In *Social Aspects of Sustainable Dryland Management,* ed. D Stiles, pp. 115–27. Chichester: Wiley

Kressel GM, Ben-David J, Abu Rabi'a K. 1991. Changes in the land usage by the Negev Bedouin since the mid-19th Century. *Nomadic Peoples* 28:28–55

Kuznar LA. 1991. Transhumant goat pastoralism in the High Sierra of the South Central Andes: human responses to environmental and social uncertainty. *Nomadic Peoples* 28:93–104

Lamprey HF. 1976. *The UNEP-MAB Integrated Project in Arid Lands: Phase III.* Reg. Proj. Doc. FP/1101-77. Nairobi: UNEP

Lamprey HF. 1983. Pastoralism yesterday and

today: the overgrazing problem. In *Tropical Savannas,* ed. F Bourliere, pp. 643–66. Amsterdam: Elsevier Sci.

Lancaster WO. 1986. *The Rwala Bedouin Today.* Cambridge: Cambridge Univ. Press

Lane C. 1994. Pastures lost: alienation of Barabaig land in the context of land policy and legislation in Tanzania. *Nomadic Peoples* 34/35:81–94

Lane C. 1996. *Pastures Lost: Barabaig Economy, Resource Tenure, and the Alienation of Land in Tanzania.* Nairobi: Initiatives Publ.

Li O, Ma R, Simpson JR. 1993. Changes in the nomadic pattern and its impact on the Inner Mongolia steppe grasslands ecosystem. *Nomadic Peoples* 33:63–72

Little MA, Leslie PW, eds. 1997. *Turkana Pastoral Nomads: Biobehavioral and Ecological Conditions of their Lives.* Oxford: Oxford Univ. Press

Little PD. 1985. Absentee herd owners and part-time pastoralists: The political economy of resource use in northern Kenya. *Hum. Ecol.* 13(2):136–51

Little PD. 1987a. Land use conflicts in the agricultural/pastoral borderlands: the case of Kenya. See Little & Horowitz 1987a, pp. 195–211

Little PD. 1987b. Domestic production and regional markets in Northern Kenya. *Am. Ethn.* 14:295–308

Little PD. 1994a. The social context of land degradation ("desertification") in dry regions. In *Population and Environment: Rethinking the Debate,* ed. L Arizpe, MP Stone, DC Major, pp. 209–51. Boulder: Westview

Little PD. 1994b. Maidens and milk markets: the sociology of dairy marketing in southern Somalia. See Fratkin et al 1994, pp. 165–84

Little PD, Horowitz MM, eds. 1987a. *Lands at Risk in the Third World.* Boulder: Westview

Little PD, Horowitz MM. 1987b. Introduction: social science perspectives on land, ecology, and development. See Little & Horowitz 1987a, pp. 1–16

Manger LO. 1988. Traders, farmers and pastoralists: economic adaptations and environmental problems in the Southern Nuba Mountains of the Sudan. In *The Ecology of Survival,* ed. DH Johnson, DM Anderson, pp. 155–72. London: Lester Crook

Manger LO, Harir S, Krywinski K, Vetaas OR. 1996. *Survival on Meagre Resources: Hadendowa Pastoralism in the Red Sea Hills.* Uppsala: Nord. Afr. Inst.

Marx E. 1977. The tribe as a unit of subsistence: nomadic pastoralism in the Middle East. *Am. Anthropol.* 79(2):343–63

Marx E, Shmueli E, eds. 1984. *The Changing Bedouin.* London: Tavistock

McCabe JT. 1990. Turkana pastoralism: a case against the tragedy of the commons. *Hum. Econ.* 18:81–103

McCabe JT, Perkin S, Schofield S. 1992. Can conservation and development be coupled among pastoral people? An examination of the Maasai of the Ngorongoro Conservation Area, Tanzania. *Hum. Organ.* 51(4): 353–66

Mearns R. 1996. Community, collective action and common grazing: the case of post-socialist Mongolia. *J. Dev. Stud.* 32(3): 297–339

Meir A. 1988. Nomads and the state: the spatial dynamics of centrifugal and centripetal forces among the Israeli Negev Bedouin. *Polit. Geogr. Q.* 7(3):251–70

Meir A. 1996. Territoriality among the Negev Bedouin in transition from nomadism to sedentarism. See Fabietti & Salzman 1996, pp. 187–207

Michael BJ. 1987. Milk production and sales by the Hawazma (Baggara) of Sudan: implications for gender roles. *Res. Ecol. Anthropol.* 9:105–41

Mohamed-Salih MA. 1991. Livestock development or pastoral development? In *When the Grass Is Gone: Development Intervention in African Arid Lands,* ed. PTW Baxter, pp. 37–57. Uppsala: Scand. Inst. Afr. Stud.

Mohamed-Salih MA. 1992. Agro-pastoralists' response to agricultural policies: the predicament of the Baggara, Western Sudan. In *Agricultural Transformation and Social Change in Africa,* ed. B Nett, V Wulf, A Diarra, pp. 153–72. Frankfurt: Lang

Mohamed-Salih MA, Baker J, Baekers J, eds. 1995. *The Migration Experience in Africa.* Uppsala: Scand. Inst. Afr. Stud.

Nathan MA, Fratkin EM, Roth EA. 1996. Sedentism and child health among Rendille pastoralists of Northern Kenya. *Soc. Sci. Med.* 43(4):503–15

Nicholson SE. 1986. Climate, drought and famine in Africa. In *Food in Sub-Saharan Africa,* ed. A Hansen, DE McMillan, pp. 107–28. Boulder: Lynne Rienner

Oba G. 1994. *The Role of Indigenous Range Management Knowledge for Desertification Control in Northern Kenya.* Uppsala: Environ. Pol. Soc.

O'Leary MF. 1984. Ecological villains or economic victims: the case of the Rendille of Northern Kenya. *UNEP Desertif. Control Bull.* 11:17–21

O'Leary MF. 1990. Drought and change amongst Northern Kenya nomadic pastoralists: the case of Rendille and Gabra. In *From Water to World-Making: African Models in Arid Lands*, ed. G Palsson, pp. 151–74. Uppsala: Scand. Inst. Afr. Stud.

Oxby C. 1975. *Pastoral Nomads and Development*. London: Int. Afr. Inst.

Peters PE. 1994. *Dividing the Commons: Politics, Policy and Culture in Botswana*. Charlottesville VA: Univ. Press Va.

Potkanski T. 1993. Decollectivisation of the Mongolian pastoral economy (1991–92): some economic and social consequences. *Nomadic Peoples* 33:123–35

Potkanski T. 1994. *Property Concepts, Herding Patterns and Management of Natural Resources Among the Ngorongoro and Salei Maasai of Tanzania*. Past. Land. Ten. Ser., Drylands Prog. No. 6. London: Int. Inst. Environ. Dev.

Prins HHT. 1992. The pastoral road to extinction: competition between wildlife and traditional pastoralism in East Africa. *Environ. Conserv.* 19(2):117–23

Rao A. 1995. From bondsmen to middlemen: hired shepherds and pastoral politics. *Anthropos* 90:149–67

Roth EA. 1990. Modeling Rendille household herd composition. *Hum. Ecol.* 18(4): 441–55

Roth EA. 1996. Traditional pastoral strategies in a modern world: An example from northern Kenya. *Hum. Organ.* 55:219–24

Salzman PC. 1974. Tribal chiefs as middlemen: the politics of encapsulation in the Middle East. *Anthropol. Q.* 47:203–10

Salzman PC. 1979. Inequality and oppression in nomadic society. In *Pastoral Production and Society*, ed. Equippe Ecologie, pp. 429–46. Cambridge: Cambridge Univ. Press

Salzman PC. 1980. Processes of sedentarization as adaptation and response. In *When Nomads Settle: Processes of Sedentarization as Adaptation and Response*. New York: Praeger

Salzman PC. 1996. Peasant pastoralism. See Fabietti & Salzman 1996, pp. 149–66

Salzman PC, Galaty JG, eds. 1990. *Nomads in a Changing World*. Naples: Inst. Univ. Orient.

Sandford S. 1983. *Management of Pastoral Development in the Third World*. Chichester: Wiley

Schlee G. 1990. Holy grounds. In *Property, Poverty, and People*, ed. PTW Baxter, R Hogg, pp. 45–54. Manchester: Univ. Manchester

Schlee G. 1995. Local war and its impact on ethnic and religious identification in Southern Ethiopia. *Geojournal* 36(1):7–17

Schmitz J. 1993. Anthropologie des conflits fonciers et hydropolitique du fleuve Sénégal (1975–1991). *Cah. Sci. Hum.* 29(4): 591–623

Scholz F. 1992. *Nomadismus Bibliographie*. Berlin: Das Arabische Buch

Schwartz HJ. 1993. Pastoral production systems in the dry lowlands of Eastern Africa. See Baumann et al 1993, pp. 1–15

Scoones I. 1988. *Sustainable Pastoralism in Africa: An Annotated Bibliography*. London: IIED

Scoones I. 1992. Coping with drought: Responses of herders and livestock in contrasting savanna environments in Zimbabwe. *Hum. Ecol.* 20(3):293–314

Scoones I, Graham O. 1994. New directions for pastoral development in Africa. *Dev. Pract.* 4:188–98

Shipton P. 1990. African famines and food security: Anthropological perspectives. *Annu. Rev. Anthropol.* 19:353–94

Simpson JR, Evangelou P, eds. 1984. *Livestock Development in Subsaharan Africa: Constraints, Prospects, Policy*. Boulder: Westview

Simpson JR, Sullivan GM. 1984. Planning for institutional change in utilization of Sub-Saharan Africa's common property range resources. *Afr. Stud. Rev.* 27(4):61–78

Spear T, Waller R, eds. 1993. *Being Maasai*. London: Currey

Spencer P. 1988. *The Maasai of Matapato: A Study of Rituals of Rebellion*. Bloomington: Indiana Univ. Press

Sperling L. 1985. Labor recruitment among East African herders. *Labor, Capital, and Society* 18(1):68–86

Sperling L. 1987. Wage employment among Samburu pastoralists of northcentral *Res. Econ. Anthropol.* 9:167–90

Sperling L, Galaty JG. 1990. Cattle, culture, and economy: dynamics in East African pastoralism. See Galaty & Johnson 1990, pp. 69–97

Steen E. 1994. Drylands of the Third World: potential for future development. *Ambio* 23(7):458–60

Stenning D. 1959. *Savannah Nomads: A Study of the Wodaabe Pastoral Fulani of Western Bornu Province of Northern Region, Nigeria*. London: Oxford Univ. Press

Svensson TG. 1992. Right to self-determination: a basic human right concerning cultural survival. The case of the Sami and the Scandinavian state. In *Human Rights in Cross-Cultural Perspectives: A Quest for Consensus*, ed. AA An-

Na'im, pp. 363–84. Philadelphia: Univ. Pa. Press

Swift J. 1977. Sahelian pastoralists: underdevelopment, desertification and famine. *Annu. Rev. Anthropol.* 6:457–78

Swift J. 1988. *Major Issues in Pastoral Development with Special Emphasis on Selected African Countries.* Rome: FAO

Swift J. 1991. Local customary institutions as the basis for natural resource management among Boran pastoralists in Northern Kenya. *IDS Bull.* 22(4):34–37. Inst. Dev. Stud., Univ. Sussex

Swift J, Mearns R. 1993. Mongolian pastoralism on the threshold of the twenty-first century. *Nomadic Peoples* 33:3–7

Talle A. 1987. Women as heads of houses: the organization of production and the role of women among pastoral Maasai in Kenya. *Ethnos* 52(1–2):50–80

Talle A. 1988. Women at a loss: changes in Maasai pastoralism and their effects on gender relations. *Stockholm Stud. Soc. Anthropol.,* Vol. 19. Stockholm: Dep. Soc. Anthropol., Univ. Stockholm

Tapper R. 1979. *Pasture and Politics: Economics, Conflict and Ritual among Shahsevan Nomads of Northwestern Iran.* London: Academic

Templer G, Swift J, Payne P. 1993. The changing significance of risk in the Mongolian pastoral economy. *Nomadic Peoples* 33: 105–22

Turner M. 1993. Overstocking the range: a critical analysis of the environmental science of Sahelian pastoralism. *Econ. Geogr.* 69(4):402–21

UNCOD. 1977. *United Nations Conference on Desertification: Its Causes and Consequences,* ed. Secretariat UNCOD. Nairobi/ UNEP

Unruh JD. 1991. Nomadic pastoralism and irrigated agriculture in Somalia. *Geojournal* 25(1):91–108

Van den Brink R, Bromley DW, Chavas J. 1995. The economics of Cain and Abel: agro-pastoral property rights in the Sahel. *J. Dev. Stud.* 31(3):373–99

Vedeld T. 1992. *Local Institution-Building and Resource Management in the West African Sahel.* Past. Dev. Netw. Pap. 33c. London: Overseas Dev. Inst.

Vira S. 1993. *The Gujars of Uttar Pradesh: 'Neglected Victims of Progress.'* Iss. Pap., Drylands Progr., No. 41. London: Int. Inst. Environ. Dev.

Waters-Bayer A. 1985. Modernizing milk production in Nigeria: Who benefits? *Ceres* 19(5):34–39

Waters-Bayer A, Bayer W. 1994. *Planning with Pastoralists: PRA and More. A Review of Methods Focused on Africa.* Eschborn, Ger: Dtsch. Ges. Tech. Zs.arb.

Yamskov AN. 1991. Ethnic conflict in the Transcaucasus: the case of Nagarno-Karabakh. *Theory Soc.* 20:631–60

Zuppan M. 1994. Need herders and farmers quarrel? Rethinking herder-farmer models in Africa. *Rural Ext. Bull. (Univ. Sussex)* 4:12–16

Annu. Rev. Anthropol. 1997. 26:263–89

ANTIEVOLUTION AND CREATIONISM IN THE UNITED STATES

Eugenie C. Scott

The National Center for Science Education, Inc., P.O. Box 9477, Berkeley, California
94709

KEY WORDS: science, religion, creation-evolution controversy, intelligent design, evolution

---

ABSTRACT

Evolution is considered controversial by a substantial minority of Americans.
Religious opposition explains this, but this opposition is comprised of a broad
continuum of religious views. It runs from "young earth creationism" through
"old earth creationism" (including "day-age," "gap," and "progressive creationism") to "theistic evolutionism." Historically, antievolutionists have attempted to ban evolution and to present it on an equal footing with "creation
science." Scholars largely ignored antievolutionism until efforts to pass "equal
time for creation and evolution" laws stimulated both political and scholarly
activism. Lately, there are efforts to discourage the teaching of evolution by requiring teachers to read disclaimers before teaching it, to teach it as "theory,
not fact," or to present fancied "evidence against evolution." Recently, "intelligent design theory," a restatement of William Paley's Argument from Design, has surfaced. Although rejected by scientists, intelligent design arguments and publications are appearing at the college level (in nonscience
courses) as accurate representations of scientific scholarship.

INTRODUCTION

According to a 1996 poll of adult Americans conducted by the National Science Board, only 44% agreed with the statement, "Human beings, as we know
them today, developed from earlier species of animals" (National Science

263

Board). Forty percent disagreed, and 16% answered "don't know." The same survey showed that 52% of American adults either agreed or didn't know that "[t]he earliest humans lived at the same time as the dinosaurs" (32% agreed, 20% didn't know).

And yet, the National Academy of Sciences states unequivocally that:

> Evolution pervades all biological phenomena. To ignore that it occurred or to classify it as a form of dogma is to deprive the student of the most fundamental organizational concept in the biological sciences. No other biological concept has been more extensively tested and more thoroughly corroborated than the evolutionary history of organisms (National Academy of Sciences 1984).

There is a gap between the acceptance of evolution in the scientific community and its acceptance among the general public. It appears that among well-accepted scientific theories (heliocentrism, cell theory, atomic theory, plate tectonics), evolution alone is rejected by nonscientists. In a poll by the American Museum of Natural History, for example, 78% of adult Americans accepted the theory of continental drift ("continents gradually change their positions") (American Museum of Natural History 1994).

A significant variable in understanding antievolutionism is the degree to which a literal interpretation of holy texts is considered essential to theology. Thus Biblical-literalist Christians, ultraconservative Jews, and Koranic-literalist Muslims object to evolution. Because the number of Jews and Muslims in the United States is small compared with Christians, and because the most active antievolutionists are Christian, I focus on Christians in this review. Antievolution and creationism in other countries are beyond the scope of this chapter; however, useful discussions can be found in Edis (1994), Goodman (1995), Groves (1991), and Scott (1991).

Religious opposition to evolution propels antievolutionism. Although antievolutionists pay lip service to supposed scientific problems with evolution, what motivates them to battle its teaching is apprehension over the implications of evolution for religion. Conservative Christians who are strongly literalist in their views fear that if their children learn evolution, they will cease to believe in God. Without God to guide them, children will grow up to be bad people. In the words of Henry R Morris, a prominent creationist, "Evolution is at the foundation of communism, fascism, Freudianism, social darwinism, behaviorism, Kinseyism, materialism, atheism, and in the religious world, modernism and neo-orthodoxy" (Morris 1963, p. 24). Conservative Christians also believe that the child who loses faith in God also is lost to salvation. Clearly, antievolutionists' motives for opposing the teaching of evolution to their children are strong. As shown below, however, the strict literalist view is not universally held by the majority of Christians in the United States.

Rejecting evolution has a long history in America. Antievolutionism has been a political and social movement in this country for most of this century. In this review, I define terms and issues critical to an understanding of the movement and briefly discuss the history, motivations, and evolution of antievolutionism. I argue that antievolutionism has evolved from the purely religious opposition of the Scopes era to creation science, and to the present neocreationism period. The academic response to creationism has been an unusual mixture of scholarship and activism. An explosion of books and articles from the mid-1970s through the late 1980s was motivated less by scholarly interest than by efforts to oppose antievolutionists in their attempts to legally impose their views on the public education system. The actual writings themselves were overwhelmingly written not for other scholars but for members of the general public. Oddly, there have been few social-scientific analyses—anthropological, sociological, or psychological—of this antievolution movement. Unlike with other social issues—such as antiabortion or animal rights—there is a marked shortage of research on "what makes these people tick."

The review concludes with the implications of a recent development in neocreationism: the movement of antievolutionism to secular schools of higher learning.

DEFINITIONS

Evolution

"Evolution" in its most basic sense is a simple idea: Change through time has taken place. The universe has a history: The present is different from the past. Physical and chemical evolution include the formation of elements in the nuclear blast furnaces of evolving stars, the formation of galaxies, and the formation of star systems with planets. The earth has changed greatly in the past four billion years; the present is different from the past.

Darwin's "descent with modification" is the most useful definition of biological evolution. Darwinism is a specific kind of evolution: Living things descend with modification from ancestors through natural selection. In the 1940s and 1950s, classical natural selection theory coupled with genetic theory became known as the synthetic theory of evolution, or neo-Darwinism. Late-twentieth-century explanations of the rate and manner of biological evolution include Eldredge and Gould's theory of "punctuated equilibria," speculations about natural selection above (species selection) and below (selfish genes) the level of organism or population, and nonselective mechanisms bringing about evolutionary change (neutralism or non-Darwinian evolution) (Dawkins 1976, Eldredge 1989, Eldredge & Gould 1972, King & Jukes 1969, Stanley 1981). The relationship between evolution and developmental biology is an active area of research. Evolutionary biological theory has progressed beyond classical Darwinism and even neo-Darwinism, although the current consensus is that neo-Darwinism explains much, if not most, of biological evolution.

Creationism

Creationism generally refers to the idea that a supernatural entity(s) created the universe and humankind. Creation stories are extensively studied in comparative religion and in the anthropology of religion. Christian creation theology stories take a wide range of forms, from the general—"God created"—to the specific—exactly what, how, and when God created. Thus, if someone responds "yes" to the survey question "Are you a creationist?" the survey will obtain little useful information about what that person believes.

SPECIAL CREATIONISM AND DEISM   To understand the variety of creationisms, it may be useful to consider various forms or poles of Christian theology (McGrath 1994, Torrance 1981). Special Creationism and Deism can be seen to contrast the most strongly. Special Creationism is the doctrine that God created the universe and all that is in it—including human beings—as a special act, or as a series of special acts. God is seen as a personal (though not necessarily anthropomorphic) entity concerned and directly involved with His creation, and especially concerned with the doings of humankind. God also actively interacts with the universe and with humankind.

Deism, however, is the theological view that God set in motion the laws of nature and "sat back" from then on. The universe came about gradually, probably beginning with the Big Bang and the subsequent formation of stars and galaxies from swirling dust clouds, and so on to the present. In this review, the key distinction between Deism and Special Creationism is that with Deism, God "is left with nothing to do," in the words of Johnson (1990). Deists envision a far less "hands-on" God than do Special Creationists, which is a major difference and source of conflict between the two theologies. The God of the Deist is a grand and awe-inspiring force but not a God one would be inclined to supplicate. Conservative Christians, especially those defining themselves as born again, treasure a personal relationship with God, who they feel is guiding their lives. Various Christian theologies can be arranged along a continuum of belief about the personality or impersonality of God, with Deists at one end and Special Creationists at the other. Special Creationists themselves can be ranged along a continuum.

THE CREATION/EVOLUTION CONTINUUM

Most members of the public define the creation/evolution controversy dichotomously with creationists on one side and evolutionists on the other, but in truth there is a continuum of positions rather than a dichotomy (see Figure 1). The continuum reflects theological conservatism and liberalism but also reflects inversely the degree of acceptance of modern science. Special Creationists can be divided into two groups: Young Earth Creationists and Old Earth Creationists.

Young Earth Creationism

Young Earth Creationists (YECs) are Special Creationists who believe that the universe came into being only a few thousand years ago. The most conservative YECs are Flat Earthers, who accept little of the modern scientific consensus (DeFord 1931). Charles K Johnson, head of the International Flat Earth Society, headquartered in Lancaster, California, believes seriously that earth is as the ancients perceived it: circular and flat, not spherical (Schadewald 1991).

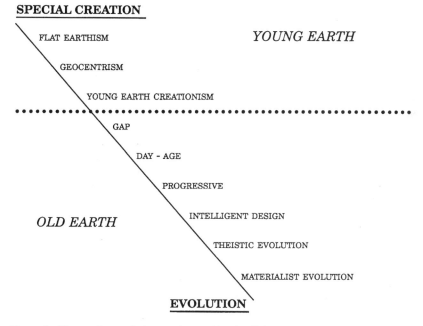

Figure 1   The creation-evolution continuum. For simplicity, statements are shown at equal spacing along a continuum. In reality, some viewpoints are closer together and some are farther apart than shown.

The earth is shaped like a coin, not a ball. The International Flat Earth Society has only about 200 members (Schadewald 1980) and is insignificant in the antievolution movement. It is an example, however, of extreme Biblical-literalist theology: The earth is flat because the Bible *says* it is flat, regardless of what science tells us.

Geocentrists are somewhat more liberal YECs. They accept that the planet is a sphere but deny that the sun is the center of the solar system. Like Flat Earthers, they reject virtually all of modern physics and chemistry as well as biology. Geocentrism is a somewhat larger but still insignificant component of modern antievolutionism. Still, at the Cleveland Bible-Science Association creationism conference in 1985, the plenary session debate was held between two Geocentrists and two Heliocentrists (Bible-Science Association 1985).

Flat Earthers and Geocentrists believe in a universe and planet that are only a few thousand years old, much as did Bishop Ussher and John Lightfoot. Technically, they are YECs, but within antievolutionist circles the term YEC is usually reserved for the followers of Henry Morris, founder and recently retired director of the Institute for Creation Research (ICR) and arguably the most influential creationist of the late twentieth century. Few of these so-called classical YECs interpret the flat-earth and geocentric passages of the Bible literally, but they reject modern physics, chemistry, and geology concerning the age of the earth. They deny biological descent with modification.

YEC AND THE INSTITUTE FOR CREATION RESEARCH   Henry Morris can be said to have defined antievolutionism in its modern form. In 1963, he and John C Whitcomb published *The Genesis Flood* (Whitcomb & Morris 1963), a seminal work that outlined a scientific rationale for Young Earth Creationism. As the title suggests, the authors accept Genesis literally, including not just the special, separate creation of human beings and all other species, but the historicity of Noah's Flood. Although efforts to make a literal interpretation of the Bible compatible with science, especially geology, occurred throughout the eighteenth and nineteenth centuries, *The Genesis Flood* was the first significant twentieth-century effort. The book made it possible for religious antievolutionists to argue that evolution was not only religiously objectionable but also scientifically flawed. Creation science was fleshed out by subsequent books and pamphlets by Morris and those inspired by him.

The ICR was founded by Morris and others in the early 1970s to promote scholarship in YEC science—especially flood geology—and to train students (Numbers 1992). It remains the flagship creationist institution to which all other YEC organizations look. It has a large publishing arm called Masterbooks, a graduate school conferring masters degrees in science and science education, and a public museum. Most other YEC organizations sell and otherwise distribute ICR books, pamphlets, filmstrips, videos, movies and other materials through their newsletters, and the movement leans heavily on Morris's writings and perspectives (Toumey 1994). The ICR also organized Back to Genesis revivals sponsored by local churches, during which ICR faculty lecture for one to three days, promoting both the theology and the science of creation science. Thousands of people attend these sessions, which are held at least once a month. Other outreach activities include radio programs broadcast on several Christian radio networks and occasional tours to the Grand Canyon and other sites.

Very little actual research is performed by ICR faculty. Publications are almost entirely on Christian apologetics. In a review of the ICR gradate school, a visiting committee of scientists concluded that "no member of the resident faculty of the ICR has continued an active and published research program since arrival at the ICR. The Institute for Creation Research can therefore not be considered to be a scientific research institution" (Wills et al 1990, p. 22).

In addition to the Institute for Creation Research, there are several other regional and national YEC organizations. Near Minneapolis is located the Bible-Science Association, which publishes a nationally distributed newsletter. Australian evangelist Ken Ham, a former ICR employee, formed his own Answers in Genesis ministry, located in Florence, Kentucky. Ham distributes the Australian four-color magazine *Creation ex Nihilo* as a premium to his members, and he also circulates a newsletter. He is currently planning to establish a Genesis Park theme park and museum in Kentucky which will present the Flood, the creation of Adam and Eve, and other elements of Genesis as historical fact.

The student group Students for Origins Research began at the University of California, Santa Barbara in 1975 and became a registered nonprofit organization in 1979. Its newspaper was distributed free on campuses around the country during the 1980s, and the organization metamorphosed in the early 1990s into Access Resource Network (ARN). Its publications have had a couple of format changes, and ARN currently publishes a journal called *Origins and Design*. Its orientation has shifted a bit from fairly strict YEC to promotion of design theory (discussed below).

Old Earth Creationism

The idea that the earth is ancient was well established in science by the mid-1800s and was not considered a radical idea in either the Church of England or the Catholic Church (Eiseley 1958). Modern YECs are not only on the fringes of modern science, they are also on the fringes of modern theology. From the mid-1700s onward, different explanations have been devised to accommodate the idea of Special Creationism with scientific data and theory showing that the earth was ancient. These views retained the critical element of Special Creation: that God is personally involved. The present may indeed be different from the past, but God was seen as the active causal agent of the observed changes.

GAP THEORY   One of the better-known accommodations of religion to science was the Gap or Restitution Theory, which claimed that there was a large temporal gap between Gen. 1:1 and Gen. 1:2 (Young 1982). Articulated from about the late eighteenth century on, Gap Theory assumes a pre-Adamic creation that was destroyed before Gen. 1:2, when God started all over again to create the world in six days and to create Adam and Eve. The gap between two separate creations allows for an accommodation of the proof of the ancient age of the earth with Special Creationism.

DAY-AGE THEORY   Another attempt to accommodate science to a literal, or mostly literal, reading of the Bible is the Day-Age Theory, which was more popular than the Gap Theory in the nineteenth and earlier part of twentieth centuries (Young 1982, p. 57). Science and religion are both accommodated by having each of the six days of creation be not a 24-h day but a long period of time, even thousands or millions of years. Many literalists have found comfort in what they regard as a rough parallel between organic evolution and Genesis, in which plants appear before animals and human beings appear last.

PROGRESSIVE CREATIONISM   Although some modern activist antievolutionists may still hold to Day-Age and Gap theories, the view held by the majority of today's Old Earth Creationists (OECs) is some form of Progressive Creationism (PC). The PC view blends Special Creationism with a fair amount of modern science. Progressive Creationists, such as Hugh Ross of Reasons to Believe ministries, have no problems with scientific data concerning the age of the earth or the long period of time it has taken for the earth to come to its current form. Ross, an astronomer with a PhD from the University of Toronto, even cites the Big Bang as evidence of the creative power of God. Although the PC view accepts modern physical science, it incorporates only parts of modern biological science.

Progressive Creationists (PCs) believe that God created "kinds" of animals that were of a higher taxonomic level than species. Most PCs accept that God created creatures containing at least as much genetic variation as a family (e.g. Felidae, Cercopithecidae) and considerable "evolution within a kind" then occurred. A created cat kind would have possessed sufficient genetic variability to differentiate into lions, tigers, leopards, pumas, bobcats, and housecats through the normal microevolutionary processes of mutation and recombination, natural selection, genetic drift, and speciation. The literature speaks of "horizontal" change, which is considered acceptable because it is within the kind. Although microevolution can explain horizontal change, evolution taking place within a kind is limited because genetic variation is limited: It is not possible to derive one kind from another. "Basic body plans," as creationists call them, are distinct from one another, and thus "vertical" changes between kinds cannot occur (Ramm 1955). In antievolution literature, vertical change equates with macroevolution, or evolution above the species level. The basic body plans of major phyla that appear in the so-called Cambrian explosion are seen by most Old Earth Creationists as evidence of Special Creation.

YECs hold similar views of created kinds, but they believe that all the kinds were created during the six, 24-h days of Genesis. Although YECs hold to the same "microevolution/horizontal"-vs-"macroevolution/vertical" dichotomy, they interpret the fossil record quite differently than such OECs as PCs. The YECs look at the patterned distribution of fossils in the geological column as merely an artifact of the formation of geological strata after the waters of Noah's Flood receded. All the kinds were created at one time, and for a variety of reasons sorted themselves out in the pattern (e.g. unicellular below multicellular, invertebrates below vertebrates) shown by paleontologists. To a PC, the distribution of fossils in the geological column is real and is the result of the special creation of different kinds at different times, followed by some differentiation within these kinds. For both YEC and OEC, however, God is a hands-on God who intervenes to produce a world that accomplishes His as yet-unknown purpose.

There rarely are sharp boundaries along a continuum. There is a sharp division between YEC and OEC but far less clarity between and among the various OEC persuasions. Even though OECs accept most of modern physics, chemistry, and geology, they are not too dissimilar to YECs in their rejection of descent with modification (the evolutionist's explanation of the fossil record).

THEISTIC EVOLUTION   In Figure 1, Progressive Creationism is followed by Theistic Evolutionism (TE), a theological view in which God created but relied more upon the laws of nature to bring about His purpose. According to TE, one species can give rise to another: Descent with modification can occur. Proponents of TE vary in whether and how much God is allowed to intervene—some Theistic Evolutionists (TEs) are close to being Deists. Other TEs see God as intervening at critical intervals during the history of life—especially in the origin of human beings—and, in turn, are closer to PCs. In one form or another, TE is the view of creation taught at the majority of mainline Protestant seminaries, and it is the official position of the Catholic church. In 1996, Pope John Paul II reiterated the Catholic TE position, according to which God created, evolution occurred, human beings may indeed have been descended from more primitive forms, and the Hand of God was required for the production of the human soul (John Paul II 1996).

MATERIALIST EVOLUTIONISM   On the continuum in Figure 1, TE is followed by Materialist Evolutionism (ME), a nonreligious view. Today, all science operates under a *methodological materialism* that assumes that scientific epistemology is limited to formulating explanations of the natural world on the basis of natural, rather than supernatural, causes. Materialist Evolutionists (MEs) go beyond science and propose that the laws of nature are not only sufficient to explain all of nature and evolution but that the supernatural does not exist. This is *philosophical materialism* (*naturalism*), the idea that there is nothing in the universe beyond matter, energy, and their interactions. This view has a long history in Western thought, but as a philosophy it is distinct from the methodological materialism that informs science in the late twentieth century. When scientists such as William Provine and Richard Dawkins present philosophical materialism as the inevitable outgrowth of science or evolution (Dawkins 1987, Provine 1988), they reinforce the view encouraged by Morris and other antievolutionists that "one cannot be an evolutionist and a Christian."

I now review the legal history of the response to antievolutionism, which stimulated the scholarly analysis of the antievolution movement that began in the mid-1970s.

LEGAL HISTORY

Creation Science

John T Scopes was tried in 1925 for violating a Tennessee law that banned the teaching of evolution. Such laws were struck down in 1968 by the Supreme Court in *Epperson* v. *Arkansas*. Of more concern for antievolutionists was the reemergence of evolution in high-school textbooks, from which the subject had been systematically deleted since about the 1930s (Grabiner & Miller 1974). After the Soviet Union beat the United States into space by launching Sputnik in the late 1950s, Congress began to pour money into upgrading public K–12 education. Beginning in 1959, the Biological Sciences Curriculum Study, a group of university scientists and master teachers, prepared a series of high-school biology textbooks that placed evolution squarely at the center of biology education. Because these books received the imprimatur of the government (they were sponsored by the National Science Foundation), they sold well and encouraged commercial publishers to rewrite their textbooks to include evolution.

The reemergence of evolution in the curriculum roused the antievolutionists to respond. In 1963, Whitcomb and Morris published *The Genesis Flood,* arguing that there were scientific data supporting a Biblical-literalist Special Creationism. The idea began to evolve that even if it were no longer possible to ban evolution, children could be given a scientific (and thus legal) alternative to evolution so they would not have to "believe" it. In 1978, a Yale law student named Wendell Bird wrote an article in the *Yale Law Review* presenting a legal justification for teaching both evolution and creation science (Bird 1978). The "equal time" movement was born.

During the early 1980s, a series of bills promoting equal time for the teaching of creation science was introduced in at least 26 state legislatures, some more than once (Scott 1994). Most of them were clones of a model bill developed by a South Carolina respiratory therapist, Paul Elwanger, which was influenced by an ICR model resolution for equal time (Morris N.d.). The bills defined creation science as including the ideas of "a worldwide flood" and other YEC mainstays, including the special creation of human beings. If so-called evolution science was taught, then creation science, its proposed parallel, must be taught as well. Arkansas and Louisiana each passed similar Elwanger-type bills, and both bills were taken to court.

ARKANSAS AND LOUISIANA   Arkansas's equal time law was declared unconstitutional in 1982 after a full trial dubbed "Scopes II." Opposing the law were leaders of many religious organizations. Joining the lead plaintiff, Methodist Rev. Bill McLean, were the bishops or other leaders of Roman Catholic, Episcopalian, African Methodist Episcopal, Presbyterians, and Southern Baptist churches, and Reform Jews (Larson 1985). The ACLU arranged pro bono representation by a leading New York law firm and assembled an all-star cast of witnesses from the fields of science, philosophy of science, education, and theology. The *McLean* v. *Arkansas* decision was a rousing victory for the anticreationists: Federal District Judge Overton not only struck down the law but declared that creation science failed as science. Having lost badly, the state did not appeal.

The failure of the Arkansas equal time law slowed but did not halt the effort to pass legislation. At virtually the same time as the Arkansas decision was being issued, Louisiana passed a similar equal time law which was challenged by both proponents and opponents: one side suing to immediately implement the law and the other requesting an injunction. The lawsuits took a long time to wend their ways through the courts, and there was no full trial as there had been in Arkansas. Finally, in 1987, the Supreme Court decided in *Edwards* v. *Aguillard* that equal time laws like Louisiana's violated the establishment clause of the First Amendment of the Constitution because they promoted an inherently religious idea: creationism (Larson 1985, Numbers 1992).

The Scholarly Response

The scientific community was appalled at the proliferation of such laws, and in 1980–1981 a loose coalition of scientists and teachers formed Committees of Correspondence in most of the states (Weinberg 1982). Led by biologist Wayne Moyer, then-director of the National Association of Biology Teachers, and retired high-school biology teacher Stanley Weinberg, this coalition evolved by 1983 into the National Center for Science Education (NCSE), which remains an organization consisting primarily of scientists who support the teaching of evolution in the public schools and oppose creation science and other religiously based attacks on evolution. Weinberg's occasional "Memorandum to Liaisons to State Committees of Correspondence," which he began in March 1981, and later, the NCSE's *Creation/Evolution Newsletter,* helped scientists and others keep abreast of legal and other developments in the antievolution movement.

In the summer of 1980, the American Humanist Association established a journal entitled *Creation/Evolution,* which was intended to provide nonscientists with understandable scientific refutations of creationist arguments. Prominent evolutionary scientists actively supported the anticreationist movement by analyzing and refuting the scientific arguments of creation science in publications read by the general public such as *Creation/Evolution, Science 82, The New Republic, Natural History,* and others. They argued that creation science argumentation characteristically pulls out odd bits of data from the mainstream scientific literature and then proclaims that these out-of-context statements are proof that evolution did not occur. Because of the arcane nature of many of these arguments, specialized knowledge from biology, astronomy, geology, biochemistry, and anthropology was needed to refute factual claims made by antievolutionists.

Scientists, many of them associated with Weinberg's Committees of Correspondence network, testified against equal time laws in their state legislatures, helping to persuade legislators not to pass such bills. The role of scientists was critical: If creationism could indeed be made scientific, then it would deserve a place in the curriculum. Scientists were the only ones qualified to judge whether creationism was in fact scientific and whether it was good scholarship. When equal time provisions were suggested in local school-board meetings, teachers greatly appreciated the input of scientists (Lewin 1981). Typical of the combined activism and scholarship of the period, one publication documented the obvious: that creation science articles were not being published in refereed journals (Scott & Cole 1985). The authors argued that documenting the missing scholarly foundation to creation science was necessary to blunt the claims being made at school boards and in court that creation science was a legitimate scientific alternative to evolution.

Most of the anticreation science books and articles appearing between 1975 and 1990 were written or edited by natural scientists rather than social scientists and focused on natural science. They criticized the failure of creation science to follow tenets of accepted scholarship as well as its distortions of empirical data (Brush 1982; Dalrymple 1983; Eldredge 1982; Futuyma 1983; Godfrey 1983, 1985; Jukes 1984; McGown 1984; Montagu 1984; Morrison 1982; Newell 1982; Strahler 1987; Wilson 1983). Creation science was readily shown to be factually wrong, conceptually confused, and based on deplorable principles of scholarship.

Philosophers of science (Kitcher 1982; Ruse 1982, 1988), historians (Larson 1985, Numbers 1982), and social scientists were not inactive at this time, however. Many joined natural scientists to lobby for keeping evolution in the curriculum and creation science out at this time. Educators and others reviewed the history of evolution in textbooks (Grabiner & Miller 1974; Nelkin 1982; Skoog 1979, 1984) while other scholars looked broadly at social, legal, and educational issues (La Follette 1983, Mayer 1982, Moyer 1981, Orlich et al 1975, Zetterberg 1983). Theologians looked with fresh interest at the question of creation theology (Frye 1983, Gilkey 1985). Lawyers and social scientists contributed to a special issue of *Science, Technology and Human Values* (La Follette 1982). On the whole, however, the sociological and anthropological analysis of antievolutionism seems to have been neglected in comparison with the outpouring of literature on the science of creationism (good analyses are McIver 1988a,b; Kehoe 1983, 1985). According to Godfrey & Cole (1996), most of the anticreationist literature produced between 1977 and 1985 (the dates of their search of computerized databases) came from natural scientists and was weighted toward analyzing the scientific claims of the creationists. Legal and political issues were the next largest category, and sociological and anthropological analysis was less than 10% of the total.

Some sought to understand the phenomenon of antievolutionism by studying and analyzing public opinion. Gallup Polls revealed that nearly half of Americans agree with the basic tenets of YEC: "God created man pretty much in his present form within the last 10,000 years" (Gallup 1982). During the 1980s, several polls of students, teachers, and even lawmakers were conducted to assess the scope and depth of antievolutionism and the acceptance of creationism. (Almquist & Cronin 1988; Ellis 1983; Eve & Harrold 1986; Zimmerman 1987a,b, 1988). Not all of these polls asked comparable questions, however, and many of them yielded ambiguous data because key terms such as evolution and creationism were not defined. Many studies were admittedly done without adequate financial support for proper sampling and sufficient sample size for statistical validity, yet all the results tended in the same direction. As Gallup had found, there was a surprisingly high rejection of a major tenet of science among the American public and an openness to teaching creation science as a matter of "fairness," even among people who were not conservative Christians.

It is doubtful whether scientists would have been involved in such analyses if the creation and evolution issue had not become politicized. There had been no secular scholarly response to Whitcomb & Morris's *The Genesis Flood* when it appeared in 1963, but a decade later when such ideas were used to justify legislation that would radically change science education in the United States, the science community did not remain silent. This response was not only individual, but institutional. The National Academy of Sciences published a widely distributed booklet for teachers that stated clearly that evolution is essential to science education and that "creationism has no place in a *science* curriculum at any level" (National Academy of Sciences 1984, p. 7). Many scientific associations, including the American Association for the Advancement of Science, the American Anthropological Association, the American Association of Physical Anthropologists, and many state academies of science passed resolutions supporting evolution and/or condemning creation science (Matsumura 1995a). Such organizations often urged their members to become involved in supporting evolution education and/or opposing creation science.

The academic community appeared to lose interest in the antievolution movement after the *McLean* and *Edwards* decisions (Godfrey & Cole 1995). Immediately after *Edwards,* prominent scientist Stephen Jay Gould proclaimed the controversy to be over (Gould 1987). Even though scholarly interest in creationism appeared to diminish, the controversy itself did not decline; it only took new forms.

After the defeat of YEC-type equal time laws, it was minimally necessary to devise new terms, if not new strategies. I refer to this period of antievolutionism after *Edwards* as Neocreationism. Equal time for creation science is still being pushed, although in the 1990s it occurs more often at the local school-board level than in the state legislatures. Over the past two years alone, NCSE has received requests for assistance from schools or school districts wrestling with equal time provisions in Alabama, California, Florida, Georgia, Illinois, Louisiana, Maine, Michigan, Montana, Nevada, New Hampshire, New York, Ohio, Oklahoma, Oregon, Pennsylvania, Texas, Washington State, and Wisconsin.

NEOCREATIONISM

Neocreationism refers to a mixed bag of antievolution strategies brought about by legal decisions against equal time laws. Although academics concluded that *Edwards* sounded the death knell for creation science, Neocreationism has evolved the avoidance of terms related to creation, such as creation science. A school district in Louisville, Ohio, which had had an equal time regulation in place before *Edwards,* rewrote the science curriculum to "avoid mention of creationism in its curriculum guide, calling it alternative theories to evolution and adding it to the science classes" (Kennedy 1992). In addition to "alternatives to evolution," the outlawing of equal time laws has resulted in the generation of many other synonyms for creation science, such as "evidence against evolution," "initial complexity theory," and "intelligent design theory."

EVIDENCE AGAINST EVOLUTION

All creation and evolution court cases in the past 30 years have been decided on the basis of the First Amendment's Establishment Clause, which calls for neutrality toward religion in public institutions. Because creationism promotes religion, it cannot be required in the curriculum. Similarly, individual teachers who sought on free-speech (academic freedom) grounds to teach creationism have lost in court: Students have a right to be free from proselytization in elementary and secondary schools (*Webster* v. *New Lennox, Peloza* v. *San Juan Capistrano*). Before *Edwards,* antievolutionists would argue that teachers should teach evolution but also teach creation science to balance it. After *Edwards,* a shift in emphasis can be seen in the neocreationist argument that when teachers teach evolution, they should teach the evidence against evolution to balance it. The wording ironically comes from *Edwards* itself, or at least from a dissenting opinion in the case. In a dissent to *Edwards,* Justice Scalia wrote that "the people of Louisiana, including those who are Christian fundamentalists, are quite entitled, as a secular matter, to have whatever scientific evidence there may be against evolution presented in their schools, just as Mr. Scopes was entitled to present whatever scientific evidence there was for it." Creationist legal strategist Wendell Bird even recommended this approach immediately after the *Edwards* decision (Bird 1987). Because the substance of creation science had always consisted of criticisms of evolution, it was easy to repackage creation science as evidence against evolution.

For example, in the spring of 1996, a bill was narrowly defeated in Ohio (Scott 1996b) to mandate the teaching of evidence against evolution. The proposed law read, in part: "Whenever a theory of the origin of human beings, other living things, or the universe that might commonly be referred to as 'evolution' is included in the instructional program provided by any school district or educational service center, both evidence and arguments supporting or consistent with the theory and evidence and arguments problematic for, inconsistent with, or not supporting the theory shall be included."

Also during the spring of 1996, Georgia's legislature considered similar legislation, which stated, in part, that "teachers shall have the right to present and critique any and all scientific theories about such origins and all facets thereof." This legislation also failed to pass, but evidence against evolution is emerging as a popular approach. It is attractive to legal specialists among the antievolutionists because it appears to avoid the Establishment Clause of the First Amendment by not obviously promoting religion. Presenting evidence against evolution per se is only bad science, which the First Amendment does not forbid.

EVOLUTION AS THEORY OR FACT

In 1996, the State of Tennessee debated and narrowly defeated a bill that would have made teachers who taught evolution as a fact—rather than as a theory—subject to dismissal for insubordination (Matsumura 1995b). In late 1995, Alabama passed a state science curriculum that required that evolution be taught "as theory rather than fact" (Scott 1995). These are not the first such cases; NCSE has records of school-board controversies or individual teachers' complaints concerning pressure to teach evolution as a theory and not fact from Alabama, Arkansas, California, Florida, Georgia, Louisiana, Pennsylvania, Texas, and Wisconsin, among other places.

The problem is that "theory" and "fact" are used differently in science and among the public. In science, a theory is a logical construct of facts, hypotheses, and laws that explains a natural phenomenon. To the general public, however, a theory is not an explanation, but a hunch or guess. To teach evolution as a theory in this sense is to teach it as something students don't have to take seriously. The State Senator in Tennessee who proposed the 1996 legislation described theories as "whims." Many a school-board meeting has erupted over evolution being presented dogmatically as fact, and letters to editors regularly fulminate with outrage over children being "forced" to "believe" in evolution.

More than one factor contributes to this vehemence. One cause is the underlying, if usually unspoken, fear many nonscientists have that "evolution means you can't believe in God." There has been no pressure for teachers to present the theories of heliocentrism, gravitation, the cell, the atom, or relativity nondogmatically, but these theories do not have consequences for some religions. People react as though they believe that when evolution is presented as a fact, it must be believed in and that students will then have to give up their faith. Most Americans do not seem to understand that Catholicism, mainline Protestantism, and all but ultraorthodox Judaism have accommodated evolution into their theologies. There are concerns about parental control as well: If parents can't control something as basic as the religious beliefs of their children, what is left?

DISCLAIMERS

In addition to calling evolution "just a theory," Neocreationists also qualify it by requiring teachers to disclaim the topic before teaching it. In 1994, the school board of Tangipahoa Parish, Louisiana, frustrated by legal restrictions against presenting creationism with evolution, compromised by requiring teachers to read a statement to students before evolution is taught, telling them that evolution "should be presented to inform students of the scientific concept and not intended to influence or dissuade the Biblical version of Creation or any other concept."

Similarly, Alabama's state board of education followed its 1995 decision that evolution must be presented as theory rather than fact by requiring all biology textbooks to have a disclaimer pasted on the inside cover that warned students that evolution was "a controversial theory" and that "No one was present when life first appeared on earth. Therefore, any statement about life's origins should be considered as theory, not fact." Similar disclaimers are being considered in other states.

A disclaimer may not obviously promote religion, but because many teachers will feel inhibited, disclaimers do discourage the teaching of evolution. Because the goal of antievolutionism is not the introduction of creationism into the curriculum but the removal of evolution from it, the teacher who omits evolution from the curriculum must be considered a victory for the antievolution side.

INTELLIGENT DESIGN

In 1989, shortly after the *Edwards* Supreme Court decision, *Of Pandas and People,* a supplemental textbook for high-school biology was published (Davis & Kenyon 1989). Its publication signified the increasing OEC influence in the neocreationist movement and introduced the term Intelligent Design (ID). ID is promoted primarily by university-based antievolutionists who tend to be PCs rather than YECs. Dean Kenyon, for example, a tenured professor of biology at San Francisco State University, and Percival Davis, who teaches at Hillsborough Community College, in Tampa, Florida, advocate ID.

ID is a lineal descendent of William Paley's Argument from Design (Paley 1803), which held that God's existence could be proved by examining his works. Paley used a metaphor: He claimed that if one found an intricately contrived watch, it was obvious that such a thing could not have come together by chance. The existence of a watch implied a watchmaker who had designed the watch with a purpose in mind. Similarly, because there is order, purpose, and design in the world, naturally there is an omniscient designer. The existence of God was proven by the presence of order and intricacy.

The vertebrate eye was Paley's classic example, well known to educated people of the nineteenth century, of design in nature. Darwin deliberately used the example of the vertebrate eye in *The Origin of Species* to demonstrate how complexity and intricate design could come about through natural selection, which of course is not a chance phenomenon. In creationist literature, evolution is synonymous with chance. In scientific accounts, there are random or chance elements in the generation of genetic variation, but natural selection, acting upon this genetic variation, is the antithesis of chance. In the PC tradition, ID allows for a fair amount of microevolution, but supporters deny that mutation and natural selection are adequate to explain the evolution of one "kind" to another, such as chordates from echinoderms, or human beings from apes. These and the origin of life are considered too complex to be explained naturally, thus ID demands that a role be left for the intelligent designer, God.

ID literature is more sophisticated than creation science literature, perhaps because it is (except for *Of Pandas and People*) usually directed toward a university audience rather than to the general public, at least up to now. One is less likely to find discussions of the vertebrate eye and more likely to find DNA structure or cellular complexity held up as too complex to have evolved by chance. *Of Pandas and People,* for example, weaves information theory into an exposition of the "linguistics" of the DNA code in an attempt to prove that DNA is so complex we can't explain it by using natural causes.

ID supporters concentrate on areas in evolutionary theory that are not yet well understood, though some of the evolutionary transitions and other phenomena that are supposedly too complex to be explained through natural causes are already partly explained, or are active areas of research. ID supporters, including YECs, emphasize the lack of "transitional fossils" between major groups, and of course connections among the phyla and subphyla will never be revealed through the fossil record (though many class transitions are). On the other hand, biochemical comparisons are allowing plausible linkages to be proposed and tested. Origin-of-life research is booming, with many working hypotheses, including a precellular DNA world preceded by an even earlier and more primitive RNA world. An especially active area in origin-of-life research involves self-organizing qualities of matter—supplementing, rather than replacing, natural selection at biochemical levels (Eigen 1992, Kauffman 1993). The relationship between living and nonliving is becoming more of a continuum and less of a dichotomy. Similarly, the more we learn about the bio-chemical, neurological, and behavioral similarities between our species and the great apes (Ruvolo 1997), with whom we shared a common ancestor, the less likely it appears that there is an unbridgeable gulf "too complex" to cross.

Antievolution at the University

One of the leading exponents of ID is Phillip Johnson, who holds an endowed chair at Boalt Hall School of Law, University of California, Berkeley. Johnson appeared on the anticreationist scene in 1991 with the publication of his book, *Darwin on Trial* (Johnson 1993). Because of Johnson's academic credentials, and because he ignored arguments about the age of the earth and was even faintly contemptuous of YEC, the book was perceived as different from tradi-tional creation science, even though no new arguments were presented. *Darwin on Trial* was reviewed by people and in journals that would never have re-viewed a publication by Morris (Gould 1992, Hull 1991, Jukes 1991). All con-cluded that Johnson lacked a solid grounding in the theory and factual basis of evolutionary science.

Although Johnson is an evolution basher, his main concern is not with whether scientific data do or do not support evolution, but with broader ques-tions of purpose and meaning. He believes in a personal God who actively in-tervenes in the world, not a Deistic God who "doesn't do anything important." Darwinism—evolution by natural selection—like all of science is done in a methodological materialistic framework. It explains the history of the world without recourse to supernatural forces. In Johnson's view, if Darwinism is true then one is forced into some sort of Deistic view of God rather than a per-sonal view, which would be theologically unbearable. Therefore evolution, and Darwinism especially, cannot be true. He is contemptuous of those who re-vise their theology on the basis of empirical evidence: "No one ever puts it the other way around: If God exists, what reason is there to believe in blind, natu-ralistic evolution in the first place?" (Bethell 1992, p. 14). In this approach, if in few others, Johnson echoes Morris, who said (referring to geological evi-dence for the Flood) that "[n]o geological difficulties, real or imagined, can be allowed to take precedence over the clear statements and necessary inference of Scripture" (Morris 1970, p. 33).

Darwinism is the focus of Johnson's complaint about the materialism of science. In his second book on this theme, *Reason in the Balance* (Johnson 1995), Johnson makes even more clear his concern that evolution and science in general, by explaining phenomena in terms of natural cause, eliminate the necessity for a deity. Of course, if science can explain phenomena using natu-ral cause, this does not mean that a believer cannot believe that God is the ultimate cause. Ironically, science can never rule out God as causal agent, precisely because of the methodological materialism Johnson decries. Johnson, however, argues against this view as too Deistic—again—God is left with nothing important to do.

Few scientists reviewed *Reason in the Balance,* mostly because it does not deal much with scientific issues and is rather more obviously theological and philosophical in nature. *Reason in the Balance* makes it clear that underlying Johnson's objection to evolution is the conflict between theism and naturalism (materialism) as philosophies. Modern scientists do explain the natural world without reference to God, but this is because by doing so scientists get better answers more quickly. Johnson conflates the methodological materialism of science with philosophical materialism: If one restricts oneself to natural explanations, one must therefore be a philosophical materialist (Scott 1993, Scott & Sager 1992). (Ironically, he is joined in this view by evolutionary biologists Provine and Dawkins!) Theism vs materialism is a legitimate philosophico-religious debate, but it is irrelevant to science. Scientists do not reject supernatural explanation out of religious animosity but out of practicality: If we can conclude that God did it, then we'll stop looking, and if there is a natural explanation, it won't be found. At one time, spirits were thought to cause disease. Most of us are glad that scientists kept looking and found microorganisms.

In 1996, Michael Behe, a biochemist at Lehigh University, published the most scholarly and scientific ID book to date, *Darwin's Black Box* (Behe 1996), which offers little comfort to typical antievolutionists. Behe accepts that natural selection produces most of the complex structural adaptations of plants and animals, and he even accepts that modern living things descended with modification from common ancestors. In a debate with Kenneth Miller, a biologist at Brown University, during the summer of 1995, Behe accepted that human beings and chimps share a common ancestor. Still, Behe asserted that there are things that can't be explained through natural processes. He claims that at the level of cell biochemistry lie "irreducibly complex" processes and structures, such as the blood-clotting cascade and the rotor motor of a microorganism's flagellum. Such structures cannot be broken down into component parts, says Behe, and therefore cannot be explained through the incremental activity of natural selection. They therefore could not have evolved, and because they could not have evolved they must have been specially created. Behe argues, as did Paley, that complexity is proof that there must be an intelligent designer, but his examples of complexity are biochemical.

Because Behe is a research scientist with a track record of legitimate publications (though not in evolutionary biology), his book has been reviewed with more seriousness than Johnson's *Darwin on Trial* (Coyne 1996, Gross 1996, Miller 1996, Orr 1996, Shreeve 1996). Although Behe claimed in *Darwin's*

Black Box that his views would sweep the scientific world in a manner comparable to the discoveries of "Newton and Einstein, Lavoisier and Schroedinger, Pasteur, and Darwin" (Behe 1996, p. 233), the response from the scientific community thus far has been decidedly tepid. Reviewers were quick to point out flaws both in reasoning and in factual and conceptual understanding.

ID proponents are not Luddites, objecting to science and its technological fruits, but they do not like naturalistic evolution. Like all conservative Christians, they insist on a significant explanatory role for God, and in life having a divinely directed purpose and meaning. To them, evolution epitomizes the offensive, strictly materialist framework in which scientists practice science today. Science itself, however, is not objected to—only its materialism in regard to theologically sensitive issues (Scott 1996b).

Allowing for the intervention of the deity in evolution, but not in the rest of science, is spelled out in an afterword addressed to teachers in *Of Pandas and People* (Hartwig & Meyer 1993). The authors argue that there are two different kinds of science: "inductive" and "historical." Supposedly, the goal of historical sciences "is not to find new laws or regularities but to reconstruct past conditions and events" (Hartwig & Meyer 1993, p. 159). This will come as a surprise to astronomers, geologists, evolutionary biologists, and anthropologists, but the authors are quite serious. They feel that it is inappropriate to allow "intelligent intervention" in inductive science because the goal is to understand the natural world as it "normally operates on it's [sic] own, i.e. *in the absence of intelligent intervention*" (italics in original). In the historical sciences, "the goal is to reconstruct past events and conditions. Thus there is no need to impose such restrictions. Quite the reverse. As we have seen, the explanation of certain artifacts or features may require reference to intelligence. Intelligent agents may have left traces of their activity in the natural world. The historical scientist need not turn a blind eye to them" (Hartwig & Meyer 1993, p. 159). Although the intelligence is not specifically identified as a personal, hands-on Christian God, it is doubtful that the authors wish teachers to teach that extraterrestrials from Alpha Centauri guided the development of life on earth.

On close inspection, historical science boils down to those scientific topics that have implications for conservative Christian theology, especially the Big Bang, the origin of life, and the origin of humankind (and to a lesser degree, but still important, the production of basic body plans during the Cambrian explosion). For these events, the door must be left open for Special Creation, the intervention of the "intelligence." So much of nature can be explained through natural processes that a direct creative role for God must be retained somewhere, or else the conservative Christian must slide toward Deism and an unacceptably impersonal God with "nothing important to do." In theology, the "God of the Gaps" problem is the problem raised by requiring direct intervention of God into the natural world. If God is the stop-gap explanation for "un-understood" natural phenomena, when natural explanations are found for them God is diminished. For this reason, Catholic and mainline Protestant theologians have rendered unto science the explanation of most aspects of the natural world. ID creates a God of the Gaps problem and is thus subject to the same theological criticisms.

Much as do their creation science predecessors, ID supporters end up defining acceptable science on the basis of preexisting religious ideology. I have discussed elsewhere the relationship of ideology (such as feminism, environmentalism, or Marxism) to scholarship, expressing reservations about whether a religiously based ideology such as Special Creationism can ever be truly scholarly (Scott 1996b). Can ID make the grade? Thus far, even if the quality of argumentation and the scientific credentials of its proponents are superior to those of creation science, there are still many indications that ID advocates are finding it difficult to approach sensitive subject matter from a scholarly, rather than an ideological, position. For example, nothing in nature should be placed off-limits to scientific inquiry merely because it has consequences for an ideology. In his contemplation of the tremendous complexity of cell phenomena, Behe considers it futile to look for natural explanations. Sadly, otherwise competent scientists associated with ID seem already to have made up their minds about what topics in the realm of the unexplained are unexplainable.

Scholarly analyses of ID have been highly critical, and it is likely that ID will not be very persuasive among scientists. Where Old Earth, ID books like Behe's and Johnson's currently are most likely to be found is in the auditoria of local school-board meetings, being held aloft as "proof" that scientists are giving up on evolution and that evolution should be taught as only a theory, or disclaimed in some way. Johnson's books and *Of Pandas and People* are already being promoted as "alternatives to evolution." In 1996, Governor Fob James of Alabama used his contingency funds to purchase copies of *Darwin on Trial* to send to every biology teacher in the state (Anonymous 1996).

Because they are Old Earthers, Neocreationists do not seem as radical or extreme as YECs, and they are more likely to be accepted by the American public. Although proponents of ID do not yet have the numbers or the money that the YEC organizations have, and although they do not have massive outreach programs aimed at the general public, they are an energetic force that will have to be reckoned with. The most active ID proponents are, in fact, associated with secular institutions of higher learning rather than with sectarian, specialized organizations such as the ICR. Their view of how to promote the "cause" is more like that of activist academics than revivalist ministers. For example, a new, ID "think tank," supported by private foundation money, has been established in Seattle as the Center for Renewal of Science and Culture and is already supporting postdoctoral students (Scott 1997).

Old Earth, ID publications by Behe, Johnson, and others will have a more profound effect on antievolutionism than creation science publications because they are being discussed at the university and college level, where the far more numerous publications of Morris are regarded primarily as curiosities. Articles and books by more moderate antievolutionists tend to be used not in science courses, but in "science studies," social problems, or philosophy courses taught by social scientists or philosophers less familiar with the facts and theory of evolution than are science faculty.

It is significant that not only evolution but the nature of science itself is being challenged. Both evolution and methodological materialism are well entrenched in science, but they are uniformly accepted neither among the general public nor in nonscientific parts of academia. There are, of course, many critiques of science in academia (e.g. Gross & Levitt 1994), and the materialistic basis of science is not uniformly embraced. In February 1997, a major secular university—the University of Texas, Austin—sponsored a conference "dedicated to fostering dialogue between naturalists and theists on the impact of metaphysical and methodological ideas on the development, interpretation, and presentation of scientific knowledge" (J Koons, personal communication). In a sense, evolution appears better buffered in academia than is philosophy of science: The Texas conference was sponsored by the philosophy department and organized around philosophical themes such as the nature of science, rather than the "truth" of evolution. There has not yet been a conference scheduled at a secular university for the purpose of discussing whether evolution occurred, and it is not likely to happen in the near future.

THE FUTURE

There are many varieties of creationism and antievolutionism extant today, and they reach different parts of the American public. At the local school-board level, there will be a continuation or even an increase in the current level of antievolutionism, including the outlawed equal time for creation science, depending on the future election of religious right–oriented school board members. However, the chief danger to evolution education comes less from teachers promoting creation science than from teachers just quietly ceasing to teach evolution because it is too controversial. Currently, high-school biology textbooks do include evolution, though they do not always get the science right (National Center for Science Education/People for the American Way 1990). Whether textbook publishers will hold the line in the face of pressure to downplay or qualify evolution remains to be seen.

In the mid to late 1990s, university-based antievolutionism is a small but growing movement. For now, participants are dwarfed in both number and effectiveness by the more public efforts of organizations such as the ICR, with its Back to Genesis road shows and media programs. YEC is still the most frequently encountered antievolutionism that K–12 teachers have to cope with, but more and more it is being augmented by "arguments against evolution," ID, or other neocreationist positions. However, because a university-based antievolution movement has great potential to reach future decision-makers (who are being educated in universities today), this component of the movement may be highly influential in the future, even if it is small today. Future generations of college graduates may think that books like those of Johnson or Behe represent modern scientific scholarship on science and evolution. This will only exacerbate the problem of antievolution at the K–12 level and in the general public: After all, members of Congress, captains of industry, and members of local school boards are almost always college graduates.

Faculty in fields with a historical component, which include astronomy, geology, biology, and anthropology, need to be explicit in their treatment of evolution so that members of the educated public understand this important scientific concept. Scientists in these fields recognize that evolution is an organizing principle in their disciplines but often fail to make this explicit to students. Biologists will, for example, teach principles of systematics and taxonomy without mentioning that the genus/species classification of organisms is possible because the splitting and branching process of evolution generates hierarchy. Astronomers will discuss galaxy formation and not use the "e-word." It is impossible to teach a physical anthropology course (or any introductory anthropology course) without teaching evolution, thus ironically it may be that most students who learn about evolution do so in departments classified as "social science" rather than natural science. This places an important responsibility upon anthropologists, who may by default be the major purveyors of evolutionary theory at the college level. We may need to spend even more time in our classes on principles of evolution than we perhaps have in the past. As members of a field that also includes the consideration of religion as part of the human way of life, anthropologists may in fact be the scientists best able to cope with the myriad aspects of the creation/evolution controversy.

The scientific establishment itself is not going to give up on evolution any more than it is going to give up on the periodic table of elements, but the amount of public support for evolution, including financial support for evolution-oriented research from federally funded organizations such as the National Science Foundation and the National Institutes of Health, may well dwindle even further if evolution loses yet more support among the general public.

Visit the *Annual Reviews home page* at
http://www.AnnualReviews.org.

Literature Cited

Almquist AJ, Cronin JE. 1988. Fact, fancy and myth on human evolution. *Curr. Anthropol.* 29(3):520–22

American Museum of Natural History. 1994. *Science and Nature Survey.* Off. Public Affairs, Am. Mus. Nat. Hist.

Anonymous. 1996. Surprise gift. No charge. *Educ. Week,* Apr. 3, p. 5

Behe M. 1996. *Darwin's Black Box: The Biochemical Challenge to Evolution.* New York: Free Press

Bethell T. 1992. Darwin in the dock. *Am. Spect.,* June, pp. 14, 16

Bible-Science Association. 1985. 1985 Bible-Sci. Assoc. Conf. Sched., Aug. 14–15, Cleveland, Ohio

Bird W. 1978. Freedom of religion and science indoctrination in public schools. *Yale Law J.* 87:515–70

Bird W. 1987. The Supreme Court decision and its meaning. *ICR Impact* Ser. 170, Aug., 4 pp.

Brush SG. 1982. Finding the age of the earth by physics or by faith? *J. Geol. Educ.* 30: 34–58

Coyne JA. 1996. God in the details. *Nature* 383:227–28

Dalrymple GB. 1983. Can the earth be dated from decay of its magnetic field? *J. Geol. Educ.* 31:124–33

Davis P, Kenyon DH, eds. 1989. *Of Pandas and People.* Dallas, TX: Haughton. 170 pp.

Dawkins R. 1976. *The Selfish Gene.* New York: Oxford. 224 pp.

Dawkins R. 1987. *The Blind Watchmaker.* New York: Norton

DeFord CS. 1991. (1931). *A Reparation: Universal Gravitation a Universal Fake.* Fairfield, WA: Ye Galleon. 62 pp.

Edis T. 1994. Islamic creationism in Turkey. *Creat./Evol.* 34:1–12

Edwards v. Aguillard, 482 U.S. 578 (1987)

Eigen M. 1992. *Steps Toward Life: A Perspective in Evolution.* Oxford: Oxford Univ. Press. 173 pp.

Eiseley L. 1958. *Darwin's Century.* Garden City, NY: Anchor. 387 pp.

Eldredge N. 1982. *The Monkey Business: A Scientist Looks at Creationism.* New York: Washington Square (Pocket Books). 157 pp.

Eldredge N. 1989. *Macroevolutionary Dynamics.* New York: McGraw-Hill. 226 pp.

Eldredge N, Gould SJ. 1972. Punctuated equilibria: an alternative to phyletic gradualism, *Models in Paleobiology,* ed. TJM Schopf, pp. 82–115. San Francisco: Freeman, Cooper. 250 pp.

Ellis WE. 1983. Biology teachers and border state beliefs. *Society* Jan./Feb:26–30

Epperson v. Arkansas, 393 U.S. 97 (1967)

Eve R, Harrold FB. 1986. Creationism, cult archaeology and other pseudoscientific beliefs: a study of college students. *Youth Soc.* 4:396–421

Eve R, Harrold FB. 1991. *The Creationist Movement in Modern America.* Boston: Twayne. 234 pp.

Frye R. 1983. *Is God a Creationist? The Religious Case Against Creation-Science.* New York: Scribner's

Futuyma DJ. 1983. *Science on Trial: The Case for Evolution.* New York: Pantheon. 251 pp.

Gallup G Jr. 1982. The Gallup poll. *The New York Times* Aug. 29, p. 22

Gilkey L. 1985. *Creationism on Trial: Evolution and God at Little Rock.* Minneapolis: Winston

Godfrey LR, ed. 1983. *Scientists Confront Creationism.* New York: Norton. 324 pp.

Godfrey LR, ed. 1985. *What Darwin Began.* Boston: Allyn & Bacon. 312 pp.

Godfrey LR, Cole JR. 1995. A Century after Darwin: scientific creationism and academe. In *Cult Archaeology and Creationism: Understanding Pseudoscientific Beliefs About the Past,* ed. FB Harrold, RA Eve, pp. 99–123. Iowa City: Univ. Iowa Press. Expanded ed.

Goodman S. 1995. Creationists in Canada. *Natl. Cent. Sci. Educ. Rep.* 15(1):10–11

Gould SJ. 1987. Creationism battle is over. *Minneap. Star & Trib.,* July 19

Gould SJ. 1992. Impeaching a self-appointed judge. *Sci. Am.* July, pp. 118–21

Grabiner JV, Miller PD. 1974. Effects of the Scopes trial. *Science* 185(4154):832–37

Gross PR. 1996. The Dissent of man. *Wall Street J.,* July, p. A11

Gross PR, Levitt N. 1994. *Higher Superstition.* Baltimore, MD: Johns Hopkins Press

Groves C. 1991. Creationism in Australia: Down but Not Out? *Natl. Cent. Sci. Educ. Rep.* 11(2):21

Hartwig MD, Meyer SC. 1993. A note to teachers. See Davis & Kenyon 1989, pp. 153–61

Hull DL. 1991. The God of the Galapagos. *Nature* 352:485–86

John Paul II. 1996. Magisterium (Message to Pontifical Academy of Sciences) L'Osservatore romano, Oct. 30, p. 3, 7

Johnson P. 1990. A reply to my critics. In *Evolution as Dogma*, ed. PE Johnson, 33–37. Found. Thought Ethics. Dallas: Haughton

Johnson P. 1993. *Darwin on Trial*, Downers Grove, IL: Inter-Varsity. 220 pp. 2nd ed.

Johnson P. 1995. *Reason in the Balance*. Downers Grove, IL: Inter-Varsity. 245 pp.

Jukes TH. 1984. The creationist challenge to science. *Nature* 308:398–400

Jukes TH. 1991. The persistent conflict. *J. Mol. Evol.* 33:205–6

Kauffman S. 1993. *The Origin of Order*. New York: Oxford Univ. Press

Kehoe A. 1983. The word of God. See Godfrey 1983, pp. 1–12

Kehoe A. 1985. Modern antievolutionism: the scientific creationists. See Godfrey 1983, pp. 165–85

Kennedy J. 1992. Teaching of creationism splits Louisville parents. *The Repository*, Sept. 30, p. B4

King JL, Jukes TH. 1969. Non-Darwinian evolution. *Science* 164:788–98

Kitcher P. 1982. *Abusing Science: The Case Against Creationism*. Cambridge: MIT Press. 213 pp.

La Follette M, ed. 1982. Introduction: creation sciences and the law. *Sci. Technol. Soc.* 40:9–10

La Follette M, ed. 1983. *Creationism, Science, and the Law*. Cambridge, MA: MIT Press

Larson EJ. 1985. *Trial and Error: The American Controversy over Creation and Evolution*. New York: Oxford. 222 pp.

Lewin R. 1981. A response to creationism evolves. *Science* 214:635–36

Matsumura MV. 1995a. *Voices for Evolution*. Berkeley, CA: Natl. Cent. Sci. Educ. 176 pp.

Matsumura MV. 1995b. Tennessee upset: "Monkey bill" law defeated. *Natl. Cent. Sci. Educ. Rep.* 15(4):6–7

Mayer W. 1982. Evolutionary theory vs. creationist doctrine. *J. Coll. Sci. Teach.* 11(5):270–76

McGown C. 1984. *In the Beginning: A Scientist Shows Why the Creationists Are Wrong*. Buffalo: Prometheus

McGrath AE. 1994. *Christian Theology: An Introduction*. Oxford: Blackwell

McIver T. 1988a. *Antievolution: An Annotated Bibliography*. Jefferson, NC: McFarland

McIver T. 1988b. Christian reconstructionism, post-millennialism, and creationism. *Creat./Evol. Newsl.* 8(1):10–17

McLean v. Arkansas, 529 F. Suppl. 1255 (1982)

Miller KR. 1996. Darwin's black box. *Rep. Natl. Cent. Sci. Educ.* 16(4):In press

Montagu A, ed. 1984. *Science and Creationism*. New York: Oxford Univ. Press. 415 pp.

Morris HR. N.d. Resolution for Equitable Treatment of Both Creation and Evolution. *Inst. Creat. Res. Impact* #26

Morris HR. 1963. *The Twilight of Evolution*. Grand Rapids, MI: Baker Book House. 103 pp.

Morris HR. 1970. *Biblical Cosmology and Modern Science*. Phillipsburg, NJ: Presbyterian and Reformed

Morrison D. 1982. Astronomy and creationism. *Mercury* Sept.-Oct., pp. 144–47

Moyer WA. 1981. Arguments for maintaining the integrity of science education. *Am. Biol. Teach.* 43(7):380–81

National Academy of Sciences. 1984. *Science and Creationism: A View from the National Academy of Sciences*. Washington, DC: Natl. Acad. Press

National Center for Science Education. People for the American Way. 1990. *Biology Textbooks 1990: The New Generation*. Washington, DC: People Am. Way. 73 pp.

National Science Board. 1996. *Science and Engineering Indicators—1996*, pp. 7-7-7-8. Washington, DC: US Gov. Print. Off., Natl. Sci. Board, pp. 96–21

Nelkin D. 1982. *The Creation Controversy: Science or Scripture in the Schools*. New York: Norton

Newell ND. 1982. *Creation and Evolution: Myth or Reality?* New York: Columbia Univ. Press

Numbers RL. 1982. Creationism in twentieth-century America. *Science* 218(4512):538–44

Numbers RL. 1992. *The Creationists*. New York: Knopf. 458 pp.

Orlich DC, Ratcliff JL, Stronck DR. 1975. Creationism in the science classroom. *Sci. Teach.* 42(5):43–45

Orr HA. 1996. Darwin v. intelligent design (again). *Boston Rev.* 21(6):28–31

Paley W. 1803. *Natural Theology: Or, Evidences of the Existence and Attributes of the Deity, Collected from the Appearances of Nature*. London: Faulder. 5th ed.

Peloza v. San Juan Capistrano Unif. Sch. Dist., 37 F. 3rd 517 (1994)

Provine W. 1988. Scientists, face it! Science and religion are incompatible. *Scientist* 2:10

Ramm B. 1955. *The Christian View of Science and Scripture.* London: Paternoster

Ruse M. 1982. Darwinism defended: a guide to the evolution controversies. Reading, MA: Addison-Wesley

Ruse M. 1988. *But Is It Science? The Philosophical Question in the Creation/Evolution Controversy.* Buffalo, NY: Prometheus. 406 pp.

Ruvolo M. 1997. Genetic diversity in hominoid primates. *Annu. Rev. Anthropol.* 26:515–40

Schadewald RJ. 1980. Earth orbits? moon landings? A Fraud! Says this prophet. *Sci. Dig.*, July, pp. 58–63

Schadewald RJ. 1991. Introduction to Charles DeFord's *Reparation.* See DeFord 1991

Scott E. 1991. Creationism in New Zealand. *Natl. Cent. Sci. Educ. Rep.* 11(2):20–21

Scott E. 1993. Review article: Darwin prosecuted. *Creat./Evol.* 33:42–47

Scott E. 1994. The Evolution of creationism: the struggle for the schools. *Nat. Hist.* 103: 10, 12–13

Scott E. 1995. State of Alabama distorts science, evolution. *Natl. Cent. Sci. Educ. Rep.* 15(4):10–11

Scott E. 1996a. Creationism, ideology, and science. In *The Flight From Science and Reason,* ed. PR Gross, N Levitt, MW Lewis. *Ann. NY Acad. Sci.* 775:505–22

Scott E. 1996b. Close Ohio vote scuttles evidence against evolution bill. *Natl. Cent. Sci. Educ. Rep.* 16(1):18

Scott E. 1997. Old earth moderates poised to spread design theory. *Rep. Natl. Cent. Sci. Educ.* 17(1):25–26

Scott E, Cole HP. 1985. The elusive scientific basis of creation science. *Q. Rev. Biol.* 60(1):21–30

Scott E, Sager TC. 1992. Review article: *Darwin on Trial,* by Phillip Johnson. *Creat./Evol.* 31:47–56

Shreeve J. 1996. Design for living. *New York Times Mag.,* Aug. 4

Skoog G. 1979. The coverage of evolution in high school biology textbooks, 1900–1977. *Sci. Educ.* 63(5):621–40

Skoog G. 1984. The coverage of evolution in high school biology textbooks published in the 1980's. *Sci. Educ.* 68(2):117–28

Stanley SM. 1981. *The New Evolutionary Timetable, Fossils, Genes, and the Origin of Species. New York:* Basic Books. 222 pp.

Strahler AN. 1987. *Science and Earth History: The Evolution/Creation Controversy.* Buffao, NY: Prometheus

Torrance TF. 1981. *Christian Theology and Scientific Culture.* Oxford: Oxford Univ. Press

Toumey C. 1994. *God's Own Scientists.* New Brunswick, NJ: Rutgers Univ. Press. 289 pp.

Webster v. New Lennon Sch. Dist., 122, 917 F. 2nd 1004 (1990)

Weinberg S. 1982. Pro-evolution public interest (letter). *BioScience* 32(3):168

Whitcomb JC, Morris HR. 1963. *The Genesis Flood: The Biblical Record and Its Scientific Implications.* Phillipsburg, NJ: Presbyterian & Reformed

Wills C, Lerner LS, Olson EC, Eimers LE, Dickerson RE. 1990. Report of visitation, Aug. 7–10, 1989, p. 22. Calif. State Dep. Educ: Private Postsecondary Educ. Div.

Wilson DB. 1983. *Did the Devil Make Darwin Do It? Modern Perspectives on the Creation-Evolution Controversy.* Ames, IA: Iowa State Univ.

Young DA. 1982. *Christianity and the Age of the Earth.* Grand Rapids, MI: Zondervan. 188 pp.

Zetterberg JP. 1983. *Evolution versus Creationism: The Public Education Controversy.* Phoenix, AZ: Oryx

Zimmerman M. 1987a. The evolution-creation controversy: opinions of Ohio high school biology teachers. *Ohio J. Sci.* 7:115–21

Zimmerman M. 1987b. Ohio school board presidents view of the evolution-creationism controversy, Part 1. *Ohio Cent. Sci. Educ. Newsl.,* Oct., pp. 1, 3, 11

Zimmerman M. 1988. Ohio school board presidents view of the evolution-creationism controversy, Part 2. *Ohio Cent. Sci. Educ. Newsl.,* Jan., pp. 1, 2

Annu. Rev. Anthropol. 1997. 26:291–312

LINGUISTIC RELATIVITY

John A. Lucy

Committee on Human Development, The University of Chicago, Chicago, Illinois
60637; e-mail: jlucy@ccp.uchicago.edu

KEY WORDS: Sapir-Whorf hypothesis, linguistic determinism, language and thought, language
and cognition, language and culture

ABSTRACT

The linguistic relativity hypothesis, the proposal that the particular language
we speak influences the way we think about reality, forms one part of the
broader question of how language influences thought. Despite long-standing
historical interest in the hypothesis, there is relatively little empirical research
directly addressing it. Existing empirical approaches are classified into three
types. 1. Structure-centered approaches begin with language differences and
ask about their implications for thought. 2. Domain-centered approaches begin
with experienced reality and ask how different languages encode it. 3.
Behavior-centered approaches begin with some practical concern and seek an
explanation in language. These approaches are compared, and recent methodological improvements highlighted. Despite empirical advances, a theoretical account needs to articulate exactly how languages interpret experiences
and how those interpretations influence thought. This will entail integrating
theory and data concerning both the general relation of language and thought
and the shaping influence of specific discursive structures and practices.

INTRODUCTION

Few ideas generate as much interest and controversy as the linguistic relativity
hypothesis, the proposal that the particular language we speak influences the
way we think about reality. The reasons are obvious: If valid it would have
widespread implications for understanding psychological and cultural life, for
the conduct of research itself, and for public policy. Yet through most of this
century, interest and controversy have not given rise to sustained programs of

291

empirical research in any of the concerned disciplines and, as a result, the validity of the proposal has remained largely in the realm of speculation. This situation has begun to change over the past decade, hence the occasion for this review.

The linguistic relativity proposal forms part of the general question of how language influences thought. Potential influences can be classed into three types or levels (Lucy 1996). The first, or semiotic, level concerns how speaking any natural language at all may influence thinking. The question is whether having a code with a symbolic component (versus one confined to iconic-indexical elements) transforms thinking. If so, we can speak of a semiotic relativity of thought with respect to other species lacking such a code. The second, or structural, level concerns how speaking one or more particular natural languages (e.g. Hopi versus English) may influence thinking. The question is whether quite different morphosyntactic configurations of meaning affect thinking about reality. If so, we can speak of a structural relativity of thought with respect to speakers using a different language. This has been the level traditionally associated with the term linguistic relativity, and this usage will be employed here. The third, or functional, level concerns whether using language in a particular way (e.g. schooled) may influence thinking. The question is whether discursive practices affect thinking either by modulating structural influences or by directly influencing the interpretation of the interactional context. If so, we can speak of a functional relativity of thought with respect to speakers using language differently. This level has been of particular interest during the second half of this century with the increasing interest in discourse-level analyses of language and can, therefore, also be conveniently referred to as discursive relativity.

Although this review concentrates on the second level—whether structural differences among languages influence thinking—it should be stressed that the other two levels are ultimately involved. Any claims about linguistic relativity of the structural sort depend on accepting a loose isofunctionality across speakers in the psychological mechanisms linking language to thinking and across languages in the everyday use of speech to accomplish acts of descriptive reference (Hymes 1966, Lucy 1996). More importantly, an adequate theoretical treatment of the second level necessarily involves engaging substantively with the other two levels (Lucy 1996; Gumperz & Levinson 1996; cf Silverstein 1976, 1979, 1981, 1985, 1993).

A number of recent publications have extensively reviewed the relevant social-science literature on linguistic relativity. Lucy (1992a) examines the historical and conceptual development of empirical research on the relation of language diversity and thought within the fields of linguistic anthropology and comparative psycholinguistics. Hill & Mannheim (1992) survey work on language and world view in anthropology, sorting out the main traditions (especially new work centered on interpretation and discourse) and indicating their connections with broader trends in anthropology. Hunt & Agnoli (1991) provide an overview of current concerns from the perspective of cognitive psychology. Finally, Gumperz & Levinson (1996) provide an eclectic overview and sampling of many of the newest directions of inquiry, again with substantial attention to discourse-level issues.

The appearance of abundance given by the long lists of references in these reviews is deceptive. Although the majority of the studies cited have some relevance to evaluating the relation between language and thought, few address the relativity proposal directly or well. In this context, there is little reason to re-inventory all these materials here. Rather, the current review provides a conceptual framework for interpreting current research by clarifying the sources and internal structure of the hypothesis, characterizing the logic of the major empirical approaches, and analyzing the needs of future research.

THE LINGUISTIC RELATIVITY HYPOTHESIS

Historical Development of Interest

Interest in the intellectual significance of the diversity of language categories has deep roots in the European tradition. Formulations recognizably related to our contemporary ones appear in England (Locke), France (Condillac, Diderot), and Germany (Hamman, Herder) during the late seventeenth and early eighteenth centuries (Aarsleff 1982, 1988; Gumperz & Levinson 1996; see also Friedrich 1986 on Vico in Italy). They were stimulated by theoretical concerns (opposition to the tenets of universal grammarians regarding the origin and status of different languages), methodological concerns (the reliability of language-based knowledge in religion and science), and practical social concerns (European efforts to consolidate national identities and cope with colonial expansion). Later, nineteenth-century work, notably that of Humboldt in Germany and Saussure in Switzerland and France, drew heavily on this earlier tradition and set the stage for twentieth-century approaches (Aarsleff 1982, 1988).

This European work was known and criticized by scholars in North America (Aarsleff 1988, Koerner 1992), and the same impulses found historically—the patent relevance of language to human sociality and intellect, the reflexive concern with the role of language in intellectual method, and the practical encounter with diversity—remain important today in motivating attention to the problem. But the linguistic relativity proposal received new impetus and reformulation there in the early twentieth century, particularly in the work of anthropological linguists Edward Sapir (1949a,b, 1964) and Benjamin

L Whorf (1956a,b) (hence the common designation of the linguistic relativity hypothesis as "the Sapir-Whorf hypothesis"). Following Boas (1966), both Sapir and Whorf emphasized direct firsthand explorations of diverse languages and rejected hierarchical, quasi-evolutionary rankings of languages and cultures—in particular the European, especially Humboldtian, obsession with the superior value of inflectional languages for the cultural or mental advancement of a people. Whorf also provided the first empirical work of consequence from a contemporary standpoint.

Surprisingly, there has been an almost complete absence of direct empirical research through most of the present century—perhaps half a dozen studies up to a decade ago (Lucy 1992a). The neglect of empirical work is so conspicuous that it must be regarded as one of the central characteristics of this area of research and warrants brief comment. One source of the neglect surely lies in the interdisciplinary nature of the problem itself which is compounded by increasing disciplinary specialization. But other, broader concerns play a role in discouraging research. Some worry that accepting linguistic relativism would effectively undermine the conduct of most of the social sciences (but see Lucy 1993a). Others fear that accepting linguistic relativism opens the door to ethical relativism (but see Fishman 1982; Lakoff 1987, p. 337). Others equate linguistic relativity with absolute linguistic determinism and dislike the implied limits to individual freedom of thought (but see Gumperz & Levinson 1996, p. 22). Anyone working on the relativity problem must be prepared to face these complicated issues and the passions and prejudices they arouse. In sum, despite long and well motivated interest in the issue, concrete research and even practical approaches to research remain remarkably undeveloped.

Formal Structure of the Hypothesis

There are a variety of specific linguistic relativity proposals, but all share three key elements linked in two relations. They all claim that certain properties of a given *language* have consequences for patterns of *thought* about *reality*. The properties of language at issue are usually morphosyntactic (but may be phonological or pragmatic) and are taken to vary in important respects. The pattern of *thought* may have to do with immediate perception and attention, with personal and social-cultural systems of classification, inference, and memory, or with aesthetic judgment and creativity. The reality may be the world of everyday experience, of specialized contexts, or of ideational tradition. These three key elements are linked by two relations: Language embodies *an interpretation* of reality and language can *influence* thought about that reality. The interpretation arises from the selection of substantive aspects of experience and their formal arrangement in the verbal code. Such selection and arrangement is, of course, necessary for language, so the crucial emphasis here is that each language involves a particular interpretation, not a common, universal one. An influence on thought ensues when the particular language interpretation guides or supports cognitive activity and hence the beliefs and behaviors dependent on it. Accounts vary in the specificity of the proposed mechanism of influence and in the degree of power attributed to it—the strongest version being a strict linguistic determinism (based, ultimately, on the identity of language and thought). A proposal of linguistic relativity thus claims that diverse interpretations of reality embodied in languages yield demonstrable influences on thought. [Hill & Mannheim (1992, pp. 383–87) discuss and endorse various criticisms of treating the relativity issue as a "hypothesis" about three discrete, identifiable, and orthogonal "variables." But if there is any interesting claim here, it is about discoverable relations between distinguishable phenomena. They implicitly acknowledge this by adopting a formulation that fits the model given here (cf Levinson 1996, p. 196).]

Such a full linguistic relativity proposal should be distinguished from several partial or more encompassing formulations that are widely prevalent. First, linguistic relativity is not the same as linguistic diversity. Without the relation to thought more generally (i.e. beyond that necessary for the act of speaking itself), it is merely linguistic diversity. Second, linguistic relativity is not the same as any influence of language on thought. Without the relation to differences among languages, we just have a common psychological mechanism shared by all (an effect at the semiotic level). Third, linguistic relativity is not the same as cultural relativity, which encompasses the full range of patterned, historically transmitted differences among communities. Linguistic relativity proposals emphasize a distinctive role for language structure in interpreting experience and influencing thought. Although such a relativity may contribute to a broader cultural relativity, it may also crosscut it. Sometimes the various elements can be technically present in a formulation but inappropriately filled. One can take as representative of language some aspect so bleached of meaning value (e.g. prefixing versus postfixing) that no interesting semantic differences suggest themselves. Or one can confound the elements by using verbal responses to assess thought or verbal stimulus materials to represent reality. Thus, in evaluating research, it is important to ask whether the various components of the hypothesis have all been represented and appropriately filled. Most existing research fails in this regard and therefore cannot address the hypothesis directly and decisively.

APPROACHES TO EMPIRICAL RESEARCH

Among the studies meeting the above criteria, there have been three approaches to research depending on which among the three key elements at issue (language, reality, thought) serves as the central orientation or point of departure for the investigation: *structure-centered, domain-centered,* and *behavior-centered.* With enough thought and labor, any of these approaches is capable of leading to a useful body of work on the hypothesis, but each also is susceptible to characteristic difficulties and derailments. The following sections characterize each approach and provide key examples that illustrate their strengths and weaknesses.

Structure-Centered Approaches

GENERAL APPROACH   A structure-centered approach begins with an observed difference between languages in their structure of meaning. The analysis characterizes the structure of meaning and elaborates the interpretations of reality implicit in them. Then evidence for the influence of these interpretations on thought is sought in speakers' behavior. The strength of the approach lies in its interpretive validity: It makes minimal assumptions beforehand about possible meanings in language and to that extent remains open to new and unexpected interpretations of reality. In a sense, this approach "listens" closely to what the language forms volunteer, pursuing various structured, crosscutting patterns of meaning and attempting to make sense of how the world must appear to someone using such categories; ideally it makes possible the characterization of the distinctive way a language interprets the world. The search for language influences likewise tends to be interpretive, searching for widespread, habitual patterns of thought and behavior—although this is not essential to the approach.

Structure-centered approaches are susceptible to several characteristic weaknesses. It is difficult to establish terms of comparison because one of the aims is to avoid taking any language or its construal of reality as a privileged frame of reference. This often leaves the proper characterization of the language pattern and of the reality at issue very underdetermined. Second, the complexity and specificity of the linguistic analysis can make comparison beyond the initial languages difficult. One practical remedy to these problems is to adopt a typological approach from the outset in characterizing the language structures and to focus particularly on referential structures where the recurrent meaning values can be more readily operationalized. In demonstrating an influence on thought, studies adopting this approach also often have difficulty providing rigorous demonstrations of significant effects, not because it is not possible but because the whole approach favors a more ethnographically rich and fluid interpretive approach.

TEMPORAL MARKING   The classic example of a language-centered approach is Whorf's pioneering work comparing Hopi and English in the 1930s (1956a;

Lucy 1985, 1992a; Lee 1991, 1996; see also Schultz 1990). Whorf argued that speakers of English treat cyclic experiences of various sorts (e.g. the passage of a day or a year) in the same grammatical frame used for ordinary object nouns. Thus, English speakers treat these cycles as object-like, as though they can be measured and counted just like tangible objects that have a form and a substance. English speakers are led by this pattern to seek the substance associated with a day, a year, and so forth, and our global, abstract notion of 'time' as a continuous, homogeneous, formless something arises to fill in the blank in this linguistic analogy. By contrast, Hopi speakers do not treat these cycles as objects but as recurrent events. Thus, although they have, as Whorf acknowledged, words for what we would recognize as temporal cycles (e.g. days, years), their formal structuration in the grammar does not give rise to the abstract notion of 'time' that we have. In Whorf's view, grouping referents and concepts as analogically "the same" for the purposes of speech leads speakers to group those referents and concepts as "the same" for thought generally as evidenced by related cultural patterns of habitual belief and behavior.

Whorf's work illustrates the characteristic analytic complexity and specificity of the linguistic analysis in a structure-centered approach. It also shows the typical tendencies to deal in an ad hoc way with providing a neutral description of reality (Whorf 1956a, pp. 141–43) and the somewhat anecdotal ethnographic evidence for linguistic influences on thought (Whorf 1956a, pp. 147–59). Despite this, his effort is exemplary in addressing all the key elements of the hypothesis.

NUMBER MARKING   The most extensive recent effort to extend and improve a structure-centered approach is my comparative study of the relation between grammatical number marking and cognition among speakers of American English and Yucatec Maya (Lucy 1992b). The study develops the linguistic analysis within a broad typological framework and provides systematic comparative assessments of individual cognition (following Carroll & Casagrande 1958).

English and Yucatec differ in their number marking patterns. First, English speakers *obligatorily* signal plural for a large number of lexical nouns, whereas Yucatec speakers *optionally* signal plural for a comparatively small number of lexical nouns. These patterns fit easily into a typological pattern visible across many languages. In nonverbal experimental tasks involving remembering and sorting, American and Yucatec speakers were sensitive to the number of various types of objects in accordance with the patterns in their grammar. Second, whereas English numerals often directly modify their associated nouns (e.g. *one candle*), Yucatec numerals must always be accompanied by a form referred to as a *numeral classifier* which provides essential information needed to count the referent [e.g. *un-tz'iit kib* 'one **long thin** wax (i.e. one candle)']. The classifiers reflect the fact that all lexical nouns in Yucatec are semantically unspecified as to essential unit. (Where our pattern is like the Maya, we use the functional equivalent of a classifier ourselves: *a cube of sugar.*) Numeral classifiers occur in a wide variety of languages throughout world, perhaps most notably in the languages of Asia—Chinese, Japanese, Thai, etc. In nonverbal experimental tasks involving classifying triads of objects that should contrast maximally in the two lexical systems, English speakers showed a corresponding preference for shape-based classifications whereas Yucatec speakers showed a corresponding preference for material-based classifications—results in line with the expectations based on the lexical structures of the two languages. In more recent research these cognitive findings have been replicated with a wider array of informants and materials, their development in childhood traced, and similar patterns found in other classifier languages (Lucy & Gaskins 1997).

This research remedies some of the traditional difficulties of structure-centered approaches by framing the linguistic analysis typologically so as to enhance comparison and by supplementing ethnographic observation with a rigorous assessment of individual thought. This then makes possible the realization of the benefits of the structure-centered approach: placing the languages at issue on an equal footing, exploring semantically significant lexical and grammatical patterns, and developing connections to related semantic patterns in the languages.

Domain-Centered Approaches

GENERAL APPROACH   A domain-centered approach begins with a certain domain of experienced reality and asks how various languages encode or construe it. Usually the analysis attempts to characterize the domain independently of language(s) and then determine how each language selects from and organizes the domain. Typically, speakers of different languages are asked to refer to "the same" materials or situations so that the different linguistic construals become clear. In a sense, this approach "asks" of each language how it would handle a given referential problem so as to reveal the distinctiveness of its functioning; ideally it makes clear the various elaborations and gaps characteristic of each language's coding of a common reality. The strength of the approach lies in its precision and control: It facilitates rapid, sure comparison among a large set of languages. The search for language influences on thought likewise tends to be focused and highly controlled, searching for detailed cognitive effects in experimental tasks—though this is not essential to the approach.

Domain-centered approaches are susceptible to several characteristic weaknesses. First, there is strong pressure to focus on domains that can be easily defined rather than on what languages typically encode. This can result in a rigorous comparison of a domain of marginal semantic relevance (e.g. a few select lexical items). Second, the high degree of domain focus, especially in elicitation procedures, tends to give a very narrow and distorted view of a language's semantic approach to a situation. Analysts typically concentrate only on those aspects of meaning that seem relevant to the domain, including or discarding elements of meaning that various languages bring to bear by applying criteria arising from the analysts' own semantic or cultural understandings of the domain. Thus the key question for any domain-centered approach is how the domain has been delineated in the first place and what the warrant is for including or excluding particular forms and meanings. Once again, a typological perspective can help establish what domains make sense to compare and what elements of meaning are routinely intercalated with them. Third, this approach tends to create bogus structures. Components of a language that lack structural unity or significance but that happen to be deployed together functionally in referring to the domain are treated as unified properties of the language. Apparent unity is often an artifact of the elicitation process. The remedy is to demonstrate structural coherence on language-internal grounds. Finally, in seeking influences on thought, studies adopting this approach often have difficulty establishing the significance of purported effects, because the approach emphasizes what it is possible to say, not what is structurally salient or habitually said.

COLOR CATEGORIES   The classic example of a domain-centered approach was developed in a series of studies of the lexical codability of colors by Eric Lenneberg and his colleagues (Brown & Lenneberg 1954, Lenneberg 1953, Lenneberg & Roberts 1956, Lucy 1992a). They showed that some colors were more codable than others in English (and later Zuni) and that the more codable colors were recognized and remembered more readily in nonlinguistic tasks. This approach to color was later continued in the well-known work on universals of basic color terms by anthropologists Brent Berlin, Paul Kay, and their collaborators (Berlin & Kay 1969, Kay & McDaniel 1978). They argued that there are cross-linguistic regularities in the encoding of color such that a small number of "basic" color terms emerge in a fairly constrained way in many languages and that these patterns stem ultimately from biological sources. This research has been widely accepted as evidence against the linguistic relativity hypothesis. In fact, the basic color term thesis deals with constraints on linguistic diversity. Addressing linguistic relativity would require assessing the impact of differences in color term systems on cognition. Despite some initial evidence that differences in color term systems do not yield differences in color cognition (Heider 1972), restudies correcting methodological flaws in this work have instead found significant language effects on memory (Lucy & Shweder 1979, 1988). Other studies reveal effects on perceptual categorization as a function of color category boundaries (Kay & Kempton 1984).

The basic color term thesis itself has come under strong criticism from the outset for having weak descriptive linguistics, a flawed elicitation methodology, and an untenable biological argument (see references in Lucy 1997, Saunders 1992, Saunders & van Brakel 1997, van Brakel 1994). Recent research has concentrated on extending and improving the cross-linguistic comparison, refining the typology, and strengthening the biological argument (Hardin & Maffi 1997; Kay et al 1991, 1997; MacLaury 1992, 1997). But little has been done to improve the quality of linguistic description.

This research reflects the typical weaknesses of domain-centered approaches: choosing a domain more for its ease of study than for its linguistic significance, being unreflective about the appropriateness of the domain for other languages, ignoring routine usage in favor of performance in a controlled task, and creating the appearance of examining a linguistic structure when none has been demonstrated on internal grounds. Because of these limitations, the studies essentially end up showing the distribution of the world's languages relative to a fixed set of parameters drawn from the Western European scientific tradition. Any gains in comparability are purchased by virtually eliminating the possibility of detecting genuine or interesting linguistic variability. Language becomes a dependent variable, a device for coding or mapping a pregiven reality, rather than a substantive contributor to its interpretation or constitution.

SPATIAL ORIENTATION   The most successful effort at a domain-centered approach has been undertaken by a research team under the direction of Stephen Levinson at the Max Planck Institute for Psycholinguistics that has been exploring the domain of space. The larger agenda of the project has been to critique the excessive reliance on English and other European languages in the field of cognitive science. Space was chosen as a domain because it has been widely regarded as invariant within philosophical, psychological, and linguistic circles and yet appeared to exhibit cross-linguistic variation (Haviland 1993, Levinson 1996a; see also Brown & Levinson 1993b, Levinson & Brown 1994). For example, speakers of modern European languages tend to favor the use of body coordinates to describe arrangements of objects (e.g. *the man is to the left of the tree*). For similar situations, speakers of other languages such as

Guugu Yiimithirr (Australian) and Tzeltal (Mayan) favor systems anchored as cardinal direction terms or topographic features respectively (e.g. *the man is to the east/uphill of the tree*).

There are, of course, other ways to refer to space both in these languages and in others, so the first task of the group was to describe the range of linguistic variation—which has turned out to be considerable (Danziger 1997, Levinson 1996a, Pederson et al 1997). The project included a dozen different languages, and for each, a linguist familiar with the language worked with informants on half a dozen elicitation tasks designed to probe spatial reference (de León 1991, Levinson 1992, Senft 1994) to compare "the meaning patterns that consistently emerge from domain-directed interactive discourse" (Pederson et al 1997, p. 9).

The second task of the project was to see whether variation in linguistic use corresponded to variation in cognition. To do this the group has exploited the sensitivity of the various spatial reference systems to rotation. If something is to the left and I turn around, it is now to the right, but if I conceive of it as to the east, then turn around, it remains to the east. Using many nonlinguistic tasks sensitive to this rotation, they find that speakers of different languages respond in ways congruent with their verbal practices (Brown & Levinson 1993a; Levinson 1992; Pederson 1993, 1995; Pederson et al 1997). Further, speakers of languages preferring extensive use of fixed coordinates show more accurate dead reckoning skills when asked to indicate the direction of familiar locations from an unfamiliar site (Levinson 1996c), suggesting that the results found in the controlled contexts may have everyday correlates.

This research has attempted to gain the advantages of precise, extensive comparison characteristic of a domain-centered approach while simultaneously avoiding its chief pitfalls by incorporating extensive linguistic description and typology into the project. Consequently, the project has achieved more serious and thorough linguistic analysis than other domain-centered approaches. The group has also supplemented controlled cognitive experimentation with naturalistic measures.

Behavior-Centered Approaches

GENERAL APPROACH   Behavior-centered approaches begin with an encounter with a marked difference in behavior, usually one that is initially inexplicable but which the researcher comes to believe has its roots in a pattern of thought arising from language practices [cf Whorf's (1956a) well-known examples of how patterns of talking contribute to accidental fires]. Ethnographic analyses that appeal heavily to language structure can be considered behavior-centered if they are also comparative (e.g. Martin 1988). Since the research does not necessarily begin with the intention of addressing the linguistic relativity question, but with a practical problem and the mode of thought giving rise to it, these studies form a heterogeneous lot. The strength of the approach lies in the significance of the behavior, which typically has clear practical consequences either for theory or to native speakers. The behavioral difference requires some explanation; if one rejects the proposed linguistic sources, another must be found.

The characteristic weakness of the approach is its ad hoc and inadequate approach to the language and reality elements, both theoretically and empirically. Some aspect of the language is identified as relevant to the behavior at issue. Although this aspect may be salient to the observer or even to speakers themselves, it need not be either structurally or functionally important in the language. Essentially, this approach "selects" structural features of the language according to a criterion of presumed relevance to a practical behavior at issue. Often no formal analysis of the language is undertaken and no comparison with other languages is attempted. When they are, both follow the same pattern of devoting attention only to elements that seem patently relevant regardless of their broader structural place and significance. Likewise, since the approach is not necessarily geared to referential semantics, the reality element may be absent altogether or receive only cursory treatment. Once again, a typological approach anchored in referential semantics would significantly improve approaches of this sort. Usually these research projects are not primarily interested in exploring the question of linguistic relativity, but rather in accounting for the noteworthy (often "deficient") behavior at issue.

COUNTERFACTUAL REASONING   A well-known example of a behavior-centered approach is Alfred Bloom's (1981, 1984) study of the relation between counterfactual markers and speakers' facility with counterfactual or hypothetical reasoning. In the course of doing research on moral reasoning, Bloom noticed that Chinese speakers had difficulty with the counterfactual questions used in such research. In searching for a reason, Bloom came to suspect that the difficulty stemmed from the way counterfactuals were marked in the Chinese language. He then designed several counterfactual reasoning experiments where he presented various controlled stories to English and Chinese speakers (with the Chinese receiving Chinese versions of the English texts) and concluded that systematic marking of counterfactuals (along with other linguistic resources) aided sustaining a theoretical mode of thought. He also discussed the disadvantages of this mode of thought from a Chinese perspective.

However, since Bloom's stimulus materials were not absolutely identical in the two cases, his approach led to a number of ambiguities. Critics (Au 1983, 1984, Liu 1985, Takano 1989; see also Cara & Politzer 1993) raised questions about the accuracy and fairness of the Chinese translations. There is no way to resolve such disputes except by appeal to what speakers would typically say about a concrete everyday situation; but this can not be tested, since the counterfactual stories by definition did not correspond to any independently observable events. Further, the differences in how much counterfactual discourse the two groups engage in and how they value it seem much more telling than any structural differences. Bloom is actually comparing a discursive register that operates over a variety of structural features and, as such, requires a discursively oriented approach (Lucy 1992a).

This study illustrates the ad hoc quality of the behavior-centered approach: The various linguistic devices have been selected because they seem relevant to the initial behavior, not because they form a coherent or salient structural aspect of the language but because of their common use in a certain discourse mode. Further, there is no anchor to reality outside of the texts. Ultimately, in such an unanchored context, it is difficult to establish that language structure contributes to the observed behavioral differences. Yet despite the ambiguity of Bloom's results, his approach succeeded in bringing together experimental work and broader cultural analysis for the first time on a problem of general interest.

OCCUPATIONAL ACCIDENTS   A recent set of studies has explored the relation between language and the incidence of occupational accidents in Finland. Occupational accident rates are substantially lower in Sweden than in Finland and among the Swedish-speaking minority within Finland despite working in the same regions with similar laws and regulations (Salminen & Hiltunen 1993, 1995; Salminen & Johansson 1996). This difference emerges even when controlling for the type, status, or hazard of the occupation or the rate or language of accident report. Researchers have attempted to account for this difference by reference to structural differences between Swedish and Finnish (Johansson & Strømnes 1995, Salminen & Hiltunen 1993).

These language differences were first analyzed by Frode J Strømnes, a Swedish experimental psychologist who became interested in why it was so difficult for him to learn Finnish. He contrasted comparable operators in the two languages and concluded that Swedish prepositions can be represented in terms of a vector geometry in a three-dimensional space whereas Finnish cases can be represented in terms of a topology in a two-dimensional space coupled with a third dimension of time (or duration) (Strømnes 1973, 1974a, 1976). Strømnes supported this analysis with a number of ingenious experiments and observations (Strømnes 1974a,b). What emerges in practical terms is a Swedish emphasis on information about movement in three-dimensional space and a Finnish emphasis on more static, Gestalt relations between borders of figures. A later study of cinematic style found that Indo-European (Swedish, Norwegian, English) productions formed coherent temporal entities in which action could be followed from beginning to end across scenes, whereas Ural-Altaic (Finnish, Hungarian, Estonian) productions showed more emphasis on static settings with only transitory movement and formed coherent person-centered entities in which scenes were linked by the emotional Gestalts of persons (Johansson & Strømnes 1995, Johansson & Salminen 1996, Strømnes et al 1982).

Based on preliminary observations of factories, the hypothesis was formed that the Finns organize the workplace in a way that favors the individual worker (person) over the temporal organization of the overall production process. Lack of attention to the overall temporal organization of the process leads to frequent disruptions in production, haste, and, ultimately, accidents (Johansson & Salminen 1996, Johansson & Strømnes 1995). At the moment, concrete evidence for this interpretation is lacking, but research on production processes is under way to test the hypothesis.

This work provides an excellent example of a behavior-centered approach that, faced with a practical behavioral difference between groups, seeks to explain it in terms of a known language difference. In comparison with Bloom's work, the linguistic variable is more coherent, the control over other contributing factors much higher, and the outcome behavior can be observed independently of language use. What is less clear, however, is the linkage between language and those behaviors.

Shifting Burdens of Proof

The research reviewed here indicates that the linguistic relativity proposal can be practically and profitably investigated in a number of ways. The linguistic variables range from small sets of lexical items to broad grammatical patterns to functional aggregates of features. The cognitive variables include the functional organization of perception, memory, categorization, and inference both in experimental and everyday settings. Some of these claims may prove ill-founded or subject to later qualification, but cumulatively they suggest that a variety of language patterns may have important influences on various aspects of thought and behavior.

In the aggregate, the studies reviewed here begin to shift the burden of proof for future research. First, they indicate that it is possible to overcome previous difficulties and to investigate the hypothesis empirically. When this is done, there is some support for the hypothesis. It is no longer sufficient to retreat behind claims that there is no favorable evidence at all or that the problem is fundamentally uninvestigable. Second, the requirements of adequate research now stand much higher. Each approach to research has its characteristic strengths: the structure-centered approach with its emphasis on linguistic form maximizes the validity of the language analysis and therefore holds the greatest potential for finding new interpretations of reality, the domain-centered approach with its emphasis on referential content maximizes the control over linguistic and cognitive comparison by anchoring both in a well-defined reality, and the behavior-centered approach with its emphasis on the everyday use or functioning of cognitive skills and orientations maximizes the real-world generalizability and practical significance of any proposed language and thought linkages. New research will have to continue the pattern of trying to achieve a workable balance among these approaches that includes an adequate representation of language, thought, and reality.

TOWARD A THEORETICAL ACCOUNT

Empirical demonstrations of the types just described move the linguistic relativity hypothesis from the realm of speculation to the realm of concrete investigation, but they are not equivalent to providing a theoretical account. Such an account must specify the conditions and mechanisms leading to relativity effects, that is, give further content to the two key relations of the hypothesis: how languages interpret reality and how languages influence thought. This involves engaging with the semiotic and discursive levels of the language and thought relation with respect to how they enable and shape structural level effects.

Interpretations of Reality

An account of how languages interpret reality constitutes an important aim of all the language sciences despite differences in opinion regarding how variable these interpretations might be (Grace 1987). To provide a general theory of how verbal categories differentially encode reality, they need to be contextualized formally, typologically, and discursively.

Formal contextualization involves assessing how meaning is distributed among the available formal resources in a language and what the implications of those placements are for the overall fashion of speaking. Traditionally the focus has been on differences such as lexical versus grammatical status, obligatoriness versus optionality, and overtness versus covertness of marking (e.g. Fishman 1960, Whorf 1956c). Future research will also have to take into account perspectival categories, such as verbal aspect, that express speaker viewpoint (Berman & Slobin 1994; cf Kay 1996, Lakoff 1987) and indexical categories, such as tense, that depend on context of use for their interpretation

(Haviland 1996, Levinson 1983, Silverstein 1976). An important issue here is whether a category type is especially salient or susceptible to secondary (or ideological) interpretation by speakers (Silverstein 1979, 1981, 1985). All these issues are fundamentally semiotic, and the significance of particular formal placement should be similar across languages.

Typological contextualization involves comparing how the system of meaning in a language compares with other languages. The distinctive quality of a given linguistic system usually only becomes clear within such a framework (Whorf 1956b). Although one might begin with only two levels, a lower, universal one and a higher language-specific one (e.g. Levinson 1997, Wierzbicka 1992), ideally such a typological framework will include a middle level where it provides substantive guidance about major patterns of structural difference across languages (Lucy 1992b).

Discursive contextualization concerns whether some patterns of use such as language standardization or schooling alter the interpretation of structural meanings (e.g. Gumperz 1982, Havránek 1964). The specific issue here is not discursive relativity as such, where the pattern of use itself embodies certain assumptions about reality (Lucy 1996), but rather the ways in which this level shapes structural meaning.

Influences on Thought

A full theory of the relation of language diversity to thought necessarily involves at least three logical components. It must distinguish between language and thought in some principled way. It must elaborate the actual mechanisms or manner of influence. And it must indicate to what extent other contextual factors affect the operation of those mechanisms.

Although almost everyone would agree that language and thought are distinct in some respects, there is no generally accepted set of criteria. Some even treat language and thought as identical at the level of conceptual or semantic representation. This is common, for example, in cognitive linguistics (e.g. Jackendoff 1983, Langacker 1987), although the implications for relativism are side-stepped by a universalist orientation (but see Lakoff 1987). Levinson (1997) provides a useful critique of such conflations of language and thought, as well as the inverse claims for a radical disjunction between the two. In distinguishing them, he places special emphasis on the structured (linear, obligatory) and social (indexical, pragmatic, public) nature of language categories in contrast to those of thought. In indicating their necessary interrelation, he emphasizes the natural processing economy of harmonizing the two. Perhaps the place where the distinction between language and thought is most debated is among those working on language acquisition and socialization, where the concern is whether language can be learned with general cognitive skills or requires specific linguistic capacities. This research on acquisition has increasingly concerned itself with language variation in recent years (e.g. Bavin 1995, Berman & Slobin 1994, Gelman & Byrnes 1991). Although the research is addressed to how language is learned, and not to linguistic relativity as such, interest in the latter has begun to grow as it becomes clear just what different interpretations of experience children must form to speak properly (Bowerman 1996, Levinson & Bowerman 1997, Ochs 1996). This research should become a major source of insight into how language and thought differ from each other and how they come to interrelate during development.

The mechanisms by which language might influence thought can be analyzed into several component elements that need to be addressed as part of developing a substantive theory. First, what is the point of impact in the linear, real-time process of thinking? Is it just "thinking for speaking" (Slobin 1996b) and otherwise without serious impact on thought? Or does speaking a language set up prior expectations about what will be seen (Whorf 1956b), play a concrete role in thought processes (Vygotsky 1987), or shape how the output of thought is interpreted, stored, or retrieved (e.g. Baddeley 1990)? Second, what is the locus of impact in terms of the functional organization of mind? Are there effects on perception, concept formation and use, logical inference, recall or recognition memory, or decision making (Lucy 1992b, Pederson et al 1997)? Are the effects at the lowest levels of cognition or only at various higher, more complex conceptual and imaginative levels (Gumperz & Levinson 1996, Hunt & Agnoli 1991, Levinson 1996b, 1997, Wierzbicka 1992; cf Friedrich 1986)? Third, what is the mode of impact, the logical dynamic governing effects? Is it analogical suggestion about the contents of experience (Whorf 1956a), a form of inner speech with residual syntagmatic and paradigmatic properties (Vygotsky 1987), heightened saliency for certain options (Brown & Lenneberg 1954), the availability of preset categories with an effect of chunking or codability (Levinson 1997; see also Brown & Lenneberg 1954, Miller 1956, Simon 1986), or perhaps via ideological reflection (Rumsey 1990, Silverstein 1981)? Finally, there is the question of the significance of impact. Are the effects large or small, easy or difficult to shed or circumvent, more or less durable or malleable as a function of verbal fluency?

The inclination of a speaker to involve language categories in thought may be affected by institutionalized discursive practices in a culture. The most obvious cases here arise in schooling (Vygotsky 1987), specialized occupations (e.g. law, science, philosophy, etc) (e.g. Mertz 1994, Havránek 1964, Silverstein 1979), and certain class strata (Bernstein 1971)—but such attitudes may also characterize an entire culture. Two particular approaches have received attention in recent years. One emphasizes the importance of linguistic ideology in shaping a community's attitude toward language structure and language practice (Hill 1985; Rumsey 1990; Silverstein 1979, 1985, 1997; Woolard & Schieffelin 1994), and the other stresses the special role of poetic or artistic works (Banfield 1978; Friedrich 1986; Lee 1985, 1993; Slobin 1996a). In both cases, structural elements are given heightened effect via reflexive activities.

CONCLUSION

The range of materials relevant to providing an adequate theoretical account of linguistic relativity is daunting. An account has to deal both with the underlying processes upon which all language and thought relations are necessarily built and with the shaping role of discourse as it is implemented in social institutions and cultural traditions. Broadening the scope of research in this way, however, should not be allowed to obscure the central reality and significance of structural differences in meaning between languages. There has long been a tendency in research on language and thought to ignore or minimize structural differences by seeing them as "mere content" either for general universal psycholinguistic processes or for the implementation of particular local discursive genres and registers. Indeed, most students receiving training in these areas today probably have little if any formal acquaintance with the details of comparative descriptive linguistics. In this context, it is important not only to reach out to other kinds of research to help formulate a theoretical account, but also to keep attending to the core problem itself, that is, the significance of differences in language structures for thought. Research on structural influences is essential both empirically and theoretically for developing a comprehensive view of the relation between language and thought at all the various levels.

ACKNOWLEDGMENTS

I thank Suzanne Gaskins for comments on an earlier draft. The section on theory profited at points from a seminar discussion at the Max Planck Institute for Psycholinguistics in 1993 with Pim Levelt, Dan Slobin, Stephen Levinson, and others.

Literature Cited

Aarsleff H. 1982. *From Locke to Saussure: Essays on the Study of Language and Intellectual History.* Minneapolis: Univ. Minn. Press

Aarsleff H. 1988. Introduction. See Humboldt 1988, pp. vii-lxv

Au TK. 1983. Chinese and English counterfactuals: the Sapir-Whorf hypothesis revisited. *Cognition* 15:155-87

Au TK. 1984. Counterfactuals: in reply to Alfred Bloom. *Cognition* 17:289-302

Baddeley A. 1990. *Human Memory.* Hillsdale, NJ: Erlbaum

Banfield A. 1978. Where epistemology, style, and grammar meet literary history: the development of represented speech and thought. *New Lit. Hist.* 9:415-54

Bavin EL. 1995. Language acquisition in crosslinguistic perspective. *Annu. Rev. Anthropol.* 24:373-96

Berlin B, Kay P. 1969. *Basic Color Terms: Their Universality and Evolution.* Berkeley: Univ. Calif. Press

Berman RA, Slobin DI. 1994. *Relating Events in Narrative: A Crosslinguistic Developmental Study.* Hillsdale, NJ: Erlbaum

Bernstein B. 1971. *Classes, Codes and Control,* Vol. 1, *Theoretical Studies Toward a Sociology of Language.* London: Routledge & Kegan Paul

Bloom AH. 1981. *The Linguistic Shaping of Thought: A Study in the Impact of Language on Thinking in China and the West.* Hillsdale, NJ: Erlbaum

Bloom AH. 1984. Caution—the words you use may affect what you say: a response to Au. *Cognition* 17:275-87

Boas F. 1966. (1911). Introduction. *Handbook of American Indian Languages,* ed. F Boas (reprint ed. P Holder), pp. 1-79. Lincoln, NE: Univ. Nebr. Press

Bowerman M. 1996. The origins of children's spatial semantic categories: cognitive versus linguistic determinants. See Gumperz & Levinson 1996, pp. 145-76

Brown P, Levinson SC. 1993a. Linguistic and nonlinguistic coding of spatial arrays: explorations in Mayan cognition. *Work. Pap. 24.* Nijmegen, Neth: Cogn. Anthropol. Res. Group

Brown P, Levinson SC. 1993b. 'Uphill' and 'downhill' in Tzeltal. *J. Linguist. Anthropol.* 3(1):46-74

Brown RW, Lenneberg EH. 1954. A study in language and cognition. *J. Abnorm. Soc. Psychol.* 49:454-56

Cara F, Politzer G. 1993. A comparison of conditional reasoning in English and Chinese. In *Cognition and Culture: A Cross-Cultural Approach to Psychology,* ed. J Altarriba, pp. 283-97. Amsterdam: North Holland

Carroll JB, ed. 1956. *Language, Thought, and Reality: Selected Writings of Benjamin Lee Whorf.* Cambridge, MA: MIT Press

Carroll JB, Casagrande JB. 1958. The function of language classifications in behavior. In *Readings in Social Psychology,* ed. E Maccoby, T Newcomb, E Hartley, pp. 18-31. New York: Holt

Danziger E. 1997. Cross-cultural studies in language and thought: Is there a metalanguage? In *The Psychology of Cultural Experience,* ed. C Moore, H Mathews. Cambridge: Cambridge Univ. Press. In press

de León L. 1991. Space games in Tzotzil: creating a context for spatial reference. *Work. Pap. 4.* Berlin: Cogn. Anthropol. Res. Group

Fishman JA. 1960. A systematization of the Whorfian hypothesis. *Behav. Sci.* 5:323-39

Fishman JA. 1982. Whorfianism of the third kind: ethnolinguistic diversity as a worldwide societal asset (The Whorfian Hypothesis: varieties of validation, confirmation, and disconfirmation II). *Lang. Soc.* 11:1-14

Friedrich P. 1986. *The Language Parallax: Linguistic Relativism and Poetic Indeterminacy.* Austin, TX: Univ. Tex. Press

Gelman SA, Byrnes JP, eds. 1991. *Perspectives on Language and Thought: Interrelations in Development.* Cambridge: Cambridge Univ. Press

Grace GW. 1987. *The Linguistic Construction of Reality.* London: Croom Helm

Gumperz JJ. 1982. *Discourse Strategies.* Cambridge: Cambridge Univ. Press

Gumperz JJ, Levinson SC, eds. 1996. *Rethinking Linguistic Relativity.* Cambridge: Cambridge Univ. Press

Hardin CL, Maffi L, eds. 1997. *Color Categories in Thought and Language.* Cambridge: Cambridge Univ. Press.

Haviland JB. 1993. Anchoring, iconicity, and orientation in Guugu Yimithirr pointing gestures. *J. Linguist. Anthropol.* 3(1):3-45

Haviland JB. 1996. Projections, transpositions, and relativity. See Gumperz & Levinson 1996, pp. 271-323

Havránek B. 1964. (1932). The functional differentiation of the standard language. In *A Prague School Reader on Esthetics, Liter-*

ary Structure, and Style, ed./transl. P Garvin, pp. 3–16. Washington, DC: Georgetown Univ. Press

Heider E. 1972. Universals in color naming and memory. *J. Exp. Psychol.* 93:10–20

Hill JH. 1985. The grammar of consciousness and the consciousness of grammar. *Am. Ethnol.* 12:725–37

Hill JH, Mannheim B. 1992. Language and world view. *Annu. Rev. Anthropol.* 21:381–406

Humboldt W von. 1988. *On Language: The Diversity of Human Language-Structure and Its Influence on the Mental Development of Mankind.* Transl. P Heath. Cambridge: Cambridge Univ. Press

Hunt E, Agnoli F. 1991. The Whorfian hypothesis: a cognitive psychology perspective. *Psychol. Rev.* 98(3):377–89

Hymes D. 1966. Two types of linguistic relativity (with examples from Amerindian ethnography). In *Sociolinguistics, Proceedings of the UCLA Sociolinguistics Conference, 1964,* ed. W Bright, pp. 114–57. The Hague: Mouton

Jackendoff R. 1983. *Semantics and Cognition.* Cambridge, MA: MIT Press

Johansson A, Salminen S. 1996. *Different languages: different information processing systems? Part I: Why can we expect differences in occupational accidents between language groups.* Presented at Int. Symp. Work Inf. Soc., Helsinki

Johansson A, Strømnes FJ. 1995. *Cultural differences in occupational accidents. Part I: Theoretical background.* Presented at Nord. Meet. Work Environ., 44th, Nantali, Finland

Kay P. 1996. Intra-speaker relativity. See Gumperz & Levinson 1996, pp. 97–114

Kay P, Berlin B, Maffi L, Merrifield W. 1997. Color naming across languages. See Hardin & Maffi 1997, pp. 320–46

Kay P, Berlin B, Merrifield W. 1991. Biocultural implications of systems of color naming. *J. Linguist. Anthropol.* 1:12–25

Kay P, Kempton W. 1984. What is the Sapir-Whorf hypothesis? *Am. Anthropol.* 86: 65–79

Kay P, McDaniel CK. 1978. The linguistic significance of the meanings of basic color terms. *Language* 54:610–46

Koerner EFK. 1992. The Sapir-Whorf hypothesis: a preliminary history and a bibliographic essay. *J. Linguist. Anthropol.* 2:173–78

Lakoff G. 1987. *Women, Fire, and Dangerous Things: What Categories Reveal about the Mind.* Chicago: Univ. Chicago Press

Langacker RW. 1987. *Foundations of Cogni-*

tive Grammar, Vol. 1, *Theoretical Prerequisites.* Stanford: Stanford Univ. Press

Lee B. 1985. Peirce, Frege, Saussure, and Whorf: the semiotic mediation of ontology. See Mertz & Parmentier 1985, pp. 99–128

Lee B. 1993. Metalanguages and subjectivities. See Lucy 1993b, pp. 365–92

Lee P. 1991. Whorf's Hopi tensors: subtle articulators in the language/thought nexus? *Cogn. Linguist.* 2(2):123–47

Lee P. 1996. *The Whorf Theory Complex: A Critical Reconstruction.* Amsterdam: Benjamins

Lenneberg EH. 1953. Cognition in ethnolinguistics. *Language* 29:463–71

Lenneberg EH, Roberts JM. 1956. The language of experience: a study in methodology. *Int. J. Am. Linguist.* 22(2):Part 2, Mem. 13

Levinson SC. 1983. *Pragmatics.* Cambridge: Cambridge Univ. Press

Levinson SC. 1992. Language and cognition: the cognitive consequences of spatial description in Guugu Yimithirr. *Work. Pap. 13.* Nijmegen, Neth: Cogn. Anthropol. Res. Group

Levinson SC. 1996a. Language and space. *Annu. Rev. Anthropol.* 25:353–82

Levinson SC. 1996b. Relativity in spatial conception and description. See Gumperz & Levinson 1996, pp. 177–202

Levinson SC. 1996c. The role of language in everyday human navigation. *Work. Pap. 38.* Nijmegen, Neth: Cogn. Anthropol. Res. Group

Levinson SC. 1997. From outer to inner space: linguistic categories and non-linguistic thinking. In *The Relationship between Linguistic and Conceptual Representation,* ed. J Nuyts, E Pederson, pp. 13–45. Cambridge: Cambridge Univ. Press

Levinson SC, Bowerman M, eds. 1997. *Language Acquisition and Conceptual Development.* Cambridge: Cambridge Univ. Press. In press

Levinson SC, Brown P. 1994. Immanuel Kant among the Tenejapans. Anthropology as empirical philosophy. *Ethos* 22(1):3–41

Liu L. 1985. Reasoning counterfactually in Chinese: Are there any obstacles? *Cognition* 21:239–70

Lucy JA. 1985. Whorf's view of the linguistic mediation of thought. See Mertz & Parmentier 1985, pp. 73–97

Lucy JA. 1992a. *Language Diversity and Thought: A Reformulation of the Linguistic Relativity Hypothesis.* Cambridge: Cambridge Univ. Press

Lucy JA. 1992b. *Grammatical Categories and*

Cognition: A Case Study of the Linguistic Relativity Hypothesis. Cambridge: Cambridge Univ. Press

Lucy JA. 1993a. Reflexive language and the human disciplines. See Lucy 1993b, pp. 1–32

Lucy JA, ed. 1993b. *Reflexive Language: Reported Speech and Metapragmatics.* Cambridge: Cambridge Univ. Press

Lucy JA. 1996. The scope of linguistic relativity: an analysis and review of empirical research. See Gumperz & Levinson 1996, pp. 37–69

Lucy JA. 1997. The linguistics of "color." See Hardin & Maffi 1997, pp. 320–46

Lucy JA, Gaskins S. 1997. Grammatical categories and the development of classification preferences: a comparative approach. See Levinson & Bowerman 1997. In press

Lucy JA, Shweder RA. 1979. Whorf and his critics: linguistic and nonlinguistic influences on color memory. *Am. Anthropol.* 81:581–615

Lucy JA, Shweder RA. 1988. The effect of incidental conversation on memory for focal colors. *Am. Anthropol.* 90:923–31

MacLaury RE. 1992. From brightness to hue: an explanatory model of color-category evolution. *Curr. Anthropol.* 33:137–36

MacLaury RE. 1997. *Color and Cognition in Mesoamerica. Constructing Categories as Vantages.* Austin, TX: Univ. Tex. Press

Mandelbaum DG, ed. 1949. *The Selected Writings of Edward Sapir in Language, Culture, and Personality.* Berkeley: Univ. Calif. Press

Martin JR. 1988. Grammatical conspiracies in Tagalog: family, face, and fate—with regard to Benjamin Lee Whorf. In *Linguistics in a Systemic Perspective,* ed. JD Benson, MJ Cummings, WS Greaves, pp. 242–300. Amsterdam: Benjamins

Mertz E. 1994. Legal language: pragmatics, poetics, and social power. *Annu. Rev. Anthropol.* 23:435–55

Mertz E, Parmentier RJ, eds. 1985. *Semiotic Mediation: Sociocultural and Psychological Perspectives.* Orlando, FL: Academic

Miller GA. 1956. The magical number seven, plus or minus two. *Psychol. Rev.* 63(2):81–97

Ochs E. 1996. Linguistic resources for socializing humanity. See Gumperz & Levinson 1996, pp. 407–37

Pederson E. 1993. Geographic and manipulable space in two Tamil linguistic systems. In *Spatial Information Theory,* ed. AU Frank, I Campari, pp. 294–311. Berlin: Springer-Verlag

Pederson E. 1995. Language as context, language as means: spatial cognition and habitual language use. *Cogn. Linguist.* 6(1):333–62

Pederson E, Danziger E, Levinson SC, Kita S, Senft G, Wilkins D. 1997. Semantic typology and spatial conceptualization. *Work. Pap. 40.* Nijmegen, Neth: Cogn. Anthropol. Res. Group

Rumsey A. 1990. Wording, meaning, and linguistic ideology. *Am. Anthropol.* 92:346–61

Salminen S, Hiltunen E. 1993. *Accident frequency of Finnish- and Swedish-speaking workers in Finland.* Presented at Nord. Sem. Safety Res., 15th, Espoo, Finland

Salminen S, Hiltunen E. 1995. *Cultural differences in occupational accidents. Part II: A case study of Finnish- and Swedish-speaking workers in Finland.* Presented at Nord. Meet. Work Environ., 44th, Naantali, Finland

Salminen S, Johansson A. 1996. *Different languages—different information processing systems? Part II: A case study of occupational accidents.* Presented at Int. Symp. Work Inf. Soc. Helsinki

Sapir E. 1949a. (1924). The grammarian and his language. See Mandelbaum 1949, pp. 150–59

Sapir E. 1949b. (1929). The status of linguistics as a science. See Mandelbaum 1949, pp. 160–66

Sapir E. 1964. (1931). Conceptual categories in primitive languages. *Language in Culture and Society: A Reader in Linguistics and Anthropology,* ed. DH Hymes, p. 128. New York: Harper & Row

Saunders B. 1992. *The invention of basic colour terms.* PhD thesis. Univ. Utrecht

Saunders B, van Brakel J. 1997. Are there nontrivial constraints on colour categorization? *Behav. Brain Sci.* In press

Schultz EA. 1990. *Dialogue at the Margins. Whorf, Bakhtin, and Linguistic Relativity.* Madison, WI: Univ. Wis. Press

Senft G. 1994. Grammaticalization of body-part terms in Kilivila. *Lang. Linguist. Melanesia* 25(1):98–99

Silverstein M. 1976. Shifters, linguistic categories, and cultural description. In *Meaning in Anthropology,* ed. K Basso, H Selby, pp. 11–55. Albuquerque, NM: Univ. N. M. Press

Silverstein M. 1979. Language structure and linguistic ideology. In *The Elements: A Parasession on Linguistic Units and Levels,* ed. P Clyne, W Hanks, C Hofbauer, pp. 193–247. Chicago: Chicago Linguist. Soc.

Silverstein M. 1981. The limits of awareness.

Work. Pap. Sociolinguist., No. 84. Austin: Southwest. Educ. Lab.

Silverstein M. 1985. Language and the culture of gender: at the intersection of structure, usage, and ideology. See Mertz & Parentier 1985, pp. 219–59

Silverstein M. 1993. Metapragmatic discourse and metapragmatic function. See Lucy 1993b, pp. 33–58

Silverstein M. 1997. Whorfianism and the linguistic imagination of nationality. In *Regimes of Language*, ed. P Kroskrity. Santa Fe, NM: Sch. Am. Res. In press

Simon HA. 1986. The parameters of human memory. In *Human Memory and Cognitive Capabilities*, ed. F Klix, H Hagendorf, pp. 299–310. Amsterdam: North Holland

Slobin DI. 1996a. From "thought and language" to "thinking for speaking." See Gumperz & Levinson 1996, pp. 70–96

Slobin DI. 1996b. Two ways to travel: verbs of motion in English and Spanish. In *Grammatical Constructions: Their Form and Meaning*, ed. M Shibitani, SA Thompson, pp. 195–220

Strømnes FJ. 1973. A semiotic theory of imagery processes with experiments on an Indo-European and a Ural-Altaic language: Do speakers of different languages experience different cognitive worlds? *Scand. J. Psychol.* 14:291–304

Strømnes FJ. 1974a. No universality of cognitive structures? Two experiments with almost-perfect one-trial learning of translatable operators in a Ural-Altaic and Indo-European language. *Scand. J. Psychol.* 15: 300–9

Strømnes FJ. 1974b. To be is not always to be.

The hypothesis of cognitive universality in the light of studies on elliptic language behavior. *Scand. J. Psychol.* 15:89–98

Strømnes FJ. 1976. *A New Physics of Inner Worlds.* Tromsø, Nor: Inst. Soc. Sci., Univ. Tromsø

Strømnes FJ, Johansson A, Hiltunen E. 1982. *The Externalized Image: A Study Showing Differences Correlating with Language Structure Between Pictorial Structure in Ural-Altaic and Indo-European Filmed Versions of the Same Plays. Plan. Res. Dep. Rep. No. 21.* Helsinki: Finn. Broadcast. Corp.

Takano Y. 1989. Methodological problems in cross-cultural studies of linguistic relativity. *Cognition* 31:141–62

van Brakel J. 1994. The *Ignis Fatuus* of semantic universalia: the case of colour. *Br. J. Philos. Sci.* 45:770–83

Vygotsky LS. 1987. (1934). Thinking and speech. In *The Collected Works of L. S. Vygotsky*, Vol. 1, *Problems of General Psychology*, ed./transl. N Minnick, pp. 39–285. New York: Plenum

Whorf BL. 1956a. (1939). The relation of habitual thought and behavior to language. See Carroll 1956, pp. 134–59

Whorf BL. 1956b. (1940). Science and linguistics. See Carroll 1956, pp. 207–19

Whorf BL. 1956c. (1945). Grammatical categories. See Carroll 1956, pp. 87–101

Wierzbicka A. 1992. *Semantics, Culture, and Cognition. Universal Human Concepts in Culture-Specific Configurations.* Oxford: Oxford Univ. Press

Woolard KA, Schieffelin BB. 1994. Language ideology. *Annu. Rev. Anthropol.* 23:55–82

Annu. Rev. Anthropol. 1997. 26:313–35

THE BIOLOGICAL STRESS RESPONSE AND LIFESTYLE:
Catecholamines and Blood Pressure

Gary D. James

Cardiovascular Center, Cornell University Medical College, New York, New York 10021

Daniel E. Brown

Department of Anthropology, University of Hawaii at Hilo, Hilo, Hawaii 96720-4091

KEY WORDS: stress, norepinephrine, epinephrine, ambulatory blood pressure, diurnal variation

ABSTRACT

Many measures in human biology that are studied as immutable traits are actually fluctuating physiological functions that adjust body systems to rapid changes in the environment. This overview discusses what has been learned about the response to the stressors inherent in continuously changing microenvironments in modern Western societies of two related physiological functions: the release of catecholamines and blood pressure. The review shows that many factors that are part of or influence lifestyle—including perception and cognitive state, the nature of the social situation, foods, stimulants and exercise—and external conditions such as temperature, continuously alter catecholamine levels and blood pressure. Because lifestyle stress may be an important selective force in human populations, studies of dynamic functions that react to it, such as catecholamine release and blood pressure, may be important in understanding the ongoing dynamics of human evolution.

INTRODUCTION

Many measures in human biology that are studied as immutable traits are actually fluctuating physiological functions that adjust body systems to rapid changes in the internal or external environment (James 1991a). The adaptive value of these functions derives from their ability to vary continuously depending on the circumstance, rather than the attainment of a single fixed state.

313

0084-6570/97/1015-0313$08.00

They help the body to maintain homeostasis in the face of transient environmental perturbations, and most likely evolved in daily conditions that were characterized by extended intervals of relative calm punctuated by brief periods of excitement, as inferred from the work of Cannon (1914) in his conceptualization of the biology of "emergency situations," which has come to be known as "fight or flight."

The daily environments experienced by human beings in modern urban societies are often typified by compartmentalization of activities and social interactions, as well as by rapid change, and differ markedly from the circumstances under which human populations spent the majority of their evolutionary time (James 1991a). Several stressful aspects of the contemporary urban environment have been noted, including but not limited to commuting, noise, pollution, overcrowding, and poor sanitation (Harrison & Jefferies 1977, Boyden 1987, James 1991a). Most stressors in urban settings are compartmentalized into microenvironments, so they are not continuously experienced (James 1991a); thus, the stresses they produce are confronted in a somewhat structured way depending upon the types and pattern of microenvironments encountered (James et al 1987, James 1991a). The pattern of microenvironmental experience over the course of a day defines a significant aspect of an individual's lifestyle and varies from person to person. From an evolutionary standpoint, successful adaptation of the individual may partially hinge upon the ability to negotiate the stressors specific to personally experienced microenvironments, which include the people, places, and things in them. However, the biological resources available for adapting to these patterned stressors are those that evolved in a daily milieu that elicited infrequent interspersions of intense physiological arousal (James et al 1989a). It is this contrast between relatively ancient biology and new environment (both social and physical) that has implicated the stresses associated with current lifestyles and the biological responses to them in the development of chronic degenerative diseases (Hinkle 1987; Sapolsky 1994; Selye 1946, 1956).

Recent advances have created the opportunity to study several biological responses to the dynamic stressors of real life. The purpose of this review is to discuss the response to lifestyle of two related fluctuating physiological functions: the release of catecholamines and blood pressure.

BIOLOGICAL ADAPTATION AND LIFESTYLE

The study of how people biologically adjust to their lifestyle is the study of how people biologically respond to the things that they do, experience, and think every day, and the stress that these things cause. The basis of bioanthropological and psychophysiological inquiry into the biological responses to this stress is the work of Hans Selye, who some fifty years ago detailed the complicated but similar reactions elicited from mammalian species when their homeostatic systems were imperiled (Selye 1946, Goodman et al 1988, Huether 1996). He described a three-stage response to noxious environmental stimuli, the first of which was an initial "alarm reaction" that involved the activation of the peripheral sympathetic-adrenal medullary system (specifically the secretion of the stress hormones epinephrine and norepinephrine) and hypothalamic pituitary-adrenocortical system (beginning a cascade that released cortisol). This was, in essence, the "fight or flight" response delineated by Cannon (1914) years before. The second was the "stage of resistance," which was defined by the local tissue adaptive responses triggered by the hormones released in stage one and reflected the maintenance of homeostasis in the face of the environmental stress. The third was a "stage of exhaustion" in which there was a gradual decline of stress resistance of the tissues that would lead to disease. Selye coined the term "general adaptation syndrome" to describe the onset and ultimate failure of the integrated neuroendocrine and physiological adaptive responses to stress. As Huether (1996) has recently pointed out, this concept of adaptive neuroendocrine adjustments leading to eventual tissue exhaustion and consequent degenerative disease has been the paradigm that has driven most research into the causes and biological consequences of stress.

Since its introduction, the concept of the general adaptation syndrome has not gone unchallenged, and has been amended and updated as it was realized that among other things, psychological perceptions of events and relationships may be as important in eliciting the syndrome as noxious environmental stimuli (Mason 1971, Goodman et al 1988, Huether 1996). It is this more recent synthesis, which includes psychological aspects of behavior, that has guided more recent bioanthropological study of the relationship between lifestyle-related stress and the physiological responses to it.

THE CATECHOLAMINES

Under stress, the sympathetic-adrenal medullary system releases into the blood epinephrine and norepinephrine, which are collectively known as catecholamines. These hormones act to prepare the individual for "fight or flight," facilitating several physiological changes such as increases in heart rate, blood pressure, mental activity, the mobilization of energy stores and cellular metabolism, and a decrease in blood flow to organs that are not needed for rapid activity (Guyton 1981). These changes may be implicated in the development of cardiovascular and other degenerative diseases, particularly if they are continuously repeated or sustained over the life of the individual (James et al 1989a) (see Figure 1).

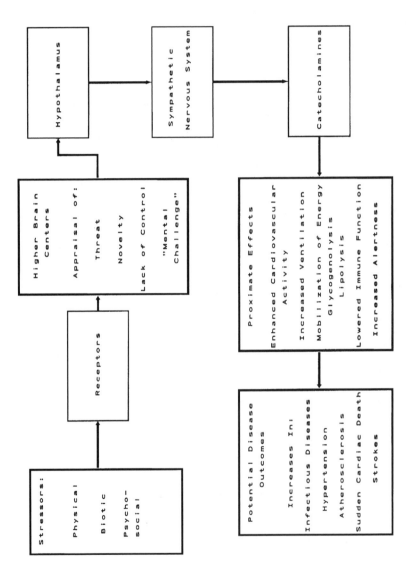

Figure 1   The sympathetic-adrenal medullary response to stress, with physiological pathways and potential outcomes noted.

The levels of circulating catecholamines are constantly adjusted to maintain homeostasis. Almost any change in the external or internal environment can increase catecholamine levels, including physical environmental factors such as cold (Johnson et al 1977, Kalita et al 1989), heat (Gorman & Proppe 1984), and high-altitude hypoxia (Hoon et al 1976, Mazzeo et al 1991). It is not our intent to review everything that affects catecholamine output. Rather, we focus on only those things that people think, do, and experience as part of their lifestyle.

Studying Catecholamine Changes

Catecholamines are studied in both plasma and urine (Akerstedt et al 1983). Plasma levels of catecholamines are catabolized from the blood rapidly; norepinephrine has a plasma half-life of about 2.5 min, whereas epinephrine has a half-life of about 1.2 min (Silverberg et al 1978, Ward et al 1983). Thus, research examining changes in plasma levels requires either multiple skin punctures over very short periods or a catheterization. Because of the invasive nature of blood collection, diurnal studies of how plasma catecholamines vary under real-life conditions are impractical. As most studies of plasma catecholamines assess the acute effects of a single life stressor, they are usually of short duration, experimental or observational in nature, and conducted under controlled conditions.

Measures of urinary catecholamines represent an estimate of average sympathetic-adrenal medullary activity over longer time periods, which have a practical minimum of about 1 h and a practical maximum of 24 h (James et al 1989a). Urinary measures are noninvasive and can therefore be used to assess the sympathetic response to real-life conditions (James et al 1989a). However, the longer period of urine collection makes it difficult to determine acute responses to specific short-term or instantaneous stressful events (James et al 1989a).

Psychological Mediators of Catecholamine Output

There are a range of factors that increase catecholamine excretion. These include mental challenges such as arithmetic tests and video games (Goldstein et al 1987, Ushiyama et al 1991) and circumstances that are characterized by uncertainty (Frankenhaeuser 1975) and that elicit anxiety and apprehension (Bridges 1974, James et al 1989a). Overstimulation of sensory systems by auditory (Welch & Welch 1969) or visual (Frankenhaeuser 1971, Wohlwill 1975) stimuli may also increase catecholamine excretion. Understimulation has been suggested to elevate catecholamine output (Frankenhaeuser 1971), but this finding may be due to the stress of isolation or confinement that often accompanies sensory deprivation experiments (Goldberger 1993).

Stress responses are further related both to the nature of the stimulus and to individual characteristics, such as personality type, motivation, attitude about the stimulus, and experience (Sokolov et al 1980). Other situational characteristics that can mediate catecholamine output include novelty (Mason 1968), threat (Lazarus & Folkman 1984), perceived control (whether it has an external or internal locus) (Dohrenwend & Dohrenwend 1970, Law et al 1994), and conflict (Crider 1970, Sokolov et al 1980). All these attributes combine stimuli with personal factors to affect catecholamine output. From an anthropological perspective, these characteristics are strongly influenced by social and cultural factors (Dohrenwend & Dohrenwend 1970, Brown 1981).

Habitual Behaviors That Increase Catecholamine Output

Smoking (Frankenhaeuser et al 1970, Reynolds et al 1981, Harrison 1995) and the ingestion of compounds such as caffeine (Ammon et al 1973, Harrison 1995) and ethyl alcohol (Myrsten et al 1971) acutely increase catecholamine output. Various dietary components may also influence catecholamine secretion. For example, in a study of middle-aged and elderly men, significant elevations of catecholamines were associated with increased total dietary energy intake (Young et al 1992). High intake levels of the amino acid tyrosine have been associated with elevated catecholamine excretion (Agharanya & Wurtman 1982), and low plasma concentration of glucose also stimulates catecholamine secretion (Santiago et al 1980). Finally, vigorous exercise will increase catecholamine levels, particularly norepinephrine, which can remain elevated for hours after exercise has ceased (Bahr et al 1991). It is interesting to note that increased physical fitness, while attenuating cardiovascular responses to stress (Herd 1991), has been associated with a greater plasma epinephrine concentration during psychological stress (Sothman et al 1988).

Catecholamine Variation and Lifestyle

Many studies in urban Western groups have shown that plasma secretion and urinary excretion of catecholamines increase in daily situations that are perceived to be stressful. These situations include driving a car (Bellet et al 1969), commuting by public transport (Lundberg 1976), various occupational and home-related activities (Levi 1964, Frankenhaeuser & Gardell 1976, Frankenhaeuser et al 1989, James et al 1993), and public speaking (Dimsdale & Moss 1980). The studies of Frankenhaeuser et al (1989) and James et al (1993) are also interesting because they show not only that catecholamine output is higher during the day at work and at home than while sleeping, but also that stressors inherent in specific daily environments such as children at home or occupational title at work (being a manager or clerical worker) can influence the pattern of daily catecholamine output (i.e. whether it is higher at work or home). Most observational studies of catecholamine variation are focused on specific situations and are generally designed to demonstrate how particular lifestyle aspects affect catecholamine output. There are relatively few studies that examine the effects of lifestyle difference on a population basis. Perhaps the best known population study was conducted by Harrison and associates (1995), who investigated lifestyle and urinary catecholamine levels among villagers in Oxfordshire, England. Urine samples were collected over three periods (morning, midday, and early evening) on a work day and a nonwork day. Comparisons across the samples showed that catecholamine excretion was significantly higher at midday and in the evening than in the morning, and average daytime excretion rates were higher on work than nonwork days. Nonmanual workers tended to have higher workday catecholamines than manual workers, and professionals and managers had higher rates than people in other occupational groups (Jenner et al 1980). Among women, epinephrine excretion rates were moderately correlated with frustration, life satisfaction, and worrying (Harrison et al 1981, Harrison 1995). In men, physical tiredness and boredom were related to low midday epinephrine excretion rates, while mental tiredness and job-related stress were associated with high excretion rates (Reynolds et al 1981). Overall, catecholamine excretion rates of men were more highly related to occupational factors, while women's rates were related to more general lifestyle issues (Harrison 1995).

Other researchers have examined cross-cultural lifestyle differences and urinary catecholamines. In a study of Filipino-American immigrants in Hawaii, those with intermediate levels of accommodation to American urban life had elevated catecholamine excretion over 24 h when compared with immigrants with either low or high levels of "Americanization" (Brown 1981, 1982). In a further study of immigrant Filipino-American women working as nurses and nurse's aides in Hawaii, norepinephrine was highest in those resident in the United States the longest (Brown et al 1997).

Studies of Samoans living in Western Samoa, American Samoa, and Hawaii examined the impact of modernization on urinary catecholamines. The first compared timed overnight and mid-morning urinary catecholamines in men from a rural village and three urban groups (manual laborers, sedentary workers, college students) from the capital city of Apia in Western Samoa. (James et al 1985, 1987). The results showed that villagers had lower mid-morning excretion rates than any of the urban groups, while overnight, the laborers and villagers had similar rates that differed from the sedentary workers and students. As many of the laborers commuted from rural villages to work in Apia, it was suggested that their overnight similarity with the villagers resulted from maintaining a more traditional lifestyle during nonwork hours (James et al 1985). The study also showed that the morning change in catecholamine levels was more directly related to stimulant and dietary intake and activity that occurred over the time of urine collection than to macro-level psychosocial phenomena determined from questionnaires (James et al 1987). Finally, differences by day of the week were found, such that subjects measured on Monday had lower catecholamine excretion rates than those measured on Friday or Saturday (James et al 1987). A second study in American Samoa found that Samoans with more traditional values and lifestyle, such as group-oriented decision making and larger social networks, tended to have lower daily urinary epinephrine levels than those with more Western lifeways (Martz et al 1984, Hanna et al 1986). The third study compared overnight, morning, and afternoon excretion rates among Samoan men and women residing in rural Western Samoa, American Samoa, and Honolulu, Hawaii (Pearson et al 1990, 1993). While no consistent group differences in average excretion rates were found (though Western Samoan rates tended to be lowest), there were substantial differences in the kinds of social behaviors associated with elevated catecholamine levels. For example, women in Western Samoa and Hawaii who spent more time in social interactions had higher epinephrine levels than women who were less social, but this association was reversed in American Samoa, where low levels of social interaction predicted higher epinephrine (Pearson et al 1993). Pearson et al (1993) also found a relatively low reproducibility in catecholamine excretion day to day among the Samoans, and suggested that this lack of continuity demonstrated the preeminent role of specific dynamic lifestyle factors in determining catecholamine levels on any given day.

Lastly, Jenner et al (1982, 1987) compared catecholamine excretion rates from several populations in two studies. In one (1982), values from "traditional" groups (the Masai and Mossi from Africa, and the Pacaa Nova Indians from the Amazon region) were found to be higher than those from Westernized English villagers from Oxfordshire, England. However, there were noted methodological problems that could have affected the results. In the other (1987), a comparison of Tokelau Islanders, Nigerians, Japanese-Americans, and Japanese revealed that the groups with more "traditional" lifestyles had lower rates of catecholamine excretion.

Other Factors That Modify Catecholamine Output

SEX   While there is little difference in urinary catecholamine excretion by gender in neutral conditions, women may respond with a lower urinary epinephrine excretion rate than men when exposed to the challenge of stressful situations (Collins & Frankenhaeuser 1978, Frankenhaeuser et al 1978, Frankenhaeuser 1983, Polefrone & Manuck 1987). One study found that during mental stress induced by taking an examination, males with high urinary cate-cholamine excretion rates had higher achievement orientation and less anxiety than other males, while females with higher catecholamine excretion rates tended to have lower self-esteem than other females (Rauste-von Wright et al 1981). This gender difference in psychological associations suggests that there may be culturally or socially mediated differences in attitude toward circum-stances that elicit stress responses. However, while these studies suggest a gender difference in sympathetic response to mental stress, others have found no gender differences in sympathetic response to mental arithmetic tests (Jones et al 1996), and few have found gender differences in stress-related in-creases in the rate of urinary norepinephrine excretion (Frankenhaeuser et al 1978).

Finally, using heart rate and blood pressure as surrogate measures of sym-pathetic response, Hastrup & Light (1984) found that women had a greater re-action to a mental stress test than men while in the luteal but not the follicular phase of their menstrual cycle. If these data are correct, one reason for the in-consistencies in gender comparisons may be that the results are confounded by menstrual cycle effects among women.

AGE   Many researchers report increases in catecholamine responses to vari-ous stressors with age (i.e. Ziegler et al 1976, Rubin et al 1982, Goldstein et al 1983, Sokolov et al 1980). However, others have found no significant age in-creases (Barnes et al 1982, Ng et al 1994). While age effects are considered to be due, in part, to physiological changes such as a decreased rate of uptake of norepinephrine by nerve cells, other considerations such as changes in physi-cal fitness, body fat, and illness prevalence may also account for some of the differences (Ng et al 1994). In addition, people of different ages have different experiences and expectations that are likely to affect their appraisal of poten-tial stressors. Finally, the effect of age on urinary catecholamine excretion may differ between the sexes (Aslan et al 1981).

BLOOD PRESSURE

Blood pressure is also continuously adjusted to maintain homeostasis. From the standpoint of the general adaptation syndrome, an acute increase in blood pres-sure may be initiated by the hormonal cascade released during the "alarm reac-tion" (James et al 1989a). Thus, anything that could affect catecholamines (noted above) could also affect blood pressure. Several studies have found asso-ciations between catecholamine excretion and blood pressure levels under real--life conditions (James et al 1985, 1993; Brown et al 1996). Blood pressure, however, is also affected by other factors. The following sections describe the nature of blood pressure and how it responds to the stressors of daily life.

Blood Pressure Defined

As the heart contracts, blood is expelled from the left ventricle into the aorta, creating a pulse wave that is dispersed throughout the cardiovascular system (Blank 1987). The maximum pressure of this pulse (that exerted against the arterial wall at the peak of contraction) is labeled systolic pressure, and the minimum pressure (that exerted when the heart is at rest, just before the next heart beat) is known as diastolic pressure (Blank 1987, O'Rourke 1990, James 1991a). As every heart contraction generates a pulse of blood, the average person may experience as many as 100,000 systolic and diastolic pressures in a 24-h day, depending on the rate at which their heart beats (James et al 1988b, James & Pecker 1994).

Arterial pressure can change substantially within seconds (Pickering & Blank 1989, James & Pecker 1994). One reason for this variability is that the blood flow needed to maintain appropriate oxygen exchange at the tissue level continuously changes with the physiological state and environmental conditions of the individual. These conditions are perpetually changing as people go about their typical daily lives (James & Pickering 1993).

Other factors can elevate seated blood pressure readings, most likely by triggering an alarm reaction to having a person take the measurement (Pickering et al 1988). These include having the measurer and subject be of opposite sex (Comstock 1957), and having a physician (an authority figure) as opposed to a nurse as the measurer (Mancia et al 1987). Because of measurer-subject interaction effects, seated readings (the most common measures in anthropological and epidemiological studies) are not likely to represent the true blood pressure of the subject, and most certainly are unrepresentative of blood pressures that occur during the ever-changing conditions over the day (James 1991a).

The Dynamic Study of Blood Pressure in Real Life

Ambulatory monitors have been developed that can be used to examine blood pressure responses to things that people do, experience, and think in everyday life. The nature of this technology is described in detail elsewhere (Pickering 1991, James 1991a, O'Brien et al 1995). In brief, however, ambulatory blood pressure monitors (of which there are several models) are portable, battery-operated devices that generally weigh less than one pound. They take blood pressure at computer-programmed intervals that can range from 5 min to 1 h (most often 15–20 min). The monitors store the readings, which after 24 h (or any time interval up to 48 h), can be downloaded into a PC for analysis using manufacturer-provided software (James & Pickering 1991, Pickering 1991).

Figure 2 shows systolic and diastolic blood pressures measured over the course of one day in a normal subject. As illustrated, there is substantial varia-

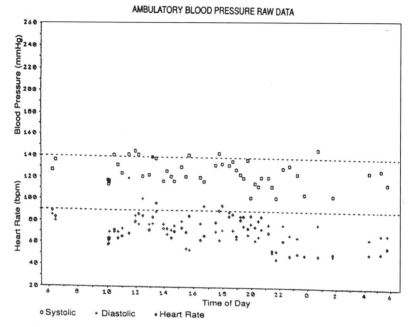

Figure 2   Graph of intermittently measured ambulatory blood pressures and heart rates in a normal subject, showing substantial daily variation independent of time (Modified from James 1991a, James & Pickering 1993).

tion in both, independent of time. In some individuals this variation may be as much as 100 mm Hg (Pickering et al 1986).

Researchers have approached the study of how lifestyle affects ambulatory blood pressures by examining factors that influence each measurement (determined from diary entries) (Van Egeren & Madarasmi 1988, Chesney & Ironson 1989, James 1991a) and by assessing whether the ambulatory pressures taken under different circumstances vary between groups who differ regarding a particular characteristic, such as smokers versus nonsmokers (Mann et al 1991) or having children or not (James et al 1989b, Pickering et al 1990). The following sections outline what has been learned about blood pressure response to habitual behavior and lifestyle.

Habitual Behavior and Blood Pressure Variation

The effects of chronic alcohol ingestion on the average daytime ambulatory pressure seems to depend on whether the person has normal or high blood pressure, with more consistent increases seen among hypertensives, and variable to no effect found among normotensives (Potter & Beevers 1984, Malhotra et al 1985, James et al 1995). The immediate effects of alcohol on blood pressure are variable, ranging from a slight decrease to an increase of 5/7 mm Hg systolic/diastolic after about 1 h of social drinking (Potter et al 1986, Stott et al 1987).

Smoking a cigarette produces an immediate increase in pressure (Cellina et al 1975). While the pressure, however, is elevated when a cigarette is smoked, evidence for a pervasive effect of smoking on average daily pressure seems to depend on age. In a study of younger smokers with normal blood pressure studied on two days (one while smoking and one while abstaining), Stewart et al (1994) found that there was little difference in the average daily pressure, although the variability of the smoking day pressure was somewhat greater. In a study comparing smokers (defined as smoking one or more packs of cigarettes per day) and nonsmokers with hypertension, Mann et al (1991) found that smokers over the age of 50 had significantly higher systolic pressures during the day than nonsmokers, but found no difference in the younger age group. They suggested that the age interaction with smoking may be because the stiffer arteries of older hypertensives may accentuate their response to nicotine. Other studies have found higher daytime pressures among smokers (Green et al 1991, James et al 1995). What is also of interest is that when sleeping pressures are compared between smokers and nonsmokers (presumably a time when smokers are not smoking), there is no difference in blood pressure (Mann et al 1991, James et al 1995).

People who do not drink coffee may experience a 10 mm Hg increase in blood pressure within about 15 min of drinking a cup, while habitual drinkers may only have a modest increase over the short term (Izzo et al 1983). Overall, caffeine has been reported to modestly increase average daily ambulatory pressure, but habituation and tolerance to caffeine over time may attenuate the effect (Jeong & Dimsdale 1990, Myers & Reeves 1991).

Finally, increasing salt in the diet tends to elevate the average level of daily ambulatory blood pressure (Gerdts et al 1994, Overlack et al 1995, James et al 1996a); however, the effect seems more accentuated in men than women (Moore et al 1991, James et al 1996a) and is not universal (Moore et al 1991, James et al 1996a). The amount of dietary salt may also affect how blood pressure varies during the day with activity. Specifically, being on a low salt diet may increase the variation associated with changing activities (James et al 1994).

Blood Pressure Variation and Lifestyle

Virtually all the studies that have examined lifestyle effects on blood pressure have been undertaken in urban Western settings (James 1991a). Most studies (i.e. Pickering et al 1982, Harshfield et al 1982, Clark et al 1987, Llabre et al 1988, Van Egeren & Madarasmi 1988, Light et al 1992, James et al 1993) show that, on average, blood pressure measured at the place of employment is higher than all other pressures during the day. This effect is independent of time of day because average work pressure has been found to be highest during the day even in night-shift workers (Sundburg et al 1988, Baumgart et al 1989).

Posture also profoundly influences daily blood pressures, with standing pressures being higher than sitting pressures and reclining pressures being lower than either standing or sitting (James et al 1986, Llabre et al 1988, Gellman et al 1990, Schwartz et al 1994). Postural effects, however, are also reflected in activity, because most activities occur in a single posture. Studies examining the effects of activity on ambulatory pressure show that physical activities such as walking or doing household chores increase it to a greater extent than activities such as reading or writing that require mental effort or other activities such as relaxing or watching TV (Clark et al 1987, Van Egeren & Madarasmi 1988, Harshfield et al 1990a, James & Pickering 1991). Personality may also interact with activity in affecting blood pressure such that individuals whose behavior is characterized by impatience, chronic time urgency, enhanced competitiveness, aggressive drive, and an inclination toward hostility [Type A personality (Rosenman 1978)] may show a greater diastolic pressure increase to activities such as driving a car, talking, walking, desk work, and attending business meetings than other non–Type A individuals (Van Egeren & Sparrow 1990). When activity has been monitored using activity (motion sensing) monitors instead of diary reports, it has been reported that the constant change in activity accounts for nearly one third of the overall variance in daily ambulatory pressure measurements (Gretler et al 1993).

Blood pressure also changes with mood, with most all moods elevating both systolic and diastolic pressure to some degree (Sokolow et al 1970, Southard et al 1986, James et al 1986, Gellman et al 1990, Schwartz et al 1994). Anger and anxiety, however, have been found to increase pressure more than happiness (James et al 1986, Schwartz et al 1994). One of the more interesting findings reported by Schwartz et al (1994) was the relative rarity of the daily experience of anger. In their study, diary reports of anger during ambulatory monitoring occurred less than 1% of the time. As anger has been postulated to play a role in the development of coronary disease and hypertension, this result suggests that it may influence these factors more through its effect on daily pressure variability than on increasing the average pressure level during a typical day (Pickering et al 1995). Finally, the situation in which moods occur may further influence how high blood pressure rises during their experience (James et al

1986, Gellman et al 1990, James & Pickering 1991). For example, anxiety may have a greater effect when it occurs away from home (James et al 1986).

The effects of microenvironment (i.e. work, home, sleep), posture, activity, and mood may also differ between men and women (James et al 1988a), by season of the year (winter or summer) (James et al 1990a), and, among men, by occupational group (James & Pickering 1991). Specifically, place of measurement, posture, and reported mood accounted for a larger percentage of the variance in blood pressures measured over the day among women and in subjects examined during November through March than among men or individuals measured during May through September. Happiness was also found to have a larger effect on the blood pressures of nonprofessional than professional men when measured away from their job or home (James & Pickering 1991).

Other Factors the Modify Blood Pressure Variation

AGE   Several studies have examined the relationship between age and the difference between awake and sleep blood pressures. Some have found no association (Drayer et al 1983, Munakata et al 1991), others have found a decreasing difference (Khoury et al 1992), while still others have found an increasing difference with age (Muneta et al 1991, James et al 1995). One reason for the variance in results among these studies is that lifestyle changes associated with age may differ among populations. Thus, in those groups where lifestyles change little, the sources and extent of daily blood pressure variability in different age groups may not differ, whereas in those groups that have clear generational transitions in lifestyle there may be significant changes in blood pressure variability. In a recent study that compared the effects of mood on daily blood pressure variation in two age cohorts of women from New York City (James et al 1996b), the influence of anger and anxiety differed markedly between younger (mean age 29) and older (mean age 52) groups. Specifically, anger had a more marked effect on blood pressure variability in the younger women (in a pattern similar to men), whereas anxiety had a greater effect in the older women. It was suggested that there may be a generational difference in how moods are reported, so the older group of women may have had a similar rise in pressure with anger, except that when they report their mood, they report themselves as being anxious because they perceive this as a more socially acceptable response (James et al 1996b).

ETHNICITY   There have been few if any studies that have examined the influences of similar or different lifestyle characteristics across ethnic groups on daily blood pressure variation, although certain psychometric characteristics such as "John Henryism" have been examined (see below). To date most research has focused on comparisons of the awake-sleep blood pressure transition in African-American and Caucasian groups. The results of this work show that in some groups (mostly from urban areas in the United States), African-Americans have a smaller average decline in both systolic and diastolic pressure from being awake to sleep (Harshfield et al 1989, 1990b; Murphy et al 1988; James 1991b). However, others have examined groups with African ancestry from Jamaica (Rowlands et al 1982), South Africa (Murphy et al 1990), and the Southern United States (Prisant et al 1991) and found no awake-sleep difference between them and Caucasian groups. More recently, James et al (1995), in a study of hypertensive patients from New York City, found that among women, smaller awake-sleep declines in systolic pressure were found among African-American women compared with Caucasian women, but among men, Caucasians were found to have smaller diastolic declines than African-Americans. Taken as a whole, these data suggest that there is no clear pattern of awake-sleep blood pressure difference between these ethnic groups, which may indicate that there are no consistent biological or lifestyle factors that differentiate them with regard to this blood pressure change. Finally, in a recent study comparing Filipino-American and Caucasian women in Hawaii (Brown et al 1995), those with Filipino-American ancestry were found to have higher average sleep diastolic pressures. This ethnic difference, however, was partially related to a greater centrality of fat deposition among the Filipino-American women.

EMPLOYMENT AND HOME STRESS   Investigations of employment-related stress and blood pressure in Western societies have generally focused on the concept of "job strain," which is defined as having high psychological job demands with low decision latitude (control over the job) (Karasek et al 1981, Pickering et al 1991). Studies from the United States and Western Europe show reasonably consistent results, in that most find some effect of job strain on blood pressure measured at work or in another daily microenvironment (Schnall et al 1990, Van Egeren 1992). Some studies, however, show no effects (Landsbergis et al 1994), whereas others show gender differences such that men have a job strain effect but women do not (Light et al 1992). It has been suggested that the effect of job strain on blood pressure may depend on cultural factors that might influence how important jobs are perceived to be (James et al 1996b). These cultural factors may partially explain gender differences. However, place of employment may also play a role. In a study of blood pressures in persons with the same job titles but who worked in different companies, Schlussel et al (1990) found that the pressures varied considerably by work venue, even though there was similar "job strain" as determined by job title. Finally, other psychological factors that define work ethic may also be important in determining occupation-related blood pressure variability. Specifically, Caucasian women and African-American men and women who were employed in high-status jobs and who exhibited the trait of high-effort coping (defined as the perception that one can meet the demands of one's environment through hard work and determination, which has been labeled "John Henry-ism") had higher pressures at work than other women or African-American men without the trait (Light et al 1995). This association was not found among Caucasian men in the study.

In further studies of working women, stress in the home environment has been found to influence blood pressure as much or more during the day than stress experienced at work (James et al 1991). The home stress effects found among women have been related to factors associated with the family such as being married or the number of children (James et al 1989b). Among women working in clerical or technical jobs who experience more stress at home than at work, the blood pressures at home may be elevated over those measured at work, so the pattern of blood pressure during the day is the exact opposite of that among women who experience more stress at work than at home (James et al 1991, Pickering et al 1990).

LIFESTYLE INCONGRUITY   Lifestyle incongruity, a concept developed by Dressler (1995), can be defined as a social context in which a high material lifestyle occurs with low occupational status. It is an important, useful, and relatively objective measure of psychosocial stress that examines the discrep-ancy between occupation and income and the amount of possessed material goods. This assessment of what might be termed "living beyond one's means" has been associated with high casual seated blood pressures in several devel-oping populations (Dressler 1982, Dressler et al 1987a,b) and among African-Americans from the Southern United States (Dressler 1990, 1991). Its effect also seems to be buffered by social resources (Dressler 1982, 1995) so that cas-ual seated blood pressures tend to be higher among people with lifestyle incon-gruity and little social support (Dressler 1991). Recently, Chin-Hong & McGarvey (1996) found that greater lifestyle incongruity was associated with lower systolic pressure in young men in Western Samoa. They proposed that the difference in pattern from previous studies resulted from specific cultural factors that define social obligations in Samoan society. While these studies suggest that lifestyle incongruity has a cardiovascular effect, how it influences daily, situationally measured ambulatory blood pressure has not been studied.

DISCUSSION

This brief report is far from encyclopedic in relating catecholamine and blood pressure responses to aspects of lifestyle. As has been noted, almost any envi-ronmental change will elicit a response, because these physiological functions maintain homeostasis. While not exhaustive, however, the review clearly shows that many things people do, think, and experience as part of their lifestyle have a profound impact on catecholamine release and blood pressure. The findings also show that real life is a complex interaction of many features, so a catecholamine or blood pressure measurement made under real-life conditions reflects a response to the complexity of the circumstance, including the subject's perceptions and cognitive state, the nature of the social situation, potential food, stimulant and exercise effects, and the ambient environmental conditions, such as temperature or altitude. Finally, the results suggest that to fully assess how lifestyle influences the body's ability to adapt, multiple measurements need to be made under the various conditions experienced during the day, because people, particularly in urban societies, live in complex ever-changing environmental conditions.

It has been noted that conducting hormonal field studies is expensive owing to the assay costs (Goodman et al 1988). Because of the cost and because the amount of data can be overwhelming and highly complex, there is some question about why studies examining physiological variability in real-life are worth doing in anthropological research. What is the payoff? The answer may lie in the fact that the stress inherent in lifestyle is a selective force that can shape the biology of populations, and hence the rate and direction of human evolution. Specifically, stress, through its effects on catecholamines, blood pressure, and other functions may contribute to cardiovascular morbidity, other degenerative conditions, and infectious disease, which will in turn ultimately affect the dynamics of population mortality (who dies and who survives) (Hinkle 1987, James 1991a). It is still not fully known how, why, or when stress causes health problems in the life of an individual.

Finally, the findings reviewed here generally consider the catecholamine and blood pressure responses to urban Western environments. Physical anthropologists need to take this technology to other societies where different lifestyles can be studied. The picture of how lifestyle affects these and other biological responses is still incomplete.

> **Visit the *Annual Reviews home page* at**
> **http://www.AnnualReviews.org.**

Literature Cited

Agharanya JC, Wurtman RJ. 1982. Effect of acute administration of large neural and other amino acids on urinary catecholamine excretion. *Life Sci.* 30:739–46

Akerstedt T, Gillberg M, Hjemdahl P, Sigurd-son K, Gustavsson I, et al. 1983. Comparison of urinary and plasma responses to mental stress. *Acta Physiol. Scand.* 117:19–26

Ammon HPT, Carlson LA, Froberg J, Karlsson C-G, Levi L. 1973. Effects of coffee and caffeine on sympatho-adreno-medullary activity, blood lipids, psychological ratings and performance. *Rep. Lab. Clin. Stress Res., No. 31.* Stockholm: Karolenska sjukhuset, Dep. Med. Psychiatry

Aslan S, Nelson L, Carruthers M, Lader M. 1981. Stress and age effects on catecholamines in normal subjects. *J. Psychosom. Res.* 25:33–41

Bahr R, Hostmark AT, Newsholme EA, Gronnerod O, Sejersted OM. 1991. Effect of exercise on recovery changes in plasma levels of FFA, glycerol, glucose and catecholamines. *Acta Physiol. Scand.* 143:105–15

Barnes RF, Raskind M, Gumbrecht G, Halter JB. 1982. The effects of age on the plasma catecholamine response to mental stress in man. *J. Clin. Endocrinol. Metab.* 54:64–69

Baumgart P, Walger P, Fuchs G, Dorst KG, Vetter H, et al. 1989. Twenty-four-hour blood pressure is not dependent on endogenous circadian rhythm. *J. Hypertens.* 7:331–34

Bellet S, Roman L, Kostis J. 1969. The effects of automobile driving on catecholamine and adrenocortical excretion. *Am. J. Cardiol.* 24:365–68

Blank SG. 1987. *The Korotkoff signal and its relationship to the arterial pressure pulse.* PhD thesis. Dep. Physiol. Biophys., Cornell Univ. Med. Coll.

Boyden S. 1987. *Western Civilization in Biological Perspective.* Oxford: Clarendon

Bridges PK. 1974. Recent physiological studies of stress and anxiety in man. *Biol. Psychiat.* 8:95–112

Brown DE. 1981. General stress in anthropological fieldwork. *Am. Anthropol.* 83: 74–92

Brown DE. 1982. Physiological stress and culture change in a group of Filipino-Americans, a preliminary investigation. *Ann. Hum. Biol.* 9:553–63

Brown DE, Jones AA, Nordloh L, James GD. 1995. Ambulatory blood pressure in nurses from two different ethnic groups in Hawaii: differences between Filipino-Americans and Caucasians. *Am. J. Phys. Anthropol.* 20(Suppl.):69–70 (Abstr.)

Brown DE, Martin LH, Mersai CT, McGuire K, James GD. 1996. Catecholamine excretion, ambulatory blood pressure and mood reports of nurses and nurses aide's in Hawaii. *Am. J. Hum. Biol.* 8:111 (Abstr.)

Brown DE, Napiha'a GM, Etrata MB, Kohagura RN, James GD. 1997. Catecholamine excretion rate and time of residence in the United States of immigrant Filipino-

American nurses and nurse's aides in Hawaii. *Am. J. Hum. Biol.* (Abstr.) 9:124

Cannon WB. 1914. The emergency function of the adrenal medulla in pain and the major emotions. *Am. J. Physiol.* 33:356–72

Cellina GU, Honour AJ, Little WA. 1975. Direct arterial pressure, heart rate, and electrocardiogram during cigarette smoking in unrestricted patients. *Am. Heart. J.* 89: 18–25

Chesney MA, Ironson GH. 1989. Diaries in ambulatory monitoring. In *Handbook of Research Methods in Cardiovascular Behavioral Medicine,* ed. N Schneiderman, SM Weiss, PG Kaufman, pp. 317–32. New York: Plenum

Chin-Hong PV, McGarvey ST. 1996. Lifestyle incongruity and adult blood pressure in Western Samoa. *Psychosom. Med.* 58: 130–37

Clark LA, Denby L, Pregibon D, Harshfield GA, Pickering TG, et al. 1987. A quantitative analysis of the effects of activity and time of day on the diurnal variations of blood pressure. *J. Chron. Dis.* 40:671–87

Collins A, Frankenhaeuser M. 1978. Stress responses in male and female engineering students. *J. Hum. Stress* 4:43–48

Comstock GW. 1957. An epidemiologic study of blood pressure levels in a biracial community in the southern United States. *Am. J. Hyg.* 65:271–315

Crider A. 1970. Experimental studies of conflict-produced stress. See Levine & Scotch 1970, pp. 165–88

Dimsdale JE, Moss J. 1980. Short-term catecholamine response to stress. *Psychosom. Med.* 42:493–97

Dohrenwend BS, Dohrenwend BP. 1970. Class and race as status-related sources of stress. See Levine & Scotch 1970, pp. 111–40

Drayer JIM, Weber MA, DeYong JL, Wyle FA. 1983. Circadian blood pressure patterns in ambulatory patients: effects of age. *Am. J. Med.* 72:493–99

Dressler WW. 1982. *Hypertension and Culture Change: Acculturation and Disease in the West Indies.* South Salem: Redgrave

Dressler WW. 1990. Lifestyle, stress, and blood pressure in a southern black community. *Psychosom. Med.* 52:182–98

Dressler WW. 1991. Social support, lifestyle incongruity, and arterial blood pressure in a southern black community. *Psychosom. Med.* 53:608–20

Dressler WW. 1995. Modeling biocultural interaction: examples from studies of stress and cardiovascular disease. *Yrbk. Phys. Anthropol.* 38:27–56

Dressler WW, Alfonso M, Chavez A, Viteri FE. 1987a. Arterial blood pressure and individual modernization in a Mexican community. *Soc. Sci. Med.* 24:679–87

Dressler WW, Santos IED, Gallagher PN, Viteri FE. 1987b. Arterial blood pressure and modernization in Brazil. *Am. Anthropol.* 89:389–409

Frankenhaeuser M. 1971. Behavior and circulating catecholamines. *Brain Res.* 31: 241–62

Frankenhaeuser M. 1975. Experimental approaches to the study of catecholamines and emotion. In *Emotions—Their Parameters and Measurement,* ed. L Levi, pp. 209–34. New York: Raven

Frankenhaeuser M. 1983. The sympathetic-adrenal and pituitary-adrenal response to challenge, comparisons between the sexes. In *Biobehavioral Bases of Coronary Heart Disease,* ed. TM Dembroski, TH Schmidt, G Blumchen, pp. 91–105. Basel: Karger

Frankenhaeuser M, Gardell B. 1976. Underload and overload in working life. A multidisciplinary approach. *J. Hum. Stress* 2: 35–46

Frankenhaeuser M, Lundberg U, Fredrikson M, Melin B, Tuomisto M, et al. 1989. Stress on and off the job as related to sex and occupational status in white-collar workers. *J. Org. Behav.* 10:321–46

Frankenhaeuser M, Myrsten A-L, Post B. 1970. Psychophysiological reactions to cigarette smoking. *Scand. J. Psychol.* 11: 237

Frankenhaeuser M, von Wright MR, Collins A, von Wright J, Sedvall G, et al. 1978. Sex differences in psychoneuroendocrine reactions to examination stress. *Psychosom. Med.* 40:334–43

Gellman M, Spitzer S, Ironson G, Llabre M, Saab P, et al. 1990. Posture, place and mood effects on ambulatory blood pressure. *Psychophysiology* 27:544–51

Gerdts E, Myking OL, Omivik P. 1994. Salt sensitive essential hypertension evaluated by 24 hour ambulatory blood pressure. *Blood Pressure* 3:375–80

Goldberger L. 1993. Sensory deprivation and overload. In *Handbook of Stress,* ed. L Goldberger, S Breznitz, pp. 333–41. New York: Free. 2nd ed.

Goldstein DS, Eisenhofer G, Sax FL, Keiser HR, Kopin IJ. 1987. Plasma norepinephrine pharmacokinetics during mental challenge. *Psychosom. Med.* 48:591–605

Goldstein DS, Lake CR, Chernow B, Ziegler MG, Coleman MD, et al. 1983. Age-dependence of hypertensive-normotensive differences in plasma norepinephrine. *Hypertension* 5:100–4

Goodman AH, Thomas RB, Swedlund AC, Armelagos GJ. 1988. Biocultural perspectives on stress in prehistoric, historical and contemporary population research. *Yrbk. Phys. Anthropol.* 31:169–202

Gorman AJ, Proppe DW. 1984. Mechanisms producing tachycardia in conscious baboons during environmental heat stress. *J. Appl. Physiol.* 56:441–46

Green MS, Harari G, Schwartz K. 1991. Cigarette smoking related to ambulatory blood pressure and heart rate. *Am. Heart. J.* 111: 932–40

Gretler DD, Carlson GF, Montano AV, Murphy MB. 1993. Diurnal blood pressure variability and physical activity measured electronically and by diary. *Am. J. Hypertens.* 6:127–33

Guyton AC. 1981. *Textbook of Medical Physiology.* Philadelphia: Saunders

Hanna JM, James GD, Martz J. 1986. Hormonal measures of stress. In *The Changing Samoans: Behavior and Health in Transition,* ed. PT Baker, JM Hanna, TS Baker, pp. 203–21. Oxford: Oxford Univ. Press

Harrison GA. 1995. *The Human Biology of the English Village.* Oxford: Oxford Univ. Press

Harrison GA, Jefferies DJ. 1977. Human biology in urban environments: a review of research strategies. *MAB Technical Notes 3,* ed. PT Baker, pp. 65–82. Paris: UNESCO

Harrison GA, Palmer CD, Jenner D, Reynolds V. 1981. Associations between rates of urinary catecholamine excretion and aspects of lifestyle among adult women in some Oxfordshire villages. *Hum. Biol.* 53: 617–33

Harshfield GA, Alpert BS, Willey ES, Somes GW, Murphy JK, et al. 1989. Race and gender influence ambulatory blood pressure patterns of adolescents. *Hypertension* 14:598–603

Harshfield GA, Hwang C, Grim CE. 1990a. Circadian variation in blacks: influence of age, gender and activity. *J. Hum. Hypertens.* 4:43–47

Harshfield GA, Pickering TG, James GD, Blank SG. 1990b. Blood pressure variability and reactivity in the natural environment. In *Blood Pressure Measurements: New Techniques in Automatic and 24-hour Indirect Monitoring,* ed. W Meyer-Sabellek, M Anlauf, R Gotzen, L Steinfield, pp. 241–51. New York: Springer-Verlag. 336 pp.

Harshfield GA, Pickering TG, Kleinert HD,

Blank S, Laragh JH. 1982. Situational variation of blood pressure in ambulatory hypertensive patients. *Psychosom. Med.* 44:237–45

Hastrup JL, Light KC. 1984. Sex differences in cardiovascular stress responses: modulation as a function of menstrual cycle phases. *J. Psychosom. Res.* 28:475–83

Herd JA. 1991. Cardiovascular responses to stress. *Physiol. Rev.* 71:305–30

Hinkle LE. 1987. Stress and disease: the concept after 50 years. *Soc. Sci. Med.* 25: 561–66

Hoon RS, Sharma SC, Balasubramanian V, Chadha KS, Mathew OP. 1976. Urinary catecholamine excretion on acute induction to high altitude (3,658 m). *J. Appl. Physiol.* 41:631–33

Huether G. 1996. The central adaptation syndrome: psychosocial stress as a trigger for adaptive modifications of brain structure and brain function. *Prog. Neurobiol.* 48: 569–612

Izzo JL, Ghosol A, Kwong T, Freeman RB, Jaenike JR. 1983. Age and prior caffeine use alter the cardiovascular and adrenomedullary responses to oral caffeine. *Am. J. Cardiol.* 52:769–73

James GD. 1991a. Blood pressure response to the daily stressors of urban environments: methodology, basic concepts and significance. *Yrbk. Phys. Anthropol.* 34: 189–210

James GD. 1991b. Race and perceived stress independently affect the diurnal variation of blood pressure in women. *Am. J. Hypertens.* 4:382–84

James GD, Baker PT, Jenner DA, Harrison GA. 1987. Variation in lifestyle characteristics and catecholamine excretion rates among young Western Samoan men. *Soc. Sci. Med.* 25:981–86

James GD, Broege PA, Schlussel YR. 1996b. Assessing cardiovascular risk and stress-related blood pressure variability in young women employed in wage jobs. *Am. J. Hum. Biol.* 8:743–49

James GD, Cates EM, Pickering TG, Laragh JH. 1989b. Parity and perceived job stress elevate blood pressure in young normotensive women. *Am. J. Hypertens.* 2: 637–39

James GD, Crews DE, Pearson J. 1989a. Catecholamines and stress. In *Human Population Biology: A Transdisciplinary Science*, ed. MA Little, JD Haas, pp. 280–95. Oxford: Oxford Univ. Press

James GD, Jenner DA, Harrison GA, Baker PT. 1985. Differences in catecholamine excretion rates, blood pressure and lifestyle among young Western Samoan men. *Hum. Biol.* 57:635–47

James GD, Moucha OP, Pickering TG. 1991. The normal hourly variation of blood pressure in women: average patterns and the effect of work stress. *J. Hum. Hypertens.* 5:505–9

James GD, Pecker MS. 1994. Aging and blood pressure. In *Biological Anthropology and Aging: Perspectives on Human Variation Over the Life Span*, ed. DE Crews, RM Garruto, pp. 321–38. Oxford: Oxford Univ. Press

James GD, Pecker MS, Pickering TG. 1996a. Sex differences in casual and ambulatory blood pressure responses to extreme changes in dietary sodium. *Blood Pressure Monitoring* 1:397–401

James GD, Pecker MS, Pickering TG, Jackson S, DiFabio B, et al. 1994. Extreme changes in dietary sodium effect the daily variability and level of blood pressure in borderline hypertensive patients. *Am. J. Hum. Biol.* 6:283–91

James GD, Pickering TG. 1991. Ambulatory blood pressure monitoring: assessing the diurnal variation of blood pressure. *Am. J. Physiol. Anthropol.* 84:343–49

James GD, Pickering TG. 1993. The influence of behavioral factors on the daily variation of blood pressure. *Am. J. Hypertens.* 6: 170–74S

James GD, Pickering TG, Yee LS, Harshfield GA, Riva S, et al. 1988b. The reproducibility of average ambulatory, home, and clinic pressures. *Hypertension* 11:545–49

James GD, Schlussel YR, Pickering TG. 1993. The association between daily blood pressure and catecholamine variability in normotensive working women. *Psychosom. Med.* 55:55–60

James GD, Toledano T, Datz G, Pickering TG. 1995. Factors influencing the awake-sleep difference in ambulatory blood pressure: main effects and sex differences. *J. Hum. Hypertens.* 9:821–26

James GD, Yee LS, Harshfield GA, Blank S, Pickering TG. 1986. The influence of happiness, anger and anxiety on the blood pressure of borderline hypertensives. *Psychosom. Med.* 48:502–8

James GD, Yee LS, Harshfield GA, Pickering TG. 1988a. Sex differences in factors affecting the daily variation of blood pressure. *Soc. Sci. Med.* 26: 1019–23

James GD, Yee LS, Pickering TG. 1990a. Winter-summer differences in the effects of emotion, posture, and place of measurement on blood pressure. *Soc. Sci. Med.* 31:1213–17

Jenner DA, Harrison GA, Day JA, Huizinga J, Salzano FM. 1982. Interpopulation comparisons of urinary catecholamines: a pilot study. *Ann. Hum. Biol.* 9:579–82

Jenner DA, Harrison GA, Prior IAM, Leonetti DL, Fujimoto WJ, et al. 1987. Interpopulation comparisons of catecholamine excretion. *Ann. Hum. Biol.* 14:1–9

Jenner DA, Reynolds V, Harrison GA. 1980. Catecholamine excretion rates and occupation. *Ergonomics* 23:237–46

Jeong D-U, Dimsdale JE. 1990. The effects of caffeine on blood pressure in the work environment. *Am. J. Hypertens.* 3:749–53

Johnson DG, Hayward JS, Jacobs TP, Collins ML, Eckerson JD, et al. 1977. Plasma norepinephrine responses of man in cold water. *J. Appl. Physiol.* 43:216–20

Jones PP, Spraul M, Matt KS, Seals DR, Skinner JS, et al. 1996. Gender does not influence sympathetic neural reactivity to stress in healthy humans. *Am. J. Physiol.* 270:H350–57

Kalita N, Tigranian K, Davydova N. 1989. Comparison of catecholamine and adrenopituitary hormone responses to cold and exercise stress in man. In *Stress: The Role of Catecholamines and Other Neurotransmitters,* ed. GR Van Loon, R Kvetnansky, R McCarty, J Axelrod, pp. 901–9. New York: Gordon & Breach

Karasek R, Baker D, Marxer F, Ahlbom A, Theorell T. 1981. Job decision latitude, job demands, and cardiovascular disease: a prospective study of Swedish men. *Am. J. Public Health* 71:694–705

Khoury S, Yarows SA, O'Brien TK, Sowers JR. 1992. Ambulatory monitoring in a nonacademic setting: effect of age and sex. *Am. J. Hypertens.* 5:616–23

Landesbergis PA, Schnall PL, Warren K, Pickering TG, Schwartz JE. 1994. Association between ambulatory blood pressure and alternative formulations of job strain. *Scand. J. Work Environ. Health* 20:349–63

Law A, Logan H, Baron RS. 1994. Desire for control, felt control, and stress: inoculation training during dental treatment. *J. Pers. Soc. Psychol.* 67:926–36

Lazarus RS, Folkman S. 1984. *Psychological Stress and the Coping Process.* New York: Springer

Levi L. 1964. The stress of everyday work as reflected in productiveness, subjective feelings, and urinary output of adrenaline and noradrenaline under salaried and piece-work conditions. *J. Psychosom. Res.* 8:189–202

Levine S, Scotch NA, eds. 1970. *Social Stress.* Chicago: Aldine

Light KC, Brownley KA, Turner JR, Hinderliter AL, Girdler SS, et al. 1995. Job status and high-effort coping influence work blood pressure in women and blacks. *Hypertension* 25:554–59

Light KC, Turner JR, Hinderliter AL. 1992. Job strain and ambulatory work blood pressure in healthy young men and women. *Hypertension* 20:214–18

Llabre M, Ironson G, Spitzer S, Gellman M, Weidler D, et al. 1988. How many blood pressure measurements are enough? An application of generalizability theory to the study of blood pressure reliability. *Psychophysiology* 25:97–106

Lundberg U. 1976. Urban commuting, crowdedness and catecholamine excretion. *J. Hum. Stress* 2:26–34

Malhotra H, Mehta SR, Mathur D, Khandelwal PD. 1985. Pressure effects of alcohol in normotensive and hypertensive subjects. *Lancet* 2:584–86

Mancia G, Parati G, Pomidossi G, Grassi G, Casadei R, et al. 1987. Alerting reaction and rise in blood pressure during management by physician and nurse. *Hypertension* 9:209–15

Mann SJ, James GD, Wang RS, Pickering TG. 1991. Elevation of ambulatory systolic pressure in hypertensive smokers. *J. Am. Med. Assoc.* 265:2226–28

Martz JM, Hanna JM, Howard SA. 1984. Stress in daily life. Evidence from Samoa. *Am. J. Phys. Anthropol.* 63:191–92

Mason JW. 1968. A review of psychoendocrine research on the sympathetic-adrenal medullary system. *Psychosom. Med.* 30:631–53

Mason JW. 1971. A re-evaluation of the concept of "non specificity" in stress theory. *J. Psychosom. Res.* 8:323–34

Mazzeo RS, Bender PR, Brooks GA, Butterfield GE, Groves BM, et al. 1991. Arterial catecholamine response during exercise with acute and chronic high-altitude exposure. *Am. J. Physiol.* 261:E419–24

Moore TJ, Halarick C, Olmedo A, Klein RC. 1991. Salt restriction lowers resting but not 24-h ambulatory pressure. *Am. J. Hypertens.* 4:410–15

Munakata M, Imai Y, Abe K, Sasaki S, Minami N, et al. 1991. Assessment of age-dependent changes in circadian rhythm in patients with essential hypertension. *J. Hypertens.* 9:407–15

Muneta S, Murakami E, Sumimoto T, Iwata T, Hiwada K, et al. 1991. Blood pressure and heart rate variability in elderly patients with isolated systolic hypertension. *J. Hum. Hypertens.* 5:393–98

Murphy MB, Nelson KS, Elliott WJ. 1988. Racial differences in diurnal blood pressure profile. *Am. J. Hypertens.* 1:55A (Abstr.)

Murphy MB, Tieger S, Sareli P, Neumann A, Fumo MA, et al. 1990. Circadian variation in blood pressure in African and American blacks, and American whites. *Am. J. Hypertens.* 3:37A (Abstr.)

Myers MG, Reeves RA. 1991. The effect of caffeine on daytime ambulatory blood pressure. *Am. J. Hypertens.* 4:427–31

Myrsten AL, Post B, Frankenhaeuser M. 1971. Catecholamine output during and after acute alcohol intoxication. *Percept. Motor Skills* 33:652–54

Ng AV, Callister R, Johnson DG, Seals DR. 1994. Sympathetic neural reactivity to stress does not increase with age in healthy humans. *Am. J. Physiol.* 267:H344–53

O'Brien E, Atkins S, Staessen J. 1995. State of the market: a review of ambulatory blood pressure monitoring devices. *Hypertension* 26:835–42

O'Rourke MF. 1990. What is blood pressure? *Am. J. Hypertens.* 3:803–10

Overlack A, Ruppert M, Kolloch R, Kraft K, Stumpe KO. 1995. Age is a major determinant of the divergent blood pressure responses to varying salt intake in essential hypertension. *Am. J. Hypertens.* 829–36

Pearson JD, Hanna JM, Fitzgerald MH, Baker PT. 1990. Modernization and catecholamine excretion of young Samoan adults. *Soc. Sci. Med.* 31:729–36

Pearson JD, James GD, Brown DE. 1993. Stress and changing lifestyles in the Pacific: physiological stress responses of Samoans in urban and rural settings. *Am. J. Hum. Biol.* 5:49–60

Pickering TG. 1991. *Ambulatory Monitoring and Blood Pressure Variability,* London: Science

Pickering TG, Blank SG. 1989. The measurement of blood pressure. In *Handbook of Research Methods in Cardiovascular Behavioral Medicine,* ed. N Schneiderman, SM Weiss, PG Kaufman, pp. 69–79. New York: Plenum

Pickering TG, Devereux RB, Gerin W, James GD, Pieper C, et al. 1990. The role of behavioral factors in white coat and sustained hypertension. *J. Hypertens.* 8:S141–47

Pickering TG, Harshfield GA, Blank S, James GD, Laragh JH, et al. 1986. Behavioral determinants of 24-hour blood pressure patterns in borderline hypertension. *J. Cardiol. Pharmacol.* 8:S89–92

Pickering TG, Harshfield GA, Kleinert HD, Blank S, Laragh JH. 1982. Blood pressure during normal daily activities, sleep and exercise. Comparison of values in normal and hypertensive subjects. *J. Am. Med. Assoc.* 247:992–96

Pickering TG, James GD, Boddie C, Harshfield GA, Blank SG, Laragh JH. 1988. How common is white coat hypertension? *J. Am. Med. Assoc.* 259:225–28

Pickering TG, James GD, Schnall PL, Schlussel YR, Pieper CF, et al. 1991. Occupational stress and blood pressure studies in working men and women. In *Women, Work and Health,* ed. M Frankenhaeuser, U Lundberg, M Chesney, pp. 171–86. New York: Plenum

Pickering TG, Schwartz JE, James GD. 1995. Ambulatory blood pressure monitoring for evaluating the relationships between lifestyle, hypertension and cardiovascular risk. *Clin. Exp. Pharmacol. Phys.* 22:226–31

Polefrone JM, Manuck SB. 1987. Gender differences in cardiovascular and neuroendocrine response to stressors. In *Gender and Stress,* ed. RC Barnett, L Biener, GK Barach, pp. 13–38. New York: Free

Potter JF, Beevers DG. 1984. Pressor effects of alcohol in hypertension. *Lancet* 1:119–22

Potter JF, Watson RDS, Skan W, Beevers DG. 1986. The pressor and metabolic effects of alcohol in normotensive subjects. *Hypertension* 8:625–31

Prisant LM, Thompson WO, Bottini PB, Carr AA, Rhodes R. 1991. Racial aspects of ambulatory blood pressure. *J. Hum. Hypertens.* 5:369–73

Rauste-von Wright M, von Wright J, Frankenhaeuser M. 1981. Relationships between sex-related psychological characteristics during adolescence and catecholamine excretion during achievement stress. *Psychophysiology* 18:362–70

Reynolds V, Jenner DA, Palmer CD, Harrison GA. 1981. Catecholamine excretion rates in relation to life-styles in the male population of Otmoor, Oxfordshire. *Ann. Hum. Biol.* 8:197–209

Rosenman RH. 1978. The interview method of assessment of the coronary-prone behavior pattern. In *Coronary-Prone Behavior,* ed. TM Dembrowski, SM Weiss, JL Sheilds, SG Haynes, M Feinlab, pp. 55–69. Berlin: Springer-Verlag

Rowlands DB, DeGiovanni J, McLeay RAB, Watson RDS, Stallard TJ, et al. 1982. Cardiovascular responses in black and white hypertensives. *Hypertension* 4:817–20

Rubin PC, Scott PJW, McLean K, Reid JL. 1982. Noradrenaline release and clearance in relation to age and blood pressure in man. *Eur J. Clin. Invest.* 12:121–25

Santiago JV, Clarke WL, Shah SD, Cryer PE. 1980. Epinephrine, norepinephrine, glucagon, and growth hormone release in association with physiological decrements in the plasma glucose concentration in normal and diabetic man. *J. Clin. Endocrinol. Metab.* 51:877–83

Sapolsky RM. 1994. *Why Zebras Don't Get Ulcers: A Guide to Stress, Stress-Related Diseases, and Coping.* New York: Freeman

Schlussel YR, Schnall PL, Zimbler M, Warren K, Pickering TG. 1990. The effect of work environments on blood pressure: evidence from seven New York organizations. *J. Hypertens.* 8:679–85

Schnall PL, Pieper C, Schwartz JE, Karasek RA, Schlussel Y, et al. 1990. The relationship between "job strain," workplace diastolic pressure, and left ventricular mass index. Results of a case-control study. *J. Am. Med. Assoc.* 263:1929–35

Schwartz JE, Warren K, Pickering TG. 1994. Mood, location and physical position as predictors of ambulatory blood pressure and heart rate: application of a multilevel random effects model. *Ann. Behav. Med.* 16:210–20

Selye H. 1946. The general adaptation syndrome and the diseases of adaptation. *J. Clin. Endocrinol.* 6:117–73

Selye H. 1956. *The Stress of Life.* New York: McGraw-Hill

Silverberg AB, Shah SD, Haymond MW, Cryer PE. 1978. Norepinephrine: hormone and neurotransmitter in man. *Am. J. Physiol.* 234(3):E252–56

Sokolov EI, Podachin VP, Belova EV. 1980. *Emotional Stress and Cardiovascular Response.* Transl. II Khomtsov, 1983. Moscow: Mir (From Russian)

Sokolow M, Werdegar D, Perloff DB, Cowan RM, Brenenstuhl H. 1970. Preliminary studies relating portably recorded blood pressures to daily life events in patients with essential hypertension. *Bib. Psychiat.* 144:164–89

Sothmann MS, Gustafson AB, Garthwaite TL, Horn TS, Hart BA. 1988. Cardiovascular fitness and selected adrenal hormone responses to cognitive stress. *Endocrinol. Res.* 14:59–69

Southard DR, Coates TJ, Kolodner K, Parker C, Padgett NE, et al. 1986. Relationship between mood and blood pressure in the natural environment: an adolescent population. *Health Psychol.* 5:469–80

Stewart MJ, Jyothinagaram S, McGinley IM, Padfield PL. 1994. Cardiovascular effects of cigarette smoking: ambulatory blood pressure and BP variability. *J. Hum. Hypertens.* 8:19–22

Stott DJ, Ball SG, Inglis GC, Davies DL, Fraser R, et al. 1987. Effects of a single moderate dose of alcohol on blood pressure, heart rate and associated metabolic and endocrine changes. *Clin. Sci.* 73:411–16

Sundburg S, Kohvakka A, Gordin A. 1988. Rapid reversal of circadian blood pressure rhythm in shift workers. *J. Hypertens.* 6:393–96

Ushiyama K, Ogawa T, Ishii M, Ajisaka R, Sugishita Y, et al. 1991. Physiologic neuroendocrine arousal by mental arithmetic stress test in healthy subjects. *Am. J. Cardiol.* 67:101–3

Van Egeren LF. 1992. The relationship between job strain and blood pressure at work, at home and during sleep. *Psychsom. Med.* 54:337–43

Van Egeren LF, Madarasmi S. 1988. A computer assisted diary (CAD) for ambulatory blood pressure monitoring. *Am. J. Hypertens.* 1:179S–85

Van Egeren LF, Sparrow AW. 1990. Ambulatory monitoring to assess real-life cardiovascular reactivity in type A and type B subjects. *Psychosom. Med.* 52:297–306

Ward MM, Mefford IN, Parker SD, Chesney MA, Taylor CB, et al. 1983. Epinephrine and norepinephrine responses in continuously collected human plasma to a series of stressors. *Psychosom. Med.* 45:471–86

Welch BL, Welch AS, eds. 1969. *Physiological Effects of Noise.* New York: Plenum

Wohlwill JF. 1975. Behavioral response and adaptation to environmental stimulation. In *Physiological Anthropology*, ed. A Damon, pp. 295–334. New York: Oxford Univ. Press

Young JB, Troisi RJ, Weiss ST, Parker DR, Sparrow D, et al. 1992. Relationship of catecholamine excretion to body size, obesity, and nutrient intake in middle-aged and elderly men. *Am. J. Clin. Nutr.* 56:827–34

Ziegler MG, Lake CR, Kopin IJ. 1976. Plasma noradrenaline increases with age. *Nature* 261:333–35

Annu. Rev. Anthropol. 1997. 26:337–57
Copyright © 1997 by Annual Reviews Inc. All rights reserved

WHAT MAKES THE HUMAN BRAIN DIFFERENT?

Terrence W. Deacon

Department of Anthropology, Boston University, Boston, Massachusetts 02215;
e-mail: twdeacon@aol.com

KEY WORDS: brain evolution, brain size, development, intelligence, encephalization, homeotic
genes, allometry

ABSTRACT

Despite decades of research that has revolutionized the neurosciences, efforts
to explain the major features of human brain evolution are still mostly based on
superficial gross neuroanatomical features (e.g. size, sulcal patterns) and on
theories of selection for high-level functions that lack precise neurobiological
predictions (e.g. general intelligence, innate grammar). Beyond its large size
we still lack an account of what makes a human brain different. However, advances in comparative neuroanatomy, developmental biology, and genetics
have radically changed our understanding of brain development. These data
challenge classic ideas about brain size, intelligence, and the addition of new
functions, such as language, and they provide tools with which we can test hypotheses about how human brains diverge from other primate brains.

INTRODUCTION

What Is Known About Human Brain Differences?

For centuries there has been little doubt that differences in the size and structure of human brains must be responsible for our unusual mental abilities. In
search of these critical anatomical differences, generations of researchers have
compared human brains to other mammal brains with the aid of histological
and quantitative techniques. One might expect that a great deal must now be
known about the structural differences between human and nonhuman brains

337

0084-6570/97/1015-0337$08.00

but unfortunately this is far from the case. This is particularly surprising considering that the neurosciences have made incredible strides in understanding brain functions at many other levels. Although there is little doubt that human brains are unusually large for a mammal of our size (Jerison 1973, Martin & Harvey 1985), beyond this one piece of information little else is certain about the relevant anatomical differences between human and nonhuman brains. Even more disturbing is that many contemporary claims and assumptions about the nature of brain evolution in human ancestry take for granted assumptions that would be judged biologically implausible with respect to other organ systems (e.g. accretion of new structures, recapitulation, modular change).

Human brain evolution is still very much studied with the classic tools of functional morphology. This is exemplified by the two principal sources of data applied to human brain evolution research: (a) quantitative analysis of brains and brain regions, and (b) comparisons of cortical surface morphology as identifiable on endocasts of fossil crania. In the 1990s, as in the 1890s, the most active area of research on brain evolution is based on studying patterns exhibited by comparative brain size data. Beyond such global approaches, however, the search for the special features of human neurobiology has not been pursued with the same level of technical sophistication as are most questions in the rest of the neurosciences. The causes of this methodological inertia include a lack of neurobiological tools suitable for studying microstructures of living human brains, the minimalistic nature of the paleoneuroanatomical record, and, of course, the intrinsic complexity of brains in general. Almost certainly there are other nonscientific causes for this inertia, including the influence of tacit assumptions about what anatomical variables are most important, about possible mechanisms of brain evolution, and about the place of human beings in some hierarchic evolutionary scheme. The methodological limitations are not so crippling as they might first appear, however, because there is a wealth of indirect neurobiological evidence that bears on these questions too.

The review does not critique prior work in the field but instead emphasizes the relevance of the rapidly growing body of neurobiological, developmental, and molecular findings that can inform and constrain the study of human brain evolution, and that mostly have not been incorporated into current theoretical perspectives.

What Does Brain Size Tell Us?

Our large brain size in comparison with our body size is undeniable, but the causes and consequences of this difference are far from obvious. Nevertheless, it is accepted almost as fact that large brains can process more information than small brains and that having more extra brain tissue provides intellectual capacity over and above basic physiological needs. Despite a century of analysis of the correlates of gross and net brain size trends, however, the mechanisms behind these presumed relationships remain unexplained. What is known is that mammalian brains and bodies scale with respect to each other according to a highly regular relationship (Figure 1A) described by an allometric exponent[1] between 2/3 and 3/4, depending on the species sampled and the mode of computation (e.g. see Jerison 1973, Martin 1981), and that this value can be considerably lower in samples from more confined taxonomic groups (e.g. family, genus, or species level; see Martin & Harvey 1985; Figure 1B). The developmental mechanisms underlying this regularity of segmental scaling remain a matter of intense debate, and therefore the mechanisms that were modified to produce deviations from these trends (e.g. encephalization of primates and human beings) are also unclear.

The highly correlated allometry of brain and body sizes in mammals has long been thought to reflect some overarching evolutionary economy of intelligence or metabolism that holds across diverse adaptations and sizes. But theories attempting to explain this regularity have almost exclusively been based on comparative statistical studies demonstrating correlations with other physiological, ecological, taxonomic, or theoretical trends. Unfortunately, it is not possible to use correlational analyses alone to determine which, if any, of the multitude of brain size associations represent direct causal mechanisms, or even which are spurious, and the fact that there are many potentially independent correlational relationships to explain adds a further complication. One cannot, on the one hand, argue that metabolic, taxonomic, embryological, or socioecological factors are involved in producing the observed trends and, on the other hand, argue that these trends reflect comparative information processing capacities alone. The specific allometric patterns that are observed may reflect a complicated evolutionary compromise among many factors, or these factors may be indirect correlates of some more basic relationship. We cannot substantiate any conjectures about the significance of brain size trends or deviations from them without independent information concerning the mecha-

---

[1] An allometric relationship, as opposed to an isometric relationship, is one in which the sizes of two corresponding body structures do not equally change across ranges of scale, either with respect to growth or in interspecific comparisons. However, body proportions often consistently correlate with scale allowing the assessment of patterns of proportional change or difference. The assessment of allometric scaling is commonly applied to samples of log transformed data points (which linearizes geometric growth relationships) and is reported in terms of the slope and y-intercept of a best fit line (typically determined by least squares regression, major axis, or reduced major axis methods) through these points. The slope of the log transformed line is the exponent of a curve of the form $Y=aX^b$. Differences in these parameters can thus be interpreted as reflecting systematic differences in growth rates or initial/ancestral conditions.

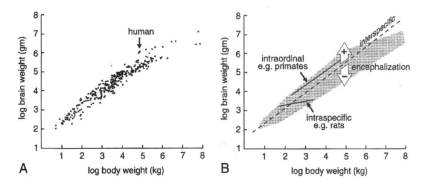

Figure 1   (*A*) Brain and body sizes in a wide selection of mammals are plotted on a log-log graph showing the almost linear distribution of points and the relative position of the human value with respect to the others. Human beings show a greater divergence from the predicted brain size for our body size than any other species. (*B*) Intraordinal (within order) and interspecific trends are superimposed on the mammalian distribution to show the shifted position of the primate trend and the flatter trend characteristic of all intraspecific brain/body scaling. Encephalization is most typically assessed with respect to the prediction for an average mammal.

nisms by which brain growth and differentiation are achieved. What kinds of developmental data would be relevant? How much are currently known? To review the developmental information applicable to these questions, it is useful to approach it hierarchically, from gross comparative assessments of brain growth processes, to developmental processes underlying regional parcellation and connectional architecture, to genetic determinants of regional differentiation of neural tissue types.

BRAIN GROWTH PATTERNS

Are Primates More Encephalized Than Other Mammals?

One of the least-questioned facts about brain evolution are the apparent advance in relative brain size among monkeys and apes as compared with most other mammals. On average, anthropoid primate brains are twice as large as would be predicted for a typical nonprimate mammal of the same body size. This comparatively greater encephalization has prompted speculation that features of the general primate adaptation may have selected for intelligence or at least removed constraints on brain expansion. A closer look, however, at the nature of this encephalization difference suggests that it may not be that simple.

The question in this case is whether it matters how this systematic proportional difference came about. Would it matter if proportionately larger brain size resulted from relatively stunted postcranial growth, as opposed to exaggerated brain growth? Consider dwarfism. Some of the most encephalized animals and human beings on the planet are dwarves. To my knowledge, there is no evidence that stunted postcranial growth contributes to augmentation of any intellectual functions, and likely the opposite is true. Although it is a source of encephalization, there are no serious contenders among encephalization theories that include dwarfism as a major factor, and yet selection on postcranial body proportions appears common in evolution as well as in selective breeding. In domestic dogs, for example, there are large differences in encephalization between large and small breeds. Small dog breeds tend to be encephalized and large dogs unencephalized, because selective breeding alters body size more extensively than brain size (Kruska 1988), a feature also evident in the pattern of intraspecific brain/body scaling. To my knowledge there is no evidence that smaller, more encephalized breeds show enhanced cognitive abilities as a result, and probably the reverse is true (Coren 1995). Could this be a model for certain forms of encephalization identified in interspecific comparisons? If so, the exclusive focus on encephalization as *brain* evolution reflects a persistent anthropocentric bias.

One obvious objection is that comparing intra- to interspecies examples of unusually high or low encephalization may not be a comparison of the same phenomenon. For example, if breed differences mostly reflect selection on postcranial features, they might not significantly correlate with differences in cognitive abilities, whereas species differences might be the result of selection influencing both brain and body size and therefore might indicate neurological differences. But comparisons of adult data alone are not sufficient to discriminate between these two possible sources of differences in relative encephalization, nor to help determine whether either effect reflects selection on brain function. An analysis that takes into account development can help.

Consider the causes of encephalization in primates. Although we cannot directly analyze the forces of selection acting on primate brains and bodies throughout their phylogenetic history, we can approach this question in much the same way we might with respect to dog breeds. We recognize that small dog encephalization is secondary to postcranial reduction because we can compare these dogs to more typical dogs and their patterns of growth. A distinct difference between brain/body growth in primates and most other mammals was first systematically analyzed by Earl Count (1947). He showed that during the prenatal growth period, most mammals grow their brains and bodies according to the same pattern with the same ratio of brain size to body size at corresponding time points, irrespective of eventual adult size (see also Holt et al 1975). The sharing of a nearly identical segmental growth pattern across wide ranges of sizes and shapes is quite remarkable and suggests that most mammals share a very conservative embryological brain growth plan (Deacon 1990a, Finlay & Darlington 1995).

The basis for this developmental regularity remains unknown, but this very conservative pattern of mammalian brain/body growth could be the major factor determining the regularity of adult brain/body patterns as well (Deacon 1990a). Similar growth curves, which are aligned during early development and merely uniformly expanded or contracted with respect to one another, could produce the pattern of brain/body allometry observed between adults of different species (Figure 2A). Below, I review genetic evidence that suggests this is the case. Although this embryonic constraint contributes to the regularity of brain/body scaling, it need not contradict additional functional arguments, but it cannot be ignored.

One deviant group, however, is the primate clade. Among anthropoids (from which most data come), brains and bodies grow along a trajectory that is parallel but shifted from that of other mammals (though cetaceans and elephants are also similarly shifted) so that at every growth stage these primates have a higher ratio of brain to body size (Count 1947, Deacon 1990a, Holt et al 1975, Martin & Harvey 1985, Sacher 1982; Figure 2A). Conservatism of the growth pattern is still evident, because growth curves still resemble those of

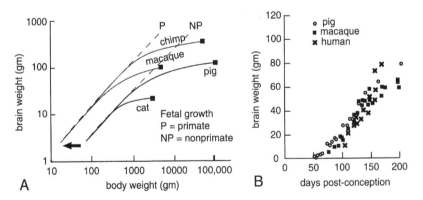

Figure 2 (*A*) The common shapes but different intercepts of developmental brain/body growth curves distinguishing primate and nonprimate mammals shown in a slightly idealized comparison of four species. The left graph schematically depicts the general pattern exhibited by brain/body growth throughout life, showing a two-phase pattern caused by the cessation of brain growth earlier than the rest of the body. P, primate fetal growth pattern; NP, nonprimate pattern; the *arrow* indicates the primate shift. (*B*) Comparison of brain growth in three mammals shows all following the same growth trajectory prenatally. This demonstrates that the left-shifted primate growth is not the result of faster brain growth but reduced body growth. Note that human beings follow this pattern also.

other mammals except for this shift. This primate shift cannot be explained in terms of postnatal growth differences and therefore must represent an independent mode of encephalization. Correspondingly, we should be suspicious of efforts to lump explanations of primate encephalization with those of encephalization in other mammal groups.

So what is the likely mechanism underlying the primate shift? It could be the result of either accelerated brain growth or decelerated postcranial growth. This latter question can be resolved by comparing absolute growth rates as opposed to relative growth rates. Data for this comparison have also been available for decades (e.g. Dickerson & Dobbing 1967, Dobbing & Sands 1973, Holt et al 1975, Widdowson 1981). When brain and body growth rates are compared between species on the same time scale, primate and nonprimate species differ in total body growth rates but not brain growth rates (Figure 2B). For example, prenatal brain growth in human beings, macaques, and pigs proceeds at essentially the same rate, whereas body growth rates for macaques and human beings overlap but are significantly below those for pigs. This appears to be generalizable to most comparisons between primates, on the one hand, and ungulates, carnivores, and rodents on the other. The clear implication is that primate encephalization is the result of a shift in *post*cranial growth processes, not a modification of brain growth!

While this has been hinted at in a number of studies over the past few years (Deacon 1990a, Holt et al 1975, Passingham 1985, Sacher 1982), there does not appear to be wide appreciation of its consequences for interpretations of primate (and human, see below) encephalization. If primates have big brains merely because they have small bodies, we cannot presume that this represents an evolutionary trend driven by cognitive demands. Indeed, primate encephalization is in this one respect analogous to the encephalization produced by dwarfism, where it does not appear to produce a cognitive advantage. But this comparison is also superficial. Unlike the way dwarfism affects postnatal brain/body growth patterns, the primate shift is the result of a cranial/postcranial growth difference that can be followed back to very early embryonic stages. Therefore, the effects of the primate shift in growth are a factor throughout all stages of brain development. This is undoubtedly an important difference, and it is the subject of the last section of this review.

Is Human Encephalization an Extension of the Primate Trend?

Before considering the likely significance of the timing of brain and body growth processes on brain function, it is informative to compare human encephalization to these other forms. Here, again, the comparison of ontogenetic growth processes provides critical information. Although in texts on human evolution it is generally suggested that the hominid increase in brain size continues a trend characteristic of primates in general, the ontogenetic comparison demonstrates that in terms of underlying mechanism this is not the case. Human brain/body growth does not deviate from that of other primates during the prenatal phase; it merely prolongs this phase in a way consistent with size differences in general, except that the human brain/body growth curve is truncated along the postnatal phase (Figure 3). Superficially, this resembles the pattern characteristic of dwarfism: typical brain growth with truncated postnatal somatic growth. But when brain and body growth rates are compared with similar-sized primates (e.g. chimpanzees) it is apparent that for the size of the adult body, human beings do not have stunted growth. The difference is that human brains grow as though they were in an ape with a very much larger body (in excess of 1000 lbs). The locus of the ontogenetic deviation from the typical primate pattern is within the head. This is also clearly demonstrated by the fossil record. Hominid body sizes have not decreased to produce human encephalization. Stature increased significantly during the transition from *Australopithecus* to *Homo*. The difference in growth process that produces increased primate encephalization over and above that typical of most other mammals is not the same as that which produces increased human encephalization over and above the typical primate pattern. Human brains and bodies grow at a rate that would be predicted for the adult sizes reached by each, respectively, except that human brains continue to grow as though in a much larger body longer

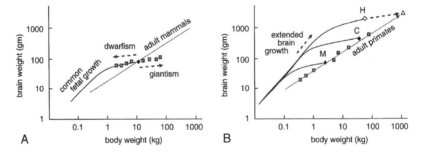

Figure 3   Somewhat idealized graphs showing the human brain/body growth pattern as compared with the pattern seen in dwarfism (*A*) and with other species of primates (*B*) (H, human; C, chimpanzee; M, macaque monkey). *Squares* and *diamonds* indicate adult values of brain and body weight. Dwarfism and giantism diverge from more typical growth curves after most brain growth is complete. Human fetal growth follows the fetal primate trajectory, but the fetal brain growth phase is comparatively extended (*dashed arrows*). The *triangle* in (*B*) indicates body growth predicted in a typical ape with human brain size. Human body growth is similar to the chimpanzee pattern, but brain growth continues as if in a larger primate.

than would be expected for our postcranial growth. This human pattern is distinct from dwarfism or the primate postcranial reduction.

Comparing the evolutionary causes and correlates of encephalization across each of these major species differences runs the risk of analogizing entirely unrelated phenomena. Quite different growth processes are responsible for the encephalization of chimpanzees, Chihuahuas, and human beings with respect to their respective phylogenetic contexts. Unless we can say with certainty that only the resulting size relationships matter for questions of brain organization and brain function, we are not justified in using cross-species correlations between encephalization and other adaptational variables to extrapolate the causes of human brain evolution. Until we understand the functional consequences of these developmental differences, we can only treat such correlations as interesting coincidences. Assumptions about the significance of differences in encephalization, about the relevance or irrelevance of total brain size, and even about the centrality of encephalization to human cognitive evolution are all placed in doubt by these differences. We need an explanation of the mechanisms behind these different modes of growth and an account of their effects on brain organization before we can go beyond merely correlative stories.

The deviation in size of the human brain is the most robust clue to what is unique, but it is not clear that increased relative brain size itself is the only or even the primary feature that is represented by this difference. The question is whether encephalization achieved by substantially different modifications of brain and body growth produces different neural architectures with different functional consequences. There are good reasons to suspect that it does.

DEVELOPMENTAL NEUROBIOLOGY

How Species-Specific Are Neural Circuit Plans?

Although quantitative differences in overall brain size stand out as obvious markers of primate and human evolutionary trends, it has long been assumed that species behavioral and cognitive differences might also be mediated by the presence or absence of distinctive brain structures and by species-specific differences of connection patterns. Beyond general questions of brain growth, the obvious question is, What is the level of detail and specificity of the information that distinguishes patterns of cells and connections in one species brain from another? Is there developmental evidence demonstrating species-unique developmental signals that are responsible for unique adult structures? Many structural and connectional details seem highly similar in the brains of different mammals, and have suggested that there is considerable connectional conservatism across mammals. Only recently have we begun to discover why.

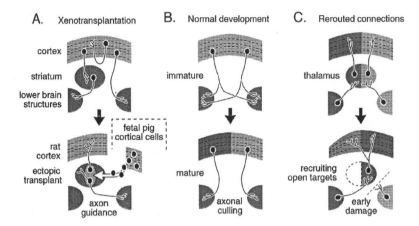

Figure 4   Evidence for conserved axonal guidance and Darwinian competitive processes in brain development. (*A*) Transplanting cortical cells from a pig fetus into an adult rat brain shows that both species use the same signals to guide axon growth to targets. *Top:* normal connections (Isacson & Deacon 1996). *Bottom:* Despite placing the graft into an inappropriate location, axons find appropriate targets. (*B*) During normal development of cortical output connections, axons are initially overproduced and nonspecific (*top*), and are later culled (*bottom*) (O'Leary 1992). (*C*) Removing inputs destined for specific thalamic targets can allow other inputs to take over the vacated region and induce this part of the thalamus to transmit different sensory information to the cortex, thus changing its functional organization (Frost & Metin 1985, Sur et al 1988).

Although common sense suggests that quite different signals might underlie different species' neural circuit designs, recent studies of axonal growth and guidance suggest otherwise. In fact, initial axonal growth from one brain structure into others may be even more conservative in evolution than the trends in brain and body growth. Although few of the molecular details are currently known, already there is evidence that highly conserved proteins (such as the netrins and homeotic gene products) guide axons along specific pathways in distantly homologous structures in animals as different as roundworms, insects, and mammals (e.g. Friedman & O'Leary 1996, Kennedy et al 1994, Colamarino & Tessier-Lavigne 1995). Further indirect evidence for conservative connectional signaling has been provided by transplantation experiments where tissue from one species' brain is allowed to grow in another species' brain. Experiments in which Japanese quail embryos were dissected and part of their very immature neural tissue was grafted into the corresponding regions of embryonic chicken brains (lacking this part) have shown that not only do the grafts link up with the host brain but that individual animals born with such a chimeric brain behave in ways that indicate that the neural connections have conferred appropriate function (Balaban et al 1988, Le Douarin 1993). Further evidence that the same or highly similar signals are used to initially guide different species' neural output branches to their appropriate targets is also provided by experiments transplanting pig fetal neurons into adult rat brains. Using species-specific markers for axons, we have demonstrated that pig axons from a variety of neuronal cell types and implanted into a number of different brain structures can use rat host guidance cues to grow axons to targets that are appropriate for the transplanted cell type (Isacson & Deacon 1996). Although not highly precise in their target specificity, axons can take elaborate routes to grow around and past nontarget structures through developmentally anomalous pathways to terminate in target structures (Figure 4A).

This provides an unexpected challenge to brain evolution theories. If axon guidance signals are highly conserved from species to species, they are not likely to account for significant differences. One might counter that only these early, generic, and not highly specific growth signals are conserved and that species differences are more likely at the microscopic level, with genetic variants producing fine differences in network patterning. However, there is also evidence that much of the fine wiring of the brain that produces the complex topographies of sensory analyzers and high-level cognitive differences is not prefigured in specific genetic instructions.

Developing Brains Adapt Themselves to Bodies

It has long been suspected that during the earliest stages of development, brains are particularly sensitive to experiences. It has also been known that young brains are remarkably more resilient in recovering from major injury. Both ideas are summed up by the claim that immature brains are far more plastic than mature brains. However, what began as investigations into the mechanisms of this plasticity has led to findings that have changed our whole understanding of how brains develop. This plasticity is an artifact of a developmental process that employs a great deal of information that is extrinsic to any individual neural cell to determine location and function within the vast network of other neurons. In general terms, evolution has eliminated any redundant architectonic information that it could from the mammalian genome in favor of using free structural information ubiquitously present in the developmental context itself. This has allowed brains to be much more responsive to adaptive challenges driving major changes in morphology.

Theoretically, one might have predicted that every mutation that resulted in a modification of limb architecture, an increase or decrease in muscle mass, or a change in the size or relative position of a sensory organ, would require at least one (and possibly many) corresponding mutations of the peripheral and central nervous systems to keep it from being malfunctional. In contrast, however, it appears that no such matching pattern of mutations is necessary, and may be relatively rare. Developing neural systems adapt to the body much as species adapt to a surrounding ecosystem by utilizing overproduction, unspecified variation, competition, selective elimination, and perpetuation of only a fraction of the original variants.

There are two levels of this process that are crucial to matching the central nervous system to the needs of an unprespecified body (Cowan et al 1984, Deacon 1990b, Finlay et al 1987, Purves 1988, Wilczynski 1984). The first involves the initial overproduction of neurons that are later selectively culled away by programmed cell death (apoptosis). The second involves a related overproduction and underspecification of axonal growth and connectivity that is also subsequently pruned as axons compete with one another for limited synaptic targets (Figure 4B). Both are highly reminiscent of Darwinian selection processes and are variants of processes that are also used elsewhere in the developing embryonic body.

The importance of neuronal overproduction and programmed cell death was first demonstrated by investigations of motor neuron development in the spinal cord and in spinal ganglia (see reviews in Katz & Lasek 1983, Purves 1988, Williams & Herrup 1988). Early in fetal development, far more motor neurons are produced than will persist into maturity. All grow axons into the

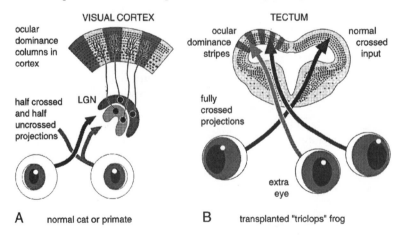

Figure 5   (*A*) Stereoscopic vision in mammals is supported by interdigitated cortical maps of the visual field from each eye. Segregation of inputs (*different shades of gray in cortex*) develops in response to patterning of inputs during development. (*B*) Spontaneous emergence of an analogous interdigitated visual field mapping in the optic tectum of a frog with a transplanted third eye (Law & Constantine-Paton 1981).

periphery, guided by relatively generic signals to a predefined class of target muscles. Once in the periphery, axons compete for connection with individual muscle fibers, which ultimately will allow only terminals from one motor neuron to develop mature neuromuscular junctions. In the ensuing competition for muscle contacts, a large fraction of motor neurons will fail to maintain any contacts, and this will eventually set in motion processes within the cell that cause it to self-destruct. Elimination of the unconnected cells produces a precise matching of muscle and motor neuron populations, post hoc. In evolutionary terms, this allows variations of neural and muscular systems to occur almost irrespective of each other (i.e. without the need for high-level regulation of different gene systems with respect to one another) and yet guarantees coordination of function. Thus, novel adaptive responses, produced by mutations that shift the distribution of muscle masses within the body, would not require any corresponding neural mutations to match, and vice versa.

Over the past decade, it has become evident that programmed cell death is a widespread phenomenon that probably plays an analogous role in matching neural populations throughout the developing brain. But this contributes more than just a matching and population sculpting function. Coupled with its corollary—axonal competition—it is a major factor in neural network pattern formation. Axonal overproduction and pruning of connections have been shown to play critical roles in circuit patterning all levels of CNS development and in the delineation of major subdivisions of cortical and subcortical structures (Figure 4B). Thus, for example, severing the optic tract at a point before complete innervation of the thalamus causes axons from other sensory systems to innervate the newly available targets and consequently alters cortical areal topography and connectivity (e.g. Frost & Metin 1985, O'Leary 1992, Sur et al 1988; Figure 4C).

The power of this "connectional Darwinism" to drive pattern formation is perhaps most vividly demonstrated by the neural adaptation for binocular visual perception. Crucial to both primate and carnivore vision is the ability to see depth by integrating information about binocular disparity, i.e. the difference in angle of gaze to the same object from each eye. The perceptual experience of depth is computed on line in the visual cortex of these mammals because of complex overlapping interdigitated projection maps arriving from each eye. This composite map is like a system of zebra stripes in which the alternating white and black bands represent the input from each eye, respectively, and in which adjoining black and white regions are receiving information about the same position in the visual field (see Figure 5A). The extent of overlap and interdigitation depends on the relative convergence of the eyes in the head, so the map pattern differs for different species and ranges from essentially no overlap in many rodent brains to nearly complete overlap in the human brain.

Given the complexity of this map structure and the precision with which it must be formed in order to function, it would seem to be a candidate for precisely prespecified organization. Shortly after this functional architecture was discovered, however, it soon became evident that its pattern could be significantly modified by simply manipulating extrinsic signals. For example, blocking visual signals from one eye during a critical period during early development could substantially bias the map so that the uncovered eye would be far more extensively represented, and if blocked long enough (or if one eye was removed), the entire primary visual cortex could become dedicated to one eye. Varieties of other developmental manipulations in animals and, more recently, computer simulations have demonstrated that this complex map architecture can be induced to develop under quite general conditions. All that is necessary are weakly topographic connection patterns and a Darwinian-like competition between axons that is biased with respect to the degree of synchrony of input signals from the two eyes. This signal patterning is provided by the only slightly different images projecting onto the two retinas.

The power of this developmental selection process to generate complex architecture is most unequivocally demonstrated in cases where the possibility of genetic instruction can be ruled out. One remarkable example is provided by a study in which additional—or third—eyes were implanted into the heads of embryonic frogs, between their existing eyes (Law & Constantine-Paton 1981). During development it was found that this extranumery eye extended axons to the optic tectum (a dorsal midbrain cortical-like structure that serves as the primary visual center in frogs) along with axons from the two normal eyes. During development this extra eye relayed information that was partially redundant with information from the closest normal eye. The result was the production of a pattern of connection with interdigitated eye-specific stripes, analogous to the ocular dominance stripes in mammal cortices (Figure 5B). Normal frogs, however, have essentially no normal binocular overlap and not even any phylogenetic history (so far as we know) of binocularity. The stripe pattern emerged de novo merely in response to the generic features of the competitive process and the systematic biases produced by input signals.

How Do Deviations in Brain Size Affect Brain Development?

How these two developmental processes might interact with relative size factors to produce brain differences is demonstrated by an animal with an extreme sensory adaptation that alters the proportions of different sensory inputs from an early stage in development. The blind mole rat (*Spalax*) lives underground its entire life and develops only tiny vestigial eyes. Recently, anatomical studies have demonstrated that ascending neural connections from the auditory and tactile sensory systems have essentially displaced visual connections in the major visual nuclei and visual cortex of this rodent (Doron & Wollberg 1994, Heil et al 1991). It is probably the case that the diminutive visual projections are simply outcompeted during early development by these other projections to produce a substantially different functional recruitment of brain structures than in a typical rodent. This demonstrates the power of quantitative reorganization of body structure to drive correlated neuronal reorganization. Even more subtle variations of the size of external receptor systems can alter normal cortical organization (e.g. Killackey et al 1994).

Depending on the extent, distribution, and timing of growth differences, we should expect that critical competitive processes will be biased differently. For example, the reduction in somatic growth that is mostly exhibited postnatally in dwarfism occurs largely after most neural developmental adaptation processes have been completed and so can be expected to have only a modest effect on the distribution of cell populations and connection patterns, whereas changes in somatic proportions that occur earlier in development (as in the blind mole rat or as in primates), should have far more significant effects on brain organization.

Currently, there is insufficient comparative neural morphological information to determine whether patterns of neural connections directly correlate with patterns of brain and body growth. We are therefore not in a position to offer more than theoretical predictions based on quite general principles and analogies to experimental conditions. However, these new developmental data provide some very important clues for guiding future research into more detailed assessments of brain structure evolution. In fact, this represents a research topic that would benefit from combining the methods of modern developmental neurobiology with traditional quantitative morphology of brain structure and growth processes. Despite a limited empirical database from which to predict the links between allometric growth trends and brain structure patterns, it may be possible to offer some educated guesses about what to expect in response to large-scale allometric deviations. The effects of primate and human encephalization are cases in point.

Consider, for example, that primate cranial/postcranial proportions are shifted from those characteristic of most other mammals from the very earliest stages of fetal growth. Because of this, disproportions in cell death patterns and axonal recruitment patterns likely ramify throughout the developing primate nervous system. In very general terms, primates ought to have proportionately less of their brains dedicated to projection systems that are directly associated with sensory and motor functions, when compared with nonprimates with similar-size brains. Nonsystematic claims to the effect that primate brains contain a smaller proportion of primary sensory and motor cortex than nonprimates have been around for generations, but systematic analysis of this and of the possible correlation with growth and body proportion relationships awaits future work. Nor are there systematic behavioral data sufficient to determine whether primates as a group exhibit different cognitive biases as a result (perhaps causing them to be less stimulus-driven during learning), as distinct from some sort of general intelligence advantage.

Finally, with respect to the human brain, the uniqueness of the pattern of human brain/body growth suggests that the pattern of internal reorganization of human brains is unlike that correlated with either form of increased encephalization due to postcranial reduction (i.e. dwarfism and the primate shift in growth). Because human brain/body proportions do not deviate from the general primate pattern during the major portion of prenatal development, it is likely that human/primate brain differences are less substantial than primate/nonprimate differences. However, the more prolonged immaturity of the brain with respect to body growth likely produces more widespread reorganization than does dwarfism. But unlike dwarfism or primate body reduction, in human beings it is the brain that is the locus of the change in growth and not postcranial structures. To appreciate this difference we are forced to go beyond simple growth and size comparisons and to consider the primary ontogenetic mechanisms underlying them.

Which Genes Are Most Relevant?

Perhaps the most revolutionary information about brain evolution and growth has come from the study of gene expression during early development. Over the past decade, the use of a molecular technique called in situ hybridization to identify specific localized RNA production in embryos has demonstrated that a diverse class of regulatory genes, generally called *homeotic* genes, interact to produce the initial segmental patterning of the body by specifying cell fates, and major growth fields. (For an overview of current research and theory in developmental genetics, including a discussion of homeotic gene function and evolution, see Raff 1996.) Perhaps the most remarkable feature of homeotic genes is their conservatism of both nucleotide sequences and developmental functions. Homeotic genes in animals as diverse as flies and human beings exhibit high levels of sequence homology, are responsible for determining body structures in corresponding locations in the developing body, and to a certain extent can even substitute for each other in cross-species transgenic experiments (for example, substituting mammal genes in mutant fly embryos to restore developmental functions). An important characteristic of homeotic genes is that they subdivide the developing body both in the dorsal-ventral axis and in the anterior-posterior axis, and into semiregular segments from anterior to posterior, providing the initial subdivision grid within which later embryonic construction will take place. The overlapping patchwork of different gene expression domains defines each subdivision in terms of an explicit combination of genes expressed only at that site, and this in turn appears to specify regional cell differentiation.

It may be possible to take advantage of the conservatism of this positional expression of homeotic genes to home in on the genes behind some of these major morphological shifts in brain growth and morphology. This approach has been successful in identifying homeotic genes associated with mutations involving other morphological abnormalities. For example, a recent study of human synpolydactyly (which produces extra digits and abnormal growth and attachment of the digits) took advantage of the known expression of the *Hox13* genes localized to the hand during its formation in other vertebrates to narrow the genetic search to that region of the genome. This ultimately led to the discovery that mutations of this gene are responsible for the morphological abnormality. By analogy, identifying the embryological locus of differences in brain-body growth relationships or brain structure relationships may provide the crucial clues to the underlying genetic differences that produce them.

Of particular relevance to the problem of brain size differences are homeotic genes that play critical roles in establishing the boundary between head structures and postcranial structures and between the midbrain and brain stem. This locus in the developing embryo has long been known to roughly correspond to the site of the initiation of neural tube formation (identified with the Spemann organizer, which is the point in the developing early embryo where mesodermal tissue initiates the formation of the neural tube from ectodermal tissue, and without which no nervous system would form). At the midbrain/ brain stem transition there is a dichotomy of developmental geometry: Behind this point, there is a regular linear pattern of gene expression. In front of it there is a less linear pattern which forms the head (partly organized with respect to more localized mesodermal structures called placodes). Not surprisingly, this point in the embryonic body seems to be a critical juncture with respect to control of cranial/postcranial growth patterns.

A few homeotic genes, initially identified by their role in fly head formation, appear to play particularly direct roles in determining where this transition between brain and brainstem will occur during development. Two relevant examples are designated *Otx1* and *Otx2* in mammals and are expressed in the brain—just in front of the midbrain/hindbrain division—at the time these embryonic decisions are made (Simeone et al 1992). Studies with frog and mouse embryos in which expression of an *Otx* gene is modified demonstrate its potential role in brain size determination. In frog embryos, the *Otx2* homologue (called *X-Otx2;* X for *Xenopus*) is initially expressed throughout the undifferentiated embryo, then progressively restricted in its expression to more and more rostral regions. Its expression, however, can be manipulated by ex-

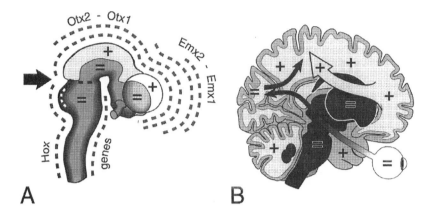

Figure 6 (*A*) Regions of the developing human embryonic brain that must have undergone additional early stem cell production to produce the adult pattern of shifted proportions of enlarged dorsal forebrain structures. The overlapping expression regions of Otx and Emx genes are indicated by *dashed lines* above the embryonic brain to show the correspondence with expanded regions (+). The *arrow* indicates the boundary between brain and brainstem with Hox genes expressed below (both dorsally and ventrally) and Otx and Emx genes expressed above (mostly restricted to dorsal structures). (*B*) Schematic diagram showing how the adult human brain diverges from allometric prediction for a "typical" primate brain. Structures indicated with "=" are roughly predictable from human body size, whereas structures indicated by "+" are greater than predicted (correspondences with embryonic brain gene expression patterns are indicated by relative lightness/darkness). The proportions of one peripheral input—the eye—with respect to the brain are shown to exemplify how this disproportion is reflected in connectional disproportions and developmental axonal competition (*dark gray arrows*—reduced—compared to *light gray arrows*—enlarged—to indicate relative numbers of projections).

ternal signals or by direct insertion of the gene product into the embryo. In embryos with higher than normal levels, this brain/body boundary develops further back, and in embryos with lower than normal levels it develops further forward on the body axis, producing relatively larger or smaller head and brain structures, respectively (Boncinelli & Mallamaci 1995). A parallel effect is seen in transgenic mouse embryos in which both *Otx2* alleles have been damaged. These embryos exhibit significant reduction and abnormalities of the developing head and brain (Matsuo et al 1995). Of course, the *Otx* genes are not the only genes involved. The expression of other genes and many other correlated molecules also contribute, and they may also influence expression of *Otx*. Nevertheless, genes such as *Otx* and their local interactions will likely provide the critical clues to the mechanisms underlying shifts in brain/body proportions.

Although we are a considerable way away from possessing sufficient comparative genetic information of this sort to answer some of the encephalization questions posed by primate and human evolution, the distinctiveness of the embryological growth patterns in each case does point to molecular correlates likely to be involved in some way. To discover which homeotic genes are involved, we need to precisely identify the locus of the divergent growth trend and then use this to narrow the search to the appropriate gene expression domain. For example, the pattern of the primate deviation from the typical mammalian brain/body growth trend suggests that a shift in the cranial/postcranial transition, such as produced by increased *Otx2* gene expression (as in experimental frogs), might be relevant, or perhaps that postcranial homeotic gene expression might be involved in body segment reduction. In human development, the locus of the difference is the brain, but does it involve the whole brain? If a more precise localization of the differences in cell production can be identified within the human brain, a better match with homeotic gene expression might be possible. This again is where morphometric studies and neural development may be able to provide complementary data.

Quantitative analyses of existing brain structure data in primates have suggested that human brain enlargement is not equally distributed among all structures, even when corrected for brain size. Although different analyses have provided conflicting predictions, and a systematic study of necessary breadth has not been done, data comparing human and nonhuman primate brain structure volumes suggest that dorsal brain structures (including cerebral cortex and cerebellar cortex) may have enlarged out of proportion to ventral brain structures (Deacon 1988, 1997). It may not be just coincidence that the *Otx* genes, as well as others implicated in brain size and normal forebrain development by experimental studies (Matsuo et al 1995, Simeone et al 1992), are differentially expressed in dorsal forebrain structures (Figure 6). Further examination of the expression of these and related genes in human as compared with other primate embryos may help to isolate the mechanisms underlying this critical human adaptation.

CONCLUSIONS

In summary, the developmental linkage between comparative brain morphometry and the competitive processes that influence the specification of axonal connectivity suggests that what is uniquely different about human brains is not just their quantitative organization, but more importantly the consequent shifts in connectivity among brain regions. Following the analogue of animals like the blind mole rat—whose central nervous system is radically modified by changes of the relative quantity of peripheral inputs—we can predict that these human disproportions of forebrain structures have produced a reorganization of connectivity from the inside out, so to speak. Two significant predictions include (*a*) an increased central projection onto visceromotor systems such as control laryngeal and respiratory muscles (essential for speech) and (*b*) an increased prefrontal cortex with more extensive and more widespread connections (likely crucial for symbolic learning and an increasing predominance of cognitive "executive" functions) (Deacon 1997). Because these neurological consequences are coupled to quantitative changes, it may also be possible to use allometric evidence from fossil material to estimate the evolutionary appearance and development of these functional capacities.

For over a century scientists have studied brain evolution as a problem of gross functional morphology. Recent developments in the neurosciences provide a wealth of new information about brain development that challenges and augments this classic approach. Presumed functional correlates of brain size differences, theories of encephalization, and the plausibility of highly modular species-specific changes all must be carefully reexamined in the context of this information. Although well-accepted claims about brain evolution in our lineage may be put in question as a result, the value of comparative morphological analysis takes on a new significance as a guide to more detailed developmental and molecular studies of the brain. Achieving this new synthesis of quantitative morphology, developmental biology, and genetics is key to unlocking the mystery of what makes human brains human.

> **Visit the *Annual Reviews* home page at**
> **http://www.AnnualReviews.org.**

Literature Cited

Balaban E, Teillet MA, Le Douarin N. 1988. Application of the quail-chick chimera system to the study of brain development and behavior. *Science* 241:1339–42

Boncinelli F, Mallamaci A. 1995. Homeobox genes in vertebrate gastrulation. *Curr. Opin. Genet. Dev.* 5:619–27

Colamarino S, Tessier-Lavigne M. 1995. The role of the floorplate in axon guidance. *Annu. Rev. Neurosci.* 18:497–529

Coren S. 1995. *The Intelligence of Dogs.* New York: Bantam Books

Count EW. 1947. Brain and body weight in man: their antecedents in growth and evolution. *Ann. NY Acad. Sci.* 46:993–1122

Cowan WM, Fawcett JW, O'Leary DDM,

Stanfield BB. 1984. Regressive events in neurogenesis. *Science* 255:1258–65

Deacon TW. 1988. Human brain evolution. II. Embryology and brain allometry. In *Intelligence and Evolutionary Biology,* ed. H Jerison, I Jerison, pp. 383–415. Berlin: Springer-Verlag

Deacon TW. 1990a. Problems of ontogeny and phylogeny in brain size evolution. *Int. J. Primatol.* 11:237–82

Deacon TW. 1990b. Rethinking mammalian brain evolution. *Am. Zool.* 30:629–705

Deacon TW. 1997. *The Symbolic Species: The Co-evolution of Language and the Brain.* New York: Norton

Dickerson JWT, Dobbing J. 1967. Prenatal

and postnatal growth and development of the central nervous system of the pig. *Proc. R. Soc. London Ser. B* 166:384–95

Dobbing J, Sands J. 1973. Quantitative growth and development of human brain. *Arch. Dis. Child.* 48:757–67

Doron N, Wollberg Z. 1994. Cross-modal neuroplasticity in the blind mole rat *Spalax ehrenbergi:* a WGA-HRP tracing study. *NeuroReport* 5:2697–701

Finlay BL, Darlington RB. 1995. Linked regularities in the development and evolution of the mammalian brain. *Science* 268: 1578–84

Finlay BL, Winkler KC, Sengelaub DR. 1987. Regressive events in brain development and scenarios for vertebrate brain evolution. *Brain Behav. Evol.* 30:102–17

Friedman G, O'Leary DDM. 1996. Retroviral misexpression of engrailed genes in the chick optic tectum perturbs the topographic targeting of retinal axons. *J. Neurosci.* 16:5490–509

Frost DO, Metin C. 1985. Induction of functional retinal projections to the somatosensory system. *Nature* 317:162–65

Heil P, Bronchti G, Scheik H. 1991. Invasion of visual cortex by the auditory system in the naturally blind mole rat. *NeuroReport* 2:735–38

Holt AB, Cheek DB, Mellits ED, Hill DE. 1975. Brain size and the relation of the primate to the nonprimate. In *Fetal and Postnatal Cellular Growth: Hormones and Nutrition,* ed. DB Cheek, pp. 23–44. New York: Wiley

Isacson O, Deacon TW. 1996. Specific axon guidance factors persist in the adult brain as demonstrated by pig neuroblasts transplanted to the rat. *Neuroscience* 75:827–37

Jerison HJ. 1973. *Evolution of the Brain and Intelligence.* New York: Academic

Katz JM, Lasek RJ. 1983. Evolution of the nervous system: role of ontogenetic mechanisms in the evolution of matching populations. *Proc. Natl. Acad. Sci. USA* 75:1349–52

Kennedy T, Serafini T, de la Torre J, Tessier-Lavigne M. 1994. Netrins are diffusable chemotropic factors for commissural axons in the embryonic spinal cord. *Cell* 78: 425–35

Killackey HP, Chiaia NL, Bennett-Clarke CA, Eck M, Rhoades RW. 1994. Peripheral influences on the size and organization of somatotopic representations in the fetal rat cortex. *J. Neurosci.* 14:1496–506

Kruska D. 1988. Mammalian domestication and its effect on brain structure and behavior. In *Intelligence and Evolutionary Biology,* ed. H Jerison, I Jerison, pp. 211–50. Berlin: Springer-Verlag

Law M, Constantine-Paton M. 1981. Anatomy and physiology of experimentally induced striped tecta. *J. Neurosci.* 1:741–59

Le Douarin NM. 1993. Embryonic neural chimaeras in the study of brain development. *Trends Neurosci.* 16:64–72

Martin RD. 1981. Relative brain size and basal metabolic rate in terrestrial vertebrates. *Nature* 293:57–60

Martin RD, Harvey PH. 1985. Brain size allometry: ontogeny and phylogeny. In *Size and Scaling in Primate Biology,* ed. W Jungers, pp. 147–73. New York: Plenum

Matsuo I, Kuratani S, Kimura C, Takeda N, Aizawa S. 1995. Mouse Otx2 functions in the formation and patterning of the rostral head. *Genes Dev.* 9:2646–58

O'Leary DDM. 1992. Development of connectional diversity and specificity in the mammalian brain by the pruning of collateral projections. *Curr. Opin. Neurobiol.* 2:707

Passingham R. 1985. Rates of brain development in mammals including man. *Brain Behav. Evol.* 26:167–75

Purves D. 1988. *Body and Brain. A Trophic Theory of Neural Connections.* Cambridge, MA: Harvard Univ. Press

Raff RA. 1996. *The Shape of Life: Genes, Development, and the Evolution of Animal Form.* Chicago: Chicago Univ. Press

Sacher GA. 1982. Brain maturation in the evolution of primates. In *Primate Brain Evolution: Methods and Concepts,* ed. E Armstrong, D Falk, pp. 97–112. New York: Plenum

Simeone A, Acampora D, Gulisano M, Stornaiuolo A, Boncinelli E. 1992. Nested expression domains of four homeobox genes in developing rostral brain. *Nature* 358: 687–90

Sur M, Garraghty PE, Roe AW. 1988. Experimentally induced visual projections into auditory thalamus and cortex. *Science* 242: 1437–41

Widdowson EM. 1981. Growth of creatures great and small. *Symp. Zool. Soc. Lond.* 46:5–17

Wilczynski W. 1984. Central neural systems subserving a homoplasous periphery. *Am. Zool.* 24:755–63

Williams RW, Herrup K. 1988. The control of neuron number. *Annu. Rev. Neurosci.* 11: 423–53

Annu. Rev. Anthropol. 1997. 26:359–84

MODELING ANCIENT POPULATION STRUCTURES AND MOVEMENT IN LINGUISTICS

Johanna Nichols

Department of Slavic Languages and Literatures, University of California, Berkeley, Berkeley, California 94720-2979; e-mail: johanna@uclink.berkeley.edu

KEY WORDS: language family, language spread, linguistic diversity, language dispersal, linguistic geography

ABSTRACT

Linguistic population structure is described in terms of language families. Geographical distributions of language families respond to climate, latitude, and economic factors. Characteristic shapes of phylogenetic descent trees for language families reflect particular types, rates, directionalities, and chronologies of spread. Languages move in predictable ways in particular geographical, economic, and social contexts. In this chapter, the linguistic prehistories of four continents are surveyed with regard to linguistic spreads, linguistic diversity, and language family origins.

INTRODUCTION

Languages enter into descent lineages, areal groupings, and typological classes. On the map they bunch up densely in some places and spread out widely in others. Over time they expand or contract in range and move in space, sometimes to great distances. They are adopted or abandoned by speech communities. Some give rise to daughter languages, some die out. Some change rapidly, some slowly. These various processes are favored or constrained by geographical and other external circumstances, and identifying them is useful in tracing linguistic prehistory and human prehistory more generally.

The most recent period of ferment in linguistic phylogeny, when principles were reviewed together with actual classification, was midcentury, when

359

works by Lamb (1959), Haas (1969), Hoenigswald (1960), and Voegelin & Voegelin (1964–1966) were produced partly in response to the bloom in field description of Native American languages. The past two decades have seen remarkable progress in the description and historical analysis of previously undescribed languages and in computational linguistics and statistical methods—as well as in archeology and human genetics—and it is time to review principles, classification, and linguistic prehistory again. Because the main obstacles to interdisciplinary communication appear to be nonlinguists' lack of understanding of how languages move and what constitutes a valid genetic grouping, most attention is given to these issues here.

Basic claims of historical linguistics are not individually referenced here; recent introductions include Crowley (1992), Hock (1991), Hock & Joseph (1996), McMahon (1994), Thomason & Kaufman (1988), and Trask (1996). No general reference work on the world's languages reflects current scientific knowledge; Moseley & Asher (1994) probably come closest. Unless otherwise indicated, all statements about numbers of languages in areas, ranges of languages, and population densities refer to the linguistic world as it was, or as it can be reconstructed, as of about 1492.

LINGUISTIC POPULATION STRUCTURE

The day-to-day work of historical-comparative linguistics can be called Neogrammarian comparison, after the self-designation of the field's theoretical founding school. It comprises the search for cognate vocabulary and regular sound correspondences within descent groups, reconstruction of ancestral sounds and words on the basis of that evidence, and the definition of subgrouping relations within the family. Neogrammarian method is called "the comparative method" in linguistics, but there is also a broader field of comparative linguistics whose concerns are not only genealogical.

Phylogenetic Trees and Linguistic Descent

The basic building block of linguistic populations is the descent group or clade. Neogrammarian comparison describes linguistic clades whose genetic relatedness is already established. Common descent is shown by shared unique innovations—features so specific and so unlikely to be diffused that their independent innovation is virtually precluded, and languages sharing them can with near-certainty be assumed to descend from a common ancestor. Genetic markers, as descent-proving features can be called, can be of three types:

1. An ordered sequence or other patterned set of form-function pairings whose overall probability of occurrence is about two orders of magnitude less

than the probability of any one language turning up in a random draw. (There are some 5000–6000 languages, hence $1/5000 \times 0.01 = 0.000002$ or two in a million). A four-consonant sequence or ordered set meets this threshold. The person prefix paradigm of the Algonquian family of North America, for example, consists of first person *ne-, second person *ke-, third person *we-, and indefinite *me- (Goddard 1975). This small but highly structured paradigm meets the threshold and is a strong genetic marker. It was recognized by Sapir (1913) and Haas (1958) as diagnostic of genetic identity between the Algonquian family and two languages of coastal California—Yurok and Wiyot (see Goddard 1975). Another genetic marker is the gender-number suffixes masculine -n, feminine -t, plural (masculine = feminine) -n in certain pronominal paradigms, which is diagnostic of Afroasiatic genetic reality (Greenberg 1960). For the computation and other examples see Nichols (1995, 1996).

2. Significantly greater than chance frequency of phoneme matchings in semantically identical words from a standard 100-word list. Tests of this type are offered by Oswalt (1991), Bender (1969), and Ringe (1992); applications of the latter are Ringe (1995a,b, 1996, 1997). (The mathematics of the significance thresholds is under revision for Ringe's test, but the basic procedure is valid.) All three use the 100-word basic vocabulary list proposed by Morris Swadesh; the first two seek greater-than-expected numbers of matching identical segments, and the third seeks greater-than-expected numbers of correspondences (not necessarily of identity) for which expected thresholds are based on the actual frequencies of segments in the two wordlists. The test of Nichols (1995) uses naturalistic ranges of phonological and semantic variation. All these are binary tests that can show that two languages are related but do not circumscribe families or identify subfamilies.

3. Although this has not been attempted, in principle a set of features—none a genetic marker by itself but all of known diachronic stability and relatively low frequency worldwide, and all demonstrably independent of each other—could as a set reach the threshold of genetic markers and serve as a diagnostic of deep genetic connection.

It is often claimed that demonstrating regular systematic sound correspondences among a set of languages (i.e. among putative cognates) constitutes demonstration of genetic relatedness. It does not. Systematic correspondences can be found among any random set of languages. It is not that systematic correspondences can be found within fixed wordlists (such as the Swadesh 100- or 200-word list) from randomly chosen languages. They cannot. Rather, a statistical wild card lurks in the assembling of putative cognate sets by the analyst. In normal stocks and families, cognates range widely in their semantics. For example, descendants of PIE *leuk- 'light, brightness' listed in Watkins (1985) include 'light,' 'moon,' 'purify,' 'meadow,' 'shine,' 'flame, fire,' 'lamp,' 'rabies,' and possibly 'lynx,' and these are only the cognates retrievable from the English vocabulary. The analyst trying to demonstrate genetic relatedness generally believes in the relatedness and is therefore motivated to pursue all plausible semantic connections. This means that the procedure for seeking cognates is a series of more or less open-ended searches each of which ends with the first success, and a search rapidly inflates the probability of finding a match (Nichols 1995, 1996). Proving genetic relatedness therefore requires that semantics be fixed or firmly controlled; hence the available heuristic methods seek out that small number of cognates whose meanings are unchanged and test whether that small number is significantly above the expected frequency. There are a number of proposed deep "families" that are said to be based on the comparative method but are actually based on premature Neogrammarian comparison and are therefore spurious (or at least unproved). Space limitations preclude reviewing them here.

All known tests give the occasional false negative when applied to known families. Greenberg's gender-number paradigm, for example (see above), is present in its entirety in three branches of Afroasiatic—Semitic, Chadic, Berber—but only partly in the others. Ringe's test fails to detect relatedness of ancient Greek to some of its sisters because the test seeks consonant correspondences and Greek has lost several consonants. For both of these families, the identity and bounds of the families can be established by other means. The false negatives are the consequence of language change, which has reshaped paradigms in Afroasiatic and eroded consonants in Greek. Because all languages constantly change and for any linguistic element there is a nonzero probability of radical mutation or complete loss, over time genetic markers become fewer in number among related languages, tests yield false negatives more often, and eventually genetic relatedness cannot be proven. Inherited elements remain in the languages, but they are statistically indistinguishable from chance resemblances, and their number also decreases over time.

This fade-out effect provides some salient thresholds in the decay of genetic markers and dissolution of families. The following are commonly recognized stages, though terminology varies. The terms used here are those of Lamb (1959), up to the level he considers to represent established relatedness.

FAMILY   This is the standard general term for a proven clade of any age. A relatively young family has a clear grammatical signature with obvious sharings of cognate morphemes in similar functions, numerous lexical cognates, and plentiful genetic markers. Families in the age range of 3500–4500 years include Kartvelian, Dravidian, Athabaskan, and Mayan. Classical Indo-European as first discovered consists of a 3500–4000-year-old core of Sanskrit, ancient Greek, and Latin. For younger families such as Romance, Germanic, Slavic, Turkic, Polynesian, Athabaskan, Algonquian, Quechuan—all around 2000 years in age—relatedness is unmistakable even to the nonlinguist, and some mutual intelligibility exists. Families aged closer to 6000 years, such as Uralic, Austronesian, and Semitic or Indo-European as judged only from modern attestations, exhibit genetic markers and cognate etyma that are not always evident to the nonspecialist.

STOCK   This is a commonly used term for a maximal reconstructable clade, i.e. the oldest families displaying regular sound correspondences and amenable to Neogrammarian comparative method. A stock usually displays several genetic markers. The oldest known stocks are about 6000 years old: e.g. Indo-European, Uralic, and Austronesian.

If a family or a language isolate has no demonstrated kin and does not enter into any demonstrable stock, then it also constitutes its own stock. For technical clarity it can be called a stock-level family or stock-level isolate. A standard reference work using terminology of this sort is Wurm & Hattori (1983). Any isolate lower group is counted as a stock when taking a census of stocks. For instance, two or three stocks are indigenous to Western Europe: Indo-European, Basque (an isolate), and, marginally, Semitic (represented by Maltese).

QUASI-STOCK   A quasi-stock is a quasi-genetic or probabilistic grouping of more than one stock which shares one or more features that are valid or promising genetic markers but which have few clear cognates and for which systematic regular sound correspondences cannot be demonstrated. Hence a quasi-stock is a probable clade but not a fully describable one and is not amenable to reconstruction. Linguistic understanding of what constitutes a promising genetic marker is still evolving and changing the received view of what is a promising quasi-stock.

The type-defining example is probably Niger-Kordofanian, a set of families and stocks mostly of sub-Saharan Africa including the Bantu family (Bendor-Samuel 1989, Greenberg 1963), discussed below. The genetic marker of Niger-Kordofanian is its complex systems of generally prefixal genders (also called concord classes), in which there are particular prefixes for particular classes and systematic correspondences between singular and plural concord classes. The system is shared widely among the daughter branches and is identifiable as a system even when individual elements are greatly changed or lost. This kind of gender system is quite specific and quite rare worldwide and thus useful as a genetic marker. Yet systematic sound correspondences and regular lexical reconstructability are absent from Niger-Kordofanian, the internal structure of the genetic tree is still in doubt (cf overview chapters in Bendor-

Samuel 1989), and whole subgroups lack the gender system. The usual interpretation is that at least the gender-using branches are sisters descendant of a lineage so ancient that little detectable shared material survives apart from the distinctive gender system.

An atypically stock-like quasi-stock is Afroasiatic, another African group established by Greenberg (1963). It consists of the families Chadic and Berber, the isolate Egyptian, the Semitic stock, a likely isolate Beja, a stock or pair of stocks Cushitic, and possibly the family Omotic (see e.g. Bender 1989, Newman 1980). The Afroasiatic quasi-stock has a distinctive grammatical signature that includes several morphological features at least two of which independently suffice statistically to show genetic relatedness beyond any reasonable doubt (the entire set is listed in Newman 1980; for statistical significance, see Newman 1980 and Nichols 1996). Hence it is routinely accepted as a genetic grouping, though uncontroversial regular correspondences cannot be found and a received reconstruction may never be possible [recent serious attempts are Orel & Stolbova (1995) and Ehret (1995); both are controversial]. Its age is quite uncertain, though clearly older than that of classic stocks like Indo-European because some of the component branches are themselves stocks of Indo-European-like age. An estimate of 10,000 years is sometimes cited (e.g. Newman 1980).

Quasi-stocks can also be detected by lexical tests. Among the several cases of clear significance for known sisters and chance-level correspondences for random pairs of languages, the pairing of Indo-European and Uralic stands out as near-significant (Ringe 1997), though there are no genetic markers in the grammatical structure.

STRUCTURAL POOL   This term, which I use ad hoc in this chapter, labels any group of stocks exhibiting some property or set of properties that is unusual or infrequent worldwide, though not so unusual or of such low probability as to be a genetic marker. The click languages of southern Africa have click consonants root-initially in most of their major-class words (nouns, verbs, adjectives) and nowhere else. This defines a structural canon type, not a genetic grouping (the click languages consist of one small family, two probable isolates, and possibly a third isolate; see below), but it is found nowhere else on earth. In fact, clicks themselves are found nowhere on earth except in these click languages and, sporadically and with a different distribution, in a few of their neighbors from the Bantu family and one Cushitic neighbor. (For clicks, see Ladefoged & Maddieson 1996.) This distribution is clearly nonrandom and testifies to some kind of historical interaction or connection among the click languages, but not to genetic relatedness.

Another structural pool is the set of stocks hugging the Pacific Rim of the Americas that exhibit personal pronoun systems with *n* in first person forms and/or *m* in the second person. Personal pronouns are normally inherited and almost never borrowed, but the *n:m* system is too small and too fraught with potential phonosymbolism and inflated probability of occurrence due to allomorphy and the cross-linguistic high frequency of nasals to be a good genetic marker. Dozens of languages and one or two dozen stocks with such systems, however, are found in the American Pacific Rim, the geographical skewing is highly significant, and other low-frequency features cluster there as well. Although not a demonstrable clade, the cluster is nonrandom and has some kind of historical identity (Nichols & Peterson 1996).

There are approximately 300 separate stocks on earth, which further comparative work may reduce to as few as 200 quasi-stocks, some of which will surely prove to be true stocks. The tests described above offer the prospect of being able to extend the fade-out point regularly to the time depth represented by the age of Afroasiatic or Indo-Uralic; reducing the world's stocks to 200 will require reaching such a time depth. (Estimates of these time depths are usually in the vicinity of 10,000 years.) Given present knowledge of language change and probability, however, descent and reconstruction will never be traceable beyond approximately 10,000 years. Methods now being developed reach back much earlier but do not trace descent. Among other things, this means that linguistics will never be able to apply phylogenetic analysis to the question of when language arose and whether all the world's languages are descended from a single ancestor.

Diversification

The rate at which languages diverge into dialects and then into daughter languages, and so on, is not constant, nor is the number of dialects or daughter languages, though whether they are relatively many or few depends on ascertainable cultural and historical factors, described below. Rates of change are accelerated by contact with other languages: The more profound the influence, the more rapid the change. There is no generally useful unit in terms of which grammar change might be measured. Lexical change is commonly measured by loss of items from a standard 100- or 200-word list of basic glosses. (Loss occurs when a word either changes meaning or drops out of use entirely.) A proposed constant rate of loss (for recent textbook summaries, see Crowley 1992; Trask 1996) makes it possible to estimate ages of families. This metric is called *glottochronology*. As the rate of vocabulary loss is not absolutely regular, accuracy is improved by computing retention percentages for larger numbers of daughter languages and by adjusting the constant for known areal effects or isolation. Embleton (1986, 1991) has proposed a different formula based on the number of adjacent languages, replacement rate in the basic word lists of the languages at issue, number of borrowings between the languages, and a measure of overall similarity between them; this method gives excellent accuracy for the language families Embleton has tested.

Glottochronology presupposes establishment of genetic relatedness and enough comparative work to distinguish cognate from noncognate vocabulary. Hence it is not valid in principle beyond the level of the stock, and even at that level it is not valid unless prior comparative work has been done.

For well-reconstructed families and under the right combination of circumstances, dating by comparison to dated archeological evidence can be quite accurate. The reconstructed Proto-Indo-European lexicon contains a sizable technical terminology for wheeled transport, terms for the major domesticated animals including the horse, but no clear terms for metals, all of which points to a date around 3500 BC (Anthony 1991, 1995; Mallory 1989). This in turn is consistent with glottochronological dates (Tischler 1973) and with the degree of differentiation exhibited by the earliest attested languages in the second and early first millennia BC.

Extinction

There are various causes of language death: the speech community is killed off, e.g. by genocide or natural disaster; the speech community is scattered; or the speech community abandons the language and shifts to another, as when Gauls shifted to Latin or Coptic speakers shifted to Arabic (for language shift, see Thomason & Kaufman 1988). The result for family trees is pruning, which may remove individual daughter languages (as when the Celtic branch of Indo-European lost Cornish through language shift to English) or entire branches (Indo-European has lost its Anatolian and Tocharian branches and others; the Afroasiatic quasi-stock has lost the Egyptian/Coptic branch). The death of a language isolate causes an entire lineage to die out, as has happened in historical times with Sumerian, Elamite, Etruscan, Iberian, northern Pictish, and no doubt countless others. Language spreads of all kinds cause extinction of languages previously in the area, usually through language shift.

Language shift usually involves an intermediate stage of society-wide bilingualism. It is favored when the target language is economically useful or functions as a vehicle of interethnic communication, or when the shifting community is accepting of linguistic variation (Hill 1996).

Language extinction by natural disaster and language shift are natural processes that have always gone on. Consequently, the branching rates in family trees drawn for surviving languages are not diversification rates but survival rates. Survival rates are less than diversification rates because there is always a nonzero probability of extinction, and this entails that older genetic groupings and more ancient nodes in family trees have, on average, fewer initial branches than younger ones. The only cross-linguistic survey of branching done so far (Nichols 1990) finds that stocks have, on average, about 1.5 initial branches; that is, many stocks are stock-level families or stock-level isolates.

Contact and Convergence

Languages whose speech communities are in contact acquire words, sounds, and even elements of grammatical structure from one another in what is known as *contact-induced change* (Thomason & Kaufman 1988). For the most part this has no impact on family tree structure or determination of descent, but in the occasional extreme case there is language mixture, in which one language can be seen as descended from two ancestral languages (examples include Mitchif, descended from both Cree and French, in southern Canada and the northern United States).

Languages long in contact can retain their discrete identities but come to re-semble each other in sound structure, lexicon, and/or grammar. The resultant structural approximation is called *convergence,* and—especially when there is extensive and stable bilingualism or multilingualism—a set of languages showing convergence is called a *linguistic area* or *Sprachbund.* Well-known examples are the Balkan peninsula, the Caucasus, the Pacific Northwest of North America, Arnhem Land in Australia, and Mesoamerica (for major case studies, see Campbell et al 1986, Emeneau 1956, Heath 1978, Masica 1976, Ross 1996). A linguistic area is a population and even in some sense a speech community. Population formation through contact is not modeled with trees; it is sometimes described as requiring a *wave model* because the diffusion and adaptation involved in convergence are propagated in geographical space (see Trask 1996, 183ff).

Structural pools are likely to be dissipated former convergence sets and/or to contain ancient sisters whose inherited commonalities have faded away be-yond the threshold of proof. At great time depths, it is impossible to distinguish between the two.

Within the geographical ranges of languages and even shallow language families, centers of political and economic importance are normally also cen-ters of dialect or language prestige and epicenters from which linguistic inno-vations spread outwards. The spread involves adoption of the innovation and abandonment of the previous locution by speakers and local speech communi-ties progressively farther from the center of innovation. Archaisms and archaic dialects then survive at the periphery of the area. (For these and other principles of linguistic geography, see Andersen 1988.) For instance, the spread of Inca empire from Cuzco also entailed the spread of a Quechuan dialect over a wider pre-Inca Quechua range. The modern result is a family tree in which one branch originated in the center of the Quechua range and the original range of the other extends both north and south (Mannheim 1985, summarizing earlier work). The same kind of geographical configuration usually accompanies the formation of a literary standard dialect. The same principle of innovating center and archaic periphery accounts for the essential geographical dynamics in all kinds of language spread and can be applied to the description of relations between languages, between families, and even between nonsisters or groupings of unknown phylogenetic status.

Genetic Density in Linguistics

Whether it is stocks, families, or languages that are counted, linguistic clades are not evenly distributed across the earth; their density shows highly significant skewings (Austerlitz 1980; Nichols 1990, 1992). The ratio of stocks to millions of square kilometers ranges from one to three for Africa and Eurasia, 10–20 for Australia and Central and South America, and over 100 for New Guinea (with its 60–80 stocks on less than a million square kilometers). The universal determinants of these differences are geographical and political-economical. Densities are higher in coastal regions, at lower latitudes, and in wetter and less seasonal climates; they are lower in continental interiors, at high latitudes, and in dryer and seasonal climates. Thus the densities of stocks or families are low, and the range of each is large, in such places as the central Eurasian steppe, the Eurasian and American arctic and subarctic, and the arid interior of Australia; they are high in (moist, tropical, mostly coastal) New Guinea, higher in California and Oregon than in Washington and British Columbia, and high in the Amazon basin. Densities are lower in complex societies, agricultural societies, and especially areas with a long history of empire; and they are higher in smaller and simpler societies. Hence they are higher in California than in Mesoamerica, and higher in Mesoamerica and the ancient Near East (both with young traditions of statehood and empire) than in the modern Near East or modern Europe. Accordingly, densities are lower where population density is higher and vice versa. Essentially, linguistic density is highest in areas where small societies can be more or less autonomous on small territories (Austerlitz 1980; Mace & Pagel 1995; Nichols 1990, 1992).

These principles apply equally well in areas of earliest human inhabitation (Africa), continents colonized early (Australia), continents colonized recently (the Americas), and formerly glaciated areas colonized recently (northern Europe, North America); to continents with no evident recent colonization (Australia) and those with evidence of multiple colonization continuing until recent millennia (New Guinea, the Americas). Thus, neither time settled nor number of colonizations has any appreciable effect on genetic density, which is determined entirely by geography, population density, and economy.

Stock density, especially as viewed over time, is the most visible attribute distinguishing two different kinds of language areas: *spread zones* and *accretion zones* (Nichols 1992, 1997c, 1998). An accretion zone (termed *residual zone* in previous works, but *residual* has an unrelated technical sense) is an area where genetic and structural diversity of languages are high and increase over time through immigration. Examples are the Caucasus, the Himalayas, the Ethiopian highlands and the northern Rift Valley, California, the Pacific Northwest of North America, Amazonia, northern Australia, and of course New Guinea. Languages appear to move into these areas more often than they move out of them. Kaufman (1990, p. 35) describes parts of South America as *sumps* or *invasion zones,* areas most of whose languages have originated elsewhere. This is a more precise notion than accretion zone: There are several different invasion zones within Amazonia, while the entirety of Amazonia can probably be described as a single accretion zone. Accretion zones generally contain representatives of major stocks in the vicinity as well as some languages with no outside kin. In the Caucasus, for instance, are found three indigenous stocks and representatives of two branches of Turkic and two branches of Indo-European.

A spread zone is an area of low density where a single language or family occupies a large range, and where diversity does not build up with immigration but is reduced by language shift and language spreading. A conspicuous spread zone is the grasslands of central Eurasia, in which, at roughly 2000-year intervals, four different spreads have carried different language families across the entire steppe and desert as well as into central Europe and Anatolia: Proto-Indo-European, Iranian, Turkic, Mongolian (discussed below). Another spread zone is central and southern Australia, in which the Pama-Nyungan quasi-stock has undergone several spreads to cover most of the continent (e.g. Evans & Jones 1997, McConvell 1996a,b). Another is northern Africa. Another is the Great Basin of the western United States, where the Numic branch of Uto-Aztecan spread from the Sierra slopes in the southwest of the range within the past two millennia (Bettinger & Baumhoff 1982, Lamb 1958, Madsen & Rhode 1994).

The dynamic of a spread zone is much like that of a dialect area. There is a locus or "center," rarely at the literal center of the range and usually at an edge, from which the language or family spreads. The locus of the various spreads on the Eurasian steppe is at the eastern edge of the range, in Central Asia; that of Pama-Nyungan is its northeastern corner; that of the Numic spread is in its southwestern corner. (These spreads are discussed below.) In a spread zone there is a general trajectory of spread: east and north in the Great Basin, west in the Eurasian steppe, south and west in Australia. At the periphery of a spread zone, remnant languages may survive from previous spreads. At the western periphery of the steppe, the Iranian language Ossetic survives from before the spread of Turkic. Possible remnants surviving from before the Numic spread are the languages of the pueblos to the east and the Maiduan and Washo languages of the Sierras to the north (Aikens 1994).

The fact that spreads are accompanied by extinction and that remnants survive, if at all, as isolates at the edges of spread zones, together with the general paucity of high-level branching structure in language families in accretion zones, explains why there are so few good candidates for quasi-stocks and so few genetic groupings of great age. Regular processes of extinction have turned the majority of stocks into isolates.

Hill (1996) proposes an anthropological dialectology that explains the different linguistic distributions of accretion and spread zones, and bunched vs extended language patterns more generally. The movement of linguistic variables of all kinds—phonemes, words, whole languages—across human populations depends on the relative dominance among speakers of two stances toward that variation: *localist* and *distributed.* The localist stance hinders the spread of variables, while the distributed stance favors them. "People with secure primary claims on essential resources are more likely to favor localist stances, while people who lack adequate primary claims and draw instead on a diverse range of secondary or indirect claims are more likely to favor distributed stances." Hence laissez-faire attitudes toward dialectal variation and weak language loyalty are favored by precarious economic circumstances.

LANGUAGE MOVEMENT AND SPREAD

Family Tree Structure and Language History

Certain family tree structures result from particular historical situations. Minimal branching—as in an isolate or stock-level shallow family—points to extinction of the rest of the family. Isolates and near-isolates are most common at edges of spreads where they represent remnants: in mountain highlands, where they are islands surrounded by languages of lowland families (e.g. Burushaski, an isolate of the Himalayas whose lower neighbors are Iranian); at coasts and continental peripheries (Basque; isolates Nivkh and Ainu in eastern Asia); between two spreads, where remnants can be trapped (Ket, the sole survivor of the Yeniseian family, trapped between Uralic to the west and Tungusic to the east); and, occasionally, as islands within spreads [Yukagir, a remnant of a former spread over much of eastern Siberia, now whittled down to small islands in northeastern Siberia as a result of Evenki and Yakut spreads; for the seventeenth-century range of Yukagir, see Levin & Potapov (1964, p. 5)].

Multiple branching at or near the root of a tree points to abrupt dispersal of the protolanguage in a large spread. The Indo-European family tree had up to a dozen major branches, all of which separated within about the first millennium of this 6000-year-old family's history (for the order of separation, see Taylor et al 1995, Warnow et al 1996). The initial diversification of the Austronesian tree may have been into three distinct Formosan branches plus Malayo-Polynesian (Pawley & Ross 1993, p. 435), pointing to rapid dispersal.

When a language family has dispersed gradually and in a more or less constant direction, its family tree assumes a distinctive, consistently left- or right-branching shape. Right and left have no theoretical place in phylogenetic trees, but for some families it is possible to exploit right and left and draw a tree that neatly projects onto a map of the daughter languages in real space. The Uralic family tree, for example, has an initial bifurcation into Finno-Ugric vs Samoyedic, and the root can be positioned over the region east of the Urals where Finno-Ugric and Samoyedic meet. Finno-Ugric bifurcates into Finnic and Ugric, and this node is positioned over the Urals where the two branches meet. Finnic bifurcates into Permian and others west (i.e. left) of the Urals; one or more branches split off farther west in the vicinity of the Volga; and finally the westernmost (leftmost) Baltic Finnic branch diversifies—into Finnish, Estonian, and others—near the Baltic coast. This is a west-branching (or left-branching) tree whose nodes and branches coincide remarkably well with the distribution of the daughter languages in real space. The westward branching is the result of consistent westward movement from a homeland in the vicinity of the Urals across northern Europe. A right-branching tree is that of the eastern Malayo-Polynesian branch of Austronesian, which when positioned over a map puts down daughter branches from progressively lower nodes as the seafaring early Austronesians moved eastward from island Southeast Asia through Melanesia and along the Solomon Island chain to the open ocean and thence out to Polynesia. For both the Uralic and the Austronesian trees, the distinctive aspect is the skewing, with the root of the tree close to one edge of the range on the map. This skewing is the result of a long-standing and consistent directionality of spread.

The projection of the root of the phylogenetic tree onto the ground in a map is known as the *center of gravity* in linguistic geography. The protohomeland of a language family is assumed to lie in the vicinity of its center of gravity (Diebold 1960, Dyen 1956, Sapir 1949), a principle that puts the homeland near the eastern edge of the range for Uralic, near the western edge for Austronesian, but in the center of the range for Slavic, which spread radially from central Europe. In spread zones, this principle works reliably only for the most recent spread. As soon as the next spread overtakes the center of gravity of the former spread, the apparent center of gravity shifts toward the far end of the range. Consider the Turkic family, whose modern center of gravity is in the western part of its range, near the middle Volga where Chuvash, the sole survivor of the Bulgar branch, meets Tatar of the other branch. The homeland, however, is known from historical sources to have been at the eastern edge of the Turkic range, near Mongolia. The Iranian family, which spread before Turkic, has two modern centers of gravity: one in the mountains south of Central Asia and one south of the Caucasus, both representing peripheral pile-ups and not the actual homeland, which was in the eastern steppe. Indo-European had early centers of gravity in central Europe, the Balkans, and western Anatolia, but these too are pile-ups and not the homeland. The modern Indo-European center of diversity is in the Balkan peninsula, and descendants of the earliest surviving offshoot, Italo-Celtic (Taylor et al 1995), are now found at the farthest periphery of the Indo-European range. [These examples from the Eurasian steppe are discussed in Nichols (1997c).] Thus family trees of early dispersants in continuing spread zones show inverted centers of gravity.

There are three known mechanisms of language spread: language shift (see Thomason & Kaufman 1988), demographic expansion (e.g. Bettinger & Baumhoff 1982, Madsen & Rhode 1994), and migration (Anthony 1990). There are probably no pure cases: Language shift is normally in response to the presence of at least a few influential immigrants; demographic expansion involves some absorption of previous population rather than extermination; and migration leads to language shift (either to or from the immigrants' language). The terms *language shift, demographic expansion,* and *migration* refer to the predominant contributor with no claim that it is exclusive. Almost all literature on language spreads assumes, at least implicitly, either demographic expansion or migration as basic mechanism, but in fact language shift is the most conservative assumption and should be the default assumption. There is no reason to believe that the mechanism of spread has any impact on the linguistic geography of the spread, but it has major implications for whether we expect to find linguistic substratum effects (which should occur with language shift but not with demographic expansion) and what degree of (biological) genetic admixture we expect to find as a consequence of spreading.

Geographical Factors

In addition to the large spread zones associated with high latitudes and arid interiors, other general tendencies of language movement can be discerned for particular geographical environments.

MOUNTAINS   Midlatitude mountains in settled agricultural areas, in historical and protohistorical times, exhibit a standard trajectory of language spread whereby lowland languages spread uphill, mountaintops are islands where remnant languages survive before being absorbed, and the mechanism of spread is "vertical bilingualism," whereby highland villagers know lowland languages but not vice versa (for the Caucasus, see Wixman 1980; for Central Asia, see Èdel'man 1980). The causal mechanism is climate: At least since the advent of the Little Ice Age in the late middle ages (Grove 1988), highland economies have been precarious, whereas the lowlands, with their longer growing seasons, are prosperous and offer markets and winter employment for the essentially transhumant male population of the highlands. Prior to the global cooling, lowlands were dry and uplands moist and warm enough for agricultural security. When highlands are economically secure, they are loci of linguistic spreads, upland dialects spread downhill, and highland clans or polities extend to form islands in lowland outposts (which can then grow into centers of dialect spread when economic fortunes shift). This generalization is based on clan origin traditions and language and dialect isoglosses in the central Caucasus (Nichols 1997b) and on evidence of highland spread of Quechua (Stark 1985) and verticality in the prehistoric and protohistorical Andes (Stanish 1992). Verticality of political economy is standardly assumed for the Andes (for more on the "vertical archipelago" of John Murra, see Masuda et al 1985), but Stanish also finds evidence for ethnic identity, and this implies language spread.

COASTLINE   Coastally adapted cultures can spread structural pools, linguistic areas, and even families far along coastlines. The various Austronesian languages of New Guinea are mostly coastal even after several millennia (see maps in Wurm & Hattori 1983). The Eskimoan spread across arctic North America to Greenland was initially entirely coastal and replaced the previous, also coastal, Dorset culture and language (Dumond 1984, Woodbury 1984). Austronesians and speakers of Eskimoan languages are coastally adapted peoples, and accordingly they have spread along coasts rather than inland. What is notable is the great extent of their coastal spreads. Earlier than these spreads is the extended spread from Beringia to South America, almost entirely along the Pacific coast, of the structural pool of languages identified by personal pronouns with first person n and second person m in addition to several other features (discussed above).

Coastal languages and language families often have discontinuous distributions. Sometimes these are due to known overwater migrations, as is the case with the various Austronesian enclaves of New Guinea. Intrusions of other languages have probably split some of the discontinuous coastal families of New Guinea (shown in Foley 1986, pp. 230–31; Wurm & Hattori 1983). The Yolngu branch of Pama-Nyungan (Australia) is isolated in northern Arnhem Land at some distance from the rest of the quasi-stock, whose distribution is otherwise monolithic (Blake 1988, Wurm & Hattori 1983), and the cause of this separation remains mysterious. Finally, accretion zones in the vicinity of coasts, like those of California and Oregon, contain languages that are geographically isolated and at some distance from their sisters; examples include the coastal Athabaskan languages of northern California and southern Oregon, distant from their relatives in Canada and Alaska. Movement of languages within accretion zones must be erratic overall and occasionally long-distance.

FOREST   The eastern forests of North America and much of pre-medieval Europe fostered sizable spreads and relatively low language diversity, comparable to that of the prairie and steppe. In seasonal and temperate climates, then, forests seem to harbor spread zones just as grasslands do. For tropical and subtropical forest the picture is less clear. High diversity is found in the Amazon basin, New Guinea, and central America, but much lower diversity is found in Africa, Southeast Asia, and eastern Australia. Perhaps the lower diversities were associated with more sedentary societies and higher population.

Economic and Political Factors

As noted above, complex societies, and especially states and empires, favor spreads and produce considerable linguistic extinction. There is a recurrent opinion in the literature that in small societies with small populations, diffusion and other influence occur easily, even to the extent that convergence can obscure family boundaries. Austerlitz (1991) notes—chiefly with reference to the Eurasian arctic and subarctic—that the combination of small population, short average lifespan, and frequent slavery and exogamy would entail a great deal of systematic multilingualism and allow for rapid vocabulary transfer. Hill (1996), citing Miller (1970), mentions that in small desert populations with shifting group membership, children would have lacked stable peer groups of age mates, the principal forum in which the individual speaker's dialect identity crystallizes. Sorensen (1985) notes the effect of linguistic and tribal exogamy in the upper Amazon. Heath (1978) and Ross (1996) present detailed case studies of the consequences of systematic bilingualism or multilingualism in Australia and New Guinea, respectively. In Australia, the consequence is a great deal of diffusion, which brings about a rough convergence piece by piece. In New Guinea, the sociolinguistic situation is different; an interethnic language influences an ethnic-specific language in vocabulary and grammar, and this gives rise to profound convergence. Hinton (1991), citing

Florence Shipek, describes systematic intertribal marriage in southern California with consequent substratal effect and language shift.

Does the initial spread of agriculture or herding result in the spread of the language of first farmers or pastoralists? Geneticists often maintain that it does and that the spread is demographic (Ammerman & Cavalli-Sforza 1984, Cavalli-Sforza et al 1994). In some cases, this may have occurred. The spread of Austronesian is widely associated with the spread of rice agriculture (Pawley & Ross 1993, pp. 442–43). However, in Mesopotamia, western Eurasia generally, and eastern North America, there is no evidence for associating any extant stock or quasi-stock with the spread of agriculture. In Mesoamerica, the likely candidate for original agriculturalists is the Mixe-Zoque stock, notable for its lack of spread (Hill 1996, Justeson & Kaufman 1993).

LINGUISTIC POPULATION HISTORIES FROM SELECTED CONTINENTS

This section is a brief survey of four continents to show how a consistent stock-based genetic classification affects statements of language distribution and language density, and how spread zones have affected language distributions. Major language spreads that have often been seen as demographic expansions or biological diffusions prove to be very ordinary cases of language shift in long-standing spread zones.

Africa

Languages of Africa are conventionally divided into four groupings, from south to north: click languages, Niger-Kordofanian, Nilo-Saharan, and Afro-asiatic [Bender (1989), Heine et al (1981), all with maps]. (In addition, on Madagascar there is Malagasy, a Western Malayo-Polynesian language with close kin in Borneo.) These four are not comparable and are not all genetic groups. The click languages include the Khoisan family in southern Africa and two or three isolates—Hadza and Sandawe in Kenya, possibly Kwadi in the southwest—and constitute a structural pool. Niger-Kordofanian is a quasi-stock, defined by the gender prefixes described above, and consists of the outlier Kordofanian family in the eastern Sahara and several west African stocks. The center of gravity for the entire quasi-stock is in west Africa, and that of the widespread Bantu family and its superordinates is in the northwest of its range (for Bantu, the vicinity of Cameroon). Three separate spreads have carried the Kordofanian outlier to the northeast, the Adamawa branch eastward in the north of the Congo basin, and the Bantu family east and south to cover most of the southern half of Africa. Thus, the distribution and prehistory of Niger-

Kordofanian suggest a long-standing epicenter of spread in west Africa, with spreads through the forest and well to the south that have obliterated any previous languages other than Khoisan in the far south. The Bantu spread is associated with the spread of the Iron Age in the east (Bouquiaux 1980), which may explain its far southern reach, but otherwise it is an unexceptional instantiation of the standing eastward language trajectory through spread-producing geography (interior forest and grassland). Its mechanism was neither migration nor expansion (Shaw et al 1993) but language shift, absorbing the results of previous spreads.

The eastern highlands of Ethiopia and Kenya and the central and northern Rift Valley are an accretion zone into which the eastern Bantu frontier has advanced and where isolate click languages, several Afroasiatic stocks, and several Nilo-Saharan stocks are found. Bender (1983) has found two other Ethiopian languages that may well be isolates. Nilo-Saharan is probably not a genetic grouping and not even a structural pool but is simply a residual grouping. A core set of its stocks identified by Bender (1983)—Nilotic, Nubian, Central Sudanic, Kunama-Ilit, Koman-Gumuz, and Kadugli—may constitute a structural pool or even a quasi-stock. The other Nilo-Saharan groups are probably unrelated families and isolates found across the Sahel and central to eastern Sahara.

The Afroasiatic quasi-stock (Diakonoff 1988, Greenberg 1963, Heine et al 1981, Newman 1980) stretches across north Africa and the Near East and into Ethiopia and Somalia. The center of gravity of Afroasiatic is in the vicinity of the Ethiopian highlands (see Blench 1993), but because the highlands are an accretion zone, the Sahara is a continuing spread zone, and Afroasiatic is ancient and an early dispersant, it can be assumed that Afroasiatic exhibits a center-of-gravity inversion with a peripheral pile-up in Ethiopia. An origin on the central to western Sahara is most likely on geographical grounds. The northwestern Sahara is where domestication of cattle and sheep is first attested (Clutton-Brock 1993; see also Phillipson 1993), and this is a logical Afroasiatic homeland.

In sum, Africa may have as many as 30 stocks and as few as 17 combined stocks and quasi-stocks. Spreads mostly from west to east have peripheralized most of the genetic and structural diversity in the eastern highlands and near the Rift Valley.

Western Eurasia

Most of this half-continent has been linguistically populated by successive rapid westward spreads originating in the steppe to the east and occurring at roughly 2000-year intervals: in reverse chronological order, Mongolian,

Turkic, Iranian, Indo-European (Nichols 1992, 1997c, 1988; for Indo-European, see also Anthony 1991, 1995; Mallory 1989). The northern forests in the same time frame have undergone only one spread, that of Uralic (bringing Estonian, Finnish, Saami, and others to northeastern Europe). The spreads mostly involved language shift, and each spread on the steppe absorbed the previous steppe languages, leaving remnants variously in central Europe, the Caucasus, and the Central Asian mountains. The Caucasus is an accretion zone with three unrelated indigenous stocks, of which Northeast Caucasian and Kartvelian have at least some structural affinities with ancient Mesopotamia and southwestern Asia, while Northwest Caucasian is radically unlike any other Eurasian stock in most respects. In far western Europe, Basque is an isolate, though with such southwest Asian affinities of structure that it could plausibly be a barely pre-Indo-European immigrant from the steppe. It is possible that no language presently found in or near Europe continues a pre-Neolithic indigene or a language of first agriculturalists.

Australia–New Guinea

The entire Australia–New Guinea landmass including the large Melanesian islands had been settled by about 40,000 BP and perhaps much earlier (Roberts & Jones 1994, White 1996). Colonization was by coastally adapted seafarers from insular southeast Asia and is believed to have been intentional and repeated. Overseas colonization has continued, and the most recent episodes are various coastal settlements of Austronesian-speaking peoples which have occurred at various times in the past four millennia (Pawley & Ross 1993, Spriggs 1995).

The entire south and east of modern Australia is a vast spread zone covered recently by languages of the Pama-Nyungan quasi-stock (Dixon 1980). Pama-Nyungan originated in the northeast of its range and spread by a combination of language shift and migration perhaps within the past six millennia (Evans & Jones 1997, McConvell 1996a,b). Northeastern Australia (southern Cape York), the likely Pama-Nyungan homeland, is a long-standing center of technological innovation (Morwood & Hobbs 1995), an area of deep divergence within Pama-Nyungan, and close to the Tangkic family, which represents a likely first sister to Pama-Nyungan (Evans 1995). The languages spoken by the first settlers of southern Australia have probably not survived, as these areas have been overrun probably more than once by spreads like that of Pama-Nyungan. The spread of Pama-Nyungan from the northeast through the drier regions does not explain why tropical Cape York and the forested eastern coastal strip are entirely Pama-Nyungan-speaking. On geographical grounds, genetic diversity should thrive in these areas. The lack of diversity suggests a dense and sedentary population.

The wetter and coastal north and northwest of Australia form an accretion zone in which a dozen or more stocks are found. These languages form a structural pool with those of coastal and especially northern New Guinea, which suggests an origin in relatively recent colonizations (Nichols 1997a). Hence it cannot be assumed that this area contains descendants of the earliest colonizers, though it contains the earliest archeological sites. Pama-Nyungan forms a structural pool with the languages of southeastern and highland New Guinea (for the New Guinea side, see Ross 1995), and on geographical and other evidence this pool is older than the coastal one. The distinction between coastal and interior strata goes back, on geographical grounds, to before the end of glaciation (Nichols 1997a).

Diffusion, multilingualism, convergence, and continent-wide areality occur on an unprecedented scale in Australia (e.g. Dixon 1980, Heath 1978). The degree of convergence even suggests genetic relatedness between Pama-Nyungan and some or all of the northern groups, at least to some investigators (Blake 1988, Dixon 1980, Evans 1988). Dixon offers potentially valid genetic markers in noun and verb paradigms, but their evidentiary value will depend on their distribution as a set among the various stocks and families. Sorting out convergence and inheritance at great time depths will require bottom-up reconstruction within genetic groupings.

The non-Austronesian languages of New Guinea and Melanesia present the greatest genetic density on earth, falling into perhaps 80 families and isolates (Foley 1986; M Donohue, unpublished surveys), the majority of which are likely to be independent stocks. Most of this diversity falls in the coastal stratum that disproportionately reflects the contributions of recent colonizations, and the Austronesian languages at least of the New Guinea mainland are fairly typical representatives of this stratum. Bilingualism in small communities has produced some cases of extreme convergence (Ross 1996), and continent-wide prevalence of certain structural features such as SOV word order (Foley 1986) also suggests convergence and certainly indicates contact-based change.

Thus in Australia–New Guinea, coastal languages have mingled and generally stayed near the coast, whereas interior language families have been decimated by spreads.

The Americas

There are about 150 separate stocks in the New World (Campbell & Mithun 1979; Goddard 1997; Kaufman 1990; Suárez 1974, 1983). Two well-described probable quasi-stocks [Hokan (Kaufman 1988), a grouping of up to a dozen stocks of California and Mexico; and Penutian, half a dozen stocks of

California and the Oregon plateau, and perhaps others] and a few other possible quasi-stocks reduce this diversity only slightly. The North American diversity is disproportionately clustered near the west coast, with several large eastward spreads extending from the coastal or intermontane west (Jacobsen 1989). The South American diversity is concentrated in the Amazon basin.

The most recent and most clearly traceable of the North American interior spreads is that of the Numic branch of Uto-Aztecan, which has spread from the Sierra foothills in the southwestern part of the Numic range to cover most of the Great Basin within the past two millennia. The anthropological literature generally assumes the spread to have been demographic expansion (Bettinger & Baumhoff 1982, Madsen & Rhode 1994), but the ecological context of the foothills-desert interface and the presumable sociolinguistics of such an interface indicate language shift (Hill 1996).

For the other two large spreads, the epicenters are also in the west, but their latitudes are uncertain. The Na-Dene stock consists of coastal Eyak and Tlingit in southern Alaska and northern British Columbia, and the widespread but young Athabaskan language family which stretches across interior Alaska and northern Canada and has coastal outliers in Oregon and northern California as well as a sizable interior outlier in Navajo and Apache of the southwestern United States. The center of gravity is on the southern Alaska coast where Tlingit, Eyak, and Alaska Athabaskan meet. Leer (1991) and Kari (1996) proposed a more southern origin, and Leer has presented evidence that unknown, now extinct coastal languages to the north were absorbed by the later Na-Dene spread. Ever since Sapir (1949), Na-Dene—the northernmost stock save Eskimo-Aleut—has been interpreted as the next-to-last entrant to the Americas, but on the evidence of linguistic geography, Na-Dene is not the latest pre-Eskimo entrant but merely the most recent subarctic spread. In any event, a shallow family like Athabaskan with a wide range in a spread zone can be assumed to have replaced earlier languages.

A still earlier spread is that of the Algic stock, represented by Yurok and Wiyot of the northern California coast (which are either independent Algic branches or a very deep branch) and the far-flung Algonquian family stretching from the western plains (e.g. Blackfoot) to the Atlantic coast (Micmac, Delaware). The center of gravity of Algonquian is in its western range (Goddard 1994), and that of Algic farther west. The Oregon-Washington plateau is a possible locus of spread, or at least a point from which Yurok and Wiyot could have moved coastward. On geographical grounds, Algic is near the Numic periphery on three sides (east, north, west) and could be the remnant of a pre-Numic spread in the Great Basin.

Whistler (1977) shows that the Penutian language families of California entered individually from the vicinity of the Oregon plateau and spread southward. The California and Oregon coastal Athabaskan languages have spread well to the south of any plausible homeland. These reconstructable histories suggest that language movement along the coast is erratic but southward overall, while the interior spreads move east and north. There is no geographical stratification that can identify the latest surviving pre-Eskimoan entrant, though it is likely to be coastal. If Proto-Athabaskan, dispersing only 2000 years ago, has daughters as far south as northern California and the Mexican border, there is no reason to assume that the necessarily much earlier pre-Eskimo entrant has remained in the north. The Pacific Rim structural pool is the result of a recent colonization episode, and its continuity essentially all around the Pacific indicates rapid spread.

CONCLUSION

Languages can move rather rapidly over human populations, and in most cases for which we have evidence, modern languages are spoken at some distance from where their ancestors originated. The combination of extinction in spread zones and convergence in accretion zones means that simple phylogenetic descent is insufficient for tracing the origin and dispersal of the world's languages and peoples. A natural task for joint linguistic-archeological investigation is tracing ancient spread zones, trajectories of movement, and densities of languages and human populations, as these have shaped modern ethnic distributions.

ACKNOWLEDGMENTS

I thank Victor Golla, James Kari, and Richard Rhodes for some bibliographical and factual references.

> **Visit the *Annual Reviews* home page at
> http://www.AnnualReviews.org.**

Literature Cited

Aikens CM. 1994. Adaptive strategies and environmental change in the Great Basin and its peripheries as determinants in the migrations of Numic-speaking peoples. See Madsen & Rhode 1994, pp. 35–43

Akazawa T, Szathmáry EJE, eds. 1996. *Prehistoric Mongoloid Dispersals.* Oxford: Oxford Univ. Press

Allen J, O'Connell JF, eds. 1995. *Transitions: Pleistocene to Holocene in Australia and Papua New Guinea. Antiquity* 69:Special No. 26

Ammerman AJ, Cavalli-Sforza LL. 1984. *The Neolithic Transition and the Genetics of Populations in Europe.* Princeton, NJ: Princeton Univ. Press

Andersen H. 1988. Center and periphery: adoption, diffusion, and spread. In *Historical Dialectology: Regional and Social*, ed. J Fisiak, pp. 39–83. Berlin: Mouton de Gruyter

Anthony DW. 1990. Migration in archeology: the baby and the bathwater. *Am. Anthropol.* 92:896–914

Anthony DW. 1991. The archeology of Indo-European origins. *J. Indo-Eur. Stud.* 19(3/4):193–222

Anthony DW. 1995. Horse, wagon, and chariot: Indo-European languages and archaeology. *Antiquity* 69:554–65

Austerlitz R. 1980. Language-family density in North America and Eurasia. *Ural-Altai. Jahrb.* 52:1–10

Austerlitz R. 1991. Alternatives in long-range comparison. See Lamb & Mitchell 1991, pp. 353–64

Bender ML. 1969. Chance CVC correspondences in unrelated languages. *Language* 45:519–36

Bender ML, ed. 1983. *Nilo-Saharan Language Studies.* East Lansing: Mich. State Univ. Press

Bender ML. 1989. Nilo-Saharan pronouns/demonstratives. In *Topics in Nilo-Saharan Linguistics*, ed. ML Bender, pp. 1–34. Hamburg: Buske

Bendor-Samuel J, ed. 1989. *The Niger-Congo Languages.* Lanham: Univ. Press Am.

Bettinger RL, Baumhoff MA. 1982. The Numic spread: Great Basin cultures in competition. *Am. Antiq.* 47(3):485–503

Blake BJ. 1988. Redefining Pama-Nyungan: toward the prehistory of Australian languages. *Aborig. Linguist.* 1:1–90

Blench RM. 1993. Recent developments in African language classification and their implications for prehistory. See Shaw et al 1993, pp. 126–38

Bouquiaux L, ed. 1980. *L'Expansion bantoue. Actes Colloq. Int. CNRS, Viviers, France, 4–16 Avril 1977.* Paris: Soc. Études Linguist. Anthropol. Fr.

Campbell L, Kaufman T, Smith-Stark TC. 1986. Mesoamerica as a linguistic area. *Language* 62:530–70

Campbell L, Mithun M, eds. 1979. *The Languages of Native America.* Austin: Univ. Tex. Press

Cavalli-Sforza LL, Menozzi P, Piazza A. 1994. *The History and Geography of Human Genes.* Princeton, NJ: Princeton Univ. Press

Clutton-Brock J. 1993. The spread of domestic animals in Africa. See Shaw et al 1993, pp. 61–70

Crowley T. 1992. *An Introduction to Historical Linguistics.* Auckland: Oxford Univ. Press. 2nd ed.

Diakonoff IM. 1988. *Afrasian Languages.* Moscow: Nauka

Diebold A. 1960. Determining the centers of dispersal of language groups. *Int. J. Am. Linguist.* 26:1–10

Dixon RMW. 1980. *The Languages of Australia.* Cambridge: Cambridge Univ. Press

Dumond DE. 1984. Prehistory: summary. See Sturtevant 1984, pp. 72–79

Durie M, Ross MD, eds. 1996. *The Comparative Method Reviewed: Regularity and Irregularity in Language Change.* New York/Oxford: Oxford Univ. Press

Dyen I. 1956. Language distribution and migration theory. *Language* 32:611–26

Edel'man DzhI. 1980. K substratnomu naslediju central'noaziatskogo jazykovogo sojuza. *Vopr. jazykozn.* 1980(5):21–32

Ehret C. 1995. *Reconstructing Proto-Afroasiatic (Proto-Afrasian): Vowels, Tone, Consonants, and Vocabulary.* Univ. Calif. Publ. Linguist. 126. Berkeley: Univ. Calif. Press

Embleton S. 1986. *Statistics in Historical Linguistics.* Bochum: Brockmeyer

Embleton S. 1991. Mathematical methods of genetic classification. See Lamb & Mitchell 1991, pp. 365–88

Emeneau MB. 1956. India as a linguistic area. *Language* 32:3–16. Reprinted in *Language and Linguistic Area*, ed. MB Emeneau, pp. 105–25. Stanford: Stanford Univ. Press

Evans ND. 1988. Arguments for Pama-Nyungan as a genetic subgroup, with particular reference to initial laminalization. *Aborig. Linguist.* 1:91–220

Evans ND. 1995. *A Grammar of Kayardild: With Historical-Comparative Notes on Tangkic.* Berlin: Mouton de Gruyter

Evans ND, Jones R. 1997. The cradle of the Pama-Nyungans. See McConvell & Evans 1997

Foley WA. 1986. *The Papuan Languages of New Guinea.* Cambridge: Cambridge Univ. Press

Goddard I. 1975. Algonquin, Wiyot, and Yurok: proving a distant genetic relationship. *Linguistics and Anthropology: In Honor of C. F. Voegelin*, ed. MD Kinkade, KL Hale, O Werner, pp. 249–62. Lisse: de Ridder

Goddard I. 1994. The west-to-east cline in Algonquian dialectology. *Actes Congr. Algonq., 25th*, ed. W Cowan, pp. 187–211. Carleton, Ott: Carleton Univ. Press

Goddard I. 1997. *Handbook of North American Indians*, Vol. 17, *Language.* Washington, DC: Smithson. Inst.

Greenberg JH. 1960. An Afro-Asiatic pattern of gender and number agreement. *J. Am. Orient. Soc.* 80(4):317–21

Greenberg JH. 1963. *The Languages of Africa.* Bloomington: Indiana Univ. Press

Grove AT. 1993. Africa's climate in the Holocene. See Shaw et al 1993, pp. 32–42

Grove J. 1988. *The Little Ice Age.* London: Methuen

Haas MR. 1958. Algonkian-Ritwan: the end of a controversy. *Int. J. Am. Linguist.* 24: 159–73

Haas MR. 1969. *The Prehistory of Languages.* The Hague: Mouton

Heath J. 1978. *Linguistic Diffusion in Arnhem Land.* Canberra: Aust. Inst. Aborig. Stud.

Heine B, Schadeberg TC, Wolff E, eds. 1981. *Die Sprachen Afrikas.* Hamburg: Buske

Hill JH. 1996. Languages on the land: toward an anthropological dialectology. David Skomp Lect., Dep. Anthropol., Indiana Univ., Mar. 21. Bloomington

Hinton L. 1991. Takic and Yuman: a study in phonological convergence. *Int. J. Am. Linguist.* 57(2):133–57

Hock HH. 1991. *Principles of Historical Linguistics.* Berlin: Mouton de Gruyter

Hock HH, Joseph BD. 1996. *Language History, Language Change, and Language Relationship. An Introduction to Historical and Comparative Linguistics.* Berlin: Mouton de Gruyter

Hoenigswald H. 1960. *Language Change and Linguistic Reconstruction.* Chicago: Univ. Chicago Press

Jacobsen WH Jr. 1989. The Pacific orientation of western North American languages. Presented at Circum-Pac. Prehist. Conf., 1st, Seattle

Justeson JS, Kaufman T. 1993. A decipherment of Epi-Olmec hieroglyphic writing. *Science* 255:606–8

Kari J. 1996. A preliminary view of hydronymic districts in Northern Athabaskan prehistory. *Names* 44(4):253–71

Kaufman T. 1988. A research program for reconstructing Proto-Hokan: first gropings. *Pap. Hokan-Penutian Lang. Workshop, 1988,* ed. S Delancey, pp. 50–168. Eugene: Dep. Linguist., Univ. Oreg.

Kaufman T. 1990. Language history in South America: what we know and how to know more. In *Amazonian Linguistics: Studies in Lowland South American Languages,* ed. DL Payne, pp. 13–73. Austin: Univ. Tex. Press

Klein HEM, Stark LR, eds. 1985. *South American Indian Languages: Retrospect and Prospect.* Austin: Univ. Tex. Press

Ladefoged P, Maddieson I. 1996. *The Sounds of the World's Languages.* Oxford: Blackwell

Lamb SM. 1958. Linguistic prehistory in the Great Basin. *Int. J. Am. Linguist.* 24(2): 95–100

Lamb SM. 1959. Some proposals for linguistic taxonomy. *Am. Linguist.* 1(2):33–49

Lamb SM, Mitchell ED, eds. 1991. *Sprung from Some Common Source: Investigations into the Prehistory of Languages.* Stanford: Stanford Univ. Press

Leer J. 1991. Evidence for a northern Northwest Coast language area: promiscuous number marking and periphrastic possessive constructions in Haida, Eyak, and Aleut. *Int. J. Am. Linguist.* 57(2):158–93

Levin MG, Potapov LP, eds. 1964. *The Peoples of Siberia.* Chicago: Univ. Chicago Press

Mace R, Pagel M. 1995. A latitudinal gradient in the density of human languages in North America. *Proc. R. Soc. London Ser. B* 261: 117–21

Madsen D, Rhode D, eds. 1994. *Across the West: Human Population Movement and the Expansion of the Numa.* Salt Lake City: Univ. Utah Press

Mallory JP. 1989. *In Search of the Indo-Europeans: Language, Archaeology, and Myth.* London: Thames & Hudson

Mannheim B. 1985. Southern Peruvian Quechua. See Klein & Stark 1985, pp. 481–515

Masica CP. 1976. *Defining a Linguistic Area: South Asia.* Chicago: Univ. Chicago Press

Masuda S, Shimada I, Morris C, eds. 1985. *Andean Ecology and Civilization.* Tokyo: Univ. Tokyo Press

McConvell P. 1996a. Backtracking to Babel: the chronology of Pama-Nyungan expansion in Australia. *Archaeol. Ocean.* 31: 125–44

McConvell P. 1996b. *Pama-Nyungan expansion: popular movement or movement of people?* Presented at Annu. Meet. Am. Anthropol. Assoc., 95th, San Francisco

McConvell P, Evans ND, eds. 1997. *Archaeology and Linguistics: Global Perspectives on Ancient Australia.* Melbourne: Oxford Univ. Press. In press

McMahon AM. 1994. *Understanding Language Change.* Cambridge: Cambridge Univ. Press

Miller W. 1970. Western Shoshoni dialects. In *Languages and Cultures of Western North America,* ed. E Swanson, pp. 17–36. Pocatello: Idaho State Univ. Press

Morwood MJ, Hobbs DR. 1995. Themes in the prehistory of tropical Australia. See Allen & O'Connell 1995, pp. 747–68

Moseley C, Asher RE, eds. 1994. *Atlas of the World's Languages.* London: Routledge

Newman P. 1980. *The Classification of Chadic within Afroasiatic.* Leiden: Universitaire Pers

Nichols J. 1990. Linguistic diversity and the first settlement of the New World. *Language* 66(3):475–521

Nichols J. 1992. *Linguistic Diversity in Space and Time.* Chicago: Univ. Chicago Press

Nichols J. 1995. Shaped by some common contingency: genetic and historical markers. Workshop Math. Methods Comp. Linguist., Inst. Res. Cogn. Sci., Univ. Pa.

Nichols J. 1996. The comparative method as heuristic. See Durie & Ross 1996, pp. 39–71

Nichols J. 1997a. Sprung from two common sources: Sahul as a linguistic area. See McConvell & Evans 1997

Nichols J. 1997b. Chechen phonology. In *Phonologies of Asia and Africa,* ed. AS Kaye, P Daniels, pp. 941–71. Bloomington, Ind: Eisenbrauns

Nichols J. 1997c. The epicenter of the Indo-European linguistic spread. In *Archaeology and Language 1: Theoretical and Methodological Orientations,* ed. RM Blench, M Spriggs, pp. 122–48. London: Routledge

Nichols J. 1998. The Eurasian spread zone and the Indo-European dispersal. In *Archaeology and Language 2,* ed. RM Blench, M Spriggs. London: Routledge. In press

Nichols J, Peterson DA. 1996. The Amerind personal pronouns. *Language* 72(2): 336–71

Orel V, Stolbova O. 1995. *Hamito-Semitic Etymological Dictionary.* Leiden: Brill

Oswalt RL. 1991. A method for assessing distant linguistic relationships. See Lamb & Mitchell 1991, pp. 389–404

Pawley A, Ross MD. 1993. Austronesian historical linguistics and culture history. *Annu. Rev. Anthropol.* 22:425–59

Phillipson DW. 1993. The antiquity of cultivation and herding in Ethiopia. See Shaw et al 1993, pp. 344–57

Ringe DA Jr. 1992. On calculating the factor of chance in language comparison. *Trans. Am. Philos. Soc.* 82:1

Ringe DA Jr. 1995a. 'Nostratic' and the factor of chance. *Diachronica* 12(1):55–74

Ringe DA Jr. 1995b. The "Mana" languages and the three-language problem. *Ocean. Linguist.* 34(1):99–122

Ringe DA Jr. 1996. The mathematics of "Amerind." *Diachronica* 13:1.135–54

Ringe DA Jr. 1997. A probabilistic evaluation of Indo-Uralic. In *Nostratic: Sifting the Evidence,* ed. B Joseph, J Salmons. Philadelphia: Benjamins. In press

Roberts RG, Jones R. 1994. Luminescence dating of sediments: new light on the human colonisation of Australia. *Austr. Aborig. Stud.* 1994(2):2–17

Ross MD. 1995. The great Papuan pronoun hunt: recalibrating our sights. In *Tales from a Concave World: Liber Amicorum Bert Voorhoeve,* ed. C Baak, M Bakker, D van der Meij, pp. 139–68. Dep. Lang. Cult. Southeast Asia Oceania, Leiden Univ.

Ross MD. 1996. Contact-induced change and the comparative method: cases from Papua New Guinea. See Durie & Ross 1996, pp. 180–217

Sapir E. 1913. Wiyot and Yurok, Algonkin languages of California. *Am. Anthropol.* 15:617–46

Sapir E. 1949. (1916). Time perspective in aboriginal American culture: a study in method. In *Selected Writings of Edward Sapir,* ed. DG Mandelbaum, pp. 389–467. Berkeley/Los Angeles: Univ. Calif. Press

Shaw T, Sinclair P, Andah B, Okpoko A, eds. 1993. *The Archaeology of Africa: Food, Metals, and Towns.* London: Routledge

Sorensen AP. 1985. An emerging Tukanoan linguistic regionality: policy pressures. See Klein & Stark 1985, pp. 140–56

Spriggs MJT. 1995. The Lapita culture and Austronesian prehistory in Oceania. In *The Austronesians: Historical and Comparative Perspectives,* ed. P Bellwood, J Fox, D Tryon, pp. 112–33. Dep. Anthropol., Res. Sch. Pac. Asian Stud., Aust. Natl. Univ.

Stanish C. 1992. *Ancient Andean Political Economy.* Austin: Univ. Tex. Press

Stark L. 1985. Ecuadorian highland Quechua: history and current status. See Klein & Stark 1985, pp. 443–80

Sturtevant WC, ed. 1984. *Handbook of North American Indians,* Vol. 5, *Arctic.* Washington, DC: Smithson. Inst.

Suárez JA. 1974. South American Indian languages. *Encycl. Br.*

Suárez JA. 1983. *The Mesoamerican Indian Languages.* Cambridge: Cambridge Univ. Press

Taylor A, Warnow T, Ringe DA Jr. 1995. Character-based reconstruction of a linguistic cladogram. *Proc. Int. Conf. Hist. Linguist.,* 12th, Manchester

Thomason S, Kaufman T. 1988. *Language Contact, Creolization, and Genetic Linguistics.* Berkeley/Los Angeles: Univ. Calif. Press

Tischler J. 1973. *Glottochronologie und Lexikostatistik. Innsbrucker Beiträge zur*

Sprachwissenschaft, Vol. 11. Innsbruck: Kowatsch

Trask RL. 1996. *Historical Linguistics.* London: Arnold

Voegelin CF, Voegelin FM. 1964–1966. Languages of the world. *Anthropol. Linguist.* 6:3–9; 7:1–2,4,7–9; 8:2–3,6–7

Warnow T, Ringe DA Jr, Taylor A. 1996. Reconstructing the evolutionary history of natural languages. *Proc. ACM-SIAM Symp. Discrete Algorithms*

Watkins C. 1985. *The American Heritage Dictionary of Indo-European Roots.* Boston: Houghton Mifflin

Whistler KW. 1977. Wintun prehistory: an interpretation based on linguistic reconstruction of plant and animal nomenclature. *Proc. Annu. Meet. Berkeley Ling. Soc.,*

3rd, ed. KW Whistler, RD Van Valin Jr, C Chiarello, JJ Jaeger, M Petruck, et al, pp. 157–74. Berkeley: Berkeley Linguist. Soc.

White JP. 1996. Paleolithic colonization in Sahul land. See Akazawa & Szathmáry 1996, pp. 303–8

Wixman R. 1980. *Language Aspects of Ethnic Patterns and Processes in the North Caucasus.* Univ. Chicago Dep. Geogr. Res. Pap. No. 191. Chicago: Univ. Chicago Press

Woodbury AC. 1984. Eskimo and Aleut languages. See Sturtevant 1984, pp. 49–63

Wurm SA, Hattori S, eds. 1983. *Language Atlas of the Pacific Area.* (Pac. Linguist. C-86). Canberra: Aust. Acad. Hum. Jpn. Acad.

Annu. Rev. Anthropol. 1997. 26:385–409
Copyright © 1997 by Annual Reviews Inc. All rights reserved

TRAFFICKING IN MEN: The Anthropology of Masculinity

Matthew C. Gutmann

Department of Anthropology, Brown University, Providence, Rhode Island 02912

KEY WORDS: masculinity, gender, difference, power, sexuality, change

---

ABSTRACT

Anthropology has always involved men talking to men about men, yet until fairly recently very few within the discipline had truly examined men *as men*. This chapter explores how anthropologists understand, utilize, and debate the category of masculinity by reviewing recent examinations of men as engendered and engendering subjects. Beginning with descriptions of four distinct ways in which masculinity is defined and treated in anthropology, special attention is paid to the relations of difference, inequality, and women to the anthropological study of masculinities, including the awkward avoidance of feminist theory on the part of many anthropologists who study manhood. Specific topics discussed include the diverse cultural economies of masculinity, the notion of cultural regions in relation to images of manhood, male friendship, machismo, masculine embodiment, violence, power, and sexual fault-lines.

CONCEPTUAL ISSUES

Anthropology has always involved men talking to men about men. Until recently, however, very few within the discipline of the "study of man" had truly examined men *as men*. Although in the past two decades the study of gender comprises the most important new body of theoretical and empirical work in the discipline of anthropology overall, gender studies are still often equated with women's studies.

It is the new examinations of men as engendered and engendering subjects that comprise the anthropology of masculinity today. There are at least four distinct ways that anthropologists define and use the concept of masculinity and the related notions of male identity, manhood, manliness, and men's roles. Marking the fluidity of these concepts, and frequently the regretable lack of theoretical rigor in approaching this issue, most anthropologists writing on this subject employ more than one of these concepts.

The first concept of masculinity holds that it is, by definition, anything that men think and do. The second is that masculinity is anything men think and do to be men. The third is that some men are inherently or by ascription considered "more manly" than other men. The final manner of approaching masculinity emphasizes the general and central importance of male-female relations, so that masculinity is considered anything that women are not.

In the anthropological literature on masculinity to date, much attention has been paid to how men in different cultural contexts perform their own and others' manhood. Herzfeld (1985, pp. 16, 47) wrote of the importance to men in a village on Crete of distinguishing between "being a good man" and "being *good at* being a man," because here it is the "performative excellence" of manliness that counts for more than merely being born male.

In his ethnographic study of "a masculine subculture" among the Sambia in New Guinea, Herdt (1994b, p. 1) seeks to present "how men view themselves as male persons, their ritual traditions, their females, and the cosmos...." The path to understanding Sambia masculinity, Herdt argued, therefore lies in paying close attention to Sambia male idioms, that is, what these men say about themselves as men. Further, in exploring male initiations among the Sambia, Herdt (1994b, p. 322) accentuates what he calls "an intense, phallic masculinity" such that the issue is not one of males striving for masculinity versus femininity but rather for a particular kind of masculinity that is, by its nature, only available to men to achieve. (See also Gregor's (1985) premise that among the Mehinaku of Brazil, as elsewhere, "male identity is anatomically based.") Nonetheless, Herdt (1994b, p. 17) wrote that while not "the public dogma" of men, for the Sambia "maleness itself emerges from femaleness."

In the first major study of manhood in anthropology, Brandes (1980) described how male identities develop in relation to women. In an examination of folklore and men in rural Andalusia, Brandes argued that even if women are not physically present with men while working or drinking, and even if they are not reflected in men's conscious thoughts, women's "presence" is a significant factor in men's own subjective understanding of what it means to be men. Discussing changing gender identities in working-class Mexico City, Gutmann (1996) also argued that most men during most of their lives view male identities in comparison with female identities.

Insufficient attention has actually been paid to men-as-men in anthropology (Godelier 1986, Ortner & Whitehead 1981), and much of what anthropologists have written about masculinity must be inferred from research on women and by extrapolation from studies on other topics.

In addition to different conceptual frameworks, two distinct topical approaches are evident in the anthropological study of masculinity. Some studies mainly treat men-only events like male initiation and sex between men, men-only organizations like men's cults, and men-only locations like men's houses and bars. Other studies include descriptions and analyses of women as integral to the broader study of manhood and masculinity. Exemplary of the first type is the widely read survey by Gilmore (1990). This study, functionalist in orientation, insists on ubiquitous if not necessarily universal male imagery in the world and on an underlying archetypal and "deep structure" of masculinity cross-culturally and transhistorically. The other approach has been to document the ambiguous and fluid nature of masculinity within particular spatial and temporal contexts, providing implicit evidence for Yanagisako & Collier's (1987) argument that there exists no unitary "man's point of view."

After tracing certain historical precedents for the contemporary study of masculinity, the review examines broader topics that anthropologists have recently related to men and manhood, such as national character; divisions of labor; family, kinship, and friendship ties; the body; and contests over power. In the absence of systematic theorization of masculinity, most studies of men-as-men in anthropology focus on only one or two of these topics, while by default they have created myriad and contradictory categories and definitions of men.

THE HISTORICAL MALE IN ANTHROPOLOGY

"An Arapesh boy grows his wife," wrote Mead (1963, p. 90). In like manner, anthropologists have historically grown their native men: Ethnographers' claims to discovering exotic (or ubiquitous) masculinity in the far reaches of the globe have always rested on the central contributions of anthropologists themselves in the creation of categories of maleness and its opposites in diverse cultural milieus. From Malinowski's (1929) interest in sexual drives (those of natives and anthropologists alike), male authority (and how it may reside in men other than the father), and the oedipal complex, to Evans-Pritchard (1974)—for whom, as Ardener (1989) famously wrote, women and cattle were both omnipresent and important, and equally mute—anthropologists have played a not insignificant role in the development and popularization of "native" definitions and distinctions regarding masculinity, femininity, homosexuality, and more. To what extent the views expressed have represented those of men, women, or anthropologists—or a combination of all these—is, in retrospect, far from clear.

As disciplinary anthropology was just taking shape, wider intellectual circles in Europe and the United States were experiencing what Mosse (1996, p. 78) calls the fin-de-siècle challenges to modern masculinity and men as the "unmarked" category: "'unmanly' men and 'unwomanly' women...were becoming ever more visible. They and the movement for women's rights threatened that gender division so crucial to the construction of modern masculinity." With all this sexual questioning, once again the call of the South Seas sirens proved too much for the impressionable Europeans. If men in Tahiti, for instance, were seen by some anthropologists as somehow freer in expressing their masculine sexuality, it was also believed that this was due in large measure to the rather childlike quality of men in these "primitive" settings.

Margaret Mead's work in the Pacific provided startling information that countered popular Western notions about adolescence and sexuality, and it threatened shibboleths there about masculinity and femininity as inherent qualities. Writing about the ambiguous and contradictory character of gender Mead (1963, p. 259) wrote: "We found the Arapesh—both men and women—displaying a personality that, out of our historically limited preoccupations, we would call maternal in its parental aspects, and feminine in its sexual aspects." In her elucidation of "the dilemma of the individual whose congenial drives are not provided for in the institutions of his culture," Ruth Benedict (1934, p. 262), too, chose to emphasize a diversity of masculinities and showed that homosexuality has historically been considered abnormal in only some societies.

Later anthropologists, including those associated in one way or another with the culture and personality school in World War II and in the 1950s, continued probing comparative similarities and differences concerning men's participation in child rearing, male personality structures, the masculine will to war, male rites of passage and socialization, penile symbolism, and more. Increasingly bifurcated models of man-woman dualisms were linked, in turn, to more "feminine" and more "masculine" national character traits (see Herman 1995). Regarding the unexamined premises of universal male domination and universal sex-role differences, no theories were as influential in the social sciences in the postwar period as those of Parsons & Bales (1955), who posited women as expressive (emotional) and men as instrumental (pragmatic, rational, and cognitive). Biology, ultimately, determined what men and women did differently in families. Generally "human nature" has been a code for the overarching importance of particular musculature and reproductive capacities, which in turn are believed by some to result inevitably in socioeconomic patterns relating to hunting and hearth (see also Friedl 1984).

Lévi-Strauss attempted to clarify certain central issues, yet it is noteworthy that in *Elementary Structures of Kinship* (1969a)—a classic that proved highly influential among the first generation of feminist anthropologists to embark on the full-fledged study of gender—he barely mentions categories such as men, masculinity, women, and femininity. Instead, men are as often as not referred to through euphemism; for instance, men are called "the givers of wives." As with early feminist anthropological studies in the 1970s, the earliest approaches to studying masculinity tended to depict an overly dichotomized world in which men were men and women were women, and women contributed as little to "making" men as men did to "making" women. Unlike these initial feminist studies of women in anthropology, however, which often sought to address, in part, women's previous "invisibility" in the canon, men have never been invisible in ethnography or theories of "mankind."

THE CULTURAL ECONOMIES OF MASCULINITY

In the past fifteen years, several ethnographies and edited volumes concerned with masculinity have appeared in English and other languages (on the latter, see Castelain-Meunier 1988, Fachel Leal 1992, Welzer-Lang & Pichevin 1992). Certain of these studies have been written by prominent anthropologists. The theoretical approaches and conclusions of these studies differ considerably, but the best have been good at asking specific questions about particular locales and historical situations, and most have avoided an ill-conceived "me-tooism" in reaction to feminist anthropology. Those who have attempted generalizations for entire "cultures" of supposedly homogeneous populations have tended to reinvent many of the same stale tags with which "men" (e.g. the men of urban Latin America, southern Spain, or the highlands of New Guinea) have often been stamped as representatives of one or another social-science paradigm.

Cultural Regions and Boundary Questions

Questions of virility and definitions of manliness have often been played out in the cultural confrontations between colonizer and colonized. As Stoler (1991, p. 56) concluded, "The demasculinization of colonized men and the hypermasculinity of European males represent principal assertions of white supremacy" (see also Fanon 1967). In part because of anthropology's own internal dynamics, and in part because of the exigencies of post–World War II empire rearrangements, the study of masculinity in anthropology has frequently been linked to cultural area studies. About "the ideals of manliness" in the circum-Mediterranean, for example, Gilmore (1990, p. 48) posited "three moral imperatives: first, impregnating one's wife; second, provisioning dependents; third, protecting the family." The argument is that these particular qualities and aims are in some significant fashion more marked in this culture area than elsewhere in the world. Anthropologists who are inclined to equate "the nation" exclusively with the men in these societies have, not surprisingly, also tended to minimize women's contributions to both masculinity and national traits. [See also Mernissi (1987) and Knauss (1987) on engendered ideals associated with Islam in the Middle East.]

In contrast, other scholars like Strathern find that in examining male-female relations some arguments about area peculiarities have been taken too far. Strathern (1988, p. 64) wrote, "Far too axiomatically, I believe, has the sex-role model held sway in anthropological analyses of [New Guinea] Highlands initiation and male-female antagonism" (see also Bowden 1984). Herdt & Stoller (1990, pp. 352–53) concluded that "[f]or the study of erotics and gender identity, cross-cultural data are still too impoverished and decontextualized to truly compare masculinity and femininity, sexual excitement, and fantasy constructs of people from different cultures." [For recent efforts in this direction, see Parker et al (1992) and Parker & Gagnon (1995).] In criticism of a free-standing "Mediterranean culture," Herzfeld (1987, p. 76) wrote that "Ethnographers may have unwittingly contributed to the creation of a stereotype" and created a self-fulfilling prophecy, an argument that may be extended to critique a cultural regionalism of masculinity.

Manhood and womanhood are culturally variable, and sexual practices and beliefs are contextual, yet cultural context does not generally equate to national culture traits. Further, most anthropologists writing about masculinity in the past two decades have found reason to discuss the transformations afoot in different cultural junctures: Herdt (1993, p. xxxii) wrote of "the egalitarian mode [that] was likely to be a cultural import of modernization" in New Guinea, while Keesing (1982, p. 16) noted potential "regional" reactions to Westernization like a possible "perpetuation or revival of male cultism." Brandes (1980, p. 11) noted that in Andalusia "social norms among people under the ages of twenty or twenty-five years seem to be departing abruptly from those held by their parents," and Herzfeld (1985) described modern "transformations" on Crete. On the whole, Gayle Rubin's (1975) emphasis on momentous transitions and changes in gender and sex relations is correct, as is her temporary reprieve from premature extermination for "the offending sex."

Throughout these ethnographic studies of men, the influence, often indirect, of certain key theoretical currents is evident, beginning with works by Marx and Freud (see Laqueur 1990) and continuing more recently with references to Foucault (1980a,b), Merleau-Ponty (1962), and Bourdieu (1990a,b; 1997).

Gender Divisions of Labor

Another element in the cultural economy of masculinity that merits attention concerns the marked differences in what men and women do in their daily chores and activities. Most ethnographers, following Durkheim's (1933) example, have sought to document these divisions of labor and on this basis make generalizations for cultural inequalities more broadly. Delaney (1991, p. 251), for example, wrote of engendered physical separation in a village in Turkey: "Besides sexual activity and eating, the only other activity in which men and women spend any extended time together is working in the *bahçe* (garden)," an indication of theologically ordained power inequalities between men and women in this area. Godelier (1986, p. 29) concluded that among the Baruya in New Guinea, gender divisions of labor presuppose rather than give rise to male dominance, as women are excluded from ownership of the land, important tools, weapons, and sacred objects among other things. A paper by Richard Lee (1968) showed that through the 1950s, at least, women's labor in gathering nuts and berries provided a far greater share of calories for the !Kung San in southern Africa than the hunting activities of the men, thereby furnishing evidence that women's contributions within this foraging society were greater not simply with respect to child rearing but in terms of adult sustenance as well. One salutary development in some recent gender studies is the attempt to describe and analyze divisions of labor not as formal and static ideal types but in their actually occurring and contradictory cultural and historical manifestations.

FAMILY

Kinship and Marriage

"Lévi-Strauss's account of the founding significance of the exchange of women," admonished Weeks (1985, p. 159), "already presupposes that it is men who, as naturally promiscuous, are in a position to exchange their women." Although certain anthropologists have presented supporting evidence unblemished by contradiction or nuance to support Lévi-Strauss's foundational theory regarding the male exchange of women, others have found reason to question such a uniform description of marriage. Exploring gender relations in nineteenth-century Malay society, Peletz (1996, p. 88) showed that "in practice, though not necessarily in local (official) ideology, men were being exchanged by women and not by other men." Conceptual attention is drawn by Peletz (1996, p. 97) in particular to Lévi-Strauss's "preoccupation with *forms* of exchange and his relative neglect of the *contents* and *strategies* of exchange."

In his work on matrifocality in Guyana, Raymond Smith (1956) reconceptualized the power dynamics within households, of heredity, and quite simply of "men's place" in the lives of many families. [For more recent treatment of these issues, see Brana Schute (1979).] Lomnitz & Pérez-Lizaur (1987) found that among the elites of Mexico City, "centralizing women" and the preeminence of the "grandfamily" reveal a great deal about the limits of male power, not only in the families themselves but more generally in the companies these families own and manage. With regard to kin terms, Carol Stack's (1974) study of African-American women in southern Illinois was among the first to challenge easy understandings of the identifiers "mother" and "father." Stack found that men's roles as fathers primarily depended not on their relations with the children but rather on the men's ongoing relations with the children's mothers.

Parenting—Fathering

Beginning with John and Beatrice Whiting's studies of child rearing in the 1950s, the meanings of fatherhood and the practices of fathers have been examined in detail cross-culturally. By documenting father absence, circumcision rites, male initiation rites, children's sleeping arrangements, status-envy, and what has been too loosely termed hypermasculinity and supermasculinity, the Whitings and their students, colleagues, and critics have written on the biological parameters within which cultural diversity may flourish in human societies (see, for example, Broude 1990, Cath et al 1989, Hollos & Leis 1989, Parker & Parker 1992, West & Konner 1976, Whiting 1963, Whiting & Whiting 1975, Whiting et al 1958).

Evidence of the variety of fathering experiences is plentiful in anthropology. Writing about rural Ireland in the 1970s, Scheper-Hughes (1979, p. 148) explained that far from being naturally inept at parenting, "men are socialized into feeling extremely inadequate and clumsy around babies." In her later work in a shantytown in northeast Brazil, Scheper-Hughes (1992, pp. 323–25) wrote that "fathers" are the men who provide babies with powdered milk, popularly referred to as "father's milk," and that through this gift the symbolic legitimacy of a child is established. Taggart's (1992) work in the Sierra Nahua region of Mexico shows that, until recently, most children slept with their father and not their mother from time of weaning until puberty. In his quantitative survey of paternal infant care among the Aka Pygmy, Hewlett (1991, p. 168) reported that "Aka fathers spend 47 percent of their day holding or within an arm's reach of their infants, and while holding the infant, [the] father is more likely than [the] mother to hug and kiss the infant." [See also Read (1952) for an early paper on the affairs of Gahuku-Gama men and Battaglia (1985) on Sabarl paternal nurturance in New Guinea.]

Gutmann (1996) draws on Lewis (1963) and others in tracing the historical pattern in rural Mexico, whereby men play a more significant role in rearing sons than is possible among urban proletarians. Nonetheless, he concluded that for numerous men and women in squatter communities in Mexico, active, consistent, and long-term parenting is a crucial element in what it means to be a man and what men do.

Highlighting issues of class and history, and the contradictions of fathering in New York City, Bourgois (1995, p. 316) quoted a young Puerto Rican man:

> I went out with this lady on 104th Street for three years; she got five kids; none of them are mine; and I used to look out for them, bro. On school days, I used to buy them their first day of school clothes, and all that shit. You shoulda seen me, how I was stealing car radios, like a madman. Breaking into cars—getting three, four, five radios in one night—just to buy them new sneakers.

Male Friendship

The subject of male spaces, men's segregation, and what Sedgwick (1985) calls homosociality has received ethnographic recognition but little systematic analysis. In men's secret houses in various societies (Poole 1982; Tuzin 1982, 1997), in male-only enclaves such as coffee houses or places to consume alcohol with others (Brandes 1987, Cowan 1990, Duneier 1992, Herzfeld 1985, Jardim 1992, Lewgoy 1992, Limón 1994, Marshall 1979), in the dependent relations of *cuatismo* and "commensal solidarity" (see Lomnitz 1977 and Papataxiarchis 1991, respectively) and unemployment among working-class youth (see Willis 1979), and in men's sports (see Alter 1992, Wacquant 1995a,b), men's exclusivity has been documented far better than it has been understood. Applying the work of Bourdieu on the body (e.g. 1990a), Wacquant's (1997) studies of "(heterosexual) *libido sexualis*" and "(homoerotic) *libido pugilistica*" among African-American boxers in Chicago are notable for theorizing about masculinity (and what makes some men more "manly") and male bodies as well as for ethnographic detail.

A central theme in discussing men's friendship is "male bonding," a term invented by the anthropologist Lionel Tiger (1984, p. 208) with the explanation that "men 'need' some haunts and/or occasions which exclude females." Despite the fact that the phrase "male bonding" has entered into common parlance in the United States as a shorthand description of male camaraderie (and is often used in a snickering manner), Tiger coined the term in an attempt to link supposedly inherent drives on the part of men (as opposed to women) to show solidarity for one another. "Male bonding," Tiger (1984, p. 135) wrote, is a trait developed over millennia, "a process with biological roots connected...to the establishment of alliances necessary for group defence and hunting."

Connell (1995, p. 46) historicizes Tiger's male bonding theory: "Since religion's capacity to justify gender ideology collapsed, biology has been called in to fill the gap." Thus, with their male genes, men are said to inherit tendencies to aggression, family life, competitiveness, political power, hierarchy, promiscuity, and the like. The influence of so "naturalized" an analysis extends far beyond the halls of anthropology and the academy to justify and promote the exclusion of women from key male domains. In the New Men's Movement in the United States (for an ethnography of this movement, see Schwalbe 1996; for its philosophy, see Bly 1990), masculinity as biological given, authenticated through genitalia and pop anthropology, is raised to the level of mystical bonding.

THE BODY

Somatic Faultlines

The erotic component to male bonding and rivalry is clearly demonstrated in many new studies on same-sex sex. Weston's (1993) paper on lesbian and gay studies in anthropology is the best review to date of how the discipline has approached this subject; here I highlight only a few additional points. Many studies in the anthropology of masculinity have as a central component the reporting and analysis of some kind of sexual relations, attractions, and fantasies between males (Almaguer 1991; Carrier 1995; Cohen 1995a,b; Herdt 1982, 1987, 1994b; Lancaster 1992, 1997a,b, 1998; Parker 1991; Roscoe 1991; Wilson 1995). Of great importance theoretically, the term "homosexuality" is increasingly out of favor, seen as too culturally narrow in meaning and implication (see Elliston 1995). As Herdt (1994a, pp. xiii–xiv) stated, "It is no longer useful to think of the Sambia as engaging in 'homosexuality,' because of the confusing meanings of this concept and their intellectual bias in the Western history of sexuality."

Major anthropological studies of men who have sexual relations with other men began with Esther Newton's (1972) study of drag queens and Joseph Carrier's 1972 dissertation on "urban Mexican male homosexual encounters" (see Carrier 1995), although other work on same-sex sex only began appearing regularly in the discipline a decade later. Also of ongoing importance is Chodorow's (1994) point that heterosexuality just as much as homosexuality is an understudied and problematic phenomenon, especially if sexuality is viewed as more than genital and reproductive bodily contact. (See also Greenberg 1988, Katz 1990, Rubin 1993.)

Many earlier studies in anthropology dealt with male bodies and sexuality (e.g. Malinowski 1929, 1955), and more recent works treated the topic if not necessarily the nomenclature of masculinity (e.g. Spiro 1982), yet only beginning in the 1970s, with the political influence of feminism, gay and lesbian studies, and the theoretical challenge of Foucault and others like Jeffrey Weeks, did anthropologists began to systematically explore the relation between material bodies and cultural relations.

Writing about sexual culture in Brazil, Parker (1991, p. 92) remarked: "It is clear that in the modern period sexuality, focused on reproduction, has become something to be managed not merely by the Catholic church or by the state, but by individuals themselves." Also reflecting on the tension between bodies and social technologies, Cohen (1995b) extends the anthropological discussion of sexual desire and bodies in the other direction in his treatment of political pornography in the North India city of Banaras. Writing about differential social suffering among men and women polio victims in China, Kohrman (1997) noted that "[f]or men, the most difficult aspects seem to be immobility," whereas for women, "their pain appears to center around bodily imperfection." One area of anthropological inquiry involving men that seems particularly scanty concerns prostitution; although there are a few ethnographic materials on male prostitutes, better ones are needed concerning men's relations with female prostitutes.

Somatic faultlines are crossed in many instances, for example, in men's ritual insinuation of themselves into the actual physical labors of reproduction through the couvade, usually analyzed as an affirmation of social paternity, an acknowledgment of the husband's role in giving birth, as revealing men's feminine qualities, and as reflecting men's desire to imitate women's reproductive abilities, i.e. "womb-envy" (see Moore 1988, p. 29; see also Paige & Paige 1981). It is interesting to compare the couvade with Ginsburg's (1990, p. 64) observations of the pro-life movement in North Dakota, where "abortion is fused with the imagery of destructive, decadent, and usually male sexuality." Such an understanding is in turn related to the relationship between sexuality and male domination: According to Godelier (1986) male sexuality among the Baruya is used to maintain the mechanisms of male domination, the production of "great men," and the ideology that justifies the social order overall (see also Godelier & Strathern 1991).

Sexual Faultlines: "Third Genders," Two-Spirit People, and Hijras

The origins of the expression "third gender," popularly employed today in cultural and gay and lesbian studies, may be traced in part to research on gender and sexual practices that cannot be easily categorized as heterosexual or homosexual. Yet all thirdness is not alike, and this formulation itself can be reified into an essentialist dogma. In his ethnohistorical account of a nineteenth-century Zuni "man-woman," Roscoe (1991, p. 2) wrote that We'wha was "a man who combined the work and social roles of men and women, an artist and a priest who dressed, at least in part, in women's clothes." Although such Native American "cross-dressing"—until recently called berdache by anthropologists—was practiced less beginning in the twentieth century, men in many tribes continued to show a preference for women's work and/or to be sexually attracted to other men. Introducing a volume meant to replace the term "berdache" with "two-spirit people," Jacobs (Jacobs et al 1997) argued that "[t]he term 'berdache' [sic] as used by anthropologists is outdated, anachronistic and does not reflect contemporary Native American conversations about gender diversity and sexualities." (For earlier work on berdache, see also Whitehead 1981 and Williams 1988.)

Writing about *hijras* in north India who may undergo castration or penectomy or be congenitally "neither man nor woman," Cohen (1995a) explained why "third genders" are themselves unreliable categories (see also Nanda 1990). Similarly, Robertson (1992, p. 422) wrote of androgyny in the Japanese theater, "Despite the workings of [a] normalizing principle, it remains the case that in Japan...neither femininity nor masculinity has been deemed the exclusive province of either female or male bodies." (On transvestism in Samoa, see Mageo 1992; on transvestism in Sardinia, see Counihan 1985.)

Objects of Bodily Lust

According to the men in rural Greece, Herzfeld (1985, p. 66) reported, women are "passive, indecisive, and unable to control either their sexuality or their tempers" (see also Herzfeld 1991). Brandes (1980, p. 77) says of Andalusia, again according to the men, that women may not be similarly considered passive, but they are known broadly "as seductresses, possessed of insatiable, lustful appetites." Brandes (1980, p. 80) also noted that men commonly feel threatened by their attraction to women "that centers primarily on the female buttocks," and through transference, many men may feel anxious about their own potential anal penetration. Dundes (1978) also offered a psychoanalytic framework for analyzing men's homoerotic preoccupations with backsides.

If generally ethnographers have concluded that few men actually equate their manhood with their genitalia, nonetheless many studies indicate that they are a favorite point of reference. Among the *hijras,* wrote Nanda (1990, p. 24), "emasculation is the major source of the ritual power," akin perhaps to what Gayle Rubin (1994, p. 79), in a critique of the degradation of psychoanalytic approaches, calls "phallus ex machina." Even more ink has been spilled in anthropology to comparatively scrutinize the symbolic role of semen. Among the Sambia, Herdt (1994b, p. 181) reported that "[f]ear of semen depletion is essential to the male viewpoint." As Herdt also famously chronicled (1994b, p.

236), the purpose of repeated oral inseminations of younger by older boys is to "create a pool of maleness." Violent and traumatic subjective experience in men's cults are analyzed by Poole (1982) as ritually induced transformations of person, self, and body among the Bimin-Kuskusmin in Papua New Guinea. Brandes (1980, p. 83) noted that in Moteros, Spain, just as mother's milk is considered to exist in limited supply, so too is semen: With each ejaculation, men get closer to their graves. Women wishing to kill their husbands have sex with them more often. (On the ramifications of semen loss for athletes, see Gregor 1985, p. 145; Monsiváis 1981, p. 113; Wacquant 1995a, p. 509.) The sacred powers of semen are also invoked among Meratus Dayaks in Indonesia with a spell to stop bullets: "You are semen. White divinity. A clotted drop. Closed with a key. Fluid iron. Fluid semen" (cited in Tsing 1993, p. 77).

POWER

Not surprisingly, a central concern in the early studies of Lewis Henry Morgan documenting cross-cultural variation was the shifting relationship between kinship and power. Typical was his comment that, "In the patriarchal family of the Roman type, paternal authority passed beyond the bounds of reason into an excess of domination" (Morgan 1985, pp. 466–67). Despite other disagreements, in most anthropological writings on masculinity to date, one common theme concerns inequality, and whether, how, and why gender inequality may characterize relations between women and men and between different men in diverse historical and cultural situations. To describe elements of male jockeying for power, and as part of seeking out the "deep structure of masculinity," David Gilmore (1990, p. 106) advanced the notion that in many if not most cultures, men, at least, share the belief that men are artificially made while women are naturally born. Thus, men must prove themselves to each other in ways that women do not (see also Dwyer 1978; Herdt 1987, p. 6; Mead 1975, p. 103). Such cross-cultural and transhistorical images regarding men are echoed in recent work by Bourdieu (1990b) on masculinity, e.g. in his statement that regardless of time or space, "among all forms of essentialism [sexism] is undoubtedly the most difficult to uproot" (p. 103), and when he (1997) declared that "the sexual act is thus represented as an act of domination, an act of possession, a 'taking' of woman by man," as if sexual positions were the same for all people at all moments.

Alpha and Mythic Males

There is ethnographic evidence for such generalizations. In rural Turkey, not only is the truly creative God symbolized as masculine, but human men are themselves said to be the ones who give life while women merely give birth (Delaney 1991). Among the nineteenth-century Tswana, through the exchange of cattle "men produced and reproduced the social substance of the collectivity—in contrast to the physical reproduction, by women, of its individual components" (Comaroff 1985, p. 60). The problem lies not with analysis of particular cultural situations, but rather with the summary that "men worldwide share the same notions" (Gilmore 1990, p. 109) about manly (active, creative) men, when such notions are based overwhelmingly on what male informants have told male ethnographers about themselves and about women.

Those writers who hold, with Lévi-Strauss (1969a, p. 496), to the foregone conclusion that the "emergence of symbolic thought must have required that women, like words, should be things that were exchanged," do not often find culturally significant differences among men and between different kinds of masculinities. In contrast to those paradigms predicated on rather homogenous images of masculinity and all-powerful men are the concepts of hegemonic and subordinate (or marginal) masculinities advanced by Connell (1987, 1995). Connell seeks to comprehensively map power inequalities, while also accounting for diverse relations between women and men and particularly the creative agency of women (see Stephen 1997) as well as men in transforming gender relations.

An important contribution of anthropological studies of masculinity has been to explore the subjective perceptions of men about being men, including the relation of being men to claiming, seeking, and exercising various forms of power over other men and over women. In this way, these studies have served to complement earlier work on the "myth of male domination" (cf Leacock 1981, Rogers 1975), and questions such as women's informal power and performative aspects of "being manly." One difficult task for the study of masculinity has been to document the variety of forms and guises of engendered power relations (à la Foucault) without losing sight of fundamental inequalities between men and women in many contexts that often may be harder to discern at a familial, small-scale level. Recognizing variety, and even complicity, does not mean forfeiting the ability to distinguish greater and lesser powers nor require subscribing to a hydraulic theory of power whereby the gain of one is necessarily the loss of the other, though it decidedly does require a clear historical framework (see di Leonardo 1979 and Sacks 1982).

Nationalism, War, and Domestic Violence

Important and innovative recent work on masculinity and violence pertains to the questions of nationalism, war, and domestic violence. War obviously exists before and outside nationalist contexts, and readers interested in men and war in tribal and other nonstate societies may contemplate Chagnon (1968) for a classic sociobiological ethnography of masculinity and warfare as well as Fried et al (1967) more generally on the anthropology of war. As to nationalism, its links to manhood in a variety of cultural contexts could not be clearer. For instance, Mosse (1996) documented the associated histories of European nationalism and masculinity, Oliven (1996) discussed Brazilian gauchos and national identity, Guy (1992) examined the historical relationship between male sexuality, family, and nationalism in Argentina.

In rural Crete, Herzfeld (1985, p. 25) described *poniria* (low cunning) as "at once an emblematic attribute of manhood and, because quintessentially *Greek,* a source of aggressive pride" and characteristic of a certain type of manhood, analogous to womanhood in opposition to official-male forms of wisdom and intelligence. Greenberg (1989) made similar points for a village in southern Mexico. Analyzing a popular depiction of postcolonial Parsi boys in India as spineless and impotent, Lurhmann (1996, pp. 132, 133) reasoned that this sexualized discourse about male inadequacies represents a displacement of anxiety because "among the Parsis the idea of impotence is associated not only with Parsi men, but with the end of empire." In very different ways, others have made connections between masculinity, violence, and formal power. In New Guinea, men influenced by the colonial message that poverty there was due primarily to male violence responded, according to Brison (1995, p. 172), either with new ambivalence about power or they tried to capitalize on their "roughness," which in both cases served to enhance the Europeans' power and prestige. For a sharp-edged ethnographic investigation of masculinity and military leaders in the United States, see Cohn (1987). On aspects of masculinity within state terror, see Nordstrom & Martin (1992).

Whether wife beating is witnessed among newlyweds (Herdt 1994b) or during a woman's first pregnancy (Gutmann 1996), whether male violence is said to prevail among particular classes historically more than others or among men who are losing their authoritarian power over women (Bourgois 1995), in anthropological writings on men, the sources of violence, if not its consequences, are often overdetermined and undertheorized except by proponents of the importance of biological-hormonal factors in human behavior, such as Konner (1982, p. 111), who wrote that the "strongest case for [biologically governed] gender difference is made in the realm of aggressive behavior." Corresponding theories drawing on political-economic, racial, gender, and cultural factors are woefully inadequate in the anthropological literature on men and violence.

Nor have male anthropologists been sufficiently active in researching some of the most difficult and important issues related to engendered violence like rape and wife beating. For a unique collection on wife beating, see Counts et al (1992). Although Gregor (1985) and others have discussed the threat of rape in tribal societies, with the exception of Bourgois's (1995) and Sanday's (1990) work on rape in the contemporary United States, few serious attempts to document and contextualize this form of male injury against women in modern societies have been made by anthropologists. [Malinowski's (1929) report on *yausa*—the "orgiastic assaults" by Trobriand women as they gang-raped a man—remains unusual in the ethnographic annals.]

WOMEN AND MASCULINITY

To reverse decades of male anthropologists rather exclusively interviewing and describing male informants, feminist anthropologists placed greater emphasis beginning in the 1970s on women and so-called "women's worlds." In good measure this was a question of "discovering" the women so notoriously absent (or "disappeared") in earlier ethnographies. Only in the 1980s did men systematically begin exploring men as engendered and engendering persons. Yet ironically, most ethnographic studies of manhood have made insufficient use of feminist contributions to our knowledge of gender and sexuality and have failed to engage sufficiently in the important debates within this discourse. In part, this illustrates what Lutz (1995) calls the "masculinization of theory," here through the evasion of what is considered theoretically unworthy. [See, for example, Gilmore's (1990, pp. 23, 166) censure of "doctrinaire Marxists" and "radical feminists."]

How to incorporate the opinions and experiences of women with respect to men and masculinity is an important concern. Some anthropologists have argued that, as men, they are severely limited in their ability to work with women. (For the differing views on this subject, see Brandes 1987; Gilmore 1990, 1991; Gregory 1984; Herdt & Stoller 1990; Keesing 1982; Streicker 1995). Gutmann (1997) argued that ethnographic investigations of men and masculinity must include research on women's ideas about and experiences with men. More than a simple statistical assertion that increasing one's sample size will sometimes increase one's understanding of a subject, and more than providing a supplement to ethnographic work with men on masculinity through adding women's voices and distinct experiences to those of men, the issue is even more that masculinities develop and transform and have little meaning except in relation to women and female identities and practices in all their similar diversity and complexity.

Some anthropologists have written of men's castration anxieties (e.g. Murphy & Murphy 1985) and mother-son intimacies (cf Gregor 1985, Spiro 1982). Writing within a Lacanian framework, Allison (1994, p. 150) said of Tokyo sex clubs, "whatever men say they need, think they're doing, and justify as necessary 'for work'…is effected symbolically and ritualistically through women and the sexuality they represent." Bloch (1986, pp. 103–4) discussed the central ambiguity of Merina male circumcision rituals as involving the identification of women with both wildness and ancestral descent. It might be argued that since Lévi-Strauss [e.g. *The Raw and the Cooked* (1969b)], all this has been obvious in anthropology: Working within this framework Sherry Ortner (1974) constructed her nature/culture model that explicitly defined men in relation to women. Yet this model is premised on the notion that although women may "control" male children, among adults it is uniformly men who culturally command women.

Thus on one level the issue of women's influence on men and masculinity has been extensively if still far from adequately discussed in the literature of mother-son bonding, Oedipal conflict, and mother-son estrangement. A further step that must be made is to link these seemingly more psychological concerns and studies to political questions of power and inequality. We need to pay attention not only to mothers' authority over male children but also to the influence of women on male adults. Stern's (1995) study of the late colonial era in Mexico is exemplary in its analysis of women's agency and aspirations in promoting "shifts in major social conventions of gender" and patriarchy within the context of a new political economy of growth and industrialization.

The recurrent theme in much anthropological writing on masculinity is that, "according to the natives," men are made and women are born. The thorough critique of this view in MacCormack & Strathern (1980) has been very influential in feminist anthropology, but unfortunately too little considered by anthropologists for whom women are largely irrelevant to constructions of masculinity. It seems worth asking, however, whether bias might not enter into some ethnographers' accounts. This is a methodological issue, and even more a conceptual one, because although it is a mistake to assume too much similarity from one cultural context to another, conclusions regarding the impossibility of a male ethnographer compiling any useful information about women, much less from women about men, seem to merit further attention. Whether women and men absent themselves from the others' presence during rituals, for example, women and men do regularly interact in other times, and they profoundly affect each others' lives and identities. We must not confuse formal roles and definitions with daily life.

Important strides have been made in studying women in a variety of cultural contexts. Corresponding studies of masculinities still lag far behind. This does not mean that ethnographies of men should be viewed, understood, or utilized primarily as a complement to women's studies. Rather, they must be developed and nurtured as integral to understanding the ambiguous relationship between multigendered differences and similarities, equalities and inequalities.

As with the study of ethnicity: one can never study one gender without studying others.

RECENT POINTS OF CONVERGENCE

Male Initiation Rites

In discussing manly rites of passage in New Guinea, Keesing (1982) finds parallels between that area and Amazonia: (*a*) the emphasis placed on *created* versus *natural* growth of boys into men, and (*b*) what men can produce—in ways that women cannot—is men. What initiation does, Keesing (1982, p. 35) wrote, is to "dramatize the change of status through symbolic rebirth—while at the same time operating directly and drastically, at a psychological level, on the bonds to women and their world, which the novices must leave behind." Debate continues about whether initiation rites represent more symbolic ruptures with mothers, and women in general, or are more tied to puberty and physiological stages of maturation; both male bodily mutilation and male seclusion from women are prominent in many recorded rites of initiation. (See also Herdt 1982, Newman & Boyd 1982, Whiting et al 1958.)

Once again, from New Guinea to Amazonia to Madagascar, women seem central to both initiation events and to various analyses explaining their significance. Comaroff (1985, p. 114) wrote of Tswana precolonial initiation rites as projecting man as "skilled human being" and woman as "incompletely socialized." Godelier (1986, p. 47) reported that among the Baruya, "it takes ten years...to separate a boy from his mother," while "it takes a little less than a fortnight to turn an adolescent into a girl ready for marriage and childrearing." Of the circumcision ceremonies among the Merina of Madagascar, Bloch (1986, p. 60) said that "the negative representation of femininity is particularly prominent." Yet elsewhere Bloch (1987, pp. 324–25) wrote of "the systematically *contradictory* nature of representations of women" among the Merina (emphasis in original). An understanding of contradiction and indeterminacy as important is often lacking in depictions of the semblance and sense of male initiation rites, though some like Dundes (1976) have written effectively about the ambivalent gender of male initiates.

Machismo

Men in Mexico, Latin America, and indeed all Spanish-speaking countries have often been characterized as uniformly macho by anthropologists, other scholars, and journalists. Despite the fact that the terms *macho,* in its modern sense, and *machismo* have short word histories, many writers from all over the world have seemed intent on discovering a ubiquitous, virulent, and "typically

Latin" machismo among men from these areas. In the 1990s, there has been a veritable "boom" in ethnographic and kindred work on machismo (see Baca-Zinn 1982, Bolton 1979, Gilmore & Gilmore 1979; and more recently, Brusco 1995, Carrier 1995, de Barbieri 1990, Gutmann 1996, Lancaster 1992, Leiner 1994, Limón 1994, Lumsden 1996, Mirandé 1997, Murray 1995, Parker 1991, Ramírez 1993).

The central claim of Brusco (1995), for example, is that evangelist Protestantism in Colombia has liberated women because it has "domesticated" men: Evangelist husbands and fathers eschew "public" machismo—drunkenness, violence, and adultery—and return to their family responsibilities. Ramírez (1993, p. 13) noted that the expression "machismo" is not used in the working-class areas he studied in Puerto Rico, yet it is commonly employed in academic and feminist circles on the island. Lancaster (1992, p. 237) reported that particular and unequal male-male sexual relations are what ultimately "grounds" the system of machismo in general in Nicaragua. Women may be ever-present in men's lives, but they do not factor into the masculinity equation for basic bodily reasons.

CONCLUSION

In any discussion of masculinity, there are potential problems, especially if the topic is reduced to possession of male genitalia or still worse if it is regarded as "for men only." In many ways arbitrary and artificial, the present review is intended to counter such typologizing. This essay has not, I trust, been read in any sense as representing "men's turn" at the scholarly tables of gender inquiry. Rather, my purpose has been to describe studies of men-as-men in the field within the context of a multigendered puzzle.

Anthropologists of various subjects will recognize the taken-for-granted nature of men and manhood in much work to date. A quick perusal of the indices to most ethnographies shows that "women" exist as a category while "men" are far more rarely listed. Masculinity is either ignored or considered so much the norm that a separate inventory is unnecessary. Then, too, "gender" often means women and not men.

"[I]n the most delicate subjects the ethnographer is bound to a large extent to depend on hearsay," Malinowski (1929, p. 283) declared, and with rare exception the situation has hardly changed since his time. How are we to understand "effeminate" Arapesh men who father their children as if they were mothers? Why do *hijras* in India seek permanent termination in their quest for "emasculation"? How and why do flirty cross-dressing men in Nicaragua (see Lancaster 1997b) exhibit "femineity"? These are questions that constitute the bodily materiality and practices of men who define themselves and are defined by others in part simply as people who are not women.

Between the performative modes in which manhood is emphasized on Crete—a readiness with words, singing, dancing, and sheep rustling (see Herzfeld 1985, p. 124)—and the attempt to invent modern hurdles for achieving manhood status (see Gilmore 1990, p. 221) lies a variety of qualities and characterizations anthropologists have labeled masculine and manly. Contrary to the assertion that men are made while women are born (albeit "in the natives' point of view") is the understanding that men are often the defenders of "nature" and "the natural order of things," while women are the ones instigating change in gender relations and much else. This is part of what Peletz (1996, p. 294) calls "the historic restructuring of male roles," as the contradictions, inequalities, and ambiguities of gender relations, ideologies, and practices in all their myriad facets and manifestations themselves prove central to the process of engendered social transformations.

ACKNOWLEDGMENTS

My thanks to Stanley Brandes, Lawrence Cohen, Meg Conkey, Michael Herzfeld, Micaela di Leonardo, Roger Lancaster, Louise Lamphere, Shirley Lindenbaum, Nancy Scheper-Hughes, Mel Spiro, Lynn Stephen, and Loïc Wacquant for comments on this essay and/or discussions on masculinity, and for Gayle Rubin's blessing to echo her earlier title, which in turn came from Emma Goldman. I wrote this paper while on a National Institutes of Health postdoctoral fellowship administered through the Prevention Research Center and the School of Public Health, University of California, Berkeley.

> **Visit the *Annual Reviews* home page** at
> **http://www.AnnualReviews.org.**

Literature Cited

Allison A. 1994. *Nightwork: Sexuality, Pleasure, and Corporate Masculinity in a Tokyo Hostess Club.* Chicago: Univ. Chicago Press

Almaguer T. 1991. Chicano men: a cartography of homosexual identity and behavior. *Differences* 3(2):75–100

Alter JS. 1992. *The Wrestler's Body: Identity and Ideology in North India.* Berkeley: Univ. Calif. Press

Ardener E. 1989. *The Voice of Prophecy and Other Essays.* London: Blackwell

Baca-Zinn M. 1982. Chicano men and masculinity. *J. Ethn. Stud.* 10(2):29–44

Battaglia D. 1985. "We feed our father": paternal nurture among the Sabarl of Papua New Guinea. *Am. Ethnol.* 12(3):427–41

Benedict R. 1934. *Patterns of Culture.* Boston: Houghton Mifflin

Bloch M. 1986. *From Blessing to Violence: History and Ideology in the Circumcision Ritual of the Merina of Madagascar.* Cambridge: Cambridge Univ. Press

Bloch M. 1987. Decent and sources of contradiction in representations of women and kinship. See Collier & Yanagisako 1987, pp. 324–37

Bly R. 1990. *Iron John: A Book About Men.* New York: Vintage

Bolton R. 1979. Machismo in motion: the ethos of Peruvian truckers. *Ethos* 7(4): 312–42

Bourdieu P. 1990a. *The Logic of Practice.* Transl. R Nice. Stanford: Stanford Univ. Press

Bourdieu P. 1990b. La domination masculine. *Actes Rech. Sci. Soc.* 84:2–31

Bourdieu P. 1997. Masculine Domination Revisited. *Berk. J. Sociol.* In press

Bourgois P. 1995. *In Search of Respect: Selling Crack in El Barrio.* Cambridge: Cambridge Univ. Press

Bowden R. 1984. Art and gender ideology in the Sepik. *Man* (N.S.) 19(3):445–58

Brana-Shute G. 1979. *On the Corner: Male Social Life in a Paramaribo Creole Neighborhood.* Prospect Heights, IL: Waveland

Brandes S. 1987. Sex roles and anthropological research in rural Andalusia. *Women's Stud.* 13:357–72

Brandes S. 1980. *Metaphors of Masculinity: Sex and Status in Andalusian Folklore.* Philadelphia: Univ. Pa. Press

Brison K. 1995. Changing constructions of masculinity in a Sepik Society. *Ethnology* 34(3):155–75

Broude GJ. 1990. Protest masculinity: a further look at the causes and the concept. *Ethos* 18(1):103–22

Brusco EE. 1995. *The Reformation of Machismo: Evangelical Conversion and Gender in Columbia.* Austin: Univ. Tex. Press

Carrier JM. 1995. *De los Otros: Intimacy and Homosexuality Among Mexican Men.* New York: Columbia Univ. Press

Castelain-Meunier C. 1988. *Les Hommes, Aujourd'hui: Virilité et identité.* Paris: Acropole

Cath SH, Gurwitt A, Gunsberg L, eds. 1989. *Fathers and Their Families.* Hillsdale, NJ: Analytic

Chagnon NA. 1968. *Yanomamo: The Fierce People.* New York: Holt, Rinehart & Winston

Chodorow NJ. 1994. *Femininities, Masculinities, Sexualities: Freud and Beyond.* Lexington: Univ. Ky. Press

Cohen L. 1995a. The pleasures of castration: the postoperative status of Hijras, Jankhas, and academics. In *Sexual Nature, Sexual Culture,* ed. PR Abramson, SD Pinkerton, pp. 276–304. Chicago: Univ. Chicago Press

Cohen L. 1995b. Holi in Banaras and the Ma-

haland of modernity. *Gay Lesbian Q.* 2: 399–424

Cohn C. 1987. Sex and death in the rational world of defense intellectuals. *Signs* 12(4) :687–718

Collier JF, Yanagisako SJ, eds. 1987. *Gender and Kinship: Essays Toward a Unified Analysis.* Stanford: Stanford Univ. Press

Comaroff J. 1985. *Body of Power, Spirit of Resistance: The Culture and History of a South African People.* Chicago: Univ. Chicago Press

Connell RW. 1987. *Gender and Power: Society, the Person and Sexual Politics.* Cambridge: Polity Press

Connell RW. 1995. *Masculinities.* Berkeley: Univ. Calif. Press

Counihan C. 1985. Transvestism and gender in a Sardinian carnival. *Anthropology* 9: 11–24

Counts DA, Brown JK, Campell JC, eds. 1992. *Sanctions and Sanctuary: Cultural Perspectives on the Beating of Wives.* Boulder, CO: Westview

Cowan JK. 1990. *Dance and the Body Politic in Northern Greece.* Princeton, NJ: Princeton Univ. Press

de Barbieri T. 1990. Sobre géneros, prácticas y valores: notas acerca de posibles erosiones del machismo en México. In *Normas y prácticas: morales y cívicas en la vida cotidiana,* ed. JM Ramírez Sáiz, pp. 83–106. Mexico City: Univ. Nac. Autón. Méx.

Delaney C. 1991. *The Seed and the Soil: Gender and Cosmology in Turkish Village Society.* Berkeley: Univ. Calif. Press

di Leonardo M. 1979. Methodology and misinterpretation of women's status in kinship studies: a case study of Goodenough and the definition of marriage. *Am. Ethnol.* 6(4):627–37

Dundes A. 1976. A psychoanalytic study of the bullroarer. *Man* (N.S.) 11:220–38

Dundes A. 1978. Into the endzone for a touchdown: a psychoanalytic consideration of American football. *West. Folk.* 37:75–88

Duneier M. 1992. *Slim's Table: Race, Respectability, and Masculinity.* Chicago: Univ. Chicago Press

Durkheim E. 1933. *The Division of Labor in Society.* Transl. G Simpson. New York: Free Press

Dwyer D. 1978. *Images and Self-images: Male and Female in Morocco.* New York: Columbia Univ. Press

Elliston DA. 1995. Erotic anthropology: "ritualized homosexuality" in Melanesia and beyond. *Am. Ethnol.* 22(4):848–67

Evans-Pritchard EE, ed. 1974. *Man and*

Woman Among the Azande. London: Faber & Faber

Fachel Leal O, ed. 1992. *Cultura e identidade masculina. Cadernos de Antropologia,* No. 7. Porto Alegre, Brazil: Univ. Fed. Rio Grande Sul

Fanon F. 1967. *Black Skin, White Masks.* Transl. CL Markmann. New York: Grove

Foucault M. 1980a. *The History of Sexuality,* Vol. 1. Transl. R Hurley. New York: Vintage

Foucault M. 1980b. *Herculine Barbin: Being the Recently Discovered Memoirs of a Nineteenth-Century French Hermaphrodite.* Transl. R McDougall. New York: Pantheon

Fried M, Harris M, Murphy R, eds. 1967. *War: The Anthropology of Armed Conflict and Aggression.* New York: Natural History

Friedl E. 1984. (1975). *Women and Men: An Anthropologist's View.* Prospect Heights, IL: Waveland

Gilmore DD. 1990. *Manhood in the Making: Cultural Concepts of Masculinity.* New Haven: Yale Univ. Press

Gilmore DD. 1991. Commodity, comity, community: male exchange in rural Andalusia. *Ethnology* 30(1):17–30

Gilmore MM, Gilmore DD. 1979. Machismo: a psychodynamic approach. *J. Psychoanal. Anthropol.* 2(3):281–300

Ginsburg F. 1990. The "word-made" flesh: the disembodiment of gender in the abortion debate. In *Uncertain Terms: Negotiating Gender in American Culture,* ed. F Ginsburg, AL Tsing, pp. 59–75. Boston: Beacon

Godelier M. 1986. *The Making of Great Men: Male Domination and Power among the New Guinea Baruya.* Cambridge: Cambridge Univ. Press

Godelier M, Strathern M, eds. 1991. *Big Men and Great Men: Personifications of Power in Melanesia.* Cambridge: Cambridge Univ. Press

Greenberg DF. 1988. *The Construction of Homosexuality.* Chicago: Univ. Chicago Press

Greenberg J. 1989. *Blood Ties: Life and Violence in Rural Mexico.* Tucson: Univ. Ariz. Press

Gregor T. 1985. *Anxious Pleasures: The Sexual Life of an Amazonian People.* Chicago: Univ. Chicago Press

Gregory JR. 1984. The myth of the male ethnographer and the woman's world. *Am. Anthropol.* 86:316–27

Gutmann MC. 1996. *The Meanings of Macho: Being a Man in Mexico City.* Berkeley: Univ. Calif. Press

Gutmann MC. 1997. "The ethnographic (g)ambit: women and the negotiation of masculinity in Mexico City. " *Am. Ethnol.* 24(4):In press

Guy DJ. 1992. *Sex and Danger in Buenos Aires: Prostitution, Family, and Nation in Argentina.* Lincoln: Univ. Nebr. Press

Herdt G, ed. 1982. *Rituals of Manhood: Male Initiation in Papua New Guinea.* Berkeley: Univ. Calif. Press

Herdt G. 1987. *The Sambia: Ritual and Gender in New Guinea.* Fort Worth: Holt, Rinehart & Winston

Herdt G. 1993. Introduction to the paperback edition. *Ritualized Homosexuality in Melanesia,* ed. G Herdt. Berkeley: Univ. Calif. Press

Herdt G. 1994a. Preface to the 1994 edition. *Guardians of the Flutes: Idioms of Masculinity.* Chicago: Univ. Chicago Press

Herdt G. 1994b. (1981). *Guardians of the Flutes: Idioms of Masculinity.* Chicago: Univ. Chicago Press

Herdt G, Stoller RJ. 1990. *Intimate Communications: Erotics and the Study of Culture.* New York: Columbia Univ. Press

Herman E. 1995. *The Romance of American Psychology: Political Culture in the Age of Experts.* Berkeley: Univ. Calif. Press

Herzfeld M. 1985. *The Poetics of Manhood: Contest and Identity in a Cretan Mountain Village.* Princeton, NJ: Princeton Univ. Press

Herzfeld M. 1987. "As in your own house": hospitality, ethnography, and the stereotype of Mediterranean society. In *Honor and Shame and the Unity of the Mediterranean,* ed. DD Gilmore, pp. 75–89. Washington, DC: Am. Anthropol. Assoc.

Herzfeld M. 1991. Silence, submission, and subversion: toward a poetics of womanhood. See Loizos & Papataxiarchis 1991, pp. 79–97

Hewlett BS. 1991. *Intimate Fathers: The Nature and Context of Aka Pygmy Paternal Infant Care.* Ann Arbor: Univ. Mich. Press

Hollos M, Leis P. 1989. *Becoming Nigerian in Ijo Society.* New Brunswick, NJ: Rutgers Univ. Press

Jacobs SE, Thomas W, Lang S, eds. 1997. *Two-Spirit People: Native American Gender Identity, Sexuality and Spirituality.* Urbana: Univ. Ill. Press

Jardim D. 1992. "Espaço social e Autosegregação Entre Homens: Gostos, Sonoridades e Masculinidade." In *Cadernos de Antropologia,* No. 7, pp. 29–42. Porto Alegre, Brazil: Univ. Fed. Rio Grande Sul

Katz J. 1990. The invention of heterosexuality. *Social. Rev.* 1:7–34

Keesing RM. 1982. Introduction. See Herdt 1982, pp. 1–43

Knauss P. 1987. *The Persistance of Patriarchy: Class, Gender, and Ideology in Twentieth Century Algeria.* New York: Praeger

Kohrman M. 1997. Motorcycles for the disabled: power, mobility, and the transformation of experience in urban China. Unpublished manuscript

Konner M. 1982. *The Tangled Wing: Biological Constraints on the Human Spirit.* New York: Harper

Lancaster RN. 1992. *Life Is Hard: Machismo, Danger, and the Intimacy of Power in Nicaragua.* Berkeley: Univ. Calif. Press

Lancaster RN. 1997a. On homosexualities in Latin America (and other places). *Am. Ethnol.* 24(1):193–202

Lancaster RN. 1997b. Gutol's performance: notes on the transvestism of everyday life. In *Sex and Sexuality in Latin America,* ed. D Balderston, DJ Guy, pp. 9–32. New York: NY Univ. Press

Lancaster RN. 1998. *The Queer Body.* Unpublished manuscript. Berkeley: Univ. Calif. Press

Laqueur T. 1990. *Making Sex: Body and Gender from the Greeks to Freud.* Cambridge: Harvard Univ. Press

Leacock E. 1981. *Myths of Male Dominance.* New York: Mon. Rev.

Lee RB. 1968. What hunters do for a living, or, how to make out on scarce resources. In *Man the Hunter,* ed. RB Lee, I DeVore, pp. 30–48. Chicago: Aldine

Leiner M. 1994. *Sexual Politics in Cuba: Machismo, Homosexuality, and AIDS.* Boulder, CO: Westview

Lévi-Strauss C. 1969a. *The Elementary Structures of Kinship.* Transl. JH Bell, JR von Sturmer, R Needham. Boston: Beacon

Lévi-Strauss C. 1969b. *The Raw and the Cooked.* Transl. J & D Weightman. New York: Harper & Row

Lewgoy B. 1992. Os Cafés na Vida Urbana de Porto Alegre (1920–1940): As Transformações em um Espaço de Sociabilidade Masculino. In *Cadernos de Antropologia,* No. 7, pp. 61–80. Porto Alegre, Brazil: Univ. Fed. Rio Grande Sul

Lewis O. 1963. (1951). *Life in a Mexican Village: Tepoztlán Restudied.* Urbana: Univ. Ill. Press

Limón J. 1994. *Dancing with the Devil: Society and Cultural Poetics in Mexican-American South Texas.* Madison: Univ. Wis. Press

Loizos P, Papataxiarchis E, eds. 1991. *Contested Identities: Gender and Kinship in Modern Greece.* Princeton, NJ: Princeton Univ. Press

Lomnitz LA. 1977. *Networks and Marginality: Life in a Mexican Shantytown.* Transl. C Lomnitz. New York: Academic

Lomnitz LA, Pérez-Lizaur M. 1987. *A Mexican Elite Family:1820–1980.* Transl. C Lomnitz. Princeton, NJ: Princeton Univ. Press

Luhrmann TM. 1996. *The Good Parsi: The Fate of a Colonial Elite in a Postcolonial Society.* Cambridge: Harvard Univ. Press

Lumsden I. 1996. *Machos, Maricones, and Gays: Cuba and Homosexuality.* Philadelphia: Temple Univ. Press

Lutz C. 1995. The gender of theory. In *Women Writing Culture,* ed. R Behar, DA Gordon, pp. 249–66. Berkeley: Univ. Calif. Press

MacCormack C, Strathern M, eds. 1980. *Nature, Culture and Gender.* Cambridge: Cambridge Univ. Press

Mageo JM. 1992. Male transvestism and cultural change in Samoa. *Am. Ethnol.* 19(3):443–59

Malinowski B. 1929. *The Sexual Life of Savages in North-Western Melanesia.* New York: Harcourt, Brace & World

Malinowski B. 1955. (1927). *Sex and Repression in Savage Society.* Cleveland: Meridian Books

Marshall M. 1979. *Weekend Warriors: Alcohol in a Micronesian Culture.* Palo Alto, CA: Mayfield

Mead M. 1963. (1935). *Sex and Temperament in Three Primitive Societies.* New York: Laurel

Mead M. 1975. (1949). *Male and Female: A Study of the Sexes in a Changing World.* New York: Morrow

Merleau-Ponty M. 1962. *Phenomenology of Perception.* Transl. C Smith. London: Routledge & Kegan Paul

Mernissi F. 1987. (1975). *Beyond the Veil: Male-Female Dynamics in a Modern Muslim Society.* Bloomington: Univ. Ind. Press

Mirandé A. 1997. *Hombres y Machos: Masculinity and Latino Culture.* Boulder, CO: Westview

Monsiváis C. 1981. *Escenas de pudor y liviandad.* Mexico City: Grijalbo

Moore HL. 1988. *Feminism and Anthropology.* Minneapolis: Univ. Minn. Press

Morgan LH. 1985. (1877). *Ancient Society.* Tucson: Univ. Ariz. Press

Mosse GL. 1996. *The Image of Man: The Creation of Modern Masculinity.* New York: Oxford Univ. Press

Murphy Y, Murphy RF. 1985. *Women of the Forest.* New York: Columbia Univ. Press. 2nd ed.

Murray SO. 1995. *Latin American Male Homosexualities.* Albuquerque: Univ. NM Press

Nanda S. 1990. *Neither Man Nor Woman: The Hijras of India.* Belmont, CA: Wadsworth

Newman PL, Boyd DJ. 1982. The making of men: ritual and meaning in Awa male initiation. See Herdt 1982, pp. 239–85

Newton E. 1972. *Mother Camp: Female Impersonators in America.* Englewood Cliffs, NJ: Prentice-Hall

Nordstrom C, Martin J, eds. 1992. *The Paths to Domination, Resistance, and Terror.* Berkeley: Univ. Calif. Press

Oliven R. 1996. *Tradition Matters: Modern Gaúcho Identity in Brazil.* New York: Columbia Univ. Press

Ortner SB. 1974. Is female to male as nature is to culture? In *Woman, Culture, and Society,* ed. MZ Rosaldo, L Lamphere, pp. 67–88. Stanford: Stanford Univ. Press

Ortner SB, Whitehead H. 1981. Accounting for sexual meanings. See Ortner & Whitehead 1981, pp. 1–27

Ortner SB, Whitehead H, eds. 1981. *Sexual Meanings: The Cultural Construction of Gender and Sexuality.* Cambridge: Cambridge Univ. Press

Paige KE, Paige JM. 1981. *The Politics of Reproductive Ritual.* Berkeley: Univ. Calif. Press

Papataxiarchis E. 1991. Friends of the heart: male commensal solidarity, gender, and kinship in Aegean Greece. See Loizos & Papataxiarchis 1991, pp. 156–79

Parker A, Russo M, Sommer D, Yaeger P, eds. 1992. *Nationalisms and Sexualities.* New York: Routledge

Parker RG. 1991. *Bodies, Pleasures, and Passions: Sexual Culture in Contemporary Brazil.* Boston: Beacon

Parker RG, Gagnon JH, eds. 1995. *Conceiving Sexuality: Approaches to Sex Research in a Postmodern World.* New York: Routledge

Parker S, Parker H. 1992. Male gender identity in the Israeli Kibbutz: reflections on "protest masculinity." *Ethos* 20(3):340–57

Parsons T, Bales RF. 1955. *Family, Socialization and Interaction Process.* New York: Free Press

Peletz MG. 1996. *Reason and Passion: Representations of Gender in a Malay Society.* Berkeley: Univ. Calif. Press

Poole FJP. 1982. The ritual forging of identity: aspects of person and self in Bimin-Kuskusmin male initiation. In Herdt 1992, pp. 99–154

Ramírez RL. 1993. *Dime capitán: Reflexiones sobre la masculinidad.* Río Piedras, Puerto Rico: Ediciones Huracán

Read KE. 1952. Nama cult of the Central Highlands, New Guinea. *Oceana* 23(1): 1–25

Robertson J. 1992. The politics of androgyny in Japan: sexuality and subversion in the theater and beyond. *Am. Ethnol.* 19(2): 419–42

Rogers SC. 1975. Female forms of power and the myth of male dominance: a model of female/male interaction in peasant society. *Am. Ethnol.* 2(4):727–55

Roscoe W. 1991. *The Zuni Man-Woman.* Albuquerque: Univ. N. M. Press

Rubin G. 1975. The traffic in women: notes on the "political economy" of sex. In *Toward an Anthropology of Women,* ed. R Reiter, pp. 157–210. New York: Mon. Rev.

Rubin G. 1993. (1982). Thinking sex: notes for a radical theory of the politics of sexuality. In *The Lesbian and Gay Studies Reader,* ed. H Abelove, MA Barale, DM Halperin, pp. 3–44. New York: Routledge

Rubin G. 1994. Sexual traffic: interview. *Differences* 6(2,3):62–99

Sacks K. 1982. (1979). *Sisters and Wives: The Past and Future of Sexual Inequality.* Urbana: Univ. Ill. Press

Sanday PR. 1990. *Fraternity Gang Rape: Sex, Brotherhood, and Privilege on Campus.* New York: NY Univ. Press

Scheper-Hughes N. 1979. *Saints, Scholars, and Schizophrenics: Mental Illness in Rural Ireland.* Berkeley: Univ. Calif. Press

Scheper-Hughes N. 1992. *Death Without Weeping: The Violence of Everyday Life in Brazil.* Berkeley: Univ. Calif. Press

Schwalbe M. 1996. *Unlocking the Iron Cage: The Men's Movement, Gender, Politics, and American Culture.* New York: Oxford Univ. Press

Sedgwick EK. 1985. *Between Men: English Literature and Male Homosocial Desire.* New York: Columbia Univ. Press

Smith R. 1956. *The Negro Family in British Guiana: Family Structure and Social Status in the Villages.* London: Routledge & Kegan Paul

Spiro ME. 1982. *Oedipus in the Trobriands.* Chicago: Univ. Chicago Press

Stack C. 1974. *All Our Kin: Strategies for Survival in a Black Community.* New York: Harper & Row

Stephen L. 1997. *Women and Social Movements in Latin America: Power from Below.* Austin: Univ. Tex. Press

Stern SJ. 1995. *The Secret History of Gender: Women, Men, and Power in Late Colonial Mexico.* Chapel Hill: Univ. N. C. Press

Stoler AL. 1991. Carnal knowledge and imperial power: gender, race, and morality in colonial Asia. In *Gender at the Crossroads of Knowledge: Feminist Anthropology in the Postmodern Era,* ed. M di Leonardo, pp. 51–101. Berkeley: Univ. Calif. Press

Strathern M. 1988. *Gender of the Gift: Problems with Women and Problems with Society in Melanesia.* Berkeley: Univ. Calif. Press

Streicker J. 1995. Policing boundaries: race, class, and gender in Cartagena, Colombia. *Am. Ethnol.* 22(1):54–74

Taggart JM. 1992. Gender segregation and cultural constructions of sexuality in two Hispanic societies. *Am. Ethnol.* 19(1): 75–96

Tiger L. 1984. (1969). *Men in Groups.* New York: Boyars

Tsing AL. 1993. *In the Realm of the Diamond Queen: Marginality in an Out-of-the-Way Place.* Princeton, NJ: Princeton Univ. Press

Tuzin DF. 1982. Ritual violence among the Ilahita Arapesh: the dynamics of moral and religious uncertainty. See Herdt 1982, pp. 321–55

Tuzin DF. 1997. *The Cassowary's Revenge: The Life and Death of Masculinity in a New Guinea Society.* Chicago: Univ. Chicago Press

Wacquant LJD. 1995a. The pugilistic point of view: how boxers think and feel about their trade. *Theory Soc.* 24(4):489–535

Wacquant LJD. 1995b. Pugs at work: bodily capital and bodily labour among professional boxers. *Body Soc.* 1(1):65–93

Wacquant LJD. 1997. The prizefighter's three bodies. Unpublished manuscript

Weeks J. 1985. *Sexuality and Its Discontents: Meanings, Myths, and Modern Sexualities.*

London: Routledge & Kegan Paul

Welzer-Lang D, Pichevin M, eds. 1992. *Des Hommes et du Masculin.* Centre de Recherches et d'Etudes Anthropologiques. Lyon: Presses Univ.

West MM, Konner MJ. 1976. The role of the father: an anthropological perspective. In *The Role of the Father in Child Development,* ed. ME Lamb, pp. 185–218. New York: Wiley

Weston K. 1993. Lesbian/gay studies in the house of anthropology. *Annu. Rev. Anthropol.* 22:339–67

Whitehead H. 1981. The bow and the burden strap: a new look at institutionalized homosexuality in native North America. See Ortner & Whitehead 1981, pp. 80–115

Whiting BB, ed. 1963. *Six Cultures: Studies of Child Rearing.* New York: Wiley

Whiting BB, Whiting JWM. 1975. *Children of Six Cultures: A Psycho-Cultural Analysis.* Cambridge: Harvard Univ. Press

Whiting JWM, Kluckhohn R, Anthony A. 1958. The function of male initiation ceremonies at puberty. In *Readings in Social Psychology,* ed. EE Maccoby, TM Newcomb, EL Hartley, pp. 359–70. New York: Holt, Rinehart & Winston

Williams W. 1988. *The Spirit and the Flesh: Sexual Diversity in American Indian Culture.* Boston: Beacon

Willis P. 1979. *Learning to Labor: How Working Class Kids Get Working Class Jobs.* New York: Columbia Univ. Press

Wilson C. 1995. *Hidden in the Blood: A Personal Investigation of AIDS in the Yucatan.* New York: Columbia Univ. Press

Yanagisako SJ, Collier JF. 1987. Toward a unified analysis of gender and kinship. See Collier & Yanagisako 1987, pp. 14–50

Annu. Rev. Anthropol. 1997. 26:411–37

PROGRAMME TO PRACTICE:
Gender and Feminism in Archaeology

Margaret W. Conkey

Archaeological Research Facility, Department of Anthropology, University of California, Berkeley, Berkeley, California 94720-3710; e-mail: conkey@qal. berkeley.edu

Joan M. Gero

Department of Anthropology, American University, Washington, DC 20016-8003; e-mail: jgero@american.edu. Formerly with the Department of Anthropology, University of South Carolina, Columbia, SC

ABSTRACT

In the past decade, archaeologists have given considerable attention to research on gender in the human past. In this review, we attempt to acknowledge much of this diverse and abundant work from an explicitly feminist perspective. We focus on reviewing a selection of approaches to gender that are anchored to specific theoretical standpoints. In addition, we highlight several approaches that challenge an archaeology of gender that does not explicitly engage with the implications of this topic for research, practice, and interpretation. From our perspective, we suggest the value of situating gender research within an explicitly feminist framework, and we draw attention to some of the important insights for archaeology from the wider field of feminist critiques of science. Last, we draw attention to the crucial implications for the practice of archaeology.

> The big, unitary Answer that levels, grades and paves reality like a superhighway is not only NOT the solution, it is at the very heart of the problem.
>
> *Utne Reader* (Jan.–Feb. 1995, p. 57)

> ...by showing "other alternatives are thinkable by no means debunks our current beliefs, it only exposes as fraudulent the absolute authority with which we think them" (Daston 1993, as cited in M.T. 1993, p. 35)

411

INTRODUCTION

In 1997, the state and fate of an archaeology of gender rest on more than any single political agenda or any monolithic approach to the topic. The intensity with which the study of gender has infused archaeological discourse and analysis in the past five years does not mean that there is now—nor is there anticipated to be—a shared orientation to the study of gender, or a single methodology for studying gender, or, perhaps more problematically, even a commonly held body of theory and data about gender (for a partial review of work on gender in archaeology before 1991, see Kehoe 1992). In fact, publications now include as diverse a set of statements and even straight-out contradictory starting assumptions as can be imagined.

This review emphasizes where a feminist-inspired archaeology sits within the discipline today and where it can potentially take the discipline as we move into the next millennium. We do not review all examples of the archaeology of gender, which, in any case, are too numerous to be accounted for individually. We also do not dwell on what is thought to be known about "women in prehistory" (but see du Cros & Smith 1993, Ehrenberg 1989, Spielman 1995), "women in history" (but see Balme & Beck 1995, Scott 1994, Seifert 1991, Walde & Willows 1991, Wall 1994), or "women in antiquity" (but see Archer et al 1994; Fantham et al 1994; Kampen 1995; Pomeroy 1975, 1991; Rabinowitz & Richlin 1993). We do not consider in any depth specific methodological approaches to reveal women (or "gender") in the archaeological record (but for an overview of diverse approaches, see Costin 1996 or Hayden 1992; for burial analysis, see Hollimon 1991, 1992; for cross-cultural regularities of gender roles, see Kent 1995; and for ethnohistory, ethnoarchaeology, iconographic research, see Arsenault 1991, Gero 1997, Miller 1988).

Rather, today's literature requires from us a more self-conscious positioning of perspectives; no single position within the larger discourse, and certainly not our own as given here, can present itself as neutral or all-encompassing or even as all-tolerant. Instead, we intend this review to move forward an explicitly feminist inquiry in archaeology, one that is committed to changing the way archaeology is practiced, the way it is presented, and the nature of archaeological interpretation.

We begin by considering how the recent explosion of interest in gender is positioned in the archaeological literature, highlighting several distinct ways of connecting empirical archaeological study to theoretical resources and arguments. We then review a selection of studies in feminist archaeology that are particularly notable for how they have opened up transformatory and imaginative possibilities for the archaeologies of the next millennium. Despite the enormous promise of these revelatory studies, we recognize internal obstacles or resistances that seem still to inhibit a full engagement in gender research in archaeology, and we raise questions about the overall effects of the increasing volume of gender research in archaeology, asking whether inquiry has been further opened to interested scholars or whether it has narrowed. Finally, we address the centrality of feminist thought—specifically the feminist critiques of science—to notions of archaeology as a science, to archaeological problem-solving, to fieldwork and data collection, and to teaching and the presentation of archaeological issues.

TAKING UP GENDER IN ARCHAEOLOGY

Locating the Corpus

The explosion of literature on archaeological gender in the past five years is concentrated in large part in published collections of papers originally presented at gender oriented conferences, or in organized speaker series (Balme & Beck 1995; Claassen 1992, 1994; du Cros & Smith 1993; Gero & Conkey 1991; Walde & Willows 1991; Wright 1996), together with similarly concentrated special gender issues of periodicals, e.g. *Historical Archaeology* [1991, 25(4)], *Norwegian Archaeological Review* [1992, 25(1)], *Plains Anthropologist* Memoir [1991, 26], *Massachusetts Archaeological Society Bulletin* [1994, 55(1)], *Journal of Anthropological Research* [1996, 51(2)], and *CRM* [1997, 20(3)]. These topic-focused special publications on gender numerically overwhelm the articles appearing singly in journals, a recognized historic pattern by which new subfields are introduced into archaeology (M Cabak, unpublished manuscript, 1989).

At the same time, almost all major North American journals have published at least one article that focuses on the archaeology of gender, including *American Anthropologist* (Moss 1993), *American Antiquity* (Wylie 1992), *Archaeology of Eastern North America* (Dent 1991), *Comparative Studies in Society and History* (Linke 1992), *Current Anthropology* (Joyce 1993b, McCafferty & McCafferty 1994), *Journal of Anthropological Archaeology* (Allen 1996, Larick 1991, Solomon 1992), *Journal of California and Great Basin Arnthropology* (McGuire & Hildebrandt 1994), *Latin American Antiquity* (Guillen 1993), *North American Archaeology* (Sassaman 1992), *Research in Economic Anthropology* (Costin 1993), *Visual Anthropology Review* (Gifford-Gonzales 1993), and *Gender, Place and Culture* (Tringham 1994). For one recent annotated bibliography, see Bacus et al (1993).

Furthermore, this is far from being a local, Americanist phenomenon. Research on gender has proceeded vigorously in many international contexts (e.g. Norway, Australia, South Africa, Germany), and international journals have regularly if sporadically included articles on gender, e.g. *Journal of European Archaeology* (Bailey 1994a, Robb 1994), *Antiquity* (Englestad 1991, Gilchrist 1991, Kehoe 1991, Meskell 1995), *Archaologie der Schweiz* (Basel) (Muller 1991), *Australian Archaeology* (McDonald 1992), *Oxford Journal of Archaeology* (Boardman 1991), *South African Archaeological Bulletin* (Mazel 1992, Wadley 1989), and *World Archaeology* (Bailey 1994b, Dobres 1995b). International interest is apparent by other measures as well: Multiple conferences (du Cros & Smith 1993; Balme & Beck 1995; Kästner & Karlisch 1991; Solomon, personal communication), thematic journals on or by women (e.g. *K.A.N.* 1985–), review articles (e.g. Dommasnes 1992), and special journal issues (Engelstad 1992) have appeared. However, French archaeologists appear perplexed by what they consider to be a historically and culturally specific Anglo-American concern with gender, a term that, they claim, has no translation into French [Coudart, personal communication; see also del Valle (1993b, p. 2) who makes a similar point for Spanish], suggesting that the genealogies of gendered anthropology are markedly Anglo-Saxon, linked to a new imperialist archaeology.

In addition to the burgeoning number of journal articles, it is increasingly the case that regional or topical edited volumes will include an article on gender (e.g. Gifford-Gonzalez's 1992 contribution to a volume on archaeozoology, or Yentsch 1991 and Spencer-Wood 1991 in a volume on inequality), and anthropological volumes on gender will sometimes include archaeological contributions (e.g. Conkey & Williams 1991, Nelson 1992, Silverblatt 1991). Moreover, gender issues are increasingly recognized as significant to other problem areas in archaeology (Dobres 1995b; Dobres & Hoffman 1994 on prehistoric technology; Hingley 1991 on social archaeology of houses; Hendon 1996 on domestic labor). Gender appears, though rarely, in Cultural Resource Management reports (e.g. Walsh et al 1994; for some discussion, or the special issue of *CRM* in 1997, see Rogers & Fowler 1994). According to Claassen, over 500 conference papers authored by over 400 individuals have been presented on gender since 1988, and over 10 conferences devoted to gender and archaeology have been held since 1987 (Claassen, personal communication), but it remains to be seen how much of the enormous oral literature will culminate in published works. A promising sign is the September 1996 announcement by the University of Pennsylvania Press of a new book series, *Regendering the Past,* devoted explicitly to gender in archaeology (e.g. Claassen & Joyce 1997).

The Gender Genre

Researchers in prehistory have embraced gender studies to resolve a wide spectrum of problems. Motivated by a rejection of the equation of human behavior with the behavior of men, a primary purpose for undertaking a gendered archaeology is to identify or assert the presence and activities of women on prehistoric sites. The value of these studies begins with a recognition of female labor in a broad range of activities (e.g. Benedict 1993), many of which were once considered exclusively male domains such as Paleoindian encampments (Chilton 1994), Paleolithic cave art (Russell 1991), Natufian transitions from foraging to agriculture (Crabtree 1991), Maya animal husbandry (Pohl 1991), or pre-Columbian Moche mortuary rituals (Arsenault 1991). Similarly, the identification of women in high prestige burials has challenged the monopolization of power by men in stratified societies (McCafferty & McCafferty 1994, Nelson 1991a). In addition, "looking for women" (indeed, finding women!) forces self-conscious attention to starting assumptions about gender, where, for instance, traditional assessments of a division of labor are examined and either adopted (Sassaman 1992, Watson & Kennedy 1991) or revised (Crabtree 1991, Duke 1991). Such "locate-the-women" projects also take up the once unshakable redundancy of gendered task "assignments" in cross-cultural perspective. For instance, by asking where women might be located in the production sequences of flaked stone tools, archaeologists have "found" women in the organization of quarrying activities (Sassaman 1997), heat treatment sequences of silicious rock, or variability in core preparation vs expedient technologies (Sassaman 1992). Looking for women also accounts for a renewed interest in iconographic representation (Levy 1995, Pollock 1991), and especially in female figurines (Bailey 1994b; Brumfiel 1996; Dobres 1992; Hamilton et al 1996; Joyce 1993a,b, 1997; Lesure 1997). The results of these studies are that women have shown up at prehistoric sites and in political and economic activities all over the globe, sometimes in the most unlikely places.

This literature contains sharply differing views of gender in human history: Males and females are interpreted as accepting and reproducing, or as resisting and redefining, their gendered social positions. Definitions of what it might have meant to be female or male at particular points in time alternate with descriptions of how gender meanings shift and undergo transformations. Gendered groups are lumped or split. The primacy of gender as determinant of social identity is sometimes emphasized. Other times, gender is subsumed under other social identities such as ethnicity, class, or occupational status. Some researchers use archaeological materials to focus on behavioral patterns (gender roles) of females and males, while others focus on gender relations and relative statuses of females and males, or on gender ideology as sets of meanings attached to being female or male (Robb 1994).

Equally notable is the continuing development and literature in archaeology that takes an explicitly gender-sensitive approach to the sociology of the field. A number of volumes deal with the previously "hidden voices"—women as archaeologists—particularly in the history of archaeology. Biographies of previously unacknowledged or underappreciated women archeologists include the work compiled in Claassen's (1994) and Reyman's (1992) edited volumes, as well as studies published elsewhere (S Bender 1991, 1992; Bishop & Lange 1991; Chilton 1992; Claassen 1993; Cordell 1991; Joiner 1992; Levine 1991; Nelson 1991b; Parezo 1993; Woodbury 1992). These reveal a surprising range of roles and strength of scholarship that women offered archaeology on many continents, sometimes as the hidden spouse but also often as a passionate but publically invisible contributor. There is also a substantive body on equity issues (in Claassen 1992, in du Cros & Smith 1993, Engelstad et al 1994, Ford & Hundt 1994, Hanen & Kelley 1992, Nelson et al 1994, Ovrevik 1991, Spielmann 1994).

Equity issues in archaeology have consistently influenced, and been influenced by, the scholarly research on gender in past human societies. In fact, studies by Smith & du Cros (1995), Wylie (1994b, 1996), and Hanen & Kelley (1992) find that the interest in engendering prehistory has been directly motivated by perceived or existing gender inequities in the modern research community (see also Whelan 1995). Meanwhile, feminist ideas, theory, or perspectives are only rarely cited as having motivated participants' interest in gender as a topic of research (Wylie 1994b, 1996).

Theoretically Anchored Positions

In this section, we highlight several theoretical approaches that have proven especially rich for engendering archaeological data and/or that present an especially well-developed theoretical position on gender. These are identified because the assumptions underlying each approach directly influence the scale of analysis, the data selected for analysis, or the interpretive meanings attached to archaeological gender research. In each case, the theoretical perspectives include a range of expressions rather than a single stance; further, they are neither mutually exclusive nor always compatible. We regret that our summaries may oversimplify to the point of distortion, but we provide additional references to persue. Ultimately, each of the six approaches represents a different way to connect empirical archaeological study with theoretical resources and arguments, a process that we strongly promote for the maturation of an engendered archaeology.

GENDER AS SOCIOBIOLOGICAL STRATEGY   Some researchers have found it useful to frame gender as the culturally mediated means by which sex groups seek to maximize their reproductive fitness by contributing more genes to the genetic constitution of future generations. Sociobiological researchers conceive of two unambiguously dichotomous sexes giving rise more or less directly to two uniformly gendered classes of individuals, males and females, whose biological sexual characteristics are modeled as presumed universals, including the (male) ability to fertilize (multiple) eggs and the (female) ability to produce single ovulation events and to physically bear children, in addition to hormonal differences, lactation, menstruation, and biological strength. Any one or a combination of several universal sex characteristics can be considered determinant of the cultural behaviors adopted by each sex group and account for why males and females are "assigned" gender-specific roles and activities. Socio-biological positions differ in the degree of determinism assigned to specific biological factors as well as in the degree of cultural conditioning and mediation that intervenes between the drive for biological fitness and the expression of gendered behaviors. Thus, highly determinant sociobiological positions include Knight's (1991) argument for the cultural implications of convergent female menstruation and the simultaneous ovulation of proximate women (see also Golub 1992; or Zeanah et al's 1995 argument for different male and female foraging strategies in the Great Basin). Hayden (1992) similarly associates "well-established" sex differences such as hormonally related aggression levels with broadly observed gender preferences for particular tasks, such as group defense. At a much less direct level of sociobiological reasoning, Costin (1996) argues that gender difference in its many diverse aspects represents a highly general means for members of each sex group, within a given cultural context, to demonstrate their appropriateness both as marriage mates and as potential parents to a mate's children.

GENDER AS SOCIAL CONSTRUCTION   The concept that gender and sex are constructed—that is, not rooted in biology or procreation nor inherently dichotomous—has been integral to feminist theory in the anthropological literature since the 1970s (see especially Kessler & McKenna 1985). But meanings of "social construction" have developed and changed, from the initial liberal feminist approaches that emphasized only the social construction of masculinity and femininity, often taken as givens [see Epstein's (1988) critique], to the French feminists' focus on psychoanalysis and politics (e.g. Irigaray 1985), to the position that challenges gender as a construction more important than, or even differentiable from, aspects of class, race, and/or ethnicity (e.g. Collins 1989, Hooks 1984), to the cultural feminists' (e.g. Butler 1990, Flax 1990) rejection of the stability of either sex or gender as categories, even as socially constructed ones, or to Lorber's (1994) recent analysis of gender as a social institution. All the variant ideas within the constructionist critique start from the assumption that the construction of our analytical categories (even the very term "gender") is deeply embedded in historical, sociocultural, ideological, and material contexts.

Archaeologically, this may take the form of questioning the "origins" of gender (e.g. Conroy 1993, Moore 1991, Whelan 1991): At what point and, more importantly, under what circumstances, did something like "gender," as a social construction, come into play in human life? What is its relationship to the (sexual) division of labor? How, archaeologically, might we recognize or identify the emergence or existence of social phenomena that look like gender? If one accepts the idea that gender is dependent upon symbolic communication systems, it is immediately problematic to assume that australopithecines or other early hominids had "gender."

There is little work within the anthropology of gender that does not take gender to be some form of social construction; perhaps only the sociobiologists reject or avoid using the concept. But the implication that necessarily follows, namely a "respect for historical difference and change" (di Leonardo 1991b, p. 29), has not always been embraced, even after such compelling studies as Laqueur (1990), Jordanova (1980), and Merchant (1980) have demonstrated the importance of historical change vis-à-vis gender and sexuality, just within Western history. While social constructivism is widespread, varying degrees of constructionism are admitted. There is justifiable concern about the radical version of the constructivist critique, which tolerates interpretations that could be labeled "nihilistic," and there is also justifiable concern for the ways in which this constructivist critique has been polarized against a conservative objectivism (Wylie 1994a,b; see also Bergman's 1995 critique of di Leonardo's oppositionality of postmodernism with political economy). Given archaeology's concern with the materiality of past human life, an important issue arising from these debates for archaeology, and one of archaeology's important contributions to them, is to probe the best means of analyzing the dialectic between human life as socially constructed and the very materiality of human life. One of the more eloquent expositions on this topic, specifically oriented toward the archaeology of gender, is by Wylie (1992; see also responses by Fotiadis 1994, Little 1994, Wylie 1994c). Above all, the idea of gender as a social construction mandates that archaeologists interrogate their starting assumptions when setting out to do an archaeology of gender.

GENDER AS AN EVOLUTIONARY PROCESS   Evolutionary models, which arrange discrete sociocultural instances in an order toward increasing complexity, may assume, and thus be useful in predicting, regular changes in the evolution of gender systems. While the egalitarian relations of foraging peoples are reiterated in nonhierarchical gender relations, an intensification of gender hierarchy is posited to correspond with each level of increased sociocultural ranking or stratification. Thus for the evolutionists, the widely observed male dominance in present-day societies is seen as anything but normal or natural.

Rather, the appearance of patriarchy is linked to the emergence or incurrence of the state, with its admission of hegemonic power relationships and overt power differentials.

Evolutionary models may follow more or less closely from Engels's descriptions of an early matriarchic period in human history (sometimes called Gynecentric Theory) later overturned by males who subverted the natural order and balance. Feminist anthropologists and ethnohistorians have used such understandings to explain the transformation of independent Naskapi women into submissive Christian wives after contact with Jesuits (Leacock 1981); the step-by-step erosion of Andean women's realms of feminine power, first through the rise of the Inka state and then as the Spanish conquest of what is now Peru intensified (Silverblatt 1987, 1991); or the undermining of Tongan women's power by the colonist invaders' transformations of social relations (Gailey 1987). There is little doubt that, given the success of archaeology with some forms of an evolutionary paradigm, the scrutiny of "gender" as part of the evolutionary transformations in the human past can and have yielded important new understandings of the transformations themselves.

GENDER AS POLITICAL ECONOMY   Although the "culture and political economy" approach is a widespread feature of much recent anthropological inquiry (see Roseberry 1988), among feminist sociocultural anthropologists this view has been promoted most vigorously by Micaela di Leonardo (1991a,b, 1993). di Leonardo (1991b, p. 27) defines five key points in her feminist culture and political economy approach (di Leonardo 1991a, but see Bergman 1995 for a critique). First, she favors a radical rejection of social evolutionism. In contrast to the evolutionist approaches noted above, she argues that "feminist anthropologists cannot locate the 'key' to male dominance over women in small-scale societies," as if these somehow represented "living history" (di Leonardo 1991b, p. 28); the approach mandates a "respect for history."

From this pour forth additional points, including the rejection of essentialism, the potent role of social constructionism (see above), and the recognition of the "embeddedness" of gender in other social divisions like hierarchy. Lastly, she argues for the imperative analysis of all forms of social inequality and the explicit recognition of the "multiple layers of context through which we perceive cultural inequalities" (1991b, p. 31).

For archaeological studies, there is much to be gained from engaging with these points and putting them to work in interpretations of the archaeological record. Foremost among those who have considered the effects of political economy on gender roles and constructs is Elizabeth Brumfiel. Brumfiel (1992) reminds archaeologists that "political economy" is not equivalent to the more traditional "subsistence economy" approach because the former recognizes the role of human agency, politics, and negotiations in economic decisions and actions. Brumfiel (1991) also draws on standard archaeological evidence such as ceramics and spindle whorls to demonstrate how Aztec women may have undertaken different strategies to negotiate the demand for production of tribute cloth. This provides an excellent example of how foregrounding gender, and in particular the role of women, in an analysis of Aztec political economy leads to more nuanced and "peopled" understanding.

Furthermore, Brumfiel's study demonstrates that there is no single "women's role" but rather several alternative strategies through which tribute can be "paid" through women's labor. Brumfiel's work is a powerful reminder against the tendency to homogenize or essentialize—in this case Aztec— "women" and forces our attention to what Moore (1993) has called "differences within" rather than to the "differences between"—as between the two genders, men and women—that are usually discussed.

GENDER AS AGENCY   Taking a cue from what has been more generally called "practice theory" (Bourdieu 1977, Ortner 1984), some scholars have come to understand gender as one of the "acts" whereby social identities are produced and are constantly "in production". Gendered subjects are produced, not born. Recent anthropological thought has recognized, first, the importance of an ongoing tension between "structure" and "agency" (after Giddens 1979 and others) and, second, "the agency of subordinated and marginalized persons to contest meanings and engage in praxis in their social worlds" (Bergman 1995, p. 235). As such, this perspective is clearly suitable for probing aspects of gender, especially in those historical circumstances in which gender, marginality, and subordination are inextricably, and perhaps inevitably, entangled.

If gender itself is taken to be produced by the goal-oriented actions and performances of individuals or groups, this opens the door, even within archaeology, to reassessments of everything from technology (as gendered labor practices, after Dobres 1995a) to sculptural choices (as producing and reaffirming conceptions of personhood, after Joyce 1993a) to apparently simple artifacts, such as the pins and spindle whorls (as markers of gendered identities, after Marcus 1994 or McCafferty & McCafferty 1991, respectively) to food preparation (Hastorf 1991).

GENDER AS PERFORMANCE   Arising largely from the work of Judith Butler (1988, 1990, 1993), the performativity view of gender dismisses gender as an essential quality or as any kind of entity that individuals can "have," and is replaced by a concept of gender as how people exhibit themselves in their actions and bodily decorations. In assuming that ongoing gender "production" is crucial, Butler directs attention to the analysis of performance as a means of analyzing this production. This is appealing in that it is a "temporally attuned approach" (Hasbrouck 1996, p. 17), one that promotes the idea that both gender and sexuality are very complex and fluid in each individual, continually in a relational flux. Moreover, in her work, and therefore differentiating her work from the earlier arguments of West & Zimmerman (1987), Butler argues that gender is constituted as a set of acts that produce the effect or appearance of a coherent substance, and that it works and derives its compelling force from the fact that people themselves mistake the gender acts they perform for the essence, coming to believe that such acts are genuine, inescapable moments of self-actualization. Thus, in Butler's terms, performatives are both generative and dissimulating, compelling certain kinds of behavior by hiding the fact that there is no essential, natural sex to which gender can refer as its starting point.

In archaeology, the performativity of gender has been explored most actively by Rosemary Joyce (1993a, 1996, 1997) showing, for instance, how the practices of inscription required in the employment of ornaments of durable materials (carved stone and ceramic beads, pendants, ear ornaments, etc) transform the open and generative shifting performances of gender to closed, prescriptional ones.

Challenges to an Archaeology of Gender

Within the explosive archaeological literature on gender, a small number of studies cross-cut the examples of theoretically anchored positions examined above and differentiate themselves by presenting the discipline with real challenges to research as usual. The assumptions, methodologies, and conclusions of such works must be taken seriously to anticipate the full potential of a feminist-inspired archaeology of gender. For instance, although Janet Spector's 1993 book, *What this Awl Means: Feminist Archaeology at a Wahpeton Dakota Village,* covers what might be expected in a traditional site report (context and background of study, methodology, data, and interpretation) it also departs radically from traditional presentations of archaeology materials. Spector (1993, p. 3) rejects an "objective, object oriented and objectifying" archaeology to position herself and other interested contemporary actors (Native Americans, crew, archaeological associates) at the center of the report. The narrative abandons the passive academic voice and the abstracted European categories imposed on Indian artifacts and insistently ties archaeological information back to the experiences of specific archaeologists (Spectors's own intellectual roots) and relationships among specific indigenous peoples (the history and experiences of the Eastern Dakota).

The reiterated use of Dakota personal names and Dakota names for things is partly (literally) how Spector forces us to consider the Wahpeton Dakota in their own terms, but Spector also plumbs ethnohistory and nineteenth-century illustrative accounts to present a richly detailed and specific reading of Dakota seasonal and gendered social life, confronting readers on another level with the enormous gulf that separates our normalizing "scientific" research from the highly individualized cultural lives that we study. Spector highlights women's activities and the relationships between men and women by examining the tasks performed by each gender, but also by presenting a fictional reconstruction of how one artifact, an incised bone awl, might have been situated and then lost in the life of one Wahpeton woman. Spector's work evokes our humility in understanding and proposing meanings for what we study in archaeology, cautioning us not to resist interpretation but rather to resist imposing meanings from outside the experiential worlds of the people we study.

Brumfiel, in her lecture as the Distinguished Archaeology Speaker at the 1991 annual meetings of the American Anthropological Association, delivered a message of considerable insight and impact, not only for the archaeology of gender but for archaeological theory more widely (Brumfiel 1992). She shows quite clearly that to take up the topic of gender is, itself, a challenge to extant theory and method. As someone trained in, skilled in, and committed to many of the tenets of "processual" archaeology, Brumfiel has particular credibility in her critique of the ecosystem approach that has long been a central feature of processual research. In this, Brumfiel challenges the usually dichotomous categories of "processual" and "postprocessual" that have come to characterize different approaches in contemporary archaeology. Instead, she argues forcefully that the analysis of social change has "been hampered" by certain components of the ecosystem approaches as used in archaeology, such as its insistence upon whole populations and whole adaptive behavioral systems as units of analysis that obscure "the visibility of gender, class, and faction in the prehistoric past." She shows that when gender, class, and faction are taken into consideration, then aspects of the prehistoric record can be explained that cannot be explained from the ecosystem perspective. Thus, the very appreciation of the importance of gender, class, and faction leads directly into a stunning critique of one fundamental processual tenet, namely, that cultures are adaptive systems.

Brumfiel (1992) also shows that the recognition of gender, class, and factions and their intersections has enormous theoretical implications. While reasserting the potential of an agent-centered or "peopled" approach, she simultaneously advocates that we can continue to pursue new versions of cross-cultural and testable models. This work is crucial to placing the archaeology of gender in several wider frameworks, including both the history of archaeological theory and the emergent emphasis in feminist research more widely on understanding the intersection among variables such as gender, race, and class.

The very category of "gender" in archaeological analysis has been challenged by Roberts (1993), with particular emphasis on the implications of gendered research for archaeology. There are two especially important aspects to her critique, a critique with which we have considerable sympathy. First, Roberts demonstrates that while social theory is central to taking up "gender" as a category of archaeological analysis, there is enormous resistance to the archaeological theorizing of gender. Because of the difficulties of importing social theory directly into archaeology, she argues, "theorizing gender will continue to be extrinsic to archaeology" (p. 17). This gives rise to the tension between those "who pursue an archaeology of gender as an end in itself (most gender case studies) and those who are critical of this approach (Conkey 1990)" (p. 18). Thus, Roberts identifies a key paradox of gender research in archaeology: "[T]hose interested in an archaeology of gender cannot afford to challenge the framework assumptions and paradigms of research practice...because an 'archaeology of gender' relies upon these things for its formulation and expression" (p. 18).

In the second aspect of her critique, Roberts makes a clear distinction between "two threads" in the use of gender as an archaeological category. She calls one "the archaeology of gender," the other "gendered archaeology." While these threads are interwoven, she says, they will necessarily have different impacts on the practice and "results" of archaeology. The archaeology of gender, while offering "crucial insights" and rectifying some gender biases, "moves toward synthesis" and does not necessarily lead to reconceptualizations. Gendered archaeology, however, "involves the interrogation of archaeological inquiry"; archaeology is shown to be a "highly-constructed form of knowledge-seeking" (Roberts 1993, p. 18). It implies that we should follow a path that is more self-reflexive and that gender, for example, must be a fully theorized concept, not just another analytical variable. She draws explicitly from feminist insights, and while advocating our attention to such, she does not advocate merely replacing our existing modes with some sort of "uniquely feminist mode," something that, in any event is itself hotly contested (e.g. Longino 1987, 1994; Stacey 1988; Wylie 1995).

Roberts (1993) herself notes that the very introduction of gender research in archaeology has contributed to two significant features of contemporary archaeology: (*a*) the recognition that archaeology is necessarily interpretive and therefore "must come to terms with other than common-sense explanations of human action" (p. 20); and (*b*) the recognition that archaeology is, more than ever, faced with developing its own distinctive understandings. This means that while there is much extrinsic to archaeology to be looked to and inspired by, gendered archaeology will necessarily need to adapt this material to the special conditions of archaeological knowledge. We endorse this view.

Critical Thoughts: The Overburden of the Cottage Industry and Other Obstacles

There is much to celebrate about the enthusiastic adoption of gender in archaeological study: New questions have been put to old data, new topics and perspectives have been brought to well-studied archaeological situations, and questions have been raised about the gendered production of both the archaeological record and archaeological knowledge (see below). But the above-discussed challenges also suggest that the explicit focus on gender in archaeology has more deeply exposed—or at least thrown into new relief—fundamental and even irreconcilable differences between what a feminist and a traditional archaeology are, and how one thus goes about doing archaeology. That is, not all archaeologists will embrace the pursuit of an archaeology of gender, even when the point is clear that not everyone must "find" gender (e.g. Dobres 1995c).

In the explosion of work in archaeology about gender, some of it draws explicitly and creatively from robust and richly developed theoretical resources, from both within and outside archaeology. But much of the literature considers gender in prehistoric studies without reconfiguring archaeology in any way, without drawing from new resources to tackle new problems, without admitting the ambiguity of archaeological data, and without repositioning the otherwise authoritative scholar in the complex web of theory, data, and archaeological practice. As Bender (1997) points out, there seems to be a rush to the pragmatic, to the empiricist studies without a simultaneous engagement with the requisite theoretical resources. To her, this makes for "rather thin gruel" (B Bender 1997). This also matters to us.

This is not to say that only archaeology has such problems. In her introduction to *Gendered Anthropology*, del Valle (1993b) notes how little of the theoretical work in gendered anthropology has impacted, much less been incorporated into, anthropology more widely, and mainstream assumptions and categories remain intact. She astutely notes that this is primarily related to the control and validation of (anthropological) knowledge, an issue to which we can only allude here (del Valle 1993b, pp. 14–16) but which is also true in archaeology.

We could expect the explosion of work in the archaeology of gender to appear in wider feminist and even anthropological treatises; there should be archaeological contributions to journals like SIGNS or to the Association for Feminist Anthropology's Silvia Forman Prize competition for an outstanding student paper. This has yet to happen. In Lorber's (1994) recent overview chapter on the archaeological contexts for understanding gender, one finds only several references to Ehrenberg's (1989) general text; no other works on the archaeology of gender are taken into account. Why is it that it is discussions of "the Goddess" (and citations of Gimbutas, e.g. 1989) that are featured in such overviews of the human past (but for critiques see Billington & Green 1996, Conkey & Tringham 1995, Meskell 1995). Why, despite the many new studies in the archaeology of gender, have most merely added gender as just another variable into an otherwise depersonalized view of the past? into an archaeological account in the passive voice? into a way of framing human life that distances and categorizes more than allowing our own positionalities to inform and generate engagements with the people of the past? We worry that the recent archaeological studies of gender have participated in narrowing the field rather than opening up our studies.

SITUATING GENDER RESEARCH: WHY FEMINISM MATTERS

It is clear by now that gender as a subject of archaeology elicits genuine concern for much needed revisions of archaeological accounts that have systematically ignored, devalued, or underestimated the roles, actions, contributions, and innovations of women. There is interest in more concentrated and informed inquiries into gender relations, gender dynamics, and explicity engendered past human societies, and for the roles and effects of gender (in its broadest senses) in human life, cultural change, and human histories. In addition, there are concerns for refocusing archaeological scrutiny to consider at least equally factions, class, gender, or other sociocultural dynamics at the human level, the concern for a more peopled past (e.g. Brumfiel 1992; McBryde 1996; Tringham 1991, 1994).

From these genuine concerns with a newly gendered and peopled past, certain additional issues are immediately implicated. From the beginning, it was apparent that rampant biases—where were the women?—were entrenched in the interpretations of past human societies. Clearly, the awareness and even shock of these and related gender biases fed on and were fed by other critiques raised by investigators like Leone (1973, 1982), Trigger (1984), or Gero et al (1983). However, subsequent archaeological studies of gender and more general critiques of the discipline have not always taken advantage of the well-established literature on gender theory and feminist critiques of science, especially as they bear on issues of interpreting human cultures and the organization of scientific practice. While Bergman (1995, p. 235) can say with confidence that feminist anthropology has been shaped by, but also has contributed to, interlinked critiques of essentialism and scientific authority, we are not so sure the same can yet be said for anthropological archaeology.

We now consider feminist resources essential to understanding the production of archaeological knowledge and the sociology of the field more generally, and the potential of gender research more specifically. These perspectives matter not merely to gender research in archaeology but to archaeology as a wider practice. The feminist literature encompasses issues that engage us in debates about the very nature of humankind: essentialism, inequality and power relationships, social categorization, political economy, rationality and ways of knowing, ideology, meaning and symbol making, materiality and agency. Most or all of these are crucial to the archaeological enterprise, whether focused on gender or not, and often offer radically innovative twists and challenges to the ways in which our conventional categories operate.

A recent and staunchly critical attack on women's studies by Patai & Koertge (1994) argued that while it might be productive to learn about women, it is downright dangerous to engage in the "radical reappraisal of all the assumptions and values found in traditional scholarship." We, however, find much merit in Sternhill's (1994) critical review of Patai & Koertge (and also of Sommers 1994), insisting that feminist thought is "supposed to be dangerous"; "radical reappraisal—rigorous, scholarly, informed—is called for."

If we want to explore a configuring of contemporary archaeology, it is simply "poor research" to ignore a large and diverse body of theoretical, analytical, and conceptual possibilities that pertain directly to and substantively inform the questions at hand. This includes the literature on gender theory, readings that span archaeological feminism (e.g. biographies of women and equity studies) and nonarchaeological feminist critiques of science. "Do I have to do the readings?" We would say the answer is, "yes."

Feminist Critiques of Science

Clearly, archaeology now admits a well-developed documentation of the social and political "entanglements," both for the practice of archaeology and for its "results" (e.g. Fotiadis 1993; Gathercole & Lowenthal 1990; Gero et al 1983; Leone 1986; Pinsky & Wylie 1989; Trigger 1980, 1989). Although no responsible archaeologist today can claim unmitigated objectivism or sociopolitical or historical innocence (Wylie 1994a,c, 1996), it is still the case that we regularly, perhaps schizophrenically, shelve our doubts and move on with assured and even definitive statements about "what the past was like."

Feminist thinking, however, has long offered a foundation for a critique of authority, symbol, the canon(s) of science, and the arrangements by which science is produced—indeed, the very nature of scientific inquiry. Feminist critiques of science raise crucial questions about who can be a "knower," about the relationships between the community of knowers and the knowledge they cooperatively produce, and about the "moralization of objectivity" (Daston & Galison 1992). Needless to say, they hardly converge on a simple solution.

Feminists have engaged in a decade of debate about the degree of revision versus rejection that would be required in today's science to make feminist-friendly those versions of objectivity that exist presently in the service of hierarchical and positivist orderings of what is to count as knowledge. Harding's "successor science" project (an insistence on irreducible difference and radical multiplicity of local knowledges) risks denying that realities can be known. Alternatively, Longino (1990, 1993) argues to preserve a modified and improved umbrella of universal scientific practice, in part because it is this very tradition, supported and carried out by a highly varied set of practitioners, that has been responsible for the unveiling of androcentrism and the devaluation of women's lots.

With such a long-standing association between feminism and science critiques, it is hardly surprising that fundamental questions about the organization of archaeological inquiry have disproportionately come from archaeologists of gender. A number of points developed out of feminist critiques of science have proved particularly powerful in interrogating archaeological practice, and we summarize some of these here, in a necessarily abbreviated form, pointing each to archaeological applications:

1. Feminists, among others, recognize that politics and the substantive products of knowledge are essentially inseparable (Code 1991, Keller 1985, Jay 1991, Rossiter 1982). Long suspicious of science as a bastion of male privilege, feminists argue that at the least the sciences betray a pervasive disinterest in concerns of women, and at worst that science, especially the social and medical sciences, reproduce and legitimize precisely the ideology of gender inequity that feminists question (Wylie 1997). Moreover, the statistical absence of women in the sciences, and the ideology that has underwritten and supported this gender distribution in the sciences, has also produced "masculinist" understandings and research conclusions.

At this very general level of critique, archaeologists have provided compelling evidence of how gendered research is coupled to specific construals of theory and of the past. Brumfiel (1993), for instance, has argued that a special high-prestige disciplinary niche is reserved for archaeological directors of large regional field projects ("big digs"), and moreover, that this prestige system generates narrow notions of class-based ideologies. Gero (1993) provides evidence that the exclusion of women from Paleoindian research has permitted a dominant paradigm to persist that focuses exclusively on hunting as the essential and definitional activity of early colonizers of the American continent.

2. Feminists, among others, have argued that rationality, with its attendant notions of separability of subject and object, dispassionate objectivity, and neutral transcendence of personal states, is a mythical conflation that never obtains in actual scientific practice and, more significantly, itself represents a metapolitics of power relations. The insistence that thinking, feeling, and willing are not separate facilities but rather underlie all informed interpretations of data has led some archaeologists to replace, or at least amplify, their purported subjectless research conclusions with richly informed fictional interpretations of what transpired in prehistory (Handsman 1991; Pollock 1991; Schrire 1995; Spector 1991, 1993; Tringham 1991). Similarly, a feminist-inspired archaeology has embraced sensuous, rather than exclusively rational or cognitive, experience as a motivating antecedent for behavior (Kus 1989); it has also focused archaeological study on sensuous domains of material life, including alcohol consumption (Lawrence-Cheney 1991, 1993), sweatlodge participation (Carman 1991), and brothel life (Seifert 1994).

3. Feminist thinking has argued for and been associated with a cognitive style that favors "intimate" knowledge and nuanced understandings of data over categorical thinking. Ambiguity in observations of data and unique expressions of phenomena are recognized and taken to be informative rather than to be dismissed as lying outside the province of "scientific" data (Haraway 1988; Keller 1983, 1985). This appreciation for the idiosyncratic and its associated tendency to distrust categorical formulations has led more specifically to an impatience with binary or dichotomous thinking (Jay 1991, Moulton 1983). Thus, archaeologists like Spector (1993) point out how common typological schemes of material inventories can bias appreciation for indigenous views, imposing foreign values and distorting native categories.

All three of these areas of feminist thought and their applications to anthropological research have been explored in Haraway's (1988) rejection of omniscient scientific knowledge, "the god trick of seeing everything from nowhere," in favor of "situated knowledges," where only the partial perspective can promise objectivity: "All Western cultural narratives about objectivity are allegories of the ideologies governing the relations of what we call mind and body, distance and responsibility. Feminist objectivity is about limited location and situated knowledge, not about transcendence and splitting of subject and object" (Haraway 1988, p. 583).

4. Feminist thinking has shared a deep commitment to challenging the status quo or, minimally, to welcoming the possibility of change in basic disciplinary arrangements. From its well-substantiated impatience with androcentric structures of knowledge and with the standard means of producing and reproducing that knowledge, feminists are eager for an alternative voice or voices to be heard. This proposition is explored more fully below.

FEMINIST PRACTICE

The implications of the feminist critique, taken seriously, point ineluctably to a recognition of the bias inherent in how archaeology is practiced, and to a dedicated effort to develop a more feminist-friendly archaeology. It is not just that archaeological institutions should be more tolerant of diverse agendas that include gender as a legitimate endeavor of research, nor that the range of variables considered relevant and the array of explanatory hypotheses considered worth testing be expanded, but more fundamentally that we reconsider the gendered arrangements by which "facts" are established and subsequently accepted as knowledge. Of course, the implicit, taken-for-granted rules of practice make it difficult to discover foundational principles and make their outcomes appear seamless, theory-neutral, and objective. If feminism, however, is to have meaning in archaeology, we must ask how to "do archaeology" as feminists (Longino 1987, p. 53). And as starting points, we suggest three broadly defined concerns that could be involved in the practical remaking of archaeology as a transformatory enterprise:

1. Feminist practice might strive to increase the visibility of human agency in knowledge production, becoming more conscious of, and making more public, the choices that accumulate into what is known about the past. Here, for instance, we might consider publishing fuller field diaries that tie investigatory decisions to specific items of new knowledge, to diminish the appearance of knowledge appearing directly and automatically from the field into textbooks. On a very different tack, we might study, with special attention, areas in the production chains of archaeological knowledge where males or females appear significantly clustered, questioning why predominantly one gender or the other is cited, or why one gender or the other participates in certain symposia or publishes in certain literatures and asking what values and priorities underpin these sortings and what kinds of knowledge they authorize.

2. Especially given the destruction and nonreplicability of archaeological sites of excavation, we might organize archaeological field projects in less hierarchical fashions, avoiding the situation of a single unchallengeable authority who pronounces judgments from the top. Instead, feminist practice might offer multiple interpretive judgments and evaluations at each nonreversible step of investigation, and coordinate multiple strategies and objectives of different co-investigators into the research of nonrenewable archaeological resources.

3. Feminist practice needs to admit ambiguity and partial or situated knowledges in its analyses; we need to find ways to value the indeterminate, the nuanced, and the specific in new narrative and historical cognitive frames,

rather than always circumscribing scientific models and categorical data. A related preliminary step that might be initiated by feminists would urge recognition that all generalized archaeological pronouncements, from taxonomic arrangements, to attributing cause-and-effect, to reconstructing climatic conditions, to interpreting past lifeways, are all interpretive activities, not entirely divorced from writing informed fictional interpretations.

"Keep Your Mind on the Prize...."

As research on women and gender comes of age in archaeology, the most pressing question we face is precisely that of how to do archaeology differently—how to do it better, more inclusively, more imaginatively—given the realization of the ways in which our thinking and practices have been confined by androcentric and many other "taken-for-granteds." Our essential premise is that an archaeology that takes feminist theory seriously is self-transformational and communal. Radical reappraisals—rigorous, scholarly, informed, purposive—emerge from feminist theory precisely because traditional assumptions and values really do look profoundly different when viewed from a woman-centered perspective. Some have wanted to call this "seeing gender everywhere," with the derogatory term "genderlirium." But "genderlirium" is an equally apt term with which to critique Western androcentricism, with its hard-headed rules for a single way of knowing and its single vision.

While archaeology enjoyed an earlier infusion of optimism from New Archaeology—the 1960s Binfordian proclamations that "we can know anything if we just ask the right questions"—we are excited by the imaginative possibilities for what archaeology can do and say if it engages with gendered archaeology (in Roberts's sense) and with much of what is under consideration in feminist thought. In our visions for archaeology, we see an increasing recognition that knowledge-making is a pluralistic enterprise with, for example, more recognition and institutional rewards for collaborative multiperspective research, teaching and writing, and increased recruitment of the many still-silenced (ethnic, gender, racial) voices that should be integral to archaeological discourse. We also envision not just tolerance for but the fostering of views—including ways of presenting and writing, and what constitutes archaeology—from many "wheres" (if not from everywhere) (after Longino 1994, Wylie 1995). We would encourage the trajectory already witnessed in the archaeology of gender to giving simultaneous attention not only to gender research about the past but also to the teaching and pedagogy of archaeology (in Claassen 1992, Wright 1996), to the practices of archaeological research (Gero 1996, Preucel & Joyce 1994), and to its institutional structures (e.g. in Nelson et al 1994).

To have a vision for an archaeology influenced by feminist concerns is not to promote a static, prescribed utopia. While one should always "keep your mind on the prize" (Collins 1994, p. 32), the feminist vision has no fixed endpoint to be achieved by a standardized set of rules (p. 32). Feminist destinations are perhaps less important than the everyday pragmatic work of moving the feminist vision along; the dignity achieved in struggling for something worthwhile may be more important than any predetermined endpoint of a feminist world. As such, we are impressed by the heretofore unimagined interest, concern, genuine thoughtfulness, and diversity of "results" from the first decade of an explicit attention to gender within archaeology.

ACKNOWLEDGMENTS

Initial inspirations and directions for this piece were offered with grace and spirit from Barbara Bender, Elizabeth Brumfiel, Ericka Englestad, Christine Hastorf, Rosemary Joyce, and Ruth Tringham at a memorable Berkeley dinner. Special gratitude and thanks to Elizabeth Brumfiel for her selfless, supportive, and superb editing, and to Rita Wright, Cathy Costin, Julia Hendon, Rosemary Joyce, Susan Evans, Michelle Marcus, Alison Wylie, and many others who kindly provided us with prepublication manuscripts. Thanks, too, to the participants of the 1994 AAA symposium, "Gender as if it really matters: feminist thinking and archaeological practice," for their thoughtful contributions to the dialogue. Joan Gero gratefully acknowledges the University of South Carolina Josephine Abney Fellowship for Feminist Research for support. While page limitations do not allow us to cite all the important papers, this itself a testimony to the vibrant state of recent scholarship.

Visit the *Annual Reviews home page* at http://www.AnnualReviews.org.

Literature Cited

Allen H. 1996. Ethnography and prehistoric archaeology in Australia. *J. Anthropol. Archeol.* 15:137–59

Archer L, Fischler S, Wyke M. 1994. *Women in Ancient Societies: An Illusion in the Night.* London: Macmillan

Arsenault D. 1991. The representation of women in Moche iconography. See Walde & Willows 1991, pp. 313–26

Bacus E, Barker AW, Bonevich JD, Dunavan SL, Fitzhugh JB, et al, eds. 1993. *A Gendered Past: A Critical Bibliography of Gender in Archaeology.* Ann Arbor, MI: Univ. Mich. Mus. Anthropol.

Bailey DW. 1994a. The representation of gender: homology or propaganda. *J. Eur. Archeol.* 2:189–202

Bailey DW. 1994b. Reading prehistoric figurines as individuals. *World Archeol.* 25: 321–31

Balme J, Beck W, eds. 1995. *Gendered Archaeology: The Second Australian Women in Archaeology Conference.* Canberra: Aust. Natl. Univ.

Bender B. 1997. Introduction. In *Gender and Material Culture: Representations of Gender from Prehistory to the Present.* London" Macmillan

Bender S. 1991. Towards a history of women in northeastern U. S. archaeology. See Walde & Willows 1991, pp. 211–16

Bender S. 1992. Marian E. White: pioneer in New York archaeology. *Bull. NY State Archeol. Assoc.* 104:14–20

Benedict JW. 1993. *Excavations at Bode's Draw: A Women's Work Area in the Mountains Near Estes Park, Colorado.* Ward, CO: Cent. Mt. Archaeol.

Bergman J. 1995. The persistence of kinship: recent contributions to feminist anthropology. *Anthropol. Q.* 68:234–40

Billington S, Green M. 1996. *The Concept of the Goddess.* London: Routledge

Bishop R, Lange F. 1991. *The Ceramic Legacy of Anna O. Shepard.* Niwot, CO: Univ. Press Colo.

Boardman J. 1991. Naked truth. *Oxford J. Archeol.* 10:119–21

Bourdieu P. 1977. *Outline of a Theory of Practice.* Cambridge: Cambridge Univ. Press

Brumfiel E. 1991. Weaving and cooking: women's production in Aztec Mexico. See Gero & Conkey 1991, pp. 224–51

Brumfiel E. 1992. Breaking and entering the ecosystem: gender, class, and faction steal the show. *Am. Anthropol.* 94(3):551–67

Brumfiel E. 1993. Review of "Ideology and Pre-Columbian Civilization," ed. A Demarest, G Conrad. *J. Anthropol. Res.* 49: 412–14

Brumfiel E. 1996. Figurines and the Aztec state: testing the effectiveness of ideological domination. See Wright 1996, pp. 143–66

Butler J. 1988. Performative acts and gender constitution: an essay in phenomenology and feminist theory. *Theatre J.* 40:519–30

Butler J. 1990. *Gender Trouble: Feminism and the Subversion of Identity.* New York: Routledge

Butler J. 1993. *Bodies That Matter: On the Discursive Limits of "Sex".* New York/London: Routledge

Carman CJ. 1991. Sweatlodge participation among Nez Perce women. See Walde & Willows 1991, pp. 159–64

Chilton E. 1992. Archaeological investigations at the Goat Island rockshelter: new light from old legacies. *Hudson Valley Reg. Rev.* 9:47–75

Chilton E. 1994. In search of paleo-women: gender implications of remains from Paleoindian sites in the Northeast. *Bull. Mass. Archeol. Soc.* 55:8–14

Claassen C, ed. 1992. *Exploring Gender Through Archaeology.* Madison, WI: Prehistory Press

Claassen C. 1993. Black and white women at Irene Mound. *South. Archeol.* 12:137–47

Claassen C, ed. 1994. *Women in Archaeology.* Philadelphia: Univ. Pa. Press

Claassen C, Joyce R, eds. 1997. *Women in Prehistory. North America and Mesoamerica.* Philadelphia: Univ. Pa. Press

Code L. 1991. *What Can She Know? Feminist Theory and the Construction of Knowledge.* Ithaca, NY: Cornell Univ. Press

Collins PH. 1989. The social construction of Black feminist thought. *SIGNS: J. Women Cult. Soc.* 14:745–73

Collins PH. 1994. Keep your mind on the prize: a review of "Theorizing Black Feminisms: The Visionary Pragamatism of Black Women," ed. SM James, APA Busia. *Women's Rev. Books* 12:32

Conkey M, Tringham R. 1995. Archaeology and the goddess: exploring the contours of feminist archaeology. See Stanton & Stewart 1995, pp. 199–247

Conkey M, Williams S. 1991. Original narratives: the political economy of gender in archaeology. See di Leonardo 1991a, pp. 102–39

Conroy LP. 1993. Female figurines of the Upper Paleolithic and the emergence of gender. See du Cros & Smith 1993, pp. 153–60

Cordell L. 1991. Sisters of sun and spade, women archaeologists in the Southwest. See Walde & Willows 1991, pp. 502–9

Costin CL. 1993. Textiles, women and political economy in late prehispanic Peru. *Res. Econ. Anthropol.* 14:3–28

Costin CL. 1996. Exploring the relationship between gender and craft in complex societies: methodological and theoretical issues of gender attribution. See Wright 1996, pp. 111–42

Crabtree P. 1991. Gender hierarchies and the division of labor in the Natufian culture of the southern Levant. See Walde & Willows 1991, pp. 384–91

Daston L. 1991. Marvelous facts and miraculous evidence in early modern Europe. *Crit. Inq.* 18:93–124

Daston L, Galison P. 1992. The image of objectivity. *Representations* 40:81–128

del Valle T, ed. 1993a. *Gendered Anthropology.* London/New York: Routledge

del Valle T. 1993b. Introduction. See del Valle 1993a, pp. 1–16

Dent RJ. 1991. Deep time in the Potomac River Valley: thoughts in Paleoindian lifeways and revisionist archaeology. *Archeol. East. North Am.* 19:23–41

di Leonardo M, ed. 1991a. *Gender at the*

Crossroads of Knowledge: Feminist Anthropology in the Post-Modern Era. Berkeley: Univ. Calif. Press

di Leonardo M. 1991b. Introduction: gender, culture and political economy, feminist anthropology in historical perspective. See di Leonardo 1991a, pp. 1–48

di Leonardo M. 1993. What a difference political economy makes: feminist anthropology in the postmodern era. Anthropol. Q. 66:76–80

Dobres M-A. 1992. Reconsidering Venus figurines: a feminist inspired re-analysis. In The Archaeology of Ideology, ed. AS Goldsmith, S Garvie, D Selin, J Smith, pp. 245–62. Calgary: Archeol. Assoc. Univ. Calgary

Dobres M-A. 1995a. Gender in the Making: Late Magdalenian Social Relations of Production in the French Midi-Pyrénées. PhD thesis. Univ. Calif., Berkeley

Dobres M-A. 1995b. Gender and prehistoric technology: on the social agency of technical strategies. World Archeol. 27:25–49

Dobres M-A. 1995c. Beyond gender attribution: some methodological issues for engendering the past. See Balme & Beck 1995, pp. 51–66

Dobres M-A, Hoffman C. 1994. Social agency and the dynamics of prehistoric technology. J. Archaeol. Method Theory 1: 211–58

Dommasnes LH. 1992. Two decades of women in prehistory and in archaeology in Norway. A review. Nor. Archeol. Rev. 25: 1–14

du Cros H, Smith L, eds. 1993. Women in Archaeology: A Feminist Critique. Canberra: Aust. Natl. Univ.

Duke P. 1991. Recognizing gender in Plains hunting groups: Is it possible or even necessary? See Walde & Willows 1991, pp. 280–83

Ehrenberg M. 1989. Women in Prehistory. Oklahoma City, OK: Univ. Okla. Press

Engelstad E. 1991. Images of power and contradiction: feminist theory and post-processual archaeology. Antiquity 65: 502–14

Engelstad E, ed. 1992. Nor. Archaeol. Rev. 25(1):1–72

Engelstad E, Mandt G, Naess J-R. 1994. Equity issues in Norwegian archaeology. See Nelson et al 1994, pp. 139–46

Epstein CF. 1988. Deceptive Distinctions: Sex, Gender and the Social Order. New Haven, CT: Yale Univ. Press

Fantham E, Foley HP, Kampen NB, Pomeroy S, Shapiro HA. 1994. Women in the Classical World: Image and Text. New York: Oxford Univ. Press

Flax J. 1990. Thinking Fragments: Psychoanalysis, Feminism, and Postmodernism in the Contemporary West. Berkeley/Los Angeles: Univ. Calif. Press

Ford A, Hundt A. 1994. Equity in academia—why the best men still win: an examination of women and men in Mesoamerican archaeology. See Nelson et al 1994, pp. 147–56

Fotiadis M. 1993. Regions of the imagination: archaeologists, local people and the archaeological record in fieldwork, Greece. J. Eur. Archeol. 1:151–70

Fotiadis M. 1994. What is archaeology's "mitigated objectivism" mitigated by? Comments on Wylie. Am. Antiq. 59(3): 545–55

Gailey C. 1987. From Kinship to Kingship: Gender Hierarchy and State Formation in the Tongan Islands. Austin, TX: Univ. Tex. Press

Gathercole P, Lowenthal D, eds. 1990. The Politics of the Past. London/Boston: Unwin Hyman

Gero J. 1993. The social world of prehistoric facts: gender and power in Paleoindian research. See du Cros & Smith 1993, pp. 31–40

Gero J. 1996. Archaeological practice and gendered encounters with field data. See Wright 1996, pp. 251–80

Gero J. 1997. La iconografia Recuay y el estudio de genero. Gaceta Andina 25/26:In press

Gero J, Conkey M, eds. 1991. Engendering Archaeology. Women and Prehistory. Oxford: Blackwell

Gero J, Lacey D, Blakey M, eds. 1983. The Socio-Politics of Archaeology. Res. Rep. No. 23, Amherst: Univ. Mass.

Giddens A. 1979. Central Problems in Social Theory: Action, Structure, and Contradiction in Social Analysis. Berkeley: Univ. Calif. Press

Gifford-Gonzalez D. 1992. Gaps in zooarchaeological analyses of butchery: Is gender an issue? In Bones to Behavior, ed. J Hudson, pp. 181–99. Carbondale: So. Ill. Univ. Cent. Archeol. Invest.

Gifford-Gonzalez D. 1993. You can hide, but you can't run: representations of women's work in illustrations of Paleolithic life. Visual Anthropol. Rev. 9:3–21

Gilchrist R. 1991. Women's archaeology? Political feminism, gender theory and historical revision. Antiquity 65:459–501

Gimbutas M. 1989. The Language of the Goddess. San Francisco: Harper & Row

Golub S. 1992. Periods: From Menarche to Menopause. London: Sage

Guillen AC. 1993. Women, rituals and social

dynamics at ancient Chalcatzingo. *Lat. Am. Antiq.* 4:209–24

Hamilton N, Marcus J, Bailey D, Haaland G, Haaland R, Ucko P. 1996. Viewpoint: Can we interpret figurines? *Cambridge Archeol. J.* 6:281–307

Handsman R. 1991. Whose art was found at Lepenski Vir? Gender relations and power in archaeology. See Gero & Conkey 1991, pp. 329–65

Hanen M, Kelley J. 1992. Gender and archaeological knowledge. In *Meta Archaeology*, ed. L Embree, pp. 195–225. Netherlands: Kluwer

Haraway D. 1988. Situated knowledges: the science question in feminism as a site of discourse in the privilege of partial perspective. *Fem. Stud.* 14:575–600

Hasbrouck J. 1996. *Gay liberation or gay colonization? Issues and suggestions for the global lesbian, gay and bisexual movement.* Presented at Annu. Meet. Am. Anthropol. Assoc., 95th, San Francisco

Hastorf C. 1991. Gender, space, and food in prehistory. See Gero & Conkey 1991, pp. 132–59

Hayden B. 1992. Observing prehistoric women. See Claassen 1992, pp. 33–48

Hendon JA. 1996. Archaeological approaches to the organization of domestic labor: household practice and domestic relations. *Annu. Rev. Anthropol.* 25:45–61

Hingley R. 1991. Domestic organization and gender relations in Iron Age and Romano-British households. In *The Social Archaeology of Houses*, ed. R Samson, pp. 125–48. Edinburgh: Edinburgh Univ. Press

Hollimon SE. 1991. Health consequences of the division of labor among the Chumash Indians of southern California. See Walde & Willows 1991, pp. 462–69

Hollimon SE. 1992. Health consequences of the division of labor among prehistoric native Americans: the chumash of southern California and the Arikara of the North Plains. See Claassen 1992, pp. 81–88

hooks b. 1984. *Feminist Theory: From Margin to Center.* Boston: South End Press

Irigaray L. 1985. (1974). *Speculum of the Other Woman.* Ithaca, NY: Cornell Univ. Press

Jay N. 1991. Gender and dichotomy: male theories of power. In *A Reader in Feminist Knowledge*, ed. S Gunew, pp. 89–106. New York: Routledge

Jordanova LJ. 1980. Natural facts: a historical perspective on science and sexuality. In *Nature, Culture, and Gender*, ed. C Mac-Cormack, M Strathern, pp. 42–69. Cambridge: Cambridge Univ. Press

Joyce RA. 1993a. *Embodying Personhood in Prehispanic Costa Rica.* Wellesley, MA: Davis Mus. Cult. Cent., Wellesley Coll.

Joyce RA. 1993b. Women's work: images of production and reproduction in pre-Hispanic southern Central America. *Curr. Anthropol.* 34:255–74

Joyce RA. 1996. *Performance and inscription: negotiating sex and gender in Classic Maya society.* Presented at Pre-Columb. Stud. Symp., Dumbarton Oaks, Washington, DC

Joyce RA. 1997. Performing gender in pre-Hispanic Central America: ornamentation, representation and the construction of the body. *RES: Anthropol. Aesthet.* In press

K. A. N. 1985–. *Kvinner i arkeologi i Norge* (Women in Archaeology in Norway). Tromsø: Univ. Norway Tromsø

Kampen NB. 1995. Looking at gender: the column of Trajan and Roman historical relief. See Stanton & Stewart 1995, pp. 46–73

Kästner S, Karlisch SM, eds. 1991. *Reader zum Symposium: Feminismus und Archäologie?!* Tübingen, Ger: Inst. Frühgesch.

Kehoe A. 1991. No possible, probable shadow of doubt. *Antiquity* 65:129–31

Kehoe A. 1992. The muted class: unshackling tradition. See Claassen 1992, pp. 23–32

Keller EF. 1983. *A Feeling for the Organism.* New York: Freeman

Keller EF. 1985. *Reflections on Gender and Science.* New Haven, CT: Yale Univ. Press

Kent S. 1995. Does sedentarization promote gender inequality? A case study from the Kalahari. *J. R. Anthropol. Inst.* 1:513–36

Kessler S, McKenna W. 1985. (1978). *Gender: An Ethnomethodological Approach.* Chicago: Univ. Chicago Press

Knight C. 1991. *Blood Relations: Menstruation and the Origins of Culture.* London: Yale Univ. Press

Kus S. 1992. Toward an archaeology of body and soul. In *Representations in Archaeology*, ed. JC Gardin, C Peebles, pp. 168–77. Bloomington: Ind. Univ. Press

Laqueur T. 1990. *Making Sex: Body and Gender from the Greeks to Freud.* Cambridge, MA: Harvard Univ. Press

Larick R. 1991. Warriors and blacksmiths: mediating ethnicity in East African spears. *J. Anthropol. Archeol.* 10:299–331

Lawrence-Cheney S. 1991. Women and alcohol: female influence on recreational patterns in the West, 1880–1890. See Walde & Willows 1991, pp. 479–89

Lawrence-Cheney S. 1993. Gender on colonial peripheries. See du Cros & Smith 1993, pp. 134–37

Leacock E. 1981. History, development, and the division of labor by sex: implications for organization. *Signs: J. Women Cult. Soc.* 7:474–91

Leone MP. 1973. Archaeology as the science of technology: Mormon town plans and fences. In *Research and Theory in Contemporary Archaeology*, ed. CL Redman, pp. 125–50. New York: Wiley

Leone MP. 1982. Some opinions about recovering mind. *Am. Antiq.* 47:742–60

Leone MP. 1986. Symbolic, structural and critical archaeology. In *American Archaeology, Past and Future*, ed. D Meltzer, J Sabloff, D Fowler, pp. 415–38. Washington, DC: Smithson. Inst. Press

Lesure R. 1997. Figurines and social identities in early sedentary societies of coastal Chiapas, Mexico, 1550–800 b. c. See Claassen & Joyce 1997, pp. 227–48

Levine MA. 1991. An historical overview of research on women in archaeology. See Walde & Willows 1991, pp. 177–86

Levy J. 1995. *Gender, power and heterarchy in middle-level societies*. Presented at Annu. Meet. Soc. Am. Archeol., 60th., Minneapolis

Linke U. 1992. Manhood, femaleness and power: a cultural analysis of prehistoric images. *Comp. Stud. Soc. Hist.* 34:579–620

Little B. 1994. Consider the hermaphroditic mind: comment on "the interplay of evidential constraints and political interests: recent archaeological research on gender." *Am. Antiq.* 59(3):539–44

Longino H. 1987. Can there be a feminist science? *Hypatia* 2:51–64

Longino H. 1990. *Science as Social Knowledge: Values and Objectivity in Science.* Princeton, NJ: Princeton Univ. Press

Longino H. 1993. Essential tensions—phase two: feminist, philosophical and social studies of science. In *A Mind of One's Own: Feminist Essays on Reason and Objectivity*, ed. L Antony, C Witt, pp. 257–72. Boulder, CO: Westview

Longino H. 1994. In search of feminist epistemology. *Monist* 77:472–85

Lorber J. 1994. *Paradoxes of Gender.* New Haven, CT: Yale Univ. Press

M. T. 1993. Challenging assumptions: Lorraine Daston. *Univ. Chicago Mag* Apr: 34–35

Marcus M. 1994. Dressed to kill: women and pins in early Iran. *Oxford Art J.* 17:3–15

Mazel A. 1992. Gender and the hunter-gatherer archaeological record: a view

from the Thukela Basin. *South Afr. Archeol. Bull.* 47:122–26

McBryde I. 1996. Past and present indivisible? In *From Prehistory to Politics: John Mulvaney and the Making of a Public Intellectual*, ed. T Bonyhady, T Griffiths, pp. 64–84. Melbourne: University Press

McCafferty SD, McCafferty GG. 1991. Spinning and weaving as female gender identity in post-Classic Mexico. In *Textile Traditions of Mesoamerica and the Andes*, ed. M Schevill, JC Berlo, E Dwyer, 2:19–44. Hamden, CT: Garland

McCafferty SD, McCafferty GG. 1994. Engendering Tomb 7 at Monte Alban: respinning an old yarn. *Curr. Anthropol.* 35: 143–66

McDonald J. 1992. The Great Mackerel rock-shelter excavation: women in the archaeological record. *Aust. Archeol.* 35:32–50

McGuire K, Hildebrandt WR. 1994. The possibilities of women and men: gender and the California milling stone horizon. *J. Calif. Great Basin Anthropol.* 16: 41–59

McGuire R, Paynter R. 1991. *The Archaeology of Inequality.* Oxford: Blackwell

Merchant C. 1980. *The Death of Nature: Women, Ecology and the Scientific Revolution.* San Francisco: Harper & Row

Meskell L. 1995. Goddesses, Gimbutas and 'New Age' archaeology. *Antiquity* 69: 74–86

Miller V, ed. 1988. *The Role of Gender in Pre-Columbian Art and Architecture.* Lanham, MD: Univ. Press Am.

Moore H. 1991. Epilogue. See Gero & Conkey 1991, pp. 407–11

Moore H. 1993. The differences within and the differences between. See del Valle 1993a, pp. 193–204

Moss M. 1993. Shellfish, gender and status on the Northwest coast: reconciling archaeological, ethnographic and ethnohistoric records of the Tlingit. *Am. Anthropol.* 95: 631–52

Moulton J. 1983. A paradigm of philosophy: the adversary method. In *Discovering Reality*, ed. S Harding, MB Hintikka, pp. 149–64. Dordrecht: Reidel

Muller F. 1991. 'Kulturelle Vielfalt': Das bild der frau in der Schweitz vor 2350 jahren. *Archaol. Schweitz* 14:115–23

Nelson M, Nelson S, Wylie A, eds. 1994. *Equity Issues for Women in Archaeology. Archaeological Papers 5.* Washington, DC: Am. Anthropol. Assoc.

Nelson S. 1991a. The 'Goddess Temple' and the status of women at Niuheliang, China. See Walde & Willows 1991, pp. 302–8

Nelson S. 1991b. Women archaeologists in Asia and the Pacific. See Walde & Willows 1991, pp. 217–19

Nelson S. 1992. Diversity of the Upper Paleolithic "Venus" figurines and archaeological mythology. In *Gender in Cross-Cultural Perspective*, ed. C Brettel, C Sargent, pp. 51–58. New York: Prentice Hall

Ortner S. 1984. Theory in anthropology since the sixties. *Comp. Stud. Soc. Hist.* 26: 126–66

Øvrevik S. 1991. *Sex ratios in archaeological organisations in Norway*. Masters thesis. Univ. Bradford, UK

Parezo N, ed. 1993. *Hidden Scholars: Women Anthropologists and the Native American Southwest*. Albuquerque: Univ. N. M. Press

Patai D, Koertge N. 1994. *Professing Feminism: Inside the Strange World of Women's Studies*. New York: New Republic/Basic Books

Pinsky V, Wylie A, eds. 1989. *Critical Traditions in Archaeology: Essays in the Philosophy, History and Sociopolitics of Archaeology*. Cambridge: Cambridge Univ. Press

Pohl M. 1991. Women, animal rearing and social status: the case of the Formative period Maya of Central America. See Walde & Willows 1991, pp. 392–99

Pollock S. 1991. Women in a men's world: images of Sumerian women. See Gero & Conkey 1991, pp. 366–87

Pomeroy SB. 1975. *Goddesses, Whores, Wives and Slaves: Women in Classical Antiquity*. New York: Schocken Books

Pomeroy SB. 1991. *Women's History and Ancient History*. Chapel Hill, NC: Univ. N. C. Press

Preucel R, Joyce RA. 1994. *Feminism, fieldwork, and the practice of archaeology*. Presented at Annu. Meet. Am. Anthropol. Assoc., 93rd, Atlanta

Rabinowitz NS, Richlin A, eds. 1993. *Feminist Theory and the Classics*. New York/London: Routledge

Reyman J, ed. 1992. *Rediscovering Our Past: Essays on the History of American Archaeology*. Aldershot, UK: Avebury

Robb J. 1994. Gender contradictions, moral coalitions and inequality in prehistoric Italy. *J. Eur. Archeol.* 2:20–49

Roberts C. 1993. A critical approach to gender as a category of analysis in archaeology. See du Cros & Smith 1993, pp. 16–21

Rogers CL, Fowler DD. 1994. *Feminist archaeology and cultural resource management*. Presented at Annu. Meet. Am. Anthropol. Assoc., 93rd, Atlanta

Roseberry W. 1988. Political economy. *Annu. Rev. Anthropol.* 17:161–85

Rossiter MW. 1982. *Women Scientists in America: Struggles and Strategies to 1940*. Baltimore: Johns Hopkins Press

Russell P. 1991. Men only? The myths about European Paleolithic artists. See Walde & Willows 1991, pp. 346–51

Sassaman KE. 1992. Lithic technology and the hunter-gatherer sexual division of labor. *North Am. Archeol.* 13:249–62

Sassaman KE. 1997. *Acquiring Stone, Acquiring Power*. Presented at Annu. Meet. Soc. Am. Archeol. 62nd, Nashville, TN

Schrire C. 1995. *Digging Through Darkness: Chronicles of an Archaeologist*. Charlottesville: Univ. Va. Press

Scott EM. 1994. *Those of Little Note: Gender, Race and Class in Historical Archaeology*. Tucson: Univ. Ariz. Press

Seifert D, ed. 1991. Gender in historical archaeology. *Hist. Archaeol.* 25(4):1–155

Seifert D. 1994. Mrs. Starr's profession. In *Those of Little Note: Gender, Race and Class in Historical Archaeology*, ed. E Scott, pp. 149–74. Tucson: Univ. Ariz. Press

Silverblatt I. 1987. *Moon, Sun and Witches: Gender Ideologies and Class in Inca and Colonial Peru*. Princeton, NJ: Princeton Univ. Press

Silverblatt I. 1991. Interpreting women in states: new feminist ethnohistories. See di Leonardo 1991a, pp. 140–71

Smith L, du Cros H. 1995. Reflections on women in archaeology. See Balme & Beck 1995, pp. 7–27

Solomon A. 1992. Gender, representation and power in San art and ethnography. *J. Anthropol. Archeol.* 11:291–329

Sommers CH. 1994. *Who Stole Feminism? How Women Have Betrayed Women*. New York: Simon & Schuster

Spector J. 1991. What this awl means. See Gero & Conkey 1991, pp. 388–406

Spector J. 1993. *What This Awl Means: Feminist Archaeology in a Wahpeton Dakota Village*. Minneapolis: Minn. Hist. Soc.

Spencer-Wood S. 1991. Toward an historical archaeology of materialistic domestic reform. See McGuire & Paynter 1991, pp. 231–86

Spielman K. 1994. *A feminist approach to archaeological field schools*. Presented at Annu. Meet. Am. Anthopol. Assoc., 93rd, Atlanta

Spielman K. 1995. The Archaeology of gender in the American Southwest. *J. Anthropol. Res.* 51

Stacey J. 1988. Can there be a feminist ethnography? *Women's Stud. Int. Forum* 11: 22–27

Stanton D, Stewart A, eds. 1995. *Feminisms in the Academy*. Ann Arbor: Univ. Mich. Press

Sternhill C. 1994. The proper study of womankind. *Women's Rev. Books* 12:1,3–4

Trigger B. 1980. Archaeology and the image of the American Indian. *Am. Antiq.* 45: 662–76

Trigger B. 1984. Alternative archaeologies: nationalist, colonialist, imperialist. *Man* 19:355–70

Trigger B. 1989. *A History of Archaeological Thought*. Cambridge: Cambridge Univ. Press

Tringham R. 1991. Households with faces: the challenge of gender in prehistoric architectural remains. See Gero & Conkey 1991, pp. 93–131

Tringham R. 1994. Engendered places in prehistory. *Gender Place Cult. Gender* 1(2): 169–203

Wadley L. 1989. Gender relations in the Thukela Basin. *South Afr. Archeol. Bull.* 44:122–26

Walde D, Willows N, eds. 1991. *The Archaeology of Gender*. Calgary: Archeol. Assoc. Univ. Calgary

Wall D. 1994. *The Archaeology of Gender: Separating the Spheres in Urban America*. New York: Plenum

Walsh L, Burke T, Markos J, Hause L. 1994. *Final Report: Archaeological Testing and Evaluations of Five Prehistoric Sites in Indian Wells Valley, Kern County, California for the Proposed Redrock 4-Lane Upgrade*. Archeol. Res. Serv., Virginia City, NV

Watson PJ, Kennedy M. 1991. The development of horticulture in the Eastern Woodlands of North America: women's role. See Gero & Conkey 1991, pp. 255–75

West C, Zimmerman DH. 1987. Doing gender. *Gender Soc.* 1:125–52

Whelan M. 1991. Gender and archaeology: mortuary studies and the search for the origins of gender differentiation. See Walde & Willows 1991, pp. 358–65

Whelan M. 1995. Beyond hearth and home on the range: feminist approaches to Plains archaeology. In *Beyond Subsistence: Plains Archaeology and the Postprocessual Critique*, ed. P Duke, MC Wilson, pp. 46–65. Tuscaloosa, AL: Univ. Ala. Press

Woodbury N. 1992. In the shadow of man, or just the shade of the lab tent? *SAA Bull.* 9:6–7

Wright R. 1996. *Gender and Archaeology*. Philadelphia: Univ. Penn. Press

Wylie A. 1992. The interplay of evidential constraints and political interests: recent archaeological research on gender. *Am. Antiq.* 57:15–35

Wylie A. 1994a. On "capturing facts alive in the past" (or present): response to Fotiadis and Little. *Am. Antiq.* 59(3):556–60

Wylie A. 1994b. *Pragmatism and politics: understanding the emergence of gender research in archaeology*. Presented as Skomp Disting. Lect. Anthropol., Indiana Univ., Bloomington

Wylie A. 1994c. Evidential constraints: pragmatic objectivism in archaeology. In *Readings in the Philosophy of Social Science*, ed. M Martin, L McIntyre, pp. 747–65. Cambridge, MA: MIT Press

Wylie A. 1995. Doing philosophy as a feminist: Longino on the search for a feminist epistemology. *Philos. Top.* 23(2):345–58

Wylie A. 1996. The constitution of archaeological evidence: gender politics and science. In *The Disunity of Science: Boundaries, Contexts, Power*, ed. P Galison, DJ Stump, pp. 311–43. Stanford, CA: Stanford Univ. Press

Wylie A. 1997. Good science, bad science or science as usual?: feminist critiques of science. In *Women in Human Evolution*, ed. LD Hager, pp. 29–55. New York/London: Routledge

Yentsch A. 1991. The symbolic divisions of pottery: sex-related attributes of English and Anglo-American household pots. See McGuire & Paynter 1991, pp. 192–230

Zeanah D, Carter J, Dugas D, Elston R, Hammett J. 1995. *An optimal foraging model of hunter-gatherer land use in the Carson Desert*. Prepared for the US Fish Wildlife Serv./US Dep. Navy. Silver City, NV: Intermountain Res.

Annu. Rev. Anthropol. 1997. 26:439–64

DOING GOOD? The Politics and Antipolitics of NGO Practices

William F. Fisher

Department of Anthropology, Harvard University, Cambridge, Massachusetts 02138

KEY WORDS: civil society, collective action, development, nongovernmental organizations, globalization

ABSTRACT

This review surveys current literature concerned with the growing numbers, changing functions, and intensifying networks of nongovernmental organizations which have had significant impacts upon globalization, international and national politics, and local lives. Studies of these changes illuminate understandings of translocal flows of ideas, knowledge, funding, and people; shed light on changing relationships among citizenry, associations, and the state; and encourage a reconsideration of connections between the personal and the political. Attention is given to the political implications of discourses about NGOs, the complex micropolitics of these associations, and the importance of situating them as evolving processes within complexes of competing and overlapping practices and discourses.

> If I knew someone was coming over with the expressed intention of doing good, I would flee.
>
> Henry David Thoreau

INTRODUCTION

In the past decade, the conception of new world orders (Edwards & Hulme 1996b, Ekins 1992, Holm & Sorenson 1995) has been encouraged by a perceived turbulence in world politics (R Kothari 1993, p. 59; Finger 1994a, p. 48; Rivera 1992; Rosenau 1990), the volatility of culturally plural societies, the acceleration of globalization (Appadurai 1991, Lash & Urry 1994), and the sense that nation-states are no longer obvious and legitimate sources of authority over civil society (Lash & Urry 1994, p. 281). During this period, local, re-

439

gional, and transnational collective action has attracted heightened attention from development practitioners, politicians, and social scientists. In the political space created by shifting interdependencies among political actors, by the globalization of capitalism and power, and by the decline of the state, growing numbers of groups loosely identified as nongovernmental organizations (NGOs) have undertaken an enormously varied range of activities, including implementing grass-roots or sustainable development, promoting human rights and social justice, protesting environmental degradation, and pursuing many other objectives formerly ignored or left to governmental agencies.[1]

Many analysts have noted and commented on the scale of this growth in NGOs (Carroll 1992, Clarke 1993, Edwards & Hulme 1996a, Farrington & Lewis 1993, Fisher 1993, Fowler 1991, Fowler & James 1995, S Kothari 1993, Princen & Finger 1994, Rademacher & Tamang 1993).[2] In the views of some observers, the third world in particular is being swept by a nongovernmental, associational, or "quiet" revolution that at least one analyst believes may "prove to be as significant to the latter twentieth century as the rise of the nation-state was to the latter nineteenth century" (Salamon 1993, p. 1, 1994, p. 109; see also Clarke 1996, Edwards & Hulme 1996a, Fisher 1993).

The potential of the global associational explosion has captivated the imagination of a wide variety of development planners, policy makers, activists, and analysts. Economists and development planners laud the role of local associations in alleviating rural poverty and helping communities adapt to modernization (Annis 1988, Bongartz et al 1992, Brown & Korten 1989, FAO 1994, Korten 1990, Padron 1987, Semboja & Therkildsen 1995, Thomson 1992, World Bank 1991, UNDP 1993); political scientists are reevaluating the role of voluntary associations in building vibrant civil societies and their impact on the relationship between society and the state (Barghouti 1994; Bratton 1989; Chazan 1992; Fowler 1991; Fox & Hernandez 1992; Frantz 1987; Ndegwa 1993, 1996; Ng'ethe & Kanyinga 1992; Sanyal 1994; Sethi 1993a,b); scholars of international relations have begun to examine the impact of NGO coalitions and networks on international politics and their role in the formation of an international civil society (Brysk 1993; Carroll 1988; Ghils 1992; Link-

---

[1]The evidence of this growth is widespread and includes the increased numbers of officially registered associations, the thousands of NGOs represented at international conferences, the increased proportion of development funding directed through NGOs, the attention paid to cooperation with NGOs by the World Bank and other international agencies, the highly publicized success of lobbying efforts of NGO coalitions, and the growing support provided to NGOs through global networks, including hundreds of World Wide Web sites.

[2]See Princen & Finger's comments on the difficulty of accurately estimating the exact dimensions of the growth of the nongovernmental sector (1994, p. 15).

enbach 1994; Lipschutz 1992; Peterson 1992; Princen 1994; Princen & Finger 1994; Shaw 1992; Sikkink 1993, 1995; Spiro 1994; Udall 1995; Wapner 1994); and some activists and analysts are reconsidering the relationship of NGOs to social movements and their ability to both empower people and contribute to alternative discourses of development and democratization (Escobar 1992, Patkar 1995, Wignaraja 1993a).

Any discussion of NGOs is further complicated by the fact that they have not only increased in number and taken on new functions, but they have also forged innovative and increasingly complex and wide-ranging formal and informal linkages with one another, with government agencies, with social movements, with international development agencies, with individual IN-GOs (international NGOs), and with transnational issue networks (Carroll 1988; Finger 1994a,b; Fisher 1995b; Lopez et al 1995; Shaw 1992; Sikkink 1993, 1995; Peterson 1992; Princen & Finger 1994). These relationships have begun to have profound impacts both on globalization and on local lives.

These changes in the nature of local and global forms of collective action intersect with issues of vital concern to anthropologists. Study of these changes not only enriches our understanding of local and translocal connections that enable and constrain flows of ideas, knowledge, funding, and people, but also invites us to reconsider both conventional notions of governance and Foucaultian ideas of governmentality and how technologies of control affect both the personal and the political, and to examine changing relationships among citizenry, associations, and the state. However, while the associational revolution has generated tremendous enthusiasm and a large new interdisciplinary literature, anthropologists, to date, have made relatively limited contributions to it. This literature as a whole is based more on faith than fact: There are relatively few detailed studies of what is happening in particular places or within specific organizations, few analyses of the impact of NGO practices on relations of power among individuals, communities, and the state, and little attention to the discourse within which NGOs are presented as the solution to problems of welfare service delivery, development, and democratization. An enhanced anthropological contribution would enrich a literature the majority of which is replete with sweeping generalizations; optimistic statements about the potentials of NGOs for delivering welfare services, implementing development projects, and facilitating democratization; and instrumental treatises on building the capacity of NGOs to perform these functions. Unpacking this literature, much of which obscures its political stance in simple categories and generalizations, requires attention to three sets of issues that have concerned some anthropologists: (*a*) how discourses about NGOs create knowledge, define sets of appropriate practices, and facilitate and encourage NGO behavior defined as appropriate; (b) how complex sets of relationships among various kinds of associations, the agencies and agents of the state, and individuals and communities have had an impact in specific locales at specific times; and (c) how we can avoid reductionist views of NGOs as fixed and generalizable entities with essential characteristics and contextualize them within evolving processes of associating.

IMAGINING NGOs

The need for unpacking the literature becomes clear when we consider the degree to which the literature on NGOs relies upon several key terms—participation, empowerment, local, and community—each of which has been given a variety of meanings and linked in different ways to analysts' perceptions of the origins, capacities, objectives, and impacts of NGOs. Ironically, with reference to these terms, NGOs have been embraced and promoted in the past decade by international development agencies like the World Bank as well as by radical critics of top-down development. Whether NGOs are seen as a progressive arm of an irresistible march toward liberal democracy that marks "the end of history," an extension of the push toward privatization, or a means to resist the imposition of Western values, knowledge, and development regimes depends on the perspective and agenda of the imaginer.

At least since the Rio Conference of 1992 (and the parallel Global Forum at which gathered representatives from over 9000 organizations from 171 countries), nothing short of miracles has been expected from NGOs (Little 1995). The optimism of the proponents of NGOs derives from a general sense of NGOs as "doing good," unencumbered and untainted by the politics of government or the greed of the market (Zivetz 1991). This is reflected in the designations that describe these associations in terms of what they are not: nongovernmental and nonprofit. NGOs are idealized as organizations through which people help others for reasons other than profit or politics (Brown & Korten 1989, Fisher 1993). This idealization of NGOs as disinterested apolitical participants in a field of otherwise implicated players has led theorists and practitioners alike to expect much of them. But as Milton Friedman has observed, "the power to do good is also the power to do harm," a process that is all the more difficult to sort out when "what one man regards as good, another may regard as harm" (Friedman 1962).

NGOs have become the "favored child" of official development agencies, hailed as the new panacea to cure the ills that have befallen the development process (Edwards & Hulme 1996a, p. 3), and imagined as a "magic bullet" which will mysteriously but effectively find its target (Dichter 1993, p. vii; Vivian 1994). Sharp criticism of previous interventionist, top-down development efforts, widespread evidence that development strategies of the past few decades have failed to adequately assist the poorest of the world's poor, and growing support for development efforts that are "sustainable" and that include the participation of intended beneficiaries have stimulated existing development agencies to search for alternative means to integrate individuals into markets, to deliver welfare services, and to involve local populations in development projects.

However, the acceptance of NGOs by the development industry has been limited, and the transfer to them of some of the responsibility for the successful implementation of development efforts is not without risk to the autonomy and existence of NGOs. Development has been a fickle industry, first embracing and then casting off a long series of enthusiastically touted new strategies. NGOs, now so widely praised, can anticipate becoming victims of the current unrealistic expectations and being abandoned as rapidly and as widely as they have been embraced.[3]

The appropriate role imagined for NGOs in development depends on the critical stance one takes toward the development industry. Critics of development can be situated within one of two general camps (Ferguson 1990).[4] The first views contemporary development processes as flawed but basically positive and inevitable (Cernea 1988; Clark 1991, 1995; Olsen 1995; Patel 1995). From this perspective, NGOs provide a means to mitigate some of the weaknesses in the development process. The second finds both the dominant development paradigm and the implementation of it fundamentally flawed (see, in particular, Escobar's influential and provocative work, 1995; see also Esteva 1987; S Kothari 1993; Patkar 1995; Rahnema 1992; Udall 1995). They see development as a historically produced discourse "which created a space in which only certain things could be said and even imagined" (Escobar 1995, p. 39). For the more radical critics, NGOs and "local" or "community" associations are valuable in so far as they are a potential source of alternative development discourses and practices. Critics from each camp may promote NGOs for their ability to facilitate participation and empowerment, but the meanings attached to these terms differ.

---

[3]There is already evidence of disillusionment with the promise of NGOs as deliverers of development and democracy. For an example, see the 1993 UNDP *Human Development Report* (UNDP 1993). Smillie & Helmich (1993, p. 15) argue that, in discussions of the potential contributions of NGOs, "it has become fashionable to move quickly from their positive attributes...to their obvious weaknesses."

[4]Of course, there are many variations within these two positions. For a fuller discussion of these issues as they affect anthropology, see Escobar (1991) and Little & Painter's (1995) response to Escobar.

The first set of critics is strongly represented in the literature on NGOs, a great portion of which takes an instrumental view of NGOs, regarding them as apolitical tools that can be wielded to further a variety of slightly modified development goals. Development agencies and international NGOs, in particular, support local NGOs for their effectiveness in pursuing the goals of what some have called a "new policy agenda," a heterogenous set of policies based on a faith in two basic values—neoliberal economics and liberal democratic theory (Biggs & Neame 1996, Edwards & Hulme 1996a, Moore 1993, Robinson 1993). As these proponents envision them, NGOs have the capacity to efficiently transfer training and skills that assist individuals and communities to compete in markets, to provide welfare services to those who are marginalized by the market, and to contribute democratization and the growth of a robust civil society, all of which are considered as critical to the success of the neoliberal economic policies (Fowler 1991, Frantz 1987, Hyden 1998).

These analysts see NGOs as everything that governments are not: unburdened with large bureaucracies, relatively flexible and open to innovation, more effective and faster at implementing development efforts, and able to identify and respond to grass-roots needs (Edwards & Hulme 1996a, Fowler 1988, FAO 1994). The common assertion that NGOs have arisen in the face of internal and external exigencies and where state-directed change has failed or faces severe limitations (Adam 1993, Ndegwa 1993) supports the view that NGOs are an important alternative to the state under some circumstances. As the World Bank (1991) has noted, NGOs "have become an important force in the development process [mitigating] the costs of developing countries' institutional weakness" (p. 135). From this perspective, "local" NGOs are a means through which impediments to development can be overcome, and international NGOs are useful insofar as they serve as intermediaries that can facilitate the work of local NGOs (see, for instance, Olsen 1995).

NGOS have also been supported by advocates of the new policy agenda because it is believed that they contribute to democratizing processes. Optimistic expectations for democratization have been boosted in the past decade by the successful challenges citizens made to formerly strong states in Eastern Europe and Latin America. But while NGOs are valued as part of a growing civil society that can engage with the state, few scholars have examined the actual contribution NGOs make either to political change and democratization or to political continuity (for exceptions, see Bongartz et al 1992, Ndegwa 1993). The connections among development, empowerment, and democratization remain speculative and rhetorical. Certainly, democratic optimism reflects a narrowly progressive view of NGOs that is not borne out by the political variety of NGOs. While prevailing policies assume that democratization is a by-product of development,[5] some analysts have argued that the objectives of development and democratization require contradictory efforts (see, for example, Carroll 1992).

The second set of development critics, those who seek alternatives to existing development paradigms, emphasize rather than downplay NGOs' potential for moral and political influence, seeing NGOs as vehicles for challenges to and transformations of relationships of power. Grass-roots organizations, in particular, are seen as engaged in a struggle for ideological autonomy from the state, political parties, and the development apparatus (Friedman 1992, Lind 1992). Activists and revolutionary theorists attribute significance to local voluntary associations not because they see these groups as part of a growing civil society that engages with the state but because they see them as part of a process that is capable of transforming the state and society.[6] They envision the emergence of alternative discourses and practices of development and anticipate the contribution of NGOs to an "insurrection of subjugated knowledges" (Foucault 1980, p. 81; see also Fisher 1993, Patkar 1995, S Kothari 1993). Seeking alternatives to development, rather than development alternatives, and skeptical about so-called democratization processes, these analysts, activists, and radical critics of neoliberal development agendas value NGOs for their ability to politicize issues that were not formerly politicized or that were ironically depoliticized through the discourses of development or "democratic" participation (R Kothari 1993, S Kothari 1993, Patkar 1995, Wignaraja 1993a).

Some of these critics of the development industry view the development apparatus as identifying "problems" that impede (or that result from) an imagined linear march of progress, and that require the intervention of government or multilateral development agencies (Escobar 1995, Ferguson 1990, Rahnema 1992). Such critics have recognized as a danger posed to NGOs the resilient ability of the development industry to absorb and transform ideas and institutions. In their view, NGOs are at risk of becoming the new "technical" solutions to development "problems," solutions that can be promoted by international development agencies in situations in which the state is seen an inhibitor (Biggs & Neame 1996).

From the perspective of these critics, the development industry's view of NGOs as efficient new instruments of development largely ignores, down-

[5]In practice, most official financial and logistical support to NGOs goes for development efforts and not democratization. On this topic, see the discussions in Edwards (1996) and Pearce (1993).

[6]NGOs seen as contributing an alternative perspective are often distinguished from more mainstream, cooperative NGOs. See, for example, the directory of alternative NGOs in South Asia compiled by Nachowitz (1990).

plays, or attempts to coopt the political role of NGOs. Through depoliticization, NGOs are in danger of becoming the new attachments to the "antipolitics" machine of development, the practices of which James Ferguson (1990)
has described in his seminal work on development in Lesotho. The description of NGOs as part of a voluntary (Brown & Korten 1989), nonprofit, independent (Fisher 1993) or "third" sector (Hulme 1994; Korten 1990; Salamon
1993, 1994) that is separate from both market and state (Wolfe 1991) contributes to the image of these associations as part of a segment of society that is
separate from politics.[7] If politics, however, is taken to refer to power-
structured relationships maintained by techniques of control, as it is by these
radical critics, then politics is not confined to institutions but pervades every
aspect of life (Foucault 1991, Gordon 1991, Kauffman 1990, Millett 1971).
Antipolitics refers to the obscuring of these relationships. Just as the "development apparatus" has generally depoliticized the need for development through
its practice of treating local conditions as "problems" that required technical
and not structural or political solutions (Ferguson 1990), it now defines problems that can be addressed via the mechanisms of NGOs rather than through
political solutions.

Whether NGOs are seen as collections of individuals engaged in what de
Tocqueville called the democratic "art of associating," or engaged in a Hegelian struggle for respect and recognition as human beings with dignity, depends a great deal on the lens through which they are viewed. Perceptions of
NGOs reflect the tensions between those who argue that new or alternative
means are needed to reach the goals of development and those who argue for a
reconception of the ends of development and an acknowledgment that the
means by which we strive for or make decisions about those ends matter as
much as the ends themselves (Escobar 1995, Ferguson 1990, Fisher 1995c).
These perceptions of NGOs are tied up with contested notions of what it means
to "do good." At stake are the very notion of the "good" and the process of deciding what it is and how to pursue it.

CONCEPTUALLY LOCATING NGOs

How is it that NGOs have come to be seen as central to such widely different
policy and political agendas? It may seem as though the analysts described

---

[7]Not surprisingly, many of these organizations and their members describe their organizations
differently, emphasizing instead positive qualities of their practices and ideology. Smitu Kothari
(1993) has observed that in India, movements with mass participation, in particular, may resent and
reject outright the externally imposed classification as NGOs and instead designate themselves as
social action groups, political action groups, or social movements.

above cannot all be talking about the same set of associations. The fact is that they are not: Divorced from ethnographic particulars, these debates hinge on two essentialized categories—civil society and NGOs—which are used in different ways by different theorists. Civil society, when it is not used as a synonym for society in general, is used to refer to "that segment of society that interacts with the state, influences the state and yet is distinct from the state" (Chazan 1992, p. 281). The term "NGO" is shorthand for a wide range of formal and informal associations. There is little agreement about what NGOs are and perhaps even less about what they should be called. The generalizations about the NGO sector obscure the tremendous diversity found within it. This diversity means that it is not a simple task to analyze the impact of NGOs at the local, national, and global levels (Carroll 1992, Fisher 1993, Fowler & James 1995, Princen & Finger 1994). Varying terminology, ideological biases, and unanalyzed assertion contribute to an obfuscation of widely varied functions and forms of organizations. How can we break down the "black box" categories of NGO and civil society and examine the way organizations so designated operate in local, regional, national, and transnational contexts? Understanding NGO practices requires that we question the selective use of examples to illustrate the claimed advantages of these organizations, unpack the asserted generalizations about the relative advantages of NGOs, and attend to the ideology and politics of both the associations and the analysts.

Associations designated as NGOs differ from one another in functions; the levels at which they operate; and organizational structures, goals, and membership. They include, but are not limited to, charitable, religious, research, human rights, and environmental organizations and range from loosely organized groups with a few unpaid staff members to organizations with multimillion dollar budgets employing hundreds. While NGOs are often purely voluntary groups with no governmental affiliation or support, some groups so designated are created and maintained by governments. The term NGOs has been applied to groups providing social welfare services; development support organizations; social action groups struggling for social justice and structural changes; support groups providing legal, research, or communications support; and locally based groups. Some are focused on a single issue or operate in a specific location. Others provide legal, research, or communications support to more locally based groups. The designation has been applied to groups with mass membership as well as claimed by small, opportunistic "brief-case" NGOs formed by members of an urban middle class to seek funding.

In an attempt to conceptually organize such diverse groups, analysts have distinguished among associations according to various sets of criteria, littering the literature with acronyms. Designations like CBOs (community-based organizations), GROs (grass-roots organizations), or POs (people's organizations) distinguish membership-based, locally autonomous groups from groups of urban intellectuals working in relatively impoverished settings as intermediary support organizations (ISOs), which are sometimes varyingly designated as MSOs (membership support organizations) or GSOs or GRSOs (grass-roots support organizations) (see, in particular, Carroll 1992, Fisher 1993, Korten 1987, 1990). Other acronyms call attention to the varying autonomy of NGOs, distinguishing fully autonomous NGOs from government-organized or -supported groups or GONGOs (Brown & Korten 1989, Ching 1994), quasi-autonomous NGOs or QUANGOs (Sinaga 1995), and donor-organized NGOs or DONGOs. Still other distinctions are made among NNGOs (NGOs in Northern or industrialized countries), SNGOs (NGOs based in Southern or developing countries), and INGOs (international NGOs). Acronyms like VOs (voluntary organizations) and PVOs (private voluntary organizations) differentiate those organizations that are nonprofit and voluntary from those with professional staffs, while others like LDAs (local development associations) identify the primary activity of the organization.[8]

The distinctions identified by these various designations can be important in specific instances, but the creation and use of acronyms remains inconsistent within the field and in any specific case often derives from a narrow objective on the part of the analyst. Categorizations that distinguish among NGOs based on function, organizational structure, and relationship to a locality or to a state are typical of that portion of the literature that addresses the means by which NGOs, or at least some categories of NGOs, can be facilitated by or built into the development arm of international and state development agencies. These categorizations are a poor basis either for forming development

---

[8]More comprehensive attempts to organize the field call attention to changes in the field and the practices of the associations over time. In an essential work on NGOs, Korten addresses the diversity of the field by distinguishing three generations of NGOs: the first committed to relief and welfare, a second attending to small-scale, local development projects, and a third consisting of community organizations interested in building coalitions (1990, pp. 115–27). Elliot (1987) has outlined a similar typology of NGOs based on distinctions among charity, development, and empowerment work. In Korten's view, first-generation relief and welfare NGOs, which predominate in the developing world, often have close ties to state and international development aid organizations and do not overtly engage in political activities. Second-generation development NGOs organize individuals locally to address issues like public health and agricultural development. These groups frequently help their constituents to overcome structural constraints, to challenge local and regional elites, and to avoid dependency relationships. Third-generation NGOs explicitly target political constraints, engaging in mobilization and "conscientization." Their focus is on coordinating communications and linkages among webs of people's organizations. These networks help to spread awareness of the practical local successes of some second-generation development strategies and to serve as catalysts for wider social movements. While these types of distinctions help to clarify the different practices of NGOs, they are still more ideal than real. In practice, these three categories or generations of NGOs are not exclusive.

policies or for guiding the pursuit of social justice. The oft-stated aim of "doing good" is undermined by an inadequate understanding of what NGOs do in specific circumstances. By constituting NGOs as an area of investigation, the discourse of development renders independent groups as objects of "scientific" study which provides and defines knowledge of these objects in such a way as to make them amenable to control. Objectifying discourse about NGOs facilitates what Charles Reilly (1992) calls their colonization by a variety of actors ranging from local elites and government agents to international agencies and INGOs (see also Jhamtani 1992).

The trick is to differentiate among various forms of organizing while avoiding reified and reductionist uses of the concept NGO. As noted above, not all NGOs operate in similar cultural, economic, and social contexts, nor do they all have the same political significance. Much of the literature on local NGOs, for instance, is concerned with those groups that are involved with challenging the state and local elites. This bias ignores the diversity of the NGO field that includes numerous examples of NGOs organized and financed by landlord, commercial, or political interests.[9] What is at issue is not what NGOs are good for, nor whether a specific association is or isn't an NGO, a QUANGO, a CONGO, a GRO, or a GSO, but an understanding of what happens in specific places and at specific times. Anthropological studies that have remained alert to specific contexts have made more significant contributions to rethinking the nature of NGO relations. Maxine Weisgrau's (1997) excellent ethnography of NGOs in northern India, for example, which focuses on the ongoing renegotiation and reinterpretation of development among NGOs, villagers, and development agents, helps us to understand what happens in a specific time and place above and beyond the stated intentions and goals for development planners and NGOs. This kind of ethnographic detail exposes the simplicity of universalizing models of and discourses about NGOs. By conceiving of NGOs as "an arena within which battles from society at large are internalized" (Clarke 1996, p. 5), rather than as a set of entities, and by focusing on fluid and changing local, regional, national, and international processes and connections, which both potentially support and suppress "an insurrection of subjugated knowledges," such studies avoid simple generalizations and reveal the rich ideological and functional diversity of NGOs.

---

[9]For example, see Silliman's (1994) discussion of the Sugar Development Foundation in the Philippines. In addition, while the focus on the Narmada conflict in India has emphasized those NGOs opposed to the construction of the Sardar Sarovar dam, the controversy has involved a wide range of NGOs with different political interests, ideologies, and strategies. Some of these NGOs have cooperated with the government and the World Bank to ensure proper implementation of resettlement policies, and some have supported the project outright (Fisher 1995a).

LINKING THE LOCAL AND THE GLOBAL

Once firmly rooted in an ethnographic understanding of the heterogeneity of histories and processes from which NGOs emerge and within which they operate, we are prepared to explore the further opportunities for and constraints on NGOs that stem from their multiple translocal connections. Shifting the emphasis from a set of organizations to a fluid web of relationships reveals the connections of NGO actions to numerous levels and fields and draws our attention to the flows of funding, knowledge, ideas, and people that move through these levels, sites, and associations (Appadurai 1991, Lash & Urry 1994). These multiple relationships include those among intermediaries, governments, constituencies, communities, leaders, elites, municipalities, state institutions, other local, national and INGOs, social movements, and NGO coalitions. As R Kothari (1993) has noted for NGOs in India's nongovernmental sector, the establishment of new linkages transcending local and even national boundaries created new and innovative possibilities for NGO practices. NGOs networks and loose coalitions now connect local, regional, national, and international levels, and at each of these levels there are additional informal linkages to governments, international funding agencies, and INGOs (Brysk 1993; Finger 1994a; Fisher 1993, 1995b; Kamarotos 1990; Leatherman et al 1994; Lipschutz 1992; Lopez et al 1995; Peterson 1992; Shaw 1992; Sikkink 1993, 1995; Udall 1995). This proliferation and interweaving creates numerous intersections that deserve anthropological attention.

Some recent studies begin by acknowledging that the different agendas and interests within complex local sites do not all originate there, nor are they all played out there (Forbes 1995, Peters 1996). These studies of NGOs, which both alert us to the complexities of local sites and direct our attention from local sites to larger contexts, are, as George Marcus (1995) has observed, both in and of the world system (see, for example, Baviskar's insightful 1995 study of adivasis along the Narmada River). Unpacking the micropolitics of NGOs is dependent upon placing these associations within larger contexts, understanding them not as local wholes subsumed within larger national and global political contexts but as fragmented sites that have multiple connections nationally and transnationally (Marcus 1995). Resistance to a particular development project, for example, is often conducted with the assistance of national coalitions and transnational issue networks of individuals and INGOs even when the agendas of these disparate players are not wholly consistent (Fisher 1995b, Patkar 1995, Princen & Finger 1994, Rich 1994, Udall 1995).

Some of the most important insights about contemporary collective action and NGOs have emerged from the literature on social movements. The best of this work tends to avoid overessentializing NGOs, to attend to the multiple subjectivities of actors, and to take into account the fragmented field within which NGOs operate. Unfortunately, the important and dynamic relationships between NGOs and social movements at the local and national levels have often been overlooked.[10] This oversight occurs in part because analysts of social movements generally stereotype NGOs as primarily social development agencies and contrast the bureaucratization or institutionalization characteristic of some NGOs with the more fluid and fragmented nature of social movements (see, for example, Frank & Fuentes 1990). This view ignores the evidence that NGOs often initiate or sustain social movements (Lehman 1990) or are the institutional vehicles that articulate protest and collective action (Diani 1992). As Clarke (1993) has demonstrated for the Philippines, some social movements are composed to a significant extent of NGO coalitions. Uniting the separate literatures that have developed around social movements on the one hand and NGOs on the other would help illuminate their complex interrelationships and also encourage us to see how these processes of association change over time (see also Diani 1992, Wignaraja 1993a). Acknowledging the commonly strong links between NGOs and social movements does not mean that NGOs should always, or even generally, be seen as progressive. As Starn (1995) has effectively argued, the motives behind the practices of individuals and associations are multiple, and both NGOs and social movements may support the state or the status quo as well as oppose it (see also Ndegwa 1993, 1996; Ng'ethe & Kanyinga 1992).

While the moniker "nongovernment organization" suggests autonomy from government organizations, NGOs are often intimately connected with their home governments in relationships that are both ambivalent and dynamic, sometimes cooperative, sometimes contentious, sometimes both simultaneously (Chazan 1992, Clarke 1993, Farrington & Lewis 1993, Ndegwa 1996, Weisgrau 1997). For example, some analysts have argued that a key factor affecting the orientation of NGOs and their ability to organize freely is sympathetic public space provided by governments (Banuri 1993, Korten 1990). This space may be provided unwillingly and only when governments are prodded by INGOs or international development agencies. In the past decade, many governments in the third world have been forced by economic necessity and international agencies to cede recognition and autonomy to NGOs (Bratton 1989, Vergara 1989). Not surprisingly, governments, on their part, have often seen NGOs as undermining state hegemony (Bratton 1989, Fowler 1991, Ng'ethe & Kanyinga 1992) and have attempted to bring them under control through government agencies set up to service them (see, for example, Clarke 1996, Rademacher & Tamang 1993). This relationship becomes even

---

[10]Some exceptions to this include Bebbington (1996), Sethi (1993a,b), and Landim (1993).

more tense when NGOs become competitors with their governments for foreign development funding or when the work of NGOs with human rights organizations to further the rights of individuals and associations places them in direct confrontation with state practices (Fowler 1991).

The relationships between NGOs and governments are so heterogenous that it is difficult to generalize about the potential impact of NGOs on the state and patterns of governance. Some analysts assert that NGOs are important new political actors who make significant contributions to political life and political change (see, in particular, Clarke's useful 1996 study), but observers disagree about the kind of impact NGOs can have. Some discuss the transformational impact of NGOs on political structures and processes (Fisher 1993) while others focus on their ability to influence legislation and public policy (Edwards 1996). The existing evidence suggests that so many factors influence the ability or desire of any particular NGO to affect policy or political structures that no easy generalization is possible. There is no simple or consistent story of good NGOs confronting evil governments. Just as the NGO field is a heterogenous one encompassing a wide range of groups with different ideological agendas, the state, too, needs to be acknowledged as a complex, heterogenous, and often fragmented actor. NGOs do not always successfully pressure local elites or local governments (Hirschman 1987, Sanyal 1994), and they are as likely to maintain the status quo as to change it (Chazan 1992, Fowler 1993, Ndegwa 1996, Starn 1995). The insufficiency of the data and the lack of clear comparative categories have led some analysts to wisely suggest abandoning as unanswerable the question about which type of NGO has greater political impact (see, for example, Clarke 1996).

Another factor that has differentially affected the relationship between Southern NGOs and their host governments is the recent proliferation of innovative linkages involving local NGOs, social movements, and transnational networks (Brysk 1993; Fisher 1995b; Kamarotos 1990; Leatherman et al 1994; Lipschutz 1992; Lopez et al 1995; Princen & Finger 1994; Shaw 1992; Sikkink 1993, 1995; Udall 1995).[11] The thickening webs of transnational networks involving Southern NGOs and transnational issue networks are cited as evidence for what some observers have identified as an emerging international civil society (Lipschutz 1992; Lopez et al 1995; Shaw 1992; Sikkink 1993, 1995). Finger (1994a) argues that the clearest example of an emerging global civil society is apparent in the international environmental movement (Princen & Finger 1994). In recent years, there has been an explosion of transnational NGO coalitions and communications networks punctuated by international confer-

---

[11]For a discussion of the effect of recent changes on the opportunities for Northern NGOs, see Dichter (1991).

ences and aided by regular use of fax and the Internet. These links bring together Northern human rights organizations, environmental activists, and Southern grass-roots groups within a "raucous, yet highly structured battleground" (Little 1995). The international campaign against the World Bank–funded Sardar Saro-var project on the Narmada river in India is one example of an effective coalition of Southern NGOs and a transnational network (Aufderheide & Rich 1988, Pat-kar 1995, Rich 1994, Udall 1995, Fisher 1995a). In the view of some theorists, specific campaigns that come together for a short time and then dissolve are enabled by an amorphous collection of networks that constitute a more durable "imagined" or "virtual" community of activists and associations.[12]

More studies on the flows of information among these networks would clar-ify when and why local struggles become international and in which cases they do not; what encourages and constrains the internationalization of local inter-ventions; and how the international and the local appropriate, commodify, and affect one another. The flows among sites are not seamless, smooth, or consis-tent, and organizational structures may function as points that constrict as well as encourage flows of money, people, information, development workers, bu-reaucrats, and activists. Not all Southern coalitions have been able to avail them-selves of transnational networks, and coalitions of northern NGOs have selec-tively assisted Southern groups, depending upon the utility of specific issues for furthering their own agendas. The Narmada campaign is a case in point, se-lected by Northern NGOs as an appropriate conflict to facilitate a strategy link-ing coalitions of environmentalists from both the North and South, and from capital city and grass roots, to lobby political forces with influence over devel-opment banks (Aufderheide & Rich 1988, Rich 1994, Udall 1995).

These translocal and transnational connections entail risk as well as opportu-nity, however. On the one hand they may offer Southern NGOs increased lever-age and autonomy in their struggle with national governments, while on the other hand, they expose these NGOs to direction or control by other sources. The fact is that the heterogeneity of the NGO field makes it easy for political forces to establish or coopt NGOs. One of the ways this occurs is through fund-ing. Funding of both Northern and Southern NGOs by development agencies, for example, has increased so much that NGOs not dependent on official aid for the majority of their budgets may be the exception rather than the rule (Ed-wards & Hulme 1996a). The dependency of local SNGOs and GROs on the un-

[12]Despite growing evidence of widespread "imagined" communities of principle-based, transnational issue networks and idealistic predictions of a growing global community, some observers argue that it is difficult to conceive of a single international civil society. In their view, it is more significant that national borders have remained enforced and national loyalties have not been superseded by global loyalties (Peterson 1992).

certain largess of donors has several direct and indirect effects (Desai & Howes 1996, Edwards 1996, Gariyo 1996, Hellinger 1987, Lara 1990, Smillie 1995, Smillie & Helmich 1993). It redirects accountability toward funders and away from the group's grass-roots constituencies (Biggs & Neame 1996, Covey 1996, Edwards & Hulme 1996a, Fisher 1994b, Fowler 1996, Fox & Hernandez 1992, Smith 1987, Tandon 1994, Zadek & Gatward 1996): NGOs become contractors, constituencies become customers, and members become clients. Extranational connections entail another danger by exposing NGOs to attacks within their own countries, raising questions about whether they "legitimately" represent their constituents (Bratton 1989). In India, for example, NGOs with foreign connections have sometimes been regarded as antinationalist agents of capitalism and Western political and cultural values (Karat 1988).

The vulnerability of their position as beneficiaries of outside funding and support may make NGOs less willing to advocate positions that run counter to those taken by the agencies funding them or their home governments (Clarke 1996). Multilateral development agencies (MLAs) tend to select for funding those NGOs that are MLA-friendly (Pratt & Stone 1995). The efforts of these selected NGOs are diverted away from social mobilization and toward the provision of services and development initiatives. This process has a ripple effect when well-funded SNGOs are able to provide more employment opportunities and attract qualified individuals away from other local NGOs that continue to focus on empowerment and social mobilization (Pearce 1993). In the views of some observers, the degree of cooptation of NGOs by development agencies through funding and joint initiatives is so advanced that NGOs are destined to become the organizational mechanism for an international welfare system, doomed to be little more than the frontmen for the "lords of poverty" (Farrington & Bebbington 1993, Fowler 1996, Hancock 1989).

THE MICROPOLITICS OF NGOs

Amid their wide range of translocal connections, all NGO practices remain discursively constructed through reference to the "local." Yet while a notion of the local remains centrally important to the legitimacy of NGOs, it is frustratingly illusive (Forbes 1995, Peters 1996, Ribot 1996a). NGOs are praised and valued for connections to local communities and the grass roots, whether these connections are direct, or indirect through the GROs they service. Their acceptance as legitimate NGOs depends on their connections to or usefulness for local constituencies (Edwards & Hulme 1996a). The concept of the local is central to the pursuit of the varyingly interpreted, contemporary development objectives of participation and empowerment (Vettivel 1993). The embracing of these objectives by the development establishment and the use of national and international intermediary NGOs to facilitate, fund, promote, and provide planning and organization assistance to so-called grass-roots organizations have resulted in the paradoxical attempt to generate participation through a top-down process of planning and organization (Chambers 1995).

Like other popular and politicized buzzwords of development (Fisher 1995c), participation and empowerment are given different meanings by different actors (Rahnema 1992). In the view of radical development critics, development policies may now stress participation (often confusing it with empowerment), but this is little more than a rhetorical flourish and is not reflected in actual or actualizable goals. As Chambers (1995) has noted, top-down planning, top-down funding, and upwards accountability negate participation. Rather than regarding participation as a general good, we need to ask in each instance in which "participation" is a claimed objective, "what responsibilities are being devolved and to whom?" These critics question the practices pursued under the rubrics of participation and empowerment: Incorporation into existing economic markets and political systems may bring advantages, but incorporation also brings new encumbrances and dependencies. Governments and development agencies express support for NGOs and participation even as they find ways to fit these new elements into old models of governance or development. Thus, the pursuit of participation by development agencies frequently fails to live up to their rhetoric, which seems to promote it and yet can amount to no more than the restructuring of control (Ribot 1996). Development agencies may allow an NGO to "represent" indigenous people at decisions taken in Washington, DC, or elsewhere, but the selection of some NGO to stand in for people is quite different from ensuring that decisions affecting the lives and resources of indigenous people are not taken without their informed consent.

To be sure, studies of specific cases have demonstrated that particular NGOs can be said to stimulate effective local participation and set objectives that contribute to the political empowerment of marginalized groups. See, for example, Ahuja's (1994) study of an NGO engaged in rural development work, Marulasiddaiah's (1994) study of Swasti, Wacker's (1994) discussion of Kikuyu women, and Viswanath's (1991) account of women's groups in India.

However, there is considerable evidence that NGOs frequently fail to live up to the expectations development agencies have of them (Bebbington & Thiele 1993; Carroll 1992; Farrington & Lewis 1993; Fowler 1991, 1993; Hashemi & Schuler 1992; Hogg 1992; Lehman 1990; Riddell & Robinson 1995; Vivian 1994; Wellard & Copestake 1993). Why, then, does the development establishment continue to support them? As Ferguson (1990) demonstrated for development interventions in Lesotho, it may be that the unspoken or unintended consequences of development support for NGOs serve the purposes of governments and development agencies.

NGOs cannot be understood as a forum in which real people are social and political actors without attention to the micropolitics of these groups. But while the need for local participation has become an article of faith in many quarters, particularly among the development community (Annis 1988, Korten 1990), most contemporary studies of the "thickening of civil society" (Fox 1992) do not include systematic analyses of power relationships within the groups and associations of civil society and the forms and channels of participation that affect power relationships.

NGOs are vulnerable to all the problems that befall other kinds of institutions, including the dangers of routinization and the gradual conversion of democratic to oligarchic rule. Weisgrau (1997) and Mehta (1996) have analyzed NGO practices in Rajasthan to show how the relationships between organizations and their constituents come to replicate older patron/client patterns. Baviskar (1995) has detailed the gap between the rhetoric of NGOs (in her case, the Narmada Bachao Andolan) and the failure of these organizations to live up to their own egalitarian rhetoric (see also Bebbington & Thiele 1993, Carroll 1992). The tendency of organizations to drift from participatory to oligarchic political structures has been presented by some institutional analysts as an "iron law of oligarchy" (Fisher 1994a, Fox 1992, Michels 1959, Uphoff 1996). Cases that support this "law" raise questions bound to trouble those who look for the transformative possibilities of NGOs: Are NGOs doomed to repeat the patterns of the societies within which they emerge? Can they empower without simultaneously victimizing? Can they enable as well as constrain? Can they do good without doing wrong?

One way to answer these questions is through a conception of civil society not as a sector that contests the will of governments but as a "vector of agonistic contentions over governmental relations" (Gordon 1991, p. 23). This emphasis on the way NGOs contribute to civil society by fueling ongoing contentions rather than merely through the multiplication and differentiation of structures (Clarke 1996) refocuses our attention on the processes and not merely the institutions of civil society. The recent expansion in the numbers of associations and the struggle for new linkages and truths support Adam Ferguson's processual view of society as an entity that repeatedly tears itself apart and endlessly remakes itself (Ferguson 1995; see also Gordon 1991). Some theorists find optimism in this expansion of civil society precisely because they see the transformation of civil society leading to transformation of the state, not the other way around. Empowerment, Rajni Kothari (1986) has argued, emerges through a decentralized self-government. In his view, "conscientization" and the struggle for new alternatives (and alternative truths) produce a new class of activists.

The view of observers like Rajni Kothari is built upon several significant assumptions about the connections of individuals, society, and the state and the possibilities for transforming them. First, this view sees macrogovernmental rationalities emerging from the articulation of microprograms and technologies of power (Simon 1995). Those holding this view see modern governmental mechanisms and rationalities as simultaneously directed at individualizing and totalizing; that is, they are about governing or making governable both individuals and society (Gordon 1991). Foucault's view of modern civil society as "the concrete ensemble within which...economic men need to be positioned in order to be adequately manageable" also emphasizes the constraints that microlevel practices place upon the individual, and the shape they give to macrolevel governmental rationalities (quoted in Gordon 1991, p. 23).

Second, while this view acknowledges the participation of NGOs in a coherent general policy of order, it also holds out the possibility of changing that policy by changing the micropractices and the discourse from which they emerge. The process within which NGOs participate can contribute to social restructuring around and under the state and the market, undermining traditional foundations and forcing adaptations to changed practices and circumstances. This change requires and emerges from the "forging together, wrenching apart and recreation of discourses which break with their predecessors" (Adam 1993, p. 329). The framing of calls for sustainable development and social justice is an instance of what Foucault has called "the strategic reversibility" of power relations, a means by which the terms of governmental practice can be turned into focuses of resistance (see also Gordon 1991). Change rests on the ability of individuals and associations to challenge the terms of governmental "truths" and struggle to change the limits of what is "thinkable." "Change the way people think," argued Stephen Biko, "and things will never be the same."

One perspective on how this change can be brought about is contributed by analysts and activists interested in the connection between personal and social change. These scholars follow Foucault insofar as they "analyze institutions from the standpoint of power relations rather than vice versa" (Foucault 1983, p. 222). In part, their analysis considers the relationship between the attempts of individuals to free themselves from the constraints of cultural or class backgrounds and attempts to empower or liberate others. The focus on personal and societal emancipation turns their attention to "the technologies of domination over others and those of the self." Changing the self and changing society both require a rejection of the representation of self imposed by relationships with others. Individuals and groups struggle for the freedom to define themselves and their relationships with others on their own terms, an effort Carmichael & Hamilton (1967) called "the first necessity of a free people and the first right any oppressor must suspend" (p. 35). The work of some empowerment NGOs contributes to this emancipatory process through the politicization of previously depoliticized realms and issues—for example, issues concerning gender or the environment. They turn issues that directly engage the self, subjective experience, and daily life into crucial sites of political contestation. The identity politics that emerge from this process are a means by which local groups maintain tenuous autonomy and reduce their susceptibility to cooptation and colonialization by external political actors. They are what Kauffman has described as a "liberating new synthesis of the personal and the political" (Kauffman 1990, p. 67).

This perspective emphasizes the tight relationship between ethics and politics. Many NGOs and the translocal coalitions they participate in are "inspired by a particular vision of the society they wish to develop" (Tandon 1994, p. 53; see also Brown & Korten 1989, Fisher 1993). These values differ—they may see themselves humanizing the policies of structural adjustment, helping constituents adjust to top-down development projects, or inducing changes in social and economic orders—but they are not value neutral: Their primary motivations are beliefs about what is right and wrong (Sikkink 1995). Although NGOs may present ethical judgments as neutral standards of judgment that stand outside political contest (see Simon 1995, p. 67), these judgments are essentially political.

In this view, power is exercised through the strategic manipulation of the options of the Other. Power is thus less a confrontation between two adversaries than it is a question of government, in which to govern is to structure the field of possible actions of others (Ferguson 1990). The relationship of NGOs to this practice of governing is complex. Since, as noted above, NGOs differ radically from one another in nature and composition, it follows that NGOs may emerge from, contribute to, or challenge the moral regulation inherent in governing.

In practice, specific NGOs may move in either democratic or oligarchic directions, depending on their constituencies and their particular circumstances. NGOs may serve both as extensions of regimes or practice, like development, and as sources of alternatives to such regimes. The transformative potential of the NGO sector may emerge less from ordered and controlled participation than from relatively chaotic sets of multiple opportunities and interdependencies. Liberty, argued Foucault (1986), is "a practice... never assured by the institutions and laws that are intended to guarantee it" (p. 245). Foucault further argued that "it can never be inherent in the structure of things to guarantee the *exercise* of freedom" (my emphasis). Some NGOs face routinization, bureaucratization, and institutionalization that encourage the drift toward oligarchy or sap them of their creative potential, while other NGOs are in a process of permanent resistance against that which is "never inherently evil but always dangerous" (see Gordon 1991, p. 47; Simon 1995, p. 87).

Thus, the objective of empowerment or "liberty" may not be served by institution building or perpetuating existent organizations, and may even be undermined by bureaucratization. It may be inappropriate to regard the fluidity of the NGO field as a weakness or the impermanence of any give NGO as a failure. Rather, we might look for permanence in the rebellious process from which many NGOs emerge and within which some NGOs remain engaged. NGOs and social movements may come and go, but the space created in their passing may contribute to new activism that builds up after them. For a particularly interesting account of a conscious effort to avoid the dangers that come with formal organization and engagement with the state, see Esteva (1987).

CONCLUSION

The growth of a multicentric world and the practices of growing numbers of nonstate national and transnational actors have had significant impact on the sites and communities that have been the focus of anthropological research. Understanding what is happening within and through organizations such as NGOs and adapting to the changing conditions within which they operate present challenges to anthropological researchers. Community-based organizations may be close to the traditional sites of anthropological concerns, but the networks and alliances they increasingly have come to form open up new sites for ethnographic research, and the wide cast of these networks, which may appear only through chaotic public spectacles of ritual performance like international conferences, call for innovative research methodologies. As researchers, we need to reconsider how to approach problems located in or flowing through multiple sites. Additional work by anthropologists will not only contribute to knowledge of what NGOs are doing but will also provide insights into anthropological conceptions of communities, local and translocal networks, technologies of control, and the political role of intellectuals. The challenge is to consider nongovernmental organizations as one specific possible form of collective action and human community and to set the stage for a comparative analysis of the different configurations these forms of collective action have taken and are taking in a complexly woven field of translocal flows.

> Visit the *Annual Reviews home page* at
> http://www.AnnualReviews.org.

Literature Cited

Adam BD. 1993. Post-Marxism and the new social movements. *Can. Rev. Soc. Anthropol.* 30(3):316–36

Ahuja K. 1994. Mobilization of rural women through voluntary efforts—a case study. *Stud. Third World Soc.* 51:1–10

Annis S. 1988. Can small-scale development be large-scale policy? In *Direct to the*

Poor: Grassroots Development in Latin America, ed. S Annis, P Hakim, pp. 209–18. Boulder: Reinner

Appadurai A. 1991. Global ethnoscapes: notes and queries for a transnational anthropology. In *Recapturing Anthropology: Working in the Present,* ed. R Fox, pp. 191–210. Santa Fe: Sch. Am. Res.

Aufderheide P, Rich B. 1988. Environmental reform and the multilateral banks. *World Policy J.* 5(2):300–21

Banuri T. 1993. The landscape of diplomatic conflicts. In *Global Ecology: A New Arena of Global Conflict,* ed. W Sachs, pp. 49–67. London: Zed

Barghouti M. 1994. *Palestinian NGOs and Their Role in Building a Civil Society.* Union Palest. Med. Relief Comm., West Bank

Baviskar A. 1995. *In the Belly of the River: Tribal Conflicts over Development in the Narmada Valley.* Delhi: Oxford

Bebbington AJ. 1996. Movements, modernizations, and markets. In *Liberation Ecologies: Environment, Development, Social Movements,* ed. R Peet, M Watts, pp. 86–109. London: Routledge

Bebbington AJ, Thiele G. 1993. *NGOs and the State in Latin America: Rethinking Roles in Sustainable Agricultural Development.* London: Routledge

Biggs SD, Neame AD. 1996. Negotiating room to maneuver: reflections concerning NGO autonomy and accountability with the new policy agenda. See Edwards & Hulme 1996a, pp. 40–52

Bongartz H, Dahal MK, Aditya A, Dahal DR. 1992. *Foreign Aid and the Role of NGOs in the Development Process of Nepal.* Kathmandu: Nepal Found. Adv. Stud.

Bratton M. 1989. The politics of NGO-government relations in Africa. *World Dev.* 17(4):569–87

Brown LD, Korten D. 1989. The role of voluntary organizations in development. IDR Work. Pap. No. 8. Boston: Inst. Dev. Res./Boston Univ. Sch. Manage.

Brysk A. 1993. From above and below: social movements, the international system, and human rights in Argentina. *Comp. Pol. Stud.* 26(3):259–85

Burchell G, Gordon C, Miller P, eds. 1991. *The Foucault Effect: Studies in Governmentality.* Chicago: Univ. Chicago Press

Carmichael S, Hamilton CV. 1967. *Black Power: The Politics of Liberation in America.* New York: Vintage

Carroll JE, ed. 1988. *International Environmental Diplomacy.* Cambridge: Cambridge Univ. Press

Carroll TF. 1992. *Intermediary NGOs: The Supporting Link in Grassroots Development.* West Hartford, CT: Kumarian

Cernea M. 1988. Nongovernmental organizations and local development. *Discuss. Pap. No. 40.* Washington, DC: World Bank

Chambers R. 1995. NGOs and development: the primacy of the personal. *Inst. Dev. Stud. Work. Pap. 14.* Brighton, Engl.

Chazan N. 1992. Africa's democratic challenge. *World Policy J.* 9(2):279–307

Ching F. 1994. Is it an NGO, or a GONGO?: new Chinese body rebuts U. S. report on human rights. *Far East. Econ. Rev.* (July 7)

Clark J. 1991. *Democratizing Development: The Role of Voluntary Organizations.* London: Earthscan

Clark J. 1995. The state, popular participation, and the voluntary sector. *World Dev.* 23(4):593–602

Clarke G. 1993. People power? Nongovernmental organizations and Philippine politics since 1986. *Philipp. Q. Cult. Soc.* 21:231–56

Clarke G. 1996. Non-governmental organisations (NGOs) and politics in the developing world. *Pap. Int. Dev. No. 20.* Swansea, Wales: Cent. Dev. Stud.

Covey JG. 1996. Accountability and effectiveness in NGO policy alliances. See Edwards & Hulme 1996a, pp. 198–214

Desai V, Howes M. 1996. Accountability and participation: a case study from Bombay. See Edwards & Hulme 1996a, pp. 101–113

Diani M. 1992. The concept of social movement. *Soc. Rev.* 40(1):1–25

Dichter T. 1991. The changing world of Northern NGOs: problems, paradoxes and possibilities. *Transnatl. Assoc.* 2:66–70

Dichter T. 1993. Forward. See Fisher 1993, pp. vii–xiv

Edwards M. 1996. Too close for comfort? the impact of official aid on nongovernmental organizations. *World Dev.* 24(6): 961–72

Edwards M, Hulme D, eds. 1996a. *Beyond the Magic Bullet: NGO Performance and Accountability in the Post-Cold War World.* West Hartford, CT: Kumarian

Edwards M, Hulme D. 1996b. Beyond the magic bullet? Lessons and conclusions. See Edwards & Hulme 1996a, pp. 254–66

Elliot C. 1987. Some aspects of relations between the North and South in the NGO sector. *World Dev.* 15(Suppl.):57–68

Ekins P. 1992. *A New World Order: Grassroots Movements for Global Change.* London: Routledge

Escobar A. 1991. Anthropology and the development encounter: the making and marketing of development anthropology. *Am. Ethnol.* 18(4):658–82

Escobar A. 1992. Reflections on "development": grassroots approaches and alternative politics in the third world. *Futures* June:411–35

Escobar A. 1995. *Encountering Development: The Making and Unmaking of the Third World.* Princeton, NJ: Princeton Univ. Press

Esteva G. 1987. Regenerating people's space. *Alternatives* 12(1):125–52

Farrington J, Bebbington A, eds. 1993. *Reluctant Partners? Nongovernmental Organizations, the State and Sustainable Agricultural Development.* London: Routledge

Farrington J, Lewis D, eds. 1993. *Non-Governmental Organisations and the State in Asia: Rethinking Roles in Sustainable Agricultural Development.* London: Routledge

Ferguson A. 1995. *An Essay on the History of Civil Society,* ed. F Ox-Salzberger. Cambridge: Cambridge Univ. Press

Ferguson J. 1990. *The Anti-Politics Machine: "Development," Depoliticization, and Bureaucratic Power in Lesotho.* Cambridge: Cambridge Univ. Press

Finger M. 1994a. NGOs and transformation: beyond social movement theory. See Princen & Finger 1994, pp. 48–66

Finger M. 1994b. Environmental NGOs in the UNCED process. See Princen & Finger 1994, pp. 186–213

Fisher J. 1993. *The Road from Rio: Sustainable Development and the Nongovernmental Movement in the Third World.* Westport, CT: Praeger

Fisher J. 1994a. Is the iron law of oligarchy rusting away in the third world? *World Dev.* 22(2):129–43

Fisher J. 1994b. Third world NGOs: a missing piece to the population puzzle. *Environment* 36(7):6–16

Fisher WF, ed. 1995a. *Toward Sustainable Development? Struggling Over India's Narmada River.* Armonk, NY: Sharpe

Fisher WF. 1995b. Development and resistance in the Narmada Valley. See Fisher 1995a, pp. 3–46

Fisher WF. 1995c. Full of sound and fury? Struggling toward sustainable development in India's Narmada Valley. See Fisher 1995a, pp. 445–61

Food and Agriculture Organization of the United Nations (FAO). 1994. *FAO Collaboration with Asian NGOs for Participatory Rural Development: The Case of ANGOC.* Rome: FAO

Forbes A. 1995. *The importance of being local: villagers, NGOs, and the World Bank in the Arun Valley, Nepal.* Presented at Annu. Meet. Am. Anthropol. Assoc., 94th, Washington, DC

Foucault M. 1980. *Power/Knowledge: Selected Interviews and Other Writings,* ed. C Gordon. New York: Pantheon

Foucault M. 1983. The subject and power. In *Michel Foucault: Beyond Structuralism and Hermeneutics,* ed. HL Dreyfus, P Rabinow, pp. 208–26. Chicago: Univ. Chicago Press

Foucault M. 1986. Space, knowledge, power. In *The Foucault Reader,* ed. P Rabinow, pp. 239–56. New York: Penguin

Foucault M. 1991. Governmentality. See Burchell et al 1991, pp. 87–104

Fowler A. 1988. NGOs in Africa: achieving comparative advantage in relief and microdevelopment. *IDS Discuss. Pap. 249.* Sussex: Inst. Dev. Stud.

Fowler A. 1991. The role of NGOs in changing state-society relations: perspectives from Eastern and Southern Africa. *Dev. Policy Rev.* 9:53–84

Fowler A. 1993. NGOs as agents of democratisation: an African perspective. *J. Int. Dev.* 5(3):325–39

Fowler A. 1996. Assessing NGO performance: difficulties, dilemmas, and a way ahead. See Edwards & Hulme 1996a, pp. 169–86

Fowler A, James R. 1995. The role of Southern NGOs in development cooperation: a review. *Occas. Pap. Ser. 1(2).* Oxford: Int. NGO Train. Res. Cent.

Fox J. 1992. Democratic rural development: leadership accountability in regional peasant organizations. *Dev. Change* 23(2):1–36

Fox J, Hernandez L. 1992. Mexico's difficult democracy: grassroots movements, NGOs, and local government. *Alternatives* 17(2):165–208

Frank AG, Fuentes M. 1990. Civil democracy: social movements in recent world history. In *Transforming the Revolution: Social Movements and the World System,* ed. S Amin, G Arrighi, A Gunder-Frank, I Wallerstein, pp. 139–80. New York: Monthly Review

Frantz TR. 1987. The Role of NGOs in the strengthening of civil society. *World Dev.* 15(Suppl.):121–27

Friedman D. 1992. *Empowerment: The Politics of Alternative Development.* Oxford: Blackwell

Friedman M. 1962. *Capitalism and Freedom.* Chicago: Univ. Chicago Press

Gariyo Z. 1996. NGOs and development in East Africa. See Edwards & Hulme 1996a, pp. 156–65

Ghils P. 1992. International civil society: international non-governmental organizations in the international system. *Int. Soc. Sci. J.* 44(3):417–31

Gordon C. 1991. Governmental rationality: an introduction. See Burchell et al 1991, pp. 1–53

Hancock G. 1989. *Lords of Poverty: The Power, Prestige, and Corruption of the International Aid Business.* New York: Atlantic Monthly Press

Hashemi S, Schuler S. 1992. *State and NGO Support Networks in Rural Bangladesh: Concepts and Coalitions for Control.* Copenhagen: Cent. Dev. Res.

Hellinger D. 1987. NGOs and the large aid donors: changing the terms of engagement. *World Dev.* 15(Suppl.):135–43

Hirschman AO. 1987. *Getting Ahead Collectively: Grassroots Experiences in Latin America.* New York: Pergamon

Hogg R. 1992. NGOs, pastoralists and the myth of community: three case studies of pastoral development from East Africa. *Nomadic Peoples* 30:122–46

Holm H, Sorenson G. 1995. *Whose World Order? Uneven Globalization and the End of the Cold War.* Boulder: Westview

Hulme D. 1994. Social development research and the third sector: NGOs as users and subjects of social enquiry. In *Rethinking Social Development: Theory, Research and Practice,* ed. D Booth, pp. 251–75. Harlow: Longman

Hyden G. 1998. State and nation under stress. In *Recovery in Africa: A Challenge for Development Cooperation in the 90s,* pp. 145–57. Stockholm: Swed. Minist. Foreign Aff. In press

Jhamtani H. 1992. The imperialism of Northern NGOs. *Earth Island J.* 7(June):10

Kamarotos AS. 1990. A view into NGO networks in human rights activities: NGO action with special reference to the UN Commission on Human Rights and its subcommission. Presented at Int. Polit. Sci. Assoc., April 10–14, Washington, DC

Karat P. 1988. *Foreign Funding and the Philosophy of Voluntary Organisations: A Factor in Imperialist Strategy.* New Delhi: Natl. Book Cent.

Kauffman LA. 1990. The anti-politics of identity. *Social. Rev.* 20(1):67–80

Korten DC. 1990. *Getting to the 21st Century: Voluntary Action and the Global Agenda.* West Hartford, CT: Kumarian

Korten DC. 1987. Third generation NGO strategies: a key to people-centered development. *World Dev.* 15(Suppl.): 145–60

Kothari R. 1986. NGOs, the state and world capitalism. *Econ. Polit. Weekly* 21(Dec): 2177–82

Kothari R. 1993. Masses, classes and the state. See Wignaraja 1993a, pp. 59–75

Kothari S. 1993. Social movements and the redefinition of democracy. In *India Briefing 1993,* ed. P Oldenburg, pp. 131–62. Boulder: Westview

Landim L. 1993. Brazilian crossroads: people's groups, walls and bridges. See Wignaraja 1993a, pp. 218–29

Lara L Jr. 1990. *The impact of foreign aid on peoples initiatives in agrarian reform.* Philipp. Peasant Inst. Res. Pap., Manila

Lash S, Urry J. 1994. *Economies of Signs and Space.* New York: Sage

Leatherman J, Pagnucco R, Smith J. 1994. International institutions and transnational social movement organizations: challenging the state in a three-level game of global transformation. *Work. Pap. Ser. Joan B. Kroc Inst. Int. Peace Stud.,* Univ. Notre Dame

Lehman D. 1990. *Democracy and Development in Latin America: Economics, Politics, and Religion in the Postwar Period.* London: Polity

Lind AC. 1992. Power, gender and development: popular women's organisations and the politics of needs in Ecuador. In *The Making of Social Movements in Latin America: Identity, Strategy, and Democracy,* ed. A Escobar, S Alvarez, pp. 139–49. Boulder: Westview

Linkenbach A. 1994. Ecological movements and the critique of development: agents and interpretors. *Thesis Eleven* 39:63–85

Lipschutz RD. 1992. Reconstructing world politics: the emergence of global civil society. *Millennium* 21(3):389–420

Little PD, Painter M. 1995. Discourse, politics, and the development process: reflections on Escobar's "Anthropology and the Development Encounter." *Am. Ethnol.* 22(3):602–9

Little PE. 1995. Ritual, power and ethnography at the Rio Earth Summit. *Crit. Anthropol.* 15(3):265–88

Lopez GA, Smith JG, Pagnucco R. 1995. The global tide. *Bull. Atomic Sci.* July/Aug.: 33–39

Marcus G. 1995. Ethnography in/out of the world system: the emergence of multisided ethnography. *Annu. Rev. Anthropol.* 24:95–117

Marulasiddaiah HM. 1994. Image of an elephant in a small mirror: Swasti—an organization for social change and development. *Stud. Third World Soc.* 51: 49–75

Mehta AS. 1996. Micro politics of voluntary action: an anatomy of change in two villages. *Cult. Surv.* 20(3):26–30

Michels R. 1959. *Political Parties.* New York: Dover

Millett K. 1971. *Sexual Politics.* New York: Avon

Moore M. 1993. Good government? Introduction. *IDS Bull.* 24(1):1–6

Nachowitz T. 1990. *An Alternative Directory of Nongovernmental Organizations in South Asia.* Syracuse: Maxwell Sch. Citizensh. Public Aff., Syracuse Univ.

Ndegwa SN. 1993. *NGOs as pluralizing agents in civil society in Kenya. Work. Pap. No. 491.* Nairobi: Inst. Dev. Stud.

Ndegwa SN. 1996. *The Two Faces of Civil Society: NGOs and Politics in Africa.* West Hartford, CT: Kumarian

Ng'ethe N, Kanyinga K. 1992. *The politics of development space: the state and NGOs in the delivery of basic services in Kenya.* Work. Pap. No. 486. Nairobi: Inst. Dev. Stud.

Olsen GR. 1995. *NGOs and the international environment in the 1990s.* Cent. Dev. Stud. Work. Pap., Copenhagen

Padron MC. 1987. Non-governmental development organizations: from development AID to development cooperation. *World Dev.* 15(Suppl.):69–77

Patel A. 1995. What do the Narmada Valley tribals want? See Fisher 1995, pp. 179–200

Patkar M. 1995. The struggle for participation and justice: a historical narrative. See Fisher 1995, pp. 157–78

Pearce J. 1993. NGOs and social change: agents or facilitators? *Dev. Practice* 3(3): 222–27

Peters P, ed. 1996. Who's local here? the politics of participation in development. *Cult. Surviv. Q.* 20(3):22–60

Peterson MJ. 1992. Transnational activity, international society and world politics. *Millennium* 21(3):371–88

Pratt B, Stone A. 1995. Multilateral agencies and NGOs: a position paper. Oxford: Int. NGO Train. Res. Cent.

Princen T. 1994. NGOs: creating a niche in environmental diplomacy. See Princen & Finger 1994b, pp. 29–47

Princen T, Finger M. 1994. *Environmental NGOs in World Politics: Linking the Local and the Global.* London/New York: Routledge

Rademacher A, Tamang D. 1993. *Democracy,*

Development and NGOs. Kathmandu: SEARCH

Rahnema M. 1992. Participation. In *The Development Dictionary,* ed. W Sachs, pp. 116–31. London: Zed

Reilly C. 1992. Foreword. See Carroll 1992, pp. x–xii

Ribot J. 1996. Participation without representation: chiefs, councils and forestry law in the West African Sahel. *Cult. Surviv.* 20(3):40–44

Rich B. 1994. *Mortgaging the Earth: The World Bank, Environmental Impoverishment, and the Crisis of Development.* Boston: Beacon

Riddel RC, Robinson M. 1995. *Non-Governmental Organizations and Rural Poverty Alleviation.* New York: Oxford Univ. Press

Rivera T. 1992. The new world order: problems and prospects for the people's movement in the Philippines. In *Beyond the Cold War,* ed. C Karagdag, A Miclat, pp. 187–94. Quezon City: People's Train. Program Phillipp. NGOs

Robinson M. 1993. Governance, democracy and conditionality: NGOs and the new policy agenda. In *Governance, Democracy And Conditionality: What Role for NGOs?* ed. A Clayton, pp.. Oxford: Int. NGO Train. Res. Cent.

Rosenau J. 1990. *Turbulence in World Politics: A Theory of Change and Continuity.* Princeton, NJ: Princeton Univ. Press

Salamon LM. 1993. *The global associational revolution: the rise of third sector on the world scene.* Occas. Pap. 15. Baltimore: Inst. Policy Stud., Johns Hopkins Univ.

Salamon LM. 1994. The rise of the nonprofit sector. *Foreign Aff.* 73(4):109–22

Sanyal B. 1994. *Cooperative autonomy: the dialectics of state-NGO relationships in developing countries.* Res. Ser. 100. Geneva: ILO

Semboja J, Therkildsen O, eds. 1995. *Service Provision Under Stress in East Africa: The State, NGOs, and People's Organizations in Kenya, Tanzania, and Uganda.* Copenhagen: Cent. Dev. Res.

Sethi H. 1993a. Survival and democracy: ecological struggles in India. See Wignaraja 1993a, pp. 122–48

Sethi H. 1993b. Action groups in the new politics. See Wignaraja 1993a, pp. 230–55

Shaw M. 1992. Global society and global responsibility: the theoretical, historical and political limits of "international society." *Millennium* 21(3):421–34

Sikkink K. 1993. Human rights, principled

issue-networks, and sovereignty in Latin America. *Int. Organ.* 47(3):411–41

Sikkink K. 1995. Non-governmental organizations and transnational issue networks in international politics. *Proc. Annu. Meet. Am. Soc. Int. Law* 89:413–15

Silliman GS. 1994. Human rights and he transition to democracy. In *Patterns of Power and Politics in the Philippines: Implications for Development*, ed. J Eder, R Youngblood, pp. 103–46. Tempe: Ariz. State Univ.

Simon J. 1995. *Foucault and the Political.* New York: Routledge

Sinaga K. 1995. *NGOs in Indonesia: A Study of the Role of Non Governmental Organizations in the Development Process.* Saarbrucken: Verlag Entwicklungspolit.

Smillie I. 1995. *The Alms Bazar: Altruism Under Fire: Non-Profit Organizations and International Development.* Ottawa: Int. Dev. Res. Cent.

Smillie I, Helmich H. 1993. *Non-Governmental Organisations and Governments: Stakeholders for Development.* Paris: Dev. Cent. Organ. Econ. Coop. Dev.

Smith BH. 1987. An agenda of future tasks for international and indigenous NGOs: views from the north. *World Dev.* 15(Suppl.): 87–93

Society for Participatory Research in Asia. *NGO-Government Relations: A Source of Life or the Kiss of Death.* New Delhi

Spiro PJ. 1994. New global communities: nongovernmental organizations in international decision-making institutions. *Wash. Q.* 18(1):45–56

Starn O. 1995. To revolt against the revolution: war and resistance in Peru's Andes. *Cult. Anthropol.* 10(4):547–80

Tandon R. 1994. Civil society, the state and the role of NGOs. In *Civil Society in the Asia-Pacific Region*, ed. I Serrano, pp. 117–36. Washington, DC: CIVICUS

Thomson A. 1992. *The World Bank and Cooperation with NGOs.* Ottawa: CODE

Udall L. 1995. The international Narmada campaign: a case of sustained advocacy. See Fisher 1995a, pp. 210–27

UNDP. 1993. *Human Development Report 1993.* New York: Oxford Univ. Press

Uphoff N. 1996. Why NGOs are not a third sector: a sectoral analysis with some thoughts on accountability, sustainability,

and evaluation. See Edwards & Hulme 1996a, pp. 23–39

Vergara C. 1989. The new context of social policy in Chile and the space for nongovernmental organisations. In *Social Policy from the Grassroots: Nongovernmental Organisations in Chile*, ed. C Downs, G Solimano, C Vergara, L Zuniga, pp. 1–8. Boulder: Westview

Vettivel SK. 1993. *Participation and Sustainable Development: Theory and Practice in Government and NGOs.* New Delhi: Vetri

Viswanath V. 1991. *NGOs and Women's Development in Rural South India: A Comparative Analysis.* Boulder: Westview

Vivian J. 1994. NGOs and sustainable development in Zimbabwe: no magic bullets. *Dev. Change* 25:181–209

Wacker C. 1994. Sustainable development through women's groups: a cultural approach to sustainable development. In *Feminist Perspectives on Sustainable Development*, ed. W Harcourt, pp. 128–42. London: Zed

Wapner P. 1994. Environmental activism and global civil society. *Dissent* 41:389–93

Weisgrau M. 1997. *Interpreting Development: Local Histories, Local Strategies.* New York: University Press Am.

Wellard K, Copestake J, eds. 1993. *Nongovernmental Organisations and the State in Africa: Rethinking Roles in Sustainable Agriculture.* London: Routledge

Wignaraja P, ed. 1993a. *New Social Movements in the South: Empowering the People.* London: Zed

Wignaraja P. 1993b. Rethinking development and democracy. See Wignaraja 1993a, pp. 4–35

Wolfe A. 1991. *Three paths to development: market, state, and civil society.* Presented at Int. Meet. NGOs UN System Agencies, Aug. 6–9, Rio de Janeiro

World Bank. 1991. *World Development Report 1991: The Challenge of Development.* Washington, DC: World Bank/Oxford Univ. Press

Zadek S, Gatward M. 1996. Transforming the transnational NGOs: Social auditing or bust? See Edwards & Hulme 1996a, pp. 226–40

Zivetz L. 1991. *Doing Good: The Australian NGO Community.* North Sydney, NSW: Allen & Unwin

Annu. Rev. Anthropol. 1997. 26:465–85

THE ARCHAEOLOGY OF ANCIENT RELIGION IN THE EASTERN WOODLANDS

James A. Brown

Department of Anthropology, Northwestern University, Evanston, Illinois 60208

KEY WORDS: cosmology, earthworks, iconographic analysis, meaning in archaeology, shamanism

ABSTRACT

Archaeology has begun to contribute to the history of spirituality in the Eastern Woodlands of North America to complement the perspectives offered by the comparative study of religions and by ethnological, folkloric, art historical, and astronomical research. Support can be found in the forms and types of ritual paraphernalia and in the associated iconography for the thesis that shamanism was a basic form of religious experience that extended back to the earliest material traces. Elaborations upon this foundation became most conspicuous during the Mississippian Period when social hierarchies developed upon an expanded, agriculturally supported population. Animal imagery changed, ancestor cults became elaborated, and cosmography took on increased importance in architecture, site layout, and mortuary rites. The canonical forms of the iconography of this period have become known as the Southeastern Ceremonial Complex. Since European contact, practices and beliefs associated with social hierarchies have disappeared or transformed.

INTRODUCTION

The study of the Eastern Woodlands religion, cosmology, and ideology (and even social organization) has remained trapped in the ethnographic present (Keyes 1994). A systematic perspective toward history was not adopted by the

465

established disciplines of ethnology, comparative religion, and comparative folklore. The impression was created that internal development is not essential to their programs—notwithstanding the practice of resorting to age area models for the construction of proxy histories, when they were convenient. No dynamic exogenous processes are envisioned, except for the effects of putative Mesoamerican inspiration. As a consequence, the deeply rooted belief that peoples north of Mesoamerica had no "history" is thereby reinforced. There are some recent exceptions to this generalization (e.g. Hultkrantz 1983, Krusche 1986), but these are largely limited in scope to a period immediately preceding the ethnographic present.

So completely have ethnohistorical characterizations of Eastern Woodlands society and religion dominated archaeological thinking that it has remained difficult for scholars of the past to break away from the constraints of what must be an incomplete if not faulty record. Post-Columbian depopulation has seriously altered precontact cultures (Galloway 1991). Dobyns (1991) has enumerated the cultural distortions and disjunctions that ensued with this process. Even in those cases where archaeologists infer the past existence of greater social and political complexity the tendency has been strong to conceive of it along lines elaborated by specific ethnohistorical types, such as the Natchez. But while there have been strides toward releasing research from the constraints that ethnographic sources place on political and social models, comparable advances cannot be claimed for inquiry into past religious practices and beliefs.

A familiarity with the archaeological record has revealed the history of North American spirituality in the Eastern Woodlands to have been more dynamic than hitherto recognized. Systematic examination of major data sets such as the engraved shell from the site of Spiro has helped (Phillips & Brown 1978, 1984). At the same time archaeologists have made open use of mythology and ethnographic material on religious beliefs and practices (e.g. Hall 1977, 1989, 1997; Prentice 1986; von Gernet & Timmins 1987) while students of comparative religion have had recourse to the systematic study of archaeological objects (e.g. Paper 1988). In eastern North America, enough is known through material vestiges to indicate that there may indeed be a history to the subject. This review of research in the Eastern Woodlands is organized along lines emphasizing the dynamic aspect of religious history.

PERSPECTIVES ON THE HISTORY OF ANCIENT RELIGION

Before archaeology developed a stake in the history of American religion this subject had long been a topic of related disciplines. Ethnology claimed an early and commanding place among them, followed later by comparative religion, folklore, and, more recently, art history and astronomical research, in both its ethnoastronomical and archaeoastronomical forms. While each has brought its own perspectives, methods of analysis, research goals, and intellectual agendas, Eastern Woodland studies have only occasionally occupied the center of attention. Now that increased interest has been directed toward historical perspectives in this area, archaeological evidence has assumed a key role in research on the topic.

Although archaeology has brought a time scale and means for placing religious history in an economic and social context, very little can be accomplished without acknowledging the contribution that all approaches have made in the past. Future research advances will continue to necessitate a multidisciplinary approach. Since none is strong on its own, all disciplinary approaches and data sources will have to be used in conjunction.

Ethnology

Ecological, functional, and evolutionary perspectives have long been the purview of ethnology. In each, the observed diversity in rites and practices has been conveniently collapsed into simplifying sociocultural dimensions, each on its own scale. The evolutionary scale was first to take hold—to be followed by sociological and psychological ones. Each could accommodate the notion, following Swanton, that rites as diverse as the sacred pipe of the Arapaho, the sacred arrows of the Cheyenne, and the stone image of the Natchez sacred shrine could be regarded as exemplars of the same idea at various levels of cultural elaboration.

The kind of reductionism identified with the structuralism of Lévi-Strauss is too antihistorical to be of utility. Because it dismisses content for an algebraic structure underlying myth, it does not deal well with the content of sacred belief (Hultkrantz 1983). The comparative sociological perspective of Victor Turner has been more fruitful (Brose et al 1985, Knight 1986). His division of ritual on an inclusive/exclusive dimension connects rituals centering on the earth and fertility with the socially most egalitarian in spirit. Because they speak to common interests and anxieties, cults of inclusiveness have a life outside of social hierarchy, class distinctions, economic control, and political centralization. They arise in the least complex of societies. In contrast, those that center upon a single individual or small group, such as ancestor cults, emphasize exclusiveness and are politically manipulative.

More directly historical has been the problem of inter-areal connections. For instance, the Prairie tribes share many features in general with the Muskogean-speaking peoples of the Southeast. These similarities have been attributed to a common heritage in an agricultural economy. The source for much of Plains Indian ritual, likewise, is visualized as a simplification of the more complex agriculturally oriented Prairie societies. More bothersome are the Pawnee, who have been singled out for attention because of customs that suggest Mesoamerican connections. Among them is a well-developed high-god concept, a conspicuous star mythology, a near priesthood presiding over important tribal bundle ceremonies, and human sacrifice to the Morning Star (Hultkrantz 1973). Although some may see these and other traits as representing a direct bridge to Mesoamerica, possibly mediated through the Pueblo Indians, others have taken a decidedly skeptical view (Griffin 1980). The Mesoamerican connection is considerably muddied by the appearance among other Prairie groups of some of the same traits in somewhat attenuated form. An alternative scenario may have existed. This is one in which the Mesoamerican traits had undergone an intermediate midcontinental development further to the East at Cahokia and other locations.

Each analytical perspective has contributed useful analogical arguments that address the problem of explaining past conditions outside of the confines of the direct historical approach. An ethnological perspective has contributed to a wide range of approaches (Hall 1989, 1997; Hudson 1984; Hudson & Tesser 1994; Kwachka 1994; Miller 1996; Murray 1991).

Comparative Religion

Comparative religion has been directly concerned with specific beliefs and practices. When informed by Native American ethnology, this research has provided a framework for prehistoric inquiry (Hultkrantz 1979, 1981, 1983, 1992; Vecsey 1988). Shamanism has been a major topic. As an evolutionary type, it has come to stand for the practice of achieving ecstasy through a deep trance. While under trance, the soul of the practitioner journeys into the upper or lower worlds (Furst 1994, Hultkrantz 1992). A second source of shamanic trance is that of communal vapor sweating in a symbolically charged sweat lodge (Paper 1990).

Other aspects of Eastern Woodland religions are likely to have an archaeological presence. These are cosmology and the structure of theistic beliefs (Hudson 1984; Hultkrantz 1973, 1981). The cult of the dead is another (Hultkrantz 1981). The dead act as intermediaries between the living and the powers above as either personal guardian spirits or masters of the game. Lineal descent is associated with such beliefs cross-culturally.

Folklore Studies

Folklore research has made use of patterning in the details of myths and ritual texts to establish likely textual histories. An important tenet has been the belief that the messages and motifs associated with myths are more stable than specific plots and episodes (Keyes 1994). Keyes concluded from his analysis of the richly detailed Apalachee Ball Game myth that "legitimizing ideologies of the elite vanish when the elite vanish. The stories may persist, but stripped of the special context and details that made them what they were. The motifs, informed by a new society with new needs, are reshuffled and restructured" (Keyes 1994, p. 110).

The Apalachee Ball Game myth is one of the few charter myths known that Keyes (1994) calls foundational to a particular ritual. The few others that are known for the Eastern Woodlands are likewise rich sources for bridging into archaeology. In contrast with later nineteenth- and twentieth-century Tunica, Yuchi, and other versions, the Apalachee Ball Game myth collected in the 1670s contained details on social hierarchy. From this myth, Keyes concluded that: (*a*) the major characters are deified and elite in the context of the myth's society, (*b*) the myth chartered at least one real social position in the Apalachee power structure, and (*c*) ceremonies performed by the Apalachee had their origins accounted for by these mythic characters.

Art History

Art historical research stresses the coherence of specific styles, their modes of representation, and their thematic development (Penney 1989, Trevelyan 1987). They are inclined toward approaching meaning through the construction of grammars of representation (Muller 1979, 1986). In terms of rule-based or other approaches, pre-Columbian figural representations are very heterogeneous. A substantial number of them have existed, and nowhere is this more evident than in the variety present in the collection embraced by the Southeastern Ceremonial Complex (SECC). Here, regional and temporal diversity is embraced in a commingling of styles. This very diversity is evidence that the complex has a long developmental history in separate regions.

The art historical approach lays great emphasis on stylization in representation without pretending that such stylizations have any inherent meaning. Nevertheless, a substantial number of literal interpretations exist in the literature.

Archaeoastronomy

Archaeoastronomy has been concerned with the astronomical basis for orientation patterns discovered in architectural features and town layouts (Krupp 1983; Williamson 1981, 1984). This research attempts to move from knowledge about the physical ordering of the universe (cosmogony) to statements about culturally specific ideational beliefs about the universe (cosmology) and their philosophical underpinnings (Williamson & Farrer 1992). Thus astronomical alignments in the Eastern Woodlands become of interest because of the global distribution of similar patterns. These patterns are thought to imply a cosmographic control over human works. The study of cosmovision (the union of cosmogony and cosmology) has also been stimulated by the corpus of large-scale excavations that has provided settlement layout information. A weakness with this approach is the sketchy information available respecting native astronomical knowledge beyond a few general principles.

ISSUES CONCERNING THE ARCHAEOLOGY OF SPIRITUALITY

When Robert Hall (1977) first raised the prospect of tracing the history of Eastern Woodlands religious practices through archaeology, the subject was widely regarded as inaccessible through material remains. Although this view remains strong, serious inquiry into the subject has been on the rise (e.g. Goldsmith et al 1992, Hall 1997). An outstanding issue yet to be resolved is whether archaeology has anything to contribute other than specific exemplifications of ethnographically documented practices and beliefs. That is, what role can archaeology play beyond a recounting of the material equipage of religious history? Lately, the theoretical problems that this challenge raises have captured a great deal of scholarly attention (Cowgill 1993, Flannery & Marcus 1993, Marcus & Flannery 1994, Renfrew & Zubrow 1994, Trigger 1995, Watson & Fotiadis 1990).

In the meantime it is commonplace for archaeological material to be interpreted directly in terms of either ethnology (Hudson 1976, 1984; Miller 1996), folklore (Lankford 1987), iconography (Brose et al 1985, Pauketat & Emerson 1991), or astronomy (Williamson & Farrer 1992). The converse is also just as prevalent. A great deal of archaeological research concerns the projection of the ethnographic present into the archaeological past. A large literature consists of such prehistoric tracings, and an even more extensive practice exists in symbolic assignment of prehistoric signs and images according to meanings gleaned from the ethnographic literature. A widespread approach, in the Eastern Woodlands and elsewhere, has been to yield to the temptation of making direct readings from Mayan, Mixtec, and Aztec texts (e.g. Brotherston 1992). Comparative ethnology is central. Ethnological connections have been vigorously defended because of the demonstrable continuities in image and artifact in the context of so many near-universal practices and beliefs (Brose et al 1985, Hall 1997, von Gernet & Timmins 1987). However, much more should be required to support any reading.

ACCESS TO MEANING THROUGH THE DIRECT HISTORICAL APPROACH

A fundamental problem revolves around the identification of meanings attached to objects in contexts that can reliably be anchored to ritual concepts and ideology known ethnologically. This problem has long resisted easy solution. One approach has been to rely on global cross-cultural studies to discover correlates of cultural complexity. Although this approach has had useful results for the Eastern Woodlands, the limitations are obvious when it comes to dealing with historically interconnected beliefs and practices. Another approach has been to argue by analogy, taking as ethnographic reference the most widespread conventions, legends, and beliefs in the conviction that if a particular practice is nearly universal within the region then the same is likely to apply to any particular case (e.g. Hultkrantz 1981, Prentice 1986, von Gernet 1992a,b, von Gernet & Timmins 1987). For instance, Hultkrantz (1979) saw in the abundance of a common symbol a common underlying significance or meaning.

A tack that is more harmonious with local tradition is to employ the direct historical approach, sometimes called "up-streaming," from the historically known to the prehistorically unknown. When restricted to a single tribe or set of closely allied tribes, this approach falls under what Hill (1994) called the method of "Tight Local Analogy." A number of connections have been offered (e.g. Choctaw, Natchez) that have potential for creating a history of religious practices. However, the pursuit of this approach has been hampered by a shortage of cases in which lines of continuity have been clearly established between cultures documented in depth [e.g. Choctaw (Galloway 1995), Natchez (Brown 1989), Iroquois (Snow 1994)].

The direct historical approach makes the logical inference that textually established forms have retained an older meaning. Furthermore, that meaning will approximate the historically known meaning or meanings the closer in time the periods are to each other. This is a principle that is well established among art historians. On the surface, this principle is not very reassuring considering the time depths that archaeologists are accustomed to. Specially ascribed meanings may have arisen or have disappeared over time. This is particularly true where a special class has co-opted a symbol to produce an ideology for its own promotion. Balancing this pessimistic note is the faith expressed generally that meanings embedded in religious ritual and practice are very conservative. Tobacco smoking is argued to be such a case (Paper 1988).

A more broadly conceived direct historical approach has been advocated by Hall (1977, 1997). Continuity of form is not required in his approach. Rather, he argues that seminal forms are connected through ethnographically established semantic equivalences among a group of contiguous and interacting societies with common historical experiences. Through this form of analogy, Hall explains the location of earthworks near bodies of water and derives the historic flat-stemmed pipe of the Prairie-Plains from the Hopewellian monitor style of approximately AD 100 (Hall 1977). A similar argument was advanced by von Gernet & Timmins (1987), who stated that "certain widely-diffused culture-historical preconditions could lead to the independent replication of specific ideas or symbols."

The direct historical approach has many weaknesses. By assuming a minimum of change it is naturally weakest where the features chosen for analysis are most easily modified through ecological change or by the impact of cultural domination. More fundamentally, the direct historical approach forces archaeologists to adopt a linear view of history in which the "purpose" of events in the past is to set the stage for conditions found in the ethnographic present.

ARCHAEOLOGICAL RESEARCH STRATEGIES

What should command our attention here are archaeological indications of a more dynamic past than what might be predicted from the ethnographic present. For this we will have to turn our attention to research perspectives that generate expectations outside of the direct historical approach.

Sacred architecture and the public use of space constitute a major source of information (Flannery & Marcus 1993). The study of shrines, their setting (including orientation), special features, and the materials found on and beneath their floors provide valuable insight into activities associated with these shrines (Coe 1995). Some notion of the potential of mound group layouts can be gathered from the collection made by Morgan (1980), although these layouts are very schematic and incorporate many undemonstrated assumptions about the regularity of surface features that remain uninvestigated by excavation or remote sensing.

Various ritual paraphernalia are a second major source. These run the gamut from shamanic equipment to cult objects. Artifact studies include smoking pipes (Emerson 1982, Jackson et al 1992, Paper 1988, Penney 1989, Prentice 1986, von Gernet & Timmins 1987), carved shrine figures (Kehoe 1997, Prentice 1986), engraved marine shell art (Brain & Phillips 1996; Phillips & Brown 1978, 1984; Smith & Smith 1989), repoussé copper (Sampson & Esarey 1993, Trevelyan 1987), negative painted pottery designs (Hilgeman 1991), and chunkey stones at Cahokia (DeBoer 1993).

The study of cosmology, religion, and ideology has been fostered by advances in the quality of information available. Representations of cult figures and mythic scenes found on various media have been studied in detail. A number of analytical compendia have been produced that pull together critically various iconographic sources. First and foremost is the shell engraving from the Spiro site (Phillips & Brown 1978, 1984). Engraved shell gorgets found throughout the Southeast (Brain & Phillips 1996) and smaller data sets have been useful (Brown & Kelly 1997; Emerson 1982, 1995). A number of typologies have been offered recently to deal with the iconographic diversity (Brose et al 1985, Hudson 1984, Knight 1986).

SHAMANIC RITUAL REPRESENTATION

The widespread distribution of isolated elements traceable to former shamanic practice has convinced many that at one time shamanic beliefs and practices were more common if not universal. Such a cultural stratum provided a logical link to Siberian customs (Furst 1994, Hultkrantz 1981, Paper 1990, von Gernet 1992b, von Gernet & Timmins 1987). Considering the antiquity of this stratum, it has to be considered as constituting an archaeological baseline.

The earliest context in which shamanism can be detected archaeologically is in the Late Archaic Period. This is a period in which societies were small in scale, the very context in which shamanism is uniquely suited. The economy was primarily centered around hunting and gathering. Artifacts that would plausibly be used by shamans make their appearance (e.g. quartz crystals, tubular smoking pipes). The widespread use of red ochre over the body is a plausibly shamanic practice. In burial plots in western Illinois, corpses were manipulated by inserting spear heads into chest cavities (Charles & Buikstra 1983).

When population grew during the Middle and Late Woodland Periods the material culture of shamanism becomes more obvious and takes on elaborate material form. Smoking pipes were embellished with animal effigies of species that could plausibly be connected with aiding the shamanic trance (Brose et al 1985, Penney 1989). The number of uneconomic small birds, otters, beavers, and frogs/toads may have been prompted by the common dream and trance experience of either flying or swimming. Pipe animals that might be seen as anomalous are the duck, the bear, and the cougar or panther. In historic times the latter two are regarded as animals imbued with special powers as top predators of the southern and northern forests. Bears have an even larger history as special animals. In the circumboreal area of the northern hemisphere, bears hold special status (Hultkrantz 1979). The bear cult is particularly prominent among the peoples inhabiting the boreal forest.

With the rise in prominence of maize as a source of food, new forms of ritual expression can be identified. Trance artifacts take on even greater degrees of expression. Large massive smoking pipes are carved with human figures in trances. Although some older forms such as frogs and owls continue, new composite beings such as the piasa (a chthonic god) become important, combining serpent, cougar, and raptorial bird.

Research conducted in recent times has reinforced the shamanic function of rock art (Conway 1992). Studies are available of Missouri rock art sites (Duncan 1993), the Gottschall site (Salzer 1987, 1993), and the northern Great Lakes area (Rajnovich 1989).

THE ROLE OF HALLUCINOGENS

Weston La Barre (1972) argued that shamanic practices had their historical origin in hallucinogenic experience. This thesis has stimulated a literature on the place of trance experience in the religious practices of eastern North America (von Gernet 1992a). Tobacco has been the center of discussion because of the ubiquity of its use. A reference to the use of *Datura* sp. in male initiation rites of an Atlantic coast group has lent further support to the belief that hallucinogenic experience was once more commonplace in the Eastern Woodlands. Tobacco has this potential whether smoked or taken in some alternative form. Native tobacco (*Nicotiana rustica*) has a higher nicotine content than commercial tobacco. The problem is whether trance inducement was central to the original use of tobacco since common usage sought only the mildest of effects (von Gernet 1992a, 1995). Citing archaeological evidence, von Gernet & Timmins (1987) argued that the appearance of birds on archaeological smoking pipes made sense if tobacco was used to achieve shamanistic out-of-body experiences (von Gernet 1992b, p. 137). Since tobacco smoking is psychoactively stimulating, the perception of flight would be a primary sensory experience. In contrast, Paper (1988) has argued for a nonhallucinatory role for tobacco because native tobacco was thought to be too weak when grown in high latitudes. What is conventionally associated may not imply functional necessity. Paper has raised an important issue by focusing on the nonhallucinogenic aspect of native ritual in the ethnographic present. Archaeology has a role here in documenting the potential complexities of tobacco and other plant-based psychoactive substance use.

The material paraphernalia of smoking for presumably ritual purposes has a long history in the Eastern Woodlands (von Gernet & Timmins 1987). The first pipes date to about 1000 BC. Charred tobacco seed residues have been identified around AD 160 for the Middle Woodland Period and later. An archaeological record of such residues is very incomplete because the microscopic seeds are not as ubiquitous as food residues. What information has accumulated is a product of the growing application of fine-grained recovery procedures for bulk flotation of archaeological sediments (Asch & Asch

1985). Trace element analysis of charred residues that could substitute have yet to be conducted.

Barring new discoveries it is noteworthy that documentation of hallucinogen use is meager. Peyote usage is relatively recent in the East (Vecsey 1988). But to the Southeast shamanic uses of jimsonweed (*Datura* sp.), peyote, and other hallucinogens are documented for the Pecos Late Archaic in the Rio Grande valley as early as AD 1 (Boyd & Dering 1996).

HISTORICAL CHANGE

Mound Building and Collective Representation

Because of their breadth of appeal, cults of inclusiveness can be identified with the earliest mound building during the Late Archaic Period. Mound building arises early (Saunders & Allen 1994), the mounds being foci of ritual activity by largely sedentary groups (Charles & Buikstra 1983, Goldstein 1995). Their use persisted into the historic period. Knight (1986, 1989) has shown that mounds themselves were regarded as sacred objects. Throughout their history, very distinct cycles of use and construction have been identified that can be likened to that of death, burial, and renewal (Brown 1996, Pauketat 1993, Schnell et al 1981). By 1000 BC patterns of interment support an interpretation of communal facilities as a means for collective representation of the dead. Secondary interment of the dead as a normal outcome of the mortuary program was a common feature of collective representation (Goldstein 1989). When the number of dead was substantial, the accumulated remains became ossuaries, whether mounded or unmounded (Brown 1996, Spence 1994).

Given the belief that mounds were sacred, the appearance of mound summit platforms on which to conduct public rites is significant. The switch from an entirely public use of this sacred space to a largely private one is even more important. Private usage is indicated by the erection of buildings within which rites could be conducted out of the public eye. In the Mississippian Period, mound summits were used for housing the chiefly elite. The archetypal example of elite mortuary usage of a mound summit is Mound C at the Fatherland site (Brown 1990). Here, the floor of the shrine was full of burial pits, containing the remains and grave goods of elite that were not disinterred, presumably because the mortuary rites were interrupted by the defeat and expulsion of the Natchez. In so appropriating such sacred space, the elite were arrogating unto themselves the power residing in mounds (Knight 1986, 1989).

A parallel history appears to apply to the sweat lodge, although little attention has been devoted to identifying this specialized structure (MacDonald 1992). The large earth lodge constructions, known most famously by the Macon earth lodge at the Ocmulgee site, may have functioned as large facilities for communal vapor sweating. Transformation of earth lodges to platform mounds has been argued for by Rudolph (1984) as part of a secular trend.

Cosmology

Hudson (1976, 1984) and Lankford (1987) have made use of myth and folklore to describe a southeastern world view that reaches into prehistory. They identify a three-tiered cosmos, in which major differences in the details seem to follow linguistic divisions. In his reconstruction of pre-Columbian belief systems, Hudson (1976, pp. 132–66) used a number of Cherokee myths. An origin of the world (cosmogony) was the focus of one myth. Two creatures were identified with the upper and lower worlds, a falcon-like bird (Tlanuwa) for the upper and a snake monster (Uktena) for the lower. The opposition between these worlds is represented in the antithetical properties of these creatures. Both the falcon and the snake predominate in archaeological imagery. Lankford (1987) identifies sun motifs, wind motifs in the looped square and woodpecker theme; the forked eye and thunderbird themes using Ojibwa material; and the horned water serpents, water-panther in Creek material.

A commonly held tenet is that the macrocosm is represented by the microcosmic. In this egocentric perspective individuals have the capacity to recreate the spiritual world in their own actions. At least two material effects ensue from this cosmological principle. First, decoration on artifacts typical of shamanic practice rely on what Brasser (1980) characterized as "self-directed" art. This term covers images that are oriented to face the user rather than to an external viewer. Examples are the Hopewellian pipe effigies that usually face the smoker. Second, actions intended to situate the cosmic center at the specific place in which a ritual is being enacted lead to very specific four- or six-point directionality. The ubiquitous cross-in-circle motif is undoubtedly a symbol of this act. Hultkrantz (1973) and many others have observed ethnographically that this cosmographic sign functions ritually in a very precise way, and that is to situate the cosmic center at the specific place in which a ritual is being enacted. Other meanings are probably derived from this ritual centering act, which can be inscribed in the earth or communicated in a variety of other manners. Just such a commonly accepted means for creating sacred space individually has probably accounted for the widespread appearance of quadrated symbolism on pottery, in domestic housing, and in the sacred hearths of the most private sacred spaces (Nabokov & Easton 1989, Pauketat & Emerson 1991).

Pantheons

Typically numerous spirits were honored as sacred among those societies for which we have extensive information (Hudson 1976, 1984; Hultkrantz 1973).

Although these mythic figures hold little divine status today, there is ample evidence that before Christian missionaries became effective, most societies had elevated certain spirits to some sort of divine status. Large pantheons held high gods and lesser divinities. Some of the most common gods are the sun, moon, thunder, and a deity connected with the underworld.

A distinctly archaeological perspective on ancient deities was provided by the archaeological discovery of red fireclay figurines from sites connected with the town of Cahokia in the American Bottom. Their context lies with shrines that date around AD 1100. The Birger figurine (see Kehoe 1997), which is the best known, has been shown by Prentice (1986) to be a mythological female figure concerned with agricultural fertility. This identification was supported by her hoeing the back of a jaguar muzzled serpent whose tail dissolved into gourds born on vines. Comparison with earth-goddess myths showed that this spirit or goddess was widely known as "Old Woman." Other fragmentary figurines represent at least one other fertility goddess (Emerson 1995, Jackson et al 1992). The meaning of these images may be more complex. Kehoe (1997) has argued that the decorated rectangular forms on which the hands of certain figurines rest may be looms or boxes with icons. In either case, these images would symbolize the integration of the community through the activity of weaving. Figurines continued to be used much later after they were converted to pipes. From a converted shrine figure and other examples in different media, Brown (1997) identified the "birdman" image of the SECC as Morning Star.

Central to the archaeological claims is the thesis that the figures depicted in stone, copper, wood, and marine shell are not about ordinary people occupying this world. Rather, they are depictions of individuals and objects in the spirit world. Although it has been commonplace for scholars to regard pre-Columbian engravings and carvings as depictions of spirit impersonation (e.g. Brose et al 1985, Hudson 1976), there is every reason to think that pre-Columbian representations were restricted similarly and that all of the pictorial materials refer to divine, spiritual, or mythical events. Although dress and artifactual accompaniments may conform to contemporary standards, this agreement accords with other artistic traditions' common means of depicting events in mythic time through forms recognized in contemporaneous material culture.

Site Layouts and Orientations

Site layouts have allowed investigation into public space utilization. Early examples (Poverty Point and various enclosures of Adena and Hopewellian cultures) employed large earthen geometric figures and enclosures (DeBoer 1997). Their size seems to be dictated by the maximum number of individuals that met there, even if only briefly. Although the size of the resident populations is a subject of dispute, many outsiders probably met at these aggregation centers at certain times; hence their shape, placement, and orientation were given greater care than ordinary villages. When maize agriculture began to support large towns, earthworks mounds and ritual structures were incorporated within the living space. A plaza surrounded by mounds and/or earthworks is an ancient architectural formula in the Eastern Woodlands. The space so delimited conforms to a basic principle of setting off a special ritual space for public use at specific times. Collective representation of a community's dead was often connected with the creation of large earthwork enclosures. Both Middle Woodland and Mississippian Period enclosures are accompanied by either mound burials or cemeteries (Riordan 1995, Sullivan et al 1995).

Alignment with the cardinal directions has been long noted (Daniel-Hartung 1981, Rolingson 1994). It is an aspect of sacred geography that covers orientations, calendars, measurement standards, and geomancy (Clay 1986, 1987; Korp 1990; Parks & Wedel 1985; Romain 1993, 1994). The American Bottom research excels in richness and diversity (Emerson 1995). Here an evolutionary unfolding of patterns in public space use have been documented (Kelly 1990). Drawing a great deal of attention at that site are the postcircle monuments ("woodhenges") that have been variously regarded as calendars or in place of solar symbols (Fowler 1991, Pauketat 1994, Rolingson 1994). The Sun Watch/Incinerator Site is another that has provided a rich source of solar sightings (Heilman & Hoefer 1981). In a survey of multiple mound groups, Rolingson (1994) found that alignments were expressed in six ways: orientation of the plaza and primary mounds, intermound alignment, house orientation, alignment across figurative earthworks, the point at which the sun strikes, and the visibility of the sun and/or stars through a narrow opening.

Although rather elaborate formulae for measured and oriented geometric earthworks were developed during Middle Woodland times (ca 50 BC to 400 AD), orientation appears to have been an older and more general characteristic used to define public space. Solstitially governed orientations of mounds and earthwork corners and entrances extend back into the Hopewellian period (Byers 1987; DeBoer 1997; Hively & Horn 1982, 1984; Romain 1994) and even to Poverty Point, ca 1000 BC (Haag 1993, Purrington & Child 1989).

Beginning perhaps as early as AD 1000, agricultural societies established complex networks of cultural relations that involved the use of common solstitial orientation of earthworks and ritual areas and sometimes common intermound measurement standards. Hall (1991) argued that towns having such common standards in their ritual architecture used these facilities in part to cement intergroup relations. Ritual adoption was one of the means for achieving such relations. Exchange of prestige goods accompanied this intersocietal interaction (Muller 1995). Sherrod & Rolingson (1987) found a subset had intermound distances laid out in a module of 47.5 m. Although the module bears the name Toltec, it was the great town of Cahokia that provided confirmation in measured distances between post holes (Fowler 1991).

At least three different positions are current (Rolingson 1994). In one, solstitial orientations represent a means for making a calendar out of stands that the sun takes at the summer and winter solstices. The idea here is that calendrical calculations are essential to successful farming in high latitudes where the window of opportunity for planting is limited (Heilman & Hoefer 1981, O'Brien & McHugh 1987). In the second, solstitially based ritual was used by the elites to legitimize their secular decision making (Smith 1992). In the third alternative, no such utilitarian purpose is present (Fowler 1991). The alignments are an effort to make the humanly built world conform with the cosmos and celestial motions. Since these are unalterable truths, human works made in concert with these geomantic principles are thereby legitimated and take on some of the sanctity of cosmic patterns. To Rolingson (1994), the utilitarian argument was undermined by the complexity with which directionality was expressed in burial rites at Cahokia Mound 72 (Fowler 1991). She stressed the cosmographical integration of the burial rites through orientation and alignments.

Most of this research has been guided by the focus on a calendrical function. The historic Pawnee have provided a rich source of material although it is easy to over-interpret the famous star chart (Chamberlain 1982, 1992; Parks 1985). They and many others world wide avail themselves of the position of the stars, particularly the Pleiades, to mark planting and midwinter ceremonies.

Cult of the Dead

The architecture of early shrines has been intensively explored. Early shrines that were relatively open were presumably open to all (Milanich et al 1984). The appearance of secluded structures exclusive in rights of access was probably followed shortly thereafter by the appearance of a priestly group (Brown 1996).

Flat-topped mounds appear much earlier than once thought in Hopewell Period contexts (Mainfort 1988). By the Mississippian Period (AD 1000) shrines become identifiable for the first time. They commonly shared the summits of flat-topped mounds with chiefly residences (Brose et al 1985, Brown 1990, Coe 1995). At Etowah and elsewhere, these shrines contained the bones of elite ancestors, shrine figures, and stores of wealth objects (Brose et al 1985, Brown 1990). In light of Natchez practices, the shrine figures probably represented ancestor deities. Although they were usually male, those from Etowah include both male and female pairs.

Southeastern Ceremonial Complex: Cults and Material Representation

The concept in its original formulation has been expanded conceptually as a consequence of the new iconographic material (Emerson 1995; Galloway 1989; Phillips & Brown 1978, 1984), while simultaneously unpacking the original definition that conflated the passage of time, different stylistic conventions and confusions contributed by intersite trade (Brose et al 1985, Knight 1986). Detailed research on representative collections has improved our understanding of the archaeological context (Brown 1996). Radiocarbon dating has supplied a chronology among four major Mississippian Period sites of the Southeast: Cahokia, Etowah, Moundville, and Spiro (Brown & Kelly 1997, King 1994). Cross-ties in a broad range of object and artifact styles are entirely congruent with this emerging chronology (Brown 1996).

Although the complex often goes by the name of Southern Cult, at least three cults can be identified by Knight (1986). One is connected with the warfare and cosmogony, a second is the platform mound itself, and a third is the temple statuary complex. Each is identified with a mutually exclusive set of artifacts and iconography. The first is well defined as a cult, centered around the birdman theme. A number of other themes are known as well (Phillips & Brown 1978). The third can be identified with the ancestor cults. The period in which cult material takes on its distinct form with canonical imagery starts around 1200 and begins to simplify between 1400 and 1450. Later material is clearly derivative, and the birdman theme becomes nearly invisible.

Preliminary work with the Mississippian Period art styles on various media indicate the existence of several geographic styles (Brown & Rogers 1989, Galloway 1989). These geographical styles are coherent on their own but share a set of themes, most notably that of the birdman, the dominant theme of the SECC. The Braden style is connected with the eastern prairie area long dominated by Siouan speaking peoples (Brown & Kelly 1997). Examples of the Braden style are found on rock faces and portable objects at the Gottschall shelter in southwestern Wisconsin (Salzer 1987, 1993) and in Missouri caves (Duncan 1993). The Cahokia site is the likely place where the Braden A form of this style, known primarily from engraved marine shell cups, probably was developed during or shortly before the Moorehead Phase (1200–1275). By 1250, this town exercised a determinative influence over much of the Southeast although Cahokia was soon to loose this leadership (Brown 1996). Another geographic style is known as the Craig style and is associated with the Caddoan-speaking peoples living at the margins of the Eastern Woodlands. The Spiro site has yielded a major document of this style (Brown & Rogers 1989). Other regional styles were produced in the southern Appalachians and other areas (Brain & Phillips 1996; Galloway 1989; Muller 1986, 1995). Each of these styles represents regional expressions of a widespread set of beliefs. Around 1400 the network began to collapse into the Southeast proper, centered around the southern Appalachians. Thus beliefs and practices that are widely thought to be restricted to Muskogean-speaking peoples and their closely affiliated neighbors were probably at one time connected to the Caddoan- and Siouan-speaking worlds as well.

THE ADVANTAGES OF HAVING A HISTORY OF EASTERN WOODLANDS RELIGION

The limitations of inquiry from a single perspective are amply illustrated by the inability to anticipate the findings of archaeologists at such sites as Cahokia and its neighborhood, the Gottschall shelter, and the iconographic material that came from the Spiro site. First there is great diversity of iconographic themes displaying provocative details that go well beyond those testified to in recent times. Second are the elaborate mortuary practices such as Mound 72 at Cahokia (Fowler 1991, Fowler et al 1997) and the Great Mortuary of Spiro (Brown 1996) that indicate a richness of cultural representation, different kinds of human sacrifice, and a diversity in the disposition of the dead to a far greater degree than present since the 1600s. Third is the degree to which attributes of Siouan gods/spirit heroes found in important mythic narratives are represented in figurative depictions on rock walls and portable artifacts of precious materials of the thirteenth and fourteenth centuries, over 500 years ago. The contemporary record has not prepared us for these revelations. Such discoveries imply great continuity of the form in hero representations, the marking in concrete physical terms of various concepts known later, and very rich belief systems that included specific cultic practices.

RESEARCH DIRECTIONS

Useful directions for future research involve the following:

1. A close attention to the contribution that iconographic analysis can make to our knowledge of shamanic practices, details of a pantheon, and other beliefs. Current analyses have shown the benefit of focusing on the patterns of substitution and equivalences found in regional versions of the SECC. Since these regional expressions appear to be tied to dominant language families, distinctions within these expressions probably comply with culturally determined usages.

2. Continued excavation of broad sections of ancient sites. Such a strategy has yielded the locations of shrines and other specialized architecture that have gone far in documenting religious practices.

3. Detailed survey and excavation of landscapes that may have been used repeatedly for ritual purposes in the past. The positioning of mounds, shrines, and various earthworks helps delineate ritual landscapes.

4. Laboratory analyses of chemical residues that can determine the nature of the concoctions placed in pipes and specialized vessels.

Visit the *Annual Reviews home page* at http://www.AnnualReviews.org.

Literature Cited

Asch DL, Asch NB. 1985. Prehistoric plant cultivation in west-central Illinois. In *Prehistoric Food Production in North America*, ed. RI Ford, pp. 149–203. *Mus. Anthropol. Univ. Michigan Anthropol. Pap. 75*

Boyd CE, Dering JP. 1996. Medicinal and hallucinogenic plants identified in the Texas Archaic. *Antiquity* 70:256–75

Brain JP, Phillips P. 1996. *Shell Gorgets.* Cambridge: Peabody Mus. Press

Brasser TJ. 1980. Self-directed pipe effigies. *Man in the Northeast* 19:95–104

Brose DS, Brown JA, Penney DW. 1985. *Ancient Art of the American Woodland Indians.* New York: Abrams

Brotherston G. 1992. *Book of the Fourth World: Reading the Native Americas through Their Literature.* Cambridge: Cambridge Univ. Press

Brown IW. 1989. Natchez Indians and the remains of a proud past. In *Natchez Before 1830*, ed. N Polk, pp. 8–28. Jackson: Univ. Miss. Press

Brown JA. 1990. Archaeology confronts history at the Natchez temple. *Southeast. Archaeol.* 9:1–10

Brown JA. 1996. The Spiro ceremonial center: the archaeology of Arkansas Valley Caddoan culture in Eastern Oklahoma. *Mem. Mus. Anthropol. Univ. Michigan 29*

Brown JA. 1997. *The Morning Star Myth in the Southeastern Ceremonial Complex.* Presented at Annu. Meet. Soc. Am. Archaeol., 62nd, Nashville, TN

Brown JA, Kelly J. 1997. Cahokia and the Southeastern Ceremonial Complex. In *Mounds, Modoc, and Mesoamerica: Papers in Honor of Melvin L. Fowler*, ed. SR Ahler. Springfield: Ill. State Mus. Sci. Pap. 55

Brown JA, Rogers JD. 1989. Linking Spiro's artistic styles: the copper connection. *Southeast. Archaeol.* 8:1–8

Byers AM. 1987. *The earth enclosures of the Central Ohio Valley.* PhD thesis. State Univ. NY Albany

Chamberlain VD. 1982. *When the Stars Came Down to Earth: Cosmology of the Skidi Pawnee Indians of North America.* Los Altos, CA: Ballena

Chamberlain VD. 1992. The chief and his council: unity and authority from the stars. See Williamson & Farrer 1992, pp. 221–35

Charles DK, Buikstra JE. 1983. Archaic mortuary sites in the central Mississippi drainage: distribution, structure, and behavioral implications. In *Archaic Hunters and Gatherers in the American Midwest*, ed. JL Phillips, JA Brown, pp. 117–45. New York: Academic

Clay RB. 1986. Adena ritual spaces. In *Early Woodland Archeology*, ed. K Farnsworth, T Emerson, pp. 581–95. Kampsville, IL: Cent. Am. Archeol.

Clay RB. 1987. Circles and ovals: two types of Adena space. *Southeast. Archaeol.* 6:46–56

Coe JL. 1995. *Town Creek Indian Mound.* Chapel Hill: Univ. N. C. Press

Conway T. 1992. The conjurer's lodge: celestial narrative from Algonkian shamans. See Williamson & Farrer 1992, pp. 236–59

Cowgill G. 1993. Distinguished lecture in archeology: beyond criticizing new archeology. *Am. Anthropol.* 95:551–73

Daniel-Hartung AL. 1981. Archaeoastronomy at a selection of Mississippian sites in the southeastern United States. See Williamson 1981, pp. 101–10

DeBoer WR. 1993. Like a rolling stone: the chunkey game and political organization in eastern North America. *Southeast. Archaeol.* 12:83–92

DeBoer WR. 1997. Ceremonial centres from the Cayapas (Esmeraldas, Ecuador) to Chillicothe (Ohio, USA). *Cambridge Archaeol. J.* 7:1

Dobyns H. 1991. New native world: links between demographic and cultural changes. In *Columbian Consequences,* Vol. 3, pp. 541–59. Washington: Smithson. Inst. Press

Duncan CD. 1993. *The petroglyphs and pictographs of missouri: a distributional, stylistic, contextual, functional and temporal analysis of the state's rock graphics.* PhD thesis. Washington Univ., St. Louis

Emerson TE. 1982. Mississippian stone images in Illinois. *Ill. Archaeol. Survey Circ.* 6

Emerson TE. 1995. *Settlement, symbolism, and hegemony in the Cahokia countryside.* PhD thesis. Univ. Wis., Madison

Flannery KV, Marcus J. 1993. Cognitive archaeology. *Cambridge Archaeol. J.* 3: 260–69

Fowler ML. 1991. Mound 72 and early Mississippian at Cahokia. In *New Perspectives on Cahokia: Views from the Periphery,* ed. JB Stoltman, pp. 1–28. Madison, WI: Prehist. Press

Fowler ML, Rose JC, Vander Leest B, Ahler SR. 1997. The mound 72 area: dedicated and sacred space in early Cahokia. *Ill. State Mus. Rep. Invest. 54*

Furst PT. 1994. Introduction: an overview of shamanism. In *Ancient Traditions,* ed G. Seaman, JS Day, pp. 1–28. Niwot, CO: Univ. Colo. Press

Galloway P, ed. 1989. *Southern Ceremonial Complex, Artifacts and Analysis: The Cottonlandia Conference.* Lincoln: Univ. Nebr. Press

Galloway P. 1991. The archaeology of ethnohistorical narrative. In *Columbian Consequences,* Vol. 3, pp. 453–69. Washington: Smithson. Inst. Press

Galloway P. 1995. *Choctaw Genesis, 1500–1700.* Lincoln: Univ. Nebr. Press

Goldsmith AS, Garvie S, Selin D, Smith J, ed. 1992. *Ancient Images, Ancient Thought: The Archaeology of Ideology.* Calgary: Univ. Calgary Archaeol. Assoc.

Goldstein LG. 1989. *The ritual of secondary disposal of the dead.* Presented at 1989 Meet. Theoretical Archaeol. Group, Newcastle upon Tyne, United Kingdom

Goldstein LG. 1995. Landscapes and mortuary practices: a case for regional perspectives. In *Regional Approaches to Mortuary Analysis,* ed. LA Beck, pp. 101–21. New York: Plenum

Griffin JB. 1980. The Mesoamerican-Southeastern U. S. connection. *Early Man* 3(2): 12–18

Haag WG. 1993. Archaeoastronomy in the Southeast. In *Archaeology of Eastern North America, Papers in Honor of Stephen Williams,* ed. JB Stoltman, pp. 103–10. Jackson: Miss. Dep. Archiv. Hist.

Hall RL. 1977. An anthropocentric perspective for eastern United States prehistory. *Am. Antiq.* 42:499–518

Hall RL. 1989. The cultural background of Mississippian symbolism. See Galloway 1989, pp. 239–78

Hall RL. 1991. Cahokia identity and interaction models of Cahokia Mississippian. In *Cahokia and the Hinterlands: Middle Mississippian Cultures of the Midwest,* ed. TE Emerson, Lewis RB, pp. 3–34. Urbana: Univ. Ill. Press

Hall RL. 1997. *An Archaeology of the Soul.* Urbana: Univ. Ill. Press

Heilman JM, Hoefer RR. 1981. Possible astronomical alignments in a Fort Ancient settlement at the Incinerator Site in Dayton, Ohio. See Williamson 1981, pp. 157–72

Hilgeman SL. 1991. Angel negative painted design structure. *Midcont. J. Archaeol.* 16 :3–33

Hill JN. 1994. Prehistoric cognition and the science of archaeology. See Renfrew & Zubrow 1994, pp. 83–92

Hiveley R, Horn R. 1982. Geometry and astronomy in prehistoric Ohio. *Archaeoastron. Suppl. J. Hist. Astron.* 4:S1–19

Hiveley R, Horn R. 1984. Hopewellian geometry and astronomy at High Bank. *Archaeoastron. Suppl. J. Hist. Astron.* 7: S85–99

Hudson C. 1976. *The Southeastern Indians.* Knoxville: Univ. Tenn. Press. 573 pp.

Hudson C. 1984. *Elements of Southeastern Indian Religion.* Leiden: Brill

Hudson C, Tesser CC, eds. 1994. *The Forgotten Centuries.* Athens: Univ. Ga. Press

Hultkrantz Å. 1973. *Prairie and Plains Indians.* Leiden: Brill

Hultkrantz Å. 1979. *The Religions of the American Indians.* Berkeley: Univ. Calif. Press

Hultkrnatz Å. 1981. *Belief and Worship in Native North America.* Syracuse, NY: Syracuse Univ. Press

Hultkrantz Å. 1983. *The Study of American Indian Religions.* Chico, CA: Scholars Press

Hultkrantz Å. 1992. *Shamanic Healing and Ritual Drama.* New York: Crossroad

Jackson DK, Fortier AC, Williams JA. 1992. *The Sponemann Site 2: The Mississippian and Oneota Occupations.* Urbana: Univ. Ill. Press

Kehoe A. 1997. *Consorting with power, weaving community.* Presented at Annu. Meet. Am. Archaeol., 62nd, Nashville, TN

Kelly JE. 1990. The emergence of Mississippian culture in the American Bottom region. In *The Mississippian Emergence,* ed. BD Smith, pp. 113–52. Washington, DC: Smithson. Inst. Press

Keyes G. 1994. Myth and social history in the early Southeast. See Kwachka 1994, pp. 106–15

King A. 1994. *Chronological placement of the Southeastern Ceremonial Complex at Etowah.* Presented at Annu. Meet. Southeast. Archaeol. Conf., 37th, Lexington, Ky.

Knight VJ. 1986. The institutional organization of Mississippian religion. *Am. Antiq.* 51:675–87

Knight VJ. 1989. Symbolism of Mississippi mounds. In *Powhatan's Mantle: Indians in the Colonial Southeast,* ed. PH Wood, GA Waselkov, MT Hotley, pp. 279–91. Lincoln: Univ. Nebr. Press

Korp M. 1990. *The Sacred Geography of the American Mound Builders.* Lewiston, NY: Mellen

Krupp EC. 1983. *Echoes of the Ancient Skies.* New York: Harper & Row

Krusche R. 1986. The origin of the mask concept in the eastern woodlands of North America. *Man Northeast* 31:1–47

Kwachka PB, ed. 1994. *Perspectives on the Southeast: Linguistics, Archaeology, and Ethnohistory.* Athens: Univ. Ga. Press

La Barre W. 1972. Hallucinogens and the shamanic origins of religion. In *Flesh of the Gods,* ed. PT Furst, pp. 261–78. New York: Praeger

Lankford GE, ed. 1987. *Native American Legends.* Little Rock, AK: August House

MacDonald RI. 1992. Ontario Iroquoian semi-subterranean sweat lodges. See Goldsmith et al 1992, pp. 323–30

Mainfort RC. 1988. Middle Woodland ceremonialism at Pinson mounds, Tennessee. *Am. Antiq.* 53:158–73

Marcus J, Flannery KV. 1994. Ancient Zapotec ritual and religion: an application of the direct historical approach. See Renfrew & Zubrow 1994, pp. 55–74

Milanich JT, Cordell AS, Knight VJ, Kohler TA, Sigler-Lavelle BJ. 1984. *McKeithen Weeden Island: The Culture of Northern Florida, A. D. 200–900.* New York: Academic

Miller J. 1996. Changing moons: a history of Caddo religion. *Plains Anthropol.* 41:243–59

Morgan WN. 1980. *Prehistoric Architecture in the Eastern United States.* Cambridge, MA: MIT Press

Muller JD. 1979. Structural studies of art styles. In *The Visual Arts, Plastic and Graphic,* ed. J Cordwell, pp. 139–211. The Hague: Mouton

Muller JD. 1986. Analysis of glyphic art. In *The Prehistoric Native American Art of Mud Glyph Cave,* ed. CH Faulkner, pp. 36–80. Knoxville: Univ. Tenn. Press

Muller JD. 1995. Regional interaction in the later Southeast. See Nassaney & Sassaman 1995, pp. 317–40

Murray D. 1991. *Forked Tongues.* London: Piter

Nabokov P, Easton R. 1989. *Native American Architecture.* Oxford: Oxford Univ. Press

Nassaney MS, Sassaman KE, ed. 1995. *Native American Interactions: Multiscalar Analyses and Interpretations in the Eastern Woodlands.* Knoxville: Univ. Tenn. Press

O'Brien PJ, McHugh WP. 1987. Mississippian solstice shrines and a Cahokia calendar; an hypothesis based on ethnohistory and archaeology. *North Am. Archaeol.* 9:227–47

Paper J. 1988. *Offering Smoke.* Moscow: Univ. Idaho Press

Paper J. 1990. "Sweat lodge": a northern native American ritual for communal shamanic trance. *Temenos* 26:85–94

Parks DR. 1985. Interpreting Pawnee star lore: Science or myth? *Am. Ind. Cult. and Res. J.* 9:53–65

Park DR, Wedel WR. 1985. Pawnee geography: historical and sacred. *Great Plains Q.* 5:143–76

Pauketat TR. 1993. Temples for Cahokia Lords. *Mem. Mus. Anthropol. Univ. Michigan 26*

Pauketat TR. 1994. *The Ascent of Chiefs.* Tuscaloosa: Univ. Ala. Press.

Pauketat TR, Emerson TE. 1991. The ideology of authority and the power of the pot. *Am. Anthropol.* 93:919–41

Penney DW. 1989. *Hopewell art.* PhD thesis. Columbia Univ., New York

Phillips P, Brown JA. 1978. *Pre-Columbian Shell Engravings from the Craig Mound at Spiro, Oklahoma,* Part 1. Cambridge, MA: Peabody Mus. Press

Phillips P, Brown JA. 1984. *Pre-Columbian Shell Engravings from the Craig Mound at Spiro, Oklahoma*, Part 2. Cambridge, MA: Peabody Mus. Press

Prentice G. 1986. An analysis of the symbolism expressed by the Birger figurine. *Am. Antiq.* 51:239–66

Purrington RD, Child CA. 1989. Poverty Point: further consideration of astronomical alignments. *Archaeoastron. Suppl. J. Hist. Astron.* 4:S1–19

Rajnovich G. 1989. Vision in the quest for medicine: an interpretation of the Indian pictographs of the Canadian Shield. *Midcont. J. Archaeol.* 14:179–225

Renfrew C, Zubrow EBW, ed. 1994. *The Ancient Mind: Elements of Cognitive Archaeology*. Cambridge: Cambridge Univ. Press.

Riordan RV. 1995. A construction sequence for a Middle Woodland hilltop enclosure. *Midcont. J. Archaeol.* 20:62–104

Rolingson MA. 1994. *Symbolic and calendric aspects of community design in eastern North America*. Presented Annu. Meet. Midwest Archaeol. Conf.

Romain WF. 1993. Hopewell ceremonial centers and geomantic influences. *Ohio Archaeol.* 43(1):35–44

Romain WF. 1994. Hopewell geometric enclosures: symbols of an ancient world view. *Ohio Archaeol.* 44(2):37–43

Rudolph JL. 1984. Earthlodges and platform mounds: changing public architecture in the southeastern United States. *Southeast. Archaeol.* 3:33–45

Salzer RJ. 1987. Preliminary report on the Gottschall site (47Ia80). *Wis. Archeol.* 68: 419–72

Salzer RJ. 1993. Oral literature and archaeology. *Wis. Archeol.* 80–119

Sampson KW, Esarey D. 1993. A survey of elaborate Mississippian copper artifacts from Illinois. *Ill. Archaeol.* 5:452–80

Saunders JW, Allen T. 1994. Hedgepeth Mounds, an Archaic mound complex in north-central Louisiana. *Am. Antiq.* 59: 471–89

Schnell FT, Knight VJ, Schnell GS. 1981. *Cemochechobee*. Gainesville: Univ. Presses Fla.

Sherrod PC, Rolingson MA. 1987. Surveyors of the ancient Mississippi Valley. *Ark. Archeol. Surv. Res. Ser.* 28

Smith BD. 1992. Mississippian elites and solar alignments: a reflection of managerial necessity, or levers of social inequality? In *Lords of the Southeast*, ed. AW Barker, TR

Pauketat, pp. 11–30. Archaeol. Pap. Am. Anthropol. Assoc. 3

Smith MT, Smith JB. 1989. Engraved shell masks in North America. *Southeast. Archaeol.* 8:9–18

Snow DR. 1994. *The Iroquois*. London: Blackwell

Spence MW. 1994. Mortuary programmes of the early Ontario Iroquoians. *Ont. Archaeol.* 58:6–26

Sullivan LP, Neusius SW, Neusius PD. 1995. Earthworks and mortuary sites on Lake Erie: believe it or not at the Ripley site. *Midcont. J. Archaeol.* 20:115–42

Trevelyan AM. 1987. *Prehistoric native American copperwork from the eastern United States*. PhD thesis. Univ. Calif, Los Angeles

Trigger BG. 1995. Expanding middle-range theory. *Antiq.* 69:449–58

Vecsey C. 1988. *Imagine Ourselves Richly: Mythic Narratives of North American Indians*. New York: Crossroad

von Gernet A. 1992a. Hallucinogens and the origins of the Iroquoian pipe/tobacco/smoking complex. In *Proceedings of the 1989 Smoking Pipe Conference*, ed. CF Hayes, pp. 171–85. Rochester, NY: Rochester Mus. Sci. Cent.

von Gernet A. 1992b. New directions in the construction of prehistoric Amerindian belief systems. See Goldsmith et al 1992, pp. 133–39

von Gernet A. 1995. Nicotian dreams: the prehistory and early history of tobacco in eastern North America. In *Consuming Habits*, ed. J Goodman, PE Lovejoy, A Sherratt, pp. 67–87. London: Routledge

von Gernet A, Timmins P. 1987. Pipes and parakeets: constructing meaning in an early Iroquoian context. In *Archaeology as Long-Term History*, ed. I Hodder, pp. 31–42. Cambridge: Cambridge Univ. Press

Watson PJ, Fotiadis M. 1990. The razor's edge: symbolic-structuralist archeology and the expansion of archeological inference. *Am. Anthropol.* 92:613–29

Williamson RA, ed. 1981. *Archaeoastronomy in the Americas*. Los Altos, CA: Ballena

Williamson RA. 1984. *Living the Sky: The Cosmos of the American Indian*. Norman: Univ. Okla. Press

Williamson RA, Farrer CR, ed. 1992. *Earth and Sky: Visions of the Cosmos in Native American Folklore*. Albuquerque: Univ. N. M. Press

Annu. Rev. Anthropol. 1997. 26:487–514

EUROPEANIZATION

John Borneman and Nick Fowler

Department of Anthropology, McGraw 203, Cornell University, Ithaca, New York
14853

KEY WORDS: European Union, tourism, sex, language, money, sport, nation-state

ABSTRACT

As a strategy of self-representation and a device of power, Europeanization is
fundamentally reorganizing territoriality and peoplehood, the two principles
of group identification that have shaped modern European order. It is the result
of a new level and intensity of integration that has been a reaction to the destruction of this century's first and second world wars and the collapse of the
cold-war division of Europe into an East and West. Driven above all by the organizational and administrative power of the European Union (EU), Europeanization is still distinct from the EU. Neither Europeanization nor the EU will
replace the nation-state, which, for now, remains a superior form for organizing democratic participation and territoriality. Nonetheless, they will likely
force states to yield some questions of sovereignty—above all, military, political, and economic—to the EU or other transnational bodies. Nations are now
being brought into new relations with each other, creating new alliances and
enmities, and are even recreating themselves. The authors explore five domains of practice where the process of Europeanization might be fruitfully
studied: language, money, tourism, sex, and sport. They suggest dealing with
the EU as a continental political unit of a novel order and with Europeanization
pragmatically as both a vision and a process.

INTRODUCTION

The people in Europe currently identify with 32 different European nations
and speak 67 languages (not counting dialects). They have created a European
currency (the Euro), flag, and newspaper (the *European*); European television

487

0084-6570/97/1015-0487$08.00

stations (the English SKY, the French-German Arté) and universities; a European Champions League for soccer, film festival, parliament, court, and law; and a "Eurovision" song festival. A few items, such as languages, have been around a long time, but most others on this partial list are less than a century old. These new things are the result of a new level and intensity of integration that has been a reaction to the destruction of this century's first and second world wars. The two hot wars were followed by the cold-war vision of a Europe formally divided by two "secular spirits" into an East and West. In addition, this cold-war vision is now increasingly seen as an interregnum, a disturbance, and perhaps an amalgam of wounds, but ultimately as a suspension of the Real. For some of these peoples, the Real is Europe before World War I, a continent consisting primarily of competing national interests, without the internal divisions wrought by international working-class movements. For others, there is a sense in which the Real itself is now haunted by a spirit yet to take form. The relatively positive specter of an Americanization of Europe and the negative specter of a Sovietization of Europe are being replaced by the anxiety of a Europeanization. But how can Europe become more European?

For reasons both external and internal to Europe, Europeanization is now an accelerated process and a set of effects that are redefining forms of identification with territory and people. Externally, Europeanization is spurred on by the end of a post–World War II continental triangulation, where "Europe" stood between the United States and the Soviet Union—the two Superpowers, as they were known—who picked over its corpse and fought to interpret its precious and infamous past and to determine the conditions of its resurrection. With the disintegration of the Soviet Union and the decline in US dominance, Europe has entered adolescence, cut loose for resignification. With no immanent invaders, no New World, no colonies, no occupiers against whom it can take shape, the "mirror of man" has been turned back on itself. It can and it must now define itself. Among the most alluring alterity with which it flirts is that ancient phantasm, the Orient, marked by an anxiety over the politically and religiously explosive Middle East and rivalry with the economic juggernauts in East, South, and Southeast Asia. Both of these Oriental phantasms are, of course, already embodied within Europe by persons, ideologies, images, and material goods from those other geographies.

Internally, Europeanization is linked foremost to the organizational and administrative power of the European Union (EU). Always seen as a means to realize some ill-defined community, the EU is increasingly an end in itself. However, this circularity—the EU as both cause and effect of itself—begs the fundamental question of what it in fact is. Notwithstanding the quite limited, primarily economic goals of its 1951 predecessor—the six-country Monta Union, a "Coal and Steel Community"—the EU is now a set of explosive and indeterminate effects of late-twentieth-century social and political processes. These effects are fundamentally reorganizing territoriality and peoplehood, the two principles that have shaped modern European order.

Today, the EU works simultaneously to solidify and subsidize processes of discrete nation-making and to enforce pan-European standards on disparate parts. Both directions solicit compliance and provoke reaction, depending on the location of the actor. For example, the EU invokes the principle of territoriality both to strengthen the ability of sovereign nation-states to organize space and to create a larger sphere of European space free of some of the costly national welfare state provisions as counterweight to Japan and North America. The EU also invokes the principle of peoplehood to direct historical memories from both national and continental perspectives. Given recent innovations in the speed and means of communication and the globalization of local systems of production and exchange, the intensity and scale at which interests are organized and institutions formed are of a different order than at other historical moments, creating new possibilities of identification within and about Europe.

Most early anthropological studies of Europe were in villages (Blok 1974, Huseby-Darvas 1987, Pitt-Rivers 1954), or they linked the village to regional or global patterns (Cole & Wolf 1974, Freeman 1973, Schneider & Schneider 1976, Wolf 1982). To the extent that anthropologists have gone beyond the village or the region, they have tended to follow historians and study only the organization of the nation and national communities (Løfgren 1989). We cannot hope to cover most of this work, which nonetheless forms an essential research base for the study of Europeanization. Since "Europe" as an object of knowledge for research is still being constructed, we merely point to ways in which this object-in-the-making is and can be studied ethnographically.

HISTORICIZING EUROPEANIZATION

Europe as an entity is not a stable, sovereign, autonomous object but exists only in historical relations and fields of power (Foucault 1980, Geyer 1993). The relationship of the European to this entity is a form of identification that works simultaneously as a strategy of self-representation and a device of power. Such a strategy has always been as dependent on the externalization or creation of negative others as on the internal dynamics of group formation (Said 1978). It was crucial in achieving a "European self-consciousness," an understanding of the parameters of its powers through the creation of negative identities and the appropriation of difference for its own ends (Brague 1992, Fontana 1995, Herzfeld 1987). Such consciousness emerged in the fourteenth and fifteenth century, in response to a "Christendom weakened by internal contradiction and pressure from without" (Hay 1957, p. 96; Bance 1992, Ranum 1975), long before it appeared as a strategy in Africa, Asia, or any of the other continents. European coherence has always been tied to some external-ity, some hypostatized other—for example, the infidel, the Orient, or the East. This coherence, however, this self-consciousness, had little effect on a sense of the political unity of Europe before the second half of the sixteenth century or on a sense of the cultural unity of Europe before the seventeenth century. The development of "Europeanism," tied to values of progress, liberty, and free-dom (versus the putative lack of those values in other continents), did not ex-tend throughout the continent until the end of the eighteenth century when, in 1796, Edmund Burke could finally declare, "No European can be a complete exile in any part of Europe" (cited in Hay 1957, p. 123).

To create a Europe with which one could identify, where one did not feel in "complete exile" in any part, required the construction of similar institutions within which an identification *like* or *as* the Other would be possible. Such Europeans could then imagine themselves as resembling or replacing one an-other (Fuss 1995). In terms of political organization, this has meant the use of the nation-state model, a model that links a territorial form of political organi-zation (states) with a particular form of peoplehood (nations) (Gellner 1983, Grillo 1980). An ethnography of a state and the principle of territorial sover-eignty must necessarily focus on very different units of analysis than one of a nation.

Although peoples and religions are never discrete and bounded, the depend-ence of states on the principle of territorial sovereignty mandates such an as-sumption. States therefore have strong interests in generating, exacerbating, and institutionalizing differences with neighbors or neighboring states (Erik-son 1993). Especially in the past several centuries, the identity of European states has been intricately tied to standing armies and the deployment of mili-tary machines, frequently for economic purposes (Tilly 1993). With the grad-ual replacement of monarchic rule by self-identified democratic polities, lead-ers required constant justification for the huge budget drains necessary to sup-port standing armies. Hence they institutionalized different kinds of pretexts (e.g. national integrity and honor, national economic power, national security) for intervention or war. Territoriality, which was initially merely a top-down strategic solution to religious hatred, became a form of bottom-up self-identification and the principle of national and international order, supported by a conglomeration of interested parties (Borneman 1997).

The concept of statehood remains the central principle asserted in much in-ternational law, and it generates most of the categories used by scholars of in-ternational relations. The 1933 Montevideo Convention defined the criteria for statehood as having (*a*) a permanent population, (*b*) a defined territory, (*c*) government, and (*d*) the capacity to enter into relations with other states (Article 1, League of Nations Treaty Series No. 881). In practice, however, only the first two criteria have been consistently upheld by the United Nations and already existing nation-states. This concept of statehood politicizes and unifies ethnically mixed and territorially dispersed populations by conflating the two criteria in such categories as national sovereignty and national integrity, which are then appealed to in justifying war against external or internal enemies.

The nation form has another parallel but separate history (Grillo 1980, Johnson 1993, Schulze 1996). Initially taken up as a political program in the French Revolution and subsequently written into the United Nations Charter (Balibar 1991, Brubaker 1992, Hobsbawm 1990), the nation form grew out of transformed empires and tribes during European state formation (Kantorowicz 1957). This transformation of diverse peoples into unified nations was rarely accomplished without intermittent purges, cleansings, or other kinds of homogenizing processes. From the late-fifteenth to the early-seventeenth centuries, all modern Western European states have engaged in variant forms of this "generic process leading to the formation of victim groups." Spain was the first, expelling unconverted Jews in 1492, perennially persecuting and finally expelling residents of identifiable Muslim descent in 1609, and between 1577 and 1630, expelling its Protestants, who at that time comprised 14% of the overall population. For the "purifiers," the economic consequences of these "cleansings" were disastrous (Zolberg 1983, pp. 31–32, 35).

In the twentieth century, national consolidations and the creation of victim groups reached new heights, especially with the advent of fascist ideologies in Europe. The peace treaties concluding World War I "lumped together many peoples in single states, called some of them 'state people' and entrusted them with the government, silently assumed that others (such as the Slovaks in Czechoslovakia, or the Croats and Slovenes in Yugoslavia) were equal partners in the government, which they of course were not, and with equal arbitrariness created out of the remnant a third group of nationalities called 'minorities.'" The result was to make it seem to the stateless and the minorities that the treaties were "an arbitrary game which handed out rule to some and servitude to others"; the newly created states regarded the treaties "as an open breach of promise and discrimination" and subsequently ignored them. Hence the two conditions of West European nation-states—"homogeneity of population and rootedness in the soil"—were introduced into Eastern and Southern Europe (Arendt 1958, pp. 149–50).

M Rainer Lepsius (1988b, pp. 256–69) has argued that despite the wars, revolutions, and massive repressions that the nation-state has created, it has offered particular advantages to West European states, including the institutionalization of peaceful conflict-solving through the rule of law, guarantees of individual freedom, the organization of interests through parliamentary democracies, and the integration of national economic development in the world economy. In each of these measures, the multiethnic, autocratic East-Central European states have been at a permanent disadvantage vis-à-vis their West European counterparts. Religious and territorial fragmentation and the inability to centralize decision-making and organize power democratically have contributed to a relative political and economic backwardness. Moreover, while a proto-nation-state model spread throughout Western Europe in the seventeenth and eighteenth centuries, Central Europe was ruled by the Hapsburg monarchy until after World War I, and Eastern Europe was liberated from Soviet domination only after 1989. Hence it should come as no surprise that most East Europeans, including peoples in the former Yugoslavia, seek to join Europe by building nation-states along what they understand as the West European model (Gal 1991, Hayden 1996).

European state building and nation formation and the development of the EU should not be elided with Europeanization, for these processes do not always work in tandem (Lepsius 1988a,b). Countries such as Norway and Poland, for example, may become more European even though they do not belong to the EU, while certain members of the EU, such as Britain, may resist Europeanization. The EU, which today is admittedly the major institutional push behind Europeanization, also deviates in essential ways from the nation-state political form. Above all, it must rely on its member states to organize its own elections and to enforce its edicts. Moreover, the EU does not have at its disposal the several centuries in which European states consolidated their nations; it must create identifications at a time when the epic form of belonging is dubious as a viable political project (MacDonald 1995). Durable versions of peoplehood may no longer be possible to organize, as they were in nineteenth- and early-twentieth-century states, as though individuals were merely a function of the plot assigned to them by their national fate (Bhabha 1990). In any case, the EU has neither fate nor plot to work with. Its appeal rests firmly on individualism and freedom, values that unsettle many national plots but upon which the process of Europeanization also depends. To the extent the EU, through its central bank, takes away the monopoly on taxation and the ability to make war still enjoyed by its member states, it is just as likely that individuals will resent as they will identify with this new authority (Tilly 1990, p. 85).

Europeanization has little to which it can appeal outside of future-oriented narratives of individualism and the market. If people become Europeans, their identities no longer turn around categories of religion, folk, or national defense but around categories of exchange, difference, and value (cf Segal 1991). Unlike belonging to the nation, which has a specific cultural content, identification with Europe is an empty sign. Europe has no Spirit, in the Hegelian sense, since, unlike the nation-state, it does not live off the dead (Anderson 1983).

States conjure up ghosts who have lived and died for the nation and its territory, but within Europe there are no European graveyards, much as there is no European food or sex. Alternately, it is unlikely that Europeanization means simply the replacement of older tyrannies of self and nation by a tyranny of present markets, or of God by the Euro, as many French intellectuals fear.

In short, historicizing Europe involves tracing backward through time the two ostensibly contradictory directions in which Europe—East, West, North, South—is now pulled. For one, Western Europe is undergoing supranational, unifying processes, driven by the (Western) EU and a post-cold-war world realignment of military and economic power. These supranational processes do not replace the nation-state, which for now remains a superior form of organizing democratic participation and a territorial form of group identification. Nonetheless, they will likely force territorial states to yield some questions of sovereignty—above all, military, political, and economic—to the EU or other transnational bodies. Moreover, in this "age of information," sovereignty frequently has no identifiable locus and therefore proves less than useful in understanding the nature of power and process (Appadurai 1991, King 1991). The other direction is the reaffirmation of nation-state sovereignty and national group differences among EU members. Along both directions, East-Central Europe is engaged in a multitrajectory process to catch up to the West, creating relatively homogeneous nation-states as a precondition for entrance into the EU and submitting to supranational economic and political regimes that restrict the sovereignty of the new national states.

ETHNOLOGIZING EUROPEANIZATION

Peoples, Cultures, National Stereotypes

Tensions in the push and pull on Europe as an object of knowledge, a strategy of self-representation, and a form of identification are frequently avoided in descriptions by people—academics, intellectuals, national or cultural spokespersons—both on and outside the continent, who instead focus on the production of national and cultural stereotypes (Kaschuba 1994). We organize the following discussion around these tensions. While all identifications have to confront the power of stereotypes and caricatures, and frequently succumb to them, they are nonetheless fundamentally ambivalent. Identifications are always marked by a fascination with the possibility of resembling or, in the extreme, replacing the Other and alternately by a fear of one's need for this Other and of what is at stake in acknowledging resemblance or replacement.

In managing such tense ambivalences, both analysts of Europe and the peoples of Europe they study have relied on metaphors. The descriptive prominence of a particular metaphorical domain varies historically and by place, and identificatory metaphors tend to deteriorate into stereotyping and caricature. Stereotyping may be the most powerful tool used to manage identificatory ambivalences and to maintain a particular domain of metaphors (Fernandez 1986, Herzfeld 1997, MacDonald 1993). As European powers interact, two other metaphors have become particularly prominent: markets, projecting exchangeability and the freedom of choice on which consumer identities depend (Bergelman & Pauwels 1992, Chapman 1995), and marriage, projecting domestic stabilization and encompassment into a harmonious whole, the model around which affective life and security are organized. The micropractices involved in the "regulation of life" (Foucault 1980) rely on the disciplinary techniques of the market and marriage. But these metaphors work in two opposite directions, the former to globalize, the latter to localize. This metaphorical prominance is attributable, on the one hand, to a new obscurity about the site of political agency, sovereignty, and accountability (Habermas 1987); to the increased global penetration of bounded social units; and to the dissolution of the ability to make clear distinctions between friend and foe (obviating the utility of national militaries). On the other hand, it is due to the bourgeoisification of European everyday life, which extends far beyond those who consider themselves bourgeois (Løfgren 1989, Maier 1975).

As states increasingly yield control of their own financial markets to supranational institutions, like the EU, market metaphors become globally rather than nationally inflected identifications. Alternately, marriage—the uniting of a man and a woman into a privileged whole—remains the state's major legal instrument and nexus for regulating kinship and analogizing socially sanctioned relations between self and other (Goody 1973, 1983, 1990; Hajnal 1965; Pina-Cabral 1992; Segalen 1986; Segalen & Gullestad 1995). States resist yielding control of marriage to other political units. In the past ten years, European states have, however, extended the marital analogy—along with its legal protections, privileges, and social controls—far beyond its reproductive and property base. Especially legal experts have used kinship categories—adoption, descent, consanguinity, marriage—to regulate the growing number of cross-sex relationships that merely resemble marriages, extending the metaphor, most controversially, to same-sex relationships. The EU and its highest court have also stepped into this domain, frequently from a "human rights" perspective, to forbid certain forms of discrimination against nonmarried peoples. The struggle for control of kinship—residence, marriage, childcare, sex, intimacy, inheritance, generational obligations—in its most encompassing anthropological sense, also involves redefining social reproduction (Strathern 1992). The penetration of the market and the EU into marriage and kinship is redefining national life courses and creating the possibility for European ones.

Since the sixteenth century, the "peoples and cultures" of Europe have objectified themselves and others through a set of systematized national stereotypes, with which everyone is familiar though certainly not in agreement (Chock 1987). Initially these ideal types were drawn from classical arguments about essential categories of age, sex, and temperament (Castiglione 1976) and written to use as compliments for the reception of ambassadors at foreign courts. Soon they were based on observations and turned into epic-like "national characteristics" inferred from climate, soil, and temperament (Huarte 1976), or "habits," "style of mind," and "manners of living" which depended on place, political regime, and period (Barclay 1612). In sum, national characteristics originated with and among royalty, spread to the bourgeoisie, and only later entered folklore and everyday life, where they have taken on an independent existence and remain an essential source for nationalism (Elias 1978).

These stereotypes are now systematized in the saccharin concept of "unity in diversity," the idea of a European continent whose major characteristic is its diverse "family of nations." To the extent the nations of Europe are seen as cultural gestalts that in turn act out familial pathologies, they represent a mytho-historical model for anthropomorphic caricature, useful to essentialize and to eliminate ambiguities for both self-understanding and othering. Their further use and study will likely strengthen identification with an epic national character at the expense of more partial, heterogeneous, and ambivalent European identifications.

At another level, however, "epic" stereotypes are undergoing a novelization (Bakhtin 1981) tied more to a heterogeneous future than to a single past, as they contribute to an image of a paternalistic European family of nations (MacDonald 1996). Driven by the increasing size and power of the EU, a new and less stable hierarchy of European identifications is emerging. Nations are being brought into new relations with each other, creating new alliances and enmities, and even recreating themselves under the changing conditions of membership and action. General North/South and East/West cleavages are still used to characterize Europe, with the North considered orderly, productive, and largely Protestant; the South spontaneous, fun-loving, and largely Catholic; the East poor and underdeveloped both politically and economically; and the West rich and developed.

Europe's two most powerful nations—France and Germany—are viewed and view themselves as parents, along with a powerful third and ambiguous relative, Britain, unsettling and resettling the Franco-German alliance. As a British intellectual put it: "In the politics of Europe, monogamy is a sin and polygamy a virtue. France and Germany are joined in holy wedlock. Although they are unfaithful to each other from time to time (generally the secret assignation is with Britain), by and large it is, if not a love match, then a marriage of convenience. By comparison, Britain is a wanton woman taking her pleasure in a suite at the Savoy or in an alleyway behind Shepherd Market" (Garel-Jones 1996, p. 20). If Britain is a wanton woman, it is because she has never been able to recover from the loss of her empire and the hollow victories in the two world wars. Germany, which dominates the purse through its central bank and strong currency, is always gendered as the patriarch. Given its criminal history in this century, however, Germany would rather dissolve itself into Europe, though it has retained its faith in the Herderian project of each part contributing its own bit to history. France, like Britain, is haunted by its colonial ties but still desires to lead the Europeanization process.

Europe's peripheral nations test the ability to integrate marginal peoples into the EU. This integration process displays not only the limitations on the resolve to unify Europe but also the willingness of nations to Europeanize. For now, Greece, for example, is serving as the bad child, ignoring pan-European concerns in the Balkans; acting egotistically; and resisting major economic structural reforms with its huge public debt, high inflation, and use of EU subsidies to prop up public consumption and income redistribution. Portugal, conversely, might be called a good child, obedient to EU norms, acknowledging its dependence within the union. Since joining the EU, Portugal has followed the tough IMF monetary restructuring and stabilization plan, invested its EU subsidies into infrastructure such as freeway development—and become economically weaker, losing quality jobs and increasing its food imports.

Finally, there are distant cousins, the new wealthy nations just brought in: Sweden, Austria, and Finland. Switzerland and Norway do not appear to want to enter soon. They may be black sheep within the EU, though nonentrance may paradoxically make them more European. All the East-Central Europeans are in the difficult position of second cousins with lesser rights. The "in-transition" countries of Poland, Hungary, and the Czech Republic are the closest to entry. Other cousins, such as Bulgaria, Romania, Croatia, and Serbia, are unwelcome bastards and considered unlikely candidates. All prospective members are considered juvenile if not actively infantalized by their Western relatives and must undergo a probationary period of Europeanization before being ostensibly adopted by the family.

Perspectives on the European Union

The EU is not the only factor, nor is it always the most significant, when it is compared with other transnational regimes that affect the making of Europe, such as the Helsinki Accords on Human Rights, the United Nations, North Atlantic Treaty Organization, multinational technology projects such as Ariane,

Organization of Economic Cooperation and Security, the World Bank, or the General Agreement on Trade and Tariffs. Although macrolevel descriptions or speculative analyses alone might confirm the widespread suspicion that the "'European' edifice...remains fundamentally hollow, selfishly obsessed with fiscal rectitude and commercial advantage?" (Judt 1996, p. 9), research to date paints a more complex picture.

Historians have traditionally defined the terms for talking about the "making of Europe," meaning the construction of national histories or the tracing of objects through time. An excellent general series with this title, edited by Jacques LeGoff, is being published simultaneously in four languages, covering such topics as the sea (Mollat du Jourdin 1993), the Enlightenment (Im Hof 1994), states, nations and nationalism (Schulze 1996), Western Christendom (Brown 1996), cities (Benevelo 1995), language (Eco 1995), revolutions (Tilly 1993), and Europe and its other (Fontana 1995).

Political scientists control most research on the EU, understandably because they specialize in the analysis of governments. Yet their focus on the EU as a supragovernment among other levels of government elides two interesting anthropological questions. First, is the EU comparable to the world's recorded repertoire of past governments, or is it a distinctly new kind of political unit in human history? Second, does the expansion of the EU substantively change the nature of Europeanization? Professional anthropologists, to the extent that they do not restrict study to national stereotypes and their legacies, are situated between historians and political scientists, concerned with the making of Europe in interaction with the EU. How this location might bear on researching Europeanization is worth exploring.

Three major foci characterize the current anthropological study of the EU and Europe. The first approach is to study the EU at its centers, to examine "Eurocrats" and the administrative and political cultures of European institutions. The second is a bottom-up approach, to examine national symbols and everyday experiences in interaction with the EU. The third is a focus on spheres of interaction where peoples of Europe engage in face-to-face encounters with each other.

EU power is centered in Brussels, Strasbourg, and Luxembourg, where the EU is present as a parliament, court, and executive council. These centers are the source and symbolic center of the EU, but they are also forming a culture of their own, distinct from the national cultures they are to represent (Abélès & Bellier 1996). Some people have become identified as "Eurocrats" who speak their own mix of languages. The European Commission and other Eurobodies might be analyzed as "melting pots," with their own formal and informal politics, their own everyday work rhythms and social schedules (Abélès 1992, 1993, 1995; Abélès & Bellier 1996). Anthropologists have also taken up the

EU as a bureaucracy (Herzfeld 1992, Wright 1994), EU bureaucrats (Shore 1995), EU cultural policies (Shore 1993), the view of Europe from Brussels (Shore & Black 1992), and the EU space agency (Zabusky 1995).

A second approach is to study not the elites who make EU policies and sit in its centers but EU interactions with local communities (Boissevain 1975, Wilson & Smith 1993). Perhaps the domain where this approach has most frequently been employed is with regard to EU agricultural policy and food [e.g. Italian and French wine growers and the EU (Giordano 1987), Iberian fisherman and EU policy (LiPuma & Meltzoff 1989), Irish farmers (Shutes 1991, 1993; Wilson 1989), and Dutch and Spanish farmers (Jurjus 1993)]. There is also a growing field of studies of the ways in which the EU is appropriated in local contexts [Corsican symbolization of land as region and nation (Jaffe 1993), EU policy influence on self-image and possessions in Greece (Costa 1993), issues of EU bureaucracy and accountability in Greece (Herzfeld 1992), immigrants and transnational phenomenon (Gullick 1993, McDonough 1993), and appropriation of European symbolism in Hungary (Hofer 1994)].

Perhaps the processes of nationalism and transnationalism have been most interestingly studied at international borders (Donnan & Wilson 1994, O'Dowd & Wilson 1996, Wilson 1993b), where there are constant changes in the content of "nationalist symbols involving flags, colors, road signs, graffiti, and parades" (Wilson 1996, pp. 210–15). Contra Judt (1996), Wilson (1995, p. 14) resists identifying the EU "as principally an organization of economic integration" but instead views it as "moving between locality, region, state, and supranation." Nonetheless, he speculates that the EU is developing into a "new type of sociopolitical configuration" where "national elites and state governments and bureaucracies are losing power." In fact, "EU-building is splintering the identification of the citizen with the state" (Wilson 1993a; 1996, p. 211).

A third approach, suggested by MacDonald (1995, pp. 7, 12, 15), entails the study of "everyday encounters" and face-to-face interactions where people work with stereotypes and construct commonalities and differences. The EU, she writes, "is not inherently composed...of any mosaic or patchwork of national cultures.... It is composed of people who mutually construct their sense and boundaries of self through relations with others." Therefore we should pay more attention to "people's own perceptions of the world...if we want to understand why people behave as they do, including why they might appear to resent or resist some policies perceived to come from Brussels."

Following upon these pioneer studies, we suggest five relatively unexplored domains of practice where the process of Europeanization might be fruitfully studied: languages, money, tourism, sex, and sport. Our choice of domains is not meant to be exhaustive.

PRACTICES OF EUROPEANIZATION

Languages

The dream of an elixir that could solve the problems of European polyglottism by establishing a language of exact equivalence between words and things seems to have been exhausted. The sixteenth-century attempt to recover the language used by Adam and his descendants before the catastrophe of Babel (the contenders being Hebrew, Egyptian, Irish, and Chinese) and the twentieth-century creation of artificial languages such as Esperanto, Beginner's All-Purpose Symbolic Instruction Code (BASIC), or Pascal appear to most of us today as futile and foolish (Eco 1995). Diverse languages are now assumed, seen more as necessary reflections of different worlds than as barriers to communication.

In Europe, language unification was accomplished through public education as part of projects of national unification. Subsequently, states have become the protectors of separate national languages, with intrinsic interests in emphasizing differences between the adjacent languages of other countries and in creating the language as a symbol of national belonging and historical treasure, establishing it as a common denominator of its citizenry. Since their legitimacy was and remains tied to the "robustness" of their languages, European states are also engaged in a permanent competition for linguistic dominance within the continent and in global arenas. Nonetheless, the nature of global exchange increasingly requires people who can speak other languages. A state that does not encourage its citizenry to learn additional foreign languages will create for itself a legitimation deficit, for it will be greatly disadvantaged in economic, political, and cultural exchanges. Given this context, de Swaan (1995, p. 10) concludes that "amalgamation among European languages is unlikely, and national languages will retain almost all of their functions in their domestic context." Diglossia will prevail, with at least one foreign language added to the mother tongue. This diglossia will likely become indexical with a cosmopolitan form of Europeanization, with the identifications of monolinguals driven more by loyalties to national and provincial cultures.

In the past couple decades, there has developed a kind of stampede toward English (de Swaan 1995, p. 3) as a second language on a European and even global scale. Among Western Europeans, the "repertoire of more than three out of four multilingual speakers contains English" and, in de Swaan's (p. 9) vivid description, English is the "sun for the national planets" that circle around it, the center of the linguistic galaxy. Much as Russian enables continued communication between members of the Soviet Union's successor states and Arabic links together the North African and Middle Eastern peoples who worship Islam, English holds the EU together and is quickly becoming the connective to East-Central Europe. This situation is historically novel, quite different than European antiquity, for example, when Latin was the central language within Europe. Latin was shared only among the elites, whose monopoly on literacy prevented widespread access to sacred texts and to the discourses of power. The dynamics in the contemporary democratic political units of Europe are such that elites and masses partake in more egalitarian relationships, frequently going to the same schools and developing similar skills. This certainly does not preclude the development of hierarchies of competency and status (Bourdieu & Passeron 1977, Willis 1977), but today, access to language training, education, and information is difficult to foreclose and fix. With the growth of visual fields of "entertainment" and mass electronic communication, other kinds of symbolic capital and hierarchies are being created that evade the stratifications that run along national linguistic axes.

Because the dominance of English within Europe is so recent (Zabusky 1995), the modes by which it establishes its dominance in everyday life and ritual occasions deserve much more attention (Ammon et al 1987–1988). The lucrative global markets in music, film, and fashion immediately come to mind as modes in which English hegemony reign. In addition, the situations in which multilinguistic competence (not always involving English) is demanded or performed, particularly among tourists, participants in international political forums, and in commercial situations, are particularly revealing moments in which cosmopolitan and provincial identifications are at stake, being discarded, chosen, or shared. During the cold war, Eastern European states adopted an official policy of learning Russian as a second language, but people widely resisted this policy. It not only resulted in resistance to Russian but also prevented East-Central Europeans from learning the languages necessary for direct access to international science, technology, and entertainment. All of the states of Central Europe abandoned the Russian language policy after 1989 and abruptly switched to teaching English and German, which are now in a new competition for dominance as the second language.

Money

Much as national languages have become symbols of diverse European identities, so have national currencies served as personal identifiers and as the essential instrument of a state's monetary policies. Paralleling the search for a medium enabling universal translatability of languages, European policymakers have sought to make their national currencies convertible and exchangeable. Following the cold war, such convertibility has been more or less achieved for all European states. The proposal to introduce in the year 2002 the Euro, an EU common currency, now promises to replace the competition and adjustment between national currencies with a system of central control and regulation.

Proponents and "Euroskeptics" agree that what is at stake is sovereignty: the ability to control the relationship between politics and identifications at the national, European, or global levels. Money poses not only the central questions concerning exchange, difference, and control over value, it also postures as a transcendent, phallic authority: the measure of all value but that which itself has no measure or value (Goux 1990).

The mystical transformative power that a European currency is believed to have is reflected in the equally mystical terms used to describe it. The currency was first named the "ecu," a simple acronym for European Currency Unit, but was changed to the Euro, making it the phonetic and lexical equivalent of the prefix used to Europeanize objects, such as EuroDisney and Eurotica. Europeanization pretends to be neutral and empty of content, preserving what is best of tradition while promoting modernization and global competitiveness. Hence the Euro was initially described as a "basket currency" that would contain other currencies like Confetti Lira, the Beautiful Mark, the soft Belgian franc, or the hard Dutch guilder. In December 1996, the EU commission responsible for design of the Euro reached a decision about which icons would be represented on the paper bills. The national patrimonies appearing on national currencies, frequently in the form of heroes from foundational periods, were too contentious. Instead, the Euro will have faces of famous architectural monuments, which tend to be more continentally than nationally defined. Certainly these icons will change as the face of Europe itself changes.

Proponents of a single currency argue that it is the sine qua non of a single European market that, they believe, cannot exist with the risk of instability, competitive devaluations, inflation, and exchange rate uncertainty. Once consolidated as a market, it is believed that western Europe will be able to compete with economies as large as those of North America and Asia. Some also argue that monetary union can take place quite independently, or even without, political union. The Austrian schilling has been fixed against the deutsche mark for 13 years, and Dutch short-term interest rates have not diverged from German rates by more than 0.8% in 8 years. Yet nobody would deny that Austria and the Netherlands are sovereign states. The most vigorous proponents of the Euro, which include bankers, large companies, and many politicians, argue that its introduction will be a major political act that, while preserving national identities, will allow a genuine rebirth of Europe.

Others view plans for a single currency less optimistically. Initially coming from the political right, particularly in Great Britain, these critics see the convergence criteria laid out by the Maastricht summit as too severe, unrealistic, and threatening to national sovereignty. Still others fear that strong currencies like the deutsche mark will be replaced by a weakened, inflation-prone Euro. More recently, opposition has come from the left, most forcefully articulated by

Pierre Bourdieu and other French intellectuals. Although this criticism also focuses centrally around the issue of sovereignty, it defines sovereignty not in terms of a traditional national defense but as the protection of diverse European "civilizational" legacies: trade unions and labor rights, general unemployment benefits, and free and universal access to humanistic education. Introduction of the Euro threatens to situate all political decisions in economistic and Social Darwinistic frameworks, removing the ability of local national governments to make policy for the common good. Rational political decisions, such as for universal health care and education, are often not rational economically.

All states, including those that do not adopt the Euro, will be affected by its usage. Hence money has received much attention in the press and in parliaments throughout the continent. Varenne (1993, p. 232) has argued that "[t]he kind of existence that it [Europe] does appear to have is that of a common 'market,' a soul-less place where merchants exploit their customers.... 'Europe' reduced to a market is indeed, nothing." This insistence on "nothingness" fails to recognize that the market itself can function as cultural content to replace the interaction of national culture and politics with a different logic. If the Euro does symbolize the nothingness that is Europe, then it is a symbol of the values of exchangeability and substitutability, thereby representing cosmopolitanism as transcendence itself. A promising area for future research in both East and West Europe would be the ongoing resymbolization of money in everyday life and the ways in which regimes of credit are changing the nature and locus of sovereignty (Verdery 1996). Another line of inquiry would be into the new monetary Euro-language: how institutions and individuals translate their national currencies, together with their associated symbolisms, through the medium of what the Bavarian Minister of Environment Peter Gauweiler has coined the new "Esperanto money."

Tourism

Tourism is a privileged domain in which European identifications are created, for it is abroad that nationals find opportunities to vacation with other nationals and where they are identified by others as either nationals or Europeans. The paradigmatic approach to this topic, criticized by Crick (1989), regards indigenous societies as unwilling "hosts" and international tourists as unwelcome "guests" who destroy cultural difference (Boissevain 1996, Smith 1989). Tourism in this framework is a destroyer of culture rather than a set of complex cultural practices in itself.

In contrast to anthropology's general disdain for tourism, the European Commission has recently shown a strong interest in what it has come to define as cultural tourism in Europe (Richards 1996): "According to the European Union, 'tourism, and especially cultural tourism in a broader sense...deserve priority attention' as policy areas....(Bernadini 1992). Cultural tourism has become recognized as an important agent of economic and social change in Europe. Politicians now refer to cultural heritage as 'Italy's General Motors'...(Fanelli 1993) or as 'the oil industry of France'...(Mosser 1994)."

Having made the claim that cultural tourism deserves "policy attention," in 1991, the EU set up the European Association for Tourism and Leisure Education (ATLAS) committee to conduct a transnational study of European cultural tourism. Their first major problem was to define in any meaningful sense cultural tourism. Because of their policy orientation, there was felt to be a need to quantify the phenomenon of cultural tourism so that its economic impact, as well as its future economic potential, could be assessed. It was also recognized, however, that a quantitatively oriented definition did not sufficiently account for the many practices that could fall under the definition of cultural tourism. The definitions that ATLAS came up with were as follows (Richards 1996, p. 24):

> *Conceptual definition:* "The movement of persons to cultural attractions away from their normal place of residence, with the intention to gather new information and experiences to satisfy their cultural needs."
>
> *Technical definition:* "All movements of persons to specific cultural attractions, such as heritage sites, artistic and cultural manifestations, arts and drama outside their normal place of residence."

By drawing attention to the importance of tourism as a way of learning about the world and of satisfying "cultural needs," the definitions take tourism seriously and also implicitly acknowledge that tourists themselves take what they do seriously. The very breadth of definitions, however, limits their utility. Most limiting is the acceptance of a reified and anachronistic version of that which constitutes the object of touristic interest: culture. The technical definition equates culture with "heritage sites, artistic and cultural manifestations, arts and drama." This does not allow that cultural practices, rather than material culture artifacts or elite institutions (museums, art galleries, historical sites), are just as likely to be the object of touristic interest.

Within Europe, there is now a market-driven element in sharing experiences abroad, in losing or at least sensing the loss of national significations, which has led to the extension of the word tourism to activities outside the semantic scope of vacations. New activities abound, such as medical tourism (in pursuit of organ transplants, operations, and treatments), drug tourism (with Amsterdam the favorite site), and sex tourism. This kind of tourism generates official anxieties by creating the potential for nonnational identifications. In France, *narcotourisme* usually refers to the organized visits of elderly ladies to Dutch "coffee shops" (the English word is used in the Netherlands) to smoke pot. Tourism also extends to French youth who travel to shoot up heroin. The drug policies of the Netherlands are a total irritant to their neighbors, for though Dutch authorities seized some 246.9 tons of illegal narcotics in 1993 (compared with 63.5 tons in France, 60.5 in Belgium, and 282.2 in Germany), the Netherlands has only 1.6 drug addicts per 1000 inhabitants (compared with 1.5 in Germany, 1.7 in Belgium, and 2.6 in France) (Demetz 1996, pp. 82–84). Such examples indicate that nonnational attractions are just as likely, if not more likely, to motivate touristic interest as Renaissance paintings and Roman ruins.

Essentializing the objects of tourist interest, as the ATLAS definition does, denies their historicity and hence suspends time (Barthes 1972, p. 76). Tourists, however, perpetually play with the limitations of time as well as space, often manipulating the boundaries of one to explore the boundaries of the other, thereby bringing in to play the notion that Bakhtin (1981) has called the "chronotope." Spaces are set aside to "recreate" the past in burgeoning heritage industries, which are then set up as ways to relive this past in the present (Badone 1991, pp. 518–45). In the late 1980s, for example, the economically depressed city of Liverpool was able to reinvent itself as a tourist attraction by drawing attention to its status as the birthplace of the Beatles. Visitors to the once-derelict Albert Dock are now invited to relive the swinging 1960s in the Beatles museum housed in a former warehouse, after which they can take "ticket-to-ride tours" around the city to look at the houses in which John, Paul, George, and Ringo grew up. Tourists are not simply invited to reinvent a nostalgic version of Liverpool's past, they are invited to relive the pasts of other people. The increasing use of simulation in the tourist industry suggests the extent to which tourism is about visiting not only other places but also other times. Tourists attempt not only to see but also to visit the past, as in the case of York's Viking museum, which simulates even the smells of a village in the Middle Ages. They also attempt to visit the future, as can be illustrated by Disneyland Paris's Tomorrowland.

Since the beginning of modern tourism in the seventeenth century, travelers have been primary promulgators of cultural stereotypes, as both observers and observed. Notions of difference among European cultures are constructed and confirmed through such face-to-face contact (MacDonald 1995). Tourism might frequently be less about the construction of stereotypes than the dismantling of them, as anyone who has been to Sweden in search of a promiscuous sexual partner could testify. Future work might fruitfully address how "cultural knowledge" is itself conceptualized and generated by tourists, the ways in which tourist practices constitute attempts to gain cultural knowledge, and finally the limitations and opportunities that various tourist practices offer in this capacity.

The strong links between tourism and anthropology lead some, such as McCannell (1976), to argue that tourism is effectively an amateur version of anthropology. If this is the case, it remains to be seen whether tourism will undergo the same kind of changes that anthropology has in the twentieth century. Stereotypes of the Other produced in late-nineteenth- and early-twentieth-century anthropology have certainly been taken up as the object of interest by tourists in search of the Real. As anthropology has become more reflexive and interactive, there has also been evidence that tourism is seeking to do the same, hence the popularity of the idea of having an "experience" while abroad. In *gîte* vacations in rural France and Italy, the goal is to live like a local rather than as a colonial expatriate in the nearest Sheraton. It is no longer satisfactory simply to observe the Other; tourists now expect to interact with and even become—if only temporarily—the Other.

Sex

In the media-hyped, truthless late twentieth century, adolescence is easy for no one, not even for Europe. The peoples of Europe are now undergoing an analogous period of self-discovery, coming to terms with the maturing body of Europe, with its desires, its orifices and closures, and its sexual identifications. Increased interactions between nationals across class and status groups within and outside Europe are radically altering practices of sex. In the eyes of North Americans, Europe's sexual identity has always been, while assuredly heterosexual, uniformly and confidently permissive and pleasure driven.

For the peoples of Europe, however, these identifications are wishful projections. Europe has no single sexuality, and to the extent that sex is patterned, people in Europe do not see themselves as particularly permissive. Sexual practices are nationally defined, regulated, and policed, but they now travel with increasing speed and frequency. The opening of borders within the EU and between East and West Europe along with wide electronic and print media access to proliferating erotic images is facilitating not only political and economic integration but a Europeanization of desires and practices (cf Ariès & Béjin 1985, Bechdolf et al 1993). Today, one can enjoy a French kiss in England or "go Greek" in Sweden. Nowhere, however, can one have European sex, at least not in Europe.

The complex sexual geography of Europe is not revealed in its conservative and liberal ideologies or in its governmental prohibitions, societal repressions, and individual responses—as Foucault (1980) long ago pointed out—but in its spatial diffusion and regulation of bodily practices (Mosse 1985). Current regulatory systems, including legal regimes, that qualify and clarify which sexual practices will be permitted and encouraged and which will be restricted and forbidden are increasingly ineffective with respect to their stated goals. In terms of providing direction for research, they function at best in an ad hoc manner to index domains of conflict. In some cases, the conflict is between national legal values and EU norms, with the interactions in the "free market" generating practices that bypass or intersect in novel ways with both forms of *reglementation*. National parliamentarians frequently claim that the EU is dictating what its sexual practices should be. Such whining by national political figures usually indicates that the EU supports the position of one of their opponents. These EU dictates are regarded sometimes as too liberal (as in the case of Britain with regard to sex), sometimes as too stringent (as in the case of the Netherlands with regard to sex). In other cases, such as the use of the pill or abortion or the regulation of pornography, conflict is not between national and supranational norms but between religious and secular authorities. In all cases, sex is a central domain for negotiating and reconfiguring popular and political authority in the context of Europeanization and globalization.

The redefinition of Europe's sexual identities has involved the isolation of locations where certain kinds of sexual practices are actually legal and constitute an essential economic industry. We call these places "Eurogenous zones." They are marked by functional specialization, with cities such as Hamburg (kinky hetero sex) and Amsterdam (safer, regulated hetero sex and a large homosexual culture) within northwestern Europe, Cracow in eastern Europe (which features Europe's only lesbian sauna), and Seyches and Mykonos in southern Europe (large gay male resorts). Moreover, the zones are all well-known tourist sites, with both customers and "suppliers" often coming from elsewhere to be someone else. Since 1989, there has been a huge recruitment of women from Eastern Europe, especially Russia, Poland, the Czech Republic, and Bulgaria, to service West Europe's heterosexual male desires. The effects of this movement and these experiences on practices of kinship and intimacy have yet to be researched.

Reproductive heterosexuality within marriage remains the social and legal "regulative ideal" within all of Europe, and states offer a plethora of well-known incentives such as tax breaks and pronatal policies to encourage its practice. As with all ideals, however, not only are they difficult to enforce, the set of prohibitions on which their authority rests also tends to produce alternatives and oppositions. These oppositions are then reincorporated into the regulative mechanisms, changing in turn the initial regulative ideal. In Amsterdam, for example, the established red light districts are centered around the official licensing of heterosexual brothels. Brothel owners are now held responsible for the health of the prostitutes who work there in order to prevent the spread of AIDS and the prostitution of children.

The national regulation of social heterodoxies—often perceived as potential social problems—has therefore been achieved through an essentially geographic policy that limits certain sexual practices to clearly defined locations where they may be more effectively—even if more permissively—monitored. In turn, however, these new Eurogenous zones are available for exploration by others located elsewhere in the body of Europe. Whereas some states have called for the EU to take measures to stamp out "sex tourism," as it is called, in its "Philoxenia Programme" of European tourism promotion, Dutch ministers recently resisted legislative proposals designed to curb many of these activities. They insisted that their liberal traditions barred them from accepting, an initiative undertaken after Belgium's "paedophile murders" of 1995, a proposed agreement to ensure punishment of people who possessed, for their own use, videos and other material featuring children in sexual acts.

Examples where European legislation is seen to be too inhibiting or too permissive in relation to national sentiments might serve as "diagnostic events" (Moore 1987) for ethnographic research on processes of Europeanization. One such event happened in fall 1996 when Britain's National Heritage Secretary, Virginia Bottomly, outlawed the French hard-core pornographic television channel "Rendez-Vous," which could be received by British viewers owning "smart cards" capable of decoding the scrambled signal broadcast from Paris. Because the European Court of Justice had previously ruled that such channels could not be prevented from being beamed into Britain, however, Bottomly was forced to ban sales of the smart cards used to decode the scrambled signal. The national restriction of access to a resource already made readily available from Europe is an example of the continuing struggle between individual rights, national regulation of pleasures in the home, and how contemporary technology can affect the geographical diffusion of sexual codes. With the right technology, every home in Europe with a satellite television and a smart card is poised to become a Eurogenous zone.

Negotiations over the proliferation of new sexual practices within Europe are not, however, limited to national versus EU notions of acceptability. For example, the scathing attack on the EU made by the Pontifical Council for the Family, an advisory body under Pope John Paul II, illustrates the continuing potency of religious forces. It drew attention to Europe's "Demographic Winter"—the phenomenon of falling birth rates and declining populations—which it blamed on women's activities outside the home, the devaluation of the notion of motherhood, and the introduction of spurious rights pertaining to reproductive health, homosexuality, and abortion. Given widespread chronic unemployment throughout Europe, the Pope's alarming message of a demographic winter and a shrinking labor force has had little effect on policy.

Finally, sex is not only a device of control and power over the marginalized or the middle class but is also deployed to challenge the powerful, as can be seen by the constant interest in sexual scandals, ranging from British politicians to Princess Stephanie of Monaco. Contemporary Europe is fertile ground for engaging in the kind of analysis, called for by Foucault (1980, p. 11), of the way in which the practices of sex are "put into discourse."

Sport

Like tourism, sport promotes the physical movement of Europeans—both players and supporters—throughout Europe. Both activities result occasionally in violent interaction. Like sex, drugs, and food, sport reveals conflicts between various interest groups seeking to control its regulation and has been subject to similar conflicts between the explicit goals of the EU vis-à-vis national and local powers. Money is also central as sport becomes commoditized and various financial interests compete for control over the relationship between players, clubs, and spectators viewing games either in person or via their television sets. No other sport illustrates these developments more clearly than soccer, because no other sport has been developed to a comparable degree at the European level. For that reason, we limit our discussion to this sport. Like the EU itself, soccer is an institutionalized system of aggressive yet cooperative competition among global, national, and local entities. As such, it is the quintessential European pursuit and is fast becoming an archetypal example of Europeanization.

European soccer is a matter of everyday discussion in every European country. It has moved far from its origins as a stage for class struggle between British upper-class "public school" amateurs and industrial working-class professionals (Curtis 1993). The remarkable popularity of soccer has depended largely on the medium of television, which now expands the notion of audience, participation, and spectatorship beyond just stadium support, which also continues to be massive. As with televised pornography, European soccer is available to every European who has the technology to receive the now nightly broadcast tournament matches. Consequently, technological rather than spatial mobility is the key factor determining the extent to which Europeans can partake in this particular form of Europeanization. In some cases, the growing popularity of televised sport is leading to cultural changes in the ways in which people spend their leisure time. The lucrative benefits that television coverage offers local soccer clubs (estimated to be $2 billion until the year 2003 alone) have implications that will affect the quality of the game, as soccer games now run six nights a week. They are also having significant effects on how the game is organized as players and clubs, both local and national, compete for resources.

At the heart of this process is the Union of European Football Association, the European body that organizes and regulates competitions at the European level. UEFA, much like other administrative bodies representing noncommercial interests, is now affected by dictates of the EU originally intended to apply to the private sector. Particularly significant was the European Court of Justice's so-called Bosman decision of December 1995. UEFA argued that 6 of the 11 players on a team should have lived for a number of years in the team's country. The court ruled that Article 48 of the EU treaty guaranteed the free movement of workers between member states, and therefore removed restrictions on the nationality of players comprising a given team.

The outcome, called free agency in North America, is a genuine Europeanizing of local teams as nationals from one country play in teams of another. European Cup teams, though still representing themselves as localities by usually taking their names from the cities in which the clubs were founded, are now, at least in theory, able to build teams in which no player originates from the club's city—or even country—of origin. Soccer is thus a concrete example of how Europeanization involves identification and subsequent replacement by other nationals. For example, Manchester United's celebrated "English king of soccer," Eric Cantona, is French. The European organization of soccer is therefore undermining the locality-based rationale for identification between fans and the clubs they support: To support Manchester United is not necessarily to support a team comprised of players from Manchester or even from Britain.

Identification with the local teams is further complicated in that there is no longer a cultural or racial resemblance between the players and their primarily working- and middle-class male followers—and this at a time when the media and fans celebrate players as national heroes. The hooliganism and violence associated with many soccer fans is most frequently rationalized as solidarity with the team and defense of the home territory. With neither territorial unit nor local "people" to defend, it remains to be seen against whom the violence will be directed and how it will be rationalized in the future.

As with the the Europeanization of national currency, the Europeanization of soccer is also part of a strategy that will enable it to compete successfully in a global context. The process of identification with and replacement by the Other does not stop with Europeans within Europe, for soccer teams are increasingly drawing from the labor resources of nations lying far beyond European horizons of the present, especially from its colonial past. To name but three examples, Tijani Babangida, a member of Nigeria's gold medal–winning Olympic team, now plays for Ajax Amsterdam; the Australian Ned Zelic now plays for Auxerre; Fenerbahce's coach Sebastio Lazaroni is Brazilian.

The Bosman decision also declared that clubs can no longer collect transfer fees from players bought by other teams once the players' contracts have expired. Players can no longer be regarded as valuable assets to be sold once they have been acquired but are effectively rented rather than owned by the clubs. This adversely affects small clubs which were previously able to raise substantial revenues by selling their star players at the end of their contracts. The Scottish club Celtic, for example, was unable to collect a $3 million transfer fee when John Collins, its star player, was sold to Monaco. Celtic argued that Monaco is not part of the EU and that the Bosman ruling was therefore inapplicable. The European Court upheld its decision, however, on the basis that Monaco plays in UEFA competitions. By imposing its larger commercial goals in the realm of sport, the European Court has effectively rendered soccer players as spatially and temporally deregulated commodities to be bought and sold—or who can buy and sell themselves—like any other means of production.

Soccer's massive popularity in Europe makes it a medium for the direct experience of Europeanization. Anthropologists will find that, as with tourism, money, language, and sex, the realm of sport is one in which previously unchallenged and secure identifications are being significantly reshaped. National soccer fans have, in the past, committed violent, xenophobic, and sometimes fatal acts in their frenzied and self-styled warrior-like support of local and national teams. The ways in which individuals respond to the reorganization of their cherished national sport, given the challenges to the traditional relations of player to clubs and spectators, will tell us very little about the "illusion of Europe," but it will reveal how Europe is becoming more European.

CONCLUSION

Most American observers are ambivalent about the EU and are unaware of Europeanization, whereas our European colleagues are divided on both the institution and the process. Locked in an almost manic-depressive cycle of Europhoria and Europessimism, we might do better to drop the search for a totalizing metaphor and the analogies with a European superstate or a United States of Europe. Instead, we suggest dealing with the EU as a continental political unit of a novel order, and with Europeanization pragmatically as a spirit, a vision, and a process.

Visit the *Annual Reviews home page* at
http://www.AnnualReviews.org.

Literature Cited

Abélès M. 1992. *La Vie Quotidienne au Parlement Européen.* Paris: Hachette
Abélès M. 1993. Political anthropology of a transnational institution: the European parliament. *Fr. Polit. Soc.* 11(1):1–19
Abélès M. 1995. Pour une anthropologie des institutions. *L'Homme* 135:65–85
Abélès M, Bellier I. 1996. Administrative and political cultures in the European institutions. *Proc. Counc. Eur. Stud., 10th, Mar. 14–16, Chicago*
Ammon U, Dittmar N, Mattheier KJ, eds. 1987–1988. *Sociolinguistics: An International Handbook of the Science of Language and Society.* Berlin/New York: de Gruyter
Anderson B. 1983. *Imagined Communities: Reflections on the Origin and Spread of Nationalism.* London: Verso
Appadurai A. 1991. Disjuncture and difference in a global cultural economy. In *Global Culture: Nationalism, Globalization and Modernity,* ed. M Featherstone, pp. 295–311. London: Sage
Arendt H. 1958. (1951). *The Origin of Totalitarianism, Part Two: Imperialism.* San Diego: Harcourt Brace Jovanovich
Ariès P, Béjin A. 1985. *Western Sexuality. Practice and Precept in Past and Present Times.* Oxford: Blackwell
Badone E. 1991. Ethnography, fiction, and the meanings of the past in Brittany. *Am. Ethnol.* 18(3):518–45
Bakhtin M. 1981. *The Dialogic Imagination.* Transl. C Emerson, JM Holmquist. Austin: Univ. Tex. Press
Balibar E. 1991. The nation form: history and ideology. In *Race, Class, Nation: Ambiguous Identities,* ed. E Balibar, I Wallerstein, pp. 622–33. New York: Routledge
Bance A. 1992. The Idea of Europe. From Erasmus to ERASMUS. *J. Eur. Stud.* 22:1–19
Barclay J. 1612. (1633). *The Mirror of Minds.* London: Walkley
Barthes R. 1972. *Mythologies.* New York: Hill & Wang
Bechdolf U, Kalliopi-Hatzistrati P, Johannsen S, Knecht M, Kromer H, et al. 1993. *Watching Europe: A Media and Cultural Studies Reader.* Tübingen: Tübingen Ver. Volksk.
Benevelo L. 1995. *The European City.* Oxford: Blackwell
Bergelman J-C, Pauwels C. 1992. Audiovisual policy and cultural identity. *Media Cult. Soc.* 14(2):169–85

Bernadini G. 1992. Tourism and cultural policy in EC policy. In *Cultural Tourism and Regional Development,* ed. P Friesland, pp. 3–5. The Hague: Leeuwarden
Bhabha H, ed. 1990. *Nation and Narration.* London: Routledge
Blok A. 1974. *The Mafia of a Sicilian Village, 1860–1960.* Oxford: Blackwell
Boissevain J. 1975. Introduction: towards a social anthropology of Europe. In *Beyond Community: Social Process in Europe,* ed. J Boissevain, J Friedl, pp. 9–17. The Hague: Dep. Educ. Sci. Neth.
Boissevain J, ed. 1996. *Coping with Tourists: European Reactions to Mass Tourism.* Providence, RI: Berghahn Books
Borneman J. 1997. Towards a theory of ethnic cleansing: territorial sovereignty, heterosexuality and Europe. In *Subversions of International Order: Studies in the Political Anthropology of Culture,* pp. 273–319. Albany: South. Univ. NY Press
Bourdieu P, Passeron J-C. 1977. *Reproduction in Education, Society and Culture.* Beverly Hills, CA: Sage
Brague R. 1992. *Europe, La Voie Romaine.* Paris: Criterion
Brown P. 1996. *The Rise of Western Christendom.* Oxford: Blackwell
Brubaker R. 1992. *Citizenship and Nationhood in France and Germany.* Cambridge, MA: Harvard Univ. Press
Castiglione B. 1976. (1578). *The Book of the Courtier.* Transl. G Bull. Harmondsworth: Penguin
Chapman M. 1995. Patronage, social anthropology and Europe. See MacDonald 1995, pp. 2–8
Chock P. 1987. The irony of stereotypes: toward an anthropology of ethnicity. *Cult. Anthropol.* 2:347–68
Cole J, Wolf ER. 1974. *The Hidden Frontier.* London/New York: Academic
Costa J. 1993. The periphery of pleasure or pain: consumer culture in the EC Mediterranean of 1992. See Wilson & Smith 1993, pp. 81–98
Crick M. 1989. Representations of international tourism in the social sciences: sun, sex, sights, savings and servility. *Annu. Rev. Anthropol.* 18:307–44
Curtis B. 1993. Gazza's tears: football, masculinity and playing away in watching Europe. See Bechdoff et al 1993, pp. 79–96
Demetz J-M. 1996. Drogue: Le Doute N'erlandais. *L'Express* June:82–84

de Swaan A. 1995. *The Language Constellation of the European Union. A Perspective from the Political Sociology of Language.* Amsterdam: Amsterdam Sch. Soc. Sci.

Donnan H, Wilson T. 1994. An anthropology of frontiers. In *Border Approaches: Anthropological Perspectives on Frontiers,* ed. H Donnan, T Wilson. Lanham, MD: Univ. Press. Am.

Eco U. 1995. *The Search for the Perfect European Language.* Oxford: Blackwell

Elias N. 1978. *The Civilizing Process: The History of Manners, Sociogenetic and Psychogenetic Investigations.* Oxford: Blackwell

Erikson T. 1993. *Ethnicity and Nationalism. Anthropological Perspectives.* London: Pluto

Fanelli F. 1993. Our museums are Italy's General Motors. *Art Newsp.* 33:6–7

Fernandez J. 1986. The mission of metaphor in expressive culture. In *Persuasions and Performances, The Play of Tropes in Culture,* ed. J Fernandez, pp. 28–72. Bloomington: Indiana Univ. Press

Fontana J. 1995. *The Distorted Past: A Re-Interpretation of Europe.* Oxford: Blackwell

Foucault M. 1980. *The History of Sexuality: An Introduction.* New York: Vintage

Freeman S. 1973. Introduction to studies in rural European social organization. *Am. Anthropol.* 75:743–50

Fuss D. 1995. *Identification Papers.* New York: Routledge

Gal S. 1991. Bartók's funeral: representations of Europe in Hungarian political rhetoric. *Am. Ethnol.* 18(3):440–58

Garel-Jones T. 1996. Time to call the German's bluff. Inflation is the demon Europeans ought to fear, which means Britain must ensure the Euro works. *Daily Telegr.,* Jan. 7, p. 20

Gellner E. 1983. *Nations and Nationalism: New Perspectives on the Past.* Ithaca: Cornell Univ. Press

Geyer M. 1993. Resistance as ongoing project: visions of order, obligations to strangers, struggles for civil society. *J. Mod. Hist.* 64:S241-47

Giordano M. 1987. The 'wine war' between France and Italy: ethno-anthropological aspects of the European community. *Sociol. Rural.* 27:56–66

Goody J. 1973. *Bridewealth and Dowry in Africa and Eurasia.* Cambridge: Cambridge Univ. Press

Goody J. 1983. *The Development of the Family and Marriage in Europe.* Cambridge: Cambridge Univ. Press

Goody J. 1990. *The Oriental, the Ancient and the Primitive: Systems of Marriage and the Family in the Pre-Industrial Societies of Eurasia.* Cambridge: Cambridge Univ. Press

Goux J-J. 1990. *Symbolic Economie after Marx and Freud.* Ithaca: Cornell Univ. Press

Grillo RD, ed. 1980. *"Nation" and "State" in Europe: Anthropological Perspectives.* New York: Academic

Gullick C. 1993. Cultural values and European financial institutions. See Wilson & Smith 1993, pp. 203–21

Habermas J. 1987. *The Philosophical Discourse of Modernity.* Oxford: Oxford Univ. Press

Hajnal J. 1965. European marriage patterns in perspective. In *Population in History: Essays in Historical Demography,* ed. DV Glass, DEC Eversley, pp. 101–47. London: Arnold

Harlig J, Csaba P, eds. 1995. *When East Meets West: Sociolinguistics in the Former Socialist Bloc.* New York: Mouton de Gruyter

Hay D. 1957. *Europe: The Emergence of an Idea.* New York: Harper & Row

Hayden R. 1996. Imagined communities and real victims: self-determination and ethnic cleansing in Yugoslavia. *Am. Ethnol.* 23(4):783–801

Herzfeld M. 1987. *Anthropology Through the Looking-Glass: Critical Ethnography in the Margins of Europe.* Cambridge: Cambridge Univ. Press

Herzfeld M. 1992. *The Social Production of Indifference: The Symbolic Roots of Bureaucracy in Western Europe.* Oxford: Berg

Herzfeld M. 1997. *Cultural Intimacy. Social Poetics in the Nation State.* New York: Routledge

Hobsbawm E. 1990. *Nations and Nationalism since 1780: Programme, Myth, Reality.* Cambridge: Cambridge Univ. Press

Hofer T. 1994. *Hungarians Between "East" and "West," National Myths and Symbols.* Budapest: Mus. Ethnogr.

Huarte J. 1976. (1575). *Examen de Ingenios Para Las Ciencas.* Madrid: Ed. Nac.

Huseby-Darvas E. 1987. Elderly women in a Hungarian village: childlessness, generativity and social control. *J. Cross-Cult. Gerontol.* 2:15–42

Im Hof U. 1994. *The Enlightenment.* Oxford: Blackwell

Jaffe A. 1993. Farming styles and intermediate structures in the wake of 1992. See Wilson & Smith 1993, pp. 61–80

Johnson R. 1993. Towards a cultural theory of the nation. An English-Dutch dialogue. In

Images of the Nation. Different Meanings of Dutchness, 1870–1940, ed. A Galema, B Henkes, H te Velde, pp. 159–217. Amsterdam: Ed. Rodolphi

Judt T. 1996. Europe: the grand illusion. *NY Rev. Books* 43(12):6–9

Jurjus A. 1993. Farming styles and intermediate structures in the wake of 1992. See Wilson & Smith 1993, pp. 99–122

Kantorowicz E. 1957. *The King's Two Bodies. A Study in Medieval Political Theology.* Princeton, NJ: Princeton Univ. Press

Kaschuba W. 1994. Everyday culture. In *Aspects of European Cultural Diversity*, pp. 189–264. London: Open Univ.

King A, ed. 1991. *Culture, Globalization and the World System. Contemporary Conditions for the Representation of Identity.* London: Macmillan

Lepsius MR. 1988a. Die Europaïsche Gemeinschaft und die Zukunft des Nationalstaates. Demokratie in Deutschland: Soziologisch-historische Konstellationsanalysen. In *Interessen, Ideen und Institutionen*, ed. MR Lepsius, pp. 249–64. Göttingen: Vanderhoeck & Ruprecht

Lepsius MR. 1988b. Die Europaïsche Gemeinschaft und die Zukunft des Nationalstaate oder Nationalitätenstaat als Modell für die Weiterentwicklung der Europäischen Gemeinschaft. Demokratie in Deutschland: Soziologisch-historische Konstellationsanalysen. In *Interessen, Ideen und Institutionen*, ed. MR Lepsius, pp. 265–85. Göttingen: Vanderhoeck & Ruprecht

LiPuma E, Meltzoff SK. 1989. Toward a theory of culture and class: an Iberian example. *Am. Ethnol.* 16(2):313–34

Løfgren O. 1989. The nationalization of culture. *Ethnol. Eur: J. Eur. Ethnol.* 19:5–25

MacDonald M. 1993. The construction of difference: an anthropological approach to stereotypes. In *Inside European Identities*, ed. S McDonald, pp. 219–36. Providence/Oxford: Berg

MacDonald M, ed. 1995. *Towards an Anthropology of the European Union.* Brussels: Eur. Comm.

MacDonald M. 1996. 'Unity in diversity': some tensions in the construction of Europe. *Soc. Anthropol.* 4:47–60

Maier C. 1975. *Recasting Bourgeois Europe: Stabilizing in France, Germany and Italy in the Decade after World War One.* Princeton, NJ: Princeton Univ. Press

McCannell D. 1976. *The Tourist.* London: Macmillan

McDonough G. 1993. The face behind the door: European integration, immigration and identity. See Wilson & Smith 1993, pp. 143–65

Mollat du Jourdin M. 1993. *Europe and the Sea.* Oxford: Blackwell

Moore SF. 1987. Explaining the present: theoretical dilemmas in processual ethnography. *Am. Ethnol.* 14(4):727–51

Mosse G. 1985. *Nationalism and Sexuality.* New York: Basic Books

Mosser F. 1994. Monuments historiques et tourisme culturel. Quel projet pour quels publics? *Cah. Espace* 37:23–27

O'Dowd L, Wilson T, eds. 1996. *Borders, Nations and States. Frontiers of Sovereignty in the New Europe.* Aldershot: Avebury

Pina-Cabral J. 1992. The primary social unit in Mediterranean and Atlantic Europe. *J. Mediterr. Stud.* 2(1):25–41

Pitt-Rivers J. 1954. *The People of the Sierra.* Chicago: Univ. Chicago Press

Ranum O. 1975. *National Consciousness, History and Political Culture in Early Modern Europe.* Baltimore: Johns Hopkins Univ. Press

Richards G, ed. 1996. *Cultural Tourism in Europe.* Oxford: CAB Int.

Said E. 1978. *Orientalism.* New York: Basic Books

Schneider J, Schneider P. 1976. *Culture and Political Economy in Western Sicily.* New York: Academic

Schulze H. 1996. *States, Nations and Nationalism from the Middle Ages to The Present.* Oxford: Blackwell

Segal H. 1991. "The European." Allegories of racial purity. *Anthropol. Today* 7(5):7–9

Segalen M. 1986. *Historical Anthropology of the Family.* Cambridge: Cambridge Univ.

Segalen M, Gullestad M, eds. 1995. *La Famille en Europe: Parenté et Perpétuation Familiale.* Paris: Découverte

Shore C. 1993. Inventing the people's Europe: critical approaches to European community cultural policy. *Man* 28:779–800

Shore C. 1995. Usurpers or pioneers? EC bureaucrats and the question of European consciousness. In *Questions of Consciousness*, ed. AP Cohen, N Rapport, pp. 217–36. New York: Routledge

Shore C, Black A. 1992. The European community and the construction of Europe. *Anthropol. Today* 8(3):10–11

Shutes M. 1991. Kerry farmers and the European community: capital transitions in a rural Irish parish. *Irish J. Sociol.* 1:1–17

Shutes M. 1993. Rural communities without family farms? Family dairy farming in the post-1993 EC. See Wilson & Smith 1993, pp. 100–23

Smith V. 1989. *Hosts and Guests: The Anthropology of Tourism.* Oxford: Blackwell

Strathern M. 1992. *Reproducing the Future: Essays on Anthropology, Kinship and the New Reproductive Technologies.* New York: Routledge

Tilly C. 1990. *Coercion, Capital and European States AD 1990–1992.* Oxford: Blackwell

Tilly C. 1993. *European Revolutions, 1492–1992.* Oxford: Blackwell

Varenne H. 1993. The question of European nationalism. See Wilson & Smith 1993, pp. 223–40

Verdery K. 1996. *What Was Socialism and What Comes Next?* Princeton, NJ: Princeton Univ. Press

Willis P. 1977. *Learning to Labor: How Working Class Kids Get Working Class Jobs.* New York: Columbia Univ. Press

Wilson T. 1989. Large farms, local politics and the international arena: the Irish tax dispute of 1979. *Hum. Organ.* 48(1):60–70

Wilson T. 1993a. An anthropology of the European community. See Wilson & Smith 1993, pp. 1–24

Wilson T. 1993b. Frontiers go but boundaries remain: the Irish border as a cultural divide. See Wilson & Smith 1993, pp. 167–88

Wilson T. 1995. The anthropology of the European Union. *ECSA Newsl.* 8:12–15

Wilson T. 1996. Sovereignty, identity and borders: political anthropology and European integration. In *Borders, Nations and States: Frontiers of Sovereignty in the New Europe,* ed. L O'Dowd, T Wilson, pp. 199–219. Aldershot: Avebury

Wilson T, Smith ME, eds. 1993. *Cultural Change and the New Europe: Perspectives on the European Community.* Boulder: Westview

Wolf E. 1982. *Europe and the People Without History.* Berkeley: Univ. Calif. Press

Wright S, ed. 1994. *Anthropology of Organizations.* London/New York: Routledge

Zabusky S. 1995. *Launching Europe: An Ethnography of European Cooperation in Space Science.* Princeton, NJ: Princeton Univ. Press

Zolberg A. 1983. The formation of new states as a refugee-generating process. *Ann. Am. Acad. Polit. Soc. Sci.* 467:24–38

Annu. Rev. Anthropol. 1997. 26:515–40

GENETIC DIVERSITY IN HOMINOID PRIMATES

M. Ruvolo

Department of Anthropology, Harvard University, Cambridge, Massachusetts 02138;
e-mail: ruvolo@fas.harvard.edu

KEY WORDS: humans, primates, molecular evolution, population genetics, hominoids

ABSTRACT

Humans are only one of the species produced by the hominoid evolutionary radiation. Common and pygmy chimpanzees (our closest relatives), gorillas, orangutans, and the lesser apes also belong to this group. In humans, patterns of genetic variation are becoming increasingly better characterized by modern molecular methods. Understanding human variation in an evolutionary context, however, requires comparison of human patterns with those of other hominoids, to reveal features shared among hominoids and those unique to humans. Genetic variation among chimpanzees, gorillas, and orangutans is beginning to be characterized, so that comparisons are now possible.

From genetic data, several different kinds of information can be reconstructed, including the evolutionary relatedness of subspecies and populations, time estimates for evolutionary divergences, past population dynamics, extent of gene flow over geographical landscapes, and group social structure. Knowledge of hominoid genetic variation is also relevant to applied fields such as primate conservation and medicine.

INTRODUCTION

Why Study Genetic Diversity?

Biological anthropologists seek to understand how humans have evolved, and reconstructing the past is therefore a major component of our discipline. Among the many types of evidence available for reconstructing the past is ge-

515

netic evidence. Studying DNA from fossils is one way to understand human history, but this approach has been plagued by the often-poor quality of DNA recovered from fossil material. While advances in biochemical methods will increasingly help to circumvent this and other problems with ancient DNA studies, there is another route to studying the past using genetic evidence. This alternative approach uses patterns of genetic diversity among living organisms to reveal aspects of their evolution.

Genetic evidence can provide insights into several different aspects of evolutionary history. We can infer the patterns of relatedness among species, sub-species, and populations—who is related to whom? From the same data, we can estimate when species, subspecies, and populations diverged from each other—when did two groups last share a common ancestor? By examining the patterning of within-group and between-group genetic differences, we can gauge whether populations overlap to a large degree in genetic composition or whether they are relatively differentiated from each another. Although this type of "static" observation does not inform us about evolutionary history directly, it can be used in conjunction with other types of genetic analyses to help reconstruct the past. In addition, when populations expand or contract in size, these events leave traces in the genetic record, allowing estimation of when an event took place and by what factor the population changed in size. Genetic data can also be used to examine aspects of social structure; for example, whether there is sex-biased transfer between groups or whether affiliative associations in primate social groups are influenced by genetic relatedness. Last, we can use genetic data to investigate how morphological variation correlates with genetic variation to see how phenotypic (outwardly detectable) and genotypic traits are correlated.

What Are the Hominoids and Why Study Them?

We can gain insight into human history by widening our view to include the study of our closest primate relatives. In addition to humans (*Homo sapiens*), the living hominoids include large-bodied apes: two species of chimpanzees, the pygmy chimpanzee or bonobo (*Pan paniscus*) and the common chimpanzee (*Pan troglodytes*), the gorilla (*Gorilla gorilla*), and the orangutan (*Pongo pygmaeus*); and many species of small-bodied apes, commonly known as gibbons (genus *Hylobates*). Evolutionary relationships among hominoids have been established using genetic evidence of several different types, and this knowledge provides a backdrop for inferring aspects of human evolution. Humans are most closely related to chimpanzees, with gorillas, orangutans, and gibbons as increasingly more evolutionarily distant cousins to the group (or clade) containing humans and chimpanzees (Caccone & Powell 1989, Ruvolo

1997). In this review, I focus on the large-bodied hominoids because humans belong to this clade; almost nothing is known about the genetic diversity of small-bodied hominoids.

Because of these evolutionary relationships, special attention has been paid recently to the attributes of chimpanzees particularly and of gorillas in the attempt to reconstruct features of early human ancestors. Some degree of phylogenetic continuity is expected, i.e. some of the traits we have in common with other living hominoids exist today because we and they have inherited them from a common ancestor. Thus shared ancestry with nonhuman hominoids is an explanation for some, but obviously not all, human traits. When it was discovered that chimpanzees make and use tools (Goodall 1970), and some chimpanzee mothers instruct infants in stone tool use (Boesch 1991), this dramatically changed our views of human tool use and chimpanzee "culture" (Wrangham et al 1994). Analogously, the study of nonhuman hominoid genetic patterns can potentially revise our views of human evolution inferred from genetic evidence.

Studying nonhuman hominoids provides us with a comparative perspective for judging whether our species is like or unlike these other primates, thus helping to discover whether we are unusual in our genetic patterning or evolutionary history. The comparative approach is powerful because it gives us an evolutionary gauge for assessing human uniqueness. It is used widely throughout biological anthropology generally, which explains why primate studies are such an active research area within the subdiscipline.

OVERVIEW OF HOMINOID GENETIC DIVERSITY

Within-Group and Between-Group Diversity

A fundamental observation about human genetic diversity is that most of the variation within our species as a whole is contained within single populations (Lewontin 1972). If some catastrophic event were to occur so that only Norwegians, for example, were left on the face of the earth, close to 86% of total human genetic variation would still be preserved by them. The next largest source of variation occurs between populations within each of the so-called human races. To extend the example, if Norwegians, Greeks, Estonians, and the other populations, which make up the so-called "Caucasian race," were the only survivors, another 8% of human variation would be preserved, for a total of 94%. By far the smallest component of human variation is that which distinguishes members of difference races, approximately 6%. If we visualize human genetic variation in a Venn diagram, each circle representing a single human population would be almost as large as the circle for our entire species, and circles from different human populations (whatever their "racial" classification) would mainly overlap. This observation is the primary reason why in a genetic sense the concept of race is considered inapplicable to humans (Lewontin 1995). Defined biologically, races are "incipient species," or "kinds of animals that show no (or only slight) structural differences, although clearly separable by biological characters" (Mayr 1970). Most human genetic variation occurs within local populations, not between anthropologically defined ethnic groups or between so-called races.

The above observation was originally made using genetic information from blood groups, serum proteins, and red blood cell enzymes, all of which are proteins coded by nuclear DNA. Does this result hold generally for other regions of the human genome (the entire complement of genetic information), such as those not coding for proteins? The latest DNA evidence suggests that it does. Microsatellite loci are highly variable regions of the genome consisting of short DNA sequences (2–6 basepairs long) repeated many times in tandem. For example, the two basepair segment CA may be repeated from ten to several hundred times at a particular place (locus) on a human chromosome. Microsatellite loci are typically so variable that at any given locus every person is likely to be a heterozygote—possessing two different gene versions (alleles); for example, having a maternally inherited allele with 30 CA repeats and a paternally inherited one with 26 repeats. Microsatellite loci do not code for protein and have no known function. Because they apparently do not influence the organism's phenotype, natural selection does not act on them, and they evolve neutrally. In that sense, they could potentially portray a different picture of human genetic diversity, one free of selective effects. To the extent that human populations have been studied by microsatellite variation, the pattern observed originally with proteins holds: Most genetic variation is contained within populations, not within continental human groups or the so-called races (Barbujani et al 1997, Bowcock et al 1994).

Generally, it is difficult to find genetic markers that exist in one human population and not in others. Instead, human populations tend to differ in having varying proportions of the same allelic versions of genes; that is, most DNA variants are globally widespread and not unique to individual populations (Barbujani et al 1997, Bowcock et al 1994, Deka et al 1995). Not only are these DNA variants shared globally, but they show a pattern of clinal variation across all continents (Cavalli-Sforza et al 1994). This lack of genetic discontinuity is another reason why the concept of human races is not supported at the genetic level (Barbujani et al 1997). It is possible, by examining many genes, to assemble a panel of loci that in combination have a high probability of differentiating human populations, ethnic groups, or "races" (Bowcock et al 1994, Deka et al 1995, Shriver et al 1997). But given enough loci, any two human groups can be distinguished, even down to the level of the matriline or the individual, so this is not the critical issue for deciding whether human races can be defined genetically. The significant point is that on a locus-by-locus basis, sharp discontinuities in genetic variation are generally not observed, and when they do exist, zones of genetic discontinuity do not usually coincide with zones of morphological or continental discontinuity (Barbujani et al 1997). Discontinuities at the phenotypic level that have been used to define human races must, by implication, be due to variation at only a few loci.

Most other large-bodied hominoids are unlike humans in that they have recognizable subspecies. Subspecies are defined as groups of phenotypically similar populations living in distinct geographic parts of the species range that differ in diagnostic morphological traits (Mayr 1970). In Africa, there are three subspecies of common chimpanzees: *Pan troglodytes schweinfurthii* (the eastern long-haired variety), *P. troglodytes verus* (western masked or pale-faced), and *P. troglodytes troglodytes* (central black-faced); and three commonly recognized gorilla subspecies: *Gorilla gorilla gorilla* (western lowland), *G. gorilla beringei* (mountain), and *G. gorilla graueri* (eastern lowland). Two orangutan subspecies inhabit Asia: *Pongo pygmaeus pygmaeus* (Bornean), and *P. pygmaeus abelii* (Sumatran). Only the bonobo *Pan paniscus* and *Homo sapiens* are monotypic.

To date, hominoid species have been genetically surveyed primarily in their mitochondrial DNA (mtDNA). This type of DNA, located outside the cell's nucleus in organelles known as mitochondria, is almost exclusively maternally transmitted. mtDNA undergoes a relatively great amount of change over evolutionary time (it evolves rapidly), and this is an advantage for studying closely related taxa (defined groups of organisms) such as individuals, subspecies, and species, because they usually show mtDNA differences. Nuclear DNA, which is organized in chromosomes inside the cell's nucleus and is inherited from both parents, is more slowly evolving, and it frequently shows little or no difference among closely related taxa. Microsatellite loci discussed above are unusual nuclear loci in this regard.

Based on the number of mitochondrial haplotypes (different genetic types) in chimpanzees (Morin et al 1994), subspecies contain in the range of 21–47% of the total species diversity (M Ruvolo, unpublished results). This overlaps with the amount of genetic diversity contained within a single population: The Gombe eastern chimpanzee community (Morin et al 1994) contains 28% of the species diversity (M Ruvolo, unpublished results). Shifting the comparative basis to the subspecies level, the Gombe population (19 individuals) contains 60% of the subspecific mitochondrial variation (Morin et al 1994; M Ruvolo, unpublished results). However, an extensive survey of 281 eastern chimpanzees from 19 forests localities found an even greater proportion of subspecific variation—80–90%—contained within populations (Goldberg 1996, Goldberg & Ruvolo 1997b). Bonobos have not been studied sufficiently to make comparable diversity estimates.

Gorilla subspecies differ greatly in the total proportion of genetic diversity they contain: Western lowland gorillas have 62%, eastern lowland gorillas 23%, and mountain gorillas only 15% (Garner & Ryder 1996; M Ruvolo, unpublished results). The figure for mountain gorillas may be low because of population reduction due to poaching and habitat destruction; evidence of inbreeding supports this view (Garner & Ryder 1996). The best-sampled gorilla populations are from this subspecies; on average they contain 10% of the total species genetic diversity (Garner & Ryder 1996; M Ruvolo, unpublished results), although this is unlikely to be representative of the other gorilla subspecies.

For orangutans, only one study exists (Lu et al 1996) from which comparable estimates can be made. Using data from the two Bornean populations represented by more than 10 individuals each, orangutan populations contain 50 and 35% of the total species diversity based, respectively, on DNA fingerprint (nuclear) variation and number of mitochondrial haplotypes (M Ruvolo, unpublished observations). As a fraction of the diversity within the Bornean subspecies alone, local populations contain 60 and 69% of the nuclear and mitochondrial diversity respectively (M Ruvolo, unpublished observations). It must be emphasized that these are rough estimates based on limited data. Yet the preliminary picture of orangutan genetic diversity is very different from that found in humans, presumably due to the greater age of the orangutan species and subspecies (see discussion below) and possibly also to social system differences that do not promote as extensive a gene flow in orangutans as in humans.

Human genetic diversity is apportioned in a different manner to that observed in the other hominoid species (Figure 1). Given that humans do not have a subspecies structure, this is not unexpected. The human species pattern most resembles that in subspecies of other hominoids (Figure 1), and it is particularly like that of eastern common chimpanzees (Goldberg 1996, Goldberg & Ruvolo 1997b). What would be most informative from a comparative perspective would be to know the patterning of genetic diversity within bonobos because, like humans, they are a species without subspecies. If humans and bonobos were to share the same genetic structuring, one could then begin to view the human pattern simply as that characteristic of monotypic species; of course, data from other monotypic species would be needed to test this point further. If humans and bonobos were different, we would have to reconsider how these different patterns could have arisen. In particular, finding a smaller proportion of species variation within bonobo populations would be surprising given their limited geographic range. Unfortunately, genetic data on bonobo variation are not yet available.

Genetic Diversity within Populations as percentage of total species diversity

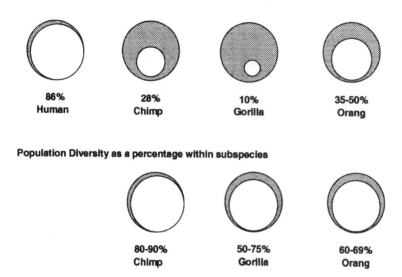

| 86% | 28% | 10% | 35-50% |
| Human | Chimp | Gorilla | Orang |

Population Diversity as a percentage within subspecies

| 80-90% | 50-75% | 60-69% |
| Chimp | Gorilla | Orang |

Figure 1 Hominoid genetic variation within single populations (*white circles*) is expressed as part of total species genetic diversity (*shaded circles, top*) and of subspecies diversity (*shaded circles, below*). Population and subspecies data illustrated are from eastern chimpanzees (Goldberg 1996, Morin et al 1994, T Goldberg & Ruvolo 1997b), Bornean orangutans (Lu et al 1996), and mountain gorillas (Garner & Ryder 1996); the mountain gorilla pattern is likely to be unrepresentative of other gorilla subspecies (see text). Human data are from Lewontin 1972.

One comparative study of hominoids claimed that humans are more variable than apes in protein variability but less variable than apes at the DNA level (Takahata 1993). However, these conclusions were based on a protein electrophoretic study (King & Wilson 1975) that used a nonrepresentative sample of common chimpanzees: Of the 35 protein loci compared (Takahata 1993), 66% were intracellular proteins surveyed in only one colony of captive chimpanzees, and these animals showed evidence of reduced genetic variability and/or inbreeding from the highly variable transferrin locus (King 1973). Another study of hominoid protein variability also found relatively low genetic variability in apes compared with humans (Bruce & Ayala 1979). Only a limited number of chimpanzees and gorillas were surveyed, however, and these were of unknown subspecies designations (Bruce & Ayala 1979), suggesting, as before, that these samples of individuals were not representative of the full species' genetic variability. The comparative data on hominoid within-species genetic variability is limited in that subspecies have not often been surveyed. Currently available evidence gives no indication that proteins and/or nuclear genes exhibit a different pattern of genetic variation from that shown by mitochondrial genes.

Evolutionary Relatedness and Divergence Times

Observations on the apportionment of genetic diversity are static and do not provide a dynamic picture of hominoid evolution over time. For the human pattern, there are two basically different ways to explain how it arose. One explanation is that large genetic differences among human populations may have existed a long time ago, built up while populations were genetically isolated; subsequently, as the human species grew larger, populations came into genetic contact and homogenization took place over time through the spread and interbreeding of people (gene flow). Thus many genetic features that previously distinguished human populations became widespread throughout the species and were no longer unique to particular groups. Alternatively, many genetic features distinguishing human populations may have never existed. The apparent genetic similarity among all humans might be due instead to our recent common ancestry. There has not been enough time for human groups to have accumulated many unique mutations differentiating populations.

Deciding between these alternative explanations can be aided by applying the concept of the "molecular clock" (Sarich & Wilson 1967, Zuckerkandl & Pauling 1962). The idea is that most molecules exhibit a constant rate of change over evolutionary time in all evolutionary lineages (Figure 2), and it is supported by evidence from amino acid sequences, immunological data, and DNA sequences. This observation was revolutionary because it provided a tool—the molecular clock—for estimating when evolutionary events had happened. Essentially, genetic difference (or genetic distance) between two species can be converted into the time since their last common ancestor, when rates of molecular change are reasonably constant. [Not all molecules exhibit rate constancy, but it is easy to test whether they do (Sarich & Wilson 1967).] [For a discussion of molecular clock calibration and its linearity with astronomical time, see Ruvolo (1995) and references therein.] In recent years, several refinements and/or limitations of the molecular clock hypothesis have been recognized (Britten 1986, Goodman 1996, Li et al 1996) that have helped in applying it more effectively. From the same type of data (genetic distances) used to support the molecular clock, evolutionary relationships among organisms can be reconstructed, because groups with a more recent common ancestor show less genetic distance than those with a more ancient ancestor. These evolutionary relationships can be summarized in the form of a phylogenetic

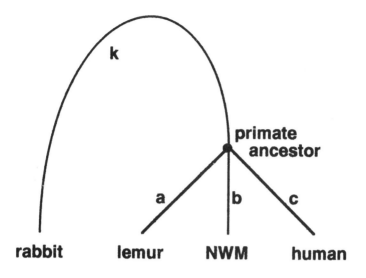

$$\text{G1 (rabbit / lemur)} = k + a$$
$$\text{G2 (rabbit / NWM)} = k + b$$
$$\text{G3 (rabbit / human)} = k + c$$

If G1 = G2 = G3, then a = b = c

If the primate ancestor lived t years ago, the rate of molecular change is
$$a\,/\,t = b\,/\,t = c\,/\,t$$
which is constant among lineages.

Figure 2   Testing for molecular rate constancy as evidence for the molecular clock. Amounts of genetic difference (or distance) between the rabbit and living species of primates [lemur, New World monkey (NWM), human] are G1, G2, G3, respectively. Each of these can be expressed as the sum of the genetic distance from rabbit to the common primate ancestor and the genetic distance from that ancestor to each primate species. If amounts of genetic distance between pairs of living species are equal (G1=G2=G3), then genetic distances from each primate species to the common ancestor are equal (a=b=c). Because these genetic differences (a, b, c) accumulated over the same period, the rate of molecular evolutionary change is constant over time in the three primate lineages. This "relative rate test" (Sarich & Wilson 1967) is capable of revealing nonconstant rates. Molecules exhibiting constant rates can have their molecular clocks calibrated using paleontological or archaeological data. A calibrated molecular clock can be used to estimate divergence times among species, subspecies, or populations.

tree. This is by no means the only method for reconstructing evolutionary trees, but it is one of several main methods generally used (Swofford et al 1996).

Current genetic evidence on humans supports the hypothesis that the common genetic ancestor of modern humans arose relatively recently, approximately 150,000–400,000 years ago (Cann et al 1987, Dorit et al 1995, Goldstein et al 1995, Hammer 1995, Hasegawa & Horai 1991, Horai et al 1995, Ruvolo et al 1993, Tishkoff et al 1996, Vigilant et al 1991, Whitfield et al 1995) and probably in Africa. Recency of the common ancestor is inferred because living humans are distinguished by very little genetic difference among them, based on molecules or genes that exhibit molecular rate constancy. This differs from the observation that human populations overlap considerably in genetic make-up, because each population could contain individuals genetically very different from one another, yet still sharing much of its diversity with other populations, if those maximally different genetic types are widespread. Although not every genetic dataset supports a recent origin (Bailey et al 1992, Maeda et al 1983, Xiong et al 1991), unanimous support is not expected under any of the alternative hypotheses of modern human origins (Ruvolo 1996). What is crucial for testing alternative hypotheses is the overall pattern of evidence from independent genetic systems, and several independent data sets from nuclear, Y-chromosomal, and mitochondrial genes support a recent origin (Ruvolo 1996). Recently, a challenge has been raised to the mtDNA evidence: mtDNA is not exclusively maternally inherited, although it is often assumed to be, and this could possibly bias inferences about human evolution (Ankel-Simons & Cummins 1996). In mice, paternal mtDNA has been detected in offspring at a frequency of one in every 10,000 copies (Gyllensten et al 1991), and individuals having a heterogeneous pool of more than one type of mtDNA are known as heteroplasmic. Could paternal leakage of mtDNA, if it exists at comparable levels in humans, change the interpretations of the mitochondrial genetic evidence for human evolution? While not impossible, this is very unlikely. Imagine the most divergent human mtDNA type, that is, the one that is most different in its DNA sequence from those of all other humans. This maximal amount of DNA sequence difference among mitochondrial types, whether large or small, is translated via molecular clock calculations into an amount of time when all humans last shared a genetic ancestor; therefore, keeping track of the most divergent mtDNA type is important for drawing inferences about human ancestry. Given its relatively great age (i.e., DNA sequence divergence), the most divergent mtDNA type probably occurs in more than one female. For paternal mtDNA leakage artifactually to reduce the age of the common genetic ancestor (thereby causing anthropologists to accept an erroneously recent origin for modern humans), all the females carrying this most divergent mtDNA type would have to mate with males having less divergent mtDNA types, and paternal leakage of mtDNA would have to occur in each case. However, simple leakage of paternal mtDNA is not sufficient; in each case, the paternal mtDNA would have to be passed on to subsequent generations exclusively, in preference to the maternal mtDNA. Replacement of one human mtDNA type by another after both co-occur heteroplasmically in a generation has been documented as a rare event (Parsons et al 1997). However the logic of this example (in order to lead to an inaccurately recent date) requires that every heteroplasmic mtDNA pool created by paternal leakage and passed on to subsequent generations must be inherited so that every grandchild (or great-grandchild, etc) receives only the paternal (less divergent, hence younger) mtDNA type, and all copies of the more ancient and more abundant (by a factor of 10^4) maternal mtDNA type are erased. The likelihood that paternal mtDNA leakage could produce a spuriously recent date for the common human mitochondrial ancestor is therefore vanishingly small, and the current interpretation of the mitochondrial evidence for modern human origins does not warrant revision because of it (contra Ankel-Simons & Cummins 1996).

Establishing place of origin for modern humans has not been straightforward from the genetic data (Hedges et al 1992, Maddison 1991, Maddison et al 1992, Templeton 1992). However, newer types of genetic analyses showing that all non-African genetic types form only a small subsample of African genetic types is compelling evidence for an African origin; these involve both mitochondrial (Penny et al 1995) and nuclear DNA data (Tishkoff et al 1996).

That early hominids (i.e. humans and their direct ancestors), *Ardipithecus, Australopithecus,* and early members of the genus *Homo,* including *Homo erectus,* are first known in Africa is undisputed, as is the fact that *Homo erectus* was the first hominid to spread out of Africa, roughly 1.8 mya. (This date for *Homo erectus*'s emergence out of Africa is almost twice as old as believed just a few years ago because of recently discovered fossils and redating of earlier finds.) Controversy centers on the fate of the non-African *H. erectus* populations: Did they go extinct? Are living humans their direct descendants? The multiregional model hypothesizes that *H. erectus* populations living in several different places in the Old World each gave rise to *Homo sapiens* and that genetic cohesion among early *H. sapiens* was maintained by gene flow (Frayer et al 1993). The extent of gene flow required for this model has not been specified, and this is problematic (Nei 1995). Under this model, the last common ancestor of modern humans was relatively ancient, close to 2 my old, before the time when some *Homo erectus* populations left Africa. An alternative hypothesis, the out-of-Africa or rapid replacement model, envisions that only one population of *H. erectus,* living in Africa, made the transition to *Homo sa-*

piens. Some of these newly evolved *Homo sapiens* then spread out of Africa and replaced the Old World *H. erectus* populations, causing their extinction. Under this model, our last common ancestor arose relatively recently in Africa (Aiello 1993, Stringer & Andrews 1988). A third model which hypothesizes hybridization between *H. erectus* and *H. sapiens* resembles the multiregional model in that the last common ancestor of modern humans would also have been relatively ancient.

The genetic data support the out-of-Africa model for modern human origins, yet it is important to bear in mind what kind of evidence could overturn this hypothesis. Finding a human population containing genetic types very different (genetically distant) from all those that have already been characterized could lead to the acceptance of a multiregional model. It has been argued that finding someone who is genetically very different from all previously studied humans is not likely, given how human variation is apportioned within populations (Ruvolo 1996). Yet the 14% of human diversity not found within individual human populations (Lewontin 1972) needs to be studied more extensively for clues to human evolutionary history, as proposed in the Human Genome Diversity Project (see Maybury-Lewis 1996). Human genetic variation in Africa appears to be greater than in other parts of the world (Cann et al 1987, Tishkoff et al 1996, Vigilant et al 1991), and this has been viewed as evidence for an African origin (Stoneking 1993). Greater African diversity is not observed with all nuclear loci, but loci not showing this pattern were for the most part originally chosen for their variability among Europeans and are thus likely to be biased against detecting variation in non-Europeans (Jorde et al 1995, Mountain & Cavalli-Sforza 1994). Given the great degree of human genetic variation within sub-Saharan Africa, more research should be focused on this geographic area. The surprising recent discovery of greater mitochondrial DNA diversity within the east African Turkana than within the rest of the world combined (Watson 1996) underscores the need to study African genetic diversity more thoroughly.

Sorting out the relatedness of human populations has also involved controversy. African populations are most distinct from non-African populations, but relatedness among non-African populations is in dispute (Cavalli-Sforza et al 1988, 1994; Nei & Roychoudhury 1993). This issue is undoubtedly complicated by the fact that the tree of human population relatedness (if we could only reconstruct it) must contain many anastomosing branches because human populations are not reproductively isolated.

The extent of human variation is low, and this can best be appreciated by comparing humans with other hominoids (Figure 3). When amounts of maximum within-species genetic difference are compared for a mitochondrial protein-coding gene, humans have the smallest degree of genetic difference

(Ruvolo et al 1994). Even the bonobo, the most poorly genetically surveyed species among the large-bodied hominoids and known from only a limited number of individuals, shows greater within-species genetic difference than found in the human species. Because amounts of genetic difference translate into time via the molecular clock, all other things being equal, this shows on a comparative scale that living humans have a more recent common ancestor than do other living hominoid species.

Looking at the hominoid evolutionary tree in broad perspective, another surprising feature concerns the relative degree of genetic difference distinguishing other species and subspecies. It is widely recognized that the chimpanzees *Pan troglodytes* and *P. paniscus* are two distinct species, differing noticeably in their morphology (especially body proportions) and in their social and sexual behavior. In contrast, gorillas have traditionally been seen as one species, as have orangutans. Yet the amount of genetic difference between gorilla subspecies and between orangutan subspecies is greater than that found between species of chimpanzees. This suggests a decoupling between genetic distance on the one hand, and morphological, behavioral, and ecological features on the other.

Within gorillas, the western lowland subspecies is highly diverse (Garner & Ryder 1996), and it is distinct from the clade consisting of mountain gorillas plus eastern lowland gorillas (Ruvolo et al 1994). The western-eastern subspecies genetic difference is slightly greater than that found between *Pan* species with DNA data (Garner & Ryder 1996, Ruvolo et al 1994) and roughly equal to it with immunological methods (Sarich 1977). MtDNA types are not shared among the subspecies; therefore, by genetic analysis in the laboratory, subspecies can be easily distinguished. This has been put to practical use in the identification of captive gorillas. In one case, a gorilla previously on display in a shopping mall was typed by mtDNA sequencing as belonging to the western lowland subspecies, and he was introduced into an appropriate social group of western lowland gorillas housed in a zoo for breeding purposes (G Amato & M Ruvolo, unpublished results).

From mtDNA sequence data, the western versus eastern gorilla groups may have diverged as long as 2.2 mya (Figure 3; Ruvolo 1996). This figure was arrived at by calibrating the molecular clock at 298,000 years for the origin of modern humans (as in Ruvolo et al 1993). On this same tree, bonobos and common chimpanzees diverged from each other roughly 2.0 mya, slightly after the gorilla subspecies. The eastern lowland gorilla subspecies may have diverged from the mountain gorilla subspecies as recently as 400,000 years ago. Both subspecies show far smaller degrees of genetic variation than do western lowland gorillas (Garner & Ryder 1996).

Orangutan subspecies are also more different genetically than species of chimpanzees. Bornean and Sumatran orangutans differ greatly in their mtDNA

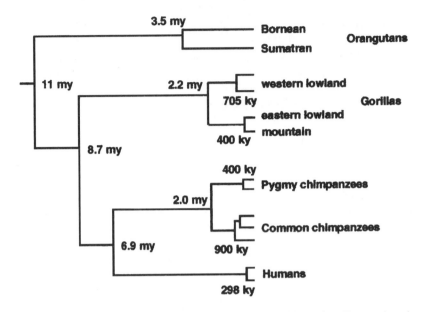

Figure 3 Hominoid evolutionary tree inferred from mitochondrial gene data. Humans show the
least variation within species and thus have a common ancestor that is more recent than that of all
other hominoid species. Orangutan subspecies are more different from one another than are the
two species of chimpanzees; the same is true for western lowland gorillas versus the other two gorilla subspecies. The tree is calibrated using 298,000 years as the divergence date for modern humans (Ruvolo et al 1993), and tree proportions are inferred from the cytochrome oxidase subunit
II gene data (Ruvolo et al 1994, Ruvolo 1996). Abbreviations: ky, thousands of years; my, millions of years. (Redrawn from Ruvolo 1996.)

(Ferris et al 1981, Lu et al 1996, Ruvolo et al 1994), total single-copy genomic
DNA (Caccone & Powell 1989), nuclear fingerprint loci (Lu et al 1996), proteins (De Boer & Khan 1982, Dugoujon et al 1984, Janczewski et al 1990, Wijinen 1982), and chromosomal structure (Seuanez et al 1979), and it is possible
to find genetic markers unique to subspecies (Ryder & Chemnick 1993). Different estimates have been made for when the subspecies diverged using data
from different genes and/or different molecular clock calibrations. Using the
same mitochondrial gene and molecular clock calibration as above (Figure 3),
orangutan subspecies are estimated to have diverged 3.5 mya (Ruvolo 1996).
This is close to the estimate of 3.2 mya based on total single-copy genomic
DNA (from data in Caccone & Powell 1989), which assumes a human-
chimpanzee divergence time of 6 my. By this same molecular clock calibration, another genetic system gives a somewhat more recent time—1.9–2.2
mya—for the split between orangutan subspecies (Lu et al 1996; M Ruvolo,

unpublished results). As reported, Lu et al (1996) estimate an orangutan sub-species divergence at 1.5–1.7 mya, but this estimate is not strictly comparable with the above because it assumes a different molecular clock calibration, with a human-chimpanzee divergence at 4.7 my. The calibration of 6 my for the human-chimpanzee divergence is probably more likely given the occurrence of *Ardipithecus* at 4.4 my and an even older fragmentary fossil thought to be homi-nid at approximately 6 my (Hill & Ward 1988). Although these genetic systems give somewhat different divergence time estimates, they agree in show-ing a relatively ancient separation between orangutan subspecies. From the one study in which hominoid subspecies are compared simultaneously by the same genetic system, it is clear that the two orangutan subspecies are the most genetically distinct hominoid subspecies identified to date (Ruvolo et al 1994).

Of the nonhuman hominoids, *Pan paniscus* is the least well-studied species, while its sister species *Pan troglodytes* has been studied most. The western subspecies *Pan troglodytes verus* is more distinctive from the other two sub-species, *P. troglodytes schweinfurthii* and *P. troglodytes troglodytes* on the ba-sis of mitochondrial DNA sequences from the control region and partial cyto-chrome *b* gene (Morin et al 1994). Genetic difference between *P. troglodytes verus* and "eastern" forms (containing *P. troglodytes schweinfurthii* and possi-bly also *P. troglodytes troglodytes*) has also been found with protein data (Goodman & Tashian 1969). The divergence time between *P. troglodytes ve-rus* and the other species has been estimated at 1.3–1.6 mya (Morin et al 1994). Another estimate for the entire common chimpanzee radiation (900,000 years) from a different mtDNA data set (Figure 3) may be low because it is based on some samples classified into subspecies according to primate importers' rec-ords; if those are inaccurate, this value would underestimate species diversity (Ruvolo et al 1994). The common chimpanzee ancestor was estimated also at 900,000 years (with 95% confidence interval 0.57–2.72 my) by Tamura & Nei (1993) from a third mtDNA region, but it is based on three individuals of un-known subspecies (from Kocher & Wilson 1991).

Is there sufficient genetic distance between the western *P. troglodytes verus* and the other two common chimpanzee subspecies to reclassify it as a separate species (Morin et al 1994)? This begs the question of what constitutes evi-dence for separate species status. Species are classically defined as "groups of interbreeding natural populations that are reproductively isolated from other such groups" (Mayr 1970). For groups living in different geographic areas, however, information on their ability to form viable hybrid offspring is rarely available. Most species have been traditionally recognized on the basis of mor-phological and behavioral data, and only more recently (since the 1960s) have those species definitions been reexamined using genetic data. Today, a combi-nation of criteria from morphology, behavior, and genetics is used to classify species and subspecies (Courtenay et al 1988, Ryder 1986) in the absence of data on reproductive behavior. Genetic distance alone, however, does not provide a yardstick for defining species or subspecies, because there is no "magic" amount of distance above which taxa are automatically considered different species and below which they are in the same species (Jolly et al 1995). The genetic basis for reproductive isolation is just beginning to be discovered in fruitflies, and it appears to involve only a few genes (Hollocher & Wu 1996). If mammals resemble fruitflies in this regard, then there could be a "genetic distance definition" of mammalian species, but one based solely on the few loci responsible for reproductive isolation. Because the genes responsible for reproductive isolation are unknown, all that we can do is compare genetic distances (at loci having nothing to do with reproductive isolation) between well-accepted species pairs and candidate species pairs. Within the hominoids, there is no pair of genetically characterized species showing less genetic difference than that between *Pan troglodytes verus* and the other two subspecies. In fact, this difference is less than that seen between the western lowland gorilla subspecies and the eastern subspecies (Garner & Ryder 1996 see Table 1). One has to go outside of the hominoids, to foxes and whales, to find species pairs with less genetic distance than that distinguishing *P. troglodytes verus* from the other subspecies (Morin et al 1994). Gathering more genetic data on chimpanzees will be useful, but it can only partially address the potentially separate species status of *Pan troglodytes verus;* other kinds of data on morphology and behavior are critical. This issue is rather academic, considering that Bornean versus Sumatran orangutan subspecies and western versus eastern subspecies of gorillas are much more different genetically from each other than are subspecies of chimpanzees. By genetic criteria, those are more compelling cases for separate species' designations. For all the nonhuman hominoids, DNA data from nuclear genes are needed to confirm the patterns of evolutionary relatedness and divergence time estimates both of which are primarily based on mitochondrial DNA.

Evidence of Past Population Expansions

Estimates of when modern humans originated rely on the amount of genetic difference between maximally different human alleles. This is only loosely related to another genetic measure, the amount of genetic difference distinguishing most pairs of human alleles; the latter measure lets us estimate when the population of modern humans expanded. It is important to note that the time of origin for modern humans could have predated the time of their population expansion (assuming one occurred) by a considerable margin. The genetic evidence can be used to estimate these two separate (but potentially coincident) events in human history.

For any population, we can measure the amount of genetic difference between all pairs of people, expressed as the number of nucleotides that are different in a stretch of DNA. If we then plot how many pairs of people show no basepair differences, one basepair difference, two basepair difference, etc, this graph will have a wave-like shape if the population underwent a size expansion or a size reduction (genetic bottleneck) sometime in the past (Rogers & Harpending 1992). From such curves, also known as mismatch analyses, we can derive information about when a population expansion or reduction occurred, the degree to which population size changed, and the initial population size (Rogers & Harpending 1992).

Mismatch analyses have been carried out on mitochondrial DNA data for humans and chimpanzees. For humans, mismatch analyses have been used to rule out the multiregional model of modern human origins (Rogers & Harpending 1992). The mismatch curve shows evidence of a population bottleneck at a time when, under the multiregional hypothesis, hominids should have been spread over vast expanses of the Old World. Mismatch analyses reconstruct the population dynamics of early modern humans and show that there would have been not enough people to maintain genetic contact required by the multiregional model (Rogers & Jorde 1995). Instead the mismatch data support a "weak Garden of Eden" model, in which the populations ultimately giving rise to modern humans diverged from one another around 100,000 years ago (a somewhat more recent date than found by other analyses of the mtDNA data), but population expansion was delayed for several tens of thousand years (Rogers & Jorde 1995). Separate times for the last common ancestor of modern humans, for the migration out of Africa, and for the major population expansion within humans are also indicated by a new method of phylogenetic analysis applied to the mitochondrial DNA data (Penny et al 1995).

The only other species for which there are comparable data is the eastern common chimpanzee *Pan troglodytes schweinfurthii*. Mismatch analysis of 37 individuals (data from Morin et al 1994) produces a curve that is not clearly unimodal but has been interpreted as showing a peak at roughly the same time as that for the human data (Rogers & Jorde 1995). From the similarities in the human and chimpanzee curves, it was suggested that population reductions took place in humans and eastern common chimpanzees at roughly the same time, and these might have both been caused by a single environmental catastrophe (Rogers & Jorde 1995). Clearly, if this were the case, gorillas ought to show some population genetic effects too, as should many other African species, including nonprimates (Ruvolo 1996). A larger mismatch analysis of 262 *P. troglodytes schweinfurthii* individuals from 19 geographically defined natural populations supports the idea that the eastern chimpanzee subspecies has undergone a recent population expansion. The time of the eastern chimpanzee expansion (Goldberg 1996, Goldberg & Ruvolo 1997b) occurred slightly before the expansion predicted for the world sample of humans (Sherry et al 1994). Furthermore, these chimpanzee mismatch analysis curves are bimodal for three individual forest populations and for the sample of eastern chimpanzees as a whole. A smaller second peak on the chimpanzee curve corresponds to an even older time of expansion than that inferred for humans, and perhaps is a remnant of an earlier eastern chimpanzee expansion (Goldberg 1996, Goldberg & Ruvolo 1997b).

Having comparable genetic data from gorillas and bonobos—and from other African species—would be valuable for understanding the patterns uncovered in human and eastern chimpanzees. This is clearly a powerful approach for uncovering past population dynamics, and one that is still being developed as a theoretical tool for understanding the past.

Inferring Primate Social Structure and Biogeographic Barriers

Studying primate species that have life spans roughly equal to our own means that researchers have to devote a good part of their lives to gain an understanding of primate life patterns. Several researchers have done this, notably Jane Goodall with common chimpanzees, Dian Fossey with mountain gorillas, and Birute Galdikas with orangutans. However, significant life events can take place in as short a time as a day, an hour, or even a few minutes. If unobserved, these events cannot be reconstructed (or only very partially so), unlike in humans where informants can report on events missed by the observer. The study of genetic variation in a population can provide some "missing pieces" of social behavior, e.g. type of sex-biased transfer among groups, extra-group matings (Gagneux et al 1997), and relatedness and origins of group members. Genetic data can also indicate distances over which gene flow occurs and reveal the existence of significant geophysical barriers to intermating among populations (Morin et al 1993).

The eastern common chimpanzee *Pan troglodytes schweinfurthii* has been most thoroughly studied with genetic data for insights about social structure. In the Gombe chimpanzee community, males are more closely related to each other than females, roughly on the order of half-siblings (Morin et al 1994). This is consistent with a pattern of females leaving the group at adolescence and males remaining in their natal group. In the Kibale Forest, Uganda, pairs of animals observed to form social affiliations most strongly do not share the same mtDNA type, indicating that they are not maternally related. In particular, pairs of cooperating males are not maternal brothers (Goldberg 1996, Goldberg & Wrangham 1997), contrary to the expectation of some behaviorists.

Individuals in the Gombe community share genetic haplotypes with other individuals living as far away as 600 km, which would imply that the extent of gene flow among populations has been considerable (Morin et al 1994). Another study of 19 forest populations of eastern chimpanzees confirms the high degree of gene flow (Goldberg 1996, Goldberg & Ruvolo 1997a). Moreover, from the observed pattern of haplotype sharing across the subspecies range, large gaps between eastern forests and major lacustrine systems have not acted as significant biogeographic barriers (Goldberg 1996, Goldberg & Ruvolo 1997a).

Within the Bornean orangutan subspecies, little genetic differentiation is seen between southern and northern populations (Lu et al 1996), even though mountains separate those populations. Thus gene flow occurs over considerable distances in at least two nonhuman hominoid subspecies. Because social interactions among relatively solitary orangutans are more difficult to observe than those among chimpanzees, and even identifying an orangutan "social group" is problematic (M Leighton, personal communication; C Knott, personal communication), having more genetic data from populations of this species should be especially helpful in elucidating their group dynamics.

Does Morphological Variation Mirror Genetic Variation?

Human morphology has a very shallow time depth. Analysis of a worldwide sample of populations of modern human skulls and fossil premodern skulls shows that, on the craniometric tree, modern humans all cluster together in a clade with only a few recent fossil humans interspersed among them (Howells 1989). Fossil humans older than approximately 10,000 years occur only in clades separate from those of living humans. African populations do not stand out as morphologically distinct from others, and few regional (i.e. "racial") differences exist. The morphological discontinuity at 10,0000 years combined with lack of regional differentiation among modern humans may be considered as support for a recent origin of modern humans in this craniometric (phenetic) study (Howells 1989). Phylogenetic analyses of cranial features provide no support for the multiregional model (Lahr 1994, Lieberman 1995), but admittedly only weak support for the replacement model (Lieberman 1995). In both types of morphological studies, homoplasy (evolutionary convergences and parallelisms) in human skull morphology has been so extensive over time that phyletic signals showing actual evolutionary relationships are virtually overwhelmed. Evaluating these results along with the genetic evidence strongly indicates that our morphologies are younger than our genes. This is not necessarily contradictory, because a genetic common ancestor of a group of individuals is almost always older than the ancestral population that gave rise to those individuals (Ruvolo 1996). Nevertheless, understanding the discrepancy between predicted times for the common ancestor of modern humans from genetic and from morphological data requires further conceptual work on the part of all biological anthropologists.

Morphological variation among the great apes has been reviewed by Uchida (1996), so only highlights are mentioned here. Some of the subspecies differences observed with genetic data are also seen in morphological traits. Among common chimpanzees, the distinctiveness of *Pan troglodytes verus* from the other two species has been observed in nonmetric traits of the teeth (Uchida 1992) and cranium (Braga 1995a,b) (though with the latter, *Pan paniscus* is more similar to *Homo sapiens* than it is to *Pan troglodytes*). Among gorillas, the western lowland subspecies is very distinctive from the other two eastern subspecies (Braga 1995a, Groves 1986, Shea & Coolidge 1988, Uchida 1992), as it is genetically. Orangutan subspecies are morphologically different, but not in metrical characters to the degree shown by their genetic differences (Groves et al 1992, Shea & Coolidge 1988, Uchida 1992). However, nonmetric cranial features show the two subspecies to be substantially different (Braga 1995a). Thus some genetic differences seen among subspecies are mirrored in morphological differences, while others are not; this demonstrates how genotypic and phenotypic systems are loosely coupled. Bonobos are morphologically less diverse than common chimpanzees (Uchida 1996), and it will be interesting to see whether the bonobo genetic pattern, when it is eventually characterized, reflects this.

OTHER APPLICATIONS

Primate Conservation

Great apes are endangered today primarily through human actions—deforestation, hunting, and poaching. Understanding their patterns of genetic variation is essential to their conservation, in the wild and in zoos. All other things being equal, it is better to conserve populations that are more rather than less genetically diverse to avoid inbreeding.

Studying genetic variation in natural populations has become vastly easier with the invention of the polymerase chain reaction (PCR). This molecular biological technique allows a researcher to genotype (genetically characterize) individuals from shed biological materials (hair, dung, urine), which can be collected in the field without disturbing group social behavior (Garner & Ryder 1992). This is far less invasive than having to anesthetize animals for blood collection. Much of the genetic research described above was performed on field-collected hairs (Morin et al 1993, Garner & Ryder 1996, Goldberg 1996,

Vigilant et al 1991). Primarily through the application of PCR methods, genetic markers that distinguish subspecies or particular populations are beginning to be discovered (Ryder 1986). These can be used to genotype animals confiscated in the illegal primate trade. These animals can then be returned to appropriate wild populations or, as in the orangutan case described above, to zoo breeding groups.

With genetic data on natural populations, corridors of gene flow—narrow tracts of land connecting forests along which animals commonly travel and exchange genes—can be identified for hominoid subspecies. Species conservationists can at least begin to incorporate this information into their plans for species survival. Of course, the most difficult part of hominoid species conservation (the financial and political aspects) is not surmounted by knowing hominoid genetic diversity patterns, but this knowledge can help in the formulation of an "optimal" species plan.

Medical Relevance

We need a better genetic understanding of our own species, not just for anthropological implications but also for use in applied fields of human biology such as medicine. Are there human populations that are genetically more diverse than others? If so, those groups should be studied more extensively to catalogue their genetic variation. This is necessary if we want to ensure, for example, that all people needing organ transplants will have an equal chance of finding appropriately matched donor organs. The observation that African-Americans have more difficulty than other Americans in finding genetically matched donor organs likely is due to their greater genetic diversity inherited from their African ancestors in HLA genes, which code for transplantation antigens and which need to match between donor and host for successful transplants (Johnson et al 1996). At the moment, this example illustrates an application benefiting only those living in countries where transplant surgery is available. Understanding the patterning and extent of human genetic variability, however, could potentially benefit people throughout the world by influencing the design of therapeutic drugs and vaccines (Weiss 1996). We cannot yet foresee all the uses of our knowledge of worldwide human genetic variation, but we should at least be aware of the possible applied benefits associated with studying human variability.

In cases where nonhuman hominoids are used as medical surrogates for humans (e.g. chimpanzees in hepatitis or AIDS studies), the need to take genetic variability into account is pressing, since a chimpanzee sample or population can vary much more genetically than those of humans. Because of their greater degree of genetic variability, chimpanzees could potentially show greater variation in their individual responses to infectious diseases and to therapeutic regimes than humans. This fact, however, is not widely appreciated in the medical community. Drawing generalizations from a few individuals is more risky if those individuals are chimpanzees or gorillas than if they are humans.

CONCLUSIONS

Among the hominoids, humans are the most well-characterized species. Our pattern of within-group and between-group genetic diversity is most similar to that found within subspecies, not species, of other hominoids. The only other large-bodied hominoid species that lacks subspecies structure is the bonobo, and it is virtually uncharacterized genetically. Considering that bonobos along with common chimpanzees are most closely related to humans, and that they differ substantially from common chimpanzees in their morphology and behavior, this is a glaring omission in our knowledge of hominoid diversity.

Some of the subspecies divisions within nonhuman hominoids are evolutionarily ancient—Bornean versus Sumatran orangutans, western lowland gorillas versus the other two eastern subspecies, and the western common chimpanzee versus the eastern and central African chimpanzee subspecies. Indeed, mitochondrial DNA lineages distinguishing individuals within one subspecies, the western lowland gorilla, are even more ancient than those of the most genetically different members of our own species. Among the hominoids, with their ancient mitochondrial lineages, we have an approximate model of what human variation might have looked like were the multiregional model correct, although perhaps with more gene flow under this model.

The relative paucity of genetic diversity within humans means that human "races" are not old or anciently derived. The phenotypic variation we observe among living humans must therefore be due to minor genetic differences. Phenotypic differences may be due to adaptation to different environments or, as Darwin believed, the result of sexual selection. Some are undoubtedly genetically based in part, but these phenotypic differences are not due to substantial portions of our genomes being different.

The value of the comparative approach in biological anthropology is twofold in revealing our similarities with other primates as well as our unique features. We cannot "run the experiment" of human evolution again. The comparative approach applied to the nonhuman hominoids shows us what the human species might have been like, but ultimately what it is not like.

ACKNOWLEDGMENTS

I thank SJ O'Brien for permission to cite work in press from his laboratory, Elizabeth Watson for permission to cite her PhD dissertation, and David Pilbeam for helpful discussion.

Visit the *Annual Reviews home page* at
http://www.AnnualReviews.org.

Literature Cited

Aiello LC. 1993. The fossil evidence for modern human origins in Africa: a revised view. *Am. Anthropol.* 95:73–96

Ankel-Simons F, Cummins JM. 1996. Misconceptions about mitochondria and mammalian fertilization: implications for theories on human evolution. *Proc. Natl. Acad. Sci. USA* 93:13859–63

Bailey WJ, Hayasaka K, Skinner CG, Kehoe S, Sieu LC, et al. 1992. Reexamination of the African hominoid trichotomy with additional sequences from the primate β-globin gene cluster. *Mol. Phylogenet. Evol.* 1:97–135

Barbujani G, Magagni A, Minch E, Cavalli-Sforza LL. 1997. An apportionment of human DNA diversity. *Proc. Natl. Acad. Sci. USA* 94:4516–19

Boesch C. 1991. Teaching among wild chimpanzees. *Anim. Behav.* 41:530–32

Bowcock AM, Ruiz-Linares A, Tomfohrde J, Minch E, Kidd JR, Cavalli-Sforza LL. 1994. High resolution of human evolutionary trees with polymorphic microsatellites. *Nature* 368:455–57

Braga J. 1995a. *Définition de certains caractères discrets crâniens chez Pongo, Gorilla et Pan. Perspectives taxonomiques et phylogénétiques.* PhD thesis. Univ. Bordeaux I, Bordeaux, France. 400 pp.

Braga J. 1995b. Variation squelettique et mesure de divergence chez les chimpanzés. Contribution de l'étude des caractères discrets. *C. R. Acad. Sci. II* 320:1025–30

Britten RJ. 1986. Rates of DNA sequence evolution differ between taxonomic groups. *Science* 231:1393–98

Bruce EJ, Ayala FJ. 1979. Phylogenetic relationships between man and the apes: electrophoretic evidence. *Evolution* 33: 1040–56

Caccone A, Powell JR. 1989. DNA divergence among hominoids. *Evolution* 45:925–42

Cann RL, Stoneking M, Wilson AC. 1987. Mitochondrial DNA and human evolution. *Nature* 325:31–36

Cavalli-Sforza LL, Menozzi P, Piazza A. 1994. *The History and Geography of Human Genes.* Princeton, NJ: Princeton Univ. Press. 1059 pp.

Cavalli-Sforza LL, Piazza A, Menozzi P,

Mountain J. 1988. Reconstruction of human evolution: bringing together genetic, archaeological, and linguistic data. *Proc. Natl. Acad. Sci. USA* 85:6002–6

Courtenay J, Groves C, Andrews P. 1988. Inter- and intra-island variation? An assessment of the differences between Bornean and Sumatran orang-utans. In *Orang-utan Biology,* ed. JH Schwartz, pp. 19–29. Oxford: Oxford Univ. Press. 383 pp.

De Boer LEM, Khan PM. 1982. Haemoglobin polymorphisms in Bornean and Sumatran orangutans. In *The Orang Utan: Its Biology and Conservation,* ed. LEM de Boer, W Junk, pp. 125–34. The Hague/Boston: Kluwer. 353 pp.

Deka R, Jin L, Shriver MD, Yu LM, DeCroo S, et al. 1995. Population genetics of dinucleotide $(dC-dA)_n \bullet (dG-dT)_n$ polymorphisms in world populations. *Am. J. Hum Genet.* 56:461–74

Dorit RL, Akashi H, Gilbert W. 1995. Absence of polymorphism at the ZFY locus on the human Y chromosome. *Science* 268:1183–86

Dugoujon JM, Blanc M, McClure HM, Lockwood E. 1984. Genetic markers of immunoglobulins in the two orangutan subspecies and their hybrids. *Folia Primatol.* 42: 188–93

Ferris SD, Brown WM, Davidson WS, Wilson AC. 1981. Extensive polymorphism in the mitochondrial DNA of apes. *Proc. Natl. Acad. Sci. USA* 78:6319–23

Frayer DW, Wolpoff MH, Thorne AG, Smith FH, Pope GG. 1993. Theories of modern human origins: the paleontological test. *Am. Anthropol.* 95:14–50

Garner KF, Ryder OA. 1992. Some applications for PCR to studies in wildlife genetics. *Symp. Zool. Soc. London* 64:167–81

Garner KF, Ryder OA. 1996. Mitochondrial DNA diversity in gorillas. *Mol. Phylogenet. Evol.* 6:39–48

Gagneux P, Woodruff DS, Boesch C. 1997. Furtive mating in female chimpanzees. *Nature* 387:358–59

Goldberg TL. 1996. *Genetics and biogeography of East African chimpanzees (Pan troglodytes schweinfurthii).* PhD thesis. Harvard Univ., Cambridge, MA. 269 pp.

Goldberg TL, Ruvolo M. 1997a. Molecular phylogenetics and historical biogeography of East African chimpanzees. *Biol. J. Linn. Soc.* In press

Goldberg TL, Ruvolo M. 1997b. The geographic apportionment of mitochondrial genetic diversity in East African chimpanzees, *Pan troglodytes schweinfurthii. Mol. Biol. Evol.* In press

Goldberg TL, Wrangham RW. 1997. Genetic correlates of social behavior in wild chimpanzees: evidence from mitochondrial DNA. *Anim. Behav.* In press

Goldstein DB, Ruiz-Linares A, Cavalli-Sforza LL, Feldman MW. 1995. An evaluation of genetic distances for use with microsatellite loci. *Genetics* 139:463–71

Goodall J. 1970. Tool-using in primates and other vertebrates. *Adv. Study Behav.* 3: 195–250

Goodman M. 1996. Epilogue: a personal account of the origins of a new paradigm. *Mol. Phylogenet. Evol.* 5:269–85

Goodman M, Tashian RE. 1969. A geographic variation in the serum transferrin and red cell phosphoglucomutase polymorphisms of chimpanzees. *Hum. Biol.* 41:237–49

Groves CP. 1986. Systematics of the great apes. In *Comparative Primate Biology. Systematics, Evolution, and Anatomy,* ed. DR Swindler, J Erwin, 1:187–217. New York: Liss. 820 pp.

Groves CP, Westwood CB, Shea BT. 1992. Unfinished business: Mahalanobis and a clockwork orang. *J. Hum. Evol.* 22:327–40

Gyllensten U, Wharton D, Josefsson A, Wilson AC. 1991. Paternal inheritance of mitochondrial DNA in mice. *Nature* 352: 255–57

Hammer MF. 1995. A recent common ancestry for human Y chromosomes. *Nature* 378:376–78

Hasegawa M, Horai S. 1991. Time of the deepest root for polymorphism in human mitochondrial DNA. *J. Mol. Evol.* 32:37–42

Hedges SB, Kumar S, Tamura K, Stoneking M. 1992. Human origins and analysis of mitochondrial DNA sequences. *Science* 255:737–39

Hill A, Ward S. 1988. Origin of the Hominidae: the record of African large hominoid evolution between 14 my and 4 my. *Yearb. Phys. Anthropol.* 31:49–83

Hollocher H, Wu C-I. 1996. The genetics of reproductive isolation in the *Drosophila simulans* clade: X vs. autosomal effects and male vs. female effects. *Genetics* 143: 1243–55

Horai S, Hayasaka K, Kondo R, Tsugane K,

Takahata N. 1995. Recent African origin of modern humans revealed by complete sequences of hominoid mitochondrial DNAs. *Proc. Natl. Acad. Sci. USA* 92: 532–36

Howells WW. 1989. Skull shapes and the map: craniometric analyses in the dispersion of modern *Homo. Pap. Peabody Mus. Archaeol. Ethnol.* Cambridge, MA: Harvard Univ. Press. 189 pp.

Janczewski DN, Goldman D, O'Brien SJ. 1990. Molecular genetic divergence of orang utan (*Pongo pygmaeus*) subspecies based on isozyme and two-dimensional gel-electrophoresis. *J. Hered.* 81:375–87

Johnson AH, Araujo H, Tang TF, Lee KW, Steiner N, Hurley DK. 1996. Cellular crossreactivity: implications for solid organ transplantation matching. *Transplantation* 61:643–48

Jolly CL, Oates JF, Disotell TR. 1995. Chimpanzee kinship. *Science* 268:185–88

Jorde LB, Bamshad MJ, Watkins WS, Zenger R, Fraley AE, et al. 1995. Origins and affinities of modern humans: a comparison of mitochondrial and nuclear genetic data. *Am. J. Hum. Genet.* 57:523–38

King M-C. 1973. *Protein polymorphisms in chimpanzee and human evolution.* PhD thesis. Univ. Calif., Berkeley. 155 pp.

King M-C, Wilson AC. 1975. Evolution at two levels in humans and chimpanzees. *Science* 188:107–16

Kocher TD, Wilson AC. 1991. Sequence evolution of mitochondrial DNA in humans and chimpanzees: control region and a protein-coding region. In *Evolution of Life: Fossils, Molecules, and Culture,* ed. S Osawa, T Honjo, pp. 391–413. Tokyo/New York: Springer-Verlag. 460 pp.

Lahr MM. 1994. The multiregional model of modern human origins: a reassessment of its morphological basis. *J. Hum. Evol.* 26: 23–56

Lewontin RC. 1972. The apportionment of human diversity. *Evol. Biol.* 6:381–98

Lewontin RC. 1995. *Human Diversity.* New York: Sci. Am. Libr. 179 pp. 2nd ed.

Li W-H, Ellsworth DL, Krushkal J, Chang BH-J, Hewett-Emmett D. 1996. Rates of nucleotide substitution in primates and rodents and the generation-time effect hypothesis. *Mol. Phylogenet. Evol.* 5: 182–87

Lieberman DE. 1995. Testing hypotheses about recent human evolution from skulls. *Curr. Anthropol.* 36:159–97

Lu Z, Karesh WB, Janczewski DN, Frazier-Taylor H, Sajuthi D, et al. 1996. Genomic differentiation among natural populations of orang utan (*Pongo pygmaeus*). *Curr. Biol.* 610:1326–36

Maddison DR. 1991. African origin of human mitochondrial DNA reexamined. *Syst. Zool.* 40:355–63

Maddison DR, Ruvolo M, Swofford DL. 1992. Geographic origins of human mitochondrial DNA: phylogenetic evidence from control region sequences. *Syst. Biol.* 41:111–24

Maeda N, Bliska JB, Smithies O. 1983. Recombination and balanced chromosome polymorphism suggested by DNA sequences 5' to the human δ-globin gene. *Proc. Natl. Acad. Sci. USA* 80:5012–16

Maybury-Lewis D, ed. 1996. *Genes, People, and Property. Cultural Survival Quarterly*, Vol. 20. Cambridge, MA: Cult. Surviv. Inc.

Mayr E. 1970. *Populations, Species, and Evolution.* Cambridge, MA: Belknap Press of Harvard Univ. Press. 453 pp.

Morin PA, Moore JJ, Chakraborty R, Jin L, Goodall J, Woodruff DS. 1994. Kin selection, social structure, gene flow, and the evolution of chimpanzees. *Science* 265:1193–201

Morin PA, Wallis J, Moore JJ, Chakraborty R, Woodruff DS. 1993. Non-invasive sampling and DNA amplification for paternity exclusion, community structure, and phylogeography in wild chimpanzees. *Primates* 3:347–56

Mountain JL, Cavalli-Sforza LL. 1994. Inference of human evolution through cladistic analysis of nuclear DNA restriction polymorphisms. *Proc. Natl. Acad. Sci. USA* 91:6515–19

Nei M. 1995. Genetic support for the out-of-Africa theory of human evolution. *Proc. Natl. Acad. Sci. USA* 92:6720–22

Nei M, Roychoudhury AK. 1993. Evolutionary relationships of human populations on a global scale. *Mol. Biol. Evol.* 10:927–43

Parsons TJ, Muniec DS, Sullivan K, Woodyatt N, Alliston-Greiner R, et al. 1997. A high observed substitution rate in the human mitochondrial DNA control region. *Nat. Genet.* 15:363–68

Penny D, Steel M, Waddell PJ, Hendy MD. 1995. Improved analyses of human mtDNA sequences support a recent African origin for *Homo sapiens. Mol. Biol. Evol.* 12:863–82

Rogers AR, Harpending H. 1992. Population growth makes waves in the distribution of pairwise genetic differences. *Mol. Biol. Evol.* 9:552–69

Rogers AR, Jorde LB. 1995. Genetic evidence

on modern human origins. *Hum. Biol.* 67:1–36

Ruvolo M. 1995. Seeing the forest and the trees. *Am. J. Phys. Anthropol.* 98:217–32

Ruvolo M. 1996. A new approach to studying modern human origins: hypothesis testing with coalescence time distributions. *Mol. Phylogenet. Evol.* 5:202–19

Ruvolo M. 1997. Molecular phylogeny of the hominoids: inferences from multiple independent DNA sequence data sets. *Mol. Biol. Evol.* 14:248–65

Ruvolo M, Pan D, Zehr S, Goldberg T, Disotell TR, et al. 1994. Gene trees and hominoid phylogeny. *Proc. Natl. Acad. Sci. USA* 91:8900–4

Ruvolo M, Zehr S, von Dornum M, Pan D, Chang B, et al. 1993. Mitochondrial COII sequences and modern human origins. *Mol. Biol. Evol.* 10:1115–35

Ryder OA. 1986. Species conservation and systematics: the dilemma of subspecies. *Trends Ecol. Evol.* 1:9–19

Ryder OA, Chemnick LG. 1993. Chromosomal and mitochondrial DNA variation in orang utans. *J. Hered.* 84:405–9

Sarich VM. 1977. Rates, sample sizes, and the neutrality hypothesis for electrophoresis in evolutionary studies. *Nature* 265:24–28

Sarich VM, Wilson AC. 1967. Immunological time scale for hominid evolution. *Science* 158:1200–3

Seuanez HN, Evans HJ, Martin DE, Fletcher J. 1979. An inversion of chromosome 2 that distinguishes between Bornean and Sumatran orangutans. *Cytogenet. Cell Genet.* 23:137–40

Shea BT, Coolidge HJ. 1988. Craniometric differentiation and systematics in the genus *Pan. J. Hum. Evol.* 17:671–85

Sherry ST, Rogers AR, Harpending H, Soodyall H, Jenkins T, Stoneking M. 1994. Mismatch distributions of mtDNA reveal recent human population expansions. *Hum. Biol.* 66:761–76

Shriver MD, Smith MW, Jin L, Marcini A, Akey JM, et al. 1997. Ethnic-affiliation estimation by use of population-specific DNA markers. *Am. J. Hum. Genet.* 60:957–64

Stoneking M. 1993. DNA and recent human evolution. *Evol. Anthropol.* 2:60–73

Stringer CB, Andrews P. 1988. Genetic and fossil evidence for the origin of modern humans. *Science* 239:1263–68

Swofford DL, Olsen GJ, Waddell PJ, Hillis DM. 1996. Phylogenetic inference. In *Molecular Systematics*, ed. DM Hillis, C Moritz, BK Mable, 11:407–514. Sunderland, MA: Sinauer. 655 pp. 2nd ed.

Takahata N. 1993. Relaxed natural selection in human populations during the Pleistocene. *Jpn. J. Genet.* 68:539–47

Tamura K, Nei M. 1993. Estimation of the number of nucleotide substitutions in the control region of mitochondrial DNA in humans and chimpanzees. *Mol. Biol. Evol.* 10:512–26

Templeton AR. 1992. Human origins and analysis of mitochondrial DNA sequences. *Science* 255:737

Tishkoff SA, Dietzsch E, Speed W, Pakstis AJ, Kidd JR, et al. 1996. Global patterns of linkage disequilibrium at the CD4 locus and modern human origins. *Science* 271:1380–87

Uchida A. 1992. *Intra-species variation among the great apes: implications for taxonomy of fossil hominids.* PhD thesis. Harvard Univ., Cambridge, MA. 325 pp.

Uchida A. 1996. What we don't know about great ape variation. *Trends Ecol. Evol.* 11:163–68

Vigilant L, Stoneking M, Harpending H, Hawkes K, Wilson AC. 1991. African populations and the evolution of human mitochondrial DNA. *Science* 253:1503–7

Watson EE. 1996. *Threads from the past: a genetic study of African ethnic groups and human origins.* PhD thesis. Massey Univ., Palmerston, NZ. 223 pp.

Weiss KM. 1996. Biological diversity is inherent in humanity. *Cult. Surv. Q.* 20:26–28

Whitfield LS, Sulston JE, Goodfellow PN. 1995. Sequence variation of the human Y chromosome. *Nature* 378:379–80

Wijinen JT, Rijksen H, de Boer LEM, Khan PM. 1982. Glucose-6-phosphate-dehydrogenase (G6PD) variation in the orang utan. In *The Orang Utan: Its Biology and Conservation,* ed. LEM de Boer, W Junk, pp. 109–18. The Hague/Boston: Kluwer. 353 pp.

Wrangham RW, de Waal FBM, McGrew WC. 1994. The challenge of behavioral diversity. In *Chimpanzee Cultures,* ed. RW Wrangham, WC McGrew, FBM de Waal, PG Heltne, pp. 1–18. Cambridge: Harvard Univ. Press. 424 pp.

Xiong W, Li W-H, Posner I, Yamamura T, Yamamoto A, et al. 1991. No severe bottleneck during human evolution: evidence from two apolipoprotein C-II deficiency alleles. *Am. J. Hum. Genet.* 48:383–89

Zuckerkandl E, Pauling L. 1962. Molecular disease, evolution, and genetic heterogeneity. In *Horizons in Biochemistry,* ed. M Kasha, B Pullman, pp. 189–225. New York: Academic. 604 pp.

Annu. Rev. Anthropol. 1997. 26:541–65
Copyright © 1997 by Annual Reviews Inc. All rights reserved

NUTRITION, ACTIVITY, AND HEALTH IN CHILDREN

Darna L. Dufour

Department of Anthropology, University of Colorado, Boulder, Colorado 80309

KEY WORDS: diet, undernutrition, obesity, energy expenditure, overnutrition

---

ABSTRACT

This chapter reviews current understanding of the associations between physical activity and nutrition in children 1 to 10 years of age. In general, both undernutrition and overnutrition are accompanied by lower levels of physical activity than in controls. In children of normal nutritional status, an association between physical activity and body composition has been difficult to demonstrate. It is clear that levels of physical activity in children are responsive to the physical and social environments, as well as to a child's nutritional status. In children of normal nutritional status, the level of physical activity increases with age in young children and then decreases in early adolescence, and males tend to be more physically active than females in a given population. Although there is a perception that children are less physically active than they were in the past, trends in physical activity through time are not known.

INTRODUCTION

Anthropologists have had a long-standing interest in diet and nutrition. Biological anthropologists have been particularly interested in questions of nutritional adaptation—that is, how humans adjust to variations in food intake as well as to particular components of the diet (Stinson 1992). Examining the components of energy balance is one approach taken to better understand nutritional adaptation in children (Zemel et al 1996). Energy balance refers to the equilibrium between energy intake (food intake) and energy expenditure. The latter includes the energy used in maintenance and growth, the thermic effect of food, and physical activity.

541

0084-6570/97/1015-0541$08.00

Physical activity, in addition to being a component of energy balance, is assumed to have intrinsic value. In children, a certain amount and variation in physical activity is considered a prerequisite to optimal growth, development, and health (Malina 1992; Saris 1985; Sunnegårdh et al 1985, 1986). Furthermore, high levels of physical activity are assumed to be protective against the development of obesity. However, the effects of physical activity on health have been difficult to determine because of the problems in defining health (Sunnegårdh et al 1985) and the methodological limitations in the measurement of physical activity. The latter has been problematical because of the competing objectives of needing to record normal activity without interfering with that activity (Davies 1996, Saris 1985).

The purpose of this chapter is to review the current understanding of the interrelationships of nutrition and physical activity in children between the ages of 1 and 10 years. Research on nutrition and physical activity in children has been focused in four broad areas. Some of the earlier and ongoing work has been directed toward understanding the effects of undernutrition on physical activity in young children. More recently, attention has been focused on describing habitual levels of physical activity in normal, apparently healthy children. A third area of interest in industrialized countries has been understanding the relationships among physical activity, fatness, and health in children. Lastly, a fourth area of interest has been in assessing physical activity as a component of total daily energy expenditure (TEE) to estimate dietary energy requirements. This last area has recently been reviewed (Torún et al 1996) and will not be covered here. I begin with a brief review of methods used to study physical activity because these are fundamental to our understanding of activity in children.

MEASURING PHYSICAL ACTIVITY IN CHILDREN

Physical activity is defined as any bodily movement produced by skeletal muscles and resulting in energy expenditure (Bouchard et al 1990). It is a large and highly variable component of energy expenditure. The other large component of energy expenditure is maintenance. This is measured as basal metabolism, or resting metabolism, and is a function of body size, body composition (especially the amount of lean tissue), and age. Growth is responsible for the continued increase in body size in children, which is reflected in the increase in basal metabolism with age. It accounts for a small fraction (about 3%) of total dietary energy needs in children 1 to 10 years of age (FAO/WHO/UNU 1985). A fourth component of energy expenditure is the thermic effect of food, i.e. the increase in metabolic rate that occurs with food intake. It is a small component of TEE. Energy balance refers to the equilibrium between food energy intake and TEE.

To assess the physical activity of children, two different types of techniques have been used. The first are techniques such as direct observation and recall questionnaires that provide a record of the kinds of physical activities engaged in. The second are techniques such as heart-rate recording and the use of stable isotopes that measure physiological responses to physical activity. Each of these techniques has strengths and limitations in the information it can provide. In general, observational and recall methods can provide useful information on the types of physical activities and the time spent in each. They are less accurate with regard to the intensity of physical activity, or in estimating TEE. The techniques measuring physiological responses provide the most accurate data on TEE. They can also provide good information on energy expenditure in activity, but yield no information on the types of activities children engage in. A detailed review of available methods has been done by Saris (1985), and a brief summary of methods suitable for use with children is provided below.

Observations and Questionnaires

Direct observation of children during specified time intervals can provide information on the type and duration of the activities engaged in. The technique is time intensive but is considered the proverbial gold standard for describing children's activities (Figure 1a). The accuracy of observers in recording the duration of activities is considered good, but their accuracy in recording the intensity of activities has been a concern. In response to this problem, Puhl et al (1990) developed the Children's Activity Rating Scale (CARS), a five-level scale that shows good reproducibility between observers. Records of children's activities can be used to estimate energy expenditure, if values for energy expenditure (from oxygen consumption) in specific activities are available (Torún 1990a). In adults, estimates of energy expenditure from activity records tend to underestimate energy expenditure obtained using other techniques (Spurr et al 1996).

The use of recall questionnaires is perhaps the most common method of studying physical activity in groups of children. In older children, this method can provide reliable information about the types of activities engaged in, but its accuracy in quantifying the duration and intensity of activity is limited (Bar-Or & Malina 1995). In addition, recall questionnaires suffer from the limitations of memory which are common in all recall methods. For young children, parents or caretakers are required to provide the information. Although questionnaires are a relatively insensitive measure of physical activity in children, they have been used by a number of investigators.

Motion Sensors

Motion sensors are devices such as pedometers that can be worn by a child and keep a count of trunk or limb movements, or devices that measure acceleration in one or more planes. Thus far these devices have not proven to be very useful

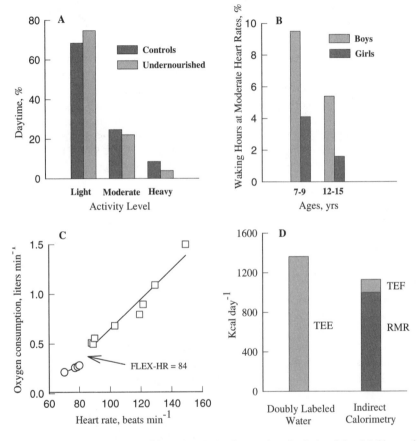

Figure 1   Data obtained using different methods of measuring physical activity. (*a*) Observed time spent in activities classified as light, moderate, and heavy by undernourished children and controls. Data replotted from Figure 4 in Torún (1990a). (*b*) Age and sex differences in time (waking hours) spent in moderate to vigorous physical activity (heart rates greater than 50% maximum oxygen consumption). Data from Livingstone et al (1992). (*c*) A heart rate oxygen consumption calibration curve. Replotted from Figure 1 in Spurr & Reina (1990). (*d*) Physical activity measured as difference between total energy expenditure (TEE, by doubly labeled water) and the sum of energy expenditure in resting (RMR) and the thermic effect of food (TEF). Data from Fontveille et al (1993a).

with children because of their low reliability and accuracy in recording some types of movement (Mukeshi et al 1990, Puhl et al 1990, Sallis et al 1992).

Heart-Rate Recording

Heart-rate recording has become one of the more popular techniques for obtaining information on the level of physical activity in children. For a group, it provides an objective assessment of intensity of physical activity, time spent at different levels of physical activity, daily patterns of physical activity, and an acceptable estimation of energy expenditure (Livingstone et al 1992). Heart rate can be recorded continuously during the normal activities of free-living children using a heart-rate cardiotachometer, such as the Polar Sport Tester TN (Polar Electro, Finland). This device uses a small transmitter with two electrodes that is attached to the child's chest using an elastic belt, and a recorder the shape of a large wrist watch that can be programmed to store heart rate at 1-min intervals for up to 16 h.

Heart-rate data can be used in several ways. One of the simplest uses is to calculate the total time spent at heart rates above resting. This, then, is assumed to be the total time the child spent in physical activity. A more interesting picture of a child's physical activity can be obtained by determining the percentage of total time the child spent at different heart rates and hence at different levels of physical activity. Levels of physical activity can be defined in terms of percent of oxygen consumption. For example, a heart rate of >140 beats/ min was approximately 50% of maximal oxygen consumption for 7- to 9-year-old Irish children and was used to define physical activity as moderate to vigorous (Figure 1b; Livingstone et al 1992).

A third use of heart-rate data is to estimate energy expenditure in groups of children. The basis of the estimate is the well-known relation between heart rate and oxygen consumption. The procedure involves measuring heart rate and oxygen consumption simultaneously in a range of activities and establishing a heart rate–oxygen consumption calibration curve (usually in the form of a regression equation). The range of activities typically used includes resting activities (lying, sitting, standing) and nonresting activities (such as a graded exercise test on a treadmill or bicycle ergometer). Because the relation between heart rate and oxygen consumption is weak in resting activities, a critical heart-rate value, called FLEX-HR is established as the mean of the highest resting and the lowest exercise heart rates (Figure 1c). At heart rates below FLEX-HR, resting metabolic rate (RMR) is used as an estimate of energy expenditure, and above FLEX-HR energy expenditure is estimated by the regression of oxygen consumption on heart rate established for each child (Spurr et al 1988). This method, the FLEX-HR method, is considered one of the best field techniques available for the objective estimate of energy expenditure in physical activity and for predicting energy expenditure in groups of free-living children (Livingstone et al 1992).

Doubly Labeled Water

The doubly labeled water (DLW) technique is considered the most accurate measure of total energy expenditure in free-living subjects. It is based on the principle that a subject given a dose of doubly labeled water ($^2H_2^{18}O$) will eliminate the hydrogen isotope ($^2H_2$) as water and the oxygen isotope (^{18}O) as both carbon dioxide and water. This differential elimination allows carbon dioxide production to be calculated and then energy expenditure from carbon dioxide production. The method provides a measure of total energy expenditure over 10–14 days. To obtain estimates of energy expenditure in physical activity, energy expenditure at rest (resting metabolic rate or RMR) and in food digestion (thermic effect of food or TEF) are usually measured separately via indirect calorimetry (oxygen consumption) and then subtracted from the total energy expenditure (Figure 1d). The method is described in detail by Schoeller et al (1986). The method is easy to use with children because it only requires that they drink a small dose of the doubly labeled water and provide some urine samples (Emons et al 1992). An important disadvantage of the method is the high purchase cost of the isotope itself.

PHYSICAL ACTIVITY IN NORMAL, APPARENTLY HEALTHY CHILDREN

Before looking at studies of physical activity in children classified as under- or overnourished, it is useful to briefly review studies of physical activity in apparently healthy children of normal nutritional status.

The first study to measure total daily energy expenditure in children was done by Spady in 1980 (Spady 1980) with 9- to 10-year-old children (n = 36) in Canada using heart-rate recorders. He found that energy expenditure in physical activity accounted for about 31% of TEE in boys and about 25% in girls. These values are considerably higher than those found in two recent studies of younger children in the United States using doubly labeled water. In a study of 4- to 6-year-olds (n = 30), Goran et al (1993) found that energy expenditure in activity was 17% of the total. This value is similar to that found by Fontvielle et al (1993a) for 5-year-old children. None of the studies found significant differences between males and females.

Two studies using heart-rate records partitioned physical activity into different levels. Gilliam et al (1981) studied a sample of 6- to 7-year-olds (n = 40) in the United States. Using heart rates of >120 beats/min as an indicator of moderate to high levels of physical activity, they found that boys and girls spent 7.7% and 6% of the day (24-h basis) at moderate to high levels of physical activity, respectively. Most of their awake time was spent in sedentary activities. Livingstone et al (1992) obtained roughly comparable results in a study of Irish children 7 to 9 years old (n = 20). The boys and girls spent 9.5% and 4.1% of their time per day in moderate to vigorous physical activity (at heart rates greater than about 137 beats/min), respectively. For the older children (12 to 15 years old) the values were 5.4% for boys and 1.6% for girls (Figure 1b). This age decline in time spent in moderate to high levels of physical activity is in agreement with other studies (Sunnegårdh et al 1985). The finding that males are more physically active than females is also in agreement with other studies in industrialized countries (Gilliam et al 1981, MacConnie et al 1982, Simons-Morton et al 1990, Spady 1980, Sunnegårdh et al 1985) and at least one developing country (Spurr & Reina 1989).

To survey a large (n = 2410), multiethnic, multiregional sample of 8-year-old US children, Simons-Morton et al (1997) used a questionnaire approach. They asked children to estimate the time spent in different kinds of activities, before and after school and during school recess, and then categorized the activities as sedentary, moderate, or vigorous with regard to energy expenditure. The boys and girls reported spending an average of 6.7% and 5.7% of total time (24-h basis) in moderate-vigorous activities, respectively. These values are in the range obtained by other investigators (Gilliam et al 1981, Livingstone et al 1992) using heart-rate techniques.

There is less quantitative information regarding the levels of physical activity of children in developing countries. Torún et al (1996) used the available literature on time allocation in a number of different societies to classify children's activities in terms of their intensity (sedentary, moderate, vigorous). From this analysis they concluded that the time spent in moderate to vigorous activities by children in urban areas of developing countries was similar to that of children in industrialized countries, and less than it is for children in rural areas of developing countries. The absolute values they report are higher than reported by other authors, a difference that might be due to the use of studies not necessarily designed to provide quantitative estimates of physical activity.

Although studies quantifying physical activity in children have given relatively little attention to the factors associated with different levels of physical activity, a number of factors appear to be important. The weather, environmental space (small urban apartment vs outside play areas), objects in the space (television vs play equipment), and other people present (peers vs adults) (McKenzie et al 1992, Super 1990). In developing countries, children's economic responsibilities (Cain 1977) and the availability of motorized transportation (Durnin 1992) also have an impact on physical activity. Adult activity levels, as well as verbal prompts from adults to be active or inactive, also affect children's activity levels (Sallis 1995). In school-age children in industrialized countries, most moderate to vigorous physical activity during nonschool hours is in organized programs (Simons-Morton et al 1997), and so the availability of such programs is a consideration. Further, it is clear from ethnographic studies that cultural definitions of age-appropriate activities for children vary, and that there are wide variations in the physical activity levels in children in different populations (Ho et al 1988, Lawrence et al 1985, Munroe et al 1983, Super 1990, Whiting & Edwards 1988).

Although researchers in industrialized countries often express concern that children are not as physically active as they should be, minimal or optimum levels of physical activity for health in children are not known (Puhl et al 1990, Torún et al 1996). In the absence of this information the tendency has been to apply adult standards, which currently specify moderate-intensity activity (heart rate >140 beats/min) for at least 20 min, three or more times per week (Simons-Morton et al 1988). This translates to about 1.3% of total time on days exercise is undertaken, and less than 1% of the time on a weekly basis. The 8-year-olds studied by Simons-Morton et al (1997) were more physically active and met the Year 2000 Objectives in the United States (Department of Health and Human Services 1991).

PHYSICAL ACTIVITY AND UNDERNUTRITION IN CHILDREN

Because physical activity is a large component of total daily energy expenditure in children, low levels of dietary energy intake associated with undernutrition would be expected to result in low levels of energy expenditure in physical activity. This section is a review of the evidence for such a reduction in physical activity seen in clinical studies and under free-living conditions.

Defining Undernutrition

Undernutrition in childhood is characterized by excessive thinness and/or low stature for age. Mild to moderate undernutrition is defined in terms of deficits in height-for-age, weight-for-height, or weight-for-age, compared with a reference (Table 1). The reference population most often used is the National Center for Health Statistics (NCHS) percentiles for the growth of children in the United States (Hamil et al 1979). These are also known as the WHO standards (WHO Working Group 1986) because the WHO has promoted their use as an international reference standard. The general acceptance of the NCHS values as a reference is based on our current understanding that the slow growth observed in underprivileged populations is due primarily to inadequate food intake, infection, and generally suboptimal environmental conditions rather than to genetic differences in growth potential (Gorstein et al 1994). The most prevalent form of undernutrition on a world-wide basis is low height-for-age, or stunting (Keller & Fillmore 1983). Low weight-for-height, or wasting, is less common. Severe undernutrition is much less prevalent than either stunting or mild to moderate wasting. Severe undernutrition refers to children who are so undernourished that they show life-threatening symptoms of severe wasting, kwashiorkor (a syndrome including growth deficit, irritability, skin lesions, and edema), or a combination of the two.

Young Children with Severe Undernutrition: Clinical Studies

Investigators noted some time ago that severely undernourished children were very inactive and did little to explore their surroundings (Trowell et al 1982). Systematic observations in Jamaica (Grantham-McGregor et al 1990) have confirmed this impression. They have also demonstrated that physical activity recovers rapidly (in just one week) with nutritional rehabilitation.

Two experiments in Guatemala demonstrated that young children respond to decreases in energy intake by decreasing their level of physical activity, and thus their total energy expenditure. In the first, Viteri & Torún (1981) observed the activity levels of severely undernourished boys (n = 5) aged 1.5 to 4.5 years during a 4-day period when the children were on a high energy–protein rehabilitation diet. They then reduced the energy and protein content of the diet to levels typically found in home diets (a reduction of 40–42% of energy and 40–50% of protein in comparison with the rehabilitation diet), waited three days, and repeated the observations of physical activity again in the same physical setting. On the lower-energy diet the children approximately doubled the time spent in sedentary play, resting and lying down, and consequently spent less time (ranging from roughly 17–56% less) in more energy-demanding activities.

The second experiment was done with boys 2–3 years of age (n = 5). The children started on a diet judged to be adequate in energy. After 40 days, energy intake was reduced by 9%, and then after another 40 days by an additional 12%. The children accommodated to the first reduction in energy intake by reducing energy expended in physical activity and to the second reduction by reducing body weight, or gain in body weight. Growth in height was not affected.

The Guatemalan experiments used very small samples, and they would probably be unrepeatable today based on current human subjects guidelines, but they demonstrated quite clearly that young children respond rapidly to reductions in energy intake by reducing physical activity and to more extreme reductions by reducing body weight or weight gain. In agreement with Torún (1994) these responses should be considered "accommodations," i.e. short-term compensatory responses, rather than adaptations.

Young Children with Mild to Moderate Undernutrition: Free-Living

Studies of physical activity in free-living (that is, living in ordinary home environments) young children with mild to moderate undernutrition have used observational techniques. Four of the five published studies focused on children 1 to 2 years of age, and the fifth included children 2 to 6 years old.

The first study to relate nutritional status to physical activity in free-living children was that of Rutishauser & Whitehead (1972). They observed the level of physical activity of Ugandan children (n = 20) and a control group of European children (n = 5) also living in Uganda. The Ugandan children had dietary energy intakes of about 70% of the recommended, and they were lighter in weight but growing in height and weight at rates similar to those of the European children. The physical activity of each of the children was observed for 5 h per day on two separate days. The results indicated that the Ugandan children spent a greater percentage of their time in sedentary activities. The control group in this study, however, was very small, and cultural differences between the Ugandan and European children could have accounted for some, if not all, of the differences found.

In the Gambia, Lawrence et al (1991) observed the activity level of Gambian children (n = 81) divided into two nutritional groups: underweight and controls. Although the differences between the two groups were in the expected direction—that is, the underweight children tended to be less physically active—only a few reached statistical significance. The investigators also reported that the Gambian children were less physically active than a comparable sample of Scottish children in Scotland. They attributed the lower levels of activity in the Gambian children to the hotter climate, the general absence of toys, the low level of stimulation provided by the caregivers, and the actual restrictions on physical activity imposed by the caregivers.

In an intervention study in rural Mexico, Chavez & Martinez (1982) compared physical activity in children receiving a nutritional supplement (n = 19) with nonsupplemented children (n = 17). The latter were characterized by moderate stunting and mild wasting. Physical activity was quantified by having an observer count foot contacts with the floor during 10-min intervals periodically throughout the day at 3-month intervals over the course of a year. The investigators found that supplemented children were three to six times more physically active than the nonsupplemented children, and the difference increased with age.

In a slightly older group of children in Guatemala, Torún (1990b) observed the physical activity of children (n = 69) aged 2 to 6 years living in the poor neighborhoods of Guatemala City. The children classified as mildly wasted spent significantly more time at sedentary and light levels of physical activity than did the children in the control group (normal weight-for-height), and significantly less time in activities classified as heavy than did the control group (Figure 1a).

A recent study in Jamaica compared the level of physical activity of stunted children (n = 78) with nonstunted (n = 26) children (Meeks Gardner et al 1990). The children were 1 to 2 years of age, and physical activity was assessed by observation. The stunted children also had significantly lower weight-for-height (mean values were 89–90% of median and indicated mild wasting) than the nonstunted, but a similar level of dietary intake. The investigators reported that stunted children spent less time in moderate to vigorous activities than did the nonstunted children. Physical activity increased with age in these children, but there were no differences related to sex. The finding of a lower level of physical activity in the stunted, mildly wasted children is consistent with the other studies reviewed above. That lack of a difference, however, in energy intake between the two groups is an unexpected finding and difficult to interpret.

The results of these studies of free-living young children are generally consistent with the results of the clinical studies; that is, children of lower body weight (for height or age) tend to be less physically active than those of normal body weight or those receiving dietary supplementation.

School-Age Children with Mild to Moderate Undernutrition

Data on the physical activity of school-age children living in areas where mild to moderate undernutrition is endemic is limited to work in Colombia, and a single study in Madagascar. In Colombia, Spurr & Reina (1989) studied energy expenditure in marginally undernourished (mild stunting and wasting) 6- to 16-year-old boys and girls and compared them with controls of normal nutritional status. On the basis of heart-rate data, it was determined that the undernourished 6- to 8-year-old boys spent significantly more time in light activities and significantly less time in activities requiring high levels of energy expenditure. The 6- to 8-year-old undernourished girls spent significantly more time in moderate activities and less in heavy activities than the controls. In the 10- to 12-year-olds (boys and girls) there was no difference between undernourished and controls.

Energy expenditure was also measured with the heart-rate technique described above. The undernourished 6- to 8-year-old boys had lower energy expenditure in physical activity than the controls; in the 10- to 12-year-old boys, however, there was no difference. The differences in energy expenditure in physical activity found in the 6- to 8-year-old boys were a function of body size, the undernourished children having a lower lean body mass (Spurr & Reina 1988a). Energy expenditure in physical activity was lower in the girls, but there were no differences between the nutritional groups.

Reasoning that differences in activity level between undernourished children and controls would be most evident under conditions that encouraged a high level of physical activity, Spurr & Reina (1988b) organized a day camp experience for the 10- to 12-year-old boys that provided athletic activities designed to increase levels of physical activity. It also provided a midday meal. In the day camp setting the energy expenditure in physical activity of the undernourished boys was less than in the normal boys in the morning. However, following the midday meal the undernourished boys showed an increased level of physical activity for a couple of hours and then a decline to levels similar to those seen in the morning. The meal effect shown in this study is intriguing, and the study bears repeating with other groups of children at different ages.

In marginally undernourished (mild stunting, mild to no wasting) girls 8 to 11 years of age, a dietary supplement in the form of a school lunch program did not affect energy expenditure in activity but did result in increased growth and fatness (Spurr & Reina 1988a).

In Madagascar, Hardenberg (1996) studied the daily activities of 6- to 9-year-old children (n = 40) living in a rural agricultural community using continuous observation for 8 h on one day in each of two seasons. Activity data for a second day was obtained by recall. Results of the study suggest that children with weight-for-heights in the low end of the normal range (< −1 standard deviations; see Table 1) spent more time in sedentary activities and less in energetically demanding manual labor than children of better nutritional status.

Summary and Conclusions

Although some of the studies reviewed above used very small samples, the findings are generally consistent and can be summarized as follows: Severely undernourished young children exhibit a depressed activity level that responds rapidly to nutritional rehabilitation. In clinical settings, young children respond rapidly to reductions in energy intake by reducing physical activity and to more extreme reductions by reducing body weight or weight gain. Free-living young children with mild to moderate undernutrition appear to spend less time in vigorous activities and more time in sedentary activities in comparison with controls in the same population. In older children, approximately 9 to 12 years of age, there is little difference in physical activity between the mildly undernourished and controls. In an experimental setting encouraging

Table 1 Commonly used measures of undernutrition and overnutrition in children 1 to 10 years of age

Measure	Comparison to NCHS/WHO[a]	Status[b]
UNDERNUTRITION		
Height-for-age	<−2 standard deviations	stunted
	90–94% 50th centile	stunted (mild)
	85–89% 50th centile	stunted (moderate)
	<85% 50th centile	stunted (severe)
Weight-for-height	<−2 standard deviations	wasted
	80–89% 50th centile	wasted (mild)
	70–79% 50th centile	wasted (moderate)
	<70% 50th centile	wasted (severe)
Weight-for-age	<−2 standard deviations	underweight
	<80% 50th centile	underweight
OVERNUTRITION		
Weight-for-age	≥120% of median	obese
Weight-for-height[c]	> standard deviations	obese
Body mass index[d]	≥85th or 95th centile	obese
Triceps skinfold, mm	≥85th centile	high adiposity
Body fat, %[e]	≥20% (boys), ≥30% (girls)	obese

[a]Comparison to NCHS reference population provides information about "relative" status only and is not used as a standard of growth (WHO Working Group 1986).

[b]Other commonly used terms for low height-for-age are low stature and growth retarded; wasting is also referred to as thinness; undernourished is also referred to as underweight. Categories (mild, moderate, severe) of stunting and wasting are from Waterlowl (1977).

[c]Recommended by the Royal College of Physicians (Gurney & Gorstein 1988).

[d]Body mass index (BMI) = weight (kg)/height(m^2).

[e]Based on increase in health risk (Dwyer & Blizzard 1996).

vigorous physical activity, however, older undernourished boys do not increase their activity levels to the same extent as control children. Their activity level does, however, show a short-term response to food energy intake in the form of a midday meal. Undernourished 8- to 11-year-old girls do not increase their overall level of physical activity in response to energy supplementation but do increase growth and fatness.

One difficulty in interpreting the studies of undernutrition in free-living children is that investigators have used different anthropometric indicators of nutritional status. Theoretically, weight-for-height should be the most sensitive indicator because it responds most rapidly to changes in the components of energy balance. Height-for-age, on the other hand, is the outcome of growth over a relatively long period, and at any given point in time children of low height-for-age could be in energy balance and growing in height at a velocity expected for their age. Weight-for-age is a composite of the other two indices and therefore more difficult to interpret.

The functional significance of the impact of mild to moderate undernutrition on physical activity has not been very well defined. We need a better understanding of how undernutrition affects children's participation in play and social activities, in school environments, and in productive activities in a given society (Hardenberg 1996, Super 1990). For example, in the study of Cali boys in the summer camp setting, it would be useful to know whether the lower level of physical activity in undernourished boys was the result of standing on the sidelines watching others play or playing a less vigorous game.

PHYSICAL ACTIVITY AND OVERNUTRITION IN CHILDREN

In industrialized countries, interest in the physical activity of children has been tied primarily to concerns with overnutrition and obesity, and secondarily to considerations of health-related fitness. The components of the latter are aerobic fitness, strength, flexibility, and leanness. Interest in the role of physical activity in obesity is particularly strong given the perceived trend toward increasing obesity in childhood in industrialized countries (Gortmaker et al 1990, Sunnegårdh et al 1985), as well as in wealthier groups in some developing countries (Gurney & Gorstein 1988, Ivanovic et al 1991, Monteiro et al 1995). In the United States, for example, body fatness (measured as triceps skinfold thickness) and obesity (triceps skinfold >85th percentile) in 6- to 17-year-olds increased between 1960 and 1980 (Gortmaker et al 1990). Interestingly, the trend toward increasing fatness and obesity evident in the skinfold data is not evident in weight-for-height (Bar-Or & Malina 1995) or body mass index (BMI) data (Harlan et al 1988). One interpretation of this discrepancy is that increases in fatness have been offset by decreases in fat-free mass, and further that such a change could occur as a consequence of decreases in physical activity and a corresponding decrease in physical fitness (Gortmaker et al 1990).

There is a general perception that levels of physical activity have declined in children in industrialized countries, but unfortunately there are few data on trends in physical activity in children. Except for leanness, measures of health-related fitness (aerobic fitness, strength, flexibility) in US children have changed very little in the past 30 years (Bar-Or & Malina 1995). If we assume that health-related fitness is associated with the level of habitual physical activity, then the lack of change in fitness measures suggests that physical activity has not declined (Bar-Or & Malina 1995). An alternative explanation is that habitual physical activity has declined, but children have been active enough to maintain aerobic fitness, strength, and flexibility (Bar-Or & Malina 1995). Overnutrition is also blamed for the increases in fatness in children. Food intake, however, has not increased in parallel with the increase in obesity. Rather, a number of studies in industrialized countries have shown lower energy intakes in children than were previously recorded (Durnin 1992, Räsänen et al 1985, Whitehead et al 1982) or have failed to show any change in intake (Albertson & Tobelmann 1993). For example, in Sweden 8-year-olds had higher body weights and higher triceps skinfolds but lower energy intakes in 1981 than they did 10 years earlier (Sunnegårdh et al 1985). These results suggest that physical activity declined during the same period.

The low level of physical activity associated with television viewing is thought to be a primary cause of the trend toward obesity in US children (Dietz & Gortmaker 1985, Gortmaker et al 1990, Gutin & Manos 1993). TV viewing has been categorized as "nonphysical activity" or "inactivity" because it is associated with very low levels of energy expenditure (Gortmaker et al 1990, Klesges et al 1993). Although the notion is intuitively attractive, and some studies have found a positive association between fatness and time spent watching TV (Dietz & Gortmaker 1985, Fontvieille et al 1993a, Gortmaker et al 1990), other studies have not (DuRant et al 1994, Goran et al 1995).

Obesity is a recognized health risk for adults. In children, obesity is associated with factors known to confer risk for obesity-related diseases in adults, although obesity does not appear to present the same risks for children themselves (Després & Lamarche 1993, Dwyer & Blizzard 1996, Pflieger et al 1994). However, given that obesity in childhood is associated with obesity in adulthood (Gutin et al 1990, Williams et al 1992), and adult obesity is a difficult condition to treat, the consensus view is that we need to prevent it in children (Troiano et al 1995).

The causes of obesity are complex (Williams & Kimm 1993). At the most basic level, however, obesity represents an accumulation of stored energy, which is a reflection of a history of positive energy balance—that is, a history of energy intake greater than energy expenditure. If the components of energy expenditure are physical activity, BMR (basal metabolic rate) and TEF (thermic effect of food), then a reduction in any one, or all of them, could contribute to a situation where expenditure is less than intake. BMR and TEF can not be considered in detail here. There is little evidence to suggest, however, that either low BMR (Bandini et al 1989, Manos et al 1993) or low TEF (Bandini et al 1990, Hultquist et al 1991, Manos et al 1993) contributes to obesity in children who are already obese. That leaves physical activity as the most likely candidate. It is clear that genetic differences play a role in the predisposition to obesity (Bouchard & Pérusse 1993, Schwartz & Seeley 1997). Nonetheless, a genetic predisposition to obesity can only be expressed in a permissive environment where energy intake is consistently or chronically greater than energy expenditure.

Measures of Overnutrition in Children

There is little agreement on how fatness or obesity should be measured in children. The commonly used measures are shown in Table 1. A number of investigators have used skinfolds, especially the triceps skinfold. This is based on the high correlation of triceps skinfold with percent body fat measured using other techniques (Roche et al 1981). The use of BMI is becoming more common. However, some investigators consider it inappropriate because it is significantly correlated with stature, especially in children, and is as much a measure of lean body mass as of fatness (Garn et al 1986). Furthermore, in children, normal values for BMI vary with age because of the rapid changes in body shape and composition that occur with development (Epstein & Higgins 1992). In all these measures, the percentile cutoffs are somewhat arbitrary in terms of health outcomes. Cutoffs for percent body fat based on an increase in risk factors for cardiovascular disease (high density lipoprotein cholesterol, fasting triglycerides, and systolic blood pressure) have recently been proposed (Dwyer & Blizzard 1996). They are 30% body fat (as a percentage of body weight) for girls and 20% for boys.

Physical Activity and Fatness

To understand the role of physical activity in regulating body weight in children, researchers have used several different approaches: (a) surveys of physical activity and fatness in groups of healthy children; (b) two-group designs in which physical activity levels in an obese and nonobese group are compared; and (c) short-term interventions aimed at increasing level of physical activity. In all these studies, energy intake is assumed to be adequate.

SURVEYS OF HEALTHY CHILDREN   In the case of healthy young children, there are five recent studies. DuRant et al (1994) observed the physical activity of 3- to 4-year-old children in three ethnic groups (Afro-Americans, Anglo-Americans, and Mexican-Americans). They found that the children who spent more time watching TV were less physically active but not fatter.

Davies et al (1995) used doubly labeled water to assess energy expenditure in activity in English children between 1.5 and 4 years of age (n = 77). They found a significant negative correlation between fatness and physical activity measured as the ratio of total energy expenditure to basal metabolic rate and as TEE minus BMR. Goran et al (1995) used recall questionnaires as well as doubly labeled water to assess physical activity in 4- to 7-year-old Mohawk (n = 26) and Anglo-American children (n = 70) during the school year. They found no relationship between energy expenditure in activity and body fatness in either group of children. Interestingly, they found energy expenditure in activity was greater in the Mohawk children, even though they watched more TV according to the recall questionnaire.

Berkowitz et al (1985) assessed the physical activity of 4- to 8-year-old children (n = 52) using motion sensors. They found no association between level of physical activity and fatness measured by triceps skinfold. They did find a negative association between high levels of physical activity and BMI, but the usefulness of BMI as a measure of adiposity in children in this age range is questionable, and hence the results are not convincing.

The only prospective study of physical activity and fatness is that of Gutin et al (1993), who studied 3- to 7-year-old children (n = 97) over a 4-year period. Analyzing the data cross-sectionally, they found that fatness (measured as skinfolds) was inversely correlated with physical activity (measured by heart rate). Analyzing the data longitudinally, however, they did not find that physical activity contributed significantly to the level of fatness in the fourth year of the study. Fatness in the fourth year of the study was largely explained by fatness in the first year and dietary energy intake. That is, fatness "tracks" well in 4- to 7-year-olds.

For older school children, there are four additional studies. Two studies (Pate et al 1990, Sunnegårdh et al 1986) used recall questionnaires to assess physical activity in large, nationally representative samples. In the Swedish study (Sunnegårdh et al 1986) of 8- to 13-year-old children there was no correlation between level of physical activity and body fatness (skinfolds), but investigators did find a tendency for higher fatness to be associated with lower levels of physical activity in both males and females. In the US study (Bouchard et al 1990) of 8- to 9-year-olds, fatness (skinfolds) was positively associated with hours of TV watching and negatively with participation in organized sports and the exercise patterns of both parents. They also found that physical activity and fitness were positively associated but that the absolute magnitude of the association was low.

A smaller study of 10-year-old Pima children (n = 43) also found a significant negative correlation between body fatness and reported participation in sports activities in the past year for boys (Fontvieille et al 1993b). The study did not, however, find any significant associations between fatness and measures of physical activity in Pima girls or in the Anglo-American comparison group.

The fourth study used heart-rate records to assess physical activity in school children (n = 76) aged 6 to 17 years during school vacation (Janz et al 1992). In this study, body fatness was inversely correlated with physical activity, but the relationship was weak. It is not clear, however, whether the investigators controlled for the effect of age. Any relationship between fatness and physical activity would be confounded by the tendency of body fat to increase (Malina 1992) and physical activity to decrease with age between 6 and 17 years.

In sum, the studies reviewed above are not entirely consistent and on the whole do not provide strong support for the idea that leanness is associated with high levels of physical activity. There are a number of factors that may help explain the inconsistent results. First, three of the four studies used recall questionnaires. Recall instruments in general have known reliability and validity problems and may not be sensitive enough to detect the relationship of interest, especially at low levels of physical activity as was the case with Pima females (Fontvieille et al 1993b). It is noteworthy that the two questionnaire studies reporting a significant negative association between fatness and physical activity (Fontvieille et al 1993b, Pate et al 1990) found it between fatness and participation in organized sports rather than between fatness and overall level of physical activity. This relationship may be an artifact of the use of recall questionnaires, if participation in formally scheduled sports activities are recalled better than more spontaneous activities. In addition, the relationship observed between leanness and participation in sports may be confounded if there is a tendency for leaner children to be involved in sports because they are leaner.

COMPARISONS OF OBESE AND NONOBESE CHILDREN   Most of the studies comparing physical activity in obese and nonobese children have focused on adolescents, and only a limited number have included older (7 to 10 years) school children. The only observational study is that of Taylor & Baranowski (1991) with 8- to 13-year olds (n = 199) in Texas. Each child was observed for two days during waking hours by a trained observer. Children in the high adiposity group were less physically active.

Results of studies using recall questionnaires are inconsistent. One study of 9- to 11-year-olds in Iowa did not find any difference between normal-weight and obese children in the time spent in light, moderate, hard, and very hard physical activities (Gazzaniga & Burns 1993). A study of 9- to 10-year-old obese (n = 55) and nonobese (n = 89) Cree children in rural Canada (Bernard et al 1995) found that obese children participated less in exercise sufficiently intense to cause them to be out of breath or perspire than did nonobese children. Further, the obese children reported spending more time watching TV than did the nonobese children.

Studies that have used heart-rate monitoring to assess physical activity in small groups of obese and nonobese children are also inconsistent. One study found a trend for obese children to spend more time sleeping and resting and less time at high levels of physical activity, but between-group differences were not significant. The other study (Maffeis et al 1996) found that obese children spent more time in sedentary activities than nonobese children.

Studies of energy expenditure in obese and nonobese children (Maffeis et al 1995, Manos et al 1993) have found few or no between-group differences. These results, however, do not necessarily indicate that obese children are as physically active as nonobese children, because energy expenditure in activity is a function of body size. Therefore, at any given level of physical activity, energy expenditure in obese children will be greater because of their greater body mass. In a pilot study of girls (n = 13), Manos et al (1993) found that energy expenditure in physical activity was higher in the obese girls, but correcting energy expenditure in activity for body weight demonstrated that the obese girls were less, not more, physically active.

In summary, studies comparing obese with nonobese school-aged children are inconclusive, but suggest that obese children are less physically active. However, we do not know if obese children are obese because of low levels of physical activity, or whether they have low levels of physical activity because they are obese. Lower levels of physical activity could be a cause, or an effect, of obesity, or both because of the likelihood of the establishment of a positive feedback loop as body weight increases. Prospective studies are needed to improve our understanding of the role of physical activity in becoming obese.

INTERVENTION STUDIES   Because of the difficulties of determining the causal pathways between physical activity and overnutrition, a number of intervention studies have been designed to determine the degree to which fatness in children can be decreased by increases in physical activity.

MacConnie et al (1982) demonstrated that the physical activity level of 7-year-old children could be increased significantly using a training program of 25 minutes of vigorous aerobic exercise four times per week for eight months. This is an adult standard of exercise intensity and equivalent to 1.7% of total time per day on four days per week. This training program did not affect the body composition of the children, all of whom were on about the 50th percentile for weight.

Burke et al (1995) reported a school-based intervention study in Western Australia with 10- to 12-year-old children that included a fitness as well as a nutrition-education component. The study demonstrated that it was possible to decrease body fatness and increase fitness. Unfortunately, in this type of study, it is difficult to disentangle the effects of physical activity on fatness from the effects of the nutritional component of the intervention.

Several intervention studies (Dwyer et al 1983, Sallis et al 1993, Walter et al 1988) have been based on school physical education programs. The results of these studies are inconsistent, but the interventions with the more vigorous levels of physical activity have shown a trend toward lower levels of fatness. These and other intervention studies (Epstein 1995) have demonstrated that the physical activity level of children can be increased through organized exercise programs. It is not clear, however, whether the increase in physical activity is offset by changes in physical activity at other times of the day or whether children increase food energy intake to compensate for the increase in energy expenditure (Gutin & Manos 1993). Studies with adults have shown that they do tend to increase energy intake (Hill et al 1995).

Interventions aimed at modifying cardiovascular disease risk factors (blood pressure, serum lipids, and glucose tolerance) in obese children using an increase in physical activity have generally shown positive effects (Brownell & Kaye 1982, Després et al 1990, Madsen et al 1993, Resnicow 1993, Widhalm et al 1978). Increased physical activity in healthy nonobese children, however, has little effect on risk factors, probably because values for these factors are in the normal range to begin with (Bar-Or & Malina 1995). Further, it is not at all clear that increased physical activity in childhood will translate into long-term benefits in cardiovascular health, because most studies have demonstrated only short-term effects (Bar-Or & Malina 1995, Livingstone et al 1992). Here, again, prospective studies are needed.

OVERVIEW AND FUTURE DIRECTIONS

Undernutrition and overnutrition in children, when sufficiently severe, are both associated with low levels of physical activity. In undernutrition, the level of physical activity appears to increase with increases in energy intake. When children are not forced to accommodate to low energy availability, the level of physical activity is probably determined by cultural and environmental factors. In overnutrition, the short-term effect of energy intake on physical activity is not clear.

The most common research design for assessing the interrelationship of nutrition and physical activity has been to use two-group designs comparing undernourished and controls, or overnourished and controls. Whether there are thresholds in under- and overnutrition at which lower levels of physical activity would be expected is unclear. The data of Torún & Viteri (1981) suggest that this is the case in severely undernourished young children. Similarly for overnutrition, there is probably some level of fatness at which physical activity is reduced because of the high cost of movement to the organism.

Assessment of physical activity in children is problematical. Further research is needed to determine the best approach for measuring both the physiological and behavioral aspects of physical activity (Bar-Or & Malina 1995). At present, heart-rate monitoring combined with observations probably provides the most useful information overall.

The level of physical activity necessary for normal growth and development, and for promoting health-related fitness and reducing health risks, is not known (Bar-Or & Malina 1995, Puhl et al 1990). In industrialized countries, the tendency has been to use an adult standard in terms of duration and intensity of activity, but this may be incompatible with the more "natural spontaneous activity patterns" of children (Livingstone et al 1992).

Finally, we do not have a very clear understanding of how social, cultural, and environmental differences affect the physical activity of children. The assumption seems to have been that some level (exactly what is unclear) of physical activity in children is biologically driven and therefore that social, cultural, and environmental differences are not relevant. It is quite clear, however, that the level of physical activity in children is a biocultural phenomenon and needs to be approached that way. In industrialized countries where food is abundant and fatness is a preoccupation of adults, physical activity in children is encouraged and even formally organized. Could adult restrictions on physical activity be operating as a behavioral accommodation to low energy availability in other places? The utility of cross-cultural comparisons is questionable until we have a clearer understanding of how cultural differences affect the physical activity of children.

Visit the *Annual Reviews home page* at http://www.AnnualReviews.org.

Literature Cited

Albertson AM, Tobelmann RC. 1993. Ten-year trend of energy intakes of American children ages 2-10 years. *Ann. NY Acad. Sci.* 699:250–52

Bandini LG, Schoeller DA, Edwards J, Young VR, Oh SH, Dietz WH. 1990. Energy expenditure during carbohydrate overfeeding in obese and nonobese adolescents. *Am. Physiol.* 256: E357–67

Bar-Or O, Malina RM. 1995. Activity, fitness and health of children and adolescents. See Cheung & Richmond 1995, pp. 79–123

Berkowitz RI, Agras WS, Korner AF, Krae-mer HC, Zeanah CH. 1985. Physical activity and adiposity: a longitudinal study from birth to childhood. *J. Pediatr.* 106: 734–38

Bernard L, Lavallée C, Gray-Donald K, Delisle H. 1995. Overweight in Cree schoolchildren and adolescents associated with diet, low physical activity, and high television viewing. *J. Am. Diet. Assoc.* 95: 800–2

Bouchard C, Pérusse L. 1993. Genetic aspects of obesity. *Annu. Rev. Nutr.* 13:337–54

Bouchard C, Shepard RJ, Stephens T, Sutton

JR, McPherson BD, eds. 1990. *Exercise, Fitness and Health: A Consensus of Current Knowledge*. Champaign, IL: Hum. Kinet.

Brownell KD, Kaye FS. 1982. A school-based behavior modification, nutrition education, and physical activity program for obese children. *Am. J. Clin. Nutr.* 35:277–83

Burke V, Beilin LJ, Milligan R, Thompson C. 1995. Assessment of nutrition and physical activity education programmes in children. *Clin. Exp. Pharmacol. Physiol.* 22:212–16

Cain M. 1977. The economic activities of children in a village in Bangladesh. *Popul. Dev. Rev.* 3:201–27

Chavez A, Martinez C. 1982. *Growing Up in a Developing Country*. Mexico: Inst. Nac. Nutr.

Cheung LWY, Richmond JB, eds. 1995. *Child Health, Nutrition and Physical Activity*. Champaign, IL: Hum. Kinet.

Davies PSW. 1996. Total energy expenditure in young children. *Am. J. Hum. Biol.* 8:183–88

Davies PSW, Gregory DJ, White A. 1995. Physical activity and body fatness in preschool children. *Int. J. Obes.* 19:6–10

Department of Health and Human Services. 1991. *Promoting Health/Preventing Disease: Year 2000 Objectives for the Nation*. Washington, DC: Public Health Serv. DHHS Publ. 91-50213

Després J-P, Bouchard C, Malina RM. 1990. Physical activity and cornary heart disease risk factors during childhood and adolescence. *Exerc. Sport Sci. Rev.* 18:243–61

Després J-P, Lamarche B. 1993. Effects of diet and physical activity on adiposity and body fat distribution: implications for the prevention of cardiovascular disease. *Nutr. Res. Rev.* 6:137–59

Dietz WH Jr, Gortmaker SL. 1985. Do we fatten our children at the television set? Obesity and television viewing in children and adolescents. *Pediatrics* 75:807–12

DuRant RH, Baranowski T, Johnson M, Thompson WO. 1994. The relationship among television watching, physical activity, and body composition of young children. *Pediatrics* 94(4):449–55

Durnin JVGA. 1992. Physical activity levels—past and present. See Norgan 1992, pp. 20–27

Dwyer T, Blizzard CL. 1996. Defining obesity in children by biological endpoint rather than population distribution. *Int. J. Obes.* 20:472–80

Dwyer T, Coonan WE, Leitch DR, Hetzel BS,

Baghurst PA. 1983. An investigation of the effects of daily physical activity on the health of primary school children in Southern Australia. *Int. J. Epidemiol.* 12:308–13

Emons HJG, Groenenboom DC, Westerterp KR, Saris WHM. 1992. Comparison of heart rate monitoring combined with indirect calorimetry and the doubly labelled water ($^2H_2{}^{18}O$) method for the measurement of energy expenditure in children. *Eur. J. Appl. Physiol.* 65:99–103

Epstein FH, Higgins M. 1992. Epidemiology of obesity. In *Obesity*, ed. P Björntorp, BN Brodoff, pp. 330–42. Philadelphia: Lippincott

Epstein LH. 1995. Exercise in the treatment of childhood obesity. *Int. J. Obes.* 19(Suppl. 4):S117–21

FAO/WHO/UNU. 1985. *Energy and Protein Requirements*. WHO Tech. Rep., Ser. 7

Fontvieille AM, Harper IT, Ferraro RT, Spraul M, Ravussin E. 1993a. Daily energy expenditure by five-year-old children, measured by doubly labeled water. *J. Pediatr.* 123:200–7

Fontvieille AM, Kriska A, Ravussin E. 1993b. Decreased physical activity in Pima Indians compared with Caucasian children. *Int. J. Obes. Relat. Metab. Disord.* 17:445–52

Garn SM, Leonard WR, Hawthorne VM. 1986. Three limitations of the body mass index. *Am. J. Clin. Nutr.* 44:996–97

Gazzaniga JM, Burns TL. 1993. Relationship between diet compostion and body fatness, with adjustment for resting energy expenditure and physical activity, in preadolescent children. *Am. J. Clin. Nutr.* 58(1):21–28

Gilliam TB, Freedson PS, Geenen DL, Shahraray B. 1981. Physical activity patterns determined by heart rate monitoring in 6–7 year-old children. *Med. Sci. Sports Exerc.* 13(1):65–67

Goran MI, Carpenter WH, Poehlman ET. 1993. Total energy expenditure in 4- to 6-yr-old children. *Am. J. Physiol.* 264:E706–11

Goran MI, Kaskoun M, Johnson R, Martinez C, Kelly B, Hood V. 1995. Energy expenditure and body fat distribution in Mohawk children. *Pediatrics* 95:89–95

Gorstein J, Sullivan K, Yip R, de Onís M, Trowbridge F, et al. 1994. Issues in the assessment of nutritional status using anthropometry. *WHO Bull.* 72:273–83

Gortmaker SL, Dietz WH Jr, Cheung LWY. 1990. Inactivity, diet, and the fattening of America. *J. Am. Diet. Assoc.* 90:1247–52

Grantham-McGregor S, Meeks Gardner JM,

Walker S, Powell C. 1990. The relationship between undernutrition, activity levels and development in young children. See Schrüch & Scrimshaw 1990, pp. 361–84

Gurney M, Gorstein J. 1988. The global prevalence of obesity—an initial overview of available data. *World Health Stat. Q.* 41: 251–54

Gutin B, Baranowski T, Manos T, Litaker M, Baranowski J, et al. 1993. Relations among fatness, physical activity, diet, resting metabolism, and fitness in 3–7 year old children. *Off. J. Am. Coll. Sports Med.* 25(5):591 (Suppl.)

Gutin B, Basch C, Shea S, Contento I, DeLozier M, et al. 1990. Blood pressure, fitness, and fatness in 5- and 6-year-old children. *J. Am. Med. Assoc.* 264:1123–27

Gutin B, Manos TM. 1993. Physical activity in the prevention of childhood obesity. *Ann. NY Acad. Sci.* 699:115–26

Hamill PVV, Dridz TA, Johnson CL, Reed RB, Roche AF, Moore WM. 1979. Physical growth: National Center for Health Statistics percentiles. *Am. J. Clin. Nutr.* 32: 607–29

Hardenberg SHB. 1996. Behavioral quality and caloric intake in Malagasy children relative to international growth references. *Am. J. Hum. Biol.* 8:207–23

Harlan WR, Landis JR, Flegal KM, Davis CS, Miller ME. 1988. Secular trends in body mass in the United States, 1960–1980. *Am. J. Epidemiol.* 128:1065–74

Hill JO, Melby C, Johnson SL, Peters JC. 1995. Physical activity and energy requirements. *Am. J. Clin. Nutr.* 62:S1059–66 (Suppl.)

Ho Z-C, Zi HM, Bo L, Ping H. 1988. Energy expenditure of preschool children in a subtropical area. *World Rev. Nutr. Diet.* 57: 75–94

Hultquist CM, Eck LH, Klesges RC, Shuster ML, Klesges L. 1991. Resting energy expenditure (REE) and thermic effect of food (TEF) in overweight and normal weight children. *Med. Sci. Sports Exerc.* 23:S74

Ivanovic D, Olivares M, Ivanovic R. 1991. Nutritional status of Chilean school children from different socioeconomic status and sex. Chile's metropolitan region. Survey 1986–1987. *Ecol. Food Nutr.* 26: 1–16

Janz KF, Golden JC, Hansen JR, Mahoney LT. 1992. Heart rate monitoring of physical activity in children and adolescents: the Muscatine study. *Pediatrics* 89:256–61

Keller W, Fillmore CM. 1983. Prevalence of protein-energy malnutrition. *World Health Stat. Q.* 36:129–67

Klesges RC, Shelton ML, Klesges LM. 1993. Effects of television on metabolic rate: potential implications for childhood obesity. *Pediatrics* 91(2):281–86

Lawrence F, Lamb WH, Lamb C, Lawrence M. 1985. A quantification of child care and infant-caregiver interaction in a West-African village. *Early Hum. Dev.* 12: 71–80

Lawrence M, Lawrence F, Durnin JVGA, Whitehead RG. 1991. A comparison of physical activity in Gambian and UK children aged 6–18 months. *Eur. J. Clin. Nutr.* 45:243–52

Livingstone MBE, Coward WA, Prentice AM, Davies PSW, Strain JJ, et al. 1992. Daily energy expenditure in free-living children: comparison of heart-rate monitoring with the doubly labeled water ($^2H_2^{18}O$) method. *Am. J. Clin. Nutr.* 56:343–52

MacConnie SE, Gilliam TB, Geenen DL, Pels AE III. 1982. Daily physical activity patterns of prepubertal children involved in a vigorous exercise program. *Int. J. Sports Med.* 3:202–7

Madsen J, Sallis JF, Rupp JW, Senn KL, Patterson TL, et al. 1993. Relationship between self-monitoring of diet and exercise change and subsequent risk factor changes in children and adults. *Patient Educ. Couns.* 21:61–69

Maffeis C, Pinelli L, Zaffanello M, Schena F, Iacumin P, Schutz Y. 1995. Daily energy expenditure in free-living conditions in obese and nonobese children: comparison of doubly labelled water ($^2H_2^{18}O$) method and heart-rate monitoring. *Int. J. Obes. Relat. Metab. Disord.* 19:671–77

Maffeis C, Zaffanello M, Pinelli L, Schutz Y. 1996. Total energy expenditure and patterns of activity in 8–10-year-old obese and nonobese children. *J. Pediatr. Gastroenterol. Nutr.* 23:256–61

McKenzie TL, Sallis JF, Nader PR, Broyles SL, Nelson JA. 1992. Anglo- and Mexican-American preschoolers at home and at recess: activity patterns and environmental influences. *J. Dev. Behav. Pediatr.* 13:173–80

Malina RM. 1992. Physical activity and behavioral development during childhood and youth. See Norgan 1992, pp. 101–20

Manos TM, Gutin B, Rhodes T, Spandorfer PR, Jackson LW, Litaker MS. 1993. Energy expenditure and intake in obese and nonobese African-American girls. *Ann. NY Acad. Sci.* 699:275–77

Meeks Gardner JM, Grantham-McGregor SM,

564   DUFOUR

Chang SM, Powell CA. 1990. Dietary intake and observed activity of stunted and nonstunted children in Kingston, Jamaica. Part II: Observed activity. *Eur. J. Clin. Nutr.* 44:585–93

Munroe RH, Munroe RL, Michelson C, Koel A, Bolton R, Bolton C. 1983. Time allocation in four societies. *Ethnology* 12: 355–70

Monteiro CA, Mondini L, Medeiros de Souza AL, Popkin BM. 1995. The nutrition transition in Brazil. *Eur. J. Clin. Nutr.* 49: 105–13

Mukeshi M, Gutin B, Anderson W, Zybert P, Basch C. 1990. Validation of the caltrac movement sensor using direct observation in young children. *Pediatr. Exerc. Sci.* 2: 249–54

Norgan NC. 1992. *Physical Activity and Health.* Cambridge: Cambridge Univ. Press

Pate RR, Dowda M, Ross JG. 1990. Associations between physical activity and physical fitness in American children. *Am. J. Dis. Child.* 144:1123–29

Pflieger KL, Treiber FA, Davis H, McCaffrey FM, Raunikar RA, Strong WB. 1994. The effect of adiposity on children's left ventricular mass and haemodynamic responses to stress. *Int. J. Obes. Relat. Metab. Disord.* 18:117–22

Puhl J, Greaves K, Hoyt M, Baranowski T. 1990. Children's activity rating scale (CARS): description and calibration. *Res. Q. Exerc. Sport* 61:26–36

Räsänen L, Ahola M, Kara R, Uhari M. 1985. Atherosclerotic precursors in Finnish children and adolescents. VIII. Food consumption and nutrient intakes. *Acta Paediatr. Scand.* 318:135–53 (Suppl.)

Resnicow K. 1993. Population versus high-risk interventions. *Ann. NY Acad. Sci.* 699: 154–66

Roche AF, Siervogel RM, Chumlea WC, Webb P. 1981. Grading fitness from limited anthropometric data. *Am. J. Clin. Nutr.* 34:31–38

Rutishauser IHE, Whitehead RG. 1972. Energy intake and expenditure in 1–3-year-old Ugandan children living in a rural environment. *Br. J. Nutr.* 28:145–52

Sallis JF. 1995. A behavioral perspective on children's physical activity. See Cheung & Richmond 1995, pp. 125–38

Sallis JF, Alcaraz JE, McKenzie TL, Hovell MF, Kolody B, Nader PR. 1992. Parental behavior in relation to physical activity and fitness in 9-year-old children. *Am. J. Dis. Child.* 146:1383–88

Sallis JF, McKenzie TL, Alcaraz JE, Kolody B, Hovell MF, Nader PR. 1993. Effects of physical education on adiposity in children. *Ann. NY Acad. Sci.* 699:127–36

Saris WHM. 1985. The asssessment and evaluation of daily physical activity in children. A review. *Acta Paediatr. Scand. Suppl.* 318:37–48

Schoeller DA, Ravssin E, Schutz Y, Acheson KJ, Baertschi P, Jequier E. 1986. Energy expenditure by doubly labelled water: validation in humans and proposed calculation. *Am. J. Physiol.* 250:R823–30

Schrüch B, Scrimshaw NS, eds. 1990. *Activity, energy expenditure and energy requirements of infants and children. Proc. IDECG Workshop, Cambridge, MA.* Lausanne: Int. Diet. Energy Consult. Group

Schwartz MW, Seeley RJ. 1997. The new biology of body weight regulation. *J. Am. Diet. Assoc.* 97:54–58

Simons-Morton BG, McKenzie TJ, Stone E, Mitchell P, Osganian V, et al. 1997. Physical activity in a multiethnic population of third graders in four states. *Am. J. Public Health* 87:45–50

Simons-Morton BG, O'Hara NM, Parcel GS, Huang IW, Baranowski T, Wilson B. 1990. Children's frequency of participation in moderate to vigorous physical activities. *Res. Q. Exerc. Sport* 61:307–14

Simons-Morton BG, Parcel GS, O'Hara NM, Blair SN, Pate RR. 1988. Health-related physical fitness in childhood: status and recommendations. *Annu. Rev. Public Health* 9:403–25

Spady DW. 1980. Total daily energy expenditure of healthy, free ranging school children. *Am. J. Clin. Nutr.* 33:766–75

Spurr GB, Dufour DL, Reina JC. 1996. Energy expenditure of urban Colombian women: a comparison of patterns and total daily expenditure by the heart rate and factorial methods. *Am. J. Clin. Nutr.* 63:870–78

Spurr GB, Prentice AM, Murgatroyd PR, Goldberg GR, Reina JC, Christman NT. 1988. Energy expenditure from minute-by-minute heart-rate recording: comparison with indirect calorimetry. *Am. J. Clin. Nutr.* 48:552–59

Spurr GB, Reina JC. 1988a. Patterns of daily energy expenditure in normal and marginally undernourished school-aged Colombian children. *Eur. J. Clin. Nutr.* 42: 819–34

Spurr GB, Reina JC. 1988b. Influence of dietary intervention on artifically increased activity in marginally undernourished Colombian boys. *Eur. J. Clin. Nutr.* 42: 835–46

Spurr GB, Reina JC. 1989. Energy expenditure/basal metabolic rate ratios in normal and marginally undernourished Colombian children 6–16 years of age. *Eur. J. Clin. Nutr.* 43:515–27

Spurr GB, Reina JC. 1990. Estimation and validation of energy expenditure obtained by the minute-by-minute measurement of heart rate. See Schrüch & Scrimshaw 1990, pp. 57–70

Stinson S. 1992. Nutritional adaptation. *Annu. Rev. Anthropol.* 21:143–70

Sunnegårdh J, Bratteby L-E, Hagman U, Samuelson G, Sjölin S. 1986. Physical activity in relation to energy intake and body fat in 8- and 13-year-old children in Sweden. *Acta Paediatr. Scand.* 75:955–63

Sunnegårdh J, Bratteby L-E, Sjölin S. 1985. Physical activity and sports involvement in 8- and 13-year-old children in Sweden. *Acta Paediatr. Scand.* 74:904–12

Super CM. 1990. The cultural regulation of infant and child activities. See Schrüch & Scrimshaw 1990, pp. 321–33

Taylor W, Baranowski T. 1991. Physical activity, cardiovascular fitness, and adiposity in children. *Res. Q. Exerc. Sport.* 62(2):157–63

Torún B. 1990a. Energy cost of various physical activities in healthy children. See Schrüch & Scrimshaw 1990, pp. 139–83

Torún B. 1990b. Short- and long-term effects of low or restricted energy intakes on the activity of infants and children. See Schrüch & Scrimshaw 1990, pp. 335–58

Torún B. 1994. Influence of malnutrition on physical activity of children and adults. In *Nutr. Sustain. Environ., Proc. 15th Int. Congr. Nutr., Adelaide,* ed. M Wahlqvist, AS Truswell, R Smith, PJ Nestel, pp. 651–54. London: Smith-Gordon

Torún B, Davies PSW, Livingstone MBE, Paolisso M, Sackett R, Spurr GB. 1996. Energy requirements and dietary energy recommendations for children and adolescents 1 to 18 years old. *Eur. J. Clin. Nutr.* 50:S37–S81 (Suppl.)

Torún B, Viteri FE. 1981. Energy requirements of preschool children and effects of varying energy intakes on protein metabolism. *UN Univ. Food Nutr. Bull.* 5:229–41 (Suppl.)

Troiano RP, Flegal KM, Kuczmarski RJ, Campbell SM, Johnson CL. 1995. Overweight prevalence and trends for children and adolescents. *Arch. Pediatr. Adolesc. Med.* 149:1085–91

Trowell HC, Davis JNP, Dean RFA. 1982. *Kwashiorkor.* A Nutrition Foundation Reprint. New York: Academic

Viteri FE, Torún B. 1981. Nutrition, physical activity, and growth. In *The Biology of Normal Human Growth,* Trans. First Karolinska Inst. Nobel Conf., ed. M Ritzén, A Aperia, K Hall, A Larsson, A Zetterberg, R Zetterström. New York: Raven

Walter HJ, Hofman A, Vaughan RD, Wynder EL. 1988. Modification of risk factors for coronary heart disease: five-year results of school-based intervention trial. *N. Engl. J. Med.* 318:1093–100

Waterlow JC. 1973. Note on the assessment and classification of protein-energy malnutrition in children. *Lancet* 2:87–89

Whitehead RG, Paul AA, Cole TJ. 1982. Trends in food energy intakes throughout childhood from one to 18 years. *Hum. Nutr. Appl. Nutr.* 36:57–62

Whiting BB, Edwards CP. 1988. *Children of Different Worlds: The Formation of Social Behavior.* Cambridge, MA: Harvard Univ. Press

WHO Working Group. 1986. Use and interpretation of anthropometric indicators of nutritional status. *WHO Bull.,* pp. 929–41

Widhalm K, Maxa E, Zyman H. 1978. Effect of diet and exercise upon the cholesterol and triglyceride content of plasma lipoproteins in overweight children. *Eur. J. Pediatr.* 127:121–26

Williams CL, Kimm SYS, eds. 1993. Prevention and treatment of childhood obesity. *Ann. NY Acad. Sci.* 699

Williams DP, Going SB, Lohman TG, Harsha DW, Srinivasan SR, et al. 1992. Body fatness and risk for elevated blood pressure, total cholesterol, and serum lipoprotein ratios in children and adolescents. *Am. J. Public Health* 82:358–63

Zemel BS, Ulijaszek SJ, Leonard W. 1996. Energetics, lifestyles and nutritional adaptation: an introduction. *Am. J. Hum. Biol.* 8:141–42

Annu. Rev. Anthropol. 1997. 26:567–90
Copyright © 1997 by Annual Reviews Inc. All rights reserved

CULTURAL POLITICS OF IDENTITY IN LATIN AMERICA

Charles R. Hale

Department of Anthropology, The University of Texas at Austin, Austin, Texas 78712

KEY WORDS: identity politics, social movements, intellectuals

---

ABSTRACT

The phrase "identity politics" has come to encapsulate a wide diversity of oppositional movements in contemporary Latin America, marking a transition away from the previous moment of unified, "national-popular" projects. This review takes a dual approach to the literature emerging from that transition, focusing on changes in both the objects of study and the analysts' lens. Four questions drive this inquiry: When did the moment of identity politics arise? What accounts for the shift? How to characterize its contents? What consequences follow for the people involved? Past answers to such questions often have tended to fall into polarized materialist and discursive theoretical camps. In contrast, this review emphasizes emergent scholarship that takes insights from both while refusing the dichotomy, and assigning renewed importance to empirically grounded and politically engaged research.

INTRODUCTION

A prospective graduate student recently visited me and provided an account of her past academic odyssey, which led her finally to opt for anthropology at Texas. All her prior work had culminated, she explained, in a plan to return home (a Latin American country) to study the politics of identity. She is far from alone. The phrase "identity politics" now figures prominently in anthropology graduate school applications and graduate seminars everywhere, as well as in many journals related to anthropology that have been founded in the past decade (*Identities, Social Identities, Cultural Studies of Latin America, Journal of Latin American Anthropology, Cultural Studies Birmingham*).

567

Even more telling is the shift that has occurred in some long-running journals, whose focus previously fit neatly within the antecedent moment of Marxist analysis, class politics, and national-popular visions of social change (e.g. *Socialist Review, NACLA, Nueva Sociedad*). Far from limited to academia, the issues at stake also animate spirited debate in the mass media, and in politics and policy, throughout the Americas.[1]

This review offers a framework to organize and think through the outpouring of work on identity politics, with a specific emphasis on Latin America. The phrase "identity politics" will refer to collective sensibilities and actions that come from a particular location within society, in direct defiance of universal categories that tend to subsume, erase, or suppress this particularity. "Location," in this sense, implies a distinctive social memory, consciousness, and practice, as well as place within the social structure.[2] To illustrate, consider a group of Nicaraguan women labor organizers who worked during the 1980s within the Sandinista Workers Union (CST). By the decade's end, these organizers had become fed up with CST's universal category "class," which allowed little room for specific attention to women's experiences as workers, and even less for critique of patriarchy. When they left the CST to form a separate organization devoted to the particular experiences, interests, and struggles of women workers, they entered the realm of identity politics (Criquillón 1995).

The review proceeds in four parts. I begin by asking when identity politics achieved prominence in Latin America and in Latin Americanist anthropology. Is it possible to specify a moment of "rupture" after which identity politics came to the fore? Next I ask how analysts account for this shift. Given the heterogeneity of the subject, is it more appropriate to pursue a series of wholly distinct explanations, rather than a single one? I then examine the character of identity politics: Does the phrase refer to a collection of practices and sensibilities that have key features in common? This will lead, finally, to a consideration of outcomes and consequences: What have people achieved through the

---

[1] This topic is entirely too extensive even to begin to cite. For a cogent recent commentary that relates public debate in the United States specifically to anthropology, see di Leonardo (1996). In this essay, she makes the interesting point that in the mainstream public eye, "identity politics" is imbued with both a "constructivist" (i.e. all histories are situated, relative truths) and "essentialist" (i.e. our history is *the* right one) contents, without addressing the substantial disparities between these two discourses. I take up this issue in what follows.

[2] This formulation is influenced by readings in the new cultural geography, the impetus for which came from Donald Moore. The literature that relates space and identity politics in this way is extensive; works that I found especially useful include Moore (1997), Massey (1994), Pile & Thrift (1995), and Gupta & Ferguson (1992).

practice of identity politics, with what impact on their lives? Rather than provide definitive answers to these questions, I frame the discussions they have generated, specify key divergences and areas of consensus, and chart the promising directions in which new research is headed. Throughout, I tack back and forth between the topic itself and the assumptions underlying anthropological analysis, drawing inspiration from others who have engaged in such critique (Coronil 1996, Kearney 1996, Taussig 1993, Williams 1989, Yúdice 1996, CA Smith 1997). By making intellectuals the objects of study as well, we keep the politics of anthropological theory on center stage and take fuller advantage of the "dual or multiple consciousness" that results (Harrison 1991).

Justifiable and enlightening for nearly any body of literature, emphasis on the entanglement of the analyst's lens and topic of study is especially crucial in this case. On the one hand, the massive and widespread evidence for a shift in the character of oppositional politics in Latin America—the "explosion" of grassroots organizations (Castañeda 1993), the rise of "new social movements" (Escobar & Alvarez 1992)—is impossible to miss. Emblematic of this shift is the surge of political activity by indigenous peoples throughout the hemisphere on the occasion of the Columbus quincentenary (Gabriel 1994, Hale 1994a, SAIIC 1992): their newly acquired national-level political influence, and their leaders' adamancy to speak for themselves. On the other hand, much writing on the topic invites skepticism. For example, Arturo Escobar (1992a, p. 82) recently wrote with annunciatory enthusiasm of new social movements, asserting that:

> up to the 1960s, identities were, in a sense, clearly defined and unproblematic. One knew who was who, so to speak, and how he or she was defined as a member of a group. One also knew what to do and how to do it (Development or Revolution, depending on one's perspective). But this is no longer true.

Assertions like this one cry out for hard-nosed historical and theoretical critique (e.g. Edelman 1996, Knight 1990). Such a neat before-after dichotomy, if relevant at all, could only reasonably apply to intellectuals well versed in paradigm hopping. When applied across the board, it leaves the distinct impression that the two realms—how people enact politics and how analysts understand these enactments—have been seriously conflated. Even more to the point are efforts to read complex social and political processes through a few purportedly emblematic literary texts, which yield predictable portrayals of Latin American societies saturated with hybridity, multiplicity, and other so-called keywords of the shift to identity politics (e.g. de la Campa 1995). Such claims culminate in the idea that Latin America has always been hybrid (e.g. Chanady 1994), an assertion that, in its very incontestability, reinforces the suspicion that changing theoretical fashions play a major role in constituting their own subject.

Yet many such critiques, instead of restoring analytical balance, often have left the debate hopelessly polarized. One need only sample the venom in the "forum" on Ahmad's (1992) work in *Public Culture* (Ahmad 1993), or reflect on the implications of Dirlik's (1994) provocative assertion that postcolonial theory came of age when third world intellectuals "arrived in First World academe," creating an "aura" that obscured the facilitating conditions of their arrival: i.e. class privilege and the "needs" of global capitalism (see also Lazarus 1991). When these critics attempt to reduce all analysis informed by postmodern theory to self-absorbed ruminations and self-interested career moves, the argument rapidly takes on an "aura" of its own. Framed as a return to "materiality," these counterarguments often allow the real subject of analysis—people struggling from the margins to gain voice and power—to vanish into thin air.

My point of departure here is that this polarized divide—between postmodern theoretical innovation and materialist reassertion—has grown steadily less important, and less useful, as an organizing framework for recent scholarship on identity politics in Latin America. It would not be difficult to find work that exemplifies those entrenched, opposing poles: identities as performative acts, politics as purely discursive battles versus hard-bitten calls for a return to the fundamental role of class struggle in history; blanket assertions of a rupture that relegates all theory "before" to the status of "totalizing Eurocentric metanarrative" versus suspiciously totalizing efforts to cast the new theory as unwitting ideological accomplice of "global capitalism." Indeed, I refer to this polarization throughout the review because it is integral to the recent intellectual history of the topic. Yet I also recast this polarization as precisely that—historical background—for two reasons. First, the flaws inherent in each pole of the debate have become mutually enabling: They are propelled more by contention with one another than by sustained empirical engagement with the subject of study. Second, most of the interesting, forward-looking research already has set its sights squarely beyond this divide, incorporating insights from both sides while rejecting the extreme terms of the polarization itself. Although one might be tempted to understand the resulting theoretical resting place as a middle ground, a synthesis of the materialist thesis and the discursive antithesis, I contend that a more radical departure is under way. The most promising work not only offers new theories of politics but sets out to explore and implement a new politics of theory (Hall 1992): skeptical of both positivist theory-building and trendy, wheel-spinning theoretical self-referentiality; methodologically rigorous, yet fully aware that all claims to objectivity are ultimately situated knowledges (Haraway 1988); and most important, oriented toward reflexive political engagement, whether focused on "subalterns" who speak, read, and write for themselves, or on powerful institutions and actors who too often in the past have avoided anthropological scrutiny.

WHEN DID THE TURN TO IDENTITY POLITICS BEGIN?

Just as some recently have protested that anthropologists were "multicultural-ists" long before the term became a lightning rod for US cultural politics (e.g. Weiner 1992), one might well claim that anthropology of Latin America was "on to" identity politics long before the phrase rose to its current heights of theoretical fashion. Consider, for example, two traditional areas of concentra-tion in Latin American anthropology—peasants and indigenous peoples. If we juxtapose these to two key features associated with identity politics—local identities shaped by global forces (Appadurai 1995), and politics as "struggles over [cultural] meanings at the level of daily life" (Escobar 1992a, p. 71; Franco 1992)—continuities come immediately to mind. At least forty years ago scholars began to place the analysis of the Latin American peasantry in a global context (Adams 1967, Mintz 1974, Wolf 1969), and sensitivity to strug-gles over cultural meanings (at least at the local level) in indigenous societies goes back even further. Michael Brown has made this latter point recently, and all the more forcefully because his work on Amazonian Indian leaders high-lights the "new politics of identity" in which they are immersed. Yet he con-cludes with a call for return to the fine-grained political ethnographies of times past, which addressed questions like: "In what ways is power created, used, ne-gotiated, and thwarted by individuals in their daily lives?" (Brown 1993, p. 320; see also Watanabe 1996). Assuming that Brown is not using hindsight to artificially resuscitate the old masters, then the similarity between his and Es-cobar's descriptions is striking: What precisely justifies the adjective "new"?

Part of the answer lies in the process of rearticulation, whereby people find new means to collectively express and pursue interests, demands, and values that have long-standing importance to them. This implied emphasis on conti-nuity must strike a delicate balance: neither imbuing people with timeless, es-sential motivations, nor assuming that these motivations come into being only when an organized effort first emerges to express them. In the case of indige-nous politics, for example, we can acknowledge the diverse forms of resistance throughout the past 500 years and note that key issues of Indian identity ad-dressed in the sixteenth century are still pertinent today (Silverblatt 1995). Yet we can also note that indigenous peoples now increasingly advance their strug-gles through a discourse that links Indian identity with rights to territory, autonomy, and peoplehood—rights that run parallel to those of the nation state itself (Albó 1991, Bonfil Batalla 1981, Conklin & Graham 1995, Jackson 1995, Sherzer & Urban 1991, Stavenhagen 1992).

A systematic analysis of rearticulation must begin with closer scrutiny of the term "identity." On my office wall hangs a poster, distributed by an organi-zation of Maya cultural activism in Guatemala, whose slogan reads: "Only when a people (*un Pueblo*) learns (*acepta*) its history and affirms (*asume*) its identity, does it have the right to define its future." This statement encapsulates a notion of identity as unique and differentiated (possessing its own historical on-tology) and inherently endowed with fundamental rights (beginning with self-determination). We might want to think about the era of "identity politics" as beginning when this particular use of the term identity became the standard, generalized idiom through which groups engage in politics with one another, the state, and other powerful adversaries (Handler 1994, Rouse 1995a).[3] Ernesto Laclau's (1977) now classic essay on populism helps to evoke and describe the previous state of affairs, when the forging of a "national-popular" bloc could theoretically reconcile the great heterogeneity of Latin American societies with the need for political unity. A national-popular bloc could encompass the whole gamut of "popular" sectors, while drawing political direction and coher-ence from a strong class-conscious leadership. Even socialism, Laclau argued, could only succeed if grounded in a convincing discourse of *lo popular*.

This vision of national-popular political transformation has been prominent in the sensibilities and strategy of twentieth-century politics in Latin America, especially in oppositional politics, through (to choose the latest possible end-point) the Sandinista electoral defeat of 1990 (Castañeda 1993, Rowe & Schelling 1991). The national-popular vision also played a key role in keeping oppositional politics within the flow of history with a "big h": a narrative that connected Latin America with Western liberal notions of economic develop-ment, membership in the community of sovereign nations, and societal mod-ernization (albeit on a path critical of capitalist exploitation and imperialism). Equally important, it empowered intellectuals to perform the crucial role of mediator: to articulate the heterogeneity of *lo popular* with the homogeneous discourse of the national-popular. The fit with Sandinista intellectuals' por-trayals of their revolution, for example, could hardly be better (Burbach & Nu-ñez 1987, Nuñez Soto 1986).

---

[3]There is a related story of intellectual genealogy to be told on the emergence of "ethnicity" and its displacement of anthropology's previous term of preference, "tribe." A glance at the literature in the early 1960s reveals a striking absence of the term "ethnicity." Over the next two decades, it became ubiquitous. In the 1990s, "ethnicity" is clearly in decline, replaced on the one hand by various uses of the term "identity" and on the other by a renaissance of interest in racism, racialization, and racial identities. For a critical analysis of the "erasure" of race from anthropology's lexicon, see Harrison (1995). Examples of the renaissance include the work of Marta Casaús Arzú (1991) and Marisol de la Cadena (1996), and the essays by Carol A Smith (1997) and Demetrio Cojtí (1997), forthcoming in *Identidades y Racismo en Guatemala*, a volume I am co-editing with Clara Arenas and Gustavo Palma of AVANCSO.

When the multiple subjects within the national-popular bloc claim their own separate rights, histories, and identities, however, this formula begins to unravel. Erosion of the national-popular project, and the crisis of intellectuals as mediators of its vision, may be the most reliable sign that identity politics have come to the fore. This implies not a stark rupture—a "before" when multiple identities fit neatly into broader categories, and an "after" when they did not; nor does it imply a uniform temporal logic, as in Wallerstein's (1995, pp. 1173, 1176) argument that the rise of identity politics can be linked to the "annunciatory and denunciatory world revolution of 1968," which starkly revealed the "total" contradiction of a world system. If we are to understand the emergence of multiple identities, then it hardly makes sense to reinscribe them within a framework in which particularity is derivative of universal, systemic forces and contradictions. The alternative logic of multiple historicities is what leads Fernando Coronil (1996) to refer to new social movements as the "spacialization of time"—that is, the claim to history emerging from a particular social location and adherence to the particular cultural political vision that follows.

Debates over the shift away from the national-popular are especially revealing in the case of the rebellion in Chiapas, which burst into the public eye in January 1994 (Nugent 1995). Should it be understood as "primarily a peasant rebellion" in response to the "politics of exclusion" brought about by the broader forces of Mexico's authoritarian regime and global economic dislocation (Collier 1994, 1995)? If so, then what role does the distinctively indigenous identity of the participants have in shaping their decision to rebel, their organization, their political objectives? Does the rebellion fit neatly within the long history of oppositional politics, directed toward capturing the aspirations of the "Mexican people" toward a newly conceived, truly democratic and representative "proyecto nacional" (García de León 1996, Valenzuela Jose 1996)? Or does it constitute a radical break with that very tradition, offering a new model for "doing politics," a movement bent more on transforming civil society than on traditional political goals like "nation building" and "taking power"? (Burbach 1994). If the latter, what are we to make of the quintessential national-popular rhetoric evident in so many Zapatista political statements, starting with the "Declaration of War" (1/1/94), which begins:

> [T]oday we say ENOUGH IS ENOUGH. We are the inheritors of the true builders of our nation....We will not die of hunger due to the insatiable ambition of a...clique of traitors...the same ones that opposed Hidalgo and Morelos, the same ones that massacred the railroad workers in 1958 and the students in 1968....

Rather than choose between these two interpretations, we might read the ubiquitous national-popular rhetoric as another indication that the shift to identity politics has been consummated. So complete is the erosion of the national-popular that it can now stage a modest return, no longer as all-encompassing political project but as another decentered, rejuvenating (though perhaps debilitated?) voice from the margins.

WHAT ACCOUNTS FOR THE SHIFT?

Any reader who has dipped even superficially into the literature on the politics of identity in Latin America will have its descriptive features well enough in mind (e.g. Mato 1994). The move from descriptive listing to explanatory analysis of the transition is much less commonly found. Collier et al (1995) provide one piece of the puzzle, in an argument that focuses on the contradictions of liberal ideology more generally (e.g. Kristeva 1993, Rouse 1995a). They point to an inherent contradiction between the universal principle of equality and the persisting marginalization of those who do not fit within the universal categories through which equality is achieved (e.g. "citizen" or "abstract individual"). This contradiction engenders political change, however, because it creates the opportunity for marginalized groups to make claims in the name of bourgeois law, albeit at the risk of reproducing the very cultural logic that once oppressed them. A gradually broadening process of inclusion results, which Collier et al point to as the cultural-juridical underpinnings for the rise of "identity politics" in contemporary times. Yet they do not explain why this process would have such intensity today. Similarly, Nina Glick Schiller et al (1992), leading analysts of "transnationalism" and its implications for identity politics (also the focus of the journal *Identities* that Glick Schiller edits) conclude in a recent essay that, "The socially constructed nature of our entire repository of terms to define and bound identity—"nationality," "race," and "ethnicity"—has just recently begun to be scrutinized adequately by social scientists. And the implications of transnationalism for hegemonic constructions of identity have yet to be analyzed."

Arjun Appadurai (1990, 1995), though cogent in his critique of both "world-systems" and "comparative-historical" approaches (the former neglects "disjuncture" and the latter "interconnectedness"), and creative in coining terms that evoke present conditions (ethnoscapes, memoryscapes, etc), also finds rigorous explanation lacking. He notes that "a strong theory of globalization, from a sociocultural point of view, is likely to require something that we certainly do not now have: a theory of intercontextual relations which incorporates our existing sense of intertexts" (1995, p. 212). How then to explain the shift, to avoid telling the story from the Eurocentric center (Wallerstein 1995), while achieving a reasonably comprehensive account? How to proceed if existing analytical tools have been rendered inadequate for the job?

Fredric Jameson's (1984, 1988) call for a "new cognitive mapping" has become a touchstone (or at least a de rigueur citation) for virtually everyone who confronts this problem, even if the resulting analyses lead in sharply contrasting directions. Jameson argues that it is wrong-headed to respond to postmodernism either with moral critique or as a cultural/theoretical option that one can embrace or reject. Instead, he takes the historical shift as a given and calls for a radically new framework to analyze "postmodern" phenomena like identity politics, combined with an insistence that the framework retain familiarly Marxist notions of causality, historical process, and, as Jameson puts it, the "social totality." Far from a flaw or contradiction, for some this combination enables rigorous explanation of the shift. Roger Rouse (1995a,b), for example, employs a series of concepts—e.g. (im)migration circuits, transnational spaces of identity formation—that are explicitly linked to a Jameson-like notion of the postmodern logic of capitalism. Rouse argues that in the present era of "transnational" capitalism, the state and bourgeoisie have responded to political opposition by encouraging people to express discontent through the idiom of identity. The politics of identity that result are easily contained, because they rest on key premises of the bourgeois edifice that they purport to challenge and, fundamentally, because they derail much more potent forms of class-based antisystemic struggle (see also Friedlander 1976, 1986; Larsen 1995; Vilas 1994)

Another group of theorists take up Jameson's call for a new cognitive mapping only after it is shorn of what Cornell West (rather provocatively) calls "a conception of totality" that "ultimately leads toward a Leninist or Leninist-like politics," a "crash course" of "pessimism" and "sectarianism" (from discussion of Jameson 1988; see also West 1986). Analysis from this perspective (e.g. García Canclini 1995, Rowe & Schelling 1991) seeks an explanation for the rise of identity politics grounded in many accounts that emerge from particular social locations and historicities. As Laclau (1994, p. 1) observes "we are witnessing a proliferation of particularistic political identities, none of which tries to ground its legitimacy and its action in a mission predetermined by universal history—whether that be mission of a universal class, or the notion of a privileged race, or an abstract principle." To the extent that Laclau does offer an inductive explanation, it is carefully framed as a matter of "social dislocation" that leaves people without a "clearly defined location in the social structure," and feeling an "originary and insurmountable lack of identity," which together engender a great need to construct one (1994, p. 2–3). Laclau's recent writings illustrate what might be called a "discursivist" approach to the rise of identity politics. He does not neglect the role of capitalist transformation in the shift (the term "social dislocation" is a reference to precisely that), but the central analytical thrust lies in the crisis and undoing of the dominant ideological frames that previously had kept identities stable, well-defined, and beyond doubt, thereby allowing the "heterogeneity of the social" to burst forth. There is a principled refusal to explain why this discursive crisis is occurring now, because to do so would force a return to the universalist "mission" from which we have just been freed.

Yet while this theoretical polarity—between the insistence on social totality versus particularity—does help to sort out alternative explanations for the shift, its utility soon reaches a point of diminishing returns. In the first place, the closer to the ground the analysis gets, the more overlapping and mutually dependent these allegedly polarized theoretical perspectives begin to appear. Moreover, there is a common tendency at both poles to leave the consciousness and agency of actors themselves obscure, theoretically evoked rather than ethnographically examined. In this vein, we might pair Cornell West's searing critique of Jameson's "totalizing" analysis with Chilean Nelly Richard's (1995, p. 221) dissent from the theoretical categories created by postmodern analysis of identity politics: "[W]omen and the Third World are categories more spoken for by postmodernity, without obliging the cultural institution to loosen its discursive monopoly over the right to speak, without ceding to them the much greater right to become autonomous subjects of enunciation...intervening (disorganizing) in the rules of discourse that determine property and pertinence (*pertenencias y pertinencias*)." If in part this is a question of, as Richard puts it, the "prestige of the authorized signature," the problem also spills over into one of theoretically driven myopia. For example, it is disquieting to see how frequently Sandinista leaders are added to the list of protagonists of "postmodern identity politics," with so little consideration of the profound conflict around precisely the features that theoretically set identity politics apart (Beverley et al 1995, Rowe & Shelling 1991). Such assertions neglect the growing body of literature focused on tensions between the Sandinista leadership's vision of the unified subject, on the one hand, and the multiple subjects of the revolutionary coalition—i.e. women (Criquillón 1995, Molyneux 1986, Randall 1994), indigenous peoples (Díaz-Polanco 1985, Gould 1997, Hale 1994b), Afro-Nicaraguans (Gordon 1998b), artisans (Field 1997), peasants (Bendaña 1991)—on the other.

A greater emphasis on ethnographic specificity offers no guarantee that a broader explanation for the shift will eventually emerge. Indeed, such work could risk falling back into a new version of the old parochialism that for so long kept anthropology on the sidelines of precisely these discussions. Yet if the work is theoretically informed and also ethnographically engaged, it stands to contribute most to a broader explanation for the shift. I'm thinking here of recent research on peasant organizing (Edelman 1996, Starn 1994), on indigenous politics (Campbell 1994, Field 1998, Jackson 1995, Rappaport 1994, Sawyer 1996, Varese 1995, Warren 1997), on religion-based social movements in Brazil (Burdick 1993), on the politics of African diasporic identities in Latin America (Gordon 1998b, Scott 1991), on the many manifestations of the women's movements (Radcliff & Westwood 1993, Stephen 1995). This work is also distinguished—though in varying ways—by the goal of achieving a relationship of dialogue, exchange, and mutual critique with the subjects of research. Neither antitheoretical nor averse to generalization, these authors are mindful of the need to tell a story in which the protagonists might recognize themselves as such, rather than as pawns in someone else's theory wars. While it is too early to know whether a "new cognitive mapping" of the shift will emerge from such research, in the meantime we are learning a lot more about what identity politics mean in a series of specific times and places.

HOW CAN IDENTITY POLITICS BE CHARACTERIZED?

The first dimension of Latin American identity politics—extrapolating from Stuart Hall's (1988) influential essay—has as its key feature a challenge to the premise that a unified subject could "represent" (both "depict" and "speak for")—heterogeneous identities and social processes. In the case of Latin American indigenous politics, for example, the landmark document is the "Declaration of Barbados," the result of a meeting in 1971 in which anthropologists (mainly Latin American Mestizos) acknowledged the rise of indigenous cultural-political militancy and called for an activist anthropology in the service of "Indian liberation" (Wright 1988). The full impact of this challenge came into play with "Barbados II," a less publicized and more tension-ridden meeting in 1979, where Indian leaders thanked anthropologists for their "solidarity" but roundly criticized them for appropriating Indian voices, for presuming to know what "Indian liberation" meant.[4] The second dimension involves critique of the internal relations of difference within any given form of political initiative, the effort to unsettle all forms of essentialism, emphasizing the invention of tradition, the hybridity of cultures, and the multiplicity of identities. These latter sensibilities are captured in the phrase "cultural politics of difference" (Alarcón 1990, Anzaldúa 1987, de Lauretis 1990, Sandoval 1990, West 1990); the most comprehensive and influential application of this argument to Latin America is Nestor García Canclini's *Culturas Híbridas* (1995; see also Escobar 1992b, Quijano 1995).

The tension between these two dimensions of identity politics in Latin America has not received sufficient attention. If García Canclini's assertion that all cultures in Latin America are now "hybrid" is meant to characterize the diverse

---

[4]This information comes from personal communication with Stefano Varese, who attended both meetings. See Varese (1994).

political sensibilities of the contemporary moment, then it surely is overstated. Many initiatives consistent with the first dimension of identity politics make recourse to unreflexive premises about "tradition" and "cultural continuity from time immemorial," not to mention assertions of bounded identities that obscure internal lines of differentiation and inequity. When assertions about the predominance of the cultural politics of difference are made across the board—especially in relation to indigenous movements, (e.g. Shapiro 1994)—they take on the flavor of theoretically driven wishful thinking. As Dirlik (1996b) has argued recently, the widespread theoretical homage paid to the "cultural politics of difference" and the equally widespread persistence of essentialism are not an awkward incongruence to be avoided or wished away, but rather a problem to be confronted and explained. A similar argument has been made in regard to the widespread resonance of Afrocentrism among African American communities and the ascendancy of "cultural politics" theoretical sensibilities in most African American academic circles (Gordon & Anderson 1997).

One response to this problem involves the notion of "strategic essentialism" (Spivak 1985), which advances the claim that people deploy essentialist political rhetoric as conscious strategies rather than eternal truths. Yet one wonders to what extent this accurately portrays how participants in many forms of identity politics actually think about what they are doing. An alternative approach might be to challenge the very dichotomy between essentialism and "constructivism," to posit that essentialism is inherent in all speech and action, and to focus instead on "who is utilizing [essentialism], how it is deployed, and where its effects are concentrated" (Fuss 1989, p. 20; see also, Scott 1991, Shohat 1992).

This call for greater attention to what essentialism means and does in specific contexts is nicely illustrated in Joanne Rappaport's work on the politics of memory in a highland indigenous community of southern Colombia. Rappaport shows, for example, how the term *recuperación* (repossession), around which the movement of indigenous militancy has crystallized, at times encompasses historical claims that could be considered essentialist, but at times also becomes "a gloss for economic innovation...regardless of whether these methods actually find their roots in the past" (1994, p. 11). This does not require one to abdicate critical analysis but proposes simply to acknowledge that the very category "essentialist"—and its supposed opposite "constructivist"—may be useful to track theoretical allegiances within the academy, but that it is insufficiently attentive to the range of ways that "essentialist" precepts are woven into political consciousness and practice, and the highly variable material consequences that result (see also Campbell 1994, Warren 1997).

Beyond noting these two dimensions in the contents of identity politics, we can also draw distinctions according to how specific political initiatives came into being. A first distinction is between subjects or identities that were once nominally included in national-popular political visions in name, even if suppressed in practice, versus those that have arisen anew, from outright neglect or suppression in the traditional political arena. Initiatives that fit the first category most clearly are those associated with the rights of women and racial or ethnic "minorities." National-popular political initiatives in contemporary Latin America invariably have made some provision for the "participation" of women in its ranks, developing some notion of the specific rights of women in the context of that initiative's overall political goals and vision. The same is true—if perhaps to a somewhat lesser extent—for the relationship with peoples of indigenous and African descent. These antecedents are crucial because they constitute a past involvement that shapes the subsequent contents of the initiative: an acknowledged debt to the Left for its role in propelling such activism, a growing frustration with the lack of responsiveness to specific political demands grounded in cultural difference, and an eventual break motivated by the perceived need for autonomy. In this sense, the longstanding debate on the problem of "double militancy" within Latin American women's organizations (Sternbach et al 1992) runs roughly parallel to the tension-ridden history of indigenous organizing within a broader Left coalition (Barre 1983, Bonfil Batalla 1981). Growing criticism of this marginalization has spawned efforts to bring to light the autonomy and agency of the groups in question at previous moments of history (e.g. Campbell 1994, Franco 1989). Although generally important and salutary corrective steps, these rereadings risk projecting uniform goals, consciousness, and identity onto people engaged in prior moments of struggle, rather than viewing each moment in historical context.

Such a history of entanglement and ambivalence does not encumber the second category: identities that received little or no recognition with prior representations of the national-popular. A prime example here is the emergence of gay and lesbian identity politics (Lancaster 1997). Other examples of the second category include emergent identities and politics revolving around environmental degradation (Martínez-Alier 1991, Sanderson 1993) and human rights activism (Schirmer 1997, Wilson 1997). While these arguably do have histories of recognition and validation within national-popular projects, they often are propelled by sharply discontinuous ideologies and political sensibilities. Human rights movements focused on the "disappeared," for example, often have emerged from discursive spaces created and validated by the dictatorships they oppose; such movements often put "conservative" premises—that women are inherently apolitical, that motherhood is inviolable—to the service of efforts to account for the missing, and to bring those responsible to justice (e.g. Perelli 1994).

A final category encompasses politics in the name of people who were once privileged signifiers of national-popular projects that have lost their allure.

One of the most ubiquitous slogans of the Sandinista revolution—"only the peasants and workers will reach the end (*llegarán hasta el final*)"—helps to make this point, if unintentionally. Peasants and workers are still around, still politically active, in some places dramatically so. But one would be hard pressed today to find a political initiative of national scope that makes peasants and workers the privileged signifier, as the Sandinistas did. These identities must now share the stage with a host of others, at best forming tenuous alliances, at worst competing for scarce international funds in an ideological climate where "Indian" causes are much more exciting and important than "peasant" ones, where funders lavish attention on any initiative with "gender" in the title yet consider workers' rights passé or even antisocial. Another prominent facet of this "decentering" is for studies of peasant or worker politics to address cross-cutting inequities of gender and race/ethnicity (Alonso 1995, Edelman 1994, Roseberry 1995, Starn 1992, Stolcke 1988). It is striking then that a fine illustration of this new analysis—Michael Kearney's *Reconceptualizing the Peasantry*—would conclude that "class differences and differentiation remain the basic theoretical and political issue" (1996, p. 173). Not long ago such an assertion would have triggered accusations of complicity with homogenizing Marxist suppression of difference, yet in this context the phrase reads as a fresh insight, a touchstone in an effort that receives high praise even from "arch postmodernists" like George Marcus. Here is another sign of theoretical clearing, an opening for research on peasant politics finally freed from the twin orthodoxies that forced us to choose between class as the last-instance answer to all analytical questions, and class as the analytical question that never even gets asked.

OUTCOMES AND CONSEQUENCES

The prospects for a theoretical clearing seem least encouraging in regard to the question of consequences. It is one thing to approach a rough consensus on the emergence of a shift, its explanation, and characterization, and quite another to do so on assessments of the consequences: what people engaged in various forms of identity politics have achieved, and can hope to achieve, with what impact on their daily lives. Here, major divergences on key concepts of power, resistance, hegemony, and structural transformation tend to surface, producing a chasm that would seem difficult to bridge. The strongest argument for the "creative renewal" potential of identity politics resides in the intrinsic value of decentralized and multifaceted political activity, a rejuvenation of the political engendered by transformations in the very meaning of "doing politics." This involves not only expanding and diversifying what counts as political—calling into question the dichotomy between public and (allegedly nonpolitical) private spheres, for example—but also innovation in the realm of strategy and tactics. The term "subversion" sheds its former meaning of "conspiring against the system" and refers instead to the art of working at the interstices, finding the inevitable cracks and contradictions in the oppressor's identity, discourse, or institutional practice, and using them to the subaltern's advantage. Even the "fragmentation of identity" and the "alienation of the self" that often come with living on the margins can be reinterpreted in this light: No longer symptoms of oppression, they can become key resources in moving toward a "third space" of "multidimensional political subjectivity" beyond the Manichean contra position of oppressor and oppressed (Bhabha 1990, de Lauretis 1990).

Yet it is not necessary to go to the extreme of celebrating fragmentation and alienation to make the case. In his critique of development, for example, Escobar (1995) offers an intriguing hypothesis that fits nicely with the "interstices" argument. Groups with greater insertion in the market, Escobar suggests, have better chances of "affirming their ways of life" (presumably by exploiting opportunities from within) than those "clinging" to conventional identities and strategies predicated on resistance from outside the political economic system. Another example is the much-needed revisionist work on the politics of conversion from Catholicism to evangelical Protestantism (Brusco 1995, Burdick 1993, Stoll 1990). Dispelling simplistic recourse to the ideological thralldom of these new religions, these analyses point to the spaces opened—for women's assertion against abusive men, for more participatory religious practice—to explain the shift. Similarly, Diane Nelson's (1996) phrase "Maya hacker" refers (among other things) to how Maya cultural activists in Guatemala have found ways to hack out a space within the national political arena, subverting the traditional-modern dichotomy that has always been used against them, and at the same time helping to dispel the impression that they are engaged in radical, frontal opposition to "the system."

From one standpoint, the "material consequences" of such political initiatives are self-evident and extensive. Merely to name forms of inequality that previously had no place in the realm of politics is in itself highly significant. The vibrancy, and in some cases substantial gains, of indigenous and women's movements throughout Latin America speak volumes on the benefits that accrue when particular identities become politicized and break out from under the tutelage of the national-popular. It is especially clear that the Pan-American indigenous movement is "gaining ground" as the title to a recent special issue of *NACLA* announces (see also, for example, Van Cott 1994). Even references to the "revitalization of civil society," though often vague and difficult to assess in a rigorous manner, point to processes that must be taken seriously. Yet it is striking that analyses in this vein are so circumspect on the question of consequences, especially in the relation to enduring political and economic inequities. In regard to new social movements, the unmediated enthusiasm has passed, replaced by more sober assessments of advances and setbacks, more carefully worded provisos that their political character "is not given in advance" but rather "rests on the articulations they may establish with other social struggles and discourses" (Escobar 1995, p. 221). Kay Warren, in a cogent and comprehensive analysis of the Maya movement and its challenge to the "unified social movement" paradigm, similarly concludes that "it is too early to know what sort of impact the Pan-Mayan movement...will have" (Warren 1997, p. 45). While in many ways it surely is too early, this conclusion also highlights a broader dilemma: discarding the "unified social movement" paradigm also means discarding unified criteria through which "impact" used to be assessed. Developing new criteria, which neither suppress nor uncritically defer to the claims of the movement itself, is a task that research on identity politics is just now beginning to confront.

In the context of this task, hard questions posed from the other side of the divide remain useful. Teresa Ebert (1993), for example, obliges us to think through the conditions under which a privileging of the cultural politics of difference might turn "ludic," concerned mostly with the aesthetic pleasures of theoretical elegance, unengaged with what Scheper-Hughes (1995) has aptly called the "political economy of suffering." Echoing general theoretical concerns (Shohat 1992, Young 1995), I have investigated the dilemmas and contradictions that result when the ostensibly progressive theories of "hybridity" and "mestizaje" travel to Guatemala and are used by elites to delegitimate Maya cultural activism (Hale 1996). Mindful of Foucault-influenced critiques of resistance (e.g. Abu-Lughod 1990, Brown 1996), Edmund T Gordon (1998a) has suggested that we work harder to draw analytical distinctions between different forms of resistance rather than jettisoning the entire concept. Finally, many scholars have argued for a more fully dialectical analysis of the global context of local resistance movements. They acknowledge the contestatory potential of movements that emerge from the interstices of the capitalist system, while at the same time pointing to the formidable limits set by that system, not so much as external constraints but as forces that constitute the very precepts on which the local itself has been predicated (Dirlik 1996a, Friedman 1990, Miyoshi 1993). Such questionings are especially constructive when they have been influenced, even partly constituted by, theoretical insights implicit in the phrase "cultural politics of difference." Then their insistence on analysis of material consequences rings true. In part reflections of theory-war fatigue, such convergences also arise from a novel set of material settings that form the underpinnings of intellectual production itself. It is therefore fitting to conclude by once more making intellectuals themselves the focus of analysis.

Following Yúdice (1996), Franco (1994), and others, I have suggested that the erosion of the national-popular has also entailed a crisis among Latin American intellectuals. A major task that this points to, but does not complete, is the systematic comparative analysis of US and Latin America–based intellectuals' responses to this crisis. I do argue that past theoretical polarities—between materialist and discursive analysis, between emphasis on social totality and particularity—have declining utility as organizing principles of such responses. This would seem to be the perspective of a third "critical modernist" position, exemplified in the work of Argentine literary critic Beatriz Sarlo (1993). The age of postmodern identity politics, for Sarlo, far from providing the basis for celebratory renewal, most accurately reflects the combined effects of commercialism and media-saturated superficiality, a politics that, having lost a sense of "scale and distance," has been reduced to "icon, image, or simulacrum." Yet her stance toward Marxist analysis, socialist politics, and the former role of the national-popular intellectual is equally critical: Gone are the days when these intellectuals could present themselves as a vanguard with a "special role of explaining the big picture" (*vocación generalizadora*) derived from the combination of broader vision and organic links to the social. In Sarlo's appraisal, intellectuals with political ambitions have nowhere to turn: They either resign themselves to obscurity and irrelevance, join the wave of privatization and become "experts," or parlay their skills in social analysis into cultural capital that wins them positions in neoliberal governments (e.g. Arturo Warman of Mexico, FH Cardoso of Brazil, JJ Brunner of Chile). Sarlo finds a limited defense against hopelessness in cultural criticism, which rests on the reassertion of aesthetic and ethical values, if not political or theoretical solutions.

Compelling in analytical acuity and in the ability to place intellectual production (including her own) in historical context, Sarlo's resting place, as Jean Franco (1994, p. 21) notes, "cannot be disentangled as easily as she would wish from the exclusionary and elitist culture of modernism." What would happen, though, if the implications of Sarlo's analysis were carried in a different direction, instead of withdrawal into the rarefied space of cultural criticism, toward direct engagement with political actors who confront the "crisis of modernity" in all its mundane, contradictory, oppressive daily manifestations? This would entail a modest form of political engagement, as skeptical as the actors themselves are apt to be of grand ideologies, political visions, or theoretical statements that neatly link local struggles to "broader realities." Within Latin America, intellectual production positioned in this way is especially apt to go unnoticed beyond the local context, precisely because the facilitating material conditions for communication of the resulting ideas are largely absent. US-based anthropologists enjoy advantages on this score, though economic privilege and northern provenance make engagement more difficult and perhaps inherently contradictory. Despite such problems, this locally engaged "critical modernist" approach is a useful place to start in building a broader analysis of identity politics, beyond the theoretical polarization of the previous moment.

One way to track this emergent trend is to look not only at theoretical allegiances but also at how the research itself is carried out. This brings into focus, for example, new forms of experimentation with collaboration and dialogue with the subjects of research, and with local organic intellectuals (Escobar et al 1997, Field 1997, Scheper-Hughes 1992), the rise in critical human rights scholarship, which in turn is grounded in human rights activism (Falla 1994, Montejo 1993, Turner 1995); a growing interest of ethnography of the powerful, with an intent to use resulting knowledge in empowering ways (e.g. Schirmer 1996); efforts to place Latin American studies in hemispheric perspective, which highlights connections between distant and nearby struggles, challenging the divide between homework and fieldwork (Hemispheric Initiative of the Americas 1993, Kearney 1990); and experimentation with the medium of presentation of the research results with hopes of moving anthropology toward effective communication beyond academia proper (Starn 1994, Turner 1992).

This empirically driven, theoretically seasoned, and politically engaged work on identity politics in Latin America offers a potential source of rejuvenation for anthropology more generally. The crisis of oppositional intellectuals in Latin America and the crisis of "ethnographic authority" among US-based anthropologists run parallel to each other. Among both groups, the role of intellectuals as intermediaries who provide data on, interpret, and theorize about the subjects of identity politics, is confronting an ever more serious challenge. How intellectuals respond to this challenge becomes an analytical and political question in its own right. Deprived of easy claims to "organic ties" with political actors "on the ground," deprived of fieldwork sites with docile, cooperative subjects, one common recourse in both cases is to withdraw. Yet the challenge also creates a mandate for reinvention: a call for intellectuals to develop methods and analytical categories that engender more constructive engagement with the multiple inequalities that organize the worlds we live in and study. This may at least help to prevent scenarios in which theoretical debate, though presenting itself as a few steps ahead of political practice, descends into self-referentiality. It will at least keep theory and activism engaged with each other, and in the best of cases could even produce ethnography that casts some light on the problems and opportunities that lie ahead.

ACKNOWLEDGMENTS

This review has grown out of a long period of collective work and discussion, although the final responsibility for its contents belongs to me alone. The initial impetus for many of the ideas and the bibliography came from the efforts of the UC Davis Group Study on the Politics of Identity in Latin America. That experience had a great formative influence on my thinking and yielded an important unpublished essay to which I refer continually. I also benefited from discussion with an excellent group of graduate students in my seminar on "Identity Politics in Contemporary Latin America" at the University of Texas. Carol Smith, Orin Starn, Ted Gordon, Charles A Hale, and Faye Harrison provided useful comments on the written text. Finally, Rodrigo Herrera worked with me extensively on the review and deserves major credit.

Literature Cited

Abu-Lughod L. 1990. The romance of resistnace: tracing transformations of power through Bedouin women. *Am. Ethnol.* 17(1):41–55

Adams RN. 1967. Nationalization. In *Social Anthropology,* Vol. 4, *Handbook of Middle American Indians,* ed. R Wauchope, pp. 469–89. Austin: Univ. Tex. Press

Ahmad A. 1992. *In Theory: Classes, Nations, Literatures.* London: Verso

Ahmad A. 1993. A response. *Public Cult.* 6: 143–91

Alarcón N. 1990. The theoretical subject(s) of This Bridge Called My Back and Anglo-American feminism. In *Making Face, Making Soul/Haciendo Caras,* ed. G Anzaldúa, pp. 356–69. San Francisco: Aunt Lute Found.

Albó X. 1991. El retorno del indio. *Rev. Andina* 2:209–345

Alonso AM. 1995. Thread of blood: colonialism, revolution, and gender on Mexico's northen frontier. Tucson: Univ. Ariz. Press

Anzaldúa G. 1987. *Borderlands/La Frontera: The New Mestiza.* San Francisco: Aunt Lute Found.

Appadurai A. 1990. Disjuncture and difference in the global cultral economy. *Public Cult.* 2(2):1–24

Appadurai A. 1995. The production of locality. In *Counterworks: Managing the Diversity of Knowledge,* ed. R Fardon, pp. 204–25. London: Routledge

Barre MC. 1983. *Ideologías Indigenistas y Movimientos Indios.* Mexico: Siglo Veintiuno

Bendaña A. 1991. *Una Tragdia Campesina.* Managua: Arte

Beverley J, Oviedo J, Aronna M, eds. 1995. *The Postmodernism Debate in Latin America.* Durham, NC: Duke Univ. Press

Bhabha H. 1990. The third space. Interview with Homi Bhabha by J Rutherford. In *Identity,* ed. J Rutherford, pp. 207–21. London: Lawrence & Wishant

Bonfil Batalla G. 1981. *Utopía y Revolución.* Mexico City: Nueva Imagen

Brown MF. 1993. *Facing the State, Facing the World: Amazonia's Native Leaders and the New Politics of Identity. L'Homme* 33(2–4):307–26

Brown MF. 1996. On resisting resistance. *Am. Anthropol.* 98(4):729–34

Brusco EE. 1995. *The Reformation of Machismo: Evangelical Conversion and Gender in Colombia.* Austin: Univ. Tex. Press

Burbach R. 1994. Roots of the postmodern rebellion in Chiapas. *New Left Rev.,* pp. 34–42

Burbach R, Nuñez O. 1987. *Fire in the Americas: Forging a Revolutionary Agenda.* London: Verso

Burdick J. 1993. *Looking for God in Brazil.* Berkeley: Univ. Calif. Press

Campbell H. 1994. *Zapotec Renaissance: Ethnic Politics and Cultural Revivalism in Southern Mexico.* Albuquerque: Univ. NM Press

Casaús A, Marta E. 1991. *Linaje y Racismo.* San José: FLACSO

Castañeda J. 1993. *Utopia Unarmed: The Latin American Left after the Cold War.* New York: Knopf

Chanady A. 1994. Latin American identity and constructions of difference. *Hisp. Issues* 10

Cojtí Cuxil D. 1997. Heterofobia y racisms Guatemalteco: perfil y estado actual. In *Racismo e Identidades en Guatemala*, ed. C Arenas, CR Hale, G Palma. Guatemala: AVANCSO. In press

Collier GA. 1994. The new politics of exclusion: antecedents to the rebellion in Mexico. *Dialect. Anthropol.* 19(1):1–44

Collier GA. 1995. *Basta! Land and the Zapatista Rebellion in Chiapas.* Oakland, CA: Food First Books

Collier JF, Mauer B, Suárez-Navaz L. 1995. Sanctioned identities: legal constructions of modern personhood. *Identities* 2(1–2): 1–27

Conklin BA, Graham LR. 1995. The shifting middle ground: Amazonian Indians and eco-politics. *Am. Anthropol.* 97(4): 695–710

Coronil F. 1996. Beyond Occidentalism: towards nonimperial geohistorical categories. *Cult. Anthropol.* 11(1):51–87

Criquillón A. 1995. The Nicaraguan women's movement: feminist reflections from within. In *New Politics of Survival: Grassroots Movements in Central America,* ed. M Sinclair, pp. 209–38. New York: Monthly Review Press

Declaration of Barbados. 1971. Declaration of Barbados. In *The Situation of the Indian in South America*, ed. W Dostal, pp. 376–81. Geneva: World Council of Indigenous Peoples

de la Cadena M. 1996. Myths, intellectuals and race/class/gender distinctions in the formation of Latin American Nations. *J. Lat. Am. Anthropol.* 2(1):112–47

de la Campa R. 1995. Postmodernism and revolution: A Central American case study. In *Late Imperial Culture,* ed. R de la Campa, EA Kaplan, M Sprinker, pp. 122–48. London: Verso

de Lauretis T. 1990. Eccentric subjects: feminist theory and historical consciousness. *Fem. Stud.* 16(1):115–148

Díaz-Polanco H. 1985. *La Cuestión Étnico-Nacional.* Mexico City: Siglo XXI

di Leonardo M. 1996. Patterns of culture wars. *The Nation* 262(14):25–29

Dirlik A. 1994. The postcolonial aura: third world criticism in the age of global capitalism. *Crit. Inq.* 20(2):328–56

Dirlik A. 1996a. The global in the local. In *Global/Local: Cultural Production and the Transnational Imaginary,* ed. R Wilson, W Dissanayake, pp. 21–45. Durham, NC: Duke Univ. Press

Dirlik A. 1996b. The past as legacy and project: postcolonial criticism in the perspective of indigenous historicism. *Am. Indian Cult. Res. J.* 20(2):1–31

Ebert T. 1993. Ludic feminism, the body, performance, and labor: bringing materialism back into feminist cultural studies. *Cult. Crit.* Winter:5–50

Edelman M. 1994. Landlords and the devil: class, ethnic, and gender dimensions of Central American peasant narratives. *Cult. Anthropol.* 9(1):58–93

Edelman M. 1996. Reconceptualizing and reconstituting peasant struggles: a new social movement in Central America. *Radical Hist. Rev.* 65(26):26–47

Edelman M. 1997. 'Campesinos' and 'Tecnicos': new peasant intellectuals in Central American Politics. In *Knowing Your Place: Rural Identity and Cultural Hierarchy,* ed. B Ching, G Creed. London: Routledge

Escobar A. 1992a. Culture, economics, and politics in Latin American social movements theory and research. See Escobar & Alvarez 1992, pp. 62–85

Escobar A. 1992b. Imagining a post-development era? Critical thought, development and social movements. *Soc. Text* 31(2):20–56

Escobar A. 1995. *Encountering Development: The Making and Unmaking of the Third World.* Princeton, NJ: Princeton Univ. Press

Escobar A, Alvarez SE. 1992. *The Making of Social Movements in Latin America: Identity, Strategy, and Democracy.* Boulder, CO: Westview

Escobar A, Rosero C, Grueso L. 1997. The process of black community organizing in the southern Pacific coast region of Colomia. In *Cultures of Politics/Politics of Cultures. Revisioning Latin American Social Movements.* Boulder: Westview. In press

Fagen R, Deere CD, Coraggio JL. 1986. *Transition and Development Problems of Third World Socialism.* New York: Monthly Review Press

Falla R. 1994. *Massacres in the Jungle.* Boulder, CO: Westview

Field L. 1997. *The Grimace of Macho Ratón.* Durham, NC: Duke Univ. Press

Franco J. 1992. Remapping culture. In *Americas: New Interpretive Essays,* ed. A Stepan, pp. 172–88. Oxford: Oxford Univ. Press

Franco J. 1989. *Plotting Women: Gender and Representation in Mexico.* New York: Columbia

Franco J. 1994. What's left of the intelligent-sia? The Uncertain future of the printed word. *NACLA* 28(2):16–21

Friedlander J. 1976. *Being Indian in Hueyapan*. New York: St. Martin's

Friedlander J. 1986. The National Institute of Mexico reinvents the Indian: the Pame example. *Am. Ethnol.* May:363–67

Friedman J. 1990. Being in the world; globalization and localization. In *Global Culture: Nationalism, Globalization and Modernity*, ed. M Featherstone. London: Sage

Fuss D. 1989. *Essentially Speaking*. New York: Routledge

Gabriel J. 1994. Initiating a movement: indigenous, black and grassroots struggles in the Americas. *Race Class* 35(3):2–20

García Canclini N. 1995. *Hybrid Cultures: Strategies for Entering and Leaving Modernity*. Minneapolis: Univ. Minn. Press

García de León A. 1996. Chiapas and the inverting of established orders. *Identities: Glob. Stud. Cult. Power* 3(1–2):261–68

Glick Schiller N, Basch L, Szanton-Blanc C. 1992. Transnationalism: a new analytic framework for understanding migration. *Ann. NY Acad. Sci.* 645:1–24

Gordon ET. 1998a. Cultural politics of black masculinity. *Transform. Anthropol.* In press

Gordon ET. 1998b. *Disparate Diasporas: Identity and Politics in an African-Nicaraguan Community*. Austin: Univ. Tex. Press. In press

Gordon ET, Anderson M. 1997. Conceptualizing the African Diaspora. *Proc. City Univ. NY Kenneth B. Clark Colloq. Ser. IRADAC.* II

Gould J. 1997. *To Die in This Way: Nicaraguan Indians and the Myth of Mestizaje, 1880–1965*. Durham, NC: Duke Univ. Press

Gupta A, Ferguson J. 1992. Beyond "culture": space, identity and the politics of difference. *Cult. Anthropol.* 7(1):6–22

Hale CR. 1994a. Between Che Guevara and the Pachamama: Mestizos, Indians and identity politics in the anti-quicentenary campaign. *Crit. Anthropol.* 14(1):9–39

Hale CR. 1994b. *Resistance and Contradiction: Miskitu Indians and the Nicaraguan State, 1894–1987*. Stanford: Stanford Univ. Press

Hale CR. 1996. Mestizaje, hybridity and the cultural politics of difference in post-revolutionary Central America. *J. Lat. Am. Anthropol.* 2(1):34–61

Hall S. 1988. New ethnicities. In *ICA Documents 7. Black Film, British Cinema*, pp. 27–31

Hall S. 1992. Cultural studies and its theoretical legacies. In *Cultural Studies*, ed. L Grossberg, pp. 277–94. London: Routledge

Handler R. 1994. Is "Identity" a useful cross-cultural concept? In *Commemorations*, ed. J Gillis, pp. 27–40. Princeton, NJ: Princeton Univ. Press

Haraway D. 1988. Situated knowledges: the science question in feminism and the privilege of partial perspective. *Fem. Stud.* 14(3):575–99

Harrison FV. 1991. *Decolonizing Anthropology: Moving Further Toward an Anthropology for Liberation*. Washington, DC: Am. Anthropol. Assoc.

Harrison FV. 1995. The persistent power of "race" in the cultural and political economy of racism. *Annu. Rev. Anthropol.* 24: 47–74

Hemispheric Initiative of the Americas. 1993. *Redrawing the Boundaries: Toward a Hemispheric Approach to "Latin America" Area Studies*. Univ. Calif., Davis

Jackson JE. 1995. Culture, genuine and spurious: the politics of Indianness in the Vaupes, Colombia. *Am. Ethnol.* 22(1):3–27

Jameson F. 1984. Postmodernism, or the cultural logic of late capitalism. *New Left Rev.* 146:53–92

Jameson F. 1988. Cognitive mapping. In *Marxism and the Interpretation of Culture*, ed. C Nelson, L Grossberg, pp. 347–60. Urbana: Univ. Ill.

Kearney M. 1990. Borders and boundaries of state and self at the end of empire. *J. Hist. Sociol.* 4(1):52–74

Kearney M. 1996. *Reconceptualizing the Peasantry: Anthropology in Global Perspective*. Boulder, CO: Westview

Knight A. 1990. Historical continuities in social movements. In *Popular Movements and Political Change in Mexico*, ed. J Foweraker, A Craig, pp. 78–102. Boulder, CO: Rienner

Kristeva J. 1993. *Nations without Nationalism*. New York: Columbia Univ. Press

Laclau E. 1977. *Politics and Ideology*. London: Verso

Laclau E. 1994. *The Making of Political Identities*. London: Verso

Laclau E, Mouffe C. 1985. Hegemony and social strategy. London: Verso

Lancaster RN. 1997. On homosexualities in Latin America (and other places). *Am. Ethnol.* 24(1):193–202

Larsen N. 1995. Postmodernism and imperialism: theory and politics in Latin America. See Beverley et al 1995, pp. 110–34

Lazarus N. 1991. Doubting the new world order: Marxism, realism, and the claims of postmodernist social theory. *Differences* 3(3)

Martínez-Alier J. 1991. Ecology and the poor: a neglected dimension of Latin American History. *J. Lat. Am. Stud.* 23(3):621–40

Massey D. 1994. *Space, Place, and Gender.* Minneapolis: Univ. Minn. Press

Mato D. 1994. *Teoría y política de la construcción de identitidades y diferencias en América Latina y el Caribe.* UNESCO: Ed. Nueva Sociedad

Mintz SW. 1974. *Caribbean Transformations.* Baltimore: Johns Hopkins Univ. Press

Miyoshi M. 1993. A borderless world? From colonialism to transnationalism and the decline of the nation state. *Crit. Inq.* 19(4): 726–51

Molyneux M. 1986. Mobilization without emancipation? Women's interests, state, and revolution. See Fagen et al 1986, pp. 280–302

Montejo V. 1993. *The dynamics of cultural resistance and tansformations: the case of Guatemalan Maya refugees in Mexico.* PhD thesis. Univ. Conn., Storrs

Moore DS. 1997. Remapping resistance: "ground for struggle" and the politics of place. In *Geographies of Resistance,* ed. S Pile, M Keith. London: Routledge. In press

Nelson DM. 1996. May hackers and the cyberspatialized nation-state: modernity, ethnostalgia, and a lizard queen in Guatemala. *Cult. Anthropol.* 11(3):287–308

Nugent D. 1995. Northern intellectuals and the EZLN. *Monthly Rev.* 47(3):124–38

Nuñez Soto O. 1986. Ideology and revolutionary politics in transitional societies. See Fagen et al 1986, pp. 231–48. New York: Monthly Rev. Press

Perelli C. 1994. The uses of conservatism: women's democratic politics in Uruguay. In *The Women's Movement in Latin America,* ed. J Jaquette, pp. 131–50. Boulder, CO: Westview

Pile S, Thrift N. 1995. *Mapping the Subject: Geographies of Cultural Transformation.* London: Routledge

Poole D. 1992. *Peru. Time of Fear.* London: Lat. Am. Bur./Monthly Review Press

Quijano A. 1995. Modernity, identity, and Utopia in Latin America. See Beverley et al 1995, pp. 201–16

Radcliffe S, Westwood S, eds. 1993. *Viva: Women and Popular Protest in Latin America.* London/New York: Routledge

Randall M. 1994. *Sandino's Daughters Revisited: Feminism in Nicaragua.* New York: Routledge

Rappaport J. 1994. *Cumbe Reborn.* Chicago: Univ. Chicago Press

Reed R. 1994. *Two rights make a wrong: indigenous peoples vs. environmental protection agencies.* Presented at Annu. Meet Am. Anthropol. Assoc., 93rd, Atlanta

Richard N. 1995. Cultural peripheries: Latin America and Postmodernist decentering. See Beverley et al 1995, pp. 217–22

Roseberry W. 1995. Latin American peasant studies in a "postcolonial" era. *J. Lat. Am. Anthropol.* 1(1):150–77

Rouse R. 1995a. Questions of identity. Personhood and collectivity in transnational migration to the United States. *Crit. Anthropol.* 15(4):351–80

Rouse R. 1995b. Thinking through transnationalism: notes on the cultural politics of class relations in contemporary United States. *Public Cult.* 7:353–402

Rowe W, Schelling V. 1991. *Memory and Modernity: Popular Culture in Latin America.* London: Verso

Said EW. 1979. *Orientalism.* New York: Vintage

SAIIC (South and Meso American Indian Information Center). 1992. *International Directory & Resource Guide: 500 Years of Resistance.* Oakland: SAIIC

Sanderson SE. 1993. Environmental politics in Latin America. In *Environmental Politics and the International Arena,* ed. S Kamienieck, pp. 223–38. Albany: SUNY Press

Sandoval C. 1990. U. S. third world feminism: the theory and method of oppositional consciousness in the postmodern world. *Genders* 10(Spring):1–24

Sarlo B. 1993. ¿Arcaicos o marginales? Situación de los intelectuales en el fin de siglo. *Punto Vista* 47:1–5

Sawyer S. 1996. Marching to nation across ethnic terrain: the 1992 Indian mobilization in lowland Ecuador. *Lat. Am. Perspect.*

Scheper-Hughes N. 1992. *Death without Weeping.* Berkeley: Univ. Calif. Press

Scheper-Hughes N. 1995. The primacy of the ethical. Propositions for a militant anthropology. *Curr. Anthropol.* 36(3):409–20

Schirmer J. 1996. The looting of democratic discourse by the Guatemalan military: implications for human rights. In *Constructing Democracy: Human Rights, Citizenship, and Society in Latin America,* ed. E Jelin, E Hershberg, pp. 85–97. Boulder, CO: Westview

Schirmer J. 1997. Universal and sustainable human rights? Special tribunals in Guatemala. In *Human Rights, Culture and Context: Anthropological perspectives,* ed. RA Wilson, pp. 161–86. Chicago: Pluto

Scott D. 1991. That event, this memory: notes on the anthropology of African diasporas in the New World. *Diaspora* 1:3:261–82

Shapiro MJ. 1994. Moral geographies and the ethics of post-sovereignty. *Public Cult.* 6:479–502

Sherzer J, Urban G. 1991. *Nation-states and Indians in Latin America.* Austin: Univ. Tex. Press

Shohat E. 1992. Notes on the post-colonial. *Soc. Text* 31/32:99–113

Silverblatt I. 1995. Becoming Indian in the Central Andes of seventeenth century Peru. In *After Colonialism: Imperial Histories and Postcolonial Displacements,* ed. G Prakash, pp. 279–98. Princeton, NJ: Princeton Univ. Press

Smith CA. 1997. A critical geneology of North American treatments of race and racism in the social analyses of Guatemala. In *Racismo e Identidades en Guatemala,* ed. C Arenas, CR Hale, G Palma. Guatemala: AVANCSO. In press

Spivak GC. 1985. Strategies of vigilance: an interview with Gayatri Chakravorti Spivak. Interview by Angela McRobbie. *Block* 10:5–9

Starn O. 1992. "I dreamed of foxes and hawks": reflections on peasant protest, new social movements, and the Rondas Campesinas of Northern Peru. See Escobar & Alvarez 1992, pp. 89–111

Starn O. 1994. Rethinking the politics of anthropology. *Curr. Anthropol.* 35(1):13–38

Stavenhagen R. 1992. Challenging the nation-state in Latin America. *J. Int. Aff.* 45(2):423–40

Stephen L. 1995. Women's rights are human rights: the merging of feminine and feminist interests among El Salvador's mothers of the disappeared (CO-MADRES). *Am. Ethnol.* 22(4):807–27

Sternbach N, Navarro-Aranguren M, Chuchryk P, Alvarez SE. 1992. Feminisms in Latin America: From Bogotá to San Bernardo. See Escobar & Alvarez 1992, pp. 207–39

Stolcke V. 1993. Is sex to gender as race is to ethnicity? In *Gendered Anthropology,* ed. T del Valle, pp. 17–37. London: Routledge

Stolcke V. 1988. *Coffee Planters, Workers, and Wives: Class Conflict and Gender Relations on Sao Paulo Coffee Plantations, 1850–1980.* New York: St. Martin's Press

Stoll D. 1990. *Is Latin America Turning Protestant? The Politics of Evangelical Growth.* Berkeley: Univ. Calif. Press

Taussig M. 1993. *Mimesis and Alterity: A Particular History of the Senses.* New York: Routledge

Turner T. 1992. Defiant images: the Kayapo appropriation of video. *Anthropol. Today* 8(6)

Turner T. 1995. An indigenous people's struggle for socially equitable and ecologically sustainable production: the Kayapo revolt against extractivism. *J. Lat. Am. Anthropol.* 1(1):98–122

Valenzuela A, José M. 1996. The Zapatista Army of National Liberation and the demands of the Mexican People. *Identities: Glob. Stud. Cult. Power* 3(1–2):253–60

Van Cott DL. 1994. Indigenous peoples and democracy in Latin America. New York: St. Martin's/Inter-Am. Dialogue

Varese S. 1995. The new environmentalist movement of Latin American indigenous people. In *Valuing Local Knowledge: Indigenous People and Intellectual Property Rights,* ed. SB Brush, D Stabinsky, pp. Washington, DC: Island

Varese S. 1994. Barbados III: On democracy and diversity. *Abya Yala News* 8(3):16–18

Vilas CM. 1994. The hour of civil society. *NACLA* 27(2):38–42

Wallerstein I. 1995. The insurmountable contradictions of liberalism: human rights and the rights of peoples in the geoculture of the modern world-system. *South Atl. Q.* 94(4):1161–78

Warren KB. 1997. *Indigenous Movements and Their Critics: Pan-Mayanism and Ethnic Resurgence in Guatemala.* Princeton, NJ: Princeton Univ. Press

Watanabe JM. 1996. Neither as they imagined nor as others intended: Mayas and anthropologists in the highlands of Guatemala since the 1960s. In *Supplement to the Handbook of Middle American Indians,* ed. JD Monaghan. Austin: Univ. Tex. Press

Weiner AB. 1992. Anthropology's lessons for cultural diversity. *Chron. Higher Educ.* July 22:B1

West C. 1986. Ethics and action in Jameson's Marxist Hermeneutics. In *Postmodernism and Politics,* ed. J Arac, pp. 123–44. Minneapolis: Univ. Minn. Press

West C. 1990. The new cultural politics of difference. In *Out There: Marginalization and Contemporary Cultures,* ed. R Ferguson, M Gever, TM Trinh, C West, pp. 19–36. Cambridge: MIT Press

Williams BF. 1989. A class act: anthropology and the race to nation across ethnic terrain. *Annu. Rev. Anthropol.* 18:401–44

Wilson R. 1997. Representing human rights violations: social contexts and subjectivities. In *Human Rights, Culture and Con-*

text, ed. R Wilson, pp. 134–60. London/Chicago: Pluto

Wolf ER. 1969. *Peasant Wars of the Twentieth Century*. Toronto: Harper & Row

Wright RM. 1988. Anthropological presuppositions of indigenous advocacy. *Annu. Rev. Anthropol.* 17:365–90

Young RJC. 1995. *Colonial Desire: Hybridity in Theory, Culture and Race*. London: Routledge

Yúdice G. 1996. Intellectuals and civil society in Latin America. *Ann. Scholar* 11(1/2): 157–74

Annu. Rev. Anthropol. 1997. 26:591–621

HISTORIES OF FEMINIST ETHNOGRAPHY

Kamala Visweswaran

Department of Anthropology, The University of Texas at Austin, Austin, Texas 78712-1086

KEY WORDS: gender analysis, feminism, women anthropologists

ABSTRACT

This review essay illustrates how changes in the conception of gender define the historical production of feminist ethnography in four distinct periods. In the first period (1880–1920), biological sex was seen to determine social roles, and gender was not seen as separable from sex, though it was beginning to emerge as an analytical category. The second period (1920–1960) marks the separation of sex from gender as sex was increasingly seen as indeterminative of gender roles. In the third period (1960–1980), the distinction between sex and gender was elaborated into the notion of a sex/gender system—the idea that different societies organized brute biological facts into particular gender regimes. By the contemporary period (1980–1996), critiques of "gender essentialism" (the reification of "woman" as a biological or universal category) suggest that the analytical separation between sex and gender is miscast because "sex" is itself a social category.

Introduction

Although the term "feminist ethnography" has only recently emerged (Abu-Lughod 1990, Stacey 1988, Visweswaran 1988), and is now included in feminist research manuals as one of a variety of interdisciplinary research methods (Reinarz 1992), its relationship to the "writing culture" critique of anthropological representation (Clifford & Marcus 1986, Marcus & Cushman 1982, Marcus & Fisher 1986) has meant that discussions of feminist ethnography have focused more on redefining the genre of ethnography than in actually exploring what is meant by "feminist." Women in the discipline, however, have long experimented with form: Elsie Clews Parsons (Babcock 1992), Ella Deloria (1988), Zora Neale Hurston (1938), and Ruth Landes (1947) are but a few examples.

591

Thus, the focus on form and genre has meant that a lineage from Elsie Clews Parsons to current feminist ethnographers has been established at the expense of a more detailed examination of what distinguishes Parsons's ethnography from that of her contemporaries or later writers.

This review proposes to redirect such discussion by looking specifically at what modifies these texts as "feminist" to assess the historical influence of feminist ethnography upon the discipline (see also Collier & Yanagisako 1989). It is an attempt to move away from the dominant terms that inform the history of anthropology—evolutionist or particularist, functionalist or structuralist, Marxist or symbolic (Ortner 1984)—to understand how gender has become an ordering category of anthropological analysis. It further attempts to use ethnography as a means of tracing shifts in the conceptualization of gender in the anthropological literature.

The question of whether the term "feminist" is appropriate to describe the thoughts and actions of women in other times and places is not an easy one (Burton 1992, Offen 1988, Riley 1990). If "feminism" has changed substantially in the past one hundred years, so too has our understanding of what constitutes gender; thus, different forms of feminism have produced different understandings of gender, where gender itself cannot be separated from the categories of race, class, or sexual identity that determine it.

Gender is today the site of considerable cross-disciplinary and transnational crisis. As Rosa Bradiotti has noted, "the sex/gender distinction, which is one of the pillars on which English-speaking feminist theory is built, makes neither epistemological nor political sense in many non-English, western-European contexts, where the notions of 'sexuality' and 'sexual difference' are used instead" (Bradiotti & Butler 1994, p. 38).

For some theorists, gender itself is a sociologism that reifies the social relations that are seen to produce it by failing to account for how the terms masculine and feminine are founded in language prior to any given social formation. The focus on sex difference, by contrast, examines how masculine and feminine are constituted differentially, insisting that "this differential is nondialectical and asymmetrical in character," where "recourse to a symbolic domain is one in which those positionalities are established and which in turn set the parameters for notions of the social" (Butler 1994, p. 18). In this view, gender is seen less as a structure of fixed relations than as a process of structuring subjectivities. While both gender and sexuality can be seen as the cultural construction of "sex," neither of which can exist before representation, the major challenge to gender as an analytic concept has come from Foucauldians who have argued that sex is not "the ground upon which culture elaborates gender." Gender is rather the "discursive origin of sex" (Morris 1995, p. 568–69); hence the focus on sex difference.

The sociologistic account of gender tends to assume that a core gender identity is produced as an effect of social construction, requiring that women not
only see themselves as a biological sex but as a social grouping with which
they must identify. Postmodern thinkers, queer theorists, and feminists of
color have led the way in advancing sexuality as both counter-paradigm and
critique of "gender essentialism." As Biddy Martin (1994, p. 105) succinctly
puts it:

> To the extent that gender is assumed to construct the ultimate ground of
> women's experience, it has in much feminist work, come to colonize every
> aspect of experience, psychological and social, as the ultimate root and ex-
> planation of that experience, consigning us, once again, to the very terms that
> we sought to exceed, expand or redefine. When an uncritical assumption of
> the category 'woman' becomes the 'subject of feminism,' then gender poli-
> tics takes the form of...the injunction to identify with/as women.

Thus, the assumption that gender comprises the core of all women's experiences produces a unified subject of identification, the need to identify
"with/as" women.

In this review essay, I attempt to provide an account of how gender has
come to signify "woman," that is, a set of social relations that produces woman
as a universal category transcending difference. I explore the linked questions
of how women are figured as subjects, and what notions of the subject underlie
the production of feminist ethnography to explain how a subject of identification is produced by particular understandings of gender at distinct historical moments. Though gender first emerged as a descriptive category for women, racial and class formations have at different historical moments worked against
gender identification, that is, the emergence of "woman" as a universal category. I thus ask how a feminist ethnography that displaces gender from its center might engage strategies of disidentification rather than identification.

Since anthropology was probably the discipline that contributed most to the
North American (or sociologistic) account of gender, I think it is valuable to
trace its operation in the feminist ethnography that produces it as an analytical
object. Working from the critique of gender essentialism, I argue that feminist
ethnography can be defined as ethnography that foregrounds the question of
social inequality vis-à-vis the lives of men, women, and children. This approach to the literature widens the subject of feminist ethnography, but the
looseness of definition is important. Although much feminist anthropology
has presumed that women were its subjects, and this review focuses largely
upon the works of women anthropologists writing about other women, I suggest at the close of this review that a broader conception of the relationship of
feminist theory to social movements means that women should not be seen as

sole subjects, authors, or audiences of feminist ethnography. Various forms of critical ethnography might thus productively be read as feminist ethnography.

As a means of gauging the historical production of feminist ethnographic texts, I propose to examine four time periods: 1880–1920, 1920–1960, 1960–1980, and 1980–1996. These periods should be considered rough approximations, not absolute chronological markers. I suggest that we use these time periods to think of gender less in terms of a progressive teleology than in terms of cycles, where it is important to note disjunctures or doubled usages of the term.

In locating this analysis as part of an ongoing retelling of the history of feminism(s) in the United States,[1] I want to emphasize the decisive role anthropology has played in shaping debates about gender in the United States. While some authors have attempted to understand how epistemologies such as feminist empiricism, standpoint theory, or postmodernism have informed feminist research (Cole & Phillips 1995) and others have concentrated on the ways that feminism has been delineated by the terms of classical political theory—liberal, radical, cultural, Marxist, or socialist (Jaggar 1988)—these categorizations are limited for understanding how anthropology as a discipline has influenced the course of feminism in this country, and how feminism has, in turn, defined itself as a movement within the limits of US history (Cott 1987, Giddens 1984).

Three paradigmatic markers have been articulated by US feminists for understanding the history of feminism(s) in this country: "first wave" or suffragist feminism, second wave, and third wave feminism. Nancy Cott's (1987) recent work holds that "feminism" did not emerge as a term of US political discourse until after 1910. What she calls the nineteenth-century "woman movement" comprised various suffrage, temperance, socialist, abolitionist, and social reform organizations. Phillippa Levine's (1987) distinction between Victorian and modern feminism, however, actually suggests that both forms are constitutive of the first wave period. Thus the first period of review, 1880–1920, roughly corresponds to the Progressive Era and marks the transition from Victorian to modern feminism, incorporating what Cott calls the first major phase of mass feminist mobilization from 1912–1919.[2] The second period of review, 1920–1960, while corresponding to a disaggregation of the women's movement (Cott 1987), also saw feminist work marked by modernist ideas and experimentation. The third period, 1960–1980, marks the onset of second wave feminism; alternately attributed to the publication of Betty

---

[1]This poses disjunction for the texts authored by non-US anthropologists discussed in this review (see Lutkehaus 1986), but other histories of feminist ethnography may yet be written.

[2]Dates for the Progressive Era are variable. I use 1920 as an endmarker because it coincides with Warren Harding's campaign for a "return to normalcy" and with what Cott terms the end of the suffrage movement and emergence of modern feminism.

Friedan's (1963) *Feminine Mystique* or to the influence of civil rights and the New Left movements (Evans 1979, Giddens 1984, King 1988), it is coterminous with a second wave of mass feminist politics between 1967 and 1974. The term "third wave feminism" is linked to the contemporary period beginning in 1980s and is still very much in contention. Some have traced its emergence to the critique by queer theorists and women of color of second wave feminism's tendency to generalize from a white, heterosexual, middle-class subject position, for again, while second wave feminism borrowed from the civil rights model, it failed to deal practically or theoretically with questions of class, sexual identity, homophobia, race, and racism within the movement (see Alarcon 1991; Combahee River Collective 1982; hooks 1984; Lorde 1984; Mohanty 1987; Moraga & Anzaldúa 1981; Sandoval 1990, 1991).

These paradigmatic markers, while they might be much refined or jettisoned altogether, are useful for understanding broad shifts in the theorization of feminist politics. We might then see the shift from first to second wave feminism as embodying the transition from an understanding of gender as a largely empirical category designating women, to an emerging form of social critique linked both to theorization of a "sex/gender" system and the development of gender "standpoint theory," the notion that women share a point of view despite cultural or class differences. I am particularly interested here in how nineteenth-century interest in the "woman question" was transformed by feminist ethnography of the second period into a "woman's point of view," much before the development of standpoint theory in the 1970s and 1980s. The shift from second wave feminism to third wave feminism can be seen in the emerging critique of the sex/gender system, and a shift away from a unified subject of consciousness in gender standpoint theory, to what has been called theories of multiple consciousness or positioning (Alarcon 1989, 1991; Anzaldúa 1987, 1991; Haraway 1988; Jones 1996a,b; Sandoval 1991).

A major theme of the first two periods was contesting stereotypes of women, despite the emphasis on cultural or racial difference prohibiting any form of identification between women. With the development of feminist standpoint theory in the 1970s and 1980s, however, gender identification or gender essentialism worked to subordinate differences of race, class, or sexual orientation (Harris 1990, Sandoval 1991, Spelman 1988, Trinh 1987). The third and fourth periods have been most marked both by the desire of feminist ethnographers to identify with their subjects as "women" and a challenge to recenter difference through textual strategies of "disidentification." If gender identification obscures difference and the workings of power, gender disidentification might expose difference and the operation of power, as part of the "rearticulation of democratic contestation" (Butler 1993, p. 4). I thus distinguish between moments of gender identification (women like "us") from moments of gender difference or disidentification (women unlike "us") vis-à-vis racial, sexual, or class positioning.

I argue that the writing of Victorian women anthropologists on Native American gender roles during the first period fomented central contradictions within the dominant evolutionary paradigm, which led to its demise. It was Elsie Clews Parsons who first foregrounded patriarchy to examine sexual inequality during the Progressive Era, and Margaret Mead who developed a distinction between sex and gender in the second period. Gayle Rubin (1975) proposed the idea of a "sex-gender" system by the mid-1970s, but in the fourth period, dual critiques of the sex/gender system and "gender essentialism" are being posited.

Although Parsons initially saw gender as an empirical category that could be documented by examining how women were treated in different societies, she did eventually develop an understanding of the cultural construction of gender. For this reason, she was one of the first feminists to argue that patriarchy was a damaging universal, not the particular evolutionary achievement of Western civilization. Second wave feminists like Robin Morgan, who propounded the universality of patriarchy or sexual asymmetry, were later critiqued by third wave feminists for ignoring that women occupied different structural positions within patriarchy depending upon group membership, or might even be subjected to multiple, interlocking patriarchies. If second wave feminists saw women as fundamentally equal in their subordination, third wave feminists insist on the inequality of women's subordination based upon the particular location of different communities in racial/class formations or heterosexual economies.

The historical perspective of this review puts it at odds with recent readings of feminist ethnography that locate the emergence of feminism in the discipline exclusively in the 1970s. This is surprising given that feminist scholars who began work in this period have already moved away from such readings (see Lamphere 1989). Nor do I believe that posing the question of a distinctly feminist ethnography presupposes an unhealthy separation of ethnography from the discipline of anthropology. To the extent that the genre of ethnography has been appropriated for other purposes and by feminists in other disciplines (Chabram 1990, Cvetkovich 1995, Frankenberg 1993, Jones 1996a,b, Newton 1993, Patai 1988, Smith & Watson 1996, Stacey 1990, Toruellas et al 1991), such a move seems to me both healthy and invigorating, not the orphan of a fraught exchange between feminist theorists and anthropologists (Gordon 1995, p. 431). In this review, I use the concepts of feminist theory to analyze the production of ethnographies about women.

In so doing, I want to move away from the question of "experimentalism"—it is clear to me that a variety of textual forms (diary, memoir, review, life history, autobiography, travelogue) have existed throughout the history of anthropological production (Behar & Gordon 1995, Tedlock 1991). My focus is thus less on "new writing" than on renewed strategies for reading. In calling for sustained attention to the works of earlier women anthropologists, then, my argument is not that feminist anthropologists of the 1970s ignored earlier work. Rather, they read it in particular ways, largely to shed light on the question of universal sexual asymmetry, less for attention to the conception of gender being advanced, or for information about self-reflexive styles of writing. My point is not that one set of readings is mistaken, only that different historical moments engender different strategies of reading. In attempting to track the intertextuality of feminist ethnography, I engage and assess those strategies of reading to understand the continuities and breaks in its production. Many other works might have been considered in this review; my objective is not to restrict what counts as "feminist ethnography" but to suggest parameters to aid in understanding what it has been and might yet become.

Since the focus of this review is upon ethnography, I review only interdisciplinary writing or work in sociocultural anthropology, linguistic anthropology, and folklore. Considerable feminist work also exists in the other subdisciplines, and I refer interested readers to those accounts (Conkey & Williams 1991, Liebowitz 1975, Zihlman 1985). Similarly, a number of reviews have periodically assessed the status of feminist scholarship in linguistic anthropology (Borker 1984, Eckert & McConnell-Ginet 1992, Gal 1991), folklore (Rosan & de Caro Jordan 1986), life history (Geiger 1986), ethnohistory (Strong 1996), and sociocultural anthropology (Atkinson 1982, Lamphere 1977, Morris 1995, Mukhopadhyay & Higgins 1988, Quinn 1977, Rapp 1979, Rogers 1978, Weston 1993), in addition to introductions for a number of recent collections (di Leonardo 1991, Ortner 1981, Rapp 1975, Rosaldo & Lamphere 1974).

I. 1880–1920: The Emergence of Gender as an Anthropological Category of Analysis[3]

When Edward Tylor addressed the Anthropological Society of Washington in 1884, he held that, "the man of the house, though he can do a great deal, cannot do it all. If his wife sympathizes with his work, and is able to do it, really half the work of investigation seems to me to fall to her, so much is to be learned through the women of the tribe, which the men will not readily disclose." Speaking in particular of Matilda Cox Stevenson's collaboration with her husband, Tylor concluded that it was a lesson not to "warn the ladies off from their proceedings, but rather to avail themselves thankfully of their help" (in Parezo

---

[3]For a fuller account of the writings of women anthropologists in this period, see Visweswaran (1997).

1993). Elsie Clews Parsons (1906) also argued that women could aid ethnology because a "woman student would have many opportunities for observing the life of women that male ethnographers have lacked" (p. 198). This suggests that early women ethnographers charged with the collection of information on women understood gender as largely an empirical or descriptive category. Still, while Alice Fletcher was interested in the study of Native American women, "hoping to add to the historical solution of the 'woman question,'" (Mark 1980, p. 67), only she, Cox Stevenson, and Parsons actually produced extensive ethnographic information about women and children, though their anthropology was not limited to this realm.

Victorian notions of sexual difference held that men and women were characterized by their biology, which in turn determined their social roles (Levine 1987, p. 129). This inseparability of sex from gender meant that the term "woman" itself was taken for granted rather than seen as something to be explained throughout much of the nineteenth century. But Erminnie Platt Smith's writing on the Iroquois, Fletcher's work on the Omaha, and Cox Stevenson's on the Zuni showed that women in "primitive" societies led lives not of degradation but of honor and respect. Such accounts challenged the Victorian evolutionary idea that Western women occupied the highest place of honor among the range of world cultures and posed a "woman question" requiring explanation. The central contradiction of Victorian evolutionism can therefore be simply stated: If the status of women was seen to be the measure of a civilization, why was it that white women were denied the vote, rights to property, and independence in a range of social activities, when "primitive" Native American women might have rights to property, a say in ritual practice, and considerable social freedom?

Still, it would not be quite accurate to say that the "woman question" sundered the logic of Victorian evolutionism. Although it had become increasingly difficult for Victorian evolutionary theory to explain away the results of emerging field-based ethnology on matrilineal societies (Cox Stevenson 1894, 1904; Fee 1975; Fletcher 1899), and this gender strain certainly contributed to its demise, high Victorianism held that while women were unequal, they were not inferior, cloaking their subordination in the glories of innate spirituality or maternal duty. In suggesting that early women anthropologists pointed to the contradiction between lowly "independent" women and highly positioned "dependent" women, then, it must be remembered that, apart from Parsons, they were not only unable to break with the conventions of Victorian society, but were to a large extent enabled by its gender ideology. Indeed, the following statements are virtually all these anthropologists have to say about the "woman question" in a rather large body of work.

Cox Stevenson (1904) wrote that "The domestic life of the Zunis might well serve as an example for the civilized world" (p. 293), and Parsons (1916) was to proclaim, "Few woman are institutionally as independent as Pueblo Indian women...particularly [ ] Zuni women (who) marry and divorce more or less at pleasure. They own their houses and their gardens. Their offspring are reckoned of their clan. Their husbands come to live with them in their family group" (p. 44). Fletcher (1883) also acknowledged that "civilization" for the Indian woman was not without its drawbacks. "Their status is one of Independence in many ways, particularly as to property. Once when our laws respecting married women were being explained to them, an Indian matron exclaimed, 'I'm glad I'm not a white woman!'" (p. 314). In a later article, "The Indian Woman and Her Problems," Fletcher (1899, p. 174) expanded:

> Under the old tribal regime, woman's industries were essential to the very life of the people, and their value was publicly recognized. While she suffered many hardships and labored early and late, her work was exalted ceremonially and she had a part in tribal functions. Her influence in the growth and development of tribal government, tribal ceremonies, and tribal power shows that her position had always been one of honor rather than one of slavery and degradation.

Even as Fletcher was concerned to argue against stereotypes of Native American women, the reverse portrait became a foil against which to judge the progress of white women, an idealized symbol of what Victorian women did not yet enjoy: independence.

In arguing for their own independence then, early women anthropologists did not argue for an end to the process that subjugated Native American women as women. In fact, the perceived "independence" of Native American women in spite of forced removal and genocide, may have worked as an ideological shield in much the same way that white women were not seen to be subjugated as *women* because they were white. Just at the moment the idea of gender difference—that is, the different social roles occupied by women in native and white cultures—might have challenged racial hierarchy, Parsons's (1916) insistence that, "The main objective of feminism in fact, may be defeminisation, the declassification of women as women, the recognition of women as human beings or personalities" (p. 54) worked to erase racial difference and inequalities between women altogether. In Parsons's writing, such a paradoxical declassification of women and subordination of difference actually shapes the emergence in her work of women as a universal category. This double movement is most present in her early writings which she characterized as "propaganda by the ethnographic method," but actually predate her entry into empirical anthropology around 1915 (see Deacon 1997, Lamphere 1989).

Much has been written of Parsons's contribution to the cultural construction of gender and her polyphonic dispersed style of writing (Babcock 1992, Deacon 1997). She has been credited with establishing an interest in "mothering as form and institution," as well as in the cross-cultural construction of sexuality through her work on the Zuni La'mana, though this designation more properly belongs to Matilda Cox Stevenson, whose descriptions of childbirth are written as unfolding social dramas,[4] and whose relationship with We'wha, Zuni "man/woman" is catalogued with affection and respect (see also Parezo 1993). Still, an understanding of how gender distinctions reflect institutional social inequality emerges more fully in Parsons's popular writings than in her ethnographic work.

Parsons's (1906) first major work, "An Ethnographical and Historical Outline of the Family," is usually forgiven its apparent evolutionism and is more often remembered for her controversial advocacy of trial marriage, whereas her problematic advocacy of birth control for classes "the least culturally developed, and therefore the least self-controlled," (p. 351) has been overlooked. As a solution to reducing the cost to the state of such criminal reproduction by its "diseased or vicious subjects," Parsons had advocated use of Galton's "eugenics certificates" (p. 344).

By 1909, however, Parsons's views of class difference seem to have been submerged in ethnographic universals about women's condition. She held that "royal ladies of the African west coast" and the queens of medieval Europe fought similar battles to establish their independence: "All these queens, nuns, and femmes de joie were the celibate or grass widow pioneers of woman's rights, the ancestresses of the modern emancipated woman" (1909, p. 758). Four years later, in *The Old-Fashioned Woman,* Parsons was again arguing that the differences between Western society and other societies were not pronounced where women were concerned (1913, p. 24):

> "Coming-out" is a custom not peculiar to civilization. Our debutantes are apt to be older, to be sure, than those elsewhere. Instead of a year or two "abroad" or in a "finishing school," savage girls usually spend but a few weeks or months in a lonely hut or in a bed or in a hammock or cage in a corner of the house or on the roof. But once "out," a debutante's life is everywhere much the same. Everywhere at this time particular attention is paid to a girl's looks.

While Parsons here articulates a form of gender identification by celebrating a practice common to diverse groups of women, in the same moment she puts under erasure the class differences of industrial society, and the very presence of working women who were not attending debutante balls but subject to eugenicist recommendations.

In her 1916 work, *Social Rule,* however, such universals had more negative connotations, for "[f]rom the domination of her family (a woman) passes under

---

[4]See her descriptions of childbirth among the Sia (1894, pp. 132–43) and Zuni (1904, pp. 294–303).

the domination of her husband and, perhaps in addition, of his family" (p. 44). Thus, at the same moment Parsons established the relative high status and autonomy of women in "primitive" cultures, her move to equalize sources of oppression between diverse groups of women makes them all subjects of the same patriarchy, effacing difference in the process. Parsons's assertion that it was patriarchal social organization that oppresses women constitutes the major break with the dominant strain of evolutionist theory that held that patriarchy was *the* form of civilized society (Fee 1975). The deployment of cultural difference to establish a universalized patriarchy is perhaps the central contribution and paradox of Parsons's ethnologically informed feminism, one which has had a troubled history in "second-wave" Anglo-American feminism, and the ideas of universal sexual asymmetry that informed the feminist anthropology of the 1970s and 1980s (cf. di Leonardo 1991, Lamphere 1989, Rapp 1975, Rosaldo 1980).

Victorian women anthropologists like Fletcher and Cox Stevenson were unable to sunder the notion that sex and gender were one and the same (though their work posed the question of separating the two). Parsons, however, in recognizing the variety of roles women played throughout histories and cultures, came close to suggesting, as Margaret Mead later did, that different sex roles might be enabled by different cultures. Parsons was thus a transitional figure, one who presaged Mead's interventions, which clearly separated sex from gender by developing a distinction between sex and sex temperament.

II. 1920–1960: Ethnographies of Race, Ethnographies of Women, and the Sex/Gender Distinction

Margaret Mead was possibly not the first social scientist to develop a distinction between biological sex and sociologically distinct gender roles, but she was certainly the first to use ethnography to do so. Her first work, *Coming of Age in Samoa,* investigated whether "the process of growth by which the girl baby becomes a grown woman," or "the sudden and conspicuous bodily changes which take place at puberty" was accompanied by an inevitable period of mental and emotional distress for the growing girl" (1928, p. 196). Mead's answer was, of course, "no." Coming of age in Samoa had none of the fraught connotations it had in the United States (p. 197).[5]

However, it was not until her comparative work in *Sex and Temperament in Three Societies* that she distinguished between sex and sex temperament in a now famous formulation (1935, p. 280): "many, if not all, of the personality traits which we have called masculine or feminine are as lightly linked to sex as are the clothing, the manners, and the form of head-dress that a society at a given period assigns to either sex." Significantly, Mead's early formulation of

---

[5]This theme was explored again in her next major work (1930), *Growing Up in New Guinea.*

gender as sex temperament was often deployed by feminist ethnographers of this period to emphasize cultural or racial difference, working against any form of gender identification.

Still, Mead's *Coming of Age in Samoa* inaugurated a period of textual production during the late 1930s to late 1940s in which "ethnographies of women," that is, texts with women as their sole or main subject, were written through the medium of the life history, "autobiography," (Landes 1971; Reichard 1934, 1939; Underhill 1979) or travel narrative (Hurston 1935, 1938; Landes 1947). Writers in this period oscillated between the empiricist assumptions of Tylor and Parsons (studying women for a more complete picture of the society) and vindicationist approaches that sought to refute cultural or gender stereotypes.

Early feminist ethnography that relied upon life history method was concerned to establish the simultaneous uniqueness and typicality of the women being written about. Ruth Landes's (1971) *Ojibwa Woman* consists of stories that Maggie Wilson narrated to her daughter about other women in the community. Although Landes describes Maggie's achievements as "boldly venturesome and resourceful," "[o]nly fragments of Maggie's life story appear in the present volume" though "[h]er major attitudes are exposed in her choice of tales…and in her turns of phrase" (p. viii). While Maggie is obviously a powerful personality and a "gifted woman," Landes struggles to justify the absence of her authorial presence by noting contradictorily, "A preliterate society masks its personalities with anonymity" (p. viii).

The insistence on making a woman both unique and typical of her culture is also found in Ruth Underhill's work. For her, "a Papago woman's history is interesting in itself, because, in this culture, there exists strongly the fear of woman's impurity with all its consequent social adjustments" (1979, p. 33). In choosing Chona as a subject, Underhill struggled to see her as typical: "She is not the aberrant type which so frequently attracts the attention of the White investigator. She accepted her culture completely, and one reason for choosing her was that she had come in contact with so many of its important phases." Still, Chona was not the "ideal Papago female type, for she was inclined to be independent and executive…" (1979, p. 34).

Autobiography, biography, and life history were often conflated to erase the narratorial presence of the white woman anthropologist, while her authorship was paradoxically underscored. Some saw themselves as neither editors nor elicitors of the life stories gathered (Landes 1971); others were more cognizant of their role in shaping the narrative. In the introduction to *Autobiography of a Papago Woman,* Ruth Underhill (1979) calls it a "memory picture," (p. 10) underscoring her role as editor of Chona's narrative, noting that her story "appears in these pages, brief and concise…" though "the writing of that simple story took three years" (p. 27). Thus, "in presenting an Indian autobiography, there still remain important questions of technique. Indian narrative style involves a repetition and a dwelling on unimportant details which confuse the White reader and make it hard for him to follow the story" (p. 3).

The devices of fiction were also used to construct the generalized subjects of life history. Gladys Reichard (1939) began *Dezba: Woman of the Desert* by noting that "Dezba is one of the 45,000 or 48,000 Navajo Indians who inhabit a vast territory from Northeastern Arizona and NorthWestern New Mexico," yet "In depicting the character of the story I have used no incidents or details which are not true. Nevertheless...the description of the actors, the relationship they bear to the author, and the episodes in which they appear are all fictional. I know no Navajo exactly like anyone here portrayed" (p. vi).

Others reflected specifically on the relationship of anthropological narrative to novelistic fiction. When Mead likened the techniques of the fieldworker to that of the novelist (cited in Lutkehaus 1995, p. 189), Kaberrry (1939) concurred that "The anthropologist needs the eye of a novelist..." (pp. 38–39). "Ethnographies of women," then, reveal considerable forethought and reflexivity about the conditions of textual production, often deliberately using "fiction" as a strategic narrative device to relay a "woman's point of view." In these texts, however, the function of a "woman's point of view" is to specify cultural difference and is not a point of identification between author, subject, and audience.

At the time of its publication, Phyllis Kaberry's (1939) *Aboriginal Woman* was heralded for of its contribution "to our knowledge of the life of Aboriginal women" and credited with disproving the "widespread idea that Aboriginal women are mere drudges, passing a life of monotony and being shamefully illtreated by their husbands" (p. xxii). Like Fletcher before her, Kaberry deployed anthropology to debunk stereotype, revealing the social construction of gender, for the Aboriginal woman had to be envisaged "as an active social personality: as a human being with all the wants, desires and needs that flesh is heir to" (p. 9). Like Mead, Kaberry was also adept at showing how culture and environment shape different notions of womanhood (p. 10):

> The country for the aboriginal woman is not so much freehold or leasehold property, but one she regards as her own because she has inherited the right to live and forage for food within its boundaries. In her patriotism, she is ready to insist that there is an abundance of game, fish, and yams, whether there is or not. To the white woman...the country is one of plains and arid hills. It seems incredible to her that the native woman can forage day, after day, wandering apparently at random in the hope of finding a few tubers.

Kaberry's perception of aboriginal women's "patriotism" in a year of drought, and awareness of her own racialization, is perhaps due to the heightened context of World War II. As racial identities were reflected through gender distinctions, so too were gender distinctions reflected through race relations. Thus the textual production of this era spanning the Depression to the end of World War II was also marked by "ethnographies of race" which more deliberately deployed a "woman's viewpoint" to foreground race relations.[6] Many works, including Zora Neale Hurston's (1938) *Tell My Horse,* which explores cross-cultural experiences of womanhood in the United States and Caribbean, or Ella Deloria's (1988) *Waterlily,* a novel about coming to womanhood in Dakota Sioux society, reveal the use of a form of gender standpoint to explore the impact of race upon the authors and those they write about, but disturb the coherence of identification between author, subject, and reader by generating multiple positionings in their texts.

Other works of this period, however, do not necessarily make women the sole subjects of analysis. Hurston's (1935) *Mules and Men* and Landes's (1947) *City of Women,* in particular, combine textual modes that enable a movement from race relations in the American South (Eatonville, Fisk University) to the analysis of race relations in Afro-Brazilian and Afro-Caribbean communities. Despite Landes's mistaken claim that racial problems in Brazil did not exist (1947, p. xxxvi), *City of Women* details her own negotiation of patriarchal racial ideologies in the United States and Brazil.

Hortense Powdermaker's (1939) *After Freedom* similarly describes her own mediating position in race relations of the US south, writing of the difficulty of working in a region of marked hostility between whites and blacks. Thus, Powdermaker (1939) is forced to account for the "woman's view" reflected in her ethnography (p. xvi):

> In the community studied, it is almost out of the question for a white woman to interview Negro men. Accordingly, the colored informants were mainly women. Since, however, the Negro family in Cottonville is so largely matriarchal, and since it would have been difficult in any situation for one person to get material of equal intimacy from members of both sexes, this was not such a serious handicap. Something of the male point of view was revealed through the women.

While Powdermaker relied upon unexamined stereotypes of the "Negro family," her writing, along with work by Landes, Hurston, Deloria, and others points to how gender distinctions are inseparable from the patriarchal race relations that produce them.

---

[6]These texts include works by sociologists working in the "Caste School of Racial Relations": John Dollard's (1937) *Caste and Class in a Southern Town,* BG Gallaghers's (1938) *American Caste and the Negro College,* and works by anthropologists, such as Davis & Gardner's (1941) *Deep South,* Melville Herskovits's (1941) *Myth of the Negro Past,* and St. Clair Drake & Horace Cayton's (1945) *Black Metropolis.*

Discussion of patriarchy sometimes worked to displace analysis of racial conflict in feminist ethnography of this period, however. Gladys Reichard's (1934) *Spider Woman* is a first person account of her own instruction in weaving over a period of four summers, but it is also staged as a series of encounters with Navajo patriarchy. Navajo men appear in her narrative as those who support her efforts to weave (especially important, since it is they who do the hard labor for setting up the looms) or those who challenge it (p. 96). Unfortunately, Reichard displays an inability to comprehend that what is for her an aesthetic pleasure or summer pastime is labor that must ultimately receive economic remuneration. When one man demands that Reichard pay his wife a large sum of money for teaching her to weave because she might in turn "teach the white women to weave so that Navajo women won't be able to earn money anymore," (p. 216) Reichard is unable to locate herself as part of a larger, white-dominated political economy, though she recognizes that the Navajo "have been exploited by whites for years" and are "on the defensive." Her dismissal of demands for correct payment is thus justified by what she sees as male domination, "corroborated by white observers and other Navajo"—that "Kinni's-Son is supported largely by the industry of his women, and he wants to be supported as well as possible" (pp. 216–17).

Despite both Reichard's and Parsons's identification with and adoption of the Spiderwoman role in Native American teachings (Weigle 1982), racial and class privilege remains unmarked in their texts. This suggests that the feminist ethnography of this period evokes a "woman's point of view" not as a subject of identification that activates woman as a universal category, but as the filter through which cultural and racial difference is both apprehended and abstracted from unequal relations of power.

III. 1960–1980: Sex/Gender Systems and Universals of Sex Oppression

Ethnographies that sought to understand the structural symbolic position of women in society began to appear in the late 1950s (Berndt 1950, Richards 1956) and continued into the 1970s and 1980s (Goodale 1971, Strathern 1972, Weiner 1976). In 1971, however, courses on the anthropology of women were taught for the first time at Stanford University, the University of Michigan, and the University of California, Santa Barbara. These courses, and others like them, properly marked the inauguration of US feminist anthropology and the books that emerged from them: Michelle Rosaldo and Louise Lamphere's (1974) *Women, Culture and Society,* Rayna Rapp's (1975) *Toward an Anthropology of Women,* and M Kay Martin and Barbara Voorhies's (1975) *Female of the Species.*

Much has already been written about the first two collections, for which Robin Morgan's (1970) *Sisterhood is Powerful* was probably a motivating, if unacknowledged force. And while second wave feminism was influenced by civil rights and other movements for racial equality (Evans 1979, Giddens 1984, King 1988), the analogy of sex oppression to race oppression was the unstated intellectual ground for these collections, allowing the submergence of racial and cultural difference in woman as a universal category.[7] In reexamining their moment of production, I want to suggest new ways of understanding the emergence and intertextuality of feminist anthropology. If it is true that the expository review was one of the first textual forms employed by this generation of feminist anthropologists (Gordon 1995), what was its relationship to ethnographic writing of this period? I argue that the first manifesto-like reviews can be read in a kind of call and response mode. In response to the call, "Are women universally the second sex?" feminist ethnographers answered equivocally "yes" and "no."

Women, Culture and Society opened with an invocation from Simone de Beauvoir and then went on to debunk the theories of "matriarchy" used as explanations for "women's past." Michelle Rosaldo and Louise Lamphere (1974) queried, "What then do anthropologists know about our heritage?" (p. 4) and concluded that since much of it was negative, "[b]y treating everywhere women's lives as interesting and problematic, we hope to loosen the hold of stereotypes that have, unfortunately, shaped our own lives (p. 15).

Like some of the Victorian era women, second wave feminist anthropologists thought that understanding the lives of women in other cultures could help them make sense of their own (Rapp 1975, p. 11). In locating feminist work in the struggle against stereotypes, the authors of these collections placed themselves in the vindicationist matriline of Fletcher, Nuttal, Hurston, Deloria, and Kaberry. Although recent reflections (Lamphere 1989) suggest that Margaret Mead was the feminist spirit behind the Rosaldo and Lamphere collection, neither *Woman, Culture and Society* nor *Toward an Anthropology of Women* detail in any substantive way the contributions of Margaret Mead. That was actually left to Martin & Voorhies (1975), who dedicated *Female of the Species* "To Margaret Mead: A continuing pioneer in the anthropological study of sex and gender." Martin & Voorhies's notion of "gender status" was indebted to Mead's work in *Sex and Temperament* and to her later notion of "sex careers" (p. 95). For them, the "biological and cultural aspects of sex" were distinguished by "features known to have a genetic basis as a person's physical sex

---

[7]Many of the Engels-influenced writers of the period used the analogy of "sex oppression" to class oppression, recalling Parsons's use of the term "sex class," but the effect was again to produce "woman" as a universal category.

or phenotypic sex" from "those features that appear to have their foundation in cultural instruction, and that reflect...a person's social sex or gender" (p. 3).

Mead was still alive at the time these works were produced; her controversial public persona, and perhaps her own apparent disavowal of feminism, made her a difficult figure for 1970s feminists to claim.[8] Betty Friedan's second wave text, *The Feminine Mystique,* also devoted an entire chapter to a critique of Mead's ideas.[9] Friedan (1963) argued that while the "feminine mystique might have taken from Margaret Mead her vision of the infinite variety of sexual patterns and the enormous plasticity of human nature, a vision based on the differences of sex and temperament she found in three primitive societies" (p. 136), what emerged from Mead's work was "a glorification of women in the female role—as defined by their sexual biological function" (p. 137).

By 1975, it was Gayle Rubin who defined the sex/gender system (again without recourse to Mead) as "the set of arrangements by which a society transforms biological sexuality into products of human activity, and in which these transformed sexual needs are satisfied" (1975, p. 159). According to her, "Every society...has a sex/gender system—a set of arrangements by which the biological raw material of human sex and procreation is shaped by human, social intervention and satisfied in a conventional manner" (1975, p. 165). It is this notion of a sex/gender system that permeates the ethnographic production of this period and the next.

Although I cannot discuss the full range of texts that use some notion of a sex/gender system, it is important to note that not all of them produce a coherent subject of identification. I have elsewhere (Visweswaran 1994) written that second wave feminist ethnographies such as Hortense Powdermaker's (1966) *Stranger and Friend,* Laura Bohannon's (1966) *Return to Laughter,* Elizabeth Fernea's (1969) *Guests of the Sheikh,* or Jean Briggs's (1970) *Never in Anger* often report the authors' assignment to the world of women, and moments of disaffection or disidentification following from the authors' inability to identify with their subjects to create a unified "woman's point of view." This group of texts powerfully suggests disjunction and discontinuity rather than progressive teleology in the historical elaboration of gender within the discipline. By contrast, most authors throughout the 1980s and 1990s enact strategies of identification with their subjects (Abu-Lughod 1987, 1993; Behar 1993; Bell 1993; Shostak 1981).

---

[8]For example, in the introduction to *Sex and Temperament,* Mead (1935) pronounced, "This study is not...a treatise on the rights of women, nor an inquiry into the basis of feminism" (p. viii). Her legacy is still contested (Foerstel & Gilliam 1992) and has only recently been reclaimed, but more for her contributions to writing (Behar & Gordon 1995, Lutkehaus 1995, Marcus & Fisher 1986, Reinharz 1991) than as the originator of the sex/gender distinction in anthropology.

[9]See Chapter 6, "The Functional Freeze, The Feminine Protest and Margaret Mead."

In noting this contrast, I want briefly to explore how feminist ethnographers of differing periods read, and reread each other's work to produce ethnographic sites of intertextuality and contestation. I am particularly interested in Eleanor Leacock's (1978) critique of Landes's (1971) work and Diane Bell's (1993) engagement with Phyllis Kaberry's (1939) work in her 1983 book *Daughters of the Dreaming.*

Leacock's (1978) critique of Ruth Landes's work is found in her classic article "Women's Status in Egalitarian Society: Implications for Social Evolution." Leacock presents Landes's work as an example of "the extent to which data can be skewed by a nonhistorical approach...based on (ethnocentric) assumptions about public-prestigious males versus private-deferent females" (p. 251). Leacock accuses Landes of providing two contradictory descriptions of women in Ojibwa society: "In one, women are extremely self-sufficient and independent and much more versatile than men." "By contrast, the second description deals with a hunting society in which women are 'inferior' and lack 'distinct training,' in which the generalization is made that 'any man is intrinsically and vastly superior to any woman...'" (p. 251).

Leacock held that if women were excluded from public decision-making (as Rosaldo and Lamphere argued) it was the result of a particular sex-gender system produced by capitalist development. The failure to identify a particular public/private dichotomy as the lens of our own sex/gender system operating through capitalism amounted, for Leacock, to a projection of false ideological categories onto others.

It is, however, possible to see Landes's descriptions of Ojibwa life as a richly woven account that conveys the complexity of women's social positioning and a productive inability to say decisively whether they are wholly independent or subordinate. I suggest that it is not the accounts that are faulty but the form of a question that asked feminists to decide conclusively one way or the other.[10]

Diane Bell, in contrast to Leacock, located herself in a line of vindicationist scholarship on aboriginal women which included Phyllis Kaberry (1939), Catherine Berndt (1950), and Jane Goodale (1971). Based on fieldwork conducted between 1976 and 1982, *Daughters of the Dreaming* is simultaneously a first-person account of "learning to be a woman" in aboriginal society (Bell 1993, pp. 21, 28, 34–35) and an account of gender relations within it. Bell de-

---

[10]Such contradictory complexity also marks Ruth Underhill's work. Remarking upon the differences between Underhill's (1938) monograph *Singing for Power,* and her 1965 study, *Red Man's Religion,* Martha Weigle (1982, pp. 172–73) notes that while Underhill's first account of Papago menstrual taboos and beliefs positions women as fearful and dangerous sites of contamination, her later account reworked the same passages in dialogical form to conclude that women's monthly social separation was a sign of sacred power.

scribes herself as "dedicated to learning a woman's point of view" (p. 33). At various points, however, her own identification with aboriginal women is punctured by moments of unease: "It was as if I had been accepted because I was a white woman and the Warlpiri had learned not to argue with whites. I was a Nakamarra, a widow, a mother, but I was also a white woman. Maybe I was a little like the welfare people" (p. 27). This is one of the few places in the text where Bell's gender identification with aboriginal women is undercut by a reflection upon the structural position of power implied in her racial positioning.

Bell clearly sees her ethnography as a kind of response to the debates about universal sexual asymmetry, noting, "I have throughout this book avoided speaking of sexual equality or inequality because I believe these concepts distort our understanding of male-female relationships in desert society" (p. 237). However, while Bell explicitly aligned herself with Leacock's position, her writing about aboriginal women was not reducible to it.[11] Like Phyllis Kaberry before her, Bell sought to underline positive yet complex images of Aboriginal women. The feminist ethnographies that emerged in response to the debates on universal sexual asymmetry, then, were remarkable for their refusal to decide the question one way or the other.

In the epilogue written 10 years after the initial publication of the book, Bell writes of her own process of identifying with the women she studied, explicitly aligning herself with the standpoint theory of Nancy Hartsock (1987) and Sandra Harding (1993). Bell's recognition of the alliance of feminist ethnography with standpoint theory is important; a larger number of feminist ethnographies are produced by standpoint theory without their authors' acknowledgment. Standpoint perspectives rely upon a notion of the sex/gender system, which assumes women are all members of the same "sex" notwithstanding different gender identifications produced by culture, for to produce a "women's standpoint," which is shared by women regardless of culture, is to rely upon the only thing women share in common: biology (see Jagger 1988, p. 377).[12]

Standpoint theory, as Catherine O'Leary (1997) so cogently argues, universalizes the category of gender so that difference is subordinated to a unified subject of identification. As standpoint theory was formalized in the 1980s, it was held that the feminist standpoint was founded "on the basis of the common threads of female experience..." (Hartsock 1987). Despite the Marxist origin of much standpoint theory, it produces gender identification between feminist

---

[11]Nor was Marjorie Shostak's (1981) *Nisa* limited to the debates about "egalitarian band societies," though it is these questions that inform her fieldwork.

[12]Interestingly enough, Dorothy Smith's (1987) early formulation of standpoint theory read Jean Brigg's ethnography not for its ruptures and disaffections (Visweswaran 1994) but for evidence of a "woman's perspective."

ethnographers and their subjects, erasing differences of race, class, or sexual orientation.[13]

Other forms of standpoint theory operate in field memoirs like Katherine Dunham's (1994) *Island Possessed,* where negritude is advanced as an existential ethnographic lens. Written in Senegal, some thirty-odd years after her first experiences in the field, it is a partial meditation of her own positioning in the scholarship on Haiti by Melville Herskovits and his students (p. 4):

> They were white and male these writers. Of my kind I was a first—a lone young woman easy to place in the clean-cut American dichotomy of color, harder to place in the complexity of Caribbean color classifications; a mulatto when occasion called for, an in-between, or "griffon" actually, I suppose; most of the time an unacceptable, which I prefer to think of as "noir"—not exactly the color black, but the quality of belonging with or being at ease with black people when in the hills or plains or anywhere, and scrambling through daily life along with them. Though the meaning of the word negritude has never been completely clear to me, here in the country of the conceiver of the concept, reflecting on my early years, I know I must have practiced, preached and lived it.

For Dunham, negritude is the standpoint that allows her to reflect upon her shifting racial position in US and Caribbean societies. The extent to which her understanding of negritude is essentialist, or only strategically so, entails a fuller discussion of racial vindicationism as a sociopolitical strategy against racism and must be balanced against her understanding of color and class difference as central to the socially constructed character of race. Like Zora Neale Hurston, Dunham deploys the ethnographic medium to reflect on her gendered racial identities in the United States and Haiti, suggesting multiple subject positionings or hyphenated consciousness. Further work might explore the extent to which black feminist standpoint theory (Collins 1990, hooks 1984, King 1988)—the notion of a "both/and orientation" derived from black women's experiences as African-Americans and as women (Collins 1990, p. 29)—is useful for understanding the ethnographies of Hurston, Dunham, and others.

IV. 1980–1996: Beyond the Sex/Gender Distinction: Critiques of Gender Essentialism

In 1980, arguably the most influential essay for feminist anthropology, and for US feminist scholarship in general, was Michelle Rosaldo's "The Use and Abuse of Anthropology: Reflections on Feminism and Cross-Cultural Under-

---

[13]Important revisions to standpoint theory have been advanced by Patricia Hill Collins (1990) and Patricia Zavella (1995) on the question of race and racial identification; some theorists also propound the notion of multiple standpoints. These versions of standpoint theory broach formulations of multiple positioning and consciousness discussed in the next section.

standing." Rosaldo (1980) began her review with a sympathetic critique of the popular feminist literature for its attempts to "catalog customs of the past in order to decide if womankind can claim through time, to have acquired or lost...power, self-esteem, autonomy and status" (p. 391). While Rosaldo insisted that "male dominance, though apparently universal, does not in actual behavioral terms, assume a universal content or universal shape" (p. 394), she held that "every social system uses the facts of biological sex to organize and explain the roles and opportunities men may enjoy, just as all known human social groups appeal to biologically based ties in the construction of familial groups and kinship bonds (p. 395) concluding that, "it would appear that certain biological facts—women's role in reproduction and, perhaps, male strength—have operated in a nonnecessary way to shape and reproduce male dominance" (p. 396). Rosaldo's critique was thus bound by the same adherence to biology of which Friedan accused Margaret Mead.

Yet Rosaldo's review attempted to address how the very argument for universal sexual asymmetry might essentialize the category of "woman" (p. 401):

> To talk of women's status is to think about a social world in ultimately dichotomous terms, wherein "woman" is universally opposed to man in the same ways in all contexts. Thus, we tend repeatedly to contrast and stress presumably given differences between women and men, instead of asking how such differences are themselves created by gender relations. In so doing, we find ourselves the victims of a conceptual tradition that discovers "essence" in the natural characteristics which distinguish us from men and then declares that women's present lot derives from what "in essence" women are....

In attempting to stress that universal facts were not reducible to biology (p. 397), and in suggesting the nonnecessary ways in which biology was read into structures of domination, Rosaldo initiated a critique of gender essentialism but was ultimately unable to achieve it because of her insistence that "'brute' biological facts have everywhere been shaped by social logics" (p. 399). Positing a direct relationship between biology and gender roles (however variously defined) runs counter to one of the central insights of queer theory, that biology may not be determinative of sexuality or sexual identification.

Judith Butler (1990) perhaps levels the critique of the sex/gender system the most succinctly:[14] "this construct called 'sex' is as culturally constructed as gender; indeed, perhaps it was always already gender, with the consequence that the distinction between sex and gender turns out to be no distinction at all. It would make no sense, then, to define gender as the cultural interpretation of

[14]I do not want to imply that there is only one critique of the sex/gender distinction; several acknowledge and work from Rubin's early distinctions (see de Lauretis 1987, Sedgewick 1990, Warner 1993).

sex, if sex itself is a gendered category" (p. 7). She concludes that "gender is not to culture as sex is to nature; gender is also the discursive/cultural means by which 'sexed nature' or a 'natural sex' is produced and established as 'prediscursive,' prior to culture, a politically neutral surface on which culture acts" (p. 7). It is worth noting that in this particular critique of the sex/gender system, sex and gender are once again seen to be indistinguishable, though in terms quite distinct from the Victorian era. In the Victorian era, biological sex was seen to entail particular social roles; in the current moment, sex is inseparable from gender because sex itself is seen to be a social category.[15]

Butler suggests that it is in performativity itself that gender operates, reembodied (or disembodied); as Mead first suggested, sexual identity can be likened to putting on or taking off a set of clothes. Gender can be seen as something people do rather than as a quality they possess, pushing the shift from gender as principle structuring social relations to forms of subjectivity a step farther. Rewriting de Beauvoir, we might say, "One is not born, one performs (or is performed as) a woman." The metaphor, while useful, also has its limitations: Subjects do not always freely choose their performances; gender, race, and class distinctions may also be performed upon them, with devastating effects.[16]

A number of feminist ethnographies now focus on the emergence of gender in performance (Harrison 1990, Jones 1996a,b, Kapchan 1996, Kondo 1995, Steedly 1993, Stewart 1996, Tsing 1993); some like Nadia Seremetakis (1991) also use a form of gender standpoint to understand the performance and poetics of particular speech genres such as the funeral lament, for "to examine death in Inner Mani is to look at Maniat society through female eyes" (p. 15).

Several have also turned to playwriting as a means of scripting ethnographic performances. Dorinne Kondo (1995) and Joni Jones (1996a,b) explore through the medium of performance what Angie Chabram (1990) has called "institutional ethnography" by locating their gender identities in the context of racialization within the United States academy. Reworking de Beauvoir's formulation of woman as other, Jones foregrounds the construction of identity in performance to ask, "What is an African American in Africa?" For Jones, performance ethnography de-essentializes notions of blackness by honoring the embodied acts of interaction and dialogue (1996a). While Dunham uses "negritude" as a means of describing the sense of ease she felt in

---

[15]Although Eve Sedgewick works from Rubin's distinctions, she concludes that gender is "the whole package of physical and cultural distinctions between men and women" (1990, p. 29). Martin (1994) has argued, "If for Sedgewick, gender becomes sex, and ineluctably follows the principles of binary division, for Butler, sex becomes gender, that is socially constructed, and the principle of binary division is itself contested, even at the level of the body" (p. 110).

[16]Butler has addressed this criticism in her subsequent (1993) book.

working with black folk in Haiti, Jones foregrounds questions of "home and field," reflecting upon her sense of unease with culturally distinct others and the difficulties of articulating a Pan-African identity. Like Kathleen Stewart (1996), Jones emphasizes the role of memory in ethnography to rework the contours between self and others, subjects and objects. In these works, gender emerges in the very performance of raced, classed, and sexed identities.

Shortly after Rosaldo's review appeared, *This Bridge Called My Back,* edited by Cherríe Moraga and Gloria Anzaldúa (1981), was published to wide acclaim. A decade later, another collection edited by Gloria Anzaldúa (1991), *Making Face/Making Soul,* was published with Norma Alarcón's critical review "The Theoretical Subjects of This Bridge Called My Back." Here Alarcón contrasted the "modal subject" of Anglo-American feminism, "an autonomous, self-making, self-determining subject, who first proceeds according to the logic of identification with regard to the subject of consciousness" (p. 357) with the subjects of *This Bridge Called My Back* displaced "across a multiplicity of discourses (feminist/lesbian, nationalist, racial, socioeconomic, historical) implying a multiplicity of positions from which they are driven to grasp or understand themselves and their relations with the real..." (p. 356).

In the wake of the critiques leveled by *This Bridge* and *Making Face,* some feminist ethnographers have evolved strategies to deal with the question of multiple positioning. Referring to themselves as "halfie" or "hyphenated" ethnographers, they describe how mixed parentage, ethnic heritage, or racial positioning have shaped their ethnographic identifications (Abu-Lughod 1993, Behar 1993, Narayan 1993, Kondo 1995, Visweswaran 1994). Others have foregrounded more radically the meaning of biracial or multiracial identity (Ajani 1994) or have attempted to understand the "social construction of whiteness" (Frankenberg 1993). Although referencing of postcolonial theory is common (Cole & Phillips 1995, Mascia-Lees et al 1989, Steedly 1993, Tsing 1993), many feminist ethnographers have been reluctant to deal explicitly with race—a marked difference from the ethnographic works of the 1930s and 1940s.

Norma Alarcón (1991) and Catherine O'Leary (1997) have both suggested that if standpoint theory works to create subjects of identification, or counteridentification, theories of multiple positioning create subjects of "disidentification." While there has been some ethnographic work that explores strategies of disidentification or multiple positioning within the text (Jones 1996a,b, Steedly 1993, Tsing 1993), the critique of gender essentialism has been slow to work itself into recent feminist writing in anthropology. Though work on feminism and postmodernism critiques gender essentialism (Alcoff 1988, Gordon 1993, Nicholson 1990), the discussion in anthropology has actually reified unproblematized notions of gender (Mascia-Lees et al 1989, Strathern 1987), perhaps because it has narrowly read the debate as one of experimental form.

Some dismiss outright the "philosophical deconstruction" of the term "woman" (Scheper-Hughes 1992), while other feminist anthropologists note that the assumptions of a unifying gender identity are "exclusionary and mystifying," cite a "few illustrious examples" of critique (Steedly 1993), and then proceed to privilege gender as the center of analysis. Notions of sisterly identification abound, and feminist ethnography continues to traffic in intimate forms of address, despite Ann Oakley's (1981) and Judith Stacey's (1988, 1990) cautions about the dangerous ground between intimacy and betrayal. The terms "friend" and "informant" are often used interchangeably in these texts; often without further reflection or comment on the intrinsic contradictions of power that are masked in such a slippage.

Working from the genre of feminist testimonial (Patai 1988, Personal Narratives Group 1989), recent feminist ethnography has elaborated a concern with "giving voice" to its subjects. Nancy Scheper-Hughes (1992) contends that in spite of "the dissonant voices in the background protesting just this choice of words" that "there is still a role for the ethnographer-writer in giving voice, as best she can, to those who have been silenced..." (p. 28). Karen McCarthy Brown (1991) similarly affirms that "the people who are being studied should be allowed to speak for themselves whenever possible..." (p. 14).

Such concerns align contemporary feminist ethnography with the life history/autobiographies of the 1930s and 1940s that sought to make the narrator transparent or absent from the text. Unlike work of the second period, however, there has been more ambivalence about the question of fiction in current work than one might expect. Although Lila Abu-Lughod's (1993) recent project is about telling stories, she is concerned to distance herself from fiction, insisting that all of the stories she recounts are "true" and that they have not been "made up." A similar caution appears in Ruth Behar's (1993) recent ethnography: "This book is not a work of fiction" (p. xiv). Even recent attempts that deploy the devices of fiction to highlight their ethnographic reporting (Brown 1991, Wolf 1990) juxtapose it with more "ethnographic" accounts (see, however, Behar & Gordon 1995, Visweswaran 1994).

Alternate forms of feminist ethnography have elaborated upon the question of culture by defining "women's culture" (Abu-Lughod 1987), women's "work culture" (Lamphere 1987, Sacks 1984, Zavella 1987), women at work (Fernandez-Kelly 1983, Kapchan 1996, Ong 1987, Quinn 1977), therapeutic culture (Cvetkovich 1995), and more recently, women's participation in popular culture (Ajani 1994, Mankekar 1993). Women's field accounts (Altorki & El-Sohl 1988) have shifted toward explicitly feminist self-reflexive narratives (Narayan 1993), and feminist work on kinship has similarly shifted from symbolic analysis (Collier & Rosaldo 1981, Collier & Yanagisako 1987, Raheja & Gold 1994, Strathern 1972) to more reflexive accounts of kin structures (Bell

1993, Trawick 1990, Weston 1991, Yanagisako 1985). In Margaret Trawick's (1990) *Notes on Love in a Tamil Family,* the unspoken part of most ethnographic research, "What Led Me to Them," explores how her own life experiences and ethnic identity resulted in fieldwork in India. Judith Stacey's (1990) *Brave New Families* is a reflection on "accidental ethnography," postmodern kin relations, "recombinant family life," feminism and fundamentalism, while Kath Weston's (1991) *Families We Choose* critiques the nuclear family to question the exile of gays and lesbians from kinship, arguing for gay families as alternate forms of family. Feminist ethnographers have also tried to detail women's speech communities, focusing on speech genres that are performed particularly by women (Abu-Lughod 1987, Kapchan 1996, Serematakis 1991), and in linguistic anthropology, feminists have turned their attention to "communities of practice" (Hall & Bucholtz 1995, Eckert & McConnell-Ginet 1992). Others have turned to neighborhood or "backyard" ethnography (Smith & Watson 1996). Work on the cultural construction of masculinity (Ajani 1994, Ebron 1991; ET Gordon, unpublished manuscript), expanding literature on gay and lesbian communities (Kennedy & Davis 1993, Lewin & Leap 1996, Newton 1993, Weston 1993), and studies on sexuality in the field (Herdt & Stoller 1990, Seizer 1995) are also recent topics of feminist ethnography. Some forms of feminist ethnography work directly from Mead's sense of anthropology as cultural critique (Ginsburg 1989, Tsing 1993), exploring the question of reproductive rights in cross-cultural contexts (Ginsburg & Tsing 1990, Jordan 1978).

Despite a variety of textual forms and strategies advanced by feminist ethnography, life histories, or life stories, continue to be popular modes for first world feminist ethnographers to write about (largely) third world subjects (Behar 1993, Brown 1991, Davison 1987, Patai 1988), who somehow reflect the entire culture. This is in marked contrast to the development of the genre of feminist biography in the discipline, where subjects like Alice Fletcher, Matilda Cox Stevenson, Elsie Clews Parsons, Ruth Benedict, Gladys Reichard, Margaret Mead, or Ruth Landes are portrayed as complex, exceptional, often heroic figures who transcend their cultures (Babcock 1992, Deacon 1997, Parezo 1993, Weigle 1982), such that their class, race, or gender prejudices are overlooked or simply ignored (see, however, Foerstel & Gilliam 1992, Mark 1980). This strongly suggests the need to understand how the very genre conventions of feminist ethnography are defined by the identification(s) of feminist anthropologists with their subjects.

Conclusion

If anthropologists like Elsie Clews Parsons, Margaret Mead, and Gayle Rubin shaped the configurations of US feminism in important ways, contemporary feminist ethnographers have been largely unresponsive to feminist challenges to gender essentialism, relying upon gender standpoint theory, which erases difference through the logic of identification. Yet if we learn to understand gender as not the endpoint of analysis but rather as an entry point into complex systems of meaning and power, then surely there are other equally valid entry points for feminist work. Gender is perhaps best understood as a heuristic device and cannot be understood a priori, apart from particular systems of representation. To mistake the category for the reality is to create gender as a sociologism, reducing it to a male/female dichotomy mistakenly constituted in advance of its operation in any system of social representation.

One of the threads running through this review concerned feminist ethnographic interest in relaying the "woman's point of view." Such vindicationist writing sought to defend women in other cultures, or used knowledge of women in other cultures to cast light on our own. Yet, as Mary John (1996) notes, this particular ethnographic relationship between (largely) Western women writing about (largely) non-Western women has produced a curious effect (pp. 116–17):

> Suddenly a new divide opens out "between feminists" and "other women"—where the assumption seems to be that feminists inhabit one world—the Western one—whereas other women live elsewhere and are *not* feminist. Why not an ethnography about being a feminist in other places?

This is where a broader conception of the relationship of feminist theory to social and nationalist movements might suggest new directions for feminist ethnographic work. Yet while feminist ethnography has emerged within the context of nationalist traditions, as a genre, it has largely failed to address itself to nationalism or state forms of power (but see Williams 1996). To take seriously the idea of writing ethnographies of feminists and feminist movements in other places means we first understand something about the shape feminism takes in other parts of the world. That these feminisms may go by other names—nationalist, Pan-Africanist, socialist, Islamist—pushes feminist anthropology to explore different forms of social inequality and the possibility that it may authorize and inscribe diverse movements for political equality (Ajani 1994; Alarcón 1991; Anzaldúa 1987, 1991; Chabram 1990; Giddens 1984; Sandoval 1991; Warner 1993; ET Gordon, unpublished manuscript), posing again, other histories of feminist ethnography.

ACKNOWLEDGMENTS

This review is dedicated to those who taught me by example that the presence of women in the discipline mattered: Jane Collier, Elizabeth Colson, Pauline Kolenda, Laura Nader, Marilyn Strathern, and Sylvia Yanagisako. I thank the organizers and participants of the Annual Conference on Feminist Anthropology and Archeology, April 27, 1996, University of Minnesota, for their instructive comments on this essay, as well as Ann Cvetkovich, Ted Gordon, Charlie Hale, Catherine O'Leary, and Katie Stewart. I thank also Faye Harrison, Louise Lamphere, and Peter Orne of the *Annual Review*. I am grateful to Jennifer Burrel and Nicolas Prat for helping to locate numerous materials for the review.

Visit the *Annual Reviews* home page at http://www.AnnualReviews.org.

Literature Cited

Abu-Lughod L. 1987. *Veiled Sentiments.* Berkeley: Univ. Calif. Press

Abu-Lughod L. 1990. Can there be a feminist ethnography? *Women Perform.* 5(1):7–27

Abu-Lughod L. 1993. *Writing Women's Worlds.* Berkeley: Univ. Calif. Press

Ajani A. 1994. *Opposing oppositional identities: fabulous boys and the refashioning of subculture theory.* MA thesis. Dep. Anthropol., Stanford Univ.

Alarcón N. 1989. The theoretical subjects of "This bridge Called My Back" and Anglo-American Feminism. See Anzaldúa 1989, pp. 356–69

Alarcón N, Albrecht L, Alexander J, eds. 1991. *The Third Wave: Feminist Perspectives on Racism.* San Francisco: Kitchen Table

Alcoff L. 1988. Cultural feminism versus poststructuralism: the identity crisis in feminist theory. *Signs* 13(3):405–36

Altorki S, El-Sohl CD, eds. 1988. *Arab Women in the Field: Studying Your Own Society.* New York: Syracuse Univ. Press

Anzaldúa G. 1987. *Borderlands/La Frontera: The New Mestiza.* San Francisco: Spinsters/Aunt Lute

Anzaldúa G, ed. 1990. *Making Face/Making Soul.* San Francisco: Aunt Lute

Atkinson J. 1982. Anthropology: review essay. *Signs* 8:236–58

Babcock B, ed. 1992. Introduction: Elsie Clews Parsons and the Pueblo construction of gender. In *Pueblo Mothers and Children: Essays by Elsie Clews Parsons, 1915–24,* ed. B Babcock, pp. 1–27. Santa Fe, NM: Ancient City

Behar R. 1993. *Translated Woman.* Boston: Beacon

Behar R, Gordon D, eds. 1995. *Women Writing Culture.* Berkeley: Univ. Calif. Press

Bell D. 1993. (1983). *Daughters of the Dreaming.* Minneapolis, MN: Univ. Minn. Press

Berndt C. 1950. Women's changing ceremonies in northern Australia. *L'Homme* 1: 1–87

Borker R. 1984. Anthropology: social and cultural perspectives. In *Women and Language in Literature and Society,* ed. S McConnell-Ginet, R Borker, N Furman, pp. 26–41. New York: Praeger

Bradiotti R, Butler J. 1994. Feminism by any other name. *Differences* 6(2–3):27–61

Brown KM. 1991. *Mama Lola.* Berkeley: Univ. Calif. Press

Burton A. 1992. "History" is now: feminist theory and the production of historical feminisms. *Women's Hist. Rev.* 1(1): 25–38

Butler J. 1990. *Gender Trouble.* New York: Routledge

Butler J. 1993. *Bodies That Matter: On the Discursive Limits of Sex.* New York: Routledge

Butler J. 1994. Against proper objects. *Differences* 6(2–3):1–26

Chabram A. 1990. Chicana/o studies as oppositional ethnography. *Cult. Stud.* 4(3): 228–47

Clifford J, Marcus G, eds. 1986. *Writing Culture.* Berkeley: Univ. Calif. Press

Cole S, Phillips L, eds. 1995. *Ethnographic Feminisms.* Ottawa: Carleton Univ. Press

Collier JF, Rosaldo M. 1981. Politics and gender in simple societies. See Ortner & Whitehead 1981a, pp. 275–329

Collier JF, Yanagisako S. 1987. *Gender and Kinship: Essays Toward a Unified Analysis.* Stanford, CA: Stanford Univ. Press

Collier JF, Yanagisako S. 1989. Theory in anthropology since feminist practice. *Crit. Anthropol.* 9(2):27–37

Collins PH. 1990. *Black Feminist Thought: Knowledge, Consciousness and the Politics of Empowerment.* Boston: Unwin Hyman

Combahee River Collective Statement. 1982. In *Home Girls: A Black Feminist Anthology*, ed. B Smith. San Francisco: Kitchen Table

Conkey M, Williams S. 1991. Original narratives: the political economy of gender in archeology. See di Leonardo 1991, pp. 102–39

Cott NF. 1987. *The Grounding of Modern Feminism.* New Haven, CT: Yale Univ. Press

Cox Stevenson M. 1894. The Sia. *Bur. Am. Ethnol., 11th, Annu. Rep. (1889–1890).* Washington, DC: US Gov. Print. Off.

Cox Stevenson M. 1904. The Zuni indians: their mythology, esoteric fraternities, and ceremonies. *Bur. Am. Ethnol., 23rd, Annu. Rep. (1901–1902).* La Casa Escuela, NM: Rio Grande

Cvetkovich A. 1995. Sexual trauma/queer memory: incest, lesbianism, and therapeutic culture. *Gay Lesbian Q. J.* 2:1–27

Davison J. 1987. *Voices from Mutira.* Boulder, CO: Reiner

Deacon D. 1997. *Elsie Clews Parsons: Inventing Modern Life.* Chicago: Univ. Chicago Press

de Lauretis T. 1987. *Technologies of Gender.* Bloomington: Univ. Ind. Press

Deloria E. 1988. *Waterlily.* Lincoln, NE: Univ. Nebr. Press

di Leonardo M, ed. 1991. *Gender at the Crossroads of Knowledge.* Berkeley: Univ. Calif. Press

Dunham K. 1994. *Island Possessed.* Chicago: Univ. Chicago Press

Ebron P. 1991. Rapping between men: performing gender. *Radic. Am.* 23(4):23–27

Eckert P, McConnell-Ginet S. 1992. Think practically and look locally: language and gender as community-based practice. *Annu. Rev. Anthropol.* 21:461–90

Evans S. 1979. *Personal Politics: The Roots of Women's Liberation in the Civil Rights Movement and the New Left.* New York: Vintage

Fee E. 1975. The sexual politics of Victorian social anthropology. In *Clio's Consciousness Raised: New Perspectives on the History of Women*, ed. M Hartman, L Banner, pp. 86–102. New York: Harper & Row

Fernandez-Kelly P. 1983. *For We Are Sold, I and My People: Women and Industry on Mexico's Frontier.* Albany: SUNY Press

Fletcher A. 1883. On Indian education and self support. *Century Mag.* 4:312–15

Fletcher A. 1899. The Indian woman and her problems. *South. Workman* May:172–76

Foerstel L, Gilliam A, eds. 1992. *Confronting the Margaret Mead Legacy: Scholarship, Empire, and the South Pacific.* Philadelphia: Temple Univ. Press

Frankenberg R. 1993. *White Women, Race Matters.* Minneapolis, MN: Univ. Minn. Press

Friedan B. 1963. *The Feminine Mystique.* New York: Norton

Gal S. 1991. Between speech and silence: the problematics of research on language and gender. See di Leonardo 1991, pp. 175–203

Geiger S. 1986. Women's life histories: method and content. *Signs* 11(2):334–51

Giddens P. 1984. *When and Where I Enter: The Impact of Black Women on Race and Sex in America.* New York: Bantam Books

Ginsburg F. 1989. *Contested Lives: The Abortion Debate in an American Community.* Berkeley: Univ. Calif. Press

Ginsburg F, Tsing A, eds. 1990. *Uncertain Terms: Negotiating Gender in American Culture.* Boston: Beacon

Goodale J. 1971. *Tiwi Wives: A Study of Women of Melville Island, Northern Australia.* Seattle: Univ. Wash. Press

Gordon D. 1993. The unhappy relationship of feminism and post-modernism in anthropology. *Anthropol. Q.* 66(3):109–17

Gordon D. 1995. Culture writing women: inscribing feminist anthropology. See Behar & Gordon 1995, pp. 429–41

Hall K, Bucholtz M, eds. 1995. *Gender Articulated: Language and the Socially Constructed Self.* New York: Routledge

Haraway D. 1988. Situated knowledges: the science question in feminism and the privilege of partial perspective *Fem. Stud.* 14: 575–99

Harding S, ed. 1987. *Feminism and Methodology.* Bloomington: Ind. Univ. Press

Harding S. 1993. Rethinking standpoint epistemology: What is "strong objectivity"? In *Feminist Epistemologies*, ed. L Alcoff, E Potter, pp. 49–82. New York: Routledge

Harris A. 1990. Race and essentialism in feminist legal theory. *Stanford Law Rev.* 42(3): 581–16

Harrison F. 1990. Three women, one struggle: anthropology, performance and pedagogy. *Transform. Anthropol.* 1:1–9

Hartsock N. 1987. (1983). The feminist standpoint: developing the ground for a specifically feminist historical materialism. See Harding 1987, pp. 157–80

Herdt GH, Stoller R. 1990. *Intimate Commu-*

nications: Erotics and the Study of Culture. New York: Columbia Univ. Press

hooks b. 1984. Feminist Theory: From Margin to Center. Boston: South End Press

Hurston ZN. 1935. Mules and Men. New York: Harper Collins

Hurston ZN. 1938. Tell My Horse. New York: Harper Collins

Jaggar AM. 1988. Feminist Politics and Human Nature. Totowa, NJ: Rowman & Littlefield

John M. 1996. Discrepant Dislocations. Berkeley: Univ. Calif. Press

Jones J. 1996a. The self as other: creating the role of Joni the ethnographer for Broken Circles. Text Perform. Q. 16:131–45

Jones J. 1996b. sista docta. In Performance in Life and Literature, ed. PH Gray, J Van Oosting, pp. 227–36. Needham Heights, MA: Allen & Bacon

Jordan B. 1978. Birth in Four Cultures: A Cross-Cultural Investigation of Childbirth in Yucatan, Holland, Sweden and the United States. Montreal: Eden

Kaberry PM. 1939. Aboriginal Woman. New York: Routledge

Kapchan D. 1996. Gender on the Market: Moroccan Women and the Revoicing of Tradition. Philadelphia: Univ. Pa. Press

Kennedy E, Davis M. 1993. Boots of Leather, Slippers of Gold. New York: Routledge

King D. 1988. Multiple jeopardy, multiple consciousness: the context of a black feminist ideology. Signs 41:1

Kondo D. 1995. Bad girls: theater, women of color, and the politics of representation. See Behar & Gordon 1995, pp. 49–64

Lamphere L. 1977. Anthropology: review essay. Signs 2(3):612–27

Lamphere L. 1987. From Working Daughters to Working Mothers: Immigrant Women in a New England Industrial Community. Ithaca: Cornell Univ. Press

Lamphere L. 1989. Feminist anthropology: the legacy of Elsie Clews Parsons. Am. Ethnol. 16:518–33

Landes R. 1971. (1938). The Ojibwa Woman: Male and Female Life Cycles Among the Ojibwa Indians of Western Ontario. New York: Norton

Landes R. 1947. City of Women. New York: Macmillan

Leacock E. 1978. Women's status in egalitarian society: implications for social evolution. Curr. Anthropol. 19:247–55, 268–75

Levine P. 1987. Victorian Feminism. London: Hutchinson

Lewin E, Leap W, eds. 1996. Doing Lesbian and Gay Anthropology: Issues in Fieldwork and Ethnography. Champaign: Univ. Ill. Press

Liebowitz L. 1975. Perspectives on the evolution of sex differences. See Rapp 1975

Lorde A. 1984. Sister Outsider. Freedom, CA: Crossing Press

Lutkehaus N. 1986. She was very Cambridge: Camilla Wedgewood and the history of women in British social anthropology. Am. Ethnol. 13(4):776–98

Lutkehaus N. 1995. Margaret Mead and the "Rustling-of-the-Wind-in-the-Palm-Trees School" of Ethnographic Writing. See Behar & Gordon 1995, pp. 186–206

Mankekar P. 1993. Television tales and a woman's rage: a nationalist recasting of Draupadi's "disrobing." Public Cult. 5:469–92

Marcus GE, Cushman D. 1982. Ethnographies as texts. Annu. Rev. Anthropol. 11: 25–69

Marcus GE, Fisher M. 1986. Anthropology as Cultural Critique. Chicago, IL: Univ. Chicago Press

Mark J. 1980. Alice Fletcher. In Four Anthropologists: An American Science in its Early Years, ed. J Mark. New York: Science History

Martin B. 1994. Sexualities without genders and other queer utopias. Diacritics 24 (2–3):104–21

Martin MK, Voorhies B. 1975. Female of the Species. New York: Columbia Univ. Press

Mascia-Lees F, Sharpe P, Ballerino Cohen C. 1989. The post-modernist turn in anthropology: cautions from a feminist perspective. Signs 15(1):7–33

Mead M. 1928. Coming of Age in Samoa. New York: Morrow

Mead M. 1930. Growing Up in New Guinea. New York: Mentor Book/New Am. Libr. World Lit.

Mead M. 1935. Sex and Temperament. New York: Morrow

Mohanty C. 1987. Feminist encounters: locating the politics of experience. Copyright 1:30–45

Moraga C, Anzaldúa G. 1981. This Bridge Called My Back. Watertown, MA: Persephone

Morgan R. 1970. Sisterhood Is Powerful. New York: Random House

Morris RC. 1995. All made up: performance theory and the new anthropology of sex and gender. Annu. Rev. Anthropol. 24: 567–92

Mukhopadhyay CC, Higgins PJ. 1988. Anthropological studies of women's status revisited: 1977–1987. Annu. Rev. Anthropol. 17:461–95

Narayan K. 1993. How native is a native anthropologist? *Am. Anthropol.* 95(3): 671–87

Newton E. 1993. *Cherry Grove, Fire Island: Sixty Years in America's First Gay and Lesbian Town.* Boston: Beacon

Nicholson L, ed. 1990. *Feminism/Postmodernism.* New York: Routledge

Oakley A. 1981. Interviewing women: a contradiction in terms? In *Doing Feminist Research,* ed. H Roberts, pp. 30–61. New York: Routledge

Offen K. 1988. On the French origin of the words feminism and feminist. *Fem. Issues* Fall:45–51

O'Leary C. 1997. Counteridentification or counterhegemony? Transforming feminist standpoint theory. *Women Polit.* In press

Ong A. 1987. *Spirits of Resistance and Capitalist Discipline: Factory Women in Malaysia.* New York: SUNY Press

Ortner S. 1984. Theory in anthropology since the sixties. *Comp. Stud. Soc. Hist.* 26: 126–66

Ortner S, Whitehead H, eds. 1981a. *Sexual Meanings: The Cultural Construction of Gender and Sexuality.* Cambridge: Cambridge Univ. Press

Ortner S, Whitehead H. 1981b. Introduction: accounting for sexual meanings. See Ortner & Whitehead 1981a, pp. 1–28

Parezo N, ed. 1993. *Hidden Scholars: Women Anthropologists and the Native Southwest.* Albuquerque: Univ. N. M. Press

Parsons EC. 1906. *The Family: An Ethnographical and Historical Outline.* New York: Putnam & Sons

Parsons EC. 1909. Higher education of women and the family. *Am. J. Sociol.* 14(6):758–65

Parsons EC. 1913. *The Old Fashioned Woman: Primitive Fancies About the Sex.* New York: Putnam & Sons

Parsons EC. 1916. *Social Rule: A Study of the Will to Power.* New York: Putnam & Sons

Patai D. 1988. *Brazilian Women Speak: Contemporary Life Stories.* New Brunswick, NJ: Rutgers Univ. Press

Personal Narrative Group. 1989. *Interpreting Women's Lives: Feminist Theory and Personal Narratives.* Bloomington: Univ. Ind. Press

Powdermaker H. 1939. *After Freedom.* New York: Viking

Quinn N. 1977. Anthropological studies on women's status. *Annu. Rev. Anthropol.* 6: 181–225

Raheja G, Gold A. 1994. *Listen to the Heron's Words: Reimagining Gender and Kinship in North India.* Berkeley: Univ. Calif. Press

Rapp R, ed. 1975. *Toward an Anthropology of Women.* New York: Mon. Rev.

Rapp R. 1979. Anthropology: review essay. *Signs* 4(3):497–513

Reichard GA. 1934. *Spider Woman.* New York: Macmillan

Reichard GA. 1939. *Dezba: Woman of the Desert.* New York: Augustin

Reinharz S. 1992. *Feminist Methods in Social Research.* Oxford Univ. Press

Richards A. 1956. *Chisungu: A Girl's Initiation Ceremony Among the Bemba of Northern Rhodesia.* London: Faber & Faber

Riley D. 1990. *Am I That Name? Feminism and the Category of "Women" in History.* Minneapolis, MN: Univ. Minn. Press

Rogers SC. 1978. Woman's place: a critical review of anthropological theory. *Comp. Stud. Soc. Hist.* 20:123–62

Rosaldo M. 1980. The use and abuse of anthropology: reflections on feminism and cross-cultural understanding. *Signs* 5: 389–417

Rosaldo M, Lamphere L, eds. 1974. *Women, Culture and Society.* Stanford, CA: Stanford Univ. Press

Rosan A, de Caro Jordan FA. 1986. Women and the study of folklore. *Signs* 11(3): 500–18

Rubin G. 1975. The traffic in women: notes on the "political economy" of sex. See Rapp 1975, pp. 157–210

Sacks K. 1984. *My Troubles Are Going to Have Trouble with Me: Everyday Trials and Triumphs of Women Workers.* New Brunswick, NJ: Rutgers Univ. Press

Sandoval C. 1990. Feminism and racism: a report on the 1981 National Women's Studies Association Conference. See Anzaldúa 1990, pp. 55–71

Sandoval C. 1991. U.S. third world feminism: the theory and method of oppositional consciousness in the post-modern world. *Genders* 10:1–24

Scheper-Hughes N. 1992. *Death Without Weeping.* Berkeley: Univ. Calif. Press

Sedgewick E. 1990. *The Epistemology of the Closet.* Berkeley: Univ. Calif. Press

Seizer S. 1995. Paradoxes of visibility in the field: rites of queer passage in anthropology. *Public Cult.* 8(1):73–100

Serematakis CN. 1991. *The Last Word: Women, Death and Divination in Inner Mani.* Chicago: Univ. Chicago Press

Shostak M. 1981. *Nisa: The Life and Words of a !Kung Woman.* Cambridge: Harvard Univ. Press

Smith D. 1987. (1974). Women's perspective as a radical critique of sociology. See Harding 1987, pp. 84–96

Smith S, Watson J. 1996. *Getting a Life: Everyday Uses of Autobiography*. Minneapolis, MN: Univ. Minn. Press

Spelman E. 1988. *The Inessential Women*. Boston: Beacon

Stacey J. 1988. Can there be a feminist ethnography? *Women's Stud. Int. Forum* 11(1): 21–27

Stacey J. 1990. *Brave New Families*. New York: Basic Books

Steedly MM. 1993. *Hanging by a Rope*. Princeton, NJ: Princeton Univ. Press

Stewart KC. 1996. *A Space on the Side of the Road: Cultural Poetics in an "Other" America*. Princeton, NJ: Princeton Univ. Press

Strathern M. 1972. *Women in Between*. London: Seminar

Strathern M. 1987. An awkward relationship: the case of feminism and anthropology. *Signs* 12(2):276–92

Strong PT. 1996. Feminist theory and the Invasion of the Heart in North America. *Ethnohistory* 43(4):683–712

Tedlock B. 1991. From participant observation to the observation of participation: the emergence of narrative ethnography. *J. Anthropol. Res.* 47(1):69–95

Torruellas R, Benmayor R, Goris A, Juarbe A. 1991. *Affirming cultural citizenship in the Puerto Rican community: critical literacy and the el barrio popular education program*. Cent. Cult. Stud. Task Force, Lang. Educ. Task Force, Hunter College, City Univ. NY

Trawick M. 1990. *Notes on Love in a Tamil Family*. Berkeley: Univ. Calif. Press

Tsing A. 1993. *In the Realm of the Diamond Queen*. Princeton, NJ: Princeton Univ. Press

Underhill RM. 1979. (1936). *Papago Woman*. Prospect Heights, IL: Waveland

Visweswaran K. 1988. Defining feminist ethnography. *Inscriptions* 3/4:27–44

Visweswaran K. 1994. *Fictions of Feminist Ethnography*. Minneapolis, MN: Univ. Minn. Press

Visweswaran K. 1997. Wild west anthropology and the disciplining of gender. In *Gender and the Origins of American Social Science,* ed. H Silverberg. Princeton, NJ: Princeton Univ. Press

Warner M, ed. 1993. *Fear of a Queer Planet*. Minneapolis, MN: Univ. Minn. Press

Weigle M. 1982. *Spiders and Spinsters*. Albuquerque: Univ. N. M. Press

Weiner A. 1976. *Women of Value, Men of Renown*. Austin: Univ. Tex. Press

Weston K. 1991. *Families We Choose*. New York: Columbia Univ. Press

Weston K. 1993. Lesbian/gay studies in the house of anthropology. *Annu. Rev. Anthropol.* 22:339–67

Williams B, ed. 1996. *Women Out of Place*. New York: Routledge

Wolf M. 1990. *A Thrice-Told Tale*. Stanford, CA: Stanford Univ. Press

Yanagisako SJ. 1985. *Transforming the Past: Tradition and Kinship among Japanese Americans*. Stanford, CA: Stanford Univ. Press

Zavella P. 1987. *Women's Work and Chicano Families: Cannery Workers of the Santa Clara Valley*. Ithaca, NY: Cornell Univ. Press

Zavella P. 1995. Feminist insider dilemmas: constructing ethnic identity with Chicana informants. In *Feminist Dilemmas in Fieldwork,* ed. D Wolf, pp. 138–59. Boulder, CO: Westview

Zihlman A. 1985. Review essay: gathering stories for hunting human nature. *Fem. Stud.* 11:364–77

AUTHOR INDEX

A

Aarsleff H, 293
Abbott S, 201
Abdoulaye R, 247
Abe K, 326
Abélès M, 497
Aboudan R, 111
Abraham M, 97, 99, 101
Abu-Lughod L, 582, 591, 607, 613
Abu Rabi'a K, 246
Acampora D, 353, 355
Acheson KJ, 546
Adam BD, 444, 457
Adams K, 83
Adams RN, 571
Aditya A, 440, 444
Adorno R, 170
Afable PO, 50
Ager D, 75
Agharanya JC, 318
Agnoli F, 293, 307
Agras WS, 557
Agrinier P, 135, 219
Ahern EM, 56
Ahlbom A, 327
Ahler SR, 481
Ahmad A, 570
Ahmed AGM, 246
Ahola M, 555
Ahuja K, 455
Aiello LC, 526
Aikens CM, 370
Aizawa S, 354, 355
Ajani A, 613–16
Ajisaka R, 316
Akashi H, 524
Akerstedt T, 316
Akey JM, 518
Alarcón N, 577, 595, 613, 616
Albertson AM, 555
Albó X, 571
Albrecht L, 595, 613, 616
Alcaraz JE, 545, 560
Alcoff L, 613
Alexander J, 595, 613, 616
Alexander RM, 192, 199
Alfonso M, 328
Algaze G, 134
Allchin FR, 89, 100
Allen H, 413
Allen T, 475

Allison A, 400
Alliston-Greiner R, 525
Almaguer T, 394
Almquist AJ, 275
Alonso AM, 580
Alper HP, 55
Alpert BS, 327
Al Sayyad N, 174
Alter JS, 393
Althusser L, 43, 44
Altorki S, 614
Altschul JH, 139, 141
Alvarez SE, 569, 579
Amanor KS, 247
Amiel D, 190
Ammerman AJ, 375
Ammon HPT, 318
Ammon U, 500
Ammons L, 246
Andah B, 376
Andersen H, 368
Anderson B, 176, 492
Anderson D, 240
Anderson M, 578
Anderson R, 170, 171
Anderson W, 545
Andrews P, 526, 530
Angenot M, 110
Angulo Villaseñor J, 134
Ankel-Simons F, 524, 525
Annis S, 440, 456
Ansari ZD, 93
Anthony A, 392, 402
Anthony DW, 366, 372, 377
Anton SC, 195
Anzaldúa G, 577, 595, 613, 616
Appadurai A, 176, 439, 450, 493, 571, 574
Appiah KA, 169, 177, 178
Arasaratnam S, 101
Araujo H, 535
Archer L, 412
Ardener E, 387
Arendt H, 491
Argemi A, 81
Ariés P, 505
Armelagos GJ, 315, 329
Armillas P, 151
Armstrong DF, 110
Arnold D, 169, 176
Arnold PJ, 135
Aronna M, 576
Aronson D, 237

Arrandale SR, 195
Arsenault D, 412, 415
Asad T, 48, 176
Asch DL, 474
Asch NB, 474
Asher RE, 360
Ashford MW Jr, 197
Aslan S, 321
Atkins S, 322
Atkinson JM, 50, 54, 55, 59, 597
Au TK, 302
Aufderheide P, 453
Augustine ST, 49
Austerlitz R, 368, 374
Austin JL, 56
Aveni AF, 134
Ayala FJ, 521
Ayanda JO, 246
Ayeni JSO, 246

B

Babcock B, 591, 599, 615
Baca-Zinn M, 403
Bachrach LK, 197
Bacus E, 413
Baddeley A, 307
Badone E, 504
Baekers J, 246
Baertschi P, 546
Baghurst PA, 560
Bahr R, 318
Bailey DW, 414, 415
Bailey WJ, 524
Bailey-Goldschmidt J, 102
Baker C, 110
Baker D, 327
Baker J, 246
Baker PT, 314, 319, 320
Bakhtin MM, 60, 495, 504
Balaban E, 347
Balandier G, 165
Balasubramanian V, 316
Baldauf RB, 83
Bales RF, 388
Balibar E, 491
Ball SG, 324
Ballerino Cohen C, 613
Balme J, 412–14
Bamshad MJ, 526
Bance A, 489
Bandaranayaka S, 99
Bandini LG, 555

SUBJECT INDEX

A

Aborigines
  feminist ethnography and, 603, 609
  gesture and, 121
"Absence of intelligent intervention"
  antievolution and creationism in United States, 283
Absolute languages
  gesture and, 116–17
Absolute value
  Marx and anthropology, 35
Abstract ideas
  gesture and, 112
Abuse
  of monuments
    government in Early Mesoamerica and, 220–22
Accidental ethnography
  feminist ethnography and, 615
Accretion zones
  ancient linguistic movement and, 369, 374, 376–77
Acharya TLA, 1–2
Acquired immunodeficiency syndrome (AIDS)
  Europeanization and, 506
  hominoid genetic diversity and, 535
  pastoralism and, 247
Action
  Marx and anthropology, 29
  religious language and, 56
Activity
  children and, 541–61
Adamawa
  ancient linguistic movement and, 375
Adaptation
  biological stress response and lifestyle, 314–15
  human brain evolution and, 340, 347–50
  pastoralism and, 237
Addressee
  religious language and, 58
Affirmative action
  practicing social anthropology in India and, 18

Africa
  ancient linguistic movement and, 363–64, 368–69, 374–76
  anthropology of colonialism and, 163, 168, 174, 177
  behavioral and phylogenetic inferences from hominid fossils, 201
  biological stress response and lifestyle, 320
  feminist ethnography and, 600, 612, 616
  government in Early Mesoamerica and, 215
  hominoid genetic diversity and, 525–26, 531, 535
  masculinity and, 391
  pastoralism and, 235–38, 242–44, 246–48, 251–54
Afroasiatic languages
  ancient linguistic movement and, 361–62, 364–65, 375–76
Age
  biological stress response and lifestyle, 321, 326
  practicing social anthropology in India and, 10
Agency
  anthropology of colonialism and, 177
  gender and feminism in archaeology, 420, 422, 426, 429
  religious language and, 47, 57, 59, 62, 64–66
  state and society at Teotihuacan, Mexico, 130
Agglutinative morphology
  gesture and, 122
Agricultural societies
  archaeology of ancient religion in North American Eastern Woodlands, 478
  pastoralism and, 246
  practicing social anthropology in India and, 19
Ahichchatra
  commerce and culture in South Asia, 89
Ainu
  ancient linguistic movement and, 370

Aka Pygmy
  masculinity and, 392
Alabama
  antievolution and creationism in United States, 276, 278–79, 284
Alaska
  ancient linguistic movement and, 374, 379
Algebraic structure
  underlying myth
    archaeology of ancient religion in North American Eastern Woodlands, 467
Algic stock
  ancient linguistic movement and, 379
Algonquin languages
  ancient linguistic movement and, 361, 363, 379
Allometry
  human brain evolution and, 337, 339, 342, 351
Alpha males
  masculinity and, 397–98
Alta Vista
  state and society at Teotihuacan, Mexico, 134
Alternate sign languages
  gesture and, 109, 120–21
Alternative histories
  anthropology of colonialism and, 168
Altun Ha
  state and society at Teotihuacan, Mexico, 135
Amazon basin
  ancient linguistic movement and, 368–69, 374, 379
  biological stress response and lifestyle, 320
  masculinity and, 402
Ambiguity
  gender and feminism in archaeology, 428–29
Amboseli Park
  pastoralism and, 243
American Bottom
  archaeology of ancient religion in North American Eastern Woodlands, 477
American Samoa
  biological stress response and lifestyle, 319–20

CUMULATIVE INDEXES

CONTRIBUTING AUTHORS, VOLUMES 18–26

CHAPTER TITLES, VOLUMES 18–26

BIOLOGICAL ANTHROPOLOGY

LINGUISTICS AND COMMUNICATIVE PRACTICES

REGIONAL STUDIES

SOCIOCULTURAL ANTHROPOLOGY

History, Theory, and Methods